AUTISM SPECTRUM DISORDER

AUTISM SPECTRUM DISORDER

Edited by

Christopher J. McDougle, MD

Director, Lurie Center for Autism
Professor of Psychiatry and Pediatrics
Massachusetts General Hospital and
MassGeneral Hospital *for* Children
Nancy Lurie Marks Professor in the Field of Autism
Harvard Medical School

OXFORD
UNIVERSITY PRESS

OXFORD
UNIVERSITY PRESS

Oxford University Press is a department of the University of Oxford. It furthers
the University's objective of excellence in research, scholarship, and education
by publishing worldwide.Oxford is a registered trade mark of Oxford University
Press in the UK and certain other countries.

Published in the United States of America by Oxford University Press
198 Madison Avenue, New York, NY 10016, United States of America.

Cataloging-in-Publication data is on file at the Library of Congress
ISBN 978-0-19-934972-2

CONTENTS

SECTION 2: ETIOLOGY

SECTION 3: TREATMENT

SECTION 4: OTHER CARE DELIVERY SERVICES AND PERSPECTIVES

FOREWORD

When I was a medical student in the mid-1980s, autism was considered a rare disorder with a prevalence of 2–4 individuals per 10,000. To my knowledge, I had never met anyone with autism. Autism was never mentioned in a lecture, and I did not encounter a patient with autism during my clinical rotations. It was not until I was a postgraduate year two (PGY- II) resident in psychiatry that I met people with autism. These were all young adults living at a residential facility in Connecticut called Ben Haven. I was there visiting the site along with my residency colleagues as part of our training experience.

Three decades later, significant changes have occurred in the field of autism, now called "autism spectrum disorder." The prevalence estimates have increased exponentially. Most of us have a colleague, classmate, or friend with a family member with an autism-related disorder. Behavioral and pharmacological treatments have been developed that are of some benefit, and educational programs and specialized schools have been created that offer services to enhance learning and to improve communication and social skills. Scientists from the fields of neuroimaging, genetics, epidemiology, cognitive neuroscience, and immunology have joined in the search for potential causes of autism.

Despite what we have learned about autism in the past 30 years, we continue to know so very little. We have conceptualized autism as a group of heterogeneous neurodevelopmental disorders rather than a single entity. The heterogeneity spans the phenotype and genotype and everything in between. This has made the identification of specific causes of autism challenging to say the least. Along these lines, individuals with autism with a similar clinical presentation may have radically different underlying pathophysiologies. This has limited our ability to match targeted treatments with particular patients. In fact, the field has made very little progress in developing therapies that result in consistent, significant improvement in what have historically been considered the core clinical domains of autism (social and communication impairment and restricted, repetitive patterns of behavior).

Thirty years ago, society had not realized that children with autism grow up and live as long as the rest of us. As a result, there has been insufficient thought about where these individuals will live, work, and go to school beyond the age of 22 years. Similarly, the amount of research involving adults with autism lags far behind that occurring in infants, toddlers, and school-age children. Practically speaking, society has little meaningful knowledge about how to provide adults with autism the basic necessities of life. This is unlikely to change until additional research helps us to address the many unanswered questions surrounding adults with autism.

This book is designed as an easy-to-use, clinically oriented, evidence-based guide for trainees and early stage clinicians. It was written with medical students, graduate students and interns in psychology, residents and fellows in neurology, psychiatry, and pediatrics, and those clinicians and researchers who have recently completed training in mind. It is intended to be read and understood during a 4- to 12-week rotation focused on autism spectrum disorder and potentially other neurodevelopmental disorders and also during review and preparation for board examinations that occur throughout professional school, postgraduate training, and for specialty-board certification after training is completed. The chapters related to clinical diagnosis and treatment aspects of autism spectrum disorder will provide a "nuts and bolts" approach on how to conduct these evaluations and interventions from a high view perspective. The chapters related to a body of scientific knowledge, such as those dedicated to neuroimaging, genetics, epidemiology, neuropathology, and immunology, highlight the relevance of the data in summary fashion and make the clinical implications of the findings explicit. Clinical case vignettes are provided wherever appropriate to aid instruction. At the end of each chapter, five "Key Points" are listed that highlight the intended takeaway message for the learner. The book concludes with chapters written by family members of adult children with autism and a young man with autism, respectively. Their perspectives convey the human aspects of living with autism, which we hope will motivate the reader to want to learn even more about the field.

It is our hope that this text provides the reader with the knowledge needed to derive maximal benefit from clinical rotations related to autism spectrum disorder and for successful preparation for board examinations. If the book helps to lead some of you toward a career related to caring for individuals with autism and their families or learning more about the biology and psychology of the syndrome, then even more will have been accomplished.

Christopher J. McDougle, MD
Boston, Massachusetts
September 1, 2015

CONTRIBUTORS

Robert E. Accordino, MD, MSc
Child and Adolescent Psychiatry Fellow
Massachusetts General Hospital/McLean
  Hospital
Boston/Belmont, MA
Harvard Medical School
Boston, MA

Matthew P. Anderson, MD, PhD
Director of Neuropathology
Beth Israel Deaconess Medical Center
Boston, MA
Associate Professor of Pathology
Harvard Medical School
Boston, MA

Fiona Baumer, MD
Chief Resident in Child Neurology
Department of Neurology
Boston Children's Hospital
Boston, MA
Harvard Medical School
Boston, MA

Harrison Brand, PhD
Research Fellow
Psychiatric and Neurodevelopmental
  Genetics Unit
Molecular Neurogenetics Unit
Center for Human Genetic Research
Massachusetts General Hospital
Boston, MA
Research Fellow in Neurology
Harvard Medical School
Boston, MA

Edward S. Brodkin, MD
Director, Adult Autism Spectrum Program
Penn Medicine
Philadelphia, PA
Associate Professor of Psychiatry
Perelman School of Medicine at the
  University of Pennsylvania
Philadelphia, PA

Kirstin Brown Birtwell, PhD
Postdoctoral Fellow in Psychology
Department of Psychiatry
Massachusetts General Hospital
Lurie Center for Autism
Lexington, MA
Postdoctoral Fellow in Psychiatry
Harvard Medical School
Boston, MA

Katelyn A. Bruno, MA, CCC-SLP
Speech and Language Pathologist
Spaulding Rehabilitation Hospital
Lurie Center for Autism
Lexington, MA

Luis M. Carcache, MD
Assistant Professor
Department of Psychiatry &
  Behavioral Health
Florida International University
School of Medicine
Miami, FL

Marji Erickson Warfield, PhD
Director and Senior Scientist
The Nathan and Toby Starr Center
 on Intellectual and Developmental
 Disabilities
The Heller School for Social Policy and
 Management
Brandeis University
Waltham, MA

Veronica P. Fleury, PhD, BCBA
Autism Spectrum Disorder Program
 Coordinator
Assistant Professor
Special Education
Department of Educational Psychology
University of Minnesota
Minneapolis, MN

Susan E. Folstein, MD
Adjunct Clinical Professor
Department of Psychiatry &
 Behavioral Health
Florida International University
School of Medicine
Miami, FL

Eric Fombonne, MD
Director of Autism Research
Institute for Development & Disability
Professor of Psychiatry
Oregon Health & Science University
Portland, OR

Leslie C. Fox, PhD
Research Assistant
Frank Porter Graham Child Development
 Institute
University of North Carolina at Chapel Hill
Chapel Hill, NC

Lawrence K. Fung, MD, PhD
Center for Interdisciplinary Brain Sciences
 Research
Instructor, Department of Psychiatry &
 Behavioral Sciences
Stanford University School of Medicine
Palo Alto, CA

Michael Gandal, MD, PhD
General Psychiatry Resident
Research Track
Department of Psychiatry and
 Biobehavioral Sciences
David Geffen School of Medicine at UCLA
Los Angeles, CA

Isobel W. Green
Harvard University
Cambridge, MA

Kristina L. Gulati, MA, CCC-SLP
Speech and Language Pathologist
Spaulding Rehabilitation Hospital
Lurie Center for Autism
Lexington, MA

Susan H. Hedges, MA
Doctoral Candidate
Frank Porter Graham Child Development
 Institute
University of North Carolina at Chapel Hill
Chapel Hill, NC

Robert L. Hendren, DO
Director, Child and Adolescent Psychiatry
Director, Autism and Neurodevelopment
 Program
UCSF Benioff Children's Hospital
San Francisco, CA
Professor and Vice Chair
Department of Psychiatry
UCSF School of Medicine
San Francisco, CA

Allison Presmanes Hill, PhD
Research Assistant Professor
Center for Spoken Language
 Understanding
Institute for Development & Disability
Department of Pediatrics
Oregon Health & Science University
Portland, OR

Jacob M. Hooker, PhD
Director of Radiochemistry
Athinoula A. Martinos Center for
  Biomedical Imaging
Massachusetts General Hospital
Charlestown, MA
Associate Professor of Radiology
Harvard Medical School
Boston, MA

Yamini J. Howe, MD
Lurie Center for Autism
MassGeneral Hospital *for* Children
Lexington, MA
Instructor in Pediatrics
Harvard Medical School
Boston, MA

Patricia Howlin, PhD
Emeritus Professor of Clinical Child
  Psychiatry
Institute of Psychiatry
King's College
London, United Kingdom
Professor of Developmental Disabilities
Brain and Mind Research Institute
University of Sydney
Sidney, Australia

Suzannah Iadarola, PhD, BCBA-D
Strong Center for Developmental
  Disabilities
Division of Neurodevelopmental and
  Behavioral Pediatrics
Assistant Professor of Pediatrics
University of Rochester Medical Center
Rochester, NY

Christen L. Kidd, MD
Resident in Psychiatry
New York-Presbyterian Hospital
Weill Cornell Medical Center
New York, NY

Kimberly Lo, MD
Triple Board Resident
Departments of Psychiatry and Pediatrics
Indiana University School of Medicine
Indianapolis, IN

Dorothy Lucci, MEd, CAGS
Program Director
Aspire
Massachusetts General Hospital
Lurie Center for Autism
Lexington, MA

Cathy Lurie
The Nancy Lurie Marks Family Foundation
Wellesley, MA

Nancy Lurie Marks, PhDhc
The Nancy Lurie Marks Family Foundation
Wellesley, MA

Iliana Magiati, PhD, DClinPsy
Assistant Professor/Chartered Clinical
  Psychologist
Department of Psychology
National University of Singapore
Singapore, Singapore

Kristin W. Malatino, PhD
Private Practice
Celebration, FL

James T. McCracken, MD
Semel Institute for Neuroscience and
  Human Behavior
Center for Autism Research and
  Treatment (CART)
Los Angeles, CA
Joseph Campbell Professor of Child
  Psychiatry and Vice Chair
Department of Psychiatry and
  Biobehavioral Sciences
David Geffen School of Medicine at UCLA
Los Angeles, CA

Christopher J. McDougle, MD
Director, Lurie Center for Autism
Massachusetts General Hospital
Lexington, MA
Nancy Lurie Marks Professor of Psychiatry
Harvard Medical School
Boston, MA

D. Scott McLeod, PhD
Executive Director
Aspire
Massachusetts General Hospital
Lurie Center for Autism
Lexington, MA
Instructor in Psychiatry
Harvard Medical School
Boston, MA

Maria Mody, PhD
Assistant Neuroscientist
Athinoula A. Martinos Center for
  Biomedical Imaging
Massachusetts General Hospital
Charlestown, MA
Lurie Center for Autism
MassGeneral Hospital *for* Children
Lexington, MA
Assistant Professor of Radiology
Harvard Medical School
Boston, MA

Tiffany J. Neal, PhD
Assistant Director
HANDS in Autism Interdisciplinary
  Training and Resource Center
Indiana University School of Medicine
Indianapolis, IN

Ann Neumeyer, MD
Medical Director, Lurie Center for Autism
MassGeneral Hospital *for* Children
Lexington, MA
Assistant Professor of Neurology
Harvard Medical School
Boston, MA

Lisa Nowinski, PhD
Staff Psychologist
Department of Psychiatry
Massachusetts General Hospital
Lurie Center for Autism
Lexington, MA
Instructor in Psychiatry
Harvard Medical School
Boston, MA

Samuel L. Odom, PhD
Director
Frank Porter Graham Child
  Development Institute
University of North Carolina at
  Chapel Hill
Chapel Hill, NC
Professor
School of Education
University of North Carolina at
  Chapel Hill
Chapel Hill, NC

Michelle L. Palumbo, MD
Lurie Center for Autism
MassGeneral Hospital *for* Children
Lexington, MA
Instructor in Pediatrics
Harvard Medical School
Boston, MA

Nigel P. Pierce, PhD
Assistant Professor
School of Education
North Carolina Central University
Durham, NC

Peter V. Rabins, MD, MPH
Member, Berman Institute of
  Bioethics
Johns Hopkins University
Baltimore, MD
Professor of Psychiatry and Behavioral
  Sciences
Johns Hopkins School of Medicine
Baltimore, MD

Allan L. Reiss, MD
Robbins Professor and Director, Center
  for Interdisciplinary Brain Sciences
  Research
Vice Chair, Department of Psychiatry &
  Behavioral Sciences
Professor of Radiology and of
  Pediatrics
Stanford University School of
  Medicine
Palo Alto, CA

Mustafa Sahin, MD, PhD
Department of Neurology
Boston Children's Hospital
Boston, MA
Associate Professor of Neurology
Harvard Medical School
Boston, MA

Clarence E. Schutt, PhD
The Nancy Lurie Marks Family Foundation
Wellesley, MA
Princeton University
Princeton, NJ

Tristram Smith, PhD
Strong Center for Developmental
  Disabilities
Division of Neurodevelopmental and
  Behavioral Pediatrics
Professor of Pediatrics
University of Rochester Medical Center
Rochester, NY

Melissa A. Sreckovic, MEd
Doctoral Candidate
Frank Porter Graham Child Development
  Institute
University of North Carolina at Chapel Hill
Chapel Hill, NC

Jennifer L. Stornelli, MOT, OTR/L
Occupational Therapist
Spaulding Rehabilitation Hospital
Lurie Center for Autism
Lexington, MA

Thayne L. Sweeten, PhD
Senior Lecturer
Department of Biology
Utah State University
Logan, UT

Naomi B. Swiezy, PhD, HSPP
Director
HANDS in Autism Interdisciplinary
  Training and Resource Center
Alan H. Cohen Family Professor of
  Psychiatry
Indiana University School of Medicine
Indianapolis, IN

Michael E. Talkowski, PhD
Director, Genomics and
  Technology Core
Psychiatric and Neurodevelopmental
  Genetics Unit
Molecular Neurogenetics Unit
Center for Human Genetic Research
Massachusetts General Hospital
Boston, MA
Assistant Professor of Neurology
Harvard Medical School
Boston, MA

Fred R. Volkmar, MD
Director, Child Study Center
Irving B. Harris Professor of Pediatrics,
  Psychiatry and Psychology
Yale University School of Medicine
New Haven, CT

Danielle Warner, MA
Community and Research Liaison
HANDS in Autism Interdisciplinary
  Training and Resource Center
Indiana University School of
  Medicine
Indianapolis, IN

John M. Williams, BFA
Winchester, MA

Brian Willoughby, PhD
Staff Psychologist
Department of Psychiatry
Massachusetts General Hospital
Learning and Emotional Assessment
  Program (LEAP)
Boston, MA
Instructor in Psychiatry
Harvard Medical School
Boston, MA

Katharine Zuckerman, MD, MPH
Assistant Professor
Division of General Pediatrics
Oregon Health & Science University
Portland, OR

Nicole R. Zürcher, PhD
Research Fellow
Athinoula A. Martinos Center for
  Biomedical Imaging
Massachusetts General Hospital
Charlestown, MA
Research Fellow in Radiology
Harvard Medical School
Boston, MA

BACKGROUND AND DIAGNOSTIC ASSESSMENT

FROM INFANTILE AUTISM TO AUTISM SPECTRUM

Evolution of the Diagnostic Concept

FRED R. VOLKMAR

HISTORICAL BACKGROUND AND AN OVERVIEW OF DIAGNOSTIC APPROACHES

Interest in both developmental and mental disorders increased markedly in the 19th century. Children with severe developmental problems (or what is now referred to as intellectual disability) became the focus both of research and of new approaches to care. Interest in so-called "feral" or "wild" children (presumably raised by animals but likely having autism) stimulated work on rehabilitation and the "nature–nurture" controversy (Wood, 1975) (Figure 1.1).

In the field of severe psychiatric disorders, the delineation of specific types of disorders in adults, such as schizophrenia (Bleuler, 1911/1950), further stimulated work on psychiatric taxonomies. The convergence of developmental factors with mental disorders in children also quickly led to extrapolation of "adult" disorders, particularly relative to what we now recognize as schizophrenia (de Sanctis, 1906/1973). In this context, the development of a new field—child psychiatry—by Leo Kanner (1935) led to diagnostic approaches unique to children.

Issues of diagnosis and classification of childhood-onset disorders began to be addressed in official diagnostic systems such as the American Psychiatric Association's *Diagnostic and Statistical Manual of Mental Disorders* (DSM), which is now in its 5th edition (DSM-5; American Psychiatric Association (APA), 2013), and the World Health Organization's *International Classification of Disease*, currently in its 10th edition (ICD-10), with both a clinical and research version (World Health Organization, 1987, 1990).

There are various purposes for classification systems, including facilitation of communication and clinical service, research, and policy/public health planning. In the United States, diagnostic labels also have importance for entitlement to service. Classification schemes face many challenges, including appropriate consideration of age and developmental aspects of syndrome expression, gender, and cultural factors. Tensions arise around the balance of comprehensive clinical coverage and research definitions—the latter of course tending to usually be more stringent (Volkmar, Schwab-Stone, & First, 2002; Rutter, 2011). Other issues arise when dealing with the complex issue of comorbidity—that is, of having

FIGURE 1.1 Victor of Aveyron (c. 1788–1828) was a French feral child who was found in 1800 after apparently spending the majority of his childhood alone in the woods. Upon his discovery, his case was taken up by a young physician, Jean Marc Gaspard Itard, who worked with the boy for five years and gave him his name, Victor. Itard was interested in determining what Victor could learn. He devised procedures to teach the boy words and recorded his progress. Based on his work with Victor, Itard broke new ground in the education of the developmentally delayed. Itard, J.M.G. (1962). Der Wilde von Aveyron [portrait]. The Wild Boy of Aveyron. New York, NY: Appleton-Century-Crofts. (Original works published 1802).

more than one disorder (Rutter, 1997). Although categorical approaches to diagnosis have tended to dominate in medicine, these are not incompatible with dimensional approaches. Increasingly, dimensional and categorical approaches have had complex relationships and, as discussed later with regard to DSM-5, have featured even more prominently in new diagnostic approaches. There are complex issues of developmental consideration for diagnostic systems in terms of both onset and impact, and the risk for other problems should not be underappreciated, particularly for early onset disorders such as autism. The advance of a multiaxial approach to diagnosis (Rutter, Shaffer, & Shepherd, 1975) led to more careful consideration of these and other factors, and the complex changes attempted in DSM-5 may or may not improve on this older approach (Rutter, 2011). Finally, the issue of consideration of etiology in diagnosis presents challenges for diagnostic systems. For example, even for a disorder such as Down syndrome (trisomy 21), there may be considerable heterogeneity in outcome. In the case of Rett's disorder—a condition included specifically in DSM-IV

(APA, 1994) because it was thought that it would likely have a specific etiology—the discovery of a genetic basis led to a decision in DSM-5 not to give the condition specific diagnostic status, presumably in part because it was believed that it is more its own distinct entity. In addition, the more "autistic-like" features of Rett's disorder were believed to be confined to the preschool years, thus making it less suitable for inclusion in the new Autism Spectrum Disorder (ASD) category. Changes in diagnostic systems present both opportunities and challenges. Opportunities arise given the potential for strongly data-based revisions to improve the diagnostic system; on the other hand, major changes have potential for disrupting ongoing studies, complicating epidemiological studies, and potentially complicating interpretation of previous research and impacting service provision.

FROM KANNER'S REPORT TO DSM-III

Although it seems likely that children with autism had been observed by others (Candland, 1995; Wolff, 2004), Kanner was the first person to recognize the condition now known as autistic disorder or ASD. In 1943, he published the classic work on this topic reporting on 11 children who Kanner believed had a congenital inability to be social (Kanner, 1943). He was careful to frame his description developmentally citing the work of Arnold Gesell at Yale University that documented how social typical infants were with others (Gesell, 1934). Kanner emphasized that the condition he described was characterized by two essential features—autism (extreme social isolation) and a need for sameness (i.e., intolerance of change) in the nonsocial world. He suggested that the condition was congenital and noted many, if not most, of the features still recognized as typical in "classic" autism (Volkmar, Reichow, & McPartland, 2012). His work also noted features such as high educational levels among parents and his impression of the potential for normal intellectual functioning. His use of the word "autism" led to a mistaken impression that the disorder was related to schizophrenia (Volkmar et al., 2012) (Figure 1.2).

Subsequent work suggested that most children with autism also had overall IQs in the intellectual deficient range even though marked scatter of abilities was sometimes observed (Goldstein, Naglieri, & Ozonoff, 2009; Harris, 2006). There was the mistaken impression in the 1950s that autism might result from some form of parental neglect, "refrigerator mothers." However, as longitudinal data were collected, the presence of distinctive features (e.g., adolescent-onset seizures) (Volkmar & Nelson, 1990), the apparently strong genetic basis of the condition (Folstein & Rutter, 1977), and differences in clinical phenomenology and onset pattern (Kolvin, 1972) clarified its strong neurobiological and genetic basis. Other work made it clear that there was no particular social class bias for autism (Wing, 1980).

As these issues were clarified in the 1960s and 1970s, research on autism began to increase. The pioneering work of a father, Bernard Rimland, helped refocus research on neurobiological mechanisms and provided the first diagnostic rating instrument for the condition (Rimland, 1964). During the 1970s, studies of treatment suggested that structured, behaviorally focused interventions were much more effective than the previously dominant unstructured, psychodynamic approaches (Rutter & Bartak, 1973).

The growing consensus on autism's validity as a diagnostic category led to the elaboration, in the late 1970s, of two sets of diagnostic guidelines. Rutter's (1978) approach emphasized abnormal social and communication development (not just due to associated intellectual disability) associated with the pattern of unusual behavioral responses (stereotyped mannerisms and difficulties with change) and early onset. In contrast, the National Society for Autistic Children's definition (Ritvo & Freeman, 1978) focused on issues such

FIGURE 1.2 Leo Kanner, M.D. was a child psychiatrist at Johns Hopkins University School of Medicine. He published the first American textbook on child psychiatry in 1935. A portrait of Leo Kanner, M.D. by Nicholas Pavloff. Reprinted with permission of the Alan Mason Chesney Medical Archives of the Johns Hopkins Medical Institutions.

as unusual rates or sequences of development and hyper/hyposensitivity to the environment. These attempts were influential given the move within psychiatry toward a more research-based diagnostic criteria approach as exemplified by the group at Washington University (Spitzer, Endicott, & Robbins, 1978). As noted previously, the advent of a multiaxial classification scheme seemed to offer considerable promise for developmental disorders, and a major re-undertaking of the DSM occurred with DSM-III (APA, 1980; Spitzer et al., 1978). Changes in approaches to diagnosis in DSM are summarized in Box 1.1.

DSM-III AND DSM-III-R

Given the body of work showing the distinctiveness of autism, a decision was made to include "infantile autism" in DSM-III (APA, 1980) as part of a new class of disorders (Pervasive Developmental Disorders (PDD)). As might be suspected, the original definition focused on the more "classic" presentation of autism, and to address developmental change, a category of "residual infantile autism" was included for cases who had once met the more rigorous "infantile autism" criteria. The definition used for infantile autism was

BOX 1.1
CHANGES IN APPROACHES TO AUTISM DIAGNOSIS FROM DSM-I TO DSM-5

DSM-I (1952) and DSM-II (1968)

Autism was not officially recognized. A limited number of diagnoses existed for childhood-onset disorders.

DSM-III (1980)

Infantile autism and residual autism were included in a new "class" of disorder (Pervasive Developmental Disorders (PDD)) along with a "late-onset" form of autism (childhood-onset PDD) and "subthreshold" PDD (atypical PDD). Advantages included use of a multiaxial approach and a research criteria approach to definition. A major disadvantage was the lack of a developmental orientation.

DSM-III-R (1987)

Autistic disorder and a new term for "subthreshold" PDD (Pervasive Developmental Disorder, Not Otherwise Specified (PDD-NOS)) were put forth. An advantage included a greater developmental orientation (polythetic criteria) but likely an overly broad diagnostic concept.

DSM-IV (1994)

In addition to autistic disorder, other conditions (Asperger's disorder, Rett's disorder, and childhood disintegrative disorder) were recognized along with PDD-NOS. Advantages for autism included convergence with the ICD-10 definition and good balance of sensitivity and specificity over IQ range as well as flexible polythetic definitions. Disadvantages included controversy regarding inclusion of "new" disorders, particularly Asperger's disorder. With the convergence of DSM-IV and ICD-10, research comparability was enhanced and resulted in an explosion of research papers.

DSM-IV-TR (text revision) (2004)

There were no changes in criteria (although there was a minor change in the description of PDD-NOS to make it clear that social difficulties have to be present). Major changes were made in the text description of Asperger's disorder.

DSM-5 (2013)

Autism spectrum disorder and the new concept of social communication disorder (the latter being a communication disorder) were put forth. Autism spectrum disorder replaces autistic disorder as well as the PDD term. Although use of "spectrum" implies broader definition, the actual definition is probably much more focused on "classic" autism, with many more able cases likely facing loss of label. As a result, a "grandfathering" rule was adopted (for cases with an older diagnosis but not for new cases). The subthreshold concept was dropped, and reliance was placed on data from diagnostic instruments rather than field trials. Adoption of a grandfathering rule effectively keeps both the old and the new system in current use, likely complicating research—particularly epidemiological and longitudinal studies.

"monothetic" (every criterion had to be met) and rather inflexible. The failure to address developmental change seemed to suggest that older and more able individuals were not significantly in need of services, and this was unfortunate. On the other hand, just the recognition of autism was an advance, as were other aspects of DSM-III (e.g., the multi-axial system). Various changes were made in the revision of DSM-III (DSM-III-R), which appeared in 1987 (APA, 1987).

In DSM-III-R, a major attempt was made to provide a more flexible and developmentally oriented set of criteria. The name of the disorder was changed to autistic disorder, and 16 detailed criteria were listed. These were grouped into three major domains of dysfunction: qualitative impairment in reciprocal social interaction and in communication, as well as restricted interests. Eight criteria from the 16 had to be present, with at least 2 from the social interaction domain and 1 each from the other two categories. The polythetic approach gave greater flexibility, although the final definition was also problematic in that the IQ level impacted the diagnosis significantly (Volkmar, Cicchetti, Bregman, & Cohen, 1992). This may have resulted from some weaknesses in the field trial used to develop the final scoring rule (Spitzer & Siegel, 1990). Unlike DSM-III, which relied heavily on historical information, DSM-III-R emphasized current examination. Unfortunately, it also became clear that it diverged significantly from the draft ICD-10 revision.

ICD-10 AND DSM-IV

The draft of the World Health Organization's ICD-10 differed from DSM-III-R in several ways. A major difference was the ICD-10 "two-book" approach with one book of clinical guidelines and a different book that presented research diagnostic criteria. Other differences existed as well, including, for autism, the tentative decision to have a rather different approach both to the diagnosis of autism and to the potential inclusion of other disorders (e.g., Asperger syndrome) as part of the overarching PDD class of conditions. It was clear that the potential for markedly different US and international approaches to diagnosis might significantly impact research, for example, in generalizing results across studies (Volkmar et al., 1992).

There were multiple facets of the DSM-IV (APA, 1994) revision process. These included reviewing specific issues and a series of commissioned literature reviews that appeared well early in the revision process. For autism, a major issue was the ICD-10's listing of other disorders in the overarching PDD category—that is, Asperger syndrome, Rett's syndrome, and childhood disintegrative disorder. There was general agreement that having some consensus between DSM-IV and ICD-10 would enhance research. Another set of papers focused on data analysis/reanalysis of differences between DSM-III-R and ICD-10 (the latter in its draft version). On balance, DSM-III-R was clearly more developmentally oriented but probably overdiagnosed autism in the more cognitively disabled and possibly underdiagnosed it in the most able (Volkmar et al., 1992). A large international field trial was undertaken in conjunction with an evaluation of the draft ICD-10 criteria (Volkmar et al., 1994). This included more than 20 sites throughout the world, with more than 100 raters providing information on nearly 1000 cases. Unlike the DSM-III-R field trial, for a case to be included, the clinician had to believe that autism was a reasonable possibility in the differential diagnosis. Information on raters was also collected. Typically, the raters had multiple sources of information available to them.

The results suggested that DSM-III-R had a high rate of false positives if significant intellectual disability was present (nearly 60%). The draft ICD-10 criteria worked well but were quite detailed and more numerous than was typical for DSM. A series of statistical analyses, including inter-rater reliability and factor analysis, were undertaken. Several different potential solutions emerged in the factor analysis. One included the traditional triad of domains of difficulty (social, communication, and restricted interests), but other potential solutions included a two-factor approach (social communication and restricted interests) and a five-factor solution (in which restricted interests criteria were sorted into three groups). Efforts were made to reduce the number of criteria in ICD-10, and the final version of DSM-IV/ICD-10 had a good balance of clinical and research utility.

In terms of compatibility with ICD-10, another set of issues for DSM-IV had to do with inclusion of other conditions within the overarching PDD category. For all these potential "new" categories, literature reviews were commissioned and, to the extent possible, data were obtained from reviews of existing data or data reanalysis and, to some extent, from the DSM-IV field trial. Two of these conditions—Rett's disorder and childhood disintegrative disorder—were characterized by developmental regression and loss of skills. For Rett's disorder, the subsequent course and other clinical features of the disorder (e.g., it appeared to be largely, if not entirely, confined to girls) were quite distinctive, although there was a period, particularly during the preschool years, when there was potential for confusion with autism (Tsai, 1997; VanAcker, Loncola, & VanAcker, 2005).

Although the decision to include it was somewhat controversial, it appeared important to include it somewhere in DSM because the genetic etiology of the condition had been identified (Gillberg, 1994; Rutter, 1994; VanAcker et al., 2005). Childhood disintegrative disorder (sometimes referred to in the past as disintegrative psychosis or Heller's syndrome) was a clearly rare condition in which children developed a relatively "classic" autism presentation but after years, sometimes many years, of normal development. Here, data from earlier studies of its differences from autism (Volkmar & Cohen, 1989) and results of data from the field trial (Volkmar et al., 1994; Volkmar & Rutter, 1995) supported its inclusion—not because it was common but because the onset was so distinctive. For Asperger's disorder, inclusion of the condition in DSM-IV was more controversial. Following its first description in 1944 (Asperger, 1944), interest in the condition was minimal until the publication of Lorna Wing's (1981) review and case series (Figure 1.3).

Subsequent to Wing's description, rather divergent views of the condition proliferated (Gillberg, 1986; Klin, McPartland, & Volkmar, 2005; Szatmari, 1991). Although not a major focus of the DSM-IV field trial, data on a number of cases with a clinician-assigned diagnosis of Asperger's disorder had been submitted, and the data suggested differences both from higher functioning autism and from PDD, Not Otherwise Specified (PDD-NOS) (Volkmar et al., 1994). After much debate, the condition was included, although ambivalence about its inclusion led to several unfortunate and problematic aspects of its definition—thus inadvertently contributing to ongoing debate about it (Bennett et al., 2008; Miller & Ozonoff, 1997; Woodbury-Smith, Klin, & Volkmar, 2005). It clearly is the case that inclusion of the condition markedly stimulated research interest (approximately 75 papers were published between 1944 and 1993, and nearly 2000 papers have been published subsequent to DSM-IV). As a practical matter, its inclusion increased compatibility with ICD-10, suggested (given better preserved verbal language and differences in clinical presentation) potentially different treatments, and, given the impression of a strong family history of similar problems in male relatives, suggested a research importance as well (Klin, Pauls, Schultz, & Volkmar, 2005).

The "subthreshold" category of PDD-NOS was included, consistent with the rest of DSM-IV, to be available for individuals whose difficulties were clinically significant and suggestive of autism without meeting full criteria for the condition. PDD-NOS (previously

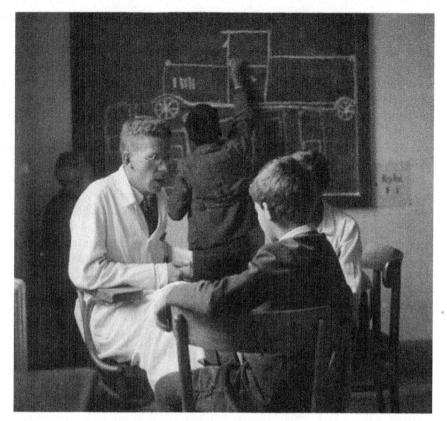

FIGURE 1.3 Univ. -Prof. Dr. Hans Asperger als junger Assistenzarzt in der Heilpädagogischen Ambulanz der Wiener Universitäts—Kinderklinik [photograph]. Fotoarchiv der ehemaligen Heilpädagogischen Station. Reprinted with permission from the private collection of Dr. Maria Asperger Felder. **Caption roughly translates to "University Professor Dr. Hans Asperger as a young doctor in the outpatient clinic of the University of Vienna, Special Education—Children's Hospital".

called atypical PDD) had its conceptual roots, in some ways, with early descriptions of unusual personality patterns characterized by unusual sensitivities and social difficulties (Rank, 1949, 1955; Towbin, 2005). It had been clear for some time that such cases significantly outnumbered those with "classic" autism, and debate centered on the degree to which these conditions were part of a broader autism phenotype (Scheeren & Stauder, 2008, Towbin, 2005).

DIMENSIONAL DIAGNOSTIC APPROACHES

Dimensional diagnostic approaches have had an increasing impact on both research and categorical approaches. This has been particularly true of DSM, for which such instruments have been used to develop new definitions. In autism, the first diagnostic checklist was developed by Rimland (1964). It has been followed by a host of other instruments—some for screening and others for formal diagnostic assessment and still others as research tools (e.g., for assessing social impairment) (Constantino et al., 2003; Coonrod & Stone, 2005;

Gillham, Carter, Volkmar, & Sparrow, 2003; Lord & Corsello, 2005). Some instruments focus specifically on special populations, such as very young children or the more cognitively able; some are based on parent or teacher report, and others are based on direct observation/interaction. For more complicated instruments, extensive training and demonstration of reliability are needed.

Challenges for dimensional approaches include the broad range of syndrome expression over both age and IQ levels. Other issues arise with regard to approach (historical information or current assessment), and still others arise relative to behaviors that are highly atypical or infrequent but important (e.g., self-injury). Some instruments allow clinical judgment to enter in, whereas others are less flexible. As a general rule, such instruments work best for school-age children and those with borderline to mild intellectual impairments. Challenges arise for the very young and for both low and high cognitive functioning individuals.

Clearly, the ability to characterize relevant clinical areas with dimensional measures has many advantages for research, particularly relative to issues of "broader phenotype." Measures of symptom severity may also be useful in monitoring progress in treatment. These issues have special relevance in DSM-5, which relied considerably on dimensional research instruments. On the one hand, the desire to use such well-standardized instruments is understandable (Regier, Narrow, Kuhl, & Kupfer, 2010). It may also create important challenges—that is, as items are moved from a highly structured and supervised research context to "real-world" settings.

MOVING TOWARD DSM-5

For DSM-5 criteria, an attempt was made to use the detailed data from research diagnostic instruments to improve on DSM-IV. Note that DSM-IV has the advantage of being consistent with ICD-10, and it provided a flexible and developmentally oriented criteria set that appeared to work well over the range of IQ and intellectual ability. Indeed, in the two decades after DSM-IV was published, there has been a truly dramatic increase in research in autism (Volkmar, 2014). It appears that having had very comparable international and US systems helped stimulate this research and comparability of findings across countries. The growing body of interest and research on autism also appeared to be associated with gradual improvement in outcome (Howlin, 2013), as well as increased understanding of basic mechanisms—both genetic (Rutter & Thapar, 2013) and neural (McPartland, Coffman, & Pelphrey, 2011).

Although research grew dramatically since DSM-IV and ICD-10 appeared, some areas of concern also arose. The DSM-IV field trial was very large and international but not truly epidemiological, and concerns were raised that the criteria proposed might be less applicable to very young children, many of whom did not always show all required features until ages 2 or 3 years (Chawarska, Klin, & Volkmar, 2008). Other issues were raised about either the validity or the definition of the DSM-IV PDD subtypes—particularly concerning Asperger's disorder (Howlin, 2003; Mayes, Calhoun, & Crites, 2001; Ozonoff & Griffith, 2000)—although, as noted previously, it is clear that diagnostic consensus is most divergent around very high functioning cases and other reports suggested both that the DSM-IV Asperger's disorder criteria could be used (Woodbury-Smith et al., 2005) and that rigorous definitions of Asperger's disorder were more likely to be associated with independent validators of the condition (IQ profiles, psychiatric history, and family history) (Klin, Volkmar, Sparrow, Ciccetti, & Rourke, 1995; Klin et al., 2005; Lincoln, Bloom, Katz, & Boksenbaum,

1998). In DSM-IV-TR (APA, 2000), the entire text for Asperger's disorder was replaced, although no changes were allowed in criteria. The diverse approaches to the diagnosis of Asperger's disorder (many originating in the 1980s, well before DSM-IV appeared) contributed to confusion on these issues. Lord (2011) suggested that assessment location was a major determinant of consistent use of Asperger's disorder. Other issues had to do with inclusion of Rett's disorder in DSM-5, given its strong genetic basis, and whether the rare condition of childhood disintegrative disorder could be reliably identified and was most appropriately included with autism. Finally, concern about the lack of an explicit approach to the definition of the broader PDD-NOS group was expressed.

DSM-5 AND AUTISM SPECTRUM DISORDER

Several overall decisions led to major changes in the approach to the diagnosis of autism in DSM-5 (APA, 2013). These included the decision to eliminate as much as possible subthreshold conditions, to move to dimensional ratings of symptoms, to no longer use the multiaxial system, and to utilize data from diagnostic instruments rather than field trials as the primary basis for testing the efficiency of criteria proposed. For autism and related disorders, the older class of PDDs was dropped in favor of a single Autism Spectrum Disorder (ASD), with a related disorder, Social Communication Disorder (SCD) (coded in the communication section of DSM-5), added. On the basis of factor analysis of a large body of data from diagnostic instruments, a decision was made to drop the traditional three-factor approach to diagnosis (social problems, communication problems, and restricted interests/behaviors) in favor of a two-factor (social–communication and restricted interests) model. The number of criteria was reduced and for the social–communication category became monothetic (the individual had to exhibit all features), whereas in the restricted and repetitive criteria, two of four symptom groupings were needed. A sensory criterion was also added to this grouping. The new SCD was defined by pragmatic difficulties and problems in the use of verbal and nonverbal communication in social situations, and although similar to PDD-NOS, the condition was included as a communication disorder rather than ASD. Changes were also made so that the severity of symptoms could be specified, and modifications were made in the approach to early onset as a diagnostic feature. As noted later, the worry that DSM-5 would disqualify individuals for a diagnosis led to an additional rule so that patients with well-established DSM-IV diagnoses on the autism spectrum could retain them, thus effectively creating two systems in current use. Given the abandonment of the multiaxial approach, specifiers could be used to indicate if a known etiological factor was present, as well as the level of need for support objectives. Other specifiers allowed for an indication of intellectual disability and language impairment. A final specifier could be used to note that catatonia was present.

Even before DSM-5 appeared, several studies were published evaluating the new approach. The focus of many such studies was how well the new approach worked in more "real-world" settings (i.e., apart from the diagnostic instruments) and whether major changes in diagnostic practice would result. These studies generally indicated that higher functioning individuals—particularly those with Asperger's disorder and PDD-NOS in DSM-IV terms—were likely to lose their diagnosis (Gibbs, Aldridge, Chandler, Witzlsperger, & Smith, 2012; Mattila et al., 2011; McPartland, Reichow, & Volkmar, 2012; Taheri & Perry, 2012; Wilson et al., 2013; Worley & Matson, 2012). This was also true, to a lesser extent, for more cognitively able individuals with autistic disorder in DSM-IV terms. Other studies raised concerns about the application of criteria to younger children, a major concern given the need for early intervention (Matson, Kozlowski, Hattier, Horovitz, & Sipes, 2012). In some ways, these results should not be viewed as surprising given that the diagnostic instruments chosen to develop the new criteria worked best (as most such instruments do) for school-age children with borderline to mild intellectual impairments. Thus, most of the studies now available suggest that DSM-5 criteria offer greater specificity but with lowered sensitivity for specific subgroups such as the more cognitively able, but socially impaired, young children and cases with the DSM-IV "PDD-NOS" diagnosis. As Tsai (2012) noted, the sensitivity and specificity that will be evident in purely clinical (i.e., rather than research) settings remain unclear. Several investigators have already made recommendations for improvements in DSM-5 (Barton, Robins, Jashar, Brennan, & Fein, 2013; Wilson et al., 2013).

Other work has addressed the change from a three- to a two-factor grouping of symptom domains (Sipes & Matson, 2014) and suggested that several different factor solutions are possible. Similarly, the DSM-IV field trial factor analysis yielded reasonable two-, three-, or five-factor solutions (Volkmar et al., 1994), but the three-factor solution was adopted in DSM-IV and ICD-10 to give the most robust set of possible combinations of criteria (more than 2000 possible combinations of the 12 criteria could result in a diagnosis of autism). The reduced number of items and factors in DSM-5 vastly reduced the number of potential combinations.

The advent of DSM-5 brings potential opportunities, as well as some concerns. The use of research instruments in research settings is clearly of great benefit—their applicability in clinical settings in which individuals do not have extensive experience or training remains unclear. The potential for creating effectively two systems (the new and the old "grandfathered" approach) can present challenges, for example, for longitudinal and epidemiological studies. Another major concern is the potential for a more stringent system to reduce access to services both for the very young and for the more cognitively able—many of whom already face challenges in securing services. Ghaziuddin (2010) has questioned the potential loss of information for research using DSM-5. Other challenges arise given pending changes in ICD-11 (currently in preparation), with the real possibility that multiple diagnostic approaches will be in current use, potentially severely compromising comparability of samples. Clearly, collapsing or removing subtypes makes it difficult to validate them (Baron-Cohen, 2009; Ghanizadeh, 2011; Mandy, Charman, & Skuse, 2011). Other investigators have raised a range of concerns. For example, Wing, Gould, and Gillberg (2011) noted a potential difficulty given nonspecificity of sensory behavior. Given all these issues, it is possible that DSM-5 groupings may become less relevant to research, as the former director of the National Institute of Mental Health has suggested (Insel, 2013).

SUMMARY

This chapter reviewed the emergence and evolution of the diagnosis and conceptualization of autism from the early work of Leo Kanner to the fifth edition of the DSM. Dimensional and categorical approaches to diagnosis were used, and the challenges and benefits of both approaches were identified. Attempts were made to consider the criteria in both the DSM and the ICD because changes were anticipated in one or the other so that commonalities could continue for the purposes of clinical and research classification of autism and related disorders throughout the world. It is hoped that the new Research Diagnostic Criteria (RDoC) for research on mental disorders will enhance the field's ability to diagnose meaningful subtypes of autism-related disorders so that targeted treatment approaches for individuals may one day be realized.

KEY POINTS

- The purposes of classification systems include facilitation of communication and clinical service, research, policy/public health planning, and entitlement to service.
- Leo Kanner, MD, was the first person to recognize and describe the condition now known as autism spectrum disorder.
- "Infantile Autism" first appeared in DSM-III as part of a new class of disorders called Pervasive Developmental Disorders.
- The diagnosis of Asperger's disorder first appeared in DSM-IV. This disorder is largely differentiated from "classic autism" based on normal language development and normal cognitive development.
- In DSM-5, the five subtypes of Pervasive Developmental Disorder were collapsed into one broad diagnostic category called Autism Spectrum Disorder.

DISCLOSURE STATEMENT

Dr. Fred R. Volkmar has nothing to disclose.

REFERENCES

American Psychiatric Association. (1980). *Diagnostic and statistical manual of mental disorders* (3rd ed.). Washington, DC: Author.

American Psychiatric Association. (1987). *Diagnostic and statistical manual of mental disorders* (3rd ed., rev.). Washington, DC: Author.

American Psychiatric Association. (1994). *Diagnostic and statistical manual of mental disorders* (4th ed.). Washington, DC: Author.

American Psychiatric Association. (2000). *Diagnostic and statistical manual of mental disorders* (4th ed., text rev.). Washington, DC: Author.

American Psychiatric Association. (2013). *Diagnostic and statistical manual of mental disorders* (5th ed.). Arlington, VA: American Psychiatric Publishing.

Asperger, H. (1944). Die "autistichen Psychopathen" im Kindersalter. *Archive fur psychiatrie und Nervenkrankheiten, 117,* 76–136.

Baron-Cohen, S. (2009, November 9). The short life of a diagnosis. *The New York Times.* Retrieved from http://www.nytimes.com

Barton, M. L., Robins, D. L., Jashar, D., Brennan, L., & Fein, D. (2013). Sensitivity and specificity of proposed DSM-5 criteria for autism spectrum disorder in toddlers. *Journal of Autism and Developmental Disorders, 43*(5), 1184–1195.

Bennett, T., Szatmari, P., Bryson, S., Volden, J., Zwaigenbaum, L., Vaccarella, L., . . . Boyle, M. (2008). Differentiating autism and Asperger syndrome on the basis of language delay or impairment. *Journal of Autism and Developmental Disorders, 38*(4), 616–625.

Bleuler, E. (1950). *Dementia praecox or the group of schizophrenias* (J. Zinkin, Trans.). New York, NY: International Universities Press. (Original work published 1911)

Candland, D. C. (1995). *Feral children and clever animals: Reflections on human nature.* New York, NY: Oxford University Press.

Chawarska, K., Klin, A., & Volkmar, F. R. (Eds.). (2008). *Autism spectrum disorders in infants and tod-dlers: Diagnosis, assessment, and treatment*. New York, NY: Guilford.

Constantino, J. N., Davis, S. A., Todd, R. D., Schindler, M. K., Gross, M. M., Brophy, S. L., . . . Reich, W. (2003). Validation of a brief quantitative measure of autistic traits: Comparison of the social responsiveness scale with the Autism Diagnostic Interview–Revised. *Journal of Autism and Developmental Disorders, 33*(4), 427–433.

Coonrod, E. E., & Stone, W. L. (2005). Screening for autism in young children. In F. R. Volkmar, A. Klin, R. Paul, & D. J. Cohen (Eds.), *Handbook of autism and pervasive developmental disorders* (3rd ed., pp. 707–729). Hoboken, NJ: Wiley.

de Sanctis, S. (1973). On some variations of dementia praecox. In S. A. Szurek & I. N. Berlin (Eds.), *Clinical studies in childhood psychosis*. New York, NY: Brunner/Mazel. (Original work published 1906)

Folstein, S., & Rutter, M. (1977). Genetic influences and infantile autism. *Nature, 265*(5596), 726–728.

Gesell, A. (1934). *Atlas of infant behavior*. New Haven, CT: Yale University Press.

Ghanizadeh, A. (2011). Can retaining Asperger syndrome in DSM-V help establish neurobiological endophenotypes? *Journal of Autism and Developmental Disorders, 41*(1), 130.

Ghaziuddin, M. (2010). Should the DSM V drop Asperger syndrome? *Journal of Autism and Developmental Disorders, 40*(9), 1146–1148.

Gibbs, V., Aldridge, F., Chandler, F., Witzlsperger, E., & Smith, K. (2012). An exploratory study comparing diagnostic outcomes for autism spectrum disorders under DSM-IV-TR with the proposed DSM-5 revision. *Journal of Autism and Developmental Disorders, 42*(8), 1750–1756.

Gillberg, C. (1986). Asperger's syndrome: Does it exist? *Psykisk Halsa, 27*(3), 184–191.

Gillberg, C. (1994). Debate and argument: Having Rett syndrome in the ICD-10 PDD category does not make sense. *Journal of Child Psychology and Psychiatry, 35*(2), 377–378.

Gillham, J. E., Carter, A. S., Volkmar, F. R., & Sparrow, S. S. (2003). Toward a developmental operational definition of autism. In M. E. Hertzig & E. A. Farber (Eds.), *Annual progress in child psychiatry and child development: 2000–2001* (pp. 363–381). New York, NY: Brunner-Routledge.

Goldstein, S., Naglieri, J. A., & Ozonoff, S. (Eds.). (2009). *Assessment of autism spectrum disorders* (pp. xiv, 384). New York, NY: Guilford.

Harris, J. C. (2006). *Intellectual disability: Understanding its development, causes, classification, evaluation, and treatment*. New York, NY: Oxford University Press.

Howlin, P. (2003). Outcome in high-functioning adults with autism with and without early language delays: Implications for the differentiation between autism and Asperger syndrome. *Journal of Autism and Developmental Disorders, 33*(1), 3–13.

Howlin, P. (2013). Outcomes in adults with autism spectrum disorders. In F. R. Volkmar, S. Rogers, R. Paul, & K. Pelphrey (Eds.), *Handbook of autism and pervasive developmental disorders* (4th ed., pp. 97–116). Hoboken, NJ: Wiley.

Insel, T. (2013, April 29). *Director's blog: Transforming diagnosis*. Retrieved from http://www.nimh.nih.gov/about/director/2013/transforming-diagnosis.shtml

Kanner, L. (1935). *Child psychiatry*. Springfield, IL: Thomas.

Kanner, L. (1943). Autistic disturbances of affective contact. *Nervous Child, 2*, 217–250.

Klin, A., McPartland, J., & Volkmar, F. R. (2005). Asperger syndrome. In F. R. Volkmar, A. Klin, R. Paul, & D. J. Cohen (Eds.), *Handbook of autism and pervasive developmental disorders* (3rd ed., pp. 88–125). Hoboken, NJ: Wiley.

Klin, A., Pauls, D., Schultz, R., & Volkmar, F. (2005). Three diagnostic approaches to Asperger syndrome: Implications for research. *Journal of Autism and Developmental Disorders, 35*(2), 221–234.

Klin, A., Volkmar, F. R., Sparrow, S. S., Cicchetti, D. V., & Rourke, B. P. (1995). Validity and neuropsychological characterization of Asperger syndrome: Convergence with nonverbal learning disabilities syndrome. *Journal of Child Psychology and Psychiatry, 36*(7), 1127–1140.

Kolvin, I. (1972). Infantile autism or infantile psychoses. *British Medical Journal, 3*(5829), 753–755.

Lincoln, A. J., Bloom, D., Katz, M., & Boksenbaum, N. (1998). Neuropsychological and neurophysiological indices of auditory processing impairment in children with multiple complex developmental disorder. *Journal of the American Academy of Child and Adolescent Psychiatry, 37*(1), 100–112.

Lord, C. (2011). Epidemiology: How common is autism? *Nature, 474*(7350), 166–168.

Lord, C., & Corsello, C. (2005). Diagnostic instruments in autism spectrum disorders. In F. R. Volkmar, A. Klin, R. Paul, & D. J. Cohen (Eds.), *Handbook of autism and pervasive developmental disorders* (3rd ed., pp. 730–771). Hoboken, NJ: Wiley.

Mandy, W. P., Charman, T., & Skuse, D. H. (2011). Testing the construct validity of proposed criteria for DSM-5 autism spectrum disorder. *Journal of the American Academy of Child and Adolescent Psychiatry, 51*(1), 41–50.

Matson, J. L., Kozlowski, A. M., Hattier, M. A., Horovitz, M., & Sipes, M. (2012). DSM-IV vs DSM-5 diagnostic criteria for toddlers with autism. *Developmental Neurorehabilitation, 15*(3), 185–190.

Mattila, M. L., Kielinen, M., Linna, S., Jussila, K., Ebeling, H., Bloigu, R., . . . Moilanen, I. (2011). Autism spectrum disorders according to DSM-IV-TR and comparison with DSM-5 draft criteria: An epidemiological study. *Journal of the American Academy of Child and Adolescent Psychiatry, 50*(6), 583–592.

Mayes, S. D., Calhoun, S. L., & Crites, D. L. (2001). Does DSM-IV Asperger's disorder exist? *Journal of Abnormal Child Psychology, 29*(3), 263–271.

McPartland, J. C., Coffman, M., & Pelphrey, K. A. (2011). Recent advances in understanding the neural bases of autism spectrum disorder. *Current Opinion in Pediatrics, 23*(6), 628–632.

McPartland, J. C., Reichow, B., & Volkmar, F. R. (2012). Sensitivity and specificity of proposed DSM-5 diagnostic criteria for autism spectrum disorder. *Journal of the American Academy of Child and Adolescent Psychiatry, 51*(4), 368–383.

Miller, J. N., & Ozonoff, S. (1997). Did Asperger's cases have Asperger's disorder? A research note. *Journal of Child Psychology and Psychiatry, 38*(2), 247–251.

Ozonoff, S., & Griffith, E. M. (2000). Neuropsychological function and the external validity of Asperger syndrome. In A. Klin & F. R. Volkmar (Eds.), *Asperger syndrome* (pp. 72–96). New York, NY: Guilford.

Rank, B. (1949). Adaptation of the psychoanalytic technique for the treatment of young children with atypical development. *American Journal of Orthopsychiatry, 19*(1), 130–139.

Rank, B. (1955). Intensive study and treatment of preschool children who show marked personality deviations, or "atypical development," and their parents. In G. Caplan (Ed.), *Emotional problems of early childhood* (pp. 491–501). Oxford, England: Basic Books.

Regier, D. A., Narrow, W. E., Kuhl, E. A., & Kupfer, D. J. (Eds.). (2010). *The conceptual evolution of DSM-5.* Arlington, VA: American Psychiatric Publishing.

Rimland, B. (1964). *Infantile autism: The syndrome and its implications for a neural theory of behavior.* New York, NY: Appleton-Century-Crofts.

Ritvo, E. R., & Freeman, B. J. (1978). Current research on the syndrome of autism: Introduction. The National Society for Autistic Children's definition of the syndrome of autism. *Journal of the American Academy of Child Psychiatry, 17*(4), 565–575.

Rutter, M. (1978). Diagnosis and definition of childhood autism. *Journal of Autism and Childhood Schizophrenia, 8*(2), 139–161.

Rutter, M. (1994). Psychiatric genetics: Research challenges and pathways forward. *American Journal of Medical Genetics, 54*(3), 185–198.

Rutter, M. (1997). Comorbidity: Concepts, claims and choices. *Criminal Behaviour and Mental Health, 7*(4), 265–285.

Rutter, M. (2011). Research review: Child psychiatric diagnosis and classification—Concepts, findings, challenges and potential. *Journal of Child Psychology and Psychiatry, 52*(6), 647–660.

Rutter, M., & Bartak, L. (1973). Special educational treatment of autistic children: A comparative study. II: Follow-up findings and implications for services. *Journal of Child Psychology and Psychiatry, 14*(4), 241–270.

Rutter, M., Shaffer, D., & Shepherd, M. (1975). *A multi-axial classification of child psychiatric disorders: An evaluation of a proposal.* Geneva: World Health Organization.

Rutter, M., & Thapar, A. (2013). Genetics of autism spectrum disorders. In F. R. Volkmar, S. Rogers, R. Paul, & K. Pelphrey (Eds.), *Handbook of autism and pervasive developmental disorders* (4th ed., pp. 411–423). Hoboken, NJ: Wiley.

Scheeren, A. M., & Stauder, J. E. A. (2008). Broader autism phenotype in parents of autistic children: Reality or myth? *Journal of Autism and Developmental Disorders, 38*(2), 276–287.

Sipes, M., & Matson, J. L. (2014). Factor structure for autism spectrum disorders with toddlers using DSM-IV and DSM-5 criteria. *Journal of Autism and Developmental Disorders, 44*(3), 636–647.

Spitzer, R. L., Endicott, J. E., & Robbins, E. (1978). Research diagnostic criteria. *Archives of General Psychiatry, 35*, 773–782.

Spitzer, R. L., & Siegel, B. (1990). The DSM-III-R field trial of pervasive developmental disorders. *Journal of the American Academy of Child and Adolescent Psychiatry, 29*(6), 855–862.

Szatmari, P. (1991). Asperger's syndrome: Diagnosis, treatment, and outcome. *Psychiatric Clinics of North America, 14*(1), 81–93.

Taheri, A., & Perry, A. (2012). Exploring the proposed DSM-5 criteria in a clinical sample. *Journal of Autism and Developmental Disorders, 42*(9), 1810–1817.

Towbin, K. E. (2005). Pervasive developmental disorder not otherwise specified. In F. R. Volkmar, A. Klin, R. Paul, & D. J. Cohen (Eds.), *Handbook of autism and pervasive developmental disorders* (3rd ed., pp. 165–200). Hoboken, NJ: Wiley.

Tsai, L. Y. (1997). Rett's syndrome: A subtype of pervasive developmental disorder? In T. A. Widiger, H. A. Pincus, R. Ross, M. B. First, & W. Davis (Eds.), *DSM-IV source book* (Vol. 3). Washington, DC: American Psychiatric Association.

Tsai, L. Y. (2012). Sensitivity and specificity: DSM-IV versus DSM-5 criteria for autism spectrum disorder. *American Journal of Psychiatry, 169*(10), 1009–1011.

VanAcker, R., Loncola, J. A., & VanAcker, E. Y. V. (2005). Rett syndrome: A pervasive developmental disorder. In F. R. Volkmar, A. Klin, R. Paul, & D. J. Cohen (Eds.), *Handbook of autism and pervasive developmental disorders* (3rd ed., pp. 126–164). Hoboken, NJ: Wiley.

Volkmar, F. (2014). Editorial: 2014 in review. *Journal of Autism and Developmental Disorders, 45*(3), 613–625.

Volkmar, F. R., Cicchetti, D. V., Bregman, J., & Cohen, D. J. (1992). Three diagnostic systems for autism: DSM-III, DSM-III–R, and ICD-10. *Journal of Autism and Developmental Disorders, 22*(4), 483–492.

Volkmar, F. R., & Cohen, D. J. (1989). Disintegrative disorder or "late onset" autism. *Journal of Child Psychology and Psychiatry and Allied Disciplines, 30*(5), 717–724.

Volkmar, F. R., Klin, A., Siegel, B., Szatmari, P., Lord, C., Campbell, M., . . . Towbin, K. (1994). Field trial for autistic disorder in DSM-IV. *American Journal of Psychiatry, 151*(9), 1361–1367.

Volkmar, F. R., & Nelson, D. S. (1990). Seizure disorders in autism. *Journal of the American Academy of Child and Adolescent Psychiatry, 29*(1), 127–129.

Volkmar, F. R., Reichow, B., & McPartland, J. (2012). Classification of autism and related conditions: Progress, challenges and opportunities. *Dialogues in Clinical Neuroscience, 14*(3), 229–237.

Volkmar, F. R., & Rutter, M. (1995). Childhood disintegrative disorder: Results of the DSM-IV autism field trial. *Journal of the American Academy of Child and Adolescent Psychiatry, 34*(8), 1092–1095.

Volkmar, F. R., Schwab-Stone, M., & First, M. (2002). Classification in child psychiatry: Principles and issues. In M. Lewis (Ed.), *Child and adolescent psychiatry: A comprehensive textbook* (3rd ed., pp. 499–506). Baltimore, MD: Williams & Wilkins.

Wilson, C. E., Gillan, N., Spain, D., Robertson, D., Roberts, G., Murphy, C. M., . . . Murphy, D. G. (2013). Comparison of ICD-10R, DSM-IV-TR and DSM-5 in an adult autism spectrum disorder diagnostic clinic. *Journal of Autism and Developmental Disorders, 43*(11), 2515–2525.

Wing, L. (1980). Childhood autism and social class: A question of selection? *British Journal of Psychiatry, 137*, 410–417.

Wing, L. (1981). Asperger's syndrome: A clinical account. *Psychological Medicine, 11*(1), 115–129.

Wing, L., Gould, J., & Gillberg, C. (2011). Autism spectrum disorders in the DSM-V: Better or worse than the DSM-IV? *Research in Developmental Disabilities, 32*(2), 768–773.

Wolff, S. (2004). The history of autism. *European Child & Adolescent Psychiatry, 13*(4), 201–208.

Wood, E. (1975). The wild boy of Aveyron ("Itard's syndrome"?). *Nursing Mirror and Midwives Journal, 140*(18), 61–63.

Woodbury-Smith, M., Klin, A., & Volkmar, F. (2005). Asperger's syndrome: A comparison of clinical diagnoses and those made according to the ICD-10 and DSM-IV. *Journal of Autism and Developmental Disorders, 35*(2), 235–240.

World Health Organization. (1987). *International classification of mental and behavioral disorders: Clinical and diagnostic guidelines. (10th ed.).—Clinical descriptions.* Geneva: Author.

World Health Organization. (1990). *International classification of mental and behavioral disorders: Diagnostic criteria for research* (10th ed.). Geneva: Author.

Worley, J. A., & Matson, J. L. (2012). Comparing symptoms of autism spectrum disorders using the current DSM-IV-TR diagnostic criteria and the proposed DSM-V diagnostic criteria. *Research in Autism Spectrum Disorders, 6*(2), 965–970.

/// 2 /// SOCIAL, COGNITIVE, AND BEHAVIORAL DEVELOPMENT OF CHILDREN AND ADOLESCENTS WITH AUTISM SPECTRUM DISORDER

KIRSTIN BROWN BIRTWELL,
BRIAN WILLOUGHBY, AND LISA NOWINSKI

INTRODUCTION

Autism spectrum disorder (ASD) is a heterogeneous neurodevelopmental condition composed of a wide "spectrum" of topographical characteristics and neuropsychological impairments. Although the ASD diagnosis has been found to be relatively stable across time (Gotham, Pickles, & Lord, 2012; Woolfenden, Sarkozy, Ridley, & Williams, 2012), developmental and functional trajectories of individuals with ASD vary considerably. Consequently, children at various developmental stages present to pediatricians, psychologists, psychiatrists, neurologists, and other health care professionals with concerns that may ultimately lead to an ASD diagnosis.

Recent research suggests that the broader phenotype of ASD may be detectable before 12 months of age (Ozonoff et al., 2014; Zwaigenbaum et al., 2005); however, ASD symptoms are typically visible between 12 and 24 months and may include delayed language development, unusual communication patterns, lack of social interest, atypical social interaction, and odd patterns of play (American Psychiatric Association (APA), 2013; Guthrie, Swineford, Nottke, & Wetherby, 2013). Nonetheless, in large community-based samples, the median age of diagnosis is older than age 4 years (Centers for Disease Control and Prevention, 2014; Shattuck et al., 2009). In some cases, in which early childhood symptoms may be more subtle, a diagnosis may not be made until late childhood or early adolescence (e.g., when increased social demands may elucidate skill deficits).

Determining the predictability and reliability of ASD over time has proven to be a challenging task for both the scientific community and the clinical community. For example, one-fourth to one-third of children with ASD experience significant social and communication skill regression in the second year of life (APA, 2013; Lord & Spence, 2006). Throughout early childhood and adolescence, the overall functional capacity among individuals diagnosed with ASD may differ extensively. For example, some children with ASD never develop functional expressive language abilities, whereas others present with superior verbal skills. Within ASD, individuals without structural language impairments have been found to present with fewer diagnostic symptoms and stronger adaptive communication, daily living, and socialization skills compared to those with structural language impairments when followed from early childhood to adolescence (Szatmari et al., 2009). Similarly, Baghdadli and colleagues (2012) demonstrated that language impairments and level of ASD symptom severity serve as risk factors for decreased social and communication functioning 10 years later. Although ASD is believed to be associated with innate neurobiological deficits that lead to chronic lifelong dysfunction, many individuals show global improvements in adolescence (McGovern & Sigman, 2005). Conversely, a small percentage of individuals deteriorate behaviorally in adolescence (APA, 2013).

Despite the heterogeneity within ASD, increased research, public awareness, and state- and federal-specific legislation and advocacy have led to important findings during the past two decades. There is still much to learn, but the field has made significant gains in understanding the social, cognitive, and behavioral developmental underpinnings of ASD.

SOCIAL FUNCTIONING

Given that social impairment is the hallmark characteristic of ASD, several researchers to date have explored how early social deficits disrupt the social and communicative developmental course. The current underlying social theories of neurodevelopment in ASD focus on the social motivation and the social cognition domains of functioning. Social motivation is an important area of focus given that these delays and disruptions are some of the first diagnostic indicators of ASD. For example, Wu and Chiang (2014) found that both typically developing infants and children aged 2–4 years with developmental delays followed a different sequence of social skill acquisition than children aged 2–4 years with ASD. Specifically, typically developing infants and developmentally delayed toddlers developed joint attention skills first, followed by object imitation and play, and referential language last, whereas children with ASD developed object imitation first, followed by responding to joint attention, play, referential language, and initiating joint attention skills last. Compared to their peers, children with ASD not only exhibit atypical social behaviors (e.g., repetitive behaviors) but also may develop different social skills at different times, further highlighting the need to more accurately identify the neurological origin of these social motivation deficiencies.

To this end, Dawson and colleagues proposed that an innate deficit in early attentional preferences for social stimuli may contribute to the larger social–behavioral profile of ASD, including attenuated joint attention, social orienting, emotion perception, imitation, and affective sharing (Bernier, Webb, & Dawson, 2006; Dawson, Meltzoff, Osterling, Rinaldi, & Brown, 1998). A central tenet to this theory is that the inherent social reward system in infant brain circuitry is disrupted, with most research to date identifying the dopaminergic system, modulated by oxytocin and vasopressin, as the central site of derailment (Rozga, Anderson, & Robins, 2011). Oxytocin, in particular, has garnered a tremendous amount of attention, with new research suggesting that deficient oxytocin function in ASD may directly contribute to decreased social motivation (Stavropoulos & Carver, 2013). Earlier research by Waterhouse, Fein, and Modahl (1996) also highlighted the importance of the amygdala and how a potentially ineffective social stimuli–emotional salience association may also contribute to decreased social motivation and initiation. Although the evidence regarding etiology is still emerging, impaired amygdala and oxytocin function appear to play important roles in the social–developmental deterioration associated with ASD.

In addition to the social motivation hypothesis, social cognitive theories, which address the inability to predict, process, and explain the behavior of others, highlight another important area of developmental disturbance in ASD. A widely accepted phenomenon, theory of mind (ToM), includes the difficulties that individuals with ASD have with perspective-taking skills and is credited to the work of Baron-Cohen, Leslie, and Frith (1985). Their work has indicated that children with ASD not only show significant delays in ToM skills but also may never acquire these skills to the extent that typical adolescents and adults do (Baron-Cohen, Jolliffe, Mortimore, & Robertson, 1997). These difficulties may explain both social and communicative deficits in ASD because meaningful and reciprocal conversation with others (a skill absent or significantly impaired in ASD) requires this ability to take the listener's perspective (Hale & Tager-Flusberg, 2005; Tager-Flusberg, 1996). Along with extensive behavioral research in ToM deficits, neuropsychological studies indicate that brain regions responsible for these skills (e.g., medial prefrontal cortex, anterior cingulate cortex, temporal poles adjacent to the amygdala, and superior temporal sulcus) may exhibit reduced activation in individuals with ASD (Rozga et al., 2011). In summary, both social motivation and social cognitive theories, and their neurobiological foundations, continue to be studied as potentially precipitating factors in the developmental emergence of ASD.

COGNITIVE FUNCTIONING

Among cognitive theories of development, executive functioning impairments and information processing models carry the most reliable empirical research support to date (Rozga et al., 2011). Executive functioning (EF) refers to a specific group of higher-level cognitive skills that are mediated by the prefrontal cortex region and required for complex problem-solving and goal-oriented behavior. EF skills include planning, organizing, working memory, cognitive flexibility, inhibition, and behavioral control, and impairments in this domain have been associated with learning disorders as well as psychiatric conditions such as attention deficit hyperactivity disorder and ASD (Corbett, Constantine, Hendren, Rocke, & Ozonoff, 2009). In ASD in particular, the restricted, repetitive, and stereotyped behaviors and interests characteristic of ASD appear to be related to the rigidity, difficulty with change, and lack of planning associated with EF deficits (Ozonoff, Pennington, & Rogers, 1991). For example, children with ASD typically have trouble when previously established routines (e.g., bedtime routine) are disrupted or rearranged. Given that EF deficits are observed across a wide variety of neurodevelopmental and learning disorders, recent research in this area has been tasked with determining what the unique ASD–EF profile may be. Some literature suggests that in individuals with ASD, cognitive and motor inhibition appears to be intact while deficits are primarily found in cognitive flexibility and attention (Ozonoff, South, & Provencal, 2005). Nonetheless, more research is needed in order to accurately determine the distinct EF profiles across diagnostic categories.

The second category of cognitive theories of development includes weak central coherence (WCC) theory (Happé & Frith, 2006) and complex information processing theories. WCC, first described by Uta Frith (1989), refers to the diminished ability to integrate smaller components of information from the environment into a more cohesive,

TABLE 2.1 Current Theories of Development in Autism Spectrum Disorder

Domain of Functioning	Theory	Summary
Social	Social motivation	Disruption in the early social reward system
	Social cognitive	Innate theory of mind (ToM) skill deficits
Cognitive	Executive functioning	Innate difficulties with higher-level cognitive skills of planning, organizing, cognitive flexibility, inhibition, and behavioral control
	Information processing	Diminished ability to integrate smaller parts into a meaningful whole and greater difficulty with complex problem-solving, skilled motor, and higher-order memory- and language-based tasks

contextually appropriate, meaningful whole. Whereas the EF theory may adequately explain the cognitive flexibility and gestalt processing deficits in ASD, the WCC model also addresses the relative visuospatial and localized attentional strengths in these individuals. In other words, individuals with ASD tend to perform well on tasks that require increased attention to detail and worse on tasks of more global, contextual attention and processing. For example, an individual with ASD may be able to recall the color of a television character's shoes or the instrument that another character was playing in a short scene but may be unable to explain the relational dynamic between the characters or the moral of the story/plot. Similarly, the complex information processing theory (Minshew & Goldstein, 1998) helps to explain both strengths and weaknesses in the ASD cognitive profile. This theory, based on a complex battery of neuropsychological tasks, suggests that individuals with ASD have greater difficulty than their typically developing peers with higher-order information processing tasks, such as complex problem solving, skilled motor tasks, concept formation, and higher-order memory and language tasks (Minshew, Webb, Williams, & Dawson, 2006). Conversely, the complex information processing theory emphasizes the rote memory, simple language, sensory perception, and visuospatial strengths of the ASD neurocognitive profile (Table 2.1).

BEHAVIORAL FUNCTIONING

In addition to social and cognitive impairments, children and adolescents with ASD commonly present with co-occurring behavioral difficulties, including behavioral dysregulation and adaptive skill deficits. Although these difficulties are common in children with ASD, the presence and severity of these symptoms may vary by several factors, including the following: the age of the child or adolescent, intelligence level, family history of mental health issues, severity of the ASD symptoms, language, and access to interventions (Levy & Perry, 2011). Similar to social and cognitive profiles, there is great heterogeneity regarding behavioral dysregulation and adaptive skills in children with ASD.

Many children with ASD are more likely than their typically developing peers to present with aggressive and/or self-injurious behaviors. For instance, Kanne and Mazurek (2011) found that 68% of children (ages 4–17 years) had behaved aggressively toward caregivers and 49% toward non-caregivers. These rates are especially high compared to those for people who have other developmental conditions but not ASD. For example, aggressive behavior has been documented in only 7–11% of children with intellectual disabilities (IDs) alone (Emerson et al., 2001). Furthermore, as per Reese, Richman, Belmont, and Morse (2005), the likelihood of aggression toward others is increased when a child with ASD demonstrates more repetitive behaviors, especially self-injurious or ritualistic behaviors, or extreme resistance to change. Behavioral dysregulation also changes across development. In young children, these behavioral symptoms may manifest as difficulties being soothed, as well as intense and prolonged outbursts (e.g., crying and temper tantrums). In older children and adolescents, difficulties with behavioral regulation may present as over-reactivity to minor problems (e.g., not getting one's own way), threatening to harm oneself (e.g., engaging in self-injury following a seemingly minor upset), and poor frustration tolerance when challenged. Of note, aggressive and disruptive behaviors are the strongest predictors of parenting stress in families of children with ASD (Baker et al., 2003).

Researchers and theorists have proposed explanations as to why behavioral regulation is a common struggle in children with ASD. For instance, Loveland (2001) notes that the regulation of one's behavior is largely dependent on perceptions regarding others' intentions, emotions, and mental states. Thus, given that social perception is a core impairment in ASD, this may lead to extreme behavioral responses that are not appropriate to the context. Furthermore, given that functional communication is also a common deficit, children with ASD may have trouble verbally expressing their needs and, instead, communicate in reactive and/or volatile ways (Goldstein, 2002). Biological explanations, such as dysfunction in the orbitofrontal–amygdala circuit in children with ASD, have also been proposed (Bachevalier & Loveland, 2006).

Adaptive skills, defined as an individual's social and practical competence to meet the demands of everyday living, are commonly impaired in children with ASD. Examples of adaptive behaviors include functional communication (e.g., indicating needs), socialization (e.g., asking a friend for a play date), and self-care skills (e.g., following a bedtime routine). Klin et al. (2007) found that the adaptive living skills of children (ages 7–18 years) with ASD were between one and three standard deviations below the population mean. The greatest adaptive impairments were in the areas of socialization and daily living skills, with communication impaired but to a lesser degree (Lee & Park, 2007). Although studies have documented adaptive skills deficits in lower-functioning children with ASD (i.e., children with a co-occurring ID), significant adaptive deficits may also be pronounced in more cognitively capable children with ASD. Furthermore, for individuals with ASD, the discrepancy between adaptive skills and intellectual ability widens with age, indicating that adaptive behavior does not keep the expected pace with chronological age or intellect (Kanne et al., 2011; Lopata et al., 2013).

CAN WE PREDICT OUTCOMES?

Given that ASD is a neurodevelopmental disorder, evidence of the diagnosis will present in early childhood; however, many factors influence the course of the disorder throughout childhood and across the lifespan. Factors such as underlying cognitive ability or IQ, language skills, social awareness and motivation to engage with others, and the presence or absence of severe dysregulation (e.g., aggression and self-injury) are thought to be important predictors of long-term outcomes. Furthermore, research continues to demonstrate that early and intensive therapy programs are effective for improving IQ, language ability, and social interactions of children with ASD (Dawson et al., 2010), thus helping to optimize outcomes for children with ASD.

The following case examples illustrate some of the social, cognitive, and behavioral developmental variability within ASD. Case 1 describes the course and outcomes for a young man who experienced a developmental regression in language skills at approximately age 2 years and never resumed speaking. Case 2 describes a relatively high functioning young man who has maintained strong verbal and cognitive abilities.

CASE STUDY 1: "SAM"

Sam is a 19-year-old young man with ASD who remains entirely nonverbal. He was born at full-term following an uncomplicated pregnancy and delivery. During the first year of life, Sam was quite colicky and difficult to soothe. He experienced frequent and extremely high fevers greater than 104°F. This required several emergency room visits to reduce the fever, although no specific cause was ever determined. By age 18 months, Sam was using a few single words consistently to express his wants and needs (e.g., "milk" and "momma"); however, his parents were concerned that he was not babbling or talking as much as his older sister had at the same age. He was evaluated by his pediatrician, who suggested that they continue to monitor his development for a while longer. Fine and gross motor development was within normal limits through the first few years of life. He sat up and started to crawl and walk at the usual times, although he tended to walk on his toes and his parents noted frequent episodes of uncontrollable "excitement" during which he would spin his body in circles with his back arched, head tilted up, and hands flapping by his side. His mother described that he could spend hours examining his collection of toy trains but never seemed interested in the train track table or other toys such as action figures or dolls.

Soon after his second birthday, Sam stopped using any words to communicate. He continued to make some noncontextual vocalizations and eventually began using some sign language, including signs for "more" and "all done." His play remained limited, and he was not interested in interacting with other children at the park or in his play group. Instead, he focused his attention on stacking or lining up toys in a nonfunctional manner. He also carried with him a favorite toy train and searched for small, round items such as buttons and coins wherever he went. He was ultimately diagnosed with ASD following a specialist evaluation and was referred for early intervention (EI) services, including 25 hours per week of intensive applied behavior analysis (ABA).

Sam continued in intensive educational programming throughout his elementary and middle school years in a specialized, substantially separate program for children with ASD. Each new skill that Sam mastered had to be systematically taught and practiced over time. He was slow to master toilet training and continues to require hand-over-hand prompting for other basic hygiene tasks, such as toothbrushing and showering. With prompting, he will follow a visual schedule, but hygiene tasks often need to be repeated by a caretaker to ensure thorough completion.

As he entered puberty, Sam began to exhibit episodes of severe self-injury and aggression. Particularly during transitions and unexpected changes in routine, he would become increasingly agitated, biting his hands and arms and hitting at people around him if they tried to redirect this behavior. These behaviors increased in frequency and intensity, ultimately requiring placement in a highly structured residential placement. With the help of his psychiatrist, behaviorist, and well-trained residential staff, his self-injury has come under much better control. He is now able to successfully participate in community outings and works 3 days per week in a medical office building helping with basic cleaning and office tasks such as stuffing envelopes with direct supervision. Sam remains nonverbal, although he recently began using an augmentative communication program on his iPad to express his wants and needs to others. Although he requires prompting to use the device consistently, he has shown proficiency in navigating the program and attempts to use the program on his own when he is getting frustrated.

CASE STUDY 2: "PETER"

Peter is an engaging 22-year-old young man who was diagnosed with ASD when he was 9 years old. He was born following an uncomplicated pregnancy and delivery. As a baby, he was happy and easy to care for. His parents describe that he would lay for hours in his crib watching the mobile spin. With regard to early developmental milestones, Peter's language development was on time to advanced. He did have some difficulty with fine motor skills, and he continues to struggle with handwriting and bilateral motor coordination.

From an early age, Peter showed interest in other children around him, although it was difficult for him to interact appropriately. At the park, he would often sit near a group of children, intently watching their play. If invited to join, he would retreat to his parents without saying anything. He rarely initiated conversation or play with his peers, but he talked quite comfortably with adults about various topics that interested him. In fact, his parents described that he often would not stop talking about his favorite video game unless he was told to do so. Occasionally, he would repetitively quote lines from his favorite movie. His peers found this bothersome, and Peter began to have increasing difficulty making and maintaining peer relationships. Over time, he became known for his depth of knowledge on particular topics such as video games, movie characters, and animals, but he continued to have difficulty relating to peers, unless the interaction centered around one of his specific areas of interest. As he got older, he struggled to control his body and often invaded the personal space of those around him. He also spoke loudly and in a monotone, robotic-like voice and needed support to monitor his speech and behavior.

In contrast to these social challenges, Peter thrived in academic settings. He was placed in advanced-level classes through middle and high school, and his teachers consistently commented on his ability to quickly learn and remember detailed information. He showed a particular affinity for animal science and biology. He has maintained a 3.5 grade point average in high school and plans to pursue an animal care degree at a local community college. Peter now has two good friends who are also interested in similar topics. Although they do not see each other outside of school, they regularly engage in role-play video games online and will message each other about the game regularly.

As demonstrated in the previous case studies, two individuals can both fully meet criteria for ASD but present rather differently throughout childhood and adolescence. These individuals' social, cognitive, and behavioral developmental profiles include a wide range of strengths and vulnerabilities. Given this heterogeneity and the numerous compelling underlying theories of psychopathology (outlined in this chapter thus far), our ability to predict long-term outcomes is somewhat limited due to these confounding factors.

CAN WE IMPROVE OUTCOMES?

The following is a common question from parents: "What can we do to reduce my child's symptoms of ASD?" As mentioned previously, the wide symptom array both within ASD and across time further complicates the answer. One key factor that has consistently been related to ASD symptom reduction and improvements in social, emotional, and adaptive outcomes is early identification and, subsequently, access to EI (Remington et al., 2007). A strong body of empirical evidence has emerged suggesting that children with ASD who enter into intensive ASD-specialized intervention services at young ages may show larger gains in cognitive and adaptive functioning than children who do not (Warren et al., 2011). Several modalities for early treatment of ASD have been developed during the past several decades. Perhaps the most well-known and well-supported intervention for children with ASD is ABA, although other methods have also been empirically validated as effective interventions. Examples of interventions beyond traditional ABA include the Early Start Denver Model (Dawson et al., 2010), Floortime (Greenspan & Wieder, 1997), and the Learning Experiences and Alternate Program for Preschoolers and Their Parents (LEAP model; Strain & Bovey, 2011).

In addition to access to EI programs for children with ASD, there is also a substantial body of research suggesting family based and contextual factors may be related to child outcomes. For instance, the literature suggests that parents of children with ASD experience higher levels of stress and depression relative to parents of neurotypical children and even compared to parents of children with other developmental disorders (Hayes & Watson, 2013; Singer, 2006). Parenting stress appears to have effects that extend beyond individual psychological functioning because parents of children with ASD report significantly higher levels of marital maladjustment (Lee et al., 2009), marital strains (Rivers & Stoneman, 2003), increased family conflict (Koegel, Schreibman, O'Neill, & Burke, 1983), and an increased number of medical and therapy appointments relative to controls (Ganz, 2007).

The stress experienced by caregivers can exacerbate their child's symptoms (Greenberg, Seltzer, Hong, & Orsmond, 2006). In addition, a number of researchers have shown that high parenting stress is predictive of fewer positive outcomes for children in intervention programs and a decreased acquisition of skills for caregivers in parent training (Hastings & Beck, 2004). Thus, outcomes of children and families may be improved when there is access to parent support programs and parent training. Examples of such programs are the EarlyBird program (Schields, 2001) and the Autism Spectrum Conditions—Enhancing Nurture and Development (ASCEND) program (Wright & Williams, 2007). This latter program is a 14-week group treatment for parents of children with ASD (ages 4–18 years) focused on parent empowerment and psychoeducation. In addition, an emerging literature on the application of mindful parenting approaches has been shown to not only decrease parenting stress but also improve aggression, noncompliance, and self-injury in children with ASD (Blackledge

& Hayes, 2006; Singh et al., 2006, 2010). Given the significant levels of caregiver stress secondary to raising a child with ASD, parent training and support groups have the potential to decrease symptoms of ASD, increase positive social and adaptive outcomes in children, and also improve overall parental and family functioning.

SUMMARY

Autism spectrum disorder is a diverse condition. The social, cognitive, and behavioral characteristics associated with ASD differ both across individuals and throughout development. Therefore, identifying the exact origin of a potential developmental disruption has been a difficult undertaking. Theories to date have inconsistently and inefficiently explained the three core deficits that characterize ASD—namely social functioning, communication and restricted, and repetitive and stereotyped behaviors. For example, social motivation theories may adequately account for social and communication deficits but fail to address the restricted, repetitive, and stereotyped behaviors that are compulsory for the full diagnosis. Conversely, emerging evidence may indicate that specific brain circuits lead to behavioral dysregulation in ASD but may not explain social and communication impairments. In addition, the paucity of longitudinal studies in these areas makes it difficult to draw clear conclusions about the developmental origin and course of promising theories such as social motivation, social cognitive, executive functioning, and information processing hypotheses.

In many ways, there is still much to discover about the developmental trajectory of ASD. Nonetheless, vital gains have been made to optimize early diagnosis and lifelong intervention strategies. Despite its largely unknown etiology, some of the most productive lines of research to date (e.g., biological and genetic findings) have been those that have pinpointed where and how the early developmental path becomes interrupted.

KEY POINTS

- Within the diagnostic category of ASD, children and adolescents present with a wide variety of social, cognitive, and behavioral characteristics.
- An individual's specific social, cognitive, and behavioral presentation can also shift significantly across development.
- Current theories of development in ASD include social motivation, social cognitive, executive functioning, and information processing models.
- Factors believed to improve outcomes include cognitive capacity, language skills, social awareness and motivation, behavior regulation skills, and, most important, initiating intervention as early in development as possible.
- Because ASD impacts not only the individual but also his or her family system and environment throughout the lifespan, treatment should include systemic interventions such as parent support and training, as well as individual treatment for the individual with ASD.

DISCLOSURE STATEMENT

Dr. Kirstin Brown Birtwell, Dr. Brian Willoughby, and Dr. Lisa Nowinski have nothing to disclose.

REFERENCES

American Psychiatric Association. (2013). *Diagnostic and statistical manual of mental disorders* (5th ed.). Arlington, VA: American Psychiatric Publishing.

Bachevalier, J., & Loveland, K. A. (2006). The orbitofrontal–amygdala circuit and self-regulation of social–emotional behavior in autism. *Neuroscience & Biobehavioral Reviews, 30*(1), 97–117.

Baghdadli, A., Assouline, B., Sonié, S., Darrou, C., Michelon, C., Assilloux, C., & Pry, R. (2012). Developmental trajectories of adaptive behaviors from early childhood to adolescence in a cohort of 152 children with autism spectrum disorders. *Journal of Autism and Developmental Disorders, 42*(7), 1314–1325.

Baker, B. L., McIntyre, L. L., Blacher, J., Crnic, K., Edelbrock, C., & Low, C. (2003). Pre-school children with and without developmental delay: Behaviour problems and parenting stress over time. *Journal of Intellectual Disability Research, 47*(4–5), 217–230.

Baron-Cohen, S., Jolliffe, T., Mortimore, C., & Robertson, M. (1997). Another advanced test of theory of mind: Evidence from very high functioning adults with autism or Asperger syndrome. *Child Psychology & Psychiatry & Allied Disciplines, 38*(7), 813–822.

Baron-Cohen, S., Leslie, A. M., & Frith, U. (1985). Does the autistic child have a "theory of mind"? *Cognition, 21*(1), 37–46.

Bernier, R., Webb, S., & Dawson, G. (2006). Understanding impairments in social engagement in autism. In P. J. Marshall & N. A. Fox (Eds.), *The development of social engagement: Neurobiological perspectives* (pp. 304–330). New York, NY: Oxford University Press.

Blackledge, J. T., & Hayes, S. C. (2006). Using acceptance and commitment training in the support for parents of children diagnosed with autism. *Child & Family Behavior Therapy, 28*, 1–18.

Centers for Disease Control and Prevention. (2014). Prevalence of autism spectrum disorder among children aged 8 years—Autism and Developmental Disabilities Monitoring Network, 11 Sites, United States, 2010. *MMWR, 63*(SS02), 1–21.

Corbett, B. A., Constantine, L. J., Hendren, R., Rocke, D., & Ozonoff, S. (2009). Examining executive functioning in children with autism spectrum disorder, attention deficit hyperactivity disorder and typical development. *Psychiatry Research, 166*(2–3), 210–222.

Dawson, G., Meltzoff, A. N., Osterling, J., Rinaldi, J., & Brown, E. (1998). Children with autism fail to orient to naturally occurring social stimuli. *Journal of Autism and Developmental Disorders, 28*(6), 479–485.

Dawson, G., Rogers, S., Munson, J., Smith, M., Winter, J., Greenson, J., . . . Varley, J. (2010). Randomized, controlled trial of an intervention for toddlers with autism: The Early Start Denver Model. *Pediatrics, 125*(1), 17–23.

Emerson, E., Kiernan, C., Alborz, A., Reeves, D., Mason, H., Swarbrick, R., et al. (2001). The prevalence of challenging behaviors: A total population study. *Research in Developmental Disabilities, 22*(1), 77–93.

Frith, U. (1989). *Autism: Explaining the Enigma.* Oxford, England: Blackwell.

Ganz, M. L. (2007). The lifetime distribution of the incremental societal costs of autism. *Archives of Pediatrics & Adolescent Medicine, 161*, 343–349.

Goldstein, H. (2002). Communication intervention for children with autism: A review of treatment efficacy. *Journal of Autism and Developmental Disorders, 32*(5), 373–396.

Gotham, K., Pickles, A., & Lord, C. (2012). Trajectories of autism severity in children using standardized ADOS scores. *Pediatrics, 130*(5), e1278–e1284.

Greenberg, J. S., Seltzer, M. M., Hong, J., & Orsmond, G. I. (2006). Bidirectional effects of expressed emotion and behavior problems and symptoms in adolescents and adults with autism. *American Journal of Mental Retardation, 111*, 229–249.

Greenspan, S. I., & Wieder, S. (1997). Developmental patterns and outcomes in infants and children with disorders in relating and communicating: A chart review of 200 cases of children with autistic spectrum diagnoses. *Journal of Developmental and Learning Disorders, 1*, 87–142.

Guthrie, W., Swineford, L. B., Nottke, C., & Wetherby, A. M. (2013). Early diagnosis of autism spectrum disorder: Stability and change in clinical diagnosis and symptom presentation. *Journal of Child Psychology and Psychiatry, 54*(5), 582–590.

Hale, C. M., & Tager-Flusberg, H. (2005). Social communication in children with autism: The relationship between theory of mind and discourse development. *Autism, 9*(2), 157–178.

Happé, F., & Frith, U. (2006). The weak coherence account: Detail-focused cognitive style in autism spectrum disorders. *Journal of Autism and Developmental Disorders, 36*(1), 5–25.

Hastings, R. P., & Beck, A. (2004). Practitioner review: Stress intervention for parents of children with intellectual disabilities. *Journal of Child Psychology and Psychiatry, 45*(8), 1338–1349.

Hayes, S. A., & Watson, S. L. (2013). The impact of parenting stress: A meta-analysis of studies comparing the experience of parenting stress in parents of children with and without autism spectrum disorders. *Journal of Autism and Developmental Disorders, 43*(3), 629–642.

Kanne, S. M., Gerber, A. J., Quirmbach, L. M., Sparrow, S. S., Cicchetti, D. V., & Saulnier, C. A. (2011). The role of adaptive behavior in autism spectrum disorders: Implications for functional outcome. *Journal of Autism and Developmental Disorders, 41*(8), 1007–1018.

Kanne, S. M., & Mazurek, M. O. (2011). Aggression in children and adolescents with ASD: Prevalence and risk factors. *Journal of Autism and Developmental Disorders, 41*(7), 926–937.

Klin, A., Saulnier, C. A., Sparrow, S. S., Cicchetti, D. V., Volkmar, F. R., & Lord, C. (2007). Social and communication abilities and disabilities in higher functioning individuals with autism spectrum disorders: The Vineland and the ADOS. *Journal of Autism and Developmental Disorders, 37*(4), 748–759.

Koegel, R. L., Schreibman, L., O'Neill, R. E., & Burke, J. C. (1983). The personality and family interaction characteristics of parents of autistic children. *Journal of Consulting and Clinical Psychology, 51*, 683–692.

Lee, G. K., Lopata, C., Volker, M. A., Thomeer, M. L., Nida, R. E., Toomey, J. A., . . . Smerbeck, A. M. (2009). Health-related quality of life of parents of children with high-functioning autism spectrum disorders. *Focus on Autism and Other Developmental Disabilities, 24*(4), 227–239.

Lee, H. J., & Park, H. R. (2007). An integrated literature review on the adaptive behavior of individuals with Asperger syndrome. *Remedial and Special Education, 28*(3), 132–139.

Levy, A., & Perry, A. (2011). Outcomes in adolescents and adults with autism: A review of the literature. *Research in Autism Spectrum Disorders, 5*(4), 1271–1282.

Lopata, C., Smith, R. A., Volker, M. A., Thomeer, M. L., Lee, G. K., & McDonald, C. A. (2013). Comparison of adaptive behavior measures for children with HFASDs. *Autism Research and Treatment, 2013*, 415989.

Lord, C., & Spence, S. (2006). Autism spectrum disorder: Phenotype and diagnosis. In S. O. Moldin & J. R. Rubenstein (Eds.), *Understanding autism: From basic neuroscience to treatment* (pp. 1–23). Boca Raton, FL: CRC Press.

Loveland, K. (2001). Toward an ecological theory of autism. In J. A. Burack, T. Charman, N. Yirmiya, & P. R. Zelazo (Eds.), *The development of autism: Perspectives from theory and research* (pp. 17–37). Mahwah, NJ: Erlbaum.

McGovern, C. W., & Sigman, M. (2005). Continuity and change from early childhood to adolescence in autism. *Journal of Child Psychology and Psychiatry, 46*(4), 401–408.

Minshew, N. J., & Goldstein, G. (1998). Autism as a disorder of complex information processing. *Mental Retardation and Developmental Disabilities Research Reviews, 4*(2), 129–136.

Minshew, N. J., Webb, S. J., Williams, D. L., & Dawson, G. (2006). Neuropsychology and neurophysiology of autism spectrum disorders. In S. O. Moldin & J. R. Rubenstein (Eds.), *Understanding autism: From basic neuroscience to treatment* (pp. 379–415). Boca Raton, FL: CRC Press.

Ozonoff, S., Pennington, B. F., & Rogers, S. J. (1991). Executive function deficits in high-functioning autistic individuals: Relationship to theory of mind. *Journal of Child Psychology and Psychiatry, 32*, 1081–1105.

Ozonoff, S., South, M., & Provencal, S. (2005). Executive functions. In F. R. Volkmar, R. Paul, A. Klin, & D. J. Cohen (Eds.), *Handbook of autism and pervasive developmental disorders* (Vol. 1, pp. 606–627). Hoboken, NJ: Wiley.

Ozonoff, S., Young, G. S., Belding, A., Hill, M., Hill, A., Hutman, T., . . . Iosif, A. (2014). The broader autism phenotype in infancy: When does it emerge? *Journal of the American Academy of Child & Adolescent Psychiatry, 53*(4), 398–407.

Reese, R. M., Richman, D. M., Belmont, J. M., & Morse, P. (2005). Functional characteristics of disruptive behavior in developmentally disabled children with and without autism. *Journal of Autism and Developmental Disorders, 35*(4), 419–428.

Remington, B., Hastings, R. P., Kovshoff, H., degli Espinosa, F., Jahr, E., Brown, T., ... Ward, N. (2007). Early intensive behavioral intervention: Outcomes for children with autism and their parents after two years. *American Journal on Mental Retardation, 112*(6), 418–438.

Rivers, J. W., & Stoneman, Z. (2003). Sibling relationships when a child has autism: Marital stress and support coping. *Journal of Autism and Developmental Disorders, 33*(4), 383–394.

Rozga, A., Anderson, S. A., & Robins, D. L. (2011). Major current neuropsychological theories of ASD. In D. Fein (Ed.), *The neuropsychology of autism* (pp. 97–120). Oxford, England: Oxford University Press.

Schields, J. (2001). National Autistic Society EarlyBird Programme: Partnership with parents. *Autism: The International Journal of Research and Practice, 5*(1), 49–56.

Shattuck, P. T., Durkin, M., Maenner, M., Newschaffer, C., Mandell, D. S., Wiggins, L., ... Cuniff, C. (2009). Timing of identification among children with an autism spectrum disorder: Findings from a population-based surveillance study. *Journal of the American Academy of Child & Adolescent Psychiatry, 48*(5), 474–483.

Singer, G. H. (2006). Meta-analysis of comparative studies of depression in mothers of children with and without developmental disabilities. *American Journal on Mental Retardation, 111*, 155–169.

Singh, N. N., Lancinoi, G. E., Winton, A. S. W., Fisher, B. C., Wahler, R. G., McAleavy, K., ... Sabaawi, M. (2006). Mindful parenting decreases aggression, noncompliance, and self-injury in children with autism. *Journal of Emotional and Behavioral Disorders, 14*, 169–177.

Singh, N. N., Lancioni, G. E., Winton, A. S. W., Singh, J., Singh, A. N., Adkins, A. D., & Wahler, R. G. (2010). Training in mindful caregiving transfers to parent–child interactions. *Journal of Child and Family Studies, 19*, 167–174.

Stavropoulos, K. K., & Carver, L. J. (2013). Research review: Social motivation and oxytocin in autism—Implications for joint attention development and intervention. *Journal of Child Psychology and Psychiatry, 54*(6), 603–618.

Strain, P. S., & Bovey, E. H. (2011). Randomized, controlled trial of the LEAP model of early intervention for young children with autism spectrum disorders. *Topics in Early Childhood Special Education, 31*(3), 133–154.

Szatmari, P., Bryson, S., Duku, E., Vaccarella, L., Zwaigenbaum, L., Bennett, T., & Boyle, M. H. (2009). Similar developmental trajectories in autism and Asperger syndrome: From early childhood to adolescence. *Journal of Child Psychology and Psychiatry, 50*(12), 1459–1467.

Tager-Flusberg, H. (1996). Current theory and research on language and communication in autism. *Journal of Autism and Developmental Disorders, 26*, 169–172.

Warren, Z., McPheeters, M. L., Sathe, N., Foss-Feig, J. H., Glasser, A., & Veenstra-VanderWeele, J. (2011). A systematic review of early intensive intervention for autism spectrum disorders. *Pediatrics, 127*(5), 1303–1311.

Waterhouse, L., Fein, D., & Modahl, C. (1996). Neurofunctional mechanism in autism. *Psychological Review, 103*(3), 457–489.

Woolfenden, S., Sarkozy, V., Ridley, G., & Williams, K. (2012). A systematic review of the diagnostic stability of Autism Spectrum Disorder. *Research in Autism Spectrum Disorders, 6*(1), 345–354.

Wright, B., & Williams, C. (2007). *Intervention and support for parents of children and young people on the autism spectrum: A resource for trainers.* London, England: Kingsley.

Wu, C., & Chiang, C. (2014). The developmental sequence of social–communicative skills in young children with autism: A longitudinal study. *Autism, 18*(4), 385–392.

Zwaigenbaum, L., Bryson, S., Rogers, T., Roberts, W., Brian, J., & Szatmari, P. (2005). Behavioral manifestation of autism in the first year of life. *International Journal of Developmental Neuroscience, 23*, 413–152.

SOCIAL, COGNITIVE, AND AFFECTIVE DEVELOPMENT OF ADULTS WITH AUTISM SPECTRUM DISORDER

PATRICIA HOWLIN AND ILIANA MAGIATI

WHAT HAPPENS TO INDIVIDUALS WITH AUTISM SPECTRUM DISORDER IN ADULTHOOD?

It is now more than 70 years since Kanner (1943) first described the syndrome that he believed was primarily characterized by an "inborn autistic disturbance of affective contact" and an "inability to relate oneself to people and situations from the beginning of life." Since then, many thousands of papers on autism have been published, and year by year we learn more about possible causes, potential treatments, and diagnostic and assessment procedures. However, despite the fact that people are *adults* with autism for many decades longer than they are *children* with autism, the focus of the vast majority of these publications is on childhood (Edwards, Watkins, Lotfizadeh, & Poling, 2012). Only a tiny proportion of studies involve adults, and fewer still have systematically investigated trajectories of development into adult life. This chapter describes what we know about adult development with respect to cognitive, social, and affective outcomes, and it highlights the need for far more, and better quality, studies in this area.

SOCIAL INTEGRATION AND INDEPENDENCE IN ADULTHOOD

One of the first accounts of what happens to adults with autism (now termed autism spectrum disorder (ASD); American Psychiatric Association, 2013) was written by Kanner himself 30 years after he published his original papers. In 1973, he reported on 96 individuals whom he had initially diagnosed as children and whom he then re-assessed when they were approximately 20–30 years of age. One of the most striking findings was the great variation in adult outcomes. Some individuals had made very little progress since first seen and were in long-stay institutional care. Others had shown improvements but, nevertheless, remained highly dependent on their families or on services for people with intellectual disabilities. In contrast, others were functioning relatively well, lived independently, and had managed to obtain academic qualifications and find employment. Several had friends or local acquaintances, and one man (a successful music composer) was married with a child. A fascinating account of one of Kanner's early cases, now in his 70s, living independently and well integrated within his rural community was published in *The Atlantic* (Donovan & Zucker, 2010).

Subsequent studies have continued to note the very wide range of outcomes in adulthood, with some individuals requiring intensive and highly specialized care throughout their lives, whereas others achieve very highly as adults. The latter group, however, tends to be in the minority, with most adults requiring substantial support and being poorly integrated within society. In a recent systematic review, Magiati, Tay, and Howlin (2014) evaluated studies that had followed up individuals with ASD as children through to adulthood. All included studies had a sample size of at least 10, and the average age of participants at follow-up was 16 years or older. A total of 25 studies published between 1984 and 2013 were identified, and although most were relatively small in size (50% comprised fewer than 50 participants), some involved several hundred individuals. The average age of participants when first assessed was 7 years, and their average age at follow-up in adulthood was 24 years (range, 17–44 years). The average IQ of the cohorts involved fell just within the borderline-average range (mean, 79.0). Despite this, social outcomes were generally reported to be "poor" or "very poor" (i.e., no friends, no job, and in residential care/living with parents). Although there was great variability between studies (with the number of participants rated as having a "good outcome"—that is, employed with or without support; having some friends; living semi/independently—ranging from 3% to 74%), at least 50% or more of participants remained highly dependent on others for their care. The majority of adults were socially isolated and had few friendships or romantic relationships. Rates of independent living and employment were also low; social independence was particularly poor for individuals with intellectual disability.

Despite variability between studies, the conclusion that the overall prognosis, up to now, for adults with ASD is poor is supported by a number of other reviews (Henninger & Taylor, 2013; Howlin & Moss, 2012; Levy & Perry, 2011). Of significant concern is the fact that although interventions and educational provisions for young children with ASD have improved markedly during recent years, these changes seem not to be reflected in significant improvements in the lives of adults.

Figures 3.1 and 3.2, for example, summarize changes in adult outcomes reported in follow-up studies conducted from the mid-1960s to 1999 compared with those completed between 2000 and 2012, as reviewed by Howlin and Moss (2012). No clearly observable improvements could be detected in the proportions of individuals living independently, in work, or in close relationships. Overall outcome ratings also indicate no major changes in the proportions rated as having "good," "fair," or "poor" social outcomes. It is true that fewer individuals now spend their adult lives in the long-stay institutions in which many of Kanner's original patients lived. Similarly, the number of individuals who continue living with their parents also seems to have declined; nevertheless, the quality and availability of adult provision remains limited. Indeed, access to services and special assistance tends to decline rapidly from secondary school onwards (Shattuck, Wagner, Narendorf, Sterzing, & Hensley, 2011). After young people with ASD exit high school, many receive no formal services and social isolation appears to increase. For example, a prevalence study of adults with ASD in the United Kingdom, including individuals of normal IQ, found that they were significantly less likely to be in work and far more likely to be economically and socially disadvantaged than their peers without ASD (Brugha et al., 2011). Data from large-scale

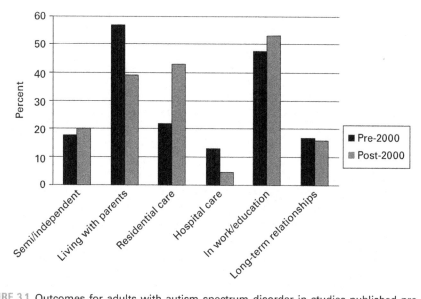

FIGURE 3.1 Outcomes for adults with autism spectrum disorder in studies published pre- and post-2000.

cohort studies in the United States confirm that, compared with their peers with intellectual, emotional, behavioral, or learning disabilities, young adults with ASD are significantly more socially isolated; thus, they are more likely never to see or be called by friends or to be invited to activities (Orsmond, Shattuck, Cooper, Sterzing, & Anderson, 2013). Taylor and Seltzer (2011) also found that day services for adults with ASD were significantly poorer than the services to which they had access when they were still in school; provision was particularly poor for adults of normal intellectual ability. It is estimated that approximately half of all young people with ASD have no vocational or educational services in the years immediately following high school (Shattuck et al., 2012), and many reviews report employment rates of 30% or less (e.g., Magiati et al., 2014). Again, even when compared with groups of individuals with other disabilities, young adults with ASD are significantly less likely

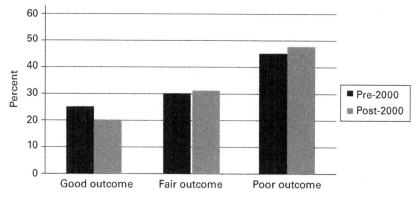

FIGURE 3.2 Overall outcome ratings for adults with autism spectrum disorder in studies published pre- and post-2000.

to be employed (Roux, Shattuck, & Cooper, 2013), and among those who are employed, jobs tend to be low-skilled, part-time, and very poorly paid (Mavranezouli et al., 2014). Moreover, these disadvantages are not just a temporary setback immediately post-school, after which individuals then go on to catch up with their peer group. Instead, educational, vocational, and employment opportunities continue to diminish, resulting in many adults having access to very limited and very poor-quality provision.

At a societal level, high levels of unemployment and dependency on government subsidies are two of the main factors contributing to the very high costs of ASD (Ganz, 2007; Knapp, Romeo, & Beecham, 2009). At a personal level, too, the costs are enormous. Without a job, most individuals have little chance of living independently and remain both economically and emotionally dependent on their families. Being unemployed also means they have little or no opportunity to meet with their peers, and this, together with the social difficulties that are core to ASD, frequently leads to increasing isolation with age. An overview of the rates of marriage and/or close friendships reported in studies of adults suggested that only approximately 20% of individuals develop intimate relationships that involve reciprocity and sharing (Howlin, 2014). Moreover, despite the high heritability of ASD (Rutter, 2013), there are no data on the numbers of individuals with ASD who have children of their own, and we know almost nothing about the difficulties they may experience or the quality of childrearing in these families. Personal accounts suggest that although individuals with ASD can succeed in maintaining close relationships and are able to parent well (Slater-Walker & Slater-Walker, 2002; Willey, 1999), successful relationships require many adaptations by both partners. Also, when difficulties are experienced, adequate support is rarely available (Lawson, 2002).

COGNITIVE AND LANGUAGE FUNCTIONING

Although for many years after Kanner it was believed that most individuals with ASD were severely cognitively and linguistically impaired, it is now recognized that a substantial minority (probably approximately 40%) are of average or above average IQ (Charman et al., 2011). There is also evidence that the majority of those with ASD acquire at least some degree of useful language, even if its development is often rather delayed (Wodka, Mathy, & Kalb, 2013). Nevertheless, there has been little research on trajectories of cognitive and language development from child to adulthood, and findings are often contradictory.

Whereas some studies report an overall decrease in IQ with age, others report general stability; still others have recorded improvements in IQ scores. However, perhaps the most consistent finding is one of great individual heterogeneity (Magiati et al., 2014). Variability is particularly evident among individuals who have an average or above average nonverbal IQ as children, but those with a childhood nonverbal IQ below 70 almost always remain in the intellectually impaired range. In a 40-year follow-up of 60 individuals who were all of average nonverbal IQ as children, Howlin, Savage, Moss, Tempier, and Rutter (2014) found that, although IQ generally remained stable over four decades, a minority showed a significant decline in cognitive ability, mostly associated with epilepsy or very severe behavioral disturbance. Although improvements in IQ can occur, these tend to be among individuals who as children had an average or above average nonverbal IQ, but whose language was initially severely delayed (Magiati et al., 2014). In their follow-up study of 85 young adults, Anderson, Liang, and Lord (2014) found average increases of more than 50 points in verbal IQ from age 2 to age 19 years among participants with a nonverbal childhood IQ of 70 or greater; those with a nonverbal childhood IQ less than 70 showed no improvement. Howlin et al. (2014) also found significant changes in verbal IQ among their cohort of individuals with average nonverbal IQ scores in childhood.

Many other studies have reported at least some improvements on tests of language over time. Nevertheless, even among individuals who do develop useful speech, scores on standardized language assessments are typically below chronological age, and functional language for the purposes of social communication tends to remain limited (Magiati et al., 2014). For example, only 35% of the 99 adults followed up by Ballaban-Gil, Rapin, Tuchman, and Shinnar (1996) achieved normal or near-normal speech fluency or comprehension; similarly, only 12% of 725 adults in the large cohort studied by Liptak, Kennedy, and Dosa (2011) were reported to be able to converse fluently.

ADAPTIVE BEHAVIOR

Although IQ is an important issue in any study of adult outcomes, it is important to be aware that in ASD, the strong positive association between IQ and adaptive functioning (e.g., self-help, social competence, daily living skills, and communication skills) that is characteristic of typical development is often disrupted. Thus, whereas in typically developing children, IQ and adaptive behavior scores tend to be at a similar level, in ASD, adaptive behavior scores may be much lower than scores on a standard IQ test (Charman et al., 2011). Data from Anderson et al. (2014) indicate that this discrepancy may be particularly marked among individuals of higher intellectual ability. For example, a young adult with ASD with an IQ in the superior range (i.e., 130 or greater) may still be unable to complete basic household or self-care tasks effectively without support. Relatively few studies have assessed adaptive behavior skills in adulthood and, again, those that have report considerable individual variability. The review by Magiati et al. (2014) suggests that although there are improvements in adaptive functioning with age, the overall level of competence in this area remains relatively low in comparison with that of peers of the same age and/or IQ. Studies of profiles of adaptive functioning also suggest that abilities in adulthood tend to be comparatively better in the domains of daily living and communication than in socialization skills (Farley et al., 2009).

MENTAL HEALTH

Given the social isolation, lack of employment, and high rates of dependence on others often experienced by adults with ASD, it might be expected that rates of mental health problems would be significantly elevated in this group. However, there are few systematic data on rates of mental health problems among adults with ASD, and the findings that are available are often inconsistent. Although some studies report that up to 84% of individuals with ASD have a diagnosable psychiatric condition (e.g., Ghaziuddin, 2005; Levy & Perry, 2011), these figures are often based on individuals attending psychiatric clinics. Data from a small number of non-referred cohorts suggest somewhat lower rates of approximately 25–30% (Howlin, 2014), but nevertheless these are still considerably higher than rates in the general population. Despite the variability in prevalence rates, there is more agreement on the types of mental health problems that are more likely to be experienced, with anxiety, depression, and obsessive–compulsive problems being the most frequently reported. In contrast, rates of schizophrenia appear to be relatively low, despite research suggesting some genetic overlap between ASD and schizophrenia (Cross-Disorder Group of the Psychiatric Genomics Consortium, 2013; Smoller, 2013).

Relatively little is known about the possible factors associated with mental health problems in ASD. For example, although there is some indication that major life events or transition points (e.g., leaving school and coping with college or employment) are associated with the onset of mental health problems (Esbensen, Greenberg, Seltzer, & Aman, 2009; Hutton, Goode, Murphy, Le Couteur, & Rutter, 2008), there have been no systematic studies in this area. There is also some evidence that individuals with ASD of higher IQ (who may have greater insight into their difficulties) are more likely to experience depression and anxiety than those with intellectual impairments (Ghaziuddin, 2005; Sterling, Dawson, Estes, & Greenson, 2008). However, other studies have found that psychiatric disorders occur equally among individuals with ASD of all intellectual ability levels (Farley et al., 2009; Hutton et al., 2008; Tsakanikos et al., 2006).

A major problem in determining rates of mental health difficulties in ASD is the scarcity of well-validated mental health measures for use in this population (Ghaziuddin, 2005). Self-report measures may be less appropriate for those individuals with ASD who have difficulties describing their inner thoughts and emotions; on the other hand, informants (e.g., caregivers, teachers, or keyworkers) may not be able to report accurately on the internal states of the adult with ASD. Diagnosis of comorbid psychopathology is further complicated by the fact that there can be overlap between ASD and symptoms associated with other mental health problems, such as obsessive–compulsive disorder or attention deficit hyperactivity disorder (ADHD). The presentation of mental health problems in individuals with ASD may also be atypical (Hutton et al., 2008). For example, the onset of depression may be characterized by an increase in stereotyped and ritualistic behaviors or in aggression and/or self-injury.

Underwood, McCarthy, and Tsakanikos (2010) highlight the lack of professionals who have expertise in diagnosing mental health problems in adults with ASD, but there is an equally great need for knowledge about effective interventions. Although there is some, albeit very limited, evidence that cognitive and/or behaviorally based therapies can be effective with this group (Bishop-Fitzpatrick, Minshew, & Eack, 2013), pharmacological interventions tend to be the most commonly used. These are of variable effectiveness; nevertheless, up to 80% of young adults with ASD in the United States are on medication, with rates of medication use increasing over time. Moreover, once medication commences, it is likely to be given long term (Esbensen et al., 2009).

CHANGES OVER TIME: SEVERITY OF AUTISM SPECTRUM DISORDER SYMPTOMS

Despite the many challenges faced by young people with ASD as they enter adult life, the one area that does seem to show positive change is the severity of their ASD-related symptoms. This pattern of steady improvement over time was first reported by Kanner, who noted that for some individuals, particularly those who became more aware of their difficulties and managed to find ways to overcome or circumvent them, mid-adolescence was often a period of marked improvement (Kanner, 1973). Similar findings were noted in the early follow-up studies of Rutter and his group (e.g., Rutter, Greenfield, & Lockyer, 1967), and many subsequent outcome studies document improvements in ASD symptoms over time. For example, in a study of more than 400 individuals with ASD who were 10–53 years old, Seltzer et al. (2003) found evidence of a decrease in ASD severity, particularly in repetitive behaviors; there were also improvements in reciprocal social interaction and in verbal and nonverbal communication. In another large-scale study of 241 young adults, Shattuck and colleagues (2007) reported significant improvements in severity of ASD symptoms (again, especially in repetitive behaviors) and in maladaptive behaviors during a 4-year period. Similar positive findings have been noted in a number of other follow-up studies (e.g., Anderson et al., 2014; Farley et al., 2009; Seltzer, Shattuck, Abbeduto, & Greenberg, 2004).

The improvements reported for cohorts of young adults also appear to continue into later adulthood. For example, Howlin, Moss, Savage, and Rutter (2013) followed up 44 adults (all of average IQ when initially diagnosed as children) from the age of 26 years to age 46 years. When assessed in their mid-forties, all still met criteria for a diagnosis of ASD, but the severity of ASD symptoms (particularly in repetitive and stereotyped behaviors) had continued to decrease during the two decades of the study. Despite these improvements in ASD symptom severity, however, social integration was often more limited than it had been for the same individuals as younger adults.

In summary, studies of trajectories of development into adulthood suggest that the majority of individuals continue to show improvements as they grow older, although social and adaptive functioning typically remain considerably impaired for many. There are also major individual differences in the extent of improvement over time. Increases in ability tend to be most marked in individuals who are less intellectually impaired, but they are also occasionally reported for those who are of very low IQ (Beadle-Brown, Murphy, Wing, Shah, & Holmes, 2000). However, the social support structures required to help adults with ASD make the best of their potential for development and to foster social inclusion and independence are too often lacking.

CAN WE PREDICT OUTCOMES IN ADULTHOOD?

Despite improvements in the severity of ASD symptoms that occur in many adults with ASD, social integration tends to remain very limited (for more details, see Magiati et al., 2014). Several follow-up studies also indicate that a minority of individuals show a significant decline in cognitive and other skills with age (Howlin et al., 2013). The highly variable outcomes of individuals with ASD in adulthood have led to exploration of childhood factors that may be related to later prognosis. On the whole, data on the association between adult outcomes and childhood variables such as the severity of symptoms in childhood or the presence of other comorbid conditions are inconsistent, and there is almost no research on the impact of other individual characteristics, genetic or socioeconomic factors, or quality of family life. The very small number of female participants in most studies precludes any conclusions about the role of gender (Magiati et al., 2014). There is evidence that the development of epilepsy is an important risk factor, whereas better language and responsiveness to joint attention are positive predictors of social and adaptive functioning some decades later (Gillespie-Lynch et al., 2012).

Only two factors—childhood IQ and the development of language by the age of 5 or 6 years—have been consistently found to be strong predictors of adult outcome. Thus, outcomes for individuals with ASD and intellectual disability and for those who do not acquire some level of useful language before school age are typically poor. Nevertheless, it is much more difficult to predict the long-term outcome for those children who are of average IQ and have developed language. Some of these individuals go on to achieve highly in their adult lives, whereas others remain dependent and a minority show an increase in difficulties and/or a decline in functioning over time (Anderson et al., 2014; Howlin et al., 2013).

For example, "Mark" and "Jonathan" are two adults followed up throughout the years by the first author. Their cases illustrate the different developmental trajectories of individuals with ASD.

CASE STUDY #1: "MARK"

Mark was diagnosed with an intellectual disability when he was 3 years old but was rediagnosed with ASD at age 4 years. At that time, he had very limited speech and severe behavioral problems. During his elementary school years, he attended an autism school, where he made good progress behaviorally and in his academic and communication skills. He was then able to transfer to a very structured, mainstream school, where his interest in mathematics was encouraged; during this time, his school and family maintained close contact with the specialized autism service.

As a young adult, Mark obtained a place in university to study mathematics, although he continued to live at home because his independence skills were still poor. Whenever problems or challenges arose (mainly involving difficulties in peer relations or having very fixed and unorthodox views about how mathematics should be taught, which brought him into conflict with his university teachers), these were managed well by professionals from the specialized autism service who supported Mark, his family, and university staff.

At the age of 24 years, Mark obtained a master's degree in mathematics, but he failed to secure employment for several years because of his inability to cope with job interviews. Professionals from the autism team then became involved in helping him find suitable employment, and subsequently Mark has remained with the same design company for 25 years. His mathematical and programming skills are much valued. The autism team has kept contact and provided advice on support and management throughout the years. The difficulties that have arisen relate mostly to communication problems (e.g., he is rapidly able to identify and correct flaws in others' programs but is poor at explaining what these errors are), poor social understanding (giving unwitting offense by standing too close to female colleagues or making personal or inappropriate remarks), or poor self-hygiene (clothing dirty or ill-kempt, infrequent bathing/shaving/hair washing, and leaving lavatory in unacceptable state). Support has involved providing direct advice and information about ASD to staff and individual counseling and practical advice and instructions to Mark (e.g., regarding hygiene or social behaviors). In this way, almost all problems have resolved rapidly, without in any way demeaning Mark's status in the workplace.

CASE STUDY #2: "JONATHAN"

In his early years, Jonathan's language development was advanced, but his behavior was very difficult to manage at home or in nursery (he was "expelled" from several nurseries because of aggression). Although he showed significant behavior problems, Jonathan's parents were unsuccessful in their attempts to obtain a diagnosis or support from child psychiatry services. Despite his very rigid behaviors and significant difficulties in social understanding and social interaction, his problems were variously attributed to his being "intellectually gifted" or to his parents' poor management skills and/or their marital problems.

During his elementary school years, Jonathan went through a series of different school placements. He was seen by an educational psychologist, but the only diagnosis given was "emotional disturbance," whereas his parents were offered intervention for marital problems. Jonathan finally settled in a small, highly structured religious school, but he remained isolated and without friends and often became aggressive because he was unable to tolerate anyone with different views/behaviors from his own. He then attended a private, highly academic mainstream school where initially he appeared to settle well. However, he subsequently had major problems with bullying (as both victim and perpetrator), was often aggressive to school staff, and became increasingly abusive to his father at home.

At the age of 15 years, he was finally seen by the child psychiatry services and diagnosed with ASD. Jonathan refused to accept this diagnosis and blamed all his difficulties on his father. He became increasingly aggressive to staff and other students at school, refused to complete homework assignments, and, following a severe incident of bullying by other students, was then homeschooled. At age 16 years, he was transferred to a specialized unit for students with Asperger's syndrome. He settled well initially, but he grew increasingly more resentful of his diagnosis of autism. Increasing physical aggression toward his parents and school staff resulted in transfer to a residential college for students with ASD at the age of 17 years. There, he viewed all other pupils and staff as inferior; he refused to follow the college's academic program and left at age 20 years.

Currently, Jonathan is 22 years old. He occasionally works in short-term jobs when he needs money. He makes "friends" easily but then rapidly alienates everyone with whom he has contact. He can be very violent toward his parents, resulting in occasional involvement with the police, and he continues to refuse any help from specialized services. Much of the time, his parents do not know where he is or what he is doing, and they are deeply fearful about his future.

What made the outcome for Mark so different from that for Jonathan? Was it the earlier diagnosis, the professional support available for him and his family during his school and college years, the fact that he was initially educated in a highly specialized autism placement, or was it because of genetic underpinnings and/or having a totally different temperament and personality?

We still know virtually nothing about the factors that influence outcome in this higher ability group, and although there are some indications that early intervention programs may make a positive difference (Anderson et al., 2014), this is an issue that requires much more systematic research. Currently, there are no longitudinal studies into adulthood to support claims (e.g., by Chasson, Harris, & Neely, 2007) that children who undergo highly intensive behavioral interventions in their pre-school years are significantly less likely to need specialist services in adult life.

CAN WE IMPROVE OUTCOMES IN ADULTHOOD?

The inadequacy of research on adults with ASD, and in particular the lack of well-controlled intervention studies, has been highlighted in two systematic reviews from the United States and United Kingdom (Lounds-Taylor et al., 2012; National Institute for Health and Clinical Excellence (NICE), 2012; see also Howlin, 2014; Piven et al., 2011). For example, in a review of psychosocial interventions for adults with ASD, Bishop-Fitzpatrick et al. (2013) found that out of a total of 1217 studies reviewed, only 13 met basic methodological requirements, and only 4 of these were randomized controlled trials. Although there are a considerable number of case studies or small case series testifying to the value of behavioral techniques for modifying behavioral difficulties or increasing functional skills, particularly in individuals with ASD and severe intellectual disabilities, there are very few well-controlled studies of other psychosocial interventions or services for individuals with ASD.

This lack of research on effective interventions for adults is particularly concerning given indications that access to adequate support networks in adulthood can have a significant impact on subsequent outcomes. The study by Farley and colleagues (2009) provides a strong argument for more cohesive community support. Compared with other adult outcome studies involving individuals of similar age and IQ, the young adults in the Farley study were more likely to be in work and to have married or to have formed close relationships, and approximately half were rated as having "good" or "very good" overall outcomes. One major factor here appears to be that almost all the participants had grown up and continue to live in communities belonging to a church organization that provides lifelong support for its members and also values the inclusion of individuals with disabilities.

The transition from school to college or from school to work can be especially challenging for individuals with ASD, and these particular life stages are often associated with an increase in psychiatric difficulties (Hutton et al., 2008). Post-school programs are needed in many different areas. Provision of sheltered or semisheltered housing, together with training and support to develop appropriate self-care and healthy living skills, is another area of (usually unmet) need. Opportunities to develop social contacts in adulthood are also crucial, but for many, as indicated in the studies by Shattuck et al. (2007) and Seltzer and colleagues (2003, 2004), such provision is generally nonexistent. Social skills interventions for adolescents and young adults show some promise in helping individuals develop greater social understanding and competence (e.g., Beaumont & Sofronoff, 2008), but very few studies have been systematically evaluated and even fewer have been tested in community settings (Bishop-Fitzpatrick et al., 2013). High-functioning adults with ASD also tend to experience a poorer quality of life compared with individuals with ADHD or other psychiatric disorders diagnosed in childhood (Barneveld, Swaab, Fagel, van Engeland, & de Sonneville, 2014). It is also evident that even when people with ASD do develop close relationships, marry, or have children of their own, both they and their families can face many challenges (Slater-Walker & Slater–Walker, 2002; Willey, 1999). However, there is very little research on interventions or support systems that can help avoid or minimize the interpersonal or social issues that may arise.

One area in which there has been some positive developments, and which potentially can have a major impact on many aspects of individuals' lives (including mental health, social relationships, financial stability, and general independence), is that of supported employment. Employment rates for individuals with ASD are known to be very low. In a review of outcome studies, Howlin and Moss (2012) found that only approximately one-third of adults were in any form of education or employment, and in cohorts including individuals of lower cognitive ability, employment rates were typically less than 25%. Because generic employment services for people with intellectual or mental disabilities rarely meet the needs of individuals with ASD, during the past two decades a number of supported employment schemes have been developed specifically for this group. These provide help to find work and offer direct support in the workplace (typically to avoid or manage social interaction problems), as well as provide guidance for work managers and colleagues to help them understand the needs, difficulties, and potential skills of employees with ASD. The number of studies evaluating the success of supported employment programs remains small (NICE, 2012; Shattuck et al., 2012), but there is growing evidence that these schemes are superior to alternative employment models (e.g., sheltered workshops) in terms of job level, pay, quality of life, and cost-effectiveness (Mavranezouli et al., 2014).

CAN THERE BE RECOVERY FROM AUTISM SPECTRUM DISORDER?

Although ASD is generally described as a lifelong disorder, there have been occasional accounts in the literature of individuals who have reportedly undergone "miracle cures," in most cases as a "result" of a specific intervention. Although most such claims lack any sound evidence base, the issue of whether some children could "recover from autism" was initially raised by Lovaas (1987), who reported that 47% of children receiving intensive behavioral treatment for more than 2 years achieved "normal intellectual and educational functioning" and were "indistinguishable" from their normal peers. These conclusions gave rise to much controversy, partly because the total sample comprised only 19 children (9 of whom were said to have possibly "recovered") and because of the very limited definition of "normal functioning" used.

However, in a series of studies, Fein and colleagues (Fein et al., 2013; Sutera et al., 2007) described a small number of children who, despite meeting full criteria for autism as preschoolers, no longer appeared to show any significant autistic impairments in adolescence. Anderson et al. (2014) also reported on a small number of individuals (8 out of a cohort of 85) who by the age of 19 years appeared to show no ASD symptoms. Neither research group refers to these individuals as "cured"; rather, they are described as having "optimal outcomes." Fein and colleagues, for example, do not rule out the possibility that these individuals might still retain some subtle deficits in social communication skills. Nevertheless, these studies, which were carefully conducted and involved detailed assessments over time, raise intriguing questions about the factors determining optimal outcomes. For example, why do other studies of adults with ASD (e.g., Farley et al., 2009; Howlin et al., 2013) fail to find individuals who no longer show any symptoms of ASD, even though several individuals in those cohorts are achieving highly? Is it because some subtle difficulties may become more apparent with age? Does the relatively early diagnosis of the Fein and Anderson cohorts make a difference, or is it the fact that more individuals in these cohorts received specialized interventions as children? Neither Fein and colleagues (Fein et al., 2013; Sutera et al., 2007) nor Anderson et al. (2014) were able to identify any specific characteristics that reliably predicted who, among individuals with an average IQ in childhood, would attain "optimal outcomes." Although less severe social impairments in infancy, better motor or other adaptive skills, and access to specialized intervention were associated with better outcomes for some, none of these variables accurately differentiated the "optimal outcome" from non-optimal outcome groups.

These studies are important in suggesting factors that are potentially associated with more positive outcomes, and the systematic testing of such hypotheses is now a significant challenge for future research. Identification of variables that modify outcome may not result in "recovery" but could well have a major impact on improving quality of life for both individuals with ASD and their families.

SUMMARY

A great deal more needs to be known about trajectories of change and outcomes of individuals with ASD in adulthood. It would be particularly informative to follow-up into adulthood those children who in the past 20–30 years have benefited from early, ASD-specific, and comprehensive educational and behavioral/developmental interventions. Only in this way can we establish whether, and to what extent, these programs result in improved adult outcomes. We also know very little about the development of females with ASD in adulthood, and virtually nothing is known about the physical, social, or mental health difficulties that older individuals with ASD may face (for a review of aging in ASD, see Happé & Charlton, 2012). For example, are rates of dementia higher or lower than those of the general population? What happens to older individuals with ASD when their parents die or can no longer care for them?

What we do know, however, is that the planning of and provision for specialized services for individuals with ASD in adulthood and older age are inadequate. Thus, studies of the effectiveness of various interventions and support services for adults with ASD in both clinical and community settings are urgently required. Finally, it is important to investigate, alongside individual and early childhood predictors, whether there are particular social or environmental factors that can enhance social integration and independence and contribute to improved outcomes for future generations of adults with ASD.

KEY POINTS

- The number of research studies published relating to the diagnosis, assessment, development, and treatment of the long-term developmental trajectories and outcomes of adults with ASD is far less than that related to children.
- Future ASD research studies should focus on the trajectory of change and outcomes of children with ASD who participated in programs and services targeting interventions specific to ASD to determine if these programs improve adult outcomes.
- ASD does not protect individuals from developing other medical and psychiatric comorbidities that can have a profound effect on their ultimate mental and social well-being.
- Society is not yet prepared to handle the influx of individuals currently diagnosed with an ASD who are yet to become adults; it is unclear how this will impact the individuals' ability to function independently and become productive members of society.
- Further studies on how to best care for and support adults with ASD in both clinical and community settings will provide a platform for improved outcomes for future generations of adults with ASD.

DISCLOSURE STATEMENT

Dr. Patricia Howlin and Dr. Iliana Magiati have nothing to disclose.

REFERENCES

American Psychiatric Association. (2013). *Diagnostic and statistical manual of mental disorders* (5th ed.). Arlington, VA: American Psychiatric Publishing.

Anderson, D. K., Liang, J. W., & Lord, C. (2014). Predicting young adult outcome among more and less cognitively able individuals with autism spectrum disorders. *Journal of Child Psychology and Psychiatry, 55*(5), 485–494.

Ballaban-Gil, K., Rapin, I., Tuchman, R., & Shinnar, S. (1996). Longitudinal examination of the behavioral, language, and social changes in a population of adolescents and young adults with autistic disorder. *Pediatric Neurology, 15*, 217–223.

Barneveld, P. S., Swaab, H., Fagel, S., van Engeland, H., & de Sonneville, L. M. J. (2014). Quality of life: A case–controlled long-term follow-up study comparing young high functioning adults with autism spectrum disorders with adults with other psychiatric disorders diagnosed in childhood. *Comprehensive Psychiatry, 55*(2), 302–310.

Beadle-Brown, J., Murphy, G., Wing, L., Shah, A., & Holmes, N. (2000). Changes in skills for people with intellectual disability: A follow-up of the Camberwell Cohort. *Journal of Intellectual Disability Research, 44*, 12–24.

Beaumont, R., & Sofronoff, K. (2008). A multi-component social skills intervention for children with Asperger syndrome: The Junior Detective Training Program. *Journal of Child Psychology and Psychiatry, 49*(7), 743–753.

Bishop-Fitzpatrick, L., Minshew, N., & Eack, S. (2013). A systematic review of psychosocial interventions for adults with autism spectrum disorders. *Journal of Autism and Developmental Disorders, 43*, 687–694.

Brugha, T. S., McManus, S., Bankart, J., Scott, F., Purdon, S., Smith, J., . . . Meltzer, H. (2011). The epidemiology of autism spectrum disorders in adults in the community in England. *Archives of General Psychiatry, 68*, 459–466.

Charman, T., Pickles, A., Simonoff, E., Chandler, S., Loucas, T., & Baird, G. (2011). IQ in children with autism spectrum disorders: Data from the Special Needs and Autism Project (SNAP). *Psychological Medicine, 41*(3), 619–627.

Chasson, G. S., Harris, G. E., & Neely, W. J. (2007). Cost comparison of early intensive behavioral intervention and special education for children with autism. *Journal of Child and Family Studies, 16*, 401–413.

Cross-Disorder Group of the Psychiatric Genomics Consortium. (2013). Genetic relationship between five psychiatric disorders estimated from genome-wide SNPs. *Nature Genetics, 45*(9), 984–994.

Donovan, J., & Zucker, C. (2010, October). Autism's first child. *The Atlantic.* Retrieved from http://www.theatlantic.com/magazine/archive/2010/10/autisms-first-child/308227

Edwards, T. L., Watkins, E. E., Lotfizadeh, A. D., & Poling, A. (2012). Intervention research to benefit people with autism: How old are the participants? *Research in Autism Spectrum Disorders, 6*, 996–999.

Esbensen, A. J., Greenberg, J. S., Seltzer, M. M., & Aman, M. G. (2009). A longitudinal investigation of psychoactive and physical medication use among adolescents and adults with autism spectrum disorders. *Journal of Autism and Developmental Disorders, 39*, 1339–1349.

Farley, M. A., McMahon, W. M., Fombonne, E., Jenson, W. R., Miller, J., Gardner, M., . . . Coon, H. (2009). Twenty-year outcome for individuals with autism and average or near-average cognitive abilities. *Autism Research, 2*, 109–118.

Fein, D., Barton, M., Eigsti, I.-M., Kelley, E., Naigles, L., Schultz, R. T, . . . Tyson, K. (2013). Optimal outcome in individuals with a history of autism. *Journal of Child Psychology and Psychiatry, 54*(2), 195–205.

Ganz, M. L. (2007). The lifetime distribution of the incremental societal costs of autism. *Archives of Pediatric and Adolescent Medicine, 61*(4), 343–349.

Ghaziuddin, M. (2005). *Mental health aspects of autism and Asperger syndrome*. London, England: Kingsley.

Gillespie-Lynch, K., Sepeta, L., Wang, Y., Marshall, S., Gomez, L., Sigman, M., & Hutman, T. (2012). Early childhood predictors of the social competence of adults with autism. *Journal of Autism and Developmental Disorders, 42*(2), 161–174.

Happé, F., & Charlton, R. A. (2012). Aging in autism spectrum disorders: A mini-review. *Gerontology, 58*, 70–78.

Henninger, N. A., & Taylor, J. L. (2013). Outcomes in adults with autism spectrum disorders: An historical perspective. *Autism, 17*(1), 103–116.

Howlin, P. (2014). Outcomes in adults with autism spectrum disorders. In F. R. Volkmar, R. Paul, S. J. Rogers, & K. A. Pelphrey (Eds.), *Handbook of autism and pervasive developmental disorders, fourth edition: Assessment, interventions, policy, the future*. Hoboken, NJ: Wiley.

Howlin, P., & Moss, P. (2012). Adults with autism spectrum disorders. *Canadian Journal of Psychiatry, 57*(5), 275–283.

Howlin, P., Moss, P., Savage, S., & Rutter, M. (2013). Social outcomes in mid to later adulthood among individuals diagnosed with autism as children. *Journal of the American Academy of Child & Adolescent Psychiatry, 52*(6), 572–558.

Howlin, P., Savage, S., Moss, P., Tempier, A., & Rutter, M. (2014). Cognitive and language skills in adults with autism: A 40-year follow-up. *Journal of Child Psychology and Psychiatry, 55*(1), 49–58.

Hutton, J., Goode, S., Murphy, M., Le Couteur, A., & Rutter, M. (2008). New-onset psychiatric disorders in individuals with autism. *Autism, 12*, 373–390.

Kanner, L. (1943). Autistic disturbances of affective contact. *Nervous Child, 2*, 217–250.

Kanner, L. (1973). *Childhood psychosis: Initial studies and new insights*. New York, NY: Winston/Wiley.

Knapp, M., Romeo, R., & Beecham, J. (2009). Economic cost of autism in the UK. *Autism, 13*(3), 317–336.

Lawson, W. (2002). *Life behind glass*. London, England: Kingsley.

Levy, A., & Perry, A. (2011). Outcomes in adolescents and adults with autism: A review of the literature. *Research in Autism Spectrum Disorders, 5*(4), 1271–1278.

Liptak, G. S., Kennedy, J. A., & Dosa, N. P. (2011). Social participation in a nationally representative sample of older youth and young adults with autism. *Journal of Developmental & Behavioral Pediatrics, 32*, 277–283.

Lounds Taylor, J., Dove, D., Veenstra-VanderWeele, J., Sathe, N. A., McPheeters, M. L., Jerome, R. N., . . . Warren, Z. (2012, June). Interventions for adolescents and young adults with autism spectrum disorders. *Comparative Effectiveness Reviews*, No. 65, AHRQ Publication No. 12-EHC063-EF. Rockville, MD: Agency for Healthcare Research and Quality.

Lovaas, O. I. (1987). Behavioral treatment and normal educational and intellectual functioning in autistic children. *Journal of Consulting and Clinical Psychology, 55*, 3–9.

Magiati, I., Tay, X. W., & Howlin, P. (2014). Cognitive, language, social and behavioral outcomes in adults with autism spectrum disorders: A systematic review of longitudinal follow-up studies in adulthood. *Clinical Psychology Review, 34*(1), 73–86.

Mavranezouli, I., Megnin-Viggar, O., Cheema, N., Howlin, P., Baron-Cohen, S., & Pilling, S. (2014). The cost-effectiveness of supported employment for adults with autism in the UK. *Autism, 18*(8), 975–984.

National Institute for Health and Clinical Excellence. (2012). *Autism: Recognition, referral, diagnosis and management of adults on the autism spectrum*, No. CG142. Available online at http://www.nice.org.uk/guidance/CG142

Orsmond, G. I., Shattuck, P., Cooper, B. P., Sterzing, P. R., & Anderson, K. A. (2013). Social participation among young adults with an autism spectrum disorder. *Journal of Autism and Developmental Disorders, 43*, 2710–2719.

Piven, J., Rabins, P., & the Autism in Older Adults Working Group. (2011). Autism spectrum disorders in older adults: Towards defining a research agenda. *Journal of the American Geriatric Society, 59*(11), 2151–2155.

Roux, A., Shattuck, P. T., & Cooper, B. P. (2013). Postsecondary employment experiences among young adults with an autism spectrum disorder. *Journal of the American Academy of Child & Adolescent Psychiatry, 52*(9), 931–939.

Rutter, M. (2013). Changing concepts and findings on autism. *Journal of Autism and Developmental Disorders, 43,* 1749–1757.

Rutter, M., Greenfeld, D., & Lockyer, L. (1967). A five to fifteen year follow-up study of infantile psychosis: II. Social and behavioral outcome. *British Journal of Psychiatry, 113,* 1183–1199.

Seltzer, M., Krauss, M., Shattuck, P., Orsmond, G., Swe, A., & Lord, C. (2003). The symptoms of autism spectrum disorders in adolescence and adulthood. *Journal of Autism and Developmental Disorders, 33,* 565–581.

Seltzer, M. M., Shattuck, P., Abbeduto, L., & Greenberg, J. S. (2004). Trajectory of development in adolescents and adults with autism. *Mental Retardation and Developmental Disabilities Research Reviews, 10,* 234–247.

Shattuck, P., Seltzer, M., Greenberg, J., Orsmond, G. I., Bolt, D., Kring, S., . . . Lord, C. (2007). Change in autism symptoms and maladaptive behaviors in adolescents and adults with an autism spectrum disorder. *Journal of Autism and Developmental Disorders, 37,* 1735–1747.

Shattuck, P., Wagner, M., Narendorf, S., Sterzing, P., & Hensley, M. (2011). Post-high school service use among young adults with autism spectrum disorder. *Archives of Pediatric Adolescent Medicine, 165*(2), 141–146.

Shattuck, P. T., Roux, A. M., Hudson, L. E., Lounds-Taylor, J., Maenner, M., & Trani, J.-F. (2012). Services for adults with an autism spectrum disorder. *Canadian Journal of Psychiatry, 57*(5), 284–291.

Slater-Walker, G., & Slater-Walker, C. (2002). *An Asperger marriage.* London, England: Kingsley.

Smoller, J. W. (2013). Disorders and borders: Psychiatric genetics and nosology. *American Journal of Medical Genetics Part B: Neuropsychiatry Genetics, 162B*(7), 559–578.

Sterling, L., Dawson, G., Estes, A., & Greenson, J. (2008). Characteristics associated with presence of depressive symptoms in adults with autism spectrum disorder. *Journal of Autism and Developmental Disorders, 38,* 1011–1018.

Sutera, S., Pandey, J., Esser, E. L., Rosenthal, M., Wilson, L., & Fein, D. (2007). Predictors of optimal outcome in toddlers diagnosed with autism spectrum disorders. *Journal of Autism and Developmental Disorders, 37,* 98–107.

Taylor, J. L., & Seltzer, M. M. (2011). Employment and post-secondary educational activities for young adults with autism spectrum disorders during the transition to adulthood. *Journal of Autism and Developmental Disorders, 41*(5), 566–574.

Tsakanikos, E., Costello, H., Holt, G., Bouras, N., Sturmey, P., & Newton, T. (2006). Psychopathology in adults with autism and intellectual disability. *Journal of Autism and Developmental Disorders, 36*(8), 1123–1129.

Underwood, L., McCarthy, J., & Tsakanikos, E. (2010). Mental health of adults with autism spectrum disorders and intellectual disability. *Current Opinion in Psychiatry, 23,* 421–426.

Willey, L. H. (1999). *Pretending to be normal: Living with Asperger's syndrome.* London, England: Kingsley.

Wodka, E. L., Mathy, P., & Kalb, L. (2013). Predictors of phrase and fluent speech in children with autism and severe language delay. *Pediatrics, 131*(4), e1128–e1134.

/// 4 /// DIFFERENTIAL DIAGNOSIS OF AUTISM SPECTRUM DISORDER ACROSS THE LIFESPAN

ISOBEL W. GREEN, CHRISTEN L. KIDD, AND ROBERT E. ACCORDINO

INTRODUCTION

When a patient presents with a suspected diagnosis of autism spectrum disorder (ASD), the clinician should thoroughly consider medical and psychiatric conditions with overlapping symptoms before making the diagnosis. The medical workup of these patients is discussed in Chapter 5. To facilitate our discussion of the differential diagnosis of ASD throughout the lifespan, we have divided the chapter between childhood and adulthood because the differential diagnosis changes considerably based on the age of the patient in question.

DIFFERENTIAL DIAGNOSIS IN CHILDHOOD

Early signs such as impaired social interaction, communication deficits, and stereotypic behavioral patterns have been consistently found in the first 2 years of life in retrospective studies of children diagnosed with ASD (Nadel & Poss, 2007). Such findings are important because early diagnosis is strongly associated with good outcome in individuals with ASD (Limon, 2007). Increased sensitivity to early signs of ASD, however, also increases the complexity of diagnosis because many early symptoms overlap significantly with those of other psychiatric conditions presenting at the same age and may be difficult to parse, especially in young children with difficulty communicating their subjective experience. Differential diagnoses continue to introduce complexity in the diagnosis of ASD throughout childhood, and clinicians should take care to consider such alternative explanations of presenting symptoms before diagnosing ASD.

Clinicians diagnose ASD on the basis of the presence of early developmental abnormalities, as well as the presence of characteristic symptoms (Bölte, Westerwald, Holtmann,

---

BOX 4.1

THE DIFFERENTIAL DIAGNOSIS OF AUTISM SPECTRUM DISORDER IN CHILDHOOD

Neurodevelopmental

Specific language impairment

Intellectual disability/global developmental delay

Mental and Behavioral

Attention deficit hyperactivity disorder

Oppositional defiant disorder

Conduct disorder

Attachment disorders

Social anxiety disorder

Major depressive disorder

Obsessive–compulsive disorder

Psychosis

Tourette's disorder

Selective mutism

Freitag, & Poustka, 2011). Differential diagnoses include symptoms that closely align with the two core symptom groups of ASD: deficient social communication and interaction and restricted, repetitive patterns of behavior or interests. Such differential diagnoses may be considered in two main areas: (1) neurodevelopmental and (2) mental and behavioral (Box 4.1). Neurodevelopmental differential diagnoses tend to involve early language development and communication deficits similar to those seen in children with ASD, whereas mental and behavioral differential diagnoses tend to mimic most closely the impaired social interaction and behavioral rigidity also characteristic of ASD.

Neurodevelopmental Disorders

Delayed speech development is the most common cause for referral to a clinician for ASD evaluation in preschool-aged children (Kuravackel & Ruble, 2014). Parents report impairment in receptive and expressive language, as well as an inability to communicate appropriately through language. Similar symptoms are seen both in specific language impairment and in global developmental delay and general intellectual disability (ID), and diagnosing clinicians should carefully consider the possibility of the child's symptoms emerging purely from a language disorder or intellectual impairment rather than ASD.

Specific Language Impairment

Specific language impairment (SLI) is diagnosed on the basis of deficits in speech production or interpretation, which impact a child's ability to interpret (receive) and produce (express) meaningful language (Prelock, Hutchins, & Glascoe, 2008). Like ASD, language disorders may also present with delayed play and imagination, as well as impaired social communication. Children with SLI, however, may be differentiated from those with ASD by the degree of deficits in social motivation: Children with SLI will generally compensate for their impoverished verbal communication by using nonverbal methods, including pointing and gesturing, and as such develop a relatively normal profile of social interaction (Macferran, Major, Fussel, & Hihg, 2011). Children with ASD, in contrast, will show consistent poverty of social interaction and a lack of empathy or interest in others.

If a child presenting with impaired use or understanding of language shows empathy and interest in social interaction (even if the experience of interaction itself is impaired) and exhibits developmentally appropriate imaginative play, the differential diagnosis of SLI should be considered. For unclear cases, specific language testing may also be useful: Verbal children with ASD tend to perform better on expressive than receptive language tests, whereas children with language deficits alone will be more likely to show greater impairment in expressive than receptive language. In addition, the level of competency detected on language tests is more likely to align with social language performance in children with pure language impairment, whereas children with ASD may well exhibit a lower level of language usage than they are shown to be capable of (National Institute for Health and Clinical Excellence (NICE), 2011).

Intellectual Disability/Global Developmental Delay

Intellectual disability is a broad diagnosis given to individuals with developmental deficits in general mental abilities. According to the fifth edition of the *Diagnostic and Statistical Manual of Mental Disorders* (DSM-5; American Psychiatric Association (APA), 2013), individuals must show the developmental onset of impairment in both intellectual and adaptive functioning, demonstrating deficiency in both areas, such as reasoning, problem solving, abstracting, and learning, and in the ability to participate and function in society at a developmentally expected level (APA, 2013, p. 37). When the diagnosis of ID is made in children too young to be administered a classic IQ test, the condition is termed ASD (Weis, 2014); because the vast majority of referrals for an assessment of ASD in intellectually/developmentally delayed children occur within the first several years of life, global developmental delay is thus pertinent to the differential diagnosis. Like children with pure global developmental delay, those with ASD show delays in language use and comprehension, lack play and social skills, and exhibit difficulty communicating with others.

In children with severe global developmental delay, impairment is likely to appear across the developmental profile; intelligence tests tend to produce a globally low measure of cognition and functioning. This profile may be used to separate children with pure global developmental delay from those with co-occurring ASD because those with ASD will likely show relative strength in areas other than language and social understanding. In addition, children with global developmental delay alone will usually show developmentally appropriate social motivation, as well as interest in peers and efforts at imitation. Children with ASD, on the other hand, will present with marked deficits in social communication, play, and flexibility, as well as the characteristic sensory sensitivity, rigidity in behavior, and hyperfocused interests seen across the autism spectrum (NICE, 2011).

Mental and Behavioral Disorders

The developmental deficits seen in the early years of ASD are soon joined by the behavioral and social correlates of the condition. These later deficits may not emerge as early as developmental impairments in speech and language comprehension, but they introduce just as much diagnostic complexity, given their high concordance of symptoms with many psychiatric conditions. Indeed, the social and communicative dysfunction and rigid, repetitive behaviors considered hallmarks of ASD may also indicate a wide variety of mood and behavioral conditions. As such, the diagnosing clinician, especially when examining children referred slightly later in childhood, should proceed methodically by considering several psychiatric conditions that align closely with the presentation of ASD before making the diagnosis of ASD.

Attention Deficit Hyperactivity Disorder

Attention deficit hyperactivity disorder (ADHD) is the most common neurobehavioral condition diagnosed in childhood (Wolraich et al., 2011). Characterized by impaired functioning or development due to persistent inattention and/or hyperactivity/impulsivity, the DSM-5 specifies that six or more symptoms of inattention and hyperactivity/impulsivity, each, must be present for diagnosis. Many of the symptoms listed in DSM-5 correlate closely with the behavioral patterns seen in individuals with ASD. Statements such as "often does not seem to listen when spoken to directly," "often does not follow through on instructions," "often runs about or climbs in situations where it is not appropriate," "often talks excessively," and "often interrupts or intrudes on others" demonstrate overlapping symptoms between ADHD and ASD (APA, 2013, p. 60).

Despite the significant concordance between profiles of childhood ADHD and ASD and recent findings of high comorbidity between the two conditions, an ADHD diagnosis remains in the differential of ASD with a profile separable from ASD with and without comorbid ADHD. Of note, whereas the DSM-IV specified the conditions as mutually exclusive, the DSM-5 allows for dual diagnosis (Leitner, 2014). A child with ADHD in the absence of ASD may present with the poor social skills and intrusive social behavior often exhibited in children with ASD but, unlike the child with ASD, will show appropriate comprehension of social norms (if not adherence to them). In addition, the child with ADHD will show appropriate social reciprocity and nonverbal communication. Although children with ADHD, like those with ASD, may engage in dangerous behavior, those with ADHD will likely show an appreciation of its potential dangers. Children with ASD, on the other hand, may show little understanding of social rules and exhibit deficits in reciprocity and nonverbal interaction. In addition, their dangerous behaviors may arise from an unawareness of common dangers rather than from impulsivity (NICE, 2011).

Oppositional Defiant Disorder

Oppositional defiant disorder (ODD), diagnosed most frequently in the preschool years, is characterized by a persistent negativity, defiance, and disobedience toward authority (Hamilton & Armando, 2008). Although it may be initially difficult to determine whether children presenting with ODD-like symptoms truly have the condition or are rather merely experiencing a "phase" of difficult behavior, individuals with ODD will maintain a reliable pattern of defiance and disobedience into later childhood and will typically show tense relations with their parents, instructors, teachers, and classmates (Hamilton & Armando, 2008). ODD's most marked presentation, therefore, is deficiency in social interaction; the defiant, disruptive behavior of children with ODD isolates them from their community (Loeber, Burke, & Pardini, 2009). Because a similar degree of social ineptitude and subsequent alienation may be seen in ASD, clinicians should carefully consider the diagnosis of ODD before confirming the diagnosis of ASD in children referred for poor social ability.

Although oppositional behavior is frequently present in children with ASD, several characteristics differentiate full ODD from the set of oppositional symptoms seen in ASD. When a child with ASD acts in opposition of others, the behavior often occurs inadvertently, as a product of hyperfocus on a personal pursuit or interest rather than in a purposeful act of defiance. When children with ASD are informed of the negative impact of their behavior on others, they are likely to become distraught. Children with ODD, on the other hand, are generally aware of the oppositional nature of their behavior and may act deliberately. In addition, children with ODD will show an ability to modulate the disruptive nature of their behavior at will, evincing a degree of social understanding beyond the child with ASD. In addition, children with ODD will generally lack the rigid, repetitive behavioral profile of ASD (NICE, 2011).

Conduct Disorder

Like ODD, conduct disorder involves marked social impairment. In individuals with conduct disorder, this impairment emerges from a persistent pattern of violation of others' basic rights and flouting of major social norms and standards. Conduct disorder is marked by aggression to people and animals, destruction of property, deceitfulness or theft, and consistent violation of societal or community rules (e.g., running away from home and skipping class in elementary school). Like ODD, childhood-onset conduct disorder may present with a level of social impairment comparable to that seen in children with ASD. Clinicians should thus consider conduct disorder in individuals referred for ASD assessment on the basis of marked social impairment.

As is the case for distinguishing children with ODD from those on the autism spectrum, individuals whose social impairment stems from conduct disorder, rather than ASD, may be differentiated on the basis of their level of social comprehension (NICE, 2011). If the child's antisocial behavior seems purposefully harmful or the child exhibits understanding of the harm he or she induces but is not distressed by this understanding, conduct disorder should be considered. As in the ODD diagnosis, the child should also be examined for signs of the stereotyped, repetitive behaviors characteristic of ASD, which are unlikely to present in conduct disorder (Efstratopoulou, Janssen, & Simons, 2012). Children with conduct disorder can also be differentiated from those with ASD through an examination of their early social communication, which generally will have developed normally in those with conduct disorder. Children with conduct disorder are also more likely to demonstrate an unimpaired "theory of mind," showing full appreciation of the fact that others have idiosyncratic mental experiences that differ from their own.

Because the assessment process for the differential diagnosis of conduct disorder closely parallels that of ODD, the diagnosing clinician may differentiate these two diagnoses by examining the specific nature of the child's antisocial behavior; children with ODD are more likely to show globally problematic peer relationships, whereas children with conduct disorder may demonstrate social competence in certain settings, associating with a deviant group (Pardini & Fite, 2010). Children with conduct disorder will also generally show a pattern of physical cruelty, theft, and deceit not characteristic of children with ODD (Loeber, Burke, Lahey, Winters, & Zera, 2000). The DSM-5's removal of the exclusion criterion for conduct disorder in children with ODD also allows for a comorbid diagnosis (APA, 2013).

Attachment Disorders

The DSM-5 specifies two distinct types of attachment disorder: disinhibited social engagement disorder and reactive attachment disorder. The disorders by definition arise in children with a history of pathogenic care, often involving abuse or neglect. Disinhibited social engagement disorder is marked by abnormally disinhibited social behavior, with affected children regularly violating social boundaries and indiscriminately attaching to and seeking comfort from strangers (Gleason et al., 2011). Reactive attachment disorder, on the other hand, is characterized by significant emotional withdrawal, with diagnosed children presenting with low levels of social responsiveness and a lack of expressed attachment behaviors even to central caregivers; children with reactive attachment disorder characteristically fail to seek or respond to comfort when upset. Symptoms of the attachment disorders align with those of ASD in that children with ASD often also show abnormal behavior at separation from and reunion with caregivers and limited response to and consideration of others' distress. In addition, children with histories of social deprivation may have developed self-soothing behaviors that are repetitive and stereotyped, as are characteristic of children with ASD (NICE, 2011).

In investigating the potential diagnosis of attachment disorder in children referred for atypical social behavior, the clinician should first consider the child's developmental history: Without a history of emotional or physical neglect or maltreatment, a diagnosis of attachment disorder cannot be made. If the degree of social deprivation is unclear or maltreatment is known to have occurred, the diagnosing clinician may examine other factors: Children with attachment disorders will show relatively typical imaginative play and will generally lack the hyperintense interests characteristic of those with ASD. To assess for reactive attachment disorder, social communication may be examined: Communication in reactive attachment disorder will appear markedly avoidant, as opposed to merely poorly regulated. To assess for disinhibited social engagement disorder, motivation behind abnormal boundaries may be examined: If intrusive behavior is distinctly attention-seeking, disinhibited social engagement disorder is indicated, whereas if the violation occurs merely out of inconsideration, ASD is more likely. The National Institute for Health and Clinical Excellence's "differential diagnosis advice for healthcare professionals" gives the example of a child climbing onto a stranger's lap: A child with disinhibited social engagement disorder will do so to seek comfort from the stranger, whereas a child with ASD is more likely to clamber over the adult to access an object that the adult is blocking (NICE, 2011).

In children referred for atypical social behavior, clinicians should solicit a developmental and social history; if children come from nurturing households, attachment disorder is not indicated. If social history is unknown or tumultuous, the diagnosing clinician may look to the child's apparent motivation behind the atypical behavior: Avoidance markedly underlying deficient social communication or boundary violations clearly driven by attention-seeking point to diagnoses of reactive attachment disorder and disinhibited social engagement disorder, respectively. In addition, children with attachment disorders may progress rapidly when placed in a consistently nurturing environment, whereas those with ASD are more likely to maintain their clinical profile (NICE, 2011).

Social Anxiety Disorder

Social anxiety disorder is characterized by a persistent, overblown fear or anxiety of social situations. Children with social anxiety disorder will appear shy and withdrawn in unfamiliar social situations, and they may show clear discomfort in interactions with others—for example, not making eye contact. They often attempt to avoid school, given the high level of social engagement the classroom requires (Stein & Stein, 2008). The deficient social profile seen in social anxiety disorder may be reminiscent of that shown by children with ASD, with symptoms of childhood social anxiety disorder such as reduced eye contact common to ASD. In addition, children with social anxiety disorder may show repetitive questioning behavior that aligns with the persistent behavioral profile of ASD (Schneier, Rodebaugh, Blanco, Lewin, & Liebowitz, 2011). As such, social anxiety disorder should be considered in the differential diagnosis of children referred for ASD screening due to impaired social interaction.

Social anxiety disorder may be readily differentiated from ASD through the assessment of social communication in familiar situations. Although children with social anxiety disorder may show impaired social communication when confronted with a novel social situation and/or strangers, when interacting with familiar individuals, they will demonstrate developmentally appropriate social communication (Bölte et al., 2011). In addition, although children with social anxiety disorder may show repetitive behaviors in the form of persistent anxious questioning, this behavior will not have the stereotyped, ritualistic quality seen in children with ASD; the response need not be exactly the same to satisfy the questioning child (NICE, 2011).

In evaluating children referred for impaired social interaction, clinicians should investigate whether the impairment is present in all social situations or only in unfamiliar or performance-based scenarios. If the child shows appropriate social functioning with familiar individuals (e.g., when among family members), social anxiety disorder, rather than ASD, is indicated. If the child shows such a capacity for typical communication and also lacks other symptoms of ASD, such as a stereotyped set of behaviors and abnormal or idiosyncratic linguistic presentation (echolalia, using minimal language, and odd phraseology), a differential diagnosis of social anxiety disorder merits strong consideration. Finally, the clinician may consider the motivation behind the child's avoidant behavior; children with social anxiety disorder will characteristically express or evince fear of judgment or critique from others as a driving factor in their avoidance, whereas children with ASD will not show this preoccupation and may in fact demonstrate markedly low concern regarding others' opinions of their behavior (NICE, 2011).

Major Depressive Disorder

Major depressive disorder (MDD) in children is characterized by the presence of a depressed mood along with a constellation of affective, neurovegetative, and cognitive symptoms such as sleep and appetite disturbance, psychomotor changes, feelings of worthlessness and guilt, anhedonia (loss of interest in activities once enjoyed), reduced energy, impaired concentration, and suicidality (APA, 2013, p. 161). The withdrawn behavior, reduced verbalization, and lack of engagement with or interest in developmentally appropriate activities that mark childhood depression may create a behavioral profile that mimics ASD. As such, the differential diagnosis of depression requires consideration in children referred for impaired social engagement (NICE, 2011).

Children affected by MDD may, during depressive episodes, show a similar pattern of social withdrawal to children on the autism spectrum, but they will lack the developmental profile of ASD, as well as other characteristic symptoms, such as stereotyped, repetitive behaviors. In addition, their social impairment will present with an episodic course and may be situational.

In children referred for an ASD evaluation due to impaired social engagement, the diagnosing clinician should obtain an early developmental history. If the child has shown periods of normalized social behavior, with only sporadic social deficiency, depression is indicated over ASD, which is characterized by a pervasive developmental course (NICE, 2011).

Obsessive–Compulsive Disorder

Obsessive–compulsive disorder (OCD) in childhood presents as patterns of obsessions and compulsions that are time-consuming and cause marked distress and impairment in daily life (APA, 2013, p. 237). Obsessions are intrusive and recurrent thoughts or impulses that provoke significant anxiety, and compulsions are ritualistic behaviors that the child performs to relieve the obsession-induced anxiety. Such rituals—common compulsions include washing, checking, and ordering—may be repeated a set number of times or until anxiety is reduced and the child feels "just right" (Kalra & Swedo, 2009). Because the obsessive, ritualistic, and repetitive behavior patterns seen in children with OCD may appear similar to the stereotyped and repetitive behaviors characteristic of children with ASD, OCD should be considered in children referred for such rigid, ritualistic behaviors.

In evaluating children referred for such behavioral patterns, clinicians should examine the patient for evidence of the other cardinal characteristic of ASD—impaired social communication. Children with OCD generally show a capacity for typical social communication (Wouters & Spek, 2011). Although those with OCD may be hindered in social interaction by the intrusiveness of obsessional thoughts and the disruptiveness of compulsions, they will show appropriate social reciprocity and appropriate consideration for others. In addition, the repetitive behaviors seen in children with OCD are generally associated with avoiding harm, whereas those observed in children with ASD tend to be associated with preserving "sameness" from day to day. Children with OCD are far more likely to be bothered by their obsessions and to perceive them in an ego-dystonic manner, as opposed to children with ASD, who will be upset only if their rituals are interrupted. Rituals associated with ASD generally do not hold the magical thinking quality of those seen in OCD (e.g., "If I tap the door handle 10 times, no planes will crash in the next minute") (NICE, 2011).

Psychosis

Psychosis refers to a group of conditions characterized by (1) disorganized thinking, (2) delusions or hallucinations, and (3) altered thought processes. Although the diagnosis of psychosis in children is made more difficult by the evolving state of a child's mind and a natural propensity toward imaginative thought, it is now recognized that children can indeed experience true psychosis, including both disconnected thoughts and pure hallucinations (Joshi & Towbin, 2002). The various childhood psychotic disorders show a broad range of clinical presentations, but there remain common symptomatic threads across the group. Atypical social interaction, notably social withdrawal and lack of friends, is often the first symptom detected, across multiple forms of psychosis (Eggers, Bunk, & Krause, 2000). The profile created by such social symptoms may look like that seen in children with ASD, so in children referred for social disengagement and withdrawal, a primary psychotic disorder should be considered. Further confounding diagnosis, developmental language and motor deficits consistent with those present in children with ASD are seen in childhood-onset schizophrenia, and children with childhood-onset schizophrenia also show stereotypies such as hand flapping (Courvoisie, Labellarte, & Riddle, 2011). As such, childhood-onset schizophrenia and other presentations on the spectrum of psychotic behavior (schizotypal disorder and schizoaffective disorder), although rare, may closely mimic ASD at least in their surface presentation. Diagnosing clinicians should always consider a diagnosis of psychosis before diagnosing ASD—although if the child is nonverbal, a determination of psychotic processes cannot be made with confidence, so clinicians should proceed with caution in evaluating language-impaired children.

Although the social and developmental presentation of children with childhood-onset schizophrenia and other psychotic disorders may mimic the social deficits seen in ASD, the two conditions are differentiated by the presence of hallucinations and delusions, which will persist as a core feature in the child with childhood-onset schizophrenia. If auditory or visual hallucinations remain present throughout childhood, and it becomes clear that such symptoms are not merely attributable to the imaginative processes of childhood, childhood-onset schizophrenia may be present (Joshi & Towbin, 2002) because persistent perceptual changes are not part of the ASD profile. In addition, although unusual thought patterns and fixations are seen in children with ASD, reality testing of children with ASD will generally show that atypical thought processes are not delusionary (Solomon, Ozonoff, Carter, & Caplan, 2008). Children with ASD perform typically on reality monitoring tasks (Farrant, Blades, & Boucher, 1998), whereas individuals with childhood-onset schizophrenia classically present with impaired reality monitoring (Subramaniam et al., 2012). Also, because psychotic symptoms will typically have a late-childhood onset (NICE, 2011), disordered communication and unusual pronunciation in younger children with ASD are more likely to be due to pragmatic language impairment (e.g., idiosyncratic or overly concrete language use and switching topics without providing context for the listener) than to delusional thoughts (Solomon et al., 2008).

Of note, before diagnosing psychosis, a clinician should carefully examine whether reports of psychotic symptoms in fact come from an overly literal interpretation of questions. When asked, for example, if he or she hears voices when no one else is in the room, a child with ASD may respond affirmatively despite having no auditory hallucinations due to the previous experience of hearing a voice when in an empty room, perhaps carrying over from a neighboring room or emitting from a television (NICE, 2011).

Tourette's Disorder

Tourette's disorder is a childhood-onset condition characterized by chronic motor and vocal tics (diagnosis requires that tics be present for at least 1 year). The motor tics observed in children with Tourette's disorder often appear similar to the stereotyped motor movements apparent in those with ASD (Volkmar, 2007), and vocal tics may involve echolalia (Ganos, Ogrzal, Schnitzler, & Münchau, 2012), which is also characteristic of children with ASD.

In a child referred for repetitive behaviors reminiscent of stereotypies, the diagnosing clinician should closely examine the behaviors to determine whether they are voluntary, rhythmic, and lingering. If the behaviors are instead involuntary, nonrhythmic, and rapid, they are not likely to be true stereotypies, and a diagnosis of Tourette's disorder, rather than ASD, may be indicated (Ozonoff, Rogers, & Hendren, 2003). In addition, children with Tourette's disorder will not show diminished capacity for social communication and reciprocity, although they may present with social isolation due to embarrassment or isolation by peers (Macferran et al., 2011).

Selective Mutism

Selective mutism is characterized by a persistent lack of speech in select social situations, despite normal speech present in other settings. Children with selective mutism will often fail to speak at school or with peers, despite communicating typically at home (Sharp,

Sherman, & Gross, 2007). The lack of social engagement seen in children with selective mutism may appear superficially similar to that arising in children with ASD, and the fact that many children with selective mutism will also have a history of language disorder or delay may also lead parents and clinicians to consider a diagnosis of ASD.

In the classroom, children with selective mutism may present very similarly to the child with ASD, given their social reticence and detachment. The child with selective mutism, however, will show entirely appropriate interaction in other situations; for instance, with family members, communication will usually be typical. In addition, a child with selective mutism will not show the stereotyped, rigid behaviors or hyperintense interests seen in ASD and will usually demonstrate appropriate nonverbal communication and normal imaginative play (NICE, 2011).

DIFFERENTIAL DIAGNOSIS IN ADULTHOOD

Recognition of ASD in adulthood presents a diagnostic challenge for several reasons. First and foremost is a universal challenge that is shared by all psychiatric and some neurological conditions—that of making a diagnosis based on behavioral criteria. Behavioral diagnoses are always more challenging and subject to discrepancies than diagnoses based on genetic, biochemical, or physical criteria, as in the examples of Huntington's disease, diabetes, and a fractured femur, respectively.

Relatively little is known about the course and manifestations of ASD in adults compared to the clinical expertise that has developed during approximately the past 25 years in the diagnosis and treatment of ASD in children and adolescents (Lehnhardt et al., 2013). Individuals with ASD can present with evolving manifestations over the course of their lifespan. According to what limited studies have found about the presentation of ASD in adults, the most prominent impairments exist in nonverbal communication and social reciprocity (Shattuck et al., 2007). Problems in verbal communication and with repetitive behaviors or stereotyped interests are less prominent. Indeed, studies have shown that of all ASD symptoms, repetitive behaviors decline most strongly with age (Seltzer et al., 2003).

Comorbidity of other psychiatric conditions also presents a challenge to the diagnosis of ASD in adults. Studies have shown that 50–70% of adults receiving a first-time diagnosis of ASD also carry or develop a diagnosis of a comorbid anxiety disorder, depression, or other psychiatric illness (Hofvander et al., 2009; Lehnhardt et al., 2013; Lugnegard, Hallerback, & Gillberg, 2011). Individuals who receive a first-time diagnosis of ASD in adulthood are more likely, by definition, to have a more subtle presentation than those whose ASD symptoms are obvious in childhood. These individuals usually have higher verbal competence and above average intelligence, and they "may achieve a comparatively high level of psychosocial functioning that often appears unremarkable, at least on the surface" (Lehnhardt et al., 2013).

Taken together, all of the previously mentioned aspects of the presentation of ASD in adulthood mean that the condition may easily be missed because it is intertwined with comorbid psychiatric symptoms or hidden behind social or cognitive compensations that come with age and experience. Therefore, the differential diagnosis for ASD in adulthood is broad, encompassing anxiety and mood disorders, personality disorders, and psychotic disorders (e.g., schizophrenia with predominant negative symptoms) (Box 4.2).

BOX 4.2

THE DIFFERENTIAL DIAGNOSIS OF AUTISM SPECTRUM DISORDER IN ADULTHOOD

Anxiety and Mood Disorders
Social anxiety disorder
Major depressive disorder with melancholic features
Obsessive–compulsive disorder
Personality Disorders
Obsessive–compulsive personality disorder
Avoidant personality disorder
Schizotypal personality disorder
Schizoid personality disorder
Psychotic Disorders
Schizophrenia with predominant negative symptoms

Anxiety and Mood Disorders

Social Anxiety Disorder

Social anxiety disorder is characterized by a fear of the scrutiny and judgment of others. In social situations—especially new, unfamiliar situations or group settings—individuals with social anxiety disorder fear that they will say or do something that will result in embarrassment or humiliation. Their fears can be so profound that these individuals will avoid most interpersonal encounters or endure them with intense physical and emotional discomfort (e.g., fear, trouble concentrating, avoiding eye contact, trembling, sweating, and heart racing) (Stein & Stein, 2008). Nevertheless, individuals with social anxiety disorder desire connection, company, and the good opinion of others.

Adults with ASD may appear similar to those with social anxiety disorder because individuals with either condition may exhibit social withdrawal in addition to being quiet in social situations. For these reasons, the diagnosis of either ASD or social anxiety disorder may be missed or delayed (Bejerot, Eriksson, & Mortberg, 2014). However, in certain situations, such as one-on-one settings with someone with whom the individual with social anxiety disorder feels comfortable, the symptoms of social anxiety will abate. In the individual with ASD, although symptoms may be less prominent in situations in which the individual feels safe and calm, the symptoms will not abate to the degree that they will in the patient with social anxiety disorder. In addition, individuals with social anxiety disorder are extremely sensitive to verbal and nonverbal signs of judgment or criticism, whereas interpreting social cues is one of the main areas of deficit in individuals with ASD. In other words, individuals with social anxiety disorder are highly attuned to nonverbal communication and social reciprocity, the precise diagnostic areas in which adults with ASD show impairment. Furthermore, individuals with ASD do not show the physical signs (e.g., tremor, sweating, and blushing) of anxiety in social situations that individuals with social anxiety disorder show.

Major Depressive Disorder With Melancholic Features

Melancholia is the term used to describe a particular type of severe depression character-ized by an almost complete loss of the capacity for pleasure and by severe neurovegetative symptoms (changes in sleep, appetite, and energy). Specifically, in addition to loss of plea-sure in all, or almost all, activities (anhedonia), it is characterized most notably by lack of mood reactivity, early morning awakening with depression worse in the mornings, marked psychomotor retardation or agitation, and significant appetite and/or weight loss (APA, 2013). It is sometimes thought to be more biologically driven and less the direct result of external stressors than other types of depression, although this etiologic aspect of melan-cholia is controversial.

An individual with melancholic depression—anhedonia, a noticeable lack of mood reactivity, and significant psychomotor slowing or agitation—might at first appear similar to an individual with ASD because of the social withdrawal and impairment generated by these particular depressive symptoms. Psychomotor slowing may appear as the impairment in eye contact, facial expressions, and gestures of social interaction evident in individuals with ASD. Similarly, anhedonia may appear as the lack of spontaneous seeking to share enjoyment, interests, or achievements seen in individuals with ASD. However, because melancholia is often an episodic, remitting illness, individuals with this type of depression, even in the midst of an episode, will be able to articulate that a fundamental change in them has occurred, as is not the case in those with ASD. Individuals with melancholic depression will have an abrupt decline in functioning associated with each episode, whereas in indi-viduals with ASD, functioning remains relatively constant, at least in the absence of serious psychiatric comorbidity.

Obsessive–Compulsive Disorder

As discussed in relation to the childhood differential diagnosis of ASD, OCD is marked by the presence of obsessions and compulsions, with the former characterized as recurrent, intrusive thoughts or impulses that cause significant anxiety, and the latter characterized as ritualistic behaviors performed to relieve the obsession-induced anxiety (APA, 2013). Common obsessions include contamination, symmetry, ordering/counting, forbidden thoughts, and harm. The compulsions undertaken to soothe obsessive processes present as rigid behavioral patterns and as such may be mistaken for the ritualistic stereotypies of individuals with ASD; as such, OCD is in the differential for adults referred for ASD assess-ment (Seibell & Hollander, 2014).

In adults referred for assessment of ASD traits who present with rigid, repetitive behav-iors, clinicians should first investigate whether the patient views his or her behaviors in an ego-syntonic or ego-dystonic manner. Unlike children with OCD, who may lack the lexi-con or insight to describe their obsessions as unreasonable (Storch et al., 2008), the vast majority of adults with OCD will readily acknowledge the irrationality of their thoughts and behaviors, despite feeling powerless to stop them (Geller et al., 2001). Individuals with ASD, on the other hand, generally view their repetitive behaviors as sensible and produc-tive (Lehnhardt et al., 2013).

As such, an ego-dystonic presentation suggests a diagnosis of OCD. In addition, empathy and social cognition are not generally impaired in individuals with OCD, so if the individual referred for repetitive behaviors presents with typical social and emotional understanding and reciprocity, OCD is further implicated and ASD is less likely.

Personality Disorders

Obsessive–Compulsive Personality Disorder

Obsessive–compulsive personality disorder (OCPD) is characterized in the DSM-5 as a condition involving impairments in self-functioning due to a rigid obsession with productivity, morality, or other personal or social codes. It also causes impairments in social functioning due to individuals' lacking empathy and hyperrigidity. Individuals with OCPD also show rigid perfectionism and inability to see more than one "correct" means of operating, as well as perseveration and inability to disengage from a task (APA, 2013). Unlike individuals with OCD, those with OCPD tend to view their compulsions in an ego-syntonic manner, believing that their self-imposed rules represent the "right and best way" to operate (International OCD Foundation, 2010). As such, individuals with OCPD tend not to report intrusive and upsetting thoughts or images, and their compulsions tend to center on achieving optimal states of, for example, productivity, morality, or order (Pinto, Steinglass, Greene, Weber, & Simpson, 2014). Because the repetitive, rigid behaviors seen in OCPD present similarly to the stereotypies of ASD, and lacking empathy and social impairment are also present in individuals with OCPD, clinicians should consider the diagnosis in adults referred for ASD assessment.

In adults presenting with the rigid behaviors and social impairment common in OCPD and ASD, clinicians should first consider the age of onset of symptoms. Because OCPD is considered an adult-onset disorder, if the individual reports behaviors extending into childhood, ASD is more likely. If the clinician confirms an adult onset of symptoms, the diagnostician may seek to differentiate between the two conditions by performing tests of effortful control and reward delay. Recent research has shown a significantly increased ability to delay gratification in individuals with OCPD compared to control participants without OCPD, with people with OCPD exhibiting a hypercapacity for self-inhibition (Pinto et al., 2014). Individuals with ASD, on the other hand, tend to show a significantly reduced ability to delay gratification and exercise effortful control, an impairment appearing across the lifespan of those with ASD (Faja & Dawson, 2015; Garon et al., 2009). As such, impairment on an effortful control and delayed gratification task would suggest ASD, whereas high performance would correlate with an OCPD diagnosis. In addition to effortful control presentation, clinicians may search for other ASD characteristics—such as impairment in nonverbal communication and sensory issues—that are not implicated in OCPD. Finally, clinicians may examine the particular profile of social impairment: Individuals with OCPD are more likely to be well-functioning in the broader community and show their most severe social deficits in intimate or familial relationships due less to social unawareness than to an unwillingness or inability to sacrifice productivity for intimacy (Costa, Samuels, Bagby, Daffin, & Norton, 2005). Those with ASD, on the other hand, generally show a more global impairment and misunderstanding of social principles.

Avoidant Personality Disorder

Avoidant personality disorder is very similar in presentation to social anxiety disorder. In fact, multiple studies have been carried out to examine whether an additional diagnosis of avoidant personality disorder in someone with social anxiety disorder adds anything helpful in terms of understanding the patient's illness (Chambless, Fydrich, & Rodebaugh, 2008; Cox, Pagura, Stein, & Sareen, 2009; Marques et al., 2012). Avoidant personality disorder is described as a "pervasive pattern of social inhibition, feelings of inadequacy, and hypersensitivity to negative evaluation, beginning by early adulthood and present in a variety of contexts" (APA, 2013, p. 673).

According to one study, although some features of avoidant personality disorder are important, a diagnosis of avoidant personality disorder in someone with generalized social anxiety disorder may have little clinical utility beyond being a marker of severity in the latter (Marques et al., 2012). However, the feature of "emotional guardedness" in avoidant personality disorder may be important in differentiating it from more severe cases of generalized social anxiety disorder. In this study, "emotional guardedness," assessed primarily by response to the Structured Clinical Interview for the DSM (SCID) scale item of "difficulty being open even with people you are close to," was found to most consistently differentiate avoidant personality disorder symptoms in patients with generalized social anxiety disorder (Marques et al., 2012).

These findings suggest that patients with avoidant personality disorder may appear even more similar to patients with ASD than do patients with social anxiety disorder alone. To differentiate avoidant personality disorder and ASD in adults, first it is important to observe patients' verbal and nonverbal communication during the interview. Patients with avoidant personality disorder may be very guarded but will be attuned, as are patients with social anxiety disorder, to social cues in a way that patients with ASD typically are not. For patients with avoidant personality disorder, although they may struggle and suffer in interpersonal relationships, particularly close ones, it is not the case that "how to make friends and socialize is a mystery," as is the case in patients with ASD (see Social Anxiety Disorder). Second, avoidant personality disorder, as with personality disorders generally, is not evident symptomatically until early adulthood, so a good psychiatric history can help enormously in differentiating avoidant personality disorder, and other personality disorders, from ASD. Finally, individuals with avoidant personality disorder will not use stereotyped or idiosyncratic language in the way that individuals with ASD may.

Schizotypal Personality Disorder

Schizotypal personality disorder is described as "a pervasive pattern of social and interpersonal deficits marked by acute discomfort with, and reduced capacity for, close relationships, as well as by cognitive or perceptual distortions and eccentricities of behavior" (APA, 2013, p. 656). Criteria for the disorder include odd or eccentric thinking, speech, and behavior, as well as "excessive social anxiety that does not diminish with familiarity and tends to be associated with paranoid fears rather than negative judgments about self" (p. 656). Criteria also include nondelusional ideas of reference, "odd beliefs or magical thinking that is inconsistent with subcultural norms," and suspiciousness or paranoid ideation.

Long-standing controversy exists about the conceptual and phenotypic overlap between ASD and the so-called schizophrenia spectrum disorders (SSD) (schizoid and schizotypal personality disorders and schizophrenia) (Barneveld et al., 2011). The conceptual blurring between the two areas began in the 1940s when Leo Kanner, in his classic paper on infantile autism, "Autistic Disturbances of Affective Contact" (Kanner, 1943), borrowed the term "autism" from Swiss psychiatrist Eugen Bleuler, who had coined it in 1911 to describe the socially withdrawn behaviors of individuals with schizophrenia. Since then, many researchers have argued about the boundaries between the two diagnostic categories. Studies in the 1970s for the most part argued that ASD and SSD were mutually exclusive categorical diagnoses with distinct developmental pathways (Barneveld et al., 2011). More recently, however, studies have shown empirical evidence for conceptual and phenotypic overlap of ASD and SSD (Barneveld et al., 2011; Hurst, Nelson-Gray, Mitchell, & Kwapil, 2007; Lugnegard et al., 2011).

The previously discussed history and recent findings demonstrate the difficulty with differentiating schizotypal personality disorder from ASD. As is evident from the criteria and previous discussion, ASD behavior traits can overlap with schizotypal ones, as has been confirmed in studies (Brugha et al., 2011; Pilling, Baron-Cohen, Megnin-Viggars, Lee, & Taylor, 2012). One study found that 40% of a group of individuals with ASD met formal criteria for schizotypal personality disorder (Barneveld et al., 2011). A key difference between the two groups is that individuals with schizotypal personality disorder have a paranoid dimension to their personality that individuals with ASD generally, although not always, do not. Patients with schizotypal personality disorder may exhibit magical thinking, nondelusional ideas of reference, and paranoid ideation, all of which are rooted in a certain suspiciousness about the motives and thinking of others. In contrast, individuals with ASD have impairments in their ability to conceptualize the mental state of others. They may be called "hypo-mentalizers," whereas individuals with schizotypal personality disorder tend to overinterpret the mental state of others in a suspicious or paranoid way and might be called "hyper-mentalizers" (Barneveld et al., 2011; Lehnhardt et al., 2013). Questioning patients along these lines, to help tease out whether this kind of mentally overinterpretive paranoid or suspicious thinking is present, will help greatly in differentiating patients with ASD from those with schizotypal personality disorder. Finally, as with all personality disorders, the patterns of the disorder generally appear during puberty or later, whereas in ASD, patterns are present from early childhood (Lehnhardt et al., 2013).

Schizoid Personality Disorder

Schizoid personality disorder is described as "a pervasive pattern of detachment from social relationships and a restricted range of expression of emotions in interpersonal settings, beginning by early adulthood and present in a variety of contexts" (APA, 2013, p. 653). Criteria for the diagnosis include "neither desires nor enjoys close relationships, including being part of a family"; "almost always chooses solitary activities"; "takes pleasure in few, if any, activities"; and "appears indifferent to the praise or criticism of others" (p. 653).

Interestingly, the term "schizoid," like the term "autism," was coined by Swiss psychiatrist Eugen Bleuler. Bleuler first used the term in 1908 to describe an individual's tendency to direct attention toward his inner life and away from the outside world. Bleuler called the exaggeration of this tendency the "schizoid personality." The existence of schizoid personality disorder as a discrete entity, however, has been controversial, and there is a paucity of empirical research validating it (Triebwasser, Chemerinski, Roussos, & Siever, 2012). It has been argued based on empirical evidence that it is not a personality disorder but, rather, a personality trait.

Individuals with schizoid personality disorder do not have a paranoid dimension to their personality, and this aspect makes it more challenging to differentiate schizoid personality disorder from ASD than it is to differentiate schizotypal personality disorder from ASD. As with schizotypal personality disorder, studies have confirmed overlap between schizoid and ASD behavioral traits (Brugha et al., 2011; Pilling et al., 2012). Therefore, if a patient fulfills criteria for schizoid personality disorder, it is probably most important to try to obtain a childhood developmental history to determine whether the patient actually has an undiagnosed ASD. If the answer is yes, the diagnosis of ASD would take precedence over the diagnosis of schizoid personality disorder because schizoid personality disorder "should not be diagnosed if the pattern of behavior occurs exclusively during the course of schizophrenia, a bipolar or depressive disorder with psychotic features, another psychotic disorder, or autism spectrum disorder" (APA, 2013, p. 656). That is, a patient cannot have a diagnosis of both ASD and schizoid personality disorder because it is understood that the schizoid symptoms are etiologically rooted in ASD and not a personality disorder. Finally, to make a diagnosis of schizoid personality disorder, it would be necessary to establish with certainty a childhood developmental history without patterns of behavior suggestive of ASD.

Psychotic Disorders

Schizophrenia With Predominant Negative Symptoms
Schizophrenia is characterized by both positive and negative symptoms of psychiatric illness. Positive symptoms are overtly psychotic; they are expressions of a loss of ability to participate with other people in a shared sense of reality. Positive symptoms include thought content not based in reality, such as paranoid delusions, and perceptual disturbances, such as auditory and visual hallucinations. Negative symptoms are not overtly psychotic. They are evidence of the loss of aspects of the sense of self. Negative symptoms include, among others, avolition, or loss of motivation, and blunted affect, or loss of emotional expressivity in facial expressions, gestures, and tone of voice. A given individual with schizophrenia can display any combination of symptoms—predominantly positive, predominantly negative, or a fairly balanced mix of both.

The presentation of schizophrenia with predominantly negative symptoms can appear similar to ASD. Negative symptoms can be described in a variety of ways, and there is a large body of research devoted to how to best characterize them. According to the most recent National Institute of Mental Health consensus statement in 2005, negative symptoms are most accurately categorized in five symptom domains: blunted affect, alogia (or poverty of speech), asociality (social withdrawal), anhedonia (loss of pleasure in activities), and avolition (loss of motivation) (Marder & Kirkpatrick, 2014). Studies have shown that although ASD and schizophrenia have different developmental trajectories, their clinical presentations at any one given time can overlap (Frith & Happe, 2005; Goldstein, Minshew, Allen, & Seaton, 2002). In particular, individuals with schizophrenia with predominantly negative symptoms have shown many of the same social deficits as individuals with ASD (Frith & Happe, 2005).

There are a few approaches that may be taken in trying to differentiate these two diagnoses. For an individual to qualify for a diagnosis of schizophrenia, he or she must at some point have had at least one of the following symptoms persisting for a significant portion of time for at least 1 month: delusions, hallucinations, or disorganized speech (e.g., "frequent derailment or incoherence") (APA, 2013, p. 99). Delusions or hallucinations persisting for this amount of time do not typically appear in ASD. The disorganized speech in schizophrenia is qualitatively different from the stereotyped and repetitive or idiosyncratic use of language in ASD. If a patient with schizophrenia, however, presents during a period of time when negative symptoms are predominant and the patient's only history of positive symptoms is disorganized speech, it may be difficult to tease out by history-taking the presence of disorganized speech if only alogia, or poverty of speech, is present on exam. If, however, a clear history of disorganized speech can be provided by a family member or close friend, this information can help to point toward a diagnosis of schizophrenia and not ASD. Of course, it is important, as in every case, to take as detailed as possible a history of childhood development because a patient with schizophrenia will not display prodromal symptoms as early as the patterns of ASD will appear in a child.

SUMMARY

The diagnosis of ASD across the lifespan remains a continuing clinical challenge, given the significant overlap between symptoms of ASD and those marking a wide variety of psychiatric conditions. Depending on the age and presentation of the patient, it may be appropriate for the clinician to consider a wide range of neurodevelopmental, anxiety, mood, personality, and psychotic disorders prior to making an ASD diagnosis. The most prominent presenting symptom should serve as a launching point for consideration of aligning differential diagnoses.

KEY POINTS

- When evaluating a child referred for possible ASD, consider both neurodevelopmental and mental and behavioral conditions based on the patient's symptoms. When evaluating an adult referred for possible ASD, consider anxiety, mood, personality, and psychotic disorders based on the patient's symptoms.
- Rather than marking a symptom as merely present, consider its particular profile in children and adults referred for possible ASD. For example, individuals with ASD will show global social impairment; those with social anxiety disorder will show impairment only in certain situations. Individuals with ASD will show inaccurate comprehension of others' mental states, but the misunderstanding will not hold the paranoid and suspicious quality seen in schizotypal personality disorder.
- Often, the holistic constellation of symptoms is more informative than the presence of any one characteristic. Search for symptom combinations: ASD diagnosis is more reliable if a child with a lack of social reciprocity also shows repetitive behaviors, nonverbal communication deficits, and intense interests.
- Move methodically through the diagnostic process. If an individual is referred for social impairment, consider, individually, each differential diagnosis involving social impairment, and compare that condition's profile to the patient's unique presentation.
- Tests outside of the usual clinical canon, such as measures of gratification delay and empathy, may be useful in parsing differential diagnoses.

DISCLOSURE STATEMENT

Dr. Robert Accordino, Dr. Isobel Green, and Dr. Christen Kidd have nothing to disclose.

REFERENCES

American Psychiatric Association. (2013). *Diagnostic and statistical manual of mental disorders* (5th ed.). Arlington, VA: American Psychiatric Publishing.

Barneveld, P. S., Pieterse, J., de Sonneville, L., van Rijn, S., Lahuis, B., van Engeland, H., & Swaab, H. (2011). Overlap of autistic and schizotypal traits in adolescents with autism spectrum disorders. *Schizophrenia Research, 126,* 231–236.

Bejerot, S., Eriksson, J. M., & Mortberg, E. (2014). Social anxiety disorder in adult autism spectrum disorder. *Psychiatry Research, 220,* 705–707.

Bölte, S., Westerwald, E., Holtmann, M., Freitag, C., & Poustka, F. (2011). Autistic traits and autism spectrum disorders: The clinical validity of two measures presuming a continuum of social communication skills. *Journal of Autism and Developmental Disorders, 41*(1), 66–72.

Brugha, T. S., McManus, S., Bankart, J., Scott, F., Purdon, S., Smith, J., ... Meltzer, H. (2011). Epidemiology of autism spectrum disorders in adults in the community in England. *Archives of General Psychiatry, 68*(5), 459–466, 647–656.

Chambless, D. L., Fydrich, T., & Rodebaugh, T. L. (2008). Generalized social phobia and avoidant personality disorder: Meaningful distinction or useless duplication? *Depression and Anxiety, 25*(1), 8–19.

Costa, P. T., Samuels, J., Bagby, M., Daffin, L., & Norton, H. (2005). Obsessive–compulsive personality disorder: A review. In M. Maj, H. S. Akiskal, J. E. Mezzich, & A. Okasha (Eds.), *Personality disorders* (pp. 405–439). New York, NY: Wiley.

Courvoisie, H., Labellarte, M. J., & Riddle, M. A. (2001). Psychosis in children: Diagnosis and treatment. *Dialogues in Clinical Neuroscience, 3*(2), 79–92.

Cox, B. J., Pagura, J., Stein, M. B., & Sareen, J. (2009). The relationship between generalized social phobia and avoidant personality disorder in a national mental health survey. *Depression and Anxiety, 26*(4), 354–362.

Eggers, C., Bunk, D., & Krause, D. (2000). Schizophrenia with onset before the age of eleven: Clinical characteristics of onset and course. *Journal of Autism and Developmental Disorders, 30,* 29–40.

Efstratopoulou, M., Janssen, R., & Simons, J. (2012). Differentiating children with attention-deficit/hyperactivity disorder, conduct disorder, learning disabilities and autistic spectrum disorders by means of their motor behavior characteristics. *Research in Developmental Disabilities, 33*(1), 196–204.

Faja, S., & Dawson, G. (2015). Reduced delay of gratification and effortful control among young children with autism spectrum disorders. *Autism, 19,* 91–101.

Farrant, A., Blades, M., & Boucher, J. (1998). Source monitoring by children with autism. *Journal of Autism and Developmental Disorders, 28*(1), 43–50.

Frith, U., & Happe, F. (2005). Autism spectrum disorder. *Current Biology, 15*(19), 786–790.

Ganos, C., Ogrzal, T., Schnitzler, A., & Münchau, A. (2012). The pathophysiology of echopraxia/echolalia: Relevance to Gilles de la Tourette's disorder. *Movement Disorders, 27*(10), 1222–1229.

Garon, N., Bryson, S. E., Zwaigenbaum, L., Smith, I. M., Brian, J., Roberts, W., & Szatmari, P. (2009). Temperament and its relationship to autistic symptoms in a high-risk infant sib cohort. *Journal of Abnormal Child Psychology, 37*(1), 59–78.

Geller, D. A., Biederman, J., Faraone, S., Agranat, A., ... Coffey, B. J. (2001). Developmental aspects of obsessive compulsive disorder: Findings in children, adolescents, and adults. *Journal of Nervous and Mental Disease, 189*(7), 471–477.

Gleason, M. M., Fox, N. A., Drury, S., Smyke, A., Egger, H. L., Nelson, C. A., III, ... Zeanah, C. H. (2011). Validity of evidence-derived criteria for reactive attachment disorder: Indiscriminately social/disinhibited and emotionally withdrawn/inhibited types. *Journal of the American Academy of Child and Adolescent Psychiatry, 8,* 216–231.

Goldstein, G., Minshew, N. J., Allen, D. N., & Seaton, B. E. (2002). High-functioning autism and schizophrenia: A comparison of an early and late onset neurodevelopmental disorder. *Archives of Clinical Neuropsychology, 17*(5), 461–475.

Hamilton, S. S., & Armando, J. (2008). Oppositional defiant disorder. *American Family Clinician, 78*(7), 861–866.

Hofvander, B., Delorme, R., Chaste, P., Nyden, A., Wentz, E., Stahlberg, O., ... Leboyer, M. (2009). Psychiatric and psychosocial problems in adults with normal-intelligence autism spectrum disorders. *BMC Psychiatry, 9,* 35.

Hurst, R. M., Nelson-Gray, R. O., Mitchell, J. T., & Kwapil, T. R. (2007). The relationship of Asperger's characteristics and schizotypal personality traits in a non-clinical adult sample. *Journal of Autism and Developmental Disorders, 37*(9), 1711–1720.

Joshi, P. T., & Towbin, K. E. (2002). Psychosis in childhood and its management. In K. L. Davis, D. Charney, J. T. Coyle, & C. Nemeroff (Eds.), *Neuropsychopharmacology: The fifth generation of progress*. Baltimore, MD: Lippincott Williams &Wilkins.

Kalra, S. K., & Swedo, S. E. (2009). Children with obsessive–compulsive disorder: Are they just "little adults"? *Journal of Clinical Investigation, 119*(4), 737–746.

Kanner, L. (1943). Autistic disturbances of affective contact. *Nervous Child, 2*, 217–250.

Kuravackel, G., & Ruble, L. (2014). Autism spectrum disorders: Reasons for treatment referrals across the developmental life span. *Journal of the Kentucky Medical Association, 12*(3), 51–56.

Lehnhardt, F., Gawronski, A., Pfeiffer, K., Kockler, H., Schilbach, L., & Vogeley, K. (2013). The investigation and differential diagnosis of Asperger syndrome in adults. *Deutsches Arzteblatt International, 110*(45), 755–763.

Leitner, Y. (2014). The co-occurrence of autism and attention deficit hyperactivity disorder in children—What do we know? *Frontiers in Human Neuroscience, 8*, 268.

Limon, A. (2007). Importance of early detection in autism spectrum disorder. *Gaceta Medica de Mexico, 143*(1), 73–78.

Loeber, R., Burke, J. D., Lahey, B. B., Winters, A., & Zera, M. (2000). Oppositional defiant and conduct disorder: A review of the past 10 years, Part I. *Journal of the American Academy of Child and Adolescent Psychiatry, 39*(12), 1468–1484.

Loeber, R., Burke, J. D., & Pardini, D. A. (2009). Perspectives on oppositional defiant disorder, conduct disorder, and psychopathic features. *Journal of Child Psychology and Psychiatry, 50*(1–2), 133–142.

Lugnegard, T., Hallerback, M. U., & Gillberg, C. (2011). Psychiatric co-morbidity in young adults with a clinical diagnosis of Asperger syndrome. *Research in Developmental Disabilities, 32*, 1910–1917.

Macferran, K., Major, N., Fussel, J., & Hihg, P. (2011). Differential and etiologic diagnosis of autism spectrum disorders. Developed for *Autism case training: A developmental–behavioral pediatrics curriculum*. Atlanta, GA: Centers for Disease Control and Prevention.

Marder, S. R., & Kirkpatrick, B. (2014). Defining and measuring negative symptoms of schizophrenia in clinical trials. *European Neuropsychopharmacology, 24*, 737–743.

Marques, L., Porter, E., Keshaviah, A., Pollack, M. H., Ameringen, M. V., Stein, M. B., & Simon, N. M. (2012). Avoidant personality disorder in individual with generalized social anxiety disorder: What does it add? *Journal of Anxiety Disorders, 26*(6), 665–672.

Nadel, S., & Poss, J. E. (2007). Early detection of autism spectrum disorders: Screening between 12 and 24 months of age. *Journal of the American Academy of Nurse Practitioners, 19*(8), 408–417.

National Institute for Health and Clinical Excellence. (2011). Appendix K. In *Autism: Recognition, referral and diagnosis of children and young people on the autism spectrum: Quick reference guide*. London, England: Author.

International OCD Foundation (201). *Obsessive compulsive personality disorder (OCPD)*. Available at http://www.ocfoundation.org/uploadedfiles/maincontent/find_help/ocpd%20fact%20sheet.pdf; accessed September 2014.

Ozonoff, S., Rogers, S., & Hendren, R. (2003). *Autism spectrum disorders: A research review for practitioners*. Washington, DC: American Psychiatric Publishing.

Pardini, D. A., & Fite, P. J. (2010). Symptoms of conduct disorder, oppositional defiant disorder, attention-deficit/hyperactivity disorder, and callous-unemotional traits as unique predictors of psychosocial maladjustment in boys: Advancing an evidence base for DSM-V. *Journal of the American Academy of Child and Adolescent Psychiatry, 49*(11), 1134–1344.

Pilling, S., Baron-Cohen, S., Megnin-Viggars, O., Lee, R., & Taylor, C. (2012). Recognition, referral, diagnosis, and management of adults with autism: Summary of NICE guidance. *British Medical Journal, 344*, e4082.

Pinto, A., Steinglass, J. E., Greene, A. L., Weber, E. U., & Simpson, H. B. (2014). Capacity to delay reward differentiates obsessive–compulsive disorder and obsessive–compulsive personality disorder. *Biological Psychiatry, 75*(8), 653–659.

Prelock, P. A., Hutchins, T., & Glascoe, F. P. (2008). Speech–language impairment: How to identify the most common and least diagnosed disability of childhood. *Medscape Journal of Medicine, 10*(6), 136.

Schneier, F. R., Rodebaugh, T. L., Blanco, C., Lewin, H., & Liebowitz, M. R. (2011). Fear and avoidance of eye contact in social anxiety disorder. *Comprehensive Psychiatry, 52*(1), 81–87.

Seibell, P. J., & Hollander, E. (2014). Management of obsessive–compulsive disorder. *F1000Prime Reports, 6,* 68.

Seltzer, M. M., Krauss, M. W., Shattuck, P. T., Orsmond, G., Swe, A., & Lord, C. (2003). The symptoms of autism spectrum disorders in adolescence and adulthood. *Journal of Autism and Developmental Disorders, 33*(6), 565–581.

Sharp, W. G., Sherman, C., & Gross, A. M. (2007). Selective mutism and anxiety: A review of the conceptualization of the disorder. *Journal of Anxiety Disorders, 24,* 568–579.

Shattuck, P. T., Seltzer, M. M., Greenberg, J. S., Orsmond, G. I., Bolt, D., Kring, S., . . . Lord, C. (2007). Change in autism symptoms and maladaptive behaviors in adolescents and adults with an autism spectrum disorder. *Journal of Autism and Developmental Disorders, 37*(9), 1735–1747.

Solomon, M., Ozonoff, S., Carter, C., & Caplan, R. (2008). Formal thought disorder and the autism spectrum: Relationship with symptoms, executive control, and anxiety. *Journal of Autism and Developmental Disorders, 38*(8), 1474–1484.

Stein, M. B., & Stein, D. J. (2008). Social anxiety disorder. *Lancet, 371,* 1115–1125.

Storch, E. A., Merlo, L. J., Larson, M. J., Marien, W. E., Geffken, G. R., Jacob, M. L., . . . Murphy, T. K. (2008). Clinical features associated with treatment-resistant pediatric obsessive–compulsive disorder. *Comprehensive Psychiatry, 49,* 35–42.

Subramaniam, K., Luks, T. L., Fisher, M., Simpson, G. V., Nagarajan, S., & Vinogradov, S. (2012). Computerized cognitive training restores neural activity within the reality monitoring network in schizophrenia. *Neuron, 73*(4), 842–853.

Triebwasser, J., Chemerinski, E., Roussos, P., & Siever, L. (2012). Schizoid personality disorder. *Journal of Personality Disorders, 26*(6), 919–926.

Volkmar, F. (2007). Autism and the pervasive developmental disorders. In A. Martin, F. R. Volkmar, & M. Lewis (Eds.), *Lewis's child and adolescent psychiatry: A comprehensive textbook.* Philadelphia, PA: Lippincott Williams & Wilkins.

Weis, R. (2014). Intellectual disability and developmental disorders in children. In *Introduction to abnormal child and adolescent psychology* (2nd ed.). Thousand Oaks, CA: Sage.

Wolraich, M., Brown, L., Brown, R. T., DuPaul, G., Earls, M., Feldman, H. M., . . . Visser, S. (2011). ADHD: Clinical practice guideline for the diagnosis, evaluation, and treatment of attention-deficit/hyperactivity disorder in children and adolescents. *Pediatrics, 128,* 1007–1022.

Wouters, S. G. M., & Spek, A. A. (2011). The use of the autism-spectrum quotient in differentiating high-functioning adults with autism, adults with schizophrenia and a neurotypical adult control group. *Research in Autism Spectrum Disorders, 5,* 1169–1175.

5

MEDICAL EVALUATION OF PATIENTS WITH AUTISM SPECTRUM DISORDER

YAMINI J. HOWE, MICHELLE L. PALUMBO, AND ANN NEUMEYER

INTRODUCTION

Autism spectrum disorder (ASD) is a highly heritable, biologically based, neurodevelopmental condition characterized by impairments in social communication and social interaction as well as restricted, repetitive patterns of behaviors (American Psychiatric Association, 2013; Hallmayer et al., 2011). This chapter addresses the medical aspects of caring for children, adolescents, and adults with ASD, focusing on important information to be obtained when taking a history and conducting a physical examination, as well as additional steps that are often necessary to complete a thorough evaluation and medical workup.

HISTORY

This section highlights key questions important to consider in taking the medical history of children, adolescents, and adults with ASD. A careful medical evaluation of patients with ASD should include taking a thorough developmental history, in addition to past medical history, review of systems, and social and family history, and it is to be generally conducted for all patients.

Developmental History

Taking a developmental history includes consideration of several developmental domains, including communication, cognition, play/leisure, motor, sensory, and emotional/behavioral. Within each domain, the clinician should be aware of the typical progression of developmental skills and elicit historical information to determine the individual patient's abilities compared with the norm. Even adolescents and adults with ASD can have challenges in simple developmental tasks that affect their functional abilities or activities of daily living. For example, skills may be highly developed in some areas (e.g., map reading) but may be quite impaired in others (e.g., maintaining oral hygiene). Therefore, a thorough and comprehensive assessment is needed in order to understand each individual's overall pattern of developmental strengths and weaknesses. Monitoring progress over time will give the clinician information necessary to tailor treatments and therapies for each individual. Furthermore, any loss of skills should alert the clinician to consider further medical or psychiatric evaluation.

Neuropsychological testing may be needed in order to inform clinical diagnosis and treatment, as well as to determine whether an individual may qualify for additional services through early intervention (or Birth-to-Three), school departments, and state-funded programs for individuals with intellectual or developmental disabilities (e.g., through a Department of Mental Retardation or Department of Developmental Services) (Ozonoff, Goodlin-Jones, & Solomon, 2005). Various aspects of cognitive function can be evaluated with neuropsychological testing. This should include verbal and nonverbal intelligence quotient (IQ), attention and executive functioning, adaptive functioning, severity of ASD symptomatology, as well as emotional and behavioral functioning.

Communication

Communication involves the ability to convey and comprehend the exchange of information with others and may be through a variety of means, including verbal, gestural, or graphic symbols (American Speech–Language–Hearing Association, 1993). Typical development of communication skills starts in infancy, when the infant learns to respond to his or her caregiver's cues and environmental stimuli through movements, facial expressions, and vocalizations. Between 6 and 12 months, verbal language progresses from babbling to production of single words. Between 12 and 18 months, vocabulary increases and speech develops to include typical prosody. The ability to share interests with others follows, including the integration of eye contact, verbalization, and gestures to direct another's attention (i.e., joint attention). Two-word combinations develop between 18 and 24 months, and by age 3 years, most are able to speak in simple sentences of three or four words.

Signs of verbal and nonverbal communication impairments for individuals with ASD may become apparent between 12 and 24 months of age, and they may present as failure to achieve language milestones. Language regression may also occur in 20–50% of children with ASD, and it typically presents as a loss of previously mastered language skills, usually beginning at approximately 18–24 months (Barger, Campbell, & McDonough, 2013; Zwaigenbaum et al., 2009). Language regression at approximately this age is considered a "hallmark" of ASD, but later onset of language regression and any motor regression is atypical and should prompt further medical workup. In addition, hearing loss may contribute to language delay, and part of the initial medical workup in a patient with possible ASD should include audiology evaluation (American Speech–Language–Hearing Association, 1991; Johnson & Myers, 2007).

Some individuals with ASD remain nonverbal, and others may develop fluent verbal abilities. Older children, adolescents, and adults who have developed more advanced language skills may have difficulty with nuances of language, such as use of irony and humor, or in engaging in reciprocal conversation. The use of verbal and nonverbal language for social interactions (known as social or pragmatic language skills) continues to be an area of weakness over the lifespan for those with ASD.

A formal evaluation by a speech–language pathologist is needed to determine the pattern of expressive, receptive, and social pragmatic skills for each patient. A speech–language pathologist can also consider alternative and augmentative communication (AAC) strategies (e.g., pictures, signs, or electronic devices) to assist in communication or aid in learning.

Medical providers and caretakers should ask about the means by which the individual communicates, verbal and/or nonverbal, and whether assistive devices are needed to ensure a successful patient encounter. Remember that a patient might use more than one mode of communication to express his or her needs or thoughts.

Cognition

Approximately 60% of children with ASD will have impairment in intellectual functioning. The Centers for Disease Control and Prevention (2014) estimates that 31% of children with ASD are classified in the range of intellectual disability (IQ ≤ 70), 23% with IQ in the borderline range (71–85), and 46% with average to above average intellectual abilities. Neuropsychological testing should be conducted on a periodic basis, starting at approximately age 5 years or early school age, in order to consider whether cognitive impairment or any learning disabilities may be present. This can be very important information for determining the most appropriate and effective school placement, outpatient treatments, or job-skills training program. Neuropsychological testing can also be helpful to determine whether academic or daily life functioning may be affected by behavioral comorbidities such as attention deficit hyperactivity disorder (ADHD) or anxiety, which may be amenable to psychopharmacological treatment. Finally, neuropsychological testing is important in determining the types and amount of services or benefits an individual may receive from the state in which he or she resides; having an intellectual disability can qualify some children and many adults for social security benefits or funding from the state's Department of Developmental Services (or Department of Mental Retardation).

Play/Leisure

Play skills in children with ASD are often delayed or discrepant with the child's developmental or cognitive level. Children may persist in enjoying play activities (e.g., play with blocks or dolls) when their peers have moved on to other areas of interest. They may have difficulty engaging others in play and knowing how to interact with peers. Referral for outpatient social skills groups or additional support for social skills may be necessary in the school setting. Older children and adults may develop highly focused interests in an unusual topic (e.g., weathervanes and lighting fixtures) that interferes with academic and/or vocational pursuits or social interactions. Questions about whether the child has friends, eats alone at school, plays alone at recess, or is invited to parties can inform the examiner about the child's social abilities.

Persistent sensory play and repetitive forms of play are also characteristic of ASD. Some patients may line up or sort objects, or they may explore the sensory aspect of items such as inspecting them at close range or shaking an object to hear a particular sound over and over.

They may just play with part of a toy (e.g., the wheels of a truck) or focus on a certain scene in a video. These behaviors may be rewarding to the patient, but they appear unusual to peers or strangers.

Motor

Individuals with ASD often have an early history of achieving motor milestones toward the later range of normal, and they may have generally low muscle tone (Jeste, 2011).

Children may appear to slouch or appear "floppy." Some children may appear weak, but asking about what the child is like when angry may help to distinguish true weakness from low tone. Many children with ASD prefer not to exercise or may not have the opportunity, which may contribute to a general deconditioned status exacerbating underlying low tone. Encouraging exercise is important for general health and well-being. Referral to occupational therapists and physical therapists is needed for careful assessment and treatment of fine and gross motor impairments, with the goals of helping individuals to attain functional skills at school as well as in daily life. Some children may get weaker with exercise or after infection or illness, and in those cases a muscle disorder (e.g., muscular dystrophy), disorder of energy metabolism, or mitochondrial disorder should be considered.

Motor stereotypies are repetitive motor movements that are voluntary, rhythmic, and apparently purposeless. They are a core feature of ASD, although they can also be seen in the general population and in other developmental disabilities (Goldman et al., 2009). Hand flapping and toe walking are common, particularly when the individual is excited or agitated.

Sensory Processing Differences

Sensory processing differences, also called sensory integration dysfunction or disorder, are a feature of ASD and have been included in the *Diagnostic and Statistical Manual of Mental Disorders*, 5th edition (DSM-5), criteria (American Psychiatric Association, 2013). Many individuals with ASD may under- or overreact to sensory stimuli. For example, caregivers may describe them as being intolerant of particular clothing, sounds, or sensations. In particular, medical providers should question parents on how avoidance of certain foods or textures may impact nutrition. As mentioned previously, it is important to establish an individual's baseline patterns of behavior because a change in sensory-seeking or repetitive behaviors can be a sign of medical illness. Occasionally, sensory-seeking behaviors may pose a safety risk. For example, if a patient is excessively mouthing or swallowing nonfood items (i.e., pica), medical workup might include screening lead levels (for those living in older homes in which lead paint was used or in high-risk geographic areas) or screening for anemia (pica can be a symptom of iron deficiency). An increase in mouthing behaviors can also be seen at times of a loose tooth or may be an indication of dental cavity, abscess, or symptoms of gastroesophageal reflux (Filipek et al., 2000).

Emotional/Behavioral Development

Psychiatric comorbidity is addressed further in Chapter 6. Understanding the individual's baseline emotional and behavioral profile is important because any change in status might alert the clinician caring for the patient's medical needs to elicit further history pertaining to potential underlying medical illness. For example, individuals may become less interactive or communicative with others in the setting of an infectious process.

Self-injurious behaviors may be related to general frustration with the inability to communicate needs in general or may be a way to indicate pain or discomfort. Worsening emotional or behavioral problems should prompt the clinician to elicit whether there may be any localizing features (e.g., self-injurious behaviors around the ear may be an expression of ear pain due to otitis media). Irritability is common in ASD and may manifest as being difficult to please, always seeming angry, or being set off by seemingly innocuous things. Before irritability is determined to represent a behavioral or psychiatric issue, however, the medical provider first needs to focus on ruling out a possible identifiable medical illness.

Past Medical History

As for all children, a careful birth and medical history should be obtained, as well as details of past medical or psychiatric facility stay and surgeries. In particular, gastrointestinal (GI) and sleep complaints are common among patients with ASD, and these are further described here. Concern for possible seizure activity and macrocephaly should also be considered, and this is addressed in more detail in Chapter 7. In addition, developmental regression with illness could be a sign of a metabolic or mitochondrial disorder and should prompt further workup.

Gastrointestinal

Children with ASD have unusually high rates of GI disorders (Coury et al., 2012). Common concerns include constipation, abdominal pain with or without diarrhea and encopresis, gastroesophageal reflux disease (GERD), and inflammation along the GI tract or colitis. Symptoms can present as behavioral changes such as insomnia, self-injurious behaviors, pica, spitting/drooling, and irritability (Buie et al., 2010). Belly pain might be expressed as tummy rubbing or pressing the belly up against objects. Rumination, or the effortless regurgitation of meals, can be a sign of a motility disorder. GERD can present as tonic neck movements in children and adults, as seen in Sandifer syndrome in infants (Lehwald et al., 2007; Nowak, Strzelczyk, Oertel, Hamer, & Rosenow, 2012). A referral back to the primary care provider or a gastroenterologist could help with further diagnosis and treatment of these conditions.

Sleep

Sleep problems are seen in 40–86% of children with ASD, which is higher than in children with other developmental delays. Sleep problems can lead to daytime behavioral difficulties in children with ASD, including inattention, impulsivity, and decreased tolerance for change (Sikora, Johnson, Clemons, & Katz, 2012). Problems may be due in part to difficulties falling asleep often related to anxiety, as well as wakefulness during the night (Goldman, Richdale, Clemons, & Malow, 2012). Insomnia may be due to core behavioral problems in ASD and/or associated comorbidities (psychiatric disorders, epilepsy, GI problems, and sleep-disordered breathing). Multiple studies have shown problems with melatonin production/regulation in individuals with ASD, and melatonin supplementation may provide benefit (Rossignol & Frye, 2011). There are other sleep disorders, such as restless leg syndrome and obstructive sleep apnea, that need to be addressed, as in a typical child. Night terrors, a brief and dramatic awakening during the first 3 hours of sleep, are often more upsetting for the parents than the child, who has no memory of the event.

Review of Systems

Clinicians should elicit a thorough review of systems, as with all patients, but should also include questions relevant to issues described in other sections of this chapter. Issues particularly pertinent to caring for individuals with ASD are presented here.

Constitutional

Does the patient have a history of recurrent severe illnesses that might suggest metabolic disease?

Head, Eyes, Ears, Nose, and Throat

Have hearing and vision been screened? Individuals with ASD may have difficulty complying with routine vision screening, and a referral to an ophthalmologist or optometrist experienced in working with individuals with developmental disabilities is often needed. A formal evaluation of hearing should also be conducted by an audiologist to rule out hearing loss as a contributing factor to language delay.

Dental

Does the patient have regular visits with a dentist? Referral to a dentist experienced in caring for those with developmental disabilities should be considered.

Respiratory/Cardiovascular

Many psychotropic medications have cardiovascular side effects, and nonverbal individuals may have difficulty expressing chest pain, so the clinician should inquire as to whether there has been any change in activity or levels of exertion.

Gastrointestinal/Genitourinary

In addition to eliciting information about bowel patterns, a delay in achieving toileting skills is common among individuals with ASD. This is often a major concern for caregivers. The clinician should also ask about enuresis.

Musculoskeletal

As mentioned previously, a delay in achieving motor milestones and advanced coordination skills is common, but myalgia, muscle weakness, and muscle pain are uncommon and should warrant further medical workup by a neurologist.

Neurological

In addition to the neurological concerns mentioned previously, a history of head trauma, headaches, seizures, or loss of consciousness is important in considering developmental progress and need for brain imaging.

Dermatologic

History of unusual birthmarks or rash might alert clinicians to screen for specific genetic or metabolic syndromes. As with all patients, eczema is common, but in particular extensive skin rash and itchiness can lead to chronic irritability and self-injurious behavior. Individuals residing in group living facilities are more likely to develop common infectious skin conditions, such as tinea pedis and common warts, that can also be irritating or painful. Those who wear diapers for extended periods are more susceptible to diaper dermatitis.

Endocrinologic

Are there symptoms to suggest thyroid disease, diabetes, or metabolic syndrome? Weight loss and weight gain are common side effects of medications.

Hematologic

With individuals who may eat a limited diet due to sensory preferences or ritualized patterns of behavior, are there symptoms suggestive for anemia due to inadequate dietary iron intake?

Immunologic

As with all patients, it is important to consider whether there is a history of asthma or allergy because allergy symptoms can lead to discomfort and affect behavior.

Sleep

As mentioned previously, taking a careful sleep history is important. Does the patient have snoring or restless sleep that might disrupt sleep? What is the usual bedtime and wake time? Where does the patient sleep? Does the patient's behavior in the night disrupt the sleep of others in the household? Does being awake at night when others are sleeping impact the patient's safety?

Social and Family History

As with all medical visits, a thorough social and family history should be obtained in order to determine what further supports are needed and to target further genetic workup. Drawing a family pedigree can be a useful way to elicit this information. This section presents additional topics to be considered as part of a careful history in individuals with ASD.

Living Situation

With whom and in what type of setting does the individual live?

Educational History

For children younger than age 3 years, it is important to elicit whether they are enrolled in early intervention (EI) or Birth-to-Three services. From age 3 to age 18–22 years, depending on the state, individuals may qualify for special education services through their local school district. With EI and school services, it is important to understand what services are being provided and what the goals are of these services, the training background of service delivery providers, and how many hours of services are being provided, as well as where the services are being delivered. If the individual is in a school setting, the provider may ask questions about class size, whether it is a private or public school, the ratio of students to teachers, and where the child receives services (e.g., at home, in a general education setting, in a smaller separate special education classroom, or individually at school).

Vocational History

At age 14 years, schools should start planning the transition from adolescent to adult services, as well as planning for vocational training needs.

Neuropsychological (described previously), educational, and/or vocational evaluations may be needed at this time. For those who are working, what level of supervision and independence does the patient have at work, and what supports are in place to ensure success?

Additional Supports

Individuals with ASD may receive funding or other supports through the state's Department of Developmental Services (or Department of Mental Retardation). Considering whether the individual has been able to receive health insurance through local Medicaid or supplemental insurance programs (e.g., Katie Beckett medical waivers in some states) is also important to understand what further resources may be available.

Legal History

Has the child or young adult ever been arrested or had interactions with the law?

Safety

Consideration of the safety of the individual's environment is important. For example, individuals who lack safety awareness may try to escape from the home, they may be at higher risk for falls if they recklessly climb up on high places such as counters or windows, and additional locks or other safety measures may be needed. Special car seats or harnesses may be needed to ensure safety in vehicles. Individuals with ASD or other developmental disabilities are also particularly prone to become targets of bullying or teasing. Furthermore, as for all individuals, eliciting whether they may have witnessed violence or whether they themselves may have been victims of physical or sexual abuse are important considerations and can lead to changes in behavior patterns (Mandell, Walrath, Manteuffel, Sgro, & Pinto-Martin, 2005).

Sexual History

Adolescents and adults with intellectual disabilities may lack awareness of appropriateness of romantic partnerships, and issues of sexuality should be addressed as for all individuals.

PHYSICAL EXAMINATION

This section discusses particular considerations for physical examination for patients with ASD; however, as with all patients, a thorough physical examination should be conducted. When conducting a general physical and neurological examination for individuals with ASD, clinicians should also take into consideration the common comorbidities presented previously and further etiological workup. Gradual exposure to medical equipment and the routines of medical visits and examinations may be needed to help patients tolerate procedures that may be stressful. Practice at home with medical equipment and collaboration with other providers, such as behavioral therapists and school nurses, may help patients feel more comfortable in the medical setting.

Vital Signs and Growth

Routine vital signs, such as heart rate and blood pressure, and growth parameters such as height, weight, and body mass index (BMI) are important clinical parameters for monitoring general health as well as medication side effects. Tachycardia and hypertension may indicate the presence of anxiety. A head circumference should be obtained and plotted on standardized curves by age. A small head size might indicate a neurogenetic disorder such as Rett syndrome, whereas a large head size might be seen with Sotos syndrome or other disorders that may warrant genetic testing.

General

A general observation of the individual's behavioral profile and developmental skills (as discussed previously) and ASD symptoms as evident in the examination room should be documented to monitor symptoms over time. A general dysmorphology examination should be conducted to guide medical and genetic workup (discussed later).

Head, Eyes, Ears, Nose, and Throat

Macrocephaly or microcephaly may be noted, as mentioned previously. The examination of the eye can reveal findings suggestive of a tic disorder with bilateral eye blinking; dilated pupils might be a sign of anxiety. A limited range of motion of the eyes might be a sign of a mitochondrial disorder. Gaze aversion and visual stereotypies should be noted if present because they are quite common in ASD. Ear examination is particularly important in individuals with ASD because they may not alert caregivers to ear pain due to a high pain tolerance or lack of an effective communication method; a foreign body or ear infection may be otherwise missed. Examination of the mouth may reveal oral motor coordination difficulties and weakness, which may accompany impaired verbal communication abilities. This might manifest as drooling or as inarticulate speech. In addition, clinicians should evaluate for tonsillar hypertrophy to rule out obstructive sleep apnea as a contributor to sleep difficulties, which are commonly seen in ASD, as mentioned previously. Dental problems such as infection or inflammation, with associated pain and discomfort, can lead to behavioral changes, as can teething in young children.

Gastrointestinal

Abdominal examination may reveal fullness suggestive of constipation or hepatosplenomegaly suggestive of a metabolic disease.

Skin

Dermatological examination should search for any neurocutaneous abnormalities suggestive of neurofibromatosis or tuberous sclerosis complex (TSC), and it should include Wood's lamp examination to search for hypopigmented macules (also called ash leaf spots). Calluses may be seen in children who have chronic self-injurious biting or gnawing. Tenting of the skin or loose ligaments can be a sign of a connective tissue disorder. In addition, the clinician should assess for evidence of skin picking or trichotillomania (hair pulling) and should monitor for superinfection of chronically irritated areas of skin.

CASE STUDY #1: "WILLIAM"

William is a 36-month-old boy who was evaluated for the diagnosis of ASD. At the age of 18 months, he had no words, poor eye contact, and no communication other than crying. At the age of 26 months, he was started in speech therapy. He then developed three words but still did not point. He was noted to engage in hand and finger stereotypies. He liked to stack toys or play with trains. He had no interest in other children. At the age of 33 months, he had a febrile seizure. Family history is notable for seizures in the father.

On physical examination, William was found to have a head circumference of 51 cm (75th percentile). He was a well-appearing boy who engaged in frequent hand-flapping behaviors. He had no eye contact with the examiner. He used no words. He cried to communicate his needs. He stared at the wheels of a toy truck and spun them frequently. His general examination was notable for three hypomelanotic macules (white or ash leaf spots) on his trunk visualized best with a Wood's lamp. There were no hypermelanotic (café au lait spots) macules. There were two ungual (nail bed) fibromas as well. The neurologic examination was otherwise notable for normal cranial nerves, although the patient was not cooperative with fundoscopy or tests of visual acuity. He was noted to have low muscle tone and yet walked on his toes.

What Can We Learn From This Case?

The important features are twofold. First, William is a child with "classic" autism, with deficits in social communication and social interaction, along with restricted, repetitive patterns of behavior such as hand flapping, fixation on parts of objects, and restricted stereotypical play. He meets DSM-5 criteria for ASD.

Second, the results of this child's physical examination (the ash leaf spots and fibromas in the nail beds) indicate he may have an underlying neurogenetic disorder, such as TSC. TSC is a genetic disorder resulting in abnormal nonmalignant tumor formation in different organs, typically the brain, eyes, skin, heart, kidneys, and lungs. The tumors seen are usually caused by mutations in either of two tumor suppressor genes: *TSC1* (located on 9q34) or *TSC2* (located on 16p13) (Borkowska, Schwartz, Kotulska, & Jozwiak, 2011; Dabora et al., 2001). There is an autosomal dominant pattern of inheritance and a high rate of associated ASD in children with TSC (approximately 43–86%) (Harrison & Bolton, 1997; Jeste, Sahin, Bolton, Ploubidis, & Humphrey, 2008). Although most children with ASD do not need neuroimaging, given these physical examination findings, it is important to refer this child to a neurologist or geneticist for further diagnostic evaluation, including an MRI of the head and kidneys and an ultrasound of the heart. Furthermore, the tumors of the brain can cause seizures, which are best managed by a neurologist.

Neurological

The neurological examination is typically reassuringly normal in individuals with ASD except for low muscle tone, which is common. The examiner should observe the patient's movements, ability to imitate, and level of communication and comprehension. One should observe the patient for motor tics as well as attention and focus because both tic disorders and ADHD are more common in individuals with ASD. General neurological examination should be conducted, including evaluation of muscle tone and bulk, gait, coordination, and performance of the Gower's maneuver in children (arising from prone to a stand) to look for proximal muscle weakness. Asymmetries in gait might indicate that the child has a focal injury or cerebral palsy. Remember that pain can also cause an asymmetric gait.

Because many individuals with ASD are toe walkers, it is important to check the heel cords to ensure that the ankles have normal range of motion and there is no tendon tightening. If so, a referral to physical therapy is indicated.

The next section further discusses laboratory and diagnostic workup for individuals with ASD. In general, an extensive diagnostic workup is not recommended for all cases of ASD, but it may be beneficial when there are concerning features on history and physical examination. For all the testing discussed next, genetic testing is the only type of testing that is routinely recommended.

GENETIC TESTING

A genetic abnormality can be identified in approximately 10–20% of cases of ASD. Currently, more than 100 genetic and genomic abnormalities have been associated with ASD (Betancur, 2011).

Small submicroscopic gene deletions or duplications are the most commonly identified abnormality (10–35%), followed by larger gene duplications or deletions that can be seen on a standard karyotype (up to 5%) and single gene mutations (<5%). Although the diagnosis of ASD remains a clinical diagnosis and genetic testing may not alter the clinical management of the patient, the results may be helpful in providing an explanation to the family, avoiding unnecessary tests, and identifying any potential comorbidities and conditions that are currently existing or may occur in the future (Schaefer et al., 2013).

The current recommendations of the American College of Medical Genetics and the American Academy of Pediatrics are to obtain a chromosomal microarray (CMA) as part of the first tier of the genetic workup (Schaefer et al., 2013; Shen et al., 2010). This is a departure from earlier guidelines that recommended ordering a karyotype. A CMA analyzes submicroscopic regions of a chromosome searching for either extra (duplication) or missing (deletion) genetic material in these regions. A karyotype examines the number of chromosomes and studies their appearance under a microscope, looking for abnormalities such as missing or extra chromosomes and abnormal shapes and sizes. Although no longer recommended as the first genetic test, ordering a karyotype may be useful in patients in whom clinical features may be indicative of a syndrome associated with a known chromosomal abnormality, such as Down syndrome or Turner syndrome (Schaefer et al., 2013).

In addition to a CMA, testing for fragile X syndrome (FXS) is recommended for both males and females who present with mild to moderate intellectual disabilities. Physical features, such as large ears, a prominent jaw, macrocephaly, and postpubertal macroorchidism in males, and a family history suggestive of an X-linked inherited disorder are often seen with this condition.

X-linked disorders, including FXS, can be seen in females; however, they are usually more mildly affected (Flore & Milunsky, 2012).

CASE STUDY #2: "JACOB"

Jacob is a 5-year-old boy from Costa Rica who came for evaluation of developmental delay with signs of ASD. Jacob had delayed developmental milestones, with sitting at the age of 15 months and walking at the age of 2 years. At the age of 3 years, he was using only three words to indicate his desire to eat or drink. He had no social greetings and used someone else's hand as a tool to gesture. He had repetitive rocking behaviors and some self-injurious behaviors with gnawing on his wrist and head slapping. He started speech therapy, as well as physical and occupational therapy, and his vocabulary improved such that he could identify many objects and express his needs with short phrases. However, he was unusually picky about eating and would only eat "white" foods such as pasta, bananas, crackers, and chips. He was not toilet trained and had chronic constipation. His mother had placed him on a gluten- and casein-free diet.

On physical examination at the age of 5 years, he was a happy and well-appearing boy with low tone in both his face and his extremities. He had a long face, large ears, and hyperextensible joints. Testicular size was normal. He had a callous on his left wrist. During the visit, he was fed crackers when he fussed. He did occasionally slap his head and gnaw on his wrist when frustrated. His eye contact was poor, and he used few spontaneous words.

Questions

What other testing would you like to order?
What are concerning features of this history and physical examination?

Testing

The features of long face, large ears, and low tone raise the question of fragile X syndrome (FXS). Although this child had already had the testing once in Costa Rica, it was repeated and found to be consistent with FXS. Remember that the large testes associated with FXS are mostly seen in postpubertal males. This diagnosis has implications for the rest of the family when there are siblings, so genetic counseling is also necessary.

Concerning features

1. Diet: The gluten-free and casein-free diet may be helpful for some children, but this and other special diets often pose nutritional challenges for children who do not get adequate calcium and vitamin D and are therefore at risk for low bone density.
2. Picky eaters are similarly at risk for poor nutrition and constipation with their low-fiber diet.
3. Incontinence: Many children with ASD, especially those who have some verbal abilities, can be toilet trained by the age of 5 years. However, chronic constipation, which is common in children with ASD and more common in children on poor diets, will impair a child's ability to toilet train. The constipation often needs to be addressed before a child can be toilet trained.

In rare cases in which findings from the history and physical examination are consistent with a syndrome associated with a single gene disorder (Table 5.1), such as phosphatase and tensin homolog (PTEN) gene mutations and Rett syndrome, it may be more appropriate to test for the specific genetic disorder in question (Flore & Milunsky, 2012; Schaefer et al., 2013).

METABOLIC TESTING

The inborn errors of metabolism (IEM) are a large heterogeneous group of disorders. These disorders result from a genetic abnormality resulting in deficits in enzymes or transport proteins required to metabolize carbohydrates, amino acids, or lipids. Toxic metabolic products accumulate and can lead to multiple organ damage, including the central nervous system (CNS) (Ghaziuddin & Al-Owain, 2013). In the United States, a large proportion of these disorders are diagnosed in infancy via universal newborn metabolic screening, commonly called the "newborn screen" or "newborn bloodspot." This generally involves a small sample of blood obtained from the newborn after birth, which is analyzed and reported by state labs. Newborn screening varies throughout the United States; therefore, it is essential to know which disorders are screened for in a particular state. However, all 50 states screen for congenital hypothyroidism, galactosemia, and phenylketonuria (PKU). The individual's pediatrician should have a copy of these results or be familiar with how the results may be obtained if he or she does not have a copy on

TABLE 5.1 Common Single Gene Disorders Associated With Autism Spectrum Disorder

Syndrome	Prevalence	Common Features	Inheritance Pattern	Genes
Neurofibromatosis-1	1/3,000 live births	Café au lait spots, neurofibromas, axillary freckling, optic glioma	Autosomal dominant	NF-1
Fragile X syndrome	16–25/100,000 live male births	Long face, large ears, postpubertal macroorchidism	X-linked dominant	FMR-1
Tuberous sclerosis complex	1/5,800 live births	Ash leaf spots; angiofibromas; cardiac, renal, and brain tumors; ungal fibromas; shagreen patch; seizures	Autosomal dominant	TSC1, TSC2
Rett syndrome	1/8,500 females by age 15 years	Microcephaly, postnatal onset, developmental regression, hand motions	X-linked dominant	MECP2
Angelman syndrome	1/ 12,000–20,000 live births	Intellectual disability, hypotonia, microcephaly, ataxia or movement disorder, seizures	Maternal inheritance usually	UBE3A
PTEN hamartoma tumor syndrome	Exact prevalence unknown	Intellectual disability, macrocephaly, skin pigment changes, skin tumors	Autosomal dominant	PTEN

Source: Adapted from Kandt (2003), Pagon et al. (1993–2014), Siegel and Smith (2010), and Toriello (2008).

TABLE 5.2 Features Suggestive of an Inborn Error of Metabolism on History and Physical Examination

Regression after the age of 3 years
Family history of an IEM
Parental consanguinity
Periods of decompensation with illness/stress
Enlarged organs
Coarse facial features
Ataxia or difficulties with coordinating voluntary muscle movements
Movement disorders
White matter changes seen with neuroimaging
Born in a country that does not have newborn screening
Cyclic vomiting
Hearing loss
Concerns on newborn screen
Acid–base or electrolyte imbalance

Source: Adapted from Flore and Milunsky (2012) and Goldman et al. (2012).

file. There is a wide array of presentations across these disorders, as well as within spe-cific disorders; however, each specific IEM has certain key features. A discussion of the specific key features specific to each disorder is beyond the scope of this chapter. There are certain features in the history and physical examination that may make the diagnosis of an IEM more likely (Table 5.2). For example, PKU, an inborn error of phenylalanine metabolism, usually presents soon after birth, whereas San Fillipo syndrome, which is a disorder of mucopolysaccharide breakdown, typically presents between the ages of 2 and 6 years (Manzi, Loizzo, Giana, & Curatolo, 2008). With the exception of the newborn screen, screening for metabolic disorders is not generally recommended for patients with ASD. As a group, the IEMs account for less than 5% of cases of ASD. The diagnostic workup of an IEM is very extensive, and the recommended initial workup is highly variable among clinicians. The workup for an IEM typically includes urine and serum amino acids, electrolyte panel, blood urea nitrogen, creatinine, liver function tests, urinalysis, complete blood count, and ammonia (Kamboj, 2008).

It is recommended that metabolic screening be reserved for children who have features such as regression with loss of milestones or cognitive skills after the age of 3 years, repeated regressions with illnesses such as fevers and colds, early onset or neonatal seizures, coarse or thick-appearing facial features, slowly progressive regression, or failure to learn any new skills during a 6-month period of time.

MITOCHONDRIAL DISORDERS

Mitochondrial disorders as a group are rare, with an estimated prevalence of 11.5 cases per 100,000. In mitochondrial disorders, the liver, brain, heart, and muscle are most com-monly affected. Mitochondria have their own DNA called mitochondrial DNA (mtDNA). Alteration of either mtDNA or nuclear DNA can cause mitochondrial disorders. Of note, mtDNA is inherited only from the mother. Furthermore, not all mtDNA is the same in a particular cell, which means that there can be a mix between normal and abnormal mtDNA; this is referred to as heteroplasmy. Hypotonia, regression after the age of 3 years, multiple organ system involvement, lactic acidosis seen on an arterial blood gas, and exacerbation of symptoms such as weakness with illnesses such as acute GI viruses are some common findings in mitochondrial disorders. Diagnostic tests for mitochondrial disorders include serum lactate, serum pyruvate, serum creatine kinase, plasma and urine acylcarnitines, urine organic acids, urine and serum amino acids, and muscle biopsy. If CNS involvement is present, cerebrospinal fluid (CSF) lactate and CSF pyruvate are recommended (Turner & Schapira, 2012). The interpretation of the results is complicated and typically best deferred to specialists in mitochondrial disorders. Testing for mitochondrial disorders is not recommended as part of the routine medical workup for ASD.

MEDICAL TESTING IN PATIENTS WITH AUTISM SPECTRUM DISORDER

Electroencephalogram

The electroencephalogram (EEG) need not be routinely obtained in patients with ASD. It should be performed only when there is a clinical suspicion of seizures, such as the patient having behaviors or spells suggestive of seizures. For example, grand mal or tonic–clonic seizures consist of arm and leg shaking with loss of consciousness and eye rolling. Petit mal seizures are characterized by brief staring spells. Focal or partial seizures might not impair consciousness and might include shaking in just one part of the body. An EEG can be quite difficult to perform in a minimally to nonverbal patient who is not able to lie still for 45 minutes or a patient who cannot tolerate the sensory aspects of the lead placement on the head. Although children with ASD do have an increased risk of seizures, the relative risk of seizures is quite low if younger than age 12 years and if there is no associated intellectual disability. A clinical study found epilepsy in 1.8% of patients without intellectual disability and younger than 12 years old, 6.1% if younger than 12 years old with intellectual disability, 8.9% if older than age 12 years and no intellectual disability, and 23.7% if older than age 12 years with intellectual disability (Woolfenden, Sarkozy, Ridley, Coory, & Williams, 2012).

Children with ASD are also known to have a higher rate of EEG abnormalities without clinical seizures and may often have "seizure-like" events with no epileptic EEG correlate. It remains unclear whether these EEG abnormalities should be treated with anticonvulsant medication in the absence of clinical seizures (Tharp, 2004; Yasuhara, 2010).

Neuroimaging

There is yet no neuroimaging test such as magnetic resonance imaging (MRI), computerized tomography, magnetic resonance spectroscopy, or positron emission tomography for the diagnosis of ASD. To date, no typical, replicable changes in the brain have been identified with MRI in ASD. Because of the need to lie still for up to 1 hour, sometimes requiring general anesthesia, it is recommended that neuroimaging only be performed in patients with an abnormal neurological examination; findings of a neurocutaneous disorder such as hypopigmented macules (ash leaf spots) on the skin, which are associated with TSC; first seizures; or a child with an unusual clinical course, such as a late regression or repeated developmental regressions.

SUMMARY

The medical and clinical care of individuals with ASD needs to be approached differently than in a typically developing child, adolescent, or adult because ASD symptomatology as well as common behavioral and medical comorbidities can affect daily life and medical treatment. This chapter recommended important questions to consider and areas on which to focus when obtaining a clinical history and physical examination. Genetic evaluation, as outlined previously, is indicated for all patients with ASD, and further medical workup should be tailored based on the individual's clinical presentation and physical findings.

KEY POINTS

- The history should be adjusted for patients with ASD to include information about communication, intelligence, school, and sensory dysfunction as well as regression.
- The physical examination of a child with ASD needs to be adjusted because of the patient's anxieties and sensory dysfunction.
- Individuals with ASD are more likely to have gastrointestinal, sleep, and neurological disorders.
- The examiner needs to focus on metabolic, neurologic, and genetic disorders that could cause ASD.
- Medical testing is not routine in patients with ASD unless specific signs or symptoms are found to warrant specific tests.

DISCLOSURE STATEMENT

Dr. Yamini J. Howe, Dr. Michelle L. Palumbo, and Dr. Ann Neumeyer have nothing to disclose.

REFERENCES

American Psychiatric Association. (2013). *Diagnostic and statistical manual of mental disorders.* 5th ed. Arlington, VA: American Psychiatric Publishing.

American Speech–Language–Hearing Association, Ad Hoc Committee on Service Delivery in the Schools. (1993). Definitions of communication disorders and variations. *ASHA Supplement, 35*(3 Suppl. 10), 40–41.

American Speech–Language–Hearing Association, Committee on Infant Hearing (1991). Guidelines for the audiologic assessment of children from birth through 36 months of age. *ASHA Supplement, 33*(5), 37–43.

Barger, B. D., Campbell, J. M., & McDonough, J. D. (2013). Prevalence and onset of regression within autism spectrum disorders: A meta-analytic review. *Journal of Autism and Developmental Disorders, 43*(4), 817–828.

Betancur, C. (2011). Etiological heterogeneity in autism spectrum disorders: More than 100 genetic and genomic disorders and still counting. *Brain Research, 1380,* 42–77.

Buie, T., Fuchs, G. J., 3rd, Furuta, G. T., et al. (2010). Recommendations for evaluation and treatment of common gastrointestinal problems in children with ASDs. *Pediatrics, 125*(Suppl. 1), S19–S29.

Borkowska, J., Schwartz, R. A., Kotulska, K., & Jozwiak, S. (2011). Tuberous sclerosis complex: Tumors and tumorigenesis. *International Journal of Dermatology 50*(1), 13–20.

Centers for Disease Control and Prevention. (2014). Prevalence of autism spectrum disorder among children aged 8 years—Autism and Developmental Disabilities Monitoring Network, 11 sites, United States, 2010. *MMWR Surveillance Summaries, 63*(Suppl. 2), 1–21.

Coury, D. L., Ashwood, P., Fasano, A., et al. (2012). Gastrointestinal conditions in children with autism spectrum disorder: Developing a research agenda. *Pediatrics, 130*(Suppl. 2), S160–S168.

Dabora, S. L., Jozwiak, S., Franz, D. N., et al. (2001). Mutational analysis in a cohort of 224 tuberous sclerosis patients indicates increased severity of TSC2, compared with TSC1, disease in multiple organs. *American Journal of Human Genetics, 68*(1), 64–80.

Filipek, P. A., Accardo, P. J., Ashwal, S., et al. (2000). Practice parameter—Screening and diagnosis of autism: Report of the Quality Standards Subcommittee of the American Academy of Neurology and the Child Neurology Society. *Neurology, 55*(4), 468–479.

Flore, L. A., & Milunsky, J. M. (2012). Updates in the genetic evaluation of the child with global developmental delay or intellectual disability. *Seminars in Pediatric Neurology, 19*(4), 173–180.

Ghaziuddin, M., & Al-Owain, M. (2013). Autism spectrum disorders and inborn errors of metabolism: An update. *Pediatric Neurology, 49*(4), 232–236.

Goldman, S., Wang, C., Salgado, M. W., Greene, P. E., Kim, M., & Rapin, I. (2009). Motor stereotypies in children with autism and other developmental disorders. *Developmental Medicine and Child Neurology, 51*(1), 30–38.

Goldman, S. E., Richdale, A. L., Clemons, T., & Malow, B. A. (2012). Parental sleep concerns in autism spectrum disorders: Variations from childhood to adolescence. *Journal of Autism and Developmental Disorders, 42*(4), 531–538.

Hallmayer, J., Cleveland, S., Torres, A., et al. (2011). Genetic heritability and shared environmental factors among twin pairs with autism. *Archives of General Psychiatry, 68*(11), 1095–1102.

Harrison, J. E., & Bolton, P. F. (1997). Annotation: Tuberous sclerosis. *Journal of Child Psychology and Psychiatry, 38*(6), 603–614.

Jeste, S. S. (2011). The neurology of autism spectrum disorders. *Current Opinion in Neurology, 24*(2), 132–139.

Jeste, S. S., Sahin, M., Bolton, P., Ploubidis, G. B., & Humphrey, A. (2008). Characterization of autism in young children with tuberous sclerosis complex. *Journal of Child Neurology, 23*(5), 520–525.

Johnson, C. P., & Myers, S. M. (2007). Identification and evaluation of children with autism spectrum disorders. *Pediatrics, 120*(5), 1183–1215.

Kamboj, M. (2008). Clinical approach to the diagnoses of inborn errors of metabolism. *Pediatrics Clinics of North America, 55*(5), 1113–1127, viii.

Kandt, R. S. (2003). Tuberous sclerosis complex and neurofibromatosis type 1: The two most common neurocutaneous diseases. *Neurologic Clinics, 21*(4), 983–1004.

Lehwald, N., Krausch, M., Franke, C., Assmann, B., Adam, R., & Knoefel, W. T. (2007). Sandifer syndrome—A multidisciplinary diagnostic and therapeutic challenge. *European Journal of Pediatric Surgery, 17*(3), 203–206.

Mandell, D. S., Walrath, C. M., Manteuffel, B., Sgro, G., & Pinto-Martin, J. A. (2005). The prevalence and correlates of abuse among children with autism served in comprehensive community-based mental health settings. *Child Abuse & Neglect, 29*(12), 1359–1372.

Manzi, B., Loizzo, A. L., Giana, G., & Curatolo, P. (2008). Autism and metabolic diseases. *Journal of Child Neurology, 23*(3), 307–314.

Nowak, M., Strzelczyk, A., Oertel, W. H., Hamer, H. M., & Rosenow, F. (2012). A female adult with Sandifer's syndrome and hiatal hernia misdiagnosed as epilepsy with focal seizures. *Epilepsy & Behavior, 24*(1), 141–142.

Ozonoff, S., Goodlin-Jones, B. L., & Solomon, M. (2005). Evidence-based assessment of autism spectrum disorders in children and adolescents. *Journal of Clinical Child and Adolescent Psychology, 34*(3), 523–540.

Pagon, R. A., Adam, M. P., Ardinger, H. H., et al. (Eds.). (1993–2014) *GeneReviews* [Internet]. Seattle, WA: University of Washington, Seattle. Available at http://www.ncbi.nlm.nih.gov/books/NBK1116.

Rossignol, D. A., & Frye, R. E. (2011). Melatonin in autism spectrum disorders: A systematic review and meta-analysis. *Developmental Medicine & Child Neurology, 53*(9), 783–792.

Schaefer, G. B., Mendelsohn, N. J.; Professional Practice and Guidelines Committee. (2013). Clinical genetics evaluation in identifying the etiology of autism spectrum disorders: 2013 guideline revisions. *Genetics in Medicine,* 2013;15(5):399–407.

Shen, Y., Dies, K. A., Holm, I. A., et al. (2010). Clinical genetic testing for patients with autism spectrum disorders. *Pediatrics, 125*(4), e727–e735.

Siegel, M. S., & Smith, W. E. (2010). Psychiatric features in children with genetic syndromes: Toward functional phenotypes. *Child & Adolescent Psychiatric Clinics of North America, 19*(2), 229–261, viii.

Sikora, D. M., Johnson, K., Clemons, T., & Katz, T. (2012). The relationship between sleep problems and daytime behavior in children of different ages with autism spectrum disorders. *Pediatrics, 130*(Suppl. 2), S83–S90.

Tharp, B. R. (2004). Epileptic encephalopathies and their relationship to developmental disorders: Do spikes cause autism? *Mental Retardation and Developmental Disabilities Research Reviews, 10*(2), 132–134.

Toriello, H. V. (2008). Role of the dysmorphologic evaluation in the child with developmental delay. *Pediatric Clinics of North America, 55*(5), 1085–1098, xi.

Turner, C., & Schapira, A. H. V. (2012). Mitochondrial disorders. In R. B. Daroff, G. M. Fenichel, J. Jankovic, & J. C. Mazziotta (Eds.), *Bradley's neurology in clinical practice* (6th ed., pp. 1473–1487). Philadelphia, PA: Saunders.

Woolfenden, S., Sarkozy, V., Ridley, G., Coory, M., & Williams, K. (2012). A systematic review of two outcomes in autism spectrum disorder—Epilepsy and mortality. *Developmental Medicine and Child Neurology, 54*(4), 306–312.

Yasuhara, A. (2010). Correlation between EEG abnormalities and symptoms of autism spectrum disorder (ASD). *Brain & Development, 32*(10), 791–798.

Zwaigenbaum, L., Bryson, S., Lord, C., et al. (2009). Clinical assessment and management of toddlers with suspected autism spectrum disorder: Insights from studies of high-risk infants. *Pediatrics, 123*(5), 1383–1391.

6

PSYCHIATRIC COMORBIDITY IN AUTISM SPECTRUM DISORDER

SUSAN E. FOLSTEIN AND LUIS M. CARCACHE

INTRODUCTION

Persons with comorbid autism spectrum disorder (ASD) have disabilities stemming not only from the clinical features necessary for diagnosis but also from comorbid psychiatric disorders and other associated abnormal behaviors. It has been known for many years that children with developmental difficulties of all kinds have a higher frequency of emotional and behavioral symptoms than typically developing children (Rutter, Graham, & Yule, 1970). These behaviors were assumed by many clinicians and scientists to be secondary to their cognitive impairments, and although this is a reasonable assumption, it led to a nihilistic attitude toward diagnosis and treatment. It is now clear that it is possible to diagnose psychiatric disorders in children with developmental disabilities, including ASD; that these disorders for the most part meet the same diagnostic criteria used in the general population (Leyfer et al., 2006); and that they respond to treatment.

The estimates of prevalence of psychiatric comorbidity vary, depending on whether the sample was drawn from a psychiatric clinic or from some other source (De Bruin, Ferdinand, Meester, De Nijs, & Verheij, 2007; Leyfer et al., 2006; Simonoff et al., 2008), but it probably occurs in the majority of persons with ASD. These conditions interfere with optimal functioning but often go undiagnosed and untreated. When anxious, depressed, overactive, or inattentive, persons with ASD are less available for teaching and less able to participate in family life and in the community. With careful observation over time, most comorbid psychiatric disorders can be diagnosed regardless of the patient's cognitive and language capacity; some are identical to those seen in persons without ASD, but others may present in unusual ways that make their identification difficult at first. Persons with ASD also have abnormal associated behaviors that do not fit easily into the psychiatric nomenclature (Dominick et al., 2007). This chapter describes the clinical features of the psychiatric disorders and abnormal associated behaviors often seen in persons with ASD, provides diagnostic pointers, and recommends psychopharmacological and behavioral treatments that may be considered. The data presented and the case examples are based on a case series of 300 clinically diagnosed patients with ASD who were systematically examined by the authors.

TAKING A HISTORY

The first and most important task is to take a thorough history, including family history of psychiatric disorder; pregnancy; problems during delivery; and medical and developmental factors, including motor, language, and social aspects. A detailed school history should inquire about attainment, peer interactions, and behavior over time. Results of other evaluations including neuropsychological testing are useful. The history of present illness should ask about episodic symptoms, as well as more chronic difficulties that occur in particular situations.

MENTAL STATUS EXAMINATION

First, note the physical appearance of the patient. There may be dysmorphic features that require further evaluation with a geneticist for syndrome identification. If a genetic disorder is diagnosed, it may have implications for other family members. Document height, weight, and head circumference, all of which may be outside the normal range. Next, note physical activity level. Many people with ASD are fidgety, and some are very hyperactive, particularly as children. Occasionally, they sit too still. Be vigilant for signs of catatonia—trouble arising from the chair, hesitancy about crossing the threshold of the doorway to your office, difficulty in deciding to pick up a pencil when you ask them to write, and becoming frozen in a particular posture.

Next, note the patient's affect. This is one of the most important observations. Anxious affect is very common and can present as it does typically in developing persons: knitted brows, fidgeting, continually looking at the parent for reassurance, handwringing, and pacing. If it is severe, the patient may not be willing to enter the room and may bang his or her head or bite him- or herself. The patient may pinch his mother or try to sit on her lap or attempt to get her to take him out of the room. If the patient has useful language, you can ask how he or she feels, but the answers may not be helpful; many persons with ASD have little insight into their internal feeling state or mood. Sometimes, if you give them some choices, they can choose one: Do you feel worried or happy? Even this approach may not accurately reflect their mood: They may try to please the examiner with their answer. The parent's history often gives more accurate information.

The next most common disturbance of affect is the one usually associated with depression. Children may sit very still and look downcast (most persons with ASD do not look at you, but they do not look downcast) and miserable. If they have useful language, they will often agree that no one likes them and that they are not good enough. Sometimes it is necessary to break the rule about asking leading questions because persons with ASD, even those with good language, often find it impossible to respond to indirect questions, particularly about feelings. Again, you may get more accurate information from the parents: They often report things the child has said that indicate low mood, including talk of suicide. The depressed mood usually represents a change, and parents may be able to link it to an approximate date. They may be able to contrast the present depressed mood with a more cheerful one from the past, albeit the patient may have had an anxious mood in some situations. Parents may not always have an accurate assessment of their child's sleep. Although some children go to their parents' bedroom if they wake in the night and get into their bed, others do not. They may have learned to stay in their room even if they are awake.

It can be difficult or impossible to decide if persons with ASD are hallucinating. They may stare into the middle distance and seem to be attending to and sometimes responding to something. However, this behavior is also seen when patients are attending to a movie that they have seen and are "playing the tape" in their heads. Staring spells may also be indicative of absence seizures. Except for more intelligent verbal patients, it is usually not possible to be certain about delusions; when present, however, they are often mood congruent and part of a depressive episode. Patients may say that people are looking at them. If asked why, they might say that it is because they are so bad. However, getting this quality of information is not always possible.

Obsessions and compulsions may also be difficult to be sure of, although occasionally very typical features of obsessive–compulsive disorder (OCD) are seen, with a distressing thought that is resisted and a related compulsive behavior that is not pleasurable but "required." OCD can also be diagnosed in nonverbal patients if a repetitive behavior seems to cause distress; in these cases, the behavior will most likely be related to checking, cleaning, grooming, or ordering and arranging. Insistence on sameness can be very similar to behavior that occurs in OCD: Things *must* be in the right place or occur as expected, and the patient is upset if something is moved or occurs out of sequence. Conversely, many of the repetitive behaviors are rewarding, such as watching the same video clip or drawing the same object repeatedly.

Testing cognition necessarily varies; sometimes the patient is both nonverbal and unable to express thoughts in writing. At a minimum, ask patients to state their name, address, and phone number; these are usually taught to them by rote. Note fine motor problems with writing. Those who have some language should be asked to read a simple passage; if they succeed, increase the difficulty to try to assess grade level. Mathematics attainment can be similarly tested. When doing this, some children become extremely anxious; many children with ASD complete their schoolwork at a slower pace. If appropriate to their level of cognition, it is instructive to do the Mini-Mental Status Examination (MMSE) (Folstein, Folstein, Whites, & Meiser, 2009). Even in fully verbal patients, the pattern of strengths and weaknesses varies tremendously, from their ability to do serial sevens rapidly to a complete inability. Patients may appear disoriented or very precise in their orientation. Handwriting is often effortful. They write very interesting sentences; a few of these are shown in Box 6.1. If using the MMSE-2, which includes symbol-digit and a story recall task, you can screen for processing speed and story memory. Almost uniformly, even the brightest patients are slow on the symbol-digit task, and they have great difficulty in recalling parts of the story that were just read to them.

PSYCHIATRIC DISORDERS

Attention deficit hyperactivity disorder (ADHD) presents the same way in individuals with ASD as in other children: hyperactivity from the time they can walk, inattention, and impulsiveness. They can be treated with the same medications used for ADHD in typical children. Some patients do not respond as expected, often becoming irritable or tearful, but this is sometimes because their restlessness and inattention are related to a mood or anxiety disorder rather than ADHD. The behaviors can be superficially similar: Children may be too anxious to listen in class; when doing homework, they get up, pace around, cry, and look worried and upset. Generally, children with ADHD sleep well compared with those

---

BOX 6.1
MMSE SENTENCES WRITTEN BY PERSONS WITH AUTISM SPECTRUM DISORDER

I honst to mommy.

I want to be a kid forever. (He just had his 21st birthday.)

Mosquitos are anoying because they bite.

Water is to keep you hydrated.

The pentagons have a diamond in the middle.

I want to move to the verdant state of Vermont.

I am going to be a quadruple instrumented.

A hexagon is a type of shape that is round.

Mr. Monkey parts is on fire!

Don't look at me.

Somtimes (sic) I dream about cheese.

I will go recycling at Villa Maria Nursing Center.

I'll just take it essy for eterything, like new friend. The reason is not to get angry at home. I'll be a good boy. I will get more friends. Bad no nothing.

---

who are anxious or depressed. Quite a number of children with ASD who present to psychiatrists have both ADHD and anxiety. If both seem to be present, consider treating the anxiety first because the inattention and pacing often improve without the use of stimulants and some children are poor eaters at baseline (stimulants can reduce appetite). However, if the hyperactivity is prominent and severe, it should be treated first. As with other children, those with ASD may not respond equally well to all the stimulants; children with ASD have the usual side effects but at a higher rate, partly because of misdiagnosis (Mahajan et al., 2012).

Anxiety in ASD is more of a trait than a state, although it does worsen in certain situations. Panic disorder is uncommon, but children with ASD may get sweaty palms, worry, appear distressed, and pace around, and they are often unable to pay attention in anxiety-provoking situations, including school. They often sleep poorly, with both initial and middle-of-the-night insomnia. Situations that commonly provoke anxiety are shown in Box 6.2 (Monroy & Folstein, 2012). The manifestations of anxiety in persons with ASD can be unusual: screaming, running away, biting themselves, or hitting their heads. They bite and damage their nails, sometimes to a pathological extent (e.g., pulling the nail out entirely) (Box 6.3).

Most persons with ASD feel least anxious at home, following their own routines and preferences. Sometimes their anxiety prevents them from going to school and family events; crowds and noise are particularly upsetting. For higher functioning children, family gatherings can provoke anxiety because of the expectation that they at least attempt to follow social conventions; for lower functioning persons, the noise and confusion often upset them. Sometimes anxiety is provoked by fears of bees, butterflies, storms, dogs, and high-pitched screams such as babies crying or little girls screaming. They can also become phobic of elevators, heights, and driving, much as can typical people.

BOX 6.2

SITUATIONS THAT OFTEN PROVOKE ANXIETY

Looking frightened

Repetitive questioning

Pacing

Cannot sit still

Having a "meltdown" (tantrum)

Biting nails

Picking scabs

Biting self

Stammer

Biting others

Anxiety can also lead to self-injurious behavior and aggression. Patients become so distressed that they bite themselves or bang their heads or lash out at others. This self-directed aggression is often treated first with atypical antipsychotics, but response is usually only partial. Occasionally, low-dose selective serotonin reuptake inhibitors (SSRIs) are helpful; patients with severe, long-standing calluses on their arms and open sores often stop injuring themselves entirely, as shown in Table 6.1 (Carbajal & Folstein, 2012). However, as discussed later, if their moods are unstable, a mood stabilizer should be considered first to prevent behavioral activation from the SSRI.

Some studies show that anxiety can be treated behaviorally in high-functioning patients with adequate language (Sofronoff, Attwood, & Hinton, 2005; Wood et al., 2009). However, if the anxiety is severe or if it is difficult for the person to understand how to self-modulate his or her anxiety, SSRIs should be considered; sometimes the dose needs

---

BOX 6.3

BEHAVIORS RELATED TO ANXIETY, IN ORDER OF FREQUENCY

Wanting to obtain an object related to a special interest

Misplaced valuable object

Excessive noise

Noisy environments

Children screaming

Loud talk with high emotional content such as parents arguing

Change in plans

Awaiting a future event

Doctor or dentist visit

TABLE 6.1 Self-Injurious Behavior: Response to SSRIs Versus Other
Medication From Retrospective Chart Review of Clinical Treatment ($N = 79$)

Response	SSRI (%)	Other Medication (%)
Worse	14	3
No change	8	53
Transient improvement	1	6
Improvement	10	28
Remission	67	10

to be very low—the usual doses can precipitate irritability, overactivity, and sleeplessness. Sometimes this behavioral activation may resemble hypomania; other times it resembles the symptoms of serotonin syndrome. Other patients respond to the usual therapeutic doses of SSRIs. Fluoxetine or sertraline are available in liquid preparations that allow very low dosing (Birmaher et al., 2003; Steingard, Zimnitzky, DeMaso, Bauman, & Bucci, 1997). If they are ineffective, other anxiolytics can be tried, such as buspirone, venlafaxine, or mirtazapine. If the mood is unstable (discussed later), patients can become hypomanic from SSRIs. If this happens (mostly in adolescents and older persons), a mood stabilizer may need to be added if some benefits were seen with the SSRI.

Anxiety from specific fears and phobias responds partly to anxiolytics, such as SSRIs, but these often have to be treated with behavioral therapy in addition to the anxiolytics. It is often helpful to use anxiolytics temporarily to make it easier for the patient to participate in the behavioral approaches that often themselves provoke anxiety and may initially make the symptoms worse.

Social anxiety is common in ASD, particularly when the patients' cognitive function allows them to realize that they are different from others. They believe that they never say the right thing and that people avoid them (Bauminger & Kasari, 2000). Sometimes they stop trying, rarely to the point of selective mutism. Others try to learn how to "pass" and may be able to participate in superficial conversation. Behavioral and psychotherapeutic approaches can occasionally be helpful.

OCD in its classical presentation is not common in ASD. It requires having an intrusive thought that the person realizes is not reasonable and that leads to compulsive behaviors related to the thought. In our case series of 300 children and adults with ASD, 15 cases were diagnosed with OCD. Not all are classical, but they share the feature of feeling compelled to do something that is not enjoyable. For example, one nonverbal boy had to touch everything that his mother had just touched. He was exhausted by this and was only happy when she sat quietly and did not touch anything. This behavior did not respond to a variety of anxiolytics, but one morning when he woke up, the touching behaviors stopped and did not recur. Usually, OCD is diagnosed in children with sufficiently developed verbal skills to describe obsessional thoughts. For example, one boy whose father worked in a hospital emergency room could not be around his father because he feared contamination; he washed his hands and body many times daily. He also did not respond to any treatments, including electroconvulsive therapy. Studies of repetitive behaviors in ASD, which occasionally meet criteria for OCD, have not found benefit of SSRIs over placebo, especially in children with ASD.

OCD in ASD is easily confused with insistence on sameness, one of the characteristic features of ASD. It differs from OCD in that the sameness is often related to a broad range of things in one individual, whereas OCD is usually related to one or two specific issues. Persons with insistence on sameness want to take the same route, do not want their belongings touched, and need to order and arrange things in a particular way. However, it can sometimes be difficult to distinguish the two if the patient has no speech or if the patient does not obviously enjoy the activities required to keep things the same. The child may become upset and aggressive if the need is violated. Although it is part and parcel of ASD, it sometimes improves with low doses of anxiolytics, but it does not disappear.

Another phenomenon that can be difficult to distinguish from OCD is the narrow range of intense interests—for example, a child who has the intense desire (the patient would call it a need) for the most recent Thomas the Tank Engine model and asks incessantly, sometimes resulting in a tantrum, until the model can be purchased. It is tempting for parents to use these intense interests as rewards for good behavior, but this can worsen the situation over time. For example, one child liked to collect stuffed animals, and his parents used them as rewards. Eventually, his whole life became consumed by making lists of stuffed animals that he wished to purchase. He followed his mother around demanding that she get all the rewards on the list. He became aggressive toward her when she refused. A behavior plan was developed that eventually stopped the behavior. He was no longer rewarded and finally gave it up as a lost cause.

Major depressive disorder (MDD) can also present in the same way as in more neurotypical people. It is not usually chronic, although it can be. There is often a clear onset, with episodes lasting on average from 1 to 6 months (Simonoff et al., 2012). The patient develops the three features of MDD: a change in mood, a change in self-attitude, and neurovegetative signs. A low mood that can be observed as a change in affect from generally cheerful (except when anxious) to downcast and sad is often present. Verbal patients may say that they are sad but are not always able to label their emotions. Their mood may also be irritable, and aggression may increase. This can also happen in hypomania; in depression, they are "irritable and miserable," and in mania (discussed later), they are "irritable and confident." Second, there is a change in self-attitude: Patients who can speak make statements such as "no one likes me," "I'm no good," and "I never do anything right." Sometimes these statements seem reasonable, given the patient's social and academic limitations, but the patient does not *usually* feel this way. These changes in self-attitude can become delusional. Also, there can be simple auditory hallucinations, usually heard inside their head, with a voice telling them that they are bad or making other derogatory remarks. Sometimes higher functioning adolescents and adults with ASD make suicide attempts or kill themselves. Drowning is a common cause of death that may sometimes be suicidal in origin; it is usually thought to be related to an epileptic seizure. Suicidal behavior can be seen in younger children: One boy put a belt around his neck when he was depressed. The third and easiest feature of depression to notice, particularly in nonverbal patients, is the neurovegetative signs of depression: worsened sleep; low energy; and loss of interest in formerly pleasurable activities, such as bowling, going to movies, riding the bus to the end of the line, or whatever they formerly enjoyed. They will usually still play video games or other activities that they find relaxing and easy. There may be more hand flapping or other repetitive motor activities. Some children lose their appetite and thus lose weight. Commonly, they dislike leaving the house, particularly for school. For example, one nonverbal child refused to get dressed and stayed in bed on school days. Self-injurious behavior may start or worsen.

Sometimes it is difficult to distinguish depression from anxiety except that depression tends to be episodic. The mid-night awakenings, tearfulness about doing homework, and irritability about particularly stressful things can be seen in both. Like MDD in typical people, depression can be seasonal; parents may attribute the change in mood to starting a new school year, leaving for vacation, or returning from vacation. These situations do occur, but change-related mood/anxiety symptoms do not usually last more than 1 or 2 weeks.

Surprisingly, there have been no double-blind, placebo-controlled trials of medications for the treatment of MDD in ASD. Thus, standard approaches to treatment of MDD in children and adults are followed, although smaller initial doses are used because of the frequency of "activation" at more standard doses. Psychiatrists who are experienced in treating depression in ASD are in agreement that SSRIs can be effective. When treating adolescents or adults with ASD, it is necessary to be vigilant about causing hypomania because their moods often become unstable at puberty.

Bipolar disorder can start at any time, as in typical persons, but it usually begins at or after puberty. The patient may have formerly been anxious or depressed or have ADHD that responded to antidepressants or stimulants, but at puberty these may stop working. The patient's mood becomes very unstable; the patient commonly has short periods of irritability during which she or he may appear to be overconfident or overbearing, followed by apologies for her or his behavior with tearfulness and remorse. When "irritable and confident," patients tell people what to do, act as if they know better, and may talk more, demand more activities, and sleep less. They may be up during the night, turning on the lights and the TV. One nonverbal patient in the case series wanted to go for endless rides in the car and visit malls. These brief high periods are usually followed by an "irritable and miserable" mood. This low mood is usually obvious from their affect, and they may cry. Unstable moods occur equally often in verbal and nonverbal patients. These alterations may not last long enough to qualify for true bipolar disorder, especially at first, as in typical adolescents.

In order to treat anxiety and depression without worsening the mood swings, it is first necessary to stabilize the mood. Because aggression is often part of the presentation, people often treat the unstable mood with risperidone or other atypical antipsychotics. These often help but have serious long-term side effects. It is usually possible to treat the mood instability with more traditional mood stabilizers, such as valproic acid or lamotrigine, or other anticonvulsants that have mood-stabilizing properties. Occasionally, particularly if the bipolar disorder has a classical presentation, lithium may be the only effective medication. Once the mood stabilizer is at a therapeutic dose (a blood level of 85 mg/dL or greater with valproic acid), antidepressants can usually be safely added for any remaining depression or anxiety. Stimulants can also be used for symptoms of ADHD once the mood is stable.

Occasionally, patients become manic or depressed only once or twice a year for a limited period of time. Because of the time-limited nature and infrequency of the episodes, it can take some time to determine if a medication led to the end of the episode or if the symptomatic improvement was the result of the patient's natural cycle.

Catatonia has been well described in ASD (Dhossche, Reti, & Wachtel, 2009; Dhossche, Wing, Ohta, & Neumarker, 2006; Kakooza-Mwesige, Wachtel, & Dhossche, 2008). If it occurs, it usually starts at or after adolescence. One adolescent patient began to follow his father around the house, copying all his motor movements. Next, he started to have trouble picking up a fork or food and became increasingly more stiff. Finally, he could not open his jaw, and he was hospitalized in order to have a nasogastric tube placed. He was treated with antipsychotics and got slightly better, but he continued to have trouble eating: He would pick up the fork and set it down several times. The catatonia, as yet undiagnosed, recurred again exactly 1 year later. After beginning and then increasing lorazepam to 8 mg/day, his symptoms resolved. Later, he became manic, and a mood stabilizer was added. The catatonia has not recurred; he remains on both medications.

Schizophrenia following an initial presentation of ASD has been well documented in case series ascertained for childhood-onset schizophrenia (Rapoport, Chavez, Greenstein, Addington, & Gogtay, 2009). Approximately one-fourth of the cases meet criteria for ASD in early life before the onset of hallucinations and delusions that characterize early onset schizophrenia. In the authors' clinical series of 300 patients with ASD, two such cases were observed. Both boys had marked delusions and hallucinations that began in adolescence and were not associated with depression or mania. One responded to aripiprazole, but the other responded only to clozapine.

Usually when an adolescent or adult with ASD has auditory hallucinations, it is in the context of MDD and there is one voice, usually heard inside the head, making deprecating comments such as "You're no good" or "Just kill yourself."

Sometimes it can be difficult to determine when an apparent voice or vision is part of a psychiatric illness or just the vivid re-experiencing of a video or movie. This sort of "eidetic imagery" that is seen in small children often persists in ASD well into adult life. If the person has no features of depression or schizophrenia, it may not need to be treated. Parents sometimes say, "He's playing his tape." Sometimes the patient can tell you what he or she is viewing.

ABNORMAL BEHAVIORS ASSOCIATED WITH AUTISM SPECTRUM DISORDER

Abnormally intense interests are common in ASD. The interests are of many types—for example, dinosaurs or other prehistoric animals, radiators, key rings, various action figures, fancy sneakers, music, and occasionally firearms. The more able patients may become real experts in their area of interest. Sometimes the interest can lead to thievery: For example, one boy took key rings from the cabinets in parking lots or valet parking desks. Usually, the interest leads to relentless pursuit of the parents until the next new thing can be purchased. Sometimes a very strong interest can lead to difficulties in convincing high-functioning adults with ASD to get a job. For example, one young man who had always been interested in sports statistics would only consider a job as a sportscaster. An interest in firearms can be dangerous. Adolescents may become interested in the technical workings of guns and hang around gun shops, where dangerous contacts can be made. One adolescent said that he wanted to join the army so he could shoot people. The interest in weapons is particularly dangerous if the patient is also depressed and isolated because it can lead to either murder or suicide. Such patients need to be closely monitored, and their parents must be sure they take their medications, even over the adolescents' objections. Obviously, guns must be removed from the house rather than encouraging the interest.

Insistence on sameness can also cause problems. Children often have meltdowns when their computer does not work, someone moves one of their possessions, or parents are unable to take the same route or follow some detail of the usual daily routine. One patient insisted that everyone leave the house on school days in the same order and wearing the same coat, taken in order from the same rack. An adult who lived in a nursing home hoarded plastic. An occupational therapist developed a therapeutic relationship with him so that together they cleared out most of the plastic from his room once a month. One day, she made a tiny, seemingly trivial, change in the monthly routine and he became aggressive toward her. Most people with ASD and problematic insistence on sameness are extremely anxious and benefit from either behavioral or pharmacological treatment.

Abnormal eating behavior is very common in persons with ASD, rarely leading to malnutrition. Mostly, they eat a very narrow range of foods of a particular type, texture, or color. Rarely do they eat fruits or vegetables. The Repetitive Behavior Scale–Revised (RBS-R) (Bodfish, Symons, Parker, & Lewis, 2000) and the Brief Autism Mealtime Behavior Inventory (BAMBI), an eating abnormality scale developed for ASD (Lukens & Linscheid, 2008), were completed by the parents of patients in the case series. The severity of abnormal eating behavior was related to several of the subscales of the RBS-R, including rituals and insistence on sameness (Almeida & Folstein, 2012).

Social naïveté is nearly universal and can lead patients into dangerous situations. Children and particularly adolescents who want to have "regular friends" will do almost anything to be allowed to hang out with them (Bauminger & Kasari, 2000). This makes them easy targets for bullying and teasing. The bullying involves anything from taking their lunch money to asking them to do the bully's math homework and getting them to approach a girl and kiss her or pull up her dress. The boys (and sometimes girls) get a laugh and the child with ASD gets into trouble. Adolescents with ASD may try very hard to "be a regular kid," usually, but not always, without much success. One boy assiduously studied how to talk to girls and have conversations on acceptable topics. Some adolescent boys with ASD approach and kiss girls, as they see other boys doing with their girlfriends between classes. This kind of behavior may be tolerated at first by kindhearted adolescent girls, knowing that the boys have ASD, but this sometimes means to the boys with ASD that the girls want a romantic relationship. They may start calling and texting, sometimes with persistence that is interpreted as stalking. These kinds of social behaviors are difficult to stop, and it may be necessary to remove these adolescents from regular public schools.

Inappropriate sexual behavior is often related to social naïveté. For example, two female adolescent patients' parents allowed them—on just one occasion—to stay home alone. Both immediately texted a boy to come over; both had unprotected sexual intercourse. It is usually necessary to disallow the use of cell phones and access to social media. The adolescents view this as very unfair, but when given access, they often make unwise choices and can get into dangerous relationships.

Pornography and masturbation are often seen in adolescent boys, and this is equally true of boys with ASD. Masturbation is usually not a problem, and the boy quickly learns that it must be done in private. A few boys, most with marked intellectual disability, continue to masturbate in inappropriate places or try to involve any female who is easily available, including their mother or schoolmates. If it becomes problematical such that the boy is excluded from school, or parents believe that they can no longer care for the adolescent at home, hormonal treatments should be considered. Sometimes sexual aggression is related to manic episodes, but often it is independent of them.

Pornography sometimes becomes problematical if the teen spends so much time on it that it interferes with other functions. Sometimes parents object not to the pornography but to the types of sites visited that show unusual (or illegal) kinds of sexual behavior. This requires very close supervision, and often it is necessary to block these types of sites.

A rigid sense of right and wrong can cause difficulties, although it is not usually dangerous. One patient was called "the enforcer" at his school because he expected perfect behavior not only from himself but also from his classmates. Sometimes, children become very upset because they see something as unjust. One boy asked to sharpen his pencil after class had started. Because other children had sharpened theirs before the class began, he thought it was not fair that he could not sharpen his pencil. He had such a meltdown over this that his mother had to take him home from school. Another young man worked for a landscape company. The company had two contracts for apartments that were across the street from each other. The company lost the contract for one of them, but the young man, soon after being diagnosed for the first time with Asperger's disorder, kept trimming hedges for both properties. After repeatedly telling him to stop this, his boss fired him. The young man harassed and threatened his former boss for unfair treatment until the man called the police. Once the police came, he stopped the behavior.

Self-injurious behavior can be extremely severe, mainly in persons with ASD and moderate or severe intellectual disability, although it can be seen in persons with normal IQ. The most common types are wrist and arm biting, head banging, and skin picking. They often result in scars from bites on the thenar eminence and wrist and in calluses on the chosen area of the skull. Others pick at their skin until it bleeds. They may get infections, including methicillin-resistant *Staphylococcus aureus*. Usually, this is related to overwhelming anxiety. It can get worse during a depressive episode.

WHEN NOTHING WORKS

Some patients seem to have atypical responses to virtually every medication. Occasional reports of unusual reactions can be related to parental anxiety about using medications so that they interpret random events as side effects. Once this is ruled out, the only recourse is trial and error. Obviously, as stressed throughout, the first step is to take a careful history and make the most likely psychiatric diagnosis. Based on that, a class of medication is chosen, starting with a low dose. However, some patients have marked side effects even at low doses or have idiosyncratic responses to many different classes of medication. Sometimes a medication has an unexpected positive effect: One girl stopped daytime enuresis when a stimulant was started for her ADHD. Another problem can be the home environment: People with ASD do not do well in noisy environments with high levels of expressed emotion. They need quiet and routine, which can sometimes be impossible to provide at home.

When aggression, sexual or physical, is severe or if the anxiety or OCD is overwhelming, patients often do better in a residential setting. In a residence, the routine is unvarying: There are very few unexpected events, and there is often less noise and confusion. Also, medication trials can be more systematic: All the doses are given, and the effects are more reliably reported.

When patients who have been doing well suddenly get worse, a medical illness should be considered first. Some persons with ASD seem not to feel or recognize pain so that cellulitis, otitis media, appendicitis, and even a broken bone can go undetected. An adolescent who liked running suddenly became irritable and uncooperative. It was eventually discovered that he had broken his ankle. After it was set, he remained upset but denied he was in pain. After starting regular pain medication, his behavior returned to baseline.

SUMMARY

Persons with ASD suffer from a variety of psychiatric disorders and abnormal associated behaviors. These interfere greatly with optimal functioning and should be diagnosed and treated. Diagnosis is fundamentally the same as for psychiatric disorders in persons without ASD, but it focuses more on history often provided by the parents and on observable manifestations of the conditions. Aggression is a prominent but nonspecific feature of many of the conditions, so diagnosis and treatment should be focused on more specific clinical features of each disorder.

KEY POINTS

- Individuals with neurodevelopmental disorders have a higher frequency of emotional and behavioral disorders than neurotypical individuals.
- The estimates of the prevalence of psychiatric comorbidity in individuals with neurodevelopmental disorders vary, but these diagnoses probably occur in the majority of persons with ASD.

- The diagnosis of psychiatric disorders in persons with ASD may rely more on the history provided by the parents and on observable manifestations of the condition compared with that of neurotypical individuals.
- It may be difficult for patients with ASD to describe their internal feeling state (mood) either because they are minimally to nonverbal or because they have little insight into their mood.
- When patients whose neuropsychiatric symptoms have been stable for some time suddenly worsen, the onset of a medical illness must be considered first.

DISCLOSURE STATEMENT

Dr. Susan E. Folstein and Dr. Luis Carcache have nothing to disclose.

REFERENCES

Almeida, N., & Folstein, S. E. (2012). Abnormal eating behaviors: Comparing the scores on the Repetitive Behavior Scale with the severity of abnormal eating behavior, using the BAMBI scale, developed for autism. Unpublished raw data.

Bauminger, N., & Kasari, C. (2000). Loneliness and friendship in high-functioning children with autism. *Child Development, 71*(2), 447–456.

Birmaher, B., Axelson, D. A., Monk, K., Kalas, C., Clark, D. B., Ehmann, M., et al. (2003). Fluoxetine for the treatment of childhood anxiety disorders. *Journal of the American Academy of Child and Adolescent Psychiatry, 42*(4), 415–423.

Bodfish, J. W., Symons, F. J., Parker, D. E., & Lewis, M. H. (2000). Varieties of repetitive behavior in autism: Comparisons to mental retardation. *Journal of Autism and Developmental Disorders, 30*(3), 237–243.

Carbajal, J., & Folstein, S. E. (2012). Self injurious behavior response to SSRI use in individuals who have autism spectrum disorders. Unpublished raw data.

De Bruin, E. L., Ferdinand, R. F., Meester, S., De Nijs, P. F., & Verheij, F. (2007). High rates of psychiatric co-morbidity in PDD-NOS. *Journal of Autism and Developmental Disorders, 37*(5), 877–886.

Dhossche, D. M., Reti, I. M., & Wachtel, L. E. (2009). Catatonia and autism: A historical review with implications for electroconvulsive therapy. *Journal of ECT, 25*(1), 19–22.

Dhossche, D. M., Wing, L., Ohta, M., & Neumarker, K.-J. (Eds.). (2006). *Catatonia in autism spectrum disorders.* San Diego, CA: Academic Press.

Dominick, K. C., Davis, N. O., Lainhart, J., Tager-Flusberg, H., & Folstein S. (2007). Atypical behaviors in children with autism and children with a history of language impairment. *Research in Developmental Disabilities, 28*(2), 145–162.

Folstein, M. F., Folstein, S. E., White, T., & Messer, M. A. (2009). *The Mini-Mental State Examination—2nd edition user's manual.* Lutz, FL: PAR.

Kakooza-Mwesige, A., Wachtel, L. E., & Dhossche, D. M. (2008). Catatonia in autism: Implications across the lifespan. *European Child & Adolescent Psychiatry, 17*(6), 327–335.

Leyfer, O. T., Folstein, S. E., Bacalman, S., Davis, N. O., Dinh, E., Morgan, J., et al. (2006). Comorbid psychiatric disorders in children with autism: Interview development and rates of disorders. *Journal of Autism and Developmental Disorders, 36*(7), 849–861.

Lukens, C. T., & Linscheid, T. R. (2008). Development and validation of an inventory to assess mealtime behavior problems in children with autism. *Journal of Autism and Developmental Disorders, 38*(2), 342–352.

Mahajan, R., Bernal, M. P., Panzer, R., Whitaker, A., Roberts, W., Handen, B., et al. (2012). Clinical practice pathways for evaluation and medication choice for attention-deficit/hyperactivity disorder symptoms in autism spectrum disorders. *Pediatrics, 130*(Suppl. 2), S125–S138.

Monroy, K., & Folstein, S. E. (2012). Situations that commonly provoke anxiety in individuals who have autism spectrum disorders. Unpublished raw data.

Rapoport, J., Chavez, A., Greenstein, D., Addington, A., & Gogtay, N. (2009). Autism-spectrum disorders and childhood onset schizophrenia: Clinical and biological contributions to a relation revisited. *Journal of the American Academy of Child and Adolescent Psychiatry, 48*(1), 10–18.

Rutter, M., Graham, P., & Yule, W. (1970). *A neuropsychiatric study in childhood.* Philadelphia, PA: Lippincott.

Simonoff, E., Jones, C. R., Pickles, A., Happé, F., Baird, G., & Charman, T. (2012). Severe mood problems in adolescents with autism spectrum disorder. *Journal of Child Psychology and Psychiatry, 53*(11), 1157–1166.

Simonoff, E., Pickles, A., Charman, T., Chandler, S., Loucas, T., & Baird, G. (2008). Psychiatric disorders in children with autism spectrum disorders: Prevalence, comorbidity, and associated factors in a population-derived sample. *Journal of the American Academy of Child and Adolescent Psychiatry, 47*(8), 921–929.

Sofronoff, K., Attwood, T., & Hinton, S. (2005). A randomized controlled trial of a CBT intervention for anxiety in children with Asperger syndrome. *Journal of Child Psychology and Psychiatry, 46*(11), 1152–1160.

Steingard, R. J., Zimnitzky, B., DeMaso, D. R., Bauman, M. L., & Bucci, J. P. (1997). Sertraline treatment of transition-associated anxiety and agitation in children with autistic disorder. *Journal of Child and Adolescent Psychopharmacology, 7*(1), 9–15.

Wood, J. J., Drahota, A., Sze, K., Har, K., Chiu, A., & Langer, D. A. (2009). Cognitive behavioral therapy for anxiety in children with autism spectrum disorders: A randomized, controlled trial. *Journal of Child Psychology and Psychiatry, 50*(3), 224–234.

/// 7 /// NEUROLOGICAL COMORBIDITIES IN AUTISM SPECTRUM DISORDER

FIONA BAUMER AND MUSTAFA SAHIN

INTRODUCTION

Clinicians have noted that, in addition to the core criteria of social and communication deficits and repetitive behaviors, children with autism spectrum disorder (ASD) also have a very high prevalence of other neurologic problems, including epilepsy, sleep disturbances, and motor disorders. These observations have raised interesting questions about the pathophysiology of ASD and are also of clinical importance to practitioners caring for these patients.

Those writing about neurologic deficits in ASD consistently raise the following three questions:

1. Do these neurologic problems directly cause the ASD phenotype? For example, do seizures or interictal discharges seen on electroencephalogram (EEG) lead to ASD symptoms?
2. Do the core features of ASD cause other neurologic problems? For example, do frequent stereotypies explain sleep disturbances?
3. Is there a common anatomic or biochemical process that gives rise to both the ASD phenotype and these other neurologic problems? If so, can these other problems be helpful in understanding the anatomy and pathophysiology of ASD?

Considering the neurologic comorbidities of ASD is clinically relevant for two important reasons. First, because patients with ASD have a high prevalence of these problems, it is important for clinicians to screen for them because they *independently* affect health and quality of life. Second, given that there may be significant interactions between these problems and the ASD phenotype, it is possible that addressing these issues will alleviate some of the symptoms of ASD.

EPILEPSY

Definitions

- **Seizures**: Excessive synchronized electrical discharges that occur in the brain, last for a certain duration, and evolve over space and/or time. Seizures may or may not have an obvious outward manifestation.
- **Interictal epileptiform discharges**: Abnormal electrical activity in the brain that does not meet all the spatial or temporal criteria of a seizure.
- **Epilepsy**: A condition of repetitive, unprovoked seizures (i.e., not brought on by illness or substance use). Epilepsy affects approximately 1% or 2% of the general population.
- **Electroencephalogram (EEG)**: A test that measures electrical activity in the brain and therefore can assess for seizures and interictal epileptiform discharges.

CASE STUDY #1: "SARA"

Sara is a girl with a diagnosis of ASD who presented to the emergency room at 3 years of age after a 5-minute episode of right eye and head deviation, drooling from the right side of her mouth, and decreased use of her right arm. After sleeping for 3 hours, Sara woke up and was back to her normal self with no focal findings on neurologic examination, so she was discharged home for outpatient workup. She had brain magnetic resonance imaging (MRI) that was normal and an EEG that demonstrated frequent generalized spike and waves activated in sleep. Given the concerning clinical event and abnormal EEG, Sara was started on levetiracetam. Two months after initiation of levetiracetam, Sara underwent a repeat EEG that continued to show multifocal spikes potentiated by sleep. There was a discussion about whether or not to increase the medication due to these abnormalities on EEG, but it was decided that this would not be helpful. Sara had developed increased irritability and violent outbursts after starting the medication, so vitamin B_6 was added empirically to try to improve the irritability with some effect.

Two years later, Sara developed new episodes of staring straight ahead, during which she was unresponsive to verbal and tactile stimuli. These occurred several times a day and did not improve after empiric increases in the levetiracetam dose. An ambulatory EEG was obtained that captured 10 such staring spells. This EEG was notable for persistence of the multifocal spikes seen previously, but there was no change in the EEG during the staring episodes, suggesting that these were unlikely to be seizures. Sara then developed additional episodes of right eye deviation and right facial twitching that continued despite maximization of the dose of levetiracetam, so the decision was made to add lamotrigine to the regimen.

Demographics

Many children with ASD go on to develop seizures during childhood, with reported prevalence rates usually cited as 30% but varying substantially among studies (5–50%)

(Maski, Jeste, & Spence, 2011). Part of this variation may be attributed to sampling techniques because population-based studies find substantially lower rates of comorbid epilepsy than do clinic-based ones. In addition, there are two peaks of seizure onset in this population—the first in early childhood and the second in adolescence—so some of the variability in reported prevalence may be related to the age of the population sampled. Given the wide range in reported prevalence, researchers have evaluated other risk factors that modulate the risk of epilepsy in ASD. The prevalence of seizure disorders certainly is highest for children with ASD and intellectual disability, approaching 21.5%, but even children with normal intelligence have an approximately 8% risk of developing epilepsy; this is substantially higher than the general population risk of 1% or 2%. Patients with ASD and known genetic conditions are also more likely to have epilepsy. For example, patients with tuberous sclerosis complex have approximately a 50% chance of developing ASD and up to a 90% lifetime risk of epilepsy. Children with "idiopathic" ASD without clear genetic variants or structural lesions, however, are still at an elevated risk of epilepsy approaching 15% (range, 13–17%). Several studies suggest that epilepsy may be more common in females with ASD than in males, but these reports were confounded by the fact that the females had lower IQs and more genetic abnormalities (Spence & Schneider, 2009).

Interictal Discharges

As EEGs have been performed more frequently in patients with ASD, another question that has arisen is the importance of interictal epileptiform discharges without seizures. These discharges have been reported in approximately 6–30% but up to 60% of children with ASD. Estimates are likely skewed because so far all studies have been performed on subjects from referred clinic samples who received an EEG because there was at least some suspicion of seizures. Therefore, population-based studies of all-comers with ASD would be required to better refine this estimate. A recent retrospective longitudinal study compared children with ASD without any EEG abnormalities, with isolated interictal epileptiform discharges, and with known epilepsy and interictal discharges. The study found that isolated discharges were more prevalent in younger children, and epilepsy was more prevalent as age increased; by early adulthood, the frequency of isolated discharges had decreased significantly. This does suggest that, much as with normally developing children, the interictal discharges may be a marker indicating a high risk for developing epilepsy (Parmeggiani et al., 2010).

Infantile Spasms

Infantile spasms are a type of brief tonic seizures that develop in the first year of life. In many cases, EEG shows not only the seizures but also a very abnormal background pattern in between seizures, which in its most severe form is called hypsarrhythmia. Infantile spasms have been highly associated with poor cognitive outcomes, including intellectual disability and ASD. One population study found that 35% of children with infantile spasms went on to develop ASD, with the vast majority of these children also showing profound intellectual disability (Saemundsen, Ludvigsson, & Rafnsson, 2007). Because infantile spasms are detected in the first year of life and ASD is not usually detected until the second or third year, there has been some question as to whether infantile spasms are more associated than other early onset seizures with a later diagnosis of ASD. To address this question, Saemundsen, Ludvigsson, and Rafnsson (2008) used a retrospective cohort study of children with infantile spasms versus other types of seizures that developed before the age of 1 year. They concluded that children with any seizure type with an obvious underlying cause—such as a brain malformation, metabolic disorder, or genetic syndrome—had a higher risk of going on to develop ASD than those previously healthy, normally developing children with "cryptogenic seizures." In general, an underlying etiology of epilepsy was more likely to be found in those with infantile spasms. Therefore, all children with seizures early in life, including those with infantile spasms, should be monitored closely for the development of ASD.

Consequences

As in any other patient, seizures in those with ASD are concerning because they can have significant health consequences and can be very socially disruptive as well. Adults with ASD and epilepsy tend to be severely disabled with very poor social functioning (Danielsson, Gillberg, Billstedt, Gillberg, & Olsson, 2005). In addition, young adults with ASD have a much higher mortality rate than the general population, and many of these deaths are attributed to epilepsy (Gillberg, Billstedt, Sundh, & Gillberg, 2010). Epilepsy-related deaths can be associated with cardiorespiratory compromise during a seizure or due to unexplained cardiorespiratory failure after a seizure—a problem known as sudden unexpected death in epilepsy (SUDEP). SUDEP is more likely in those with poorly controlled seizures (Tomson, Walczak, Sillanpaa, & Sander, 2005), which is a problem for many individuals with ASD.

Isolated epileptiform discharges have been of particular interest because the question has been raised as to whether these discharges cause autistic symptoms in some patients. This question first stemmed from the observation that epileptic encephalopathies—disorders in which seizures or persistent abnormal interictal discharges are thought to directly affect cognition—can cause regression in language skills. The most prominent example of this is Landau–Kleffner syndrome, in which healthy children have loss of language in the setting of an EEG pattern know as electrical status epilepticus of sleep (ESES) (Trevathan, 2004); see Figure 7.1 for an example of this EEG pattern. Approximately 30% of children with ASD have a pattern of "autistic regression" that includes seemingly normal development until approximately 2 years of age, after which they lose the language and social skills they had previously acquired. Researchers have hypothesized that, like language regression in Landau–Kleffner syndrome, autistic regression could also be a result of an epileptic encephalopathy. Several studies have found an association between autistic regression and interictal discharges on EEG, but the data in this field are conflicting (Chez et al., 2006; Kim, Donnelly, Tournay, Book, & Filipek, 2006; Tuchman, Alessandri, & Cuccaro, 2010; Tuchman & Rapin, 2002).

Evaluation

Patients with ASD are at risk for any type of seizures but most frequently have complex partial seizures. Because this seizure type often manifests as alteration in consciousness and unusual focal movements, it can be difficult to differentiate seizures from other behaviors seen in ASD. This can be challenging for the clinician because there is risk of both over- and underreporting of seizures by caretakers. Therefore, it is recommended that EEGs be obtained for any behavior that is clinically suspicious for seizures (Maski et al.,

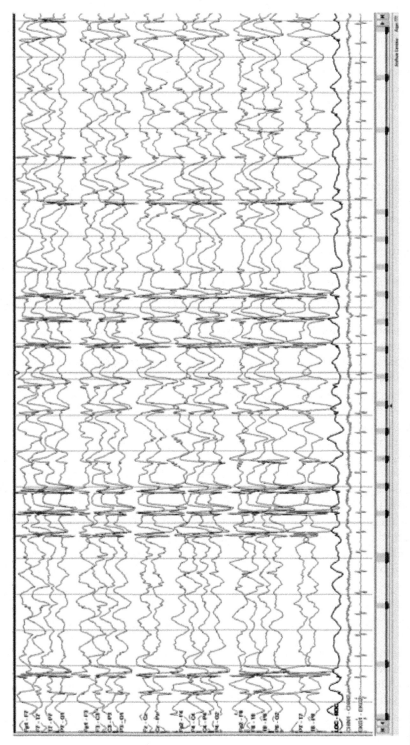

FIGURE 7.1 EEG recording of electrical status epilepticus of sleep (ESES). ESES is an EEG pattern of generalized (occurring in all leads) and frequent paroxysmal discharges or spikes that are present in greater than 85% of slow wave sleep. This pattern is often associated with developmental regression.

Source: Image courtesy of Dr. Jeffrey Bolton, Boston Children's Hospital, Boston.

2011). Ideally, an EEG should be an overnight study because there can be many epileptiform abnormalities brought out only in sleep. For any patient found to have seizures, a
thorough workup for known genetic or metabolic etiologies of ASD (i.e., tuberous sclerosis
complex, Rett's disorder, 15q11–13 duplication, MECP2 duplication, Phelan–McDermid
syndrome, and metabolic disorders) should be undertaken. At this point, although there is
not clear evidence that interictal discharges can cause autistic regression, an EEG should
also be considered in patients with ASD and an abrupt decline in language, social, or cognitive functioning (Kagan-Kushnir, Roberts, & Snead, 2005; Tuchman, Hirtz, & Mamounas,
2013; Tuchman & Rapin, 2002).

Treatment

Although treatment for epilepsy in patients with ASD will be specific to the patient and
the characteristics of his or her seizure disorder, there are some potential issues that
should be considered in advance. First, several antiepileptic drugs, especially levetiracetam and certain benzodiazepines, can cause worsening of behavioral problems. This
should be kept in mind when selecting appropriate treatment for seizures in patients with
ASD. A second issue is that those with ASD and epilepsy are much more likely to have
seizures that are refractory to treatment. In a study of patients referred to an epilepsy
clinic with idiopathic ASD (specifically, no genetic or infectious cause and no tuberous
sclerosis or history of infantile spasms), approximately one-third had treatment refractory epilepsy defined as failure to respond to two adequate trials of antiepileptic drugs.
Those with a younger age of onset of seizures were more likely to have severe, difficult-to-
treat epilepsy (Sansa et al., 2011). Often, some seizures are tolerated in patients with
ASD and treatment refractory epilepsy if the seizures do not interfere with the patient's
functioning and further treatment is limited by medication side effects. It should be kept
in mind, however, that untreated seizures increase the risk of morbidity in patients with
ASD (Danielsson et al., 2005).

Treatment of patients with isolated epileptiform discharges but without clear seizures
must be undertaken only with extreme care because it is still unclear if this will benefit the
patient. If it is believed that the onset of these discharges correlates well with a marked
change in the patient's cognitive, language, or social functioning, a short and closely
observed course of treatment can be considered. Treatment options have included medications used to treat epileptic encephalopathies such as steroids or benzodiazepines, as well
as antiepileptic medications known to decrease spikes, such as valproate. If pharmacologic
therapy is undertaken, it is critical that clinicians establish whether there is improvement
in symptoms and correlate this with an improvement in the background EEG (Tuchman
et al., 2010).

Basic Science

Given the significant comorbidity between ASD, epilepsy, and intellectual disability, much
research has focused on whether or not there is a causal relationship between these conditions or instead if there is an underlying pathology that has the potential to cause them
all. All three disorders are considered distributed processes that affect multiple neural networks. Therefore, the primary hypothesis currently under investigation is that abnormal
synaptic plasticity early in life gives rise to neural networks that can cause epilepsy and
ASD, as well as other neurologic phenotypes. On a structural level, this hypothesis has been

supported by neuropathologic examination of brains of patients with ASD that found evidence of cellular disorganization—including heterotopias, dysplasias, and abnormalities in neurogenesis and neuronal migration—similar to that seen in patients with epilepsy even though only one-third of the subjects with ASD in this group had seizures (Wegiel et al., 2010). Currently, most research in this field is directed at genetic studies of copy number variants (CNVs). CNVs are genetic deletions, duplications, and insertions in the genome, and several CNVs in genes associated with synaptic plasticity have been identified in subjects with both idiopathic epilepsy and ASD. In large genetic studies, several CNVs emerge, including duplications of chromosome 15q11–13, duplications and deletions of 16p11, and deletions of 22q11–13. Each of these is believed to be responsible for approximately 0.5–1% of sporadic cases of ASD. It is now estimated that an additional 10% of sporadic cases of ASD are caused by rare but identifiable CNVs; therefore, there is significant interest in identifying rare CNVs that lead to phenotypes of ASD and/or epilepsy (Geschwind, 2009; Tuchman & Cuccaro, 2011).

SLEEP DISORDERS

Definitions

- **Insomnia**: Difficulty initiating or maintaining sleep.
- **Sleep efficiency**: Percentage of time in bed that is spent sleeping.
- **Sleep latency**: Time to fall asleep after getting in bed.
- **Actigraphy**: A clinical test in which a small wristwatch-like device is worn and measures movement. It can be used to assess activity overnight and infer time spent asleep.
- **Polysomnography**: A multifaceted study that utilizes EEG, electrocardiogram, and respiratory monitoring to specifically assess a person's sleep, including the frequency and duration of different sleep stages, as well as respiratory problems that emerge during sleep.

CASE STUDY #1—CONTINUED

In addition to the seizures, Sara has had significant difficulty with sleep throughout her life. Starting at 2 years of age, Sara began to have temper tantrums at bedtime, during which she would jump and scream by the front door until her parents would take her for a ride in the car. While riding in the car, she was able to fall asleep and maintain sleep throughout the night. These behaviors eventually improved when the family stopped taking her on rides and implemented a more consistent bedtime routine.

Approximately 2 years later, Sara developed two new sleep problems—trouble falling asleep and inability to sleep through the night. Although she continued with the same bedtime routine, Sara would now remain awake for 60–90 minutes after being put to bed. Her neurologist prescribed melatonin to be given 1 hour before bedtime, and there was some improvement after the dose was up-titrated to 5 mg. The family also observed that Sara's trouble falling asleep was worse in the spring and fall when she had allergy symptoms, and her sleep latency improved after being started on an antihistamine medication during these seasons.

More concerning to the family, Sara began waking up at 3 am with agitated, destructive behavior. Fortuitously, one such nocturnal awakening occurred when she was undergoing her ambulatory EEG, and there was no seizure activity seen. Because her sleep seemed so disturbed immediately before these awakenings, there was concern for restless leg syndrome and a ferritin level was checked, which was 30 ng/mL. Consequently, a 4-month course of ferrous sulfate was started and continued until the ferritin level increased to greater than 50 ng/mL; on repeat testing 1 month after discontinuation of ferrous sulfate, the ferritin level remained at this level. With this intervention, Sara seemed to have fewer nighttime awakenings.

Demographics

Sleep disorders are quite common in all children but are particularly prevalent in those with ASD, even compared to patients with other developmental disorders. Based on parental surveys, it is estimated that 50–80% of children with ASD compared with approximately 10–50% of typically developing children have significant trouble sleeping. Studies relying on parental reports and actigraphy have consistently found that children with ASD have prolonged sleep latency, disrupted sleep, and early morning awakenings (Malow, 2004). Several studies have also used polysomnography to describe specific alterations in sleep architecture in patients with ASD. This research found abnormalities in, as well as a decreased amount of, rapid eye movement (REM) sleep in these patients compared with both typically developing children and IQ-matched subjects with other developmental disorders (Buckley et al., 2010; Diomedi et al., 1999; Elia et al., 2000). One group also reported subtle differences in non-REM sleep (Miano et al., 2007).

Sleep problems persist across the lifespan in patients with ASD, but the specific causes and consequences of insomnia change as children age. A survey study of 1859 patients with ASD showed that younger children demonstrated symptoms of a behavioral insomnia syndrome, consisting of more nighttime anxiety and bedtime resistance. They also had poor sleep efficiency secondary to nocturnal awakenings and parasomnias, such as sleepwalking (Kotagal & Broomall, 2012). Some of the core and associated features of ASD, including perseverative thoughts and actions and poor emotional regulation, contribute to the behavioral insomnia syndrome (Maski et al., 2011). Adolescents often manifest symptoms of circadian rhythm sleep disturbances, including a delayed sleep phase and prolonged sleep latency, leading to chronic sleep deprivation and daytime sleepiness (Goldman, Richdale, Clemons, & Malow, 2012). Research has suggested that disturbances in melatonin physiology contribute to these sleep disorders in ASD (Rossignol & Frye, 2011). In addition to insomnia, other prevalent sleep disorders in ASD include REM sleep behavior disorder that presents as aggressive or violent dream reenactment; disorders of excessive normal movements such as restless leg syndrome; and sleep problems related to other medical comorbidities, such as gastrointestinal discomfort and poor vision (Kotagal & Broomall, 2012). As in much of the typically developing population, respiratory disorders such as obstructive sleep apnea are also common, especially among obese patients.

Significance

Adequate sleep is important for memory consolidation and appropriate modulation of response to emotional stimuli, so it is therefore not surprising that the severity of disordered sleep directly correlates with symptoms of cognitive dysfunction and emotional dysregulation in children with ASD (Kotagal & Broomall, 2012). Sleep researchers theorize that REM sleep in particular is important in learning because it tends to increase after intensive educational sessions; thus, a decreased amount in ASD may cause problems in processing new information and consolidating memories (Buckley et al., 2010). In addition, there is a relevant feedback loop that develops due to poor sleep in children with ASD: Sleep deprivation leads to emotional lability and difficulty with cognitive processing that leads to bedtime resistance and perhaps worsening stereotypies or disruptive thoughts, which in turn leads to sleep deprivation. Interestingly, supporting the observation that sleep problems can precipitate or worsen autistic features, one study found that children with autistic regression were more likely than children with ASD without regression to have disordered sleep (Giannotti, Cortesi, Cerquiglini, Vagnoni, & Valente, 2011).

Evaluation

Given the prevalence of sleep disorders in patients with ASD, experts recommend that both primary physicians and specialists who work with patients with ASD screen for insomnia. This can be done with simple targeted questions such as those found on the Children's Sleep Habits Questionnaire (CSHQ) (Box 7.1), a tool that is applicable for children ages 4–10 years old. Specifically, questions about patterns of activity surrounding bedtime can help uncover behavioral insomnias, whereas exploring sleep patterns such as a consistently delayed bedtime can suggest circadian rhythm disorders. In addition, effects of sleep disorders, including daytime sleepiness or poor attention, should be assessed. The clinician should remember that sometimes sleep problems will manifest as other behavioral complaints, and he or she should inquire about sleep whenever there is a parental concern for irritability, aggression, or emotional lability (Malow et al., 2012).

BOX 7.1

CHILDREN'S SLEEP HABITS QUESTIONNAIRE (CSHQ) SCREEN FOR INSOMNIA

1. Does your child fall asleep within 20 minutes after going to bed?
2. Does your child fall asleep in the parents' or sibling's bed?
3. Does your child sleep too little?
4. Does your child awaken once during the night?
5. Do you think these behaviors are a problem?

Experts from the Sleep Committee of the Autism Treatment Network (ATN) agreed on these five screening questions based on their experience and review of the ATN database (N = 4887). The CSHQ is a 45-question tool.

If the family does endorse symptoms of insomnia, then the patient should be screened with a standard review of systems for medical problems that could contribute to disrupted sleep, including epilepsy, pain, gastrointestinal problems, nutritional deficiencies, obesity, and psychiatric conditions. Lastly, medications should be reviewed because many can affect sleep, and psychotropic medications such as selective serotonin reuptake inhibitors (SSRIs) and stimulants used to treat the behavioral problems often seen in ASD are frequent offenders. In addition, the clinician should evaluate for respiratory disorders of sleep, such as obstructive sleep apnea, and movement disorders, such as restless leg syndrome. Clinicians should have a low threshold to check a ferritin level if there is any suspicion of disrupted sleep or nighttime awakenings because low iron stores can contribute to restless leg syndrome and these movements often respond well to iron supplementation. If either respiratory problems or nocturnal seizures are suspected, the patient should be referred to a sleep specialist for consideration of polysomnography. Other reasons for referral to a sleep specialist include severe insomnia that is threatening the patient's safety due to daytime sleepiness or insomnia that does not respond to the behavioral and initial pharmacologic treatments described later (Malow et al., 2012; Maski et al., 2011). Children with ASD may have more difficulty than most completing a polysomnography because the test requires sleeping in a new environment with significant monitoring. Overall, working with a sleep specialist in a pediatric hospital may be helpful given the familiarity of the staff with working with children with behavioral disorders.

Treatment

The initial treatment for insomnia in all children includes behavioral interventions that reinforce good sleep hygiene and addressing other medical issues that may be contributing to poor sleep. Establishing a bedtime routine may be more difficult in those with ASD due to their trouble with emotional regulation and transitions, as well as confusion about parental expectations caused by deficits in language. Conversely, some children do well when given a routine due to their preference for consistency. Behavioral modifications, including behavioral extinction and positive reinforcement, may encourage more appropriate sleep patterns as well (Malow et al., 2012).

Many children with ASD eventually do require pharmacologic therapy to manage insomnia. Melatonin clearly has the most evidence in pediatric insomnia, and there are now studies that suggest that deficits in the melatonin pathway may contribute to sleep disorders in patients with ASD specifically (Rossignol & Frye, 2011). To date, the only drug for sleep disorders in patients with ASD to be studied in a blinded, placebo-controlled manner is melatonin. After a trial of melatonin, other pharmacologic agents can be offered based on the clinician's assessment and comfort level. Clonidine is frequently tried, although tolerance often develops and results in a reduced duration of action (Malow, 2004). If the patient has medical or psychiatric problems that require pharmacologic treatment, a drug that secondarily promotes sleep can be preferentially chosen. For patients with ferritin levels less than 50 ng/mL, supplementation with ferrous sulfate can be considered, although response should be monitored every 3 months to prevent iron toxicity; families should also be counseled ahead of time on the management of the gastrointestinal upset and constipation often seen with iron supplementation (Kotagal, 2012). Otherwise, referral to a pediatric sleep specialist can be considered. Regardless of the intervention, it is important that the patient be followed closely to assess the impact of the therapy on quality of sleep (Malow et al., 2012).

Basic Science

Researchers are currently exploring the physiologic basis of why people with ASD are at such high risk for developing sleep disturbances. In their review on sleep in ASD, Kotagal and Broomall (2012) summarize several such studies and particularly highlight papers examining the imbalance between inhibitory and excitatory neural activity. In general, glutamate is thought to be an excitatory neurotransmitter and γ-aminobutyric acid (GABA) an inhibitory one. Pathology studies have shown a decreased concentration of $GABA_B$ receptors in the cingulate and fusiform cortex in postmortem brain samples of patients with ASD. There has been parallel research suggesting that a decrease in GABA activity in the cingulate cortex is also present in primary insomnia. In addition, certain genetic mutations found in ASD—particularly those affecting synaptic proteins in the neurexin and neuroligin families—affect whether synapses will be glutamatergic or GABAergic and thus can tip the brain toward an excitatory state, contributing to difficulty in sleep maintenance. Finally, melatonin is important in the establishment of the GABA system in neurons, and multiple studies have demonstrated a decreased concentration of melatonin in patients with ASD. There is increasing evidence that an excess of excitation compared to inhibition in the brains of children with ASD is correlated with clinical problems such as sleep disorders or even epilepsy, although additional research is required to determine if this imbalance is truly causative. Furthermore, deeper understanding of the excitation/inhibition imbalance in the brain will be required to devise new therapeutic option.

MOTOR DISORDERS

Definitions

- **Motor delay**: Failure to meet expected gross motor milestones (independently sitting, walking, jumping, etc.) and fine motor milestones (developing a raking and then pincer grasp, manipulating objects, etc.) at the expected time.
- **Hypotonia**: Reduced resistance during passive movement of muscles, leading to postural instability or increased joint mobility.
- **Dyspraxia or apraxia**: Impairment in the ability to carry out skilled movements or gestures, despite having the desire and physical ability to perform them. Dyspraxia can affect many movements, including oral movements associated with speech, feeding, or management of secretions; hand movements such as those needed to manipulate tools or to write; and leg movements needed for a normal gait. Ideomotor apraxia is difficulty recognizing skilled gestures performed by others.
- **Stereotypies**: Repetitive, seemingly purposeless movements that can involve multiple body parts. They constitute a core diagnostic criterion in ASD and were traditionally thought to be self-stimulatory behavior, although that notion is now changing.

CASE STUDY #2: "CRAIG"

Craig is an 8-year-old boy with a history of nonverbal ASD who had multiple repetitive behaviors. Since he was much younger, he has had frequent episodes of hand waving and hand biting that occur more often when he is sleep deprived or in unusual or stressful situations. As he has gotten older, these movements have begun to interfere with his participation at school and have become more difficult to redirect. Currently, Craig has started to wake in the middle of the night and perform these behaviors, making it more difficult for him to fall back asleep. In addition, although Craig has been noted to walk on his tiptoes since he began walking at 13 months of age, he has more recently had more trouble with balance both at home and at school, with occasional falls. This was initially thought to be secondary to an infection and then to the clonidine that was started to improve his sleep, but the incoordination persisted even after the infection resolved and the medication was withdrawn.

Demographics

Repetitive behaviors are one of the core symptoms of ASD, and it has been increasingly recognized that a high percentage of people with this disorder (60–80%) have other deficits in motor skills. Of those with a genetic cause for their ASD, approximately 90% have motor delays (Geschwind, 2009). Compared with the literature investigating seizures and sleep disturbances in ASD, however, the research on motor problems to date has arrived at less cohesive conclusions. Overall, the work suggests that problems with movement in patients with ASD begin in infancy or early childhood and evolve through the lifespan. In young children with motor delay, a subsequent diagnosis of ASD is also a risk factor for persistence of motor problems throughout life (Van Waelvelde, Oostra, Dewitte, Van Den Broeck, & Jongmans, 2010).

Most research on motor dysfunction in ASD has focused on older children who have more subtle problems with gait, coordination, and praxis that persist through childhood (Ming, Brimacombe, & Wagner, 2007; Ozonoff et al., 2008). Reported gait abnormalities include toe walking and trouble with ankle movement, ataxia, incoordination, and asymmetry of stride (Calhoun, Longworth, & Chester, 2011; Esposito, Venuti, Apicella, & Muratori, 2011; Rinehart et al., 2006); of these problems, it seems that limitation in ankle motion emerges most consistently across studies as a significant problem in both children and adults with ASD (Calhoun et al., 2011; Hallett et al., 1993). At least one study utilizing gait analysis suggested gait patterns similar to that seen in Parkinson's disease, indicating basal ganglia involvement as well (Vilensky, Damasio, Maurer, 1980). Incoordination—including postural instability, difficulty with hand–eye coordination, and other difficulty in limb positioning—is strongly associated with ASD (Fournier, Hass, Naik, Lodha, & Cauraugh, 2010). Perhaps most interesting, dyspraxia, or difficulty performing skilled movements, is quite consistently reported in patients with ASD. Performance on tests of praxis, including identifying skilled movements made by others, is poorest in those subjects with the most severe social and communication deficits, suggesting a common underlying etiology between the motor and language problems (Dowell, Mahone, & Mostofsky, 2009). It has also been suggested that problems of praxis may be specific to ASD more so than to other developmental disorders that also affect motion, such as attention deficit hyperactivity disorder (MacNeil & Mostofsky, 2012).

Although motor problems in older children with ASD have long been recognized, traditional teaching was that motor function early in childhood was generally intact. More recent work, however, suggests that many infants and young children with ASD have motor problems as well. One study of 154 children with a diagnosis of ASD found that the majority of young children (63% of the 2- to 6-year-olds) had hypotonia and that this problem persisted in 38% of the older group (7- to 18-year-olds). In this study, 9% of subjects also had gross motor delay, although they all ultimately achieved their motor milestones (Ming et al., 2007). Teitelbaum and colleagues retrospectively assessed home videos of children with ASD (Teitelbaum et al., 1998) and Asperger's disorder (Teitelbaum et al., 2004), and they reported that characteristic motor differences were observable at 4–6 months of age. Further video-analysis studies have had mixed results. Esposito et al. (2011) evaluated pre-ambulatory movements as well as early gait and found asymmetry in both types of movements that were specific to ASD compared to movements in children with other forms of developmental delay or typical development. Ozonoff et al. (2008) could not replicate Teitelbaum et al.'s findings. Based on these studies, it seems that there is a high incidence of motor problems in infancy and early childhood in patients with ASD, although the specific nature of these differences in still under research.

Stereotypies are the one motor phenomenon included in the core diagnostic criteria for ASD. These repetitive, seemingly purposeless movements are now considered an environmentally mediated movement disorder. Although children with other forms of developmental delay also frequently exhibit stereotypies, they are much more common in children with ASD. In one study, 63–70% of children with ASD exhibited stereotypies compared to 18–30% of those with other forms of developmental delay. In particular, stereotypies of gait (i.e., pacing, spinning, or skipping) and hand–finger movements (shaking, tapping, waving, clapping, opening–closing, or twirling) were more specific to ASD. The incidence and severity of stereotypies correlated with lower IQ and with more significant autistic symptoms, suggesting that stereotypies are a marker of the severity of ASD (Goldman et al., 2009).

Significance

Motor problems in ASD are of special interest to researchers and clinicians because early motor development is more easily observable and quantifiable than early language or social development, and therefore such problems may allow for earlier detection of ASD. As described previously, there has been much research focusing on identifying patterns of motor dysfunction specific to ASD with overall mixed results. In general, it appears that children with motor delays early in life are at risk for having an ASD, and particular attention should be paid to screening their language and social development. Stereotypies, especially those involving the hands or gait, may be more concerning for ASD than for other forms of developmental delay. Motor symptoms are also important in children with ASD because the severity of motor deficits may be a marker of disease severity and predict development of later language or social skills. For example, there is evidence that early oral and manual motor skills are strongly correlated with later speech fluency (Bhat, Galloway, & Landa, 2012; Gernsbacher, Sauer, Geye, Schweigert, & Hill Goldsmith, 2008). In addition to permitting earlier diagnosis and serving as a marker of illness severity, motor problems in ASD may be an important therapeutic target. Researchers hypothesize that intervening early may improve not only the motor symptoms but also possibly other traits of ASD, including language and socialization, whose development could be limited by poor motor function (Jeste, 2011).

Evaluation and Treatment

Although there is a growing interest in motor problems in ASD, the evaluation and treatment of these issues has not yet been well established. Because stereotypies are a core feature of the disorder, there has been significant research on behavioral interventions to reduce their frequency with multiple forms of behavioral conditioning. Even exercise is shown to lead to some improvement. At this point, no particular form of behavioral therapy has emerged as being specifically effective in reducing stereotypies; thus, applied behavior analysis therapy is still recommended (Boyd, McDonough, & Bodfish, 2012). Psychopharmacologic treatments such as SSRIs have also been used to treat stereotypies, but their efficacy for this purpose is under question (Carrasco, Volkmar, & Bloch, 2012). Although standards of evaluation and treatment are still not formalized, clinicians should screen all children with ASD for motor deficits, including hypotonia and gross delay in younger children, as well as more subtle issues such as dyspraxia in older children.

Basic Science

Based on history and examination findings in patients with ASD, clinicians and researchers have localized motor problems to the cerebellar and frontostriatal pathways, and recent imaging research further supports this localization (Jeste, 2011). In a series of articles, Mostofsky and colleagues reported that left motor cortex and premotor cortical white matter volumes (Mostofsky, Burgess, & Gidley Larson, 2007) and basal ganglia shape (Qiu, Adler, Crocetti, Miller, & Mostofsky, 2010) were associated with poor motor performances and problems with praxis. They also found differences in cerebellar activation during motor tasks compared to controls (Mostofsky et al., 2009; Tsai et al., 2012). Recently, a consensus group reviewing the role of the cerebellum in ASD concluded that the anatomy and neurochemistry of the cerebellum are affected in a significant proportion of patients with ASD and that these changes underlie motor and some cognitive deficits in this disorder (Fatemi et al., 2012).

SUMMARY

As described in this chapter, patients with ASD are susceptible to a number of other underlying neurologic problems that can have a severe impact on daily functioning as well as general health. Although this chapter focuses on three of the more frequent and severe comorbidities, patients with ASD often face many other neurologic problems, including intellectual disability, sensory integration problems, and pain. We still do not clearly understand whether neurologic problems—such as epileptiform discharges, severely disturbed sleep, or significant apraxia—can be the cause of the core symptoms of ASD, but there is building evidence that at the very least, such problems exacerbate these symptoms by affecting attention and ability to participate in behavioral treatments usually offered to patients with ASD. Clinicians who work with patients with ASD, therefore, should not only be aware of such comorbidities but also actively screen for them because many of these are treatable conditions, such as seizures or insomnia, and caregivers may fail to mention or may not notice these issues.

KEY POINTS

- Children with ASD often have other neurological problems, such as epilepsy, disturbed sleep, or movement disorders. Screening for and addressing these problems is a shared responsibility of all medical providers caring for these patients.

- It can be difficult to distinguish seizures from unusual behaviors in children with ASD by history alone, so EEG should be considered before considering treatment.
- Many children with ASD have seizures, but even more have abnormal EEGs without clear seizures. Treatment of these abnormalities is a controversial and evolving field.
- There is a high incidence of sleep disturbances in children with ASD, and the etiology changes across the lifespan. Sleep disturbances should be considered whenever there are concerns for daytime irritability or emotional lability.
- Motor problems, including stereotypies and apraxia, can be both a marker of clinical severity and an important therapeutic target for children with ASD.

DISCLOSURE STATEMENT

Dr. Fiona Baumer has nothing to disclose.

Dr. Mustafa Sahin has served on the scientific advisory board for the Tuberous Sclerosis Alliance and has received research support from Children's Hospital Boston Translational Research Program, Autism Speaks, the Tuberous Sclerosis Alliance, Novartis Pharmaceuticals Inc., Hoffmann-La Roche, Shire, the Department of Defense/ Congressionally Directed Medical Research Program, the Nancy Lurie Marks Family Foundation, and the National Institutes of Health (NIH U01 NS082320,U54 NS092090 and P30 HD018655-31).

REFERENCES

Bhat, A. N., Galloway, J. C., & Landa, R. J. (2012). Relation between early motor delay and later communication delay in infants at risk for autism. *Infant Behavior & Development, 35*(4), 838–846.

Boyd, B. A., McDonough, S. G., & Bodfish, J. W. (2012). Evidence-based behavioral interventions for repetitive behaviors in autism. *Journal of Autism and Developmental Disorders, 42*(6), 1236–1248.

Buckley, A. W., Rodriguez, A. J., Jennison, K., Buckley, J., Thurm, A., Sato, S., et al. (2010). Rapid eye movement sleep percentage in children with autism compared with children with developmental delay and typical development. *Archives of Pediatrics and Adolescent Medicine, 164*(11), 1032–1037.

Calhoun, M., Longworth, M., & Chester, V. L. (2011). Gait patterns in children with autism. *Clinical Biomechanics (Bristol, Avon), 26*(2), 200–206.

Carrasco, M., Volkmar, F. R., & Bloch, M. H. (2012). Pharmacologic treatment of repetitive behaviors in autism spectrum disorders: Evidence of publication bias. *Pediatrics, 129*(5), e1301–e1310.

Chez, M. G., Chang, M., Krasne, V., Coughlan, C., Kominsky, M., & Schwartz, A. (2006). Frequency of epileptiform EEG abnormalities in a sequential screening of autistic patients with no known clinical epilepsy from 1996 to 2005. *Epilepsy & Behavior, 8*(1), 267–271.

Danielsson, S., Gillberg, I. C., Billstedt, E., Gillberg, C., & Olsson, I. (2005). Epilepsy in young adults with autism: A prospective population-based follow-up study of 120 individuals diagnosed in childhood. *Epilepsia, 46*(6), 918–923.

Diomedi, M., Curatolo, P., Scalise, A., Placidi, F., Caretto, F., & Gigli, G. L. (1999). Sleep abnormalities in mentally retarded autistic subjects: Down's syndrome with mental retardation and normal subjects. *Brain & Development, 21*(8), 548–553.

Dowell, L. R., Mahone, E. M., & Mostofsky, S. H. (2009). Associations of postural knowledge and basic motor skill with dyspraxia in autism: Implication for abnormalities in distributed connectivity and motor learning. *Neuropsychology, 23*(5), 563–570.

Elia, M., Ferri, R., Musumeci, S. A., Del Gracco, S., Bottitta, M., Scuderi, C., et al. (2000). Sleep in subjects with autistic disorder: A neurophysiological and psychological study. *Brain & Development*, 22(2), 88–92.

Esposito, G., Venuti, P., Apicella, F., & Muratori, F. (2011). Analysis of unsupported gait in toddlers with autism. *Brain & Development*, 33(5), 367–373.

Fatemi, S. H., Aldinger, K. A., Ashwood, P., Bauman, M. L., Blaha, C. D., Blatt, G. J., et al. (2012). Consensus paper: Pathological role of the cerebellum in autism. *Cerebellum*, 11(3), 777–807.

Fournier, K. A., Hass, C. J., Naik, S. K., Lodha, N., & Cauraugh, J. H. (2010). Motor coordination in autism spectrum disorders: A synthesis and meta-analysis. *Journal of Autism and Developmental Disorders*, 40(10), 1227–1240.

Gernsbacher, M. A., Sauer, E. A., Geye, H. M., Schweigert, E. K., & Hill Goldsmith, H. (2008). Infant and toddler oral- and manual-motor skills predict later speech fluency in autism. *Journal of Child Psychology and Psychiatry*, 49(1), 43–50.

Geschwind, D. H. (2009). Advances in autism. *Annual Review of Medicine*, 60, 367–380.

Giannotti, F., Cortesi, F., Cerquiglini, A., Vagnoni, C., & Valente, D. (2011). Sleep in children with autism with and without autistic regression. *Journal of Sleep Research*, 20(2), 338–347.

Gillberg, C., Billstedt, E., Sundh, V., & Gillberg, I. C. (2010). Mortality in autism: A prospective longitudinal community-based study. *Journal of Autism and Developmental Disorders*, 40(3), 352–357.

Goldman, S., Wang, C., Salgado, M. W., Greene, P. E., Kim, M., & Rapin, I. (2009). Motor stereotypies in children with autism and other developmental disorders. *Developmental Medicine and Child Neurology*, 51(1), 30–38.

Goldman, S. E., Richdale, A. L., Clemons, T., & Malow, B. A. (2012). Parental sleep concerns in autism spectrum disorders: Variations from childhood to adolescence. *Journal of Autism and Developmental Disorders*, 42(4), 531–538.

Hallett, M., Lebiedowska, M. K., Thomas, S. L., Stanhope, S. J., Denckla, M. B., & Rumsey, J. (1993). Locomotion of autistic adults. *Archives of Neurology*, 50(12), 1304–1308.

Jeste, S. S. (2011). The neurology of autism spectrum disorders. *Current Opinion in Neurology*, 24(2), 132–139.

Kagan-Kushnir, T., Roberts, S. W., & Snead, O. C. (2005). Screening electroencephalograms in autism spectrum disorders: Evidence-based guideline. *Journal of Child Neurology*, 20(3), 197–206.

Kim, H. L., Donnelly, J. H., Tournay, A. E., Book, T. M., & Filipek, P. (2006). Absence of seizures despite high prevalence of epileptiform EEG abnormalities in children with autism monitored in a tertiary care center. *Epilepsia*, 47(2), 394–398.

Kotagal, S. (2012). Treatment of dyssomnias and parasomnias in childhood. *Current Treatment Options in Neurology*, 14(6), 630–649.

Kotagal, S., & Broomall, E. (2012). Sleep in children with autism spectrum disorder. *Pediatric Neurology*, 47(4), 242–251.

MacNeil, L. K., & Mostofsky, S. H. (2012). Specificity of dyspraxia in children with autism. *Neuropsychology*, 26(2), 165–171.

Malow, B. A. (2004). Sleep disorders, epilepsy, and autism. *Mental Retardation and Developmental Disabilities Research Reviews*, 10(2), 122–125.

Malow, B. A., Byars, K., Johnson, K., Weiss, S., Bernal, P., Goldman, S. E., et al. (2012). A practice pathway for the identification, evaluation, and management of insomnia in children and adolescents with autism spectrum disorders. *Pediatrics*, 130(Suppl. 2), S106–S124.

Maski, K. P., Jeste, S. S., & Spence, S. J. (2011). Common neurological co-morbidities in autism spectrum disorders. *Current Opinion in Pediatrics*, 23(6), 609–615.

Miano, S., Bruni, O., Elia, M., Trovato, A., Smerieri, A., Verrillo, E., et al. (2007). Sleep in children with autistic spectrum disorder: A questionnaire and polysomnographic study. *Sleep Medicine*, 9(1), 64–70.

Ming, X., Brimacombe, M., & Wagner, G. C. (2007). Prevalence of motor impairment in autism spectrum disorders. *Brain & Development*, 29(9), 565–570.

Mostofsky, S. H., Burgess, M. P., & Gidley Larson, J. C. (2007). Increased motor cortex white matter volume predicts motor impairment in autism. *Brain*, 130(Pt. 8), 2117–2122.

Mostofsky, S. H., Powell, S. K., Simmonds, D. J., Goldberg, M. C., Caffo, B., & Pekar, J. J. (2009). Decreased connectivity and cerebellar activity in autism during motor task performance. *Brain, 132*(Pt. 9), 2413–2425.

Ozonoff, S., Young, G. S., Goldring, S., Greiss-Hess, L., Herrera, A. M., Steele, J., et al. (2008). Gross motor development, movement abnormalities, and early identification of autism. *Journal of Autism and Developmental Disorders, 38*(4), 644–656.

Parmeggiani, A., Barcia, G., Posar, A., Raimondi, E., Santucci, M., & Scaduto, M. C. (2010). Epilepsy and EEG paroxysmal abnormalities in autism spectrum disorders. *Brain & Development, 32*(9), 783–789.

Qiu, A., Adler, M., Crocetti, D., Miller, M. I., & Mostofsky, S. H. (2010). Basal ganglia shapes predict social, communication, and motor dysfunctions in boys with autism spectrum disorder. *Journal of the American Academy of Child and Adolescent Psychiatry, 49*(6), 539–551.

Rinehart, N. J., Tonge, B. J., Iansek, R., McGinley, J., Brereton, A. V., Enticott, P. G., et al. (2006). Gait function in newly diagnosed children with autism: Cerebellar and basal ganglia related motor disorder. *Developmental Medicine and Child Neurology, 48*(10), 819–824.

Rossignol, D. A., & Frye, R. E. (2011). Melatonin in autism spectrum disorders: A systematic review and meta-analysis. *Developmental Medicine and Child Neurology, 53*(9), 783–792.

Saemundsen, E., Ludvigsson, P., & Rafnsson, V. (2007). Autism spectrum disorders in children with a history of infantile spasms: A population-based study. *Journal of Child Neurology, 22*(9), 1102–1109

Saemundsen, E., Ludvigsson, P., & Rafnsson, V. (2008). Risk of autism spectrum disorders after infantile spasms: A population-based study nested in a cohort with seizures in the first year of life. *Epilepsia, 49*(11), 1865–1870.

Spence, S. J., & Schneider, M. T. (2009). The role of epilepsy and epileptiform EEGs in autism spectrum disorders. *Pediatric Research, 65*(6), 599–606.

Tomson, T., Walczak, T., Sillanpaa, M., & Sander, J. W. (2005). Sudden unexpected death in epilepsy: A review of incidence and risk factors. *Epilepsia, 46*(Suppl. 11), 54–61.

Trevathan, E. (2004). Seizures and epilepsy among children with language regression and autistic spectrum disorders. *Journal of Child Neurology, 19*(Suppl. 1), S49–S57.

Tsai, P. T., Hull, C., Chu, Y., Greene-Colozzi, E., Sadowski, A. R., Leech, J. M., et al. (2012). Autistic-like behaviour and cerebellar dysfunction in Purkinje cell Tsc1 mutant mice. *Nature, 488*(7413), 647–651.

Tuchman, R., Alessandri, M., & Cuccaro, M. (2010). Autism spectrum disorders and epilepsy: Moving towards a comprehensive approach to treatment. *Brain & Development, 32*(9), 719–730.

Tuchman, R., & Cuccaro, M. (2011). Epilepsy and autism: Neurodevelopmental perspective. *Current Neurology and Neuroscience Reports, 11*(4), 428–434.

Tuchman, R., Hirtz, D., & Mamounas, L. A. (2013). NINDS epilepsy and autism spectrum disorders workshop report. *Neurology, 81*(18), 1630–1636.

Tuchman, R., & Rapin, I. (2002). Epilepsy in autism. *Lancet Neurology, 1*(6), 352–358.

Van Waelvelde, H., Oostra, A., Dewitte, G., Van Den Broeck, C., & Jongmans, M. J. (2010). Stability of motor problems in young children with or at risk of autism spectrum disorders, ADHD, and/or developmental coordination disorder. *Developmental Medicine and Child Neurology, 52*(8), e174–e178.

Wegiel, J., Kuchna, I., Nowicki, K., Imaki, H., Marchi, E., Ma, S. Y., et al. (2010). The neuropathology of autism: Defects of neurogenesis and neuronal migration, and dysplastic changes. *Acta Neuropathologica, 119*(6), 755–770.

GENETIC DISORDERS ASSOCIATED WITH THE AUTISM SPECTRUM DISORDER PHENOTYPE

LAWRENCE K. FUNG AND ALLAN L. REISS

INTRODUCTION

Core symptoms of autism spectrum disorder (ASD)—deficits in social communication, social interaction, and the presence of restricted, repetitive patterns of behavior, interests, or activities—have been reported in a growing list of genetic diseases. This chapter provides an introduction to the genetic diseases that include ASD symptomatology as a component of the phenotype. Four major classes of genetic diseases are described: monogenic, chromosomal, metabolic, and mitochondrial. As shown in Tables 8.1 and 8.2, many genetic syndromes exhibit features of ASD. Eight are discussed in more detail in this chapter. This discussion is followed by an approach for detecting syndromic features of ASD in a diagnostic evaluation. To illustrate some of the key concepts in this chapter, two case examples of genetic diseases are presented.

Monogenic Diseases

Monogenic or single-gene diseases result from modifications in a single gene occurring in all cells in the body. More than 10,000 human diseases are estimated to be monogenic disorders. These diseases are further categorized into three main categories: dominant, recessive, and X-linked. Autosomal dominant diseases involve damage to one gene copy on non-sex chromosomes, whereas autosomal recessive diseases involve both gene copies. X-linked monogenic diseases are associated with defective genes on the X chromosome. Men carry only one copy of the X chromosome, whereas women carry two. Therefore, women with X-linked monogenic diseases are usually carriers with no symptoms or milder manifestations relative to men with X-linked diseases, who tend to have more severe symptoms.

Many syndromic ASDs belong to autosomal dominant monogenic diseases (see Table 8.1)—for example, neurofibromatosis type 1 (NF1; Garg et al., 2013), tuberous

TABLE 8.1 Partial List of Monogenic and Chromosomal Diseases Exhibiting Autism Spectrum Disorder Symptoms

Genetic Syndrome	Classification	Location of Defect	Genetic Abnormality	Reference
Bannayan–Riley–Ruvalcaba syndrome[a]	Monogenic; AD	10q23.31	Mutation in PTEN gene	Lynch et al. (2009)
CHARGE syndrome	Monogenic; AD	8q12.1–q12.2 7q21.11	Mutation in CHD7 gene Mutation in SEMA3E gene	Bergman et al. (2011)
Cohen syndrome	Monogenic; AR	8q22.2	Mutation in COH1 gene	Douzgou and Petersen (2011)
Cornelia de Lange syndrome	Monogenic; AD	5p13.2	Mutation in CDLS1 gene	Schrier et al. (2011)
Cowden syndrome[a]	Monogenic; AD	10q23	Mutation in PTEN gene	Conti et al. (2012)
Fragile X syndrome	Monogenic; X-linked	Xq27.3	Mutation in FMR1 gene	Fung et al. (2012)
Joubert syndrome	Monogenic; AR	9q34.3	Mutation in AHI1 gene	Alvarez Retuerto et al. (2008)
Lujan–Fryns syndrome	Monogenic; X-linked	Xq13.1	Mutation in MED12 gene	Lerma-Carrillo et al. (2006)
Neurofibromatosis type 1	Monogenic, AD	17q11.2	Mutation in NF1 gene	Garg et al. (2013)
Phelan–McDermid syndrome	Monogenic; AD	22q13.33	Mutation in SHANK3 gene	Sarasua et al. (2014)
Rett syndrome	Monogenic; X-linked	Xq28 14q13	Mutation in MeCP2 gene Mutation in FOXG1 gene	Castro et al. (2013)
Sotos syndrome	Monogenic; AD	5q35.2–q35.3	Mutation in NSD1 gene	Buxbaum et al. (2007)
Timothy syndrome	Monogenic; AD	12p13.33	Mutation in CACNA1C gene	Lu et al. (2012)
Tuberous sclerosis complex	Monogenic, AD	9q34 16p13	Mutation in TSC1 gene Mutation in TSC2 gene	Curatolo et al. (2010)
15q13.3 deletion syndrome	Chromosomal	15q13.3	Deletion involving CHRNA7 gene	Hoppman-Chaney et al. (2013)
15q13.3 duplication syndrome	Chromosomal	15q13.3	Duplication	Beal (2014)

TABLE 8.1 Continued

Genetic Syndrome	Classification	Location of Defect	Genetic Abnormality	Reference
16p11.2 deletion syndrome	Chromosomal	16p11.2	Deletion	Zufferey et al. (2012)
16p11.2 duplication syndrome	Chromosomal	16p11.2	Duplication	Barber et al. (2013)
22q13 duplication syndrome	Chromosomal	22q13	Duplication	Frye (2012)
Angelman syndrome	Chromosomal; imprinting	15q11-13	Maternal deletions involving *UBE3A* gene	Thibert et al. (2013)
Down syndrome	Chromosomal	Chromosome 21	Trisomy 21	Carter et al. (2007)
Prader–Willi syndrome	Chromosomal; imprinting	15q11-13	Paternal deletions involving *SNRPN* and *NDN* genes	Dykens, Lee, and Roof (2011)
Potocki–Lupski syndrome	Chromosomal	17p11.2	Duplication	Treadwell-Deering, Powell, and Potocki (2010)
Smith–Magenis syndrome	Chromosomal	17p11.2	Deletion involving *RAI1* gene	Laje et al. (2010)
Velocardiofacial syndrome	Chromosomal	22q11.21	Deletion involving haploinsufficiency of *TBX1* gene	Jonas et al. (2014)
Williams–Beuren syndrome	Chromosomal	7q11.23	Hemizygous deletion of 1.5–1.8 Mb on 7q11.23	Tordjman et al. (2013)
Williams–Beuren region duplication syndrome	Chromosomal	7q11.23	Duplication	Sanders et al. (2011)
Klinefelter (47,XXY) syndrome	Chromosomal	X chromosome	Aneuploidy	Ross et al. (2012)
47,XYY syndrome	Chromosomal	Y chromosome	Aneuploidy	Margari et al. (2014)

[a]Classified under PTEN-associated disorders.

AD, autosomal dominant; AR, autosomal recessive.

sclerosis (Curatolo, Napolioni, & Moavero, 2010), CHARGE syndrome (Bergman et al., 2011), Cornelia de Lange syndrome (Schrier et al., 2011), Phelan–McDermid syndrome (Sarasua et al., 2014), Sotos syndrome (Buxbaum et al., 2007), Timothy syndrome (Lu, Dai, Martinez-Agosto, & Cantor, 2012), phosphatase and tensin homolog (PTEN)-associated disorders (including Bannayan–Riley–Ruvalcaba syndrome) (Lynch, Lynch, McMenamin, &

TABLE 8.2 Partial List of Metabolic Diseases Exhibiting Autism Spectrum Disorder Symptoms

Genetic Syndrome	Location of Defect	Genetic Abnormality	Reference
6-*N*-trimethyllysine dioxygenase deficiency	Xq28	Mutation in *TMLHE* gene	Celestino-Soper et al. (2012)
Cerebral folate deficiency	5q11.2–q13.2	Mutation in *DHFR* gene	Ramaekers, Blau, Sequeira, Nassogne, and Quadros (2007)
Cytosolic 5′ nucleotidase superactivity	7p14.3	Mutation in *NT5C3A* gene	Page, Yu, Fontanesi, and Nyhan (1997)
Phenylketonuria	12q23.2	Mutation in *PAH* gene	Baieli, Pavone, Meli, Fiumara, and Coleman (2003)
Smith–Lemli–Opitz syndrome	11q13.4	Mutation in *DHCR7* gene	Nowaczyk and Irons (2012)
Succinic semialdehyde dehydrogenase (SSADH) deficiency	6p22.3	Mutation in *ALDH5A1* gene	Knerr, Gibson, Jakobs, and Pearl (2008)

Webb, 2009), and Cowden syndrome (Conti et al., 2012). Fewer syndromic ASDs are autosomal recessive—for example, Cohen syndrome (Douzgou & Petersen, 2011) and Joubert syndrome (Alvarez Retuerto et al., 2008). Two of the most well-known syndromic ASDs are X-linked monogenic diseases—fragile X syndrome (FXS; Fung, Quintin, Haas, & Reiss, 2012) and Rett syndrome (RTT; Castro, Mellios, & Sur, 2013).

Chromosomal Diseases

Chromosomal diseases can arise from alterations of the number of chromosomes (aneuploidy) or changes in a fragment (portion) of a chromosome. Changes of a chromosomal fragment can take the form of deletion, duplication, or translocation. Deletions and duplications are also known as copy number variations (CNVs).

Table 8.1 lists representative chromosomal diseases in which ASD symptoms commonly occur. Individuals with 47,XYY syndrome (Margari, Lamanna, Craig, Simone, & Gentile, 2014), a relatively common sex chromosome aneuploidy, often manifest ASD symptoms. ASD symptoms can also occur infrequently in association with Down syndrome(Carter, Capone, Gray, Cox, & Kaufmann, 2007). Microdeletions of small fragments of chromosomes have also been found in several syndromes associated with ASD—for example, Angelman syndrome (Thibert, Larson, Hsieh, Raby, & Thiele, 2013), Prader–Willi syndrome, Smith–Magenis syndrome (Laje et al., 2010), velocardiofacial syndrome (Jonas, Montojo, & Bearden, 2014), and Williams–Beuren syndrome (Tordjman et al., 2013). Duplications or deletions of certain regions of the DNA are known to be especially associated with ASD; for example, either duplication or deletion of 16p11.2 (Barber et al., 2013; Zufferey et al., 2012) and 15q11–q13 (Beal, 2014; Hoppman-Chaney, Wain, Seger, Superneau, & Hodge, 2013) are associated with ASD.

Metabolic Diseases

Various metabolic diseases are reported to be associated with ASD (see Table 8.2) (Schaefer & Mendelsohn, 2013). These diseases are relatively rare, and they generally present early in life. Inborn errors of metabolism include the following: carbohydrate metabolism defects, amino acid metabolism defects, organic acid disorders, fatty acid oxidation disorders, purine metabolism disorders, lysosomal storage disorders, and peroxisomal disorders. Most metabolic disorders are associated with serious medical problems, such as seizures, extrapyramidal symptoms, and failure to thrive. Developmental regression is common for children with metabolic diseases. The ability to diagnose metabolic diseases has had a major impact on public health. The most notable example is neonatal screening for phenylketonuria (PKU), a genetic disorder in which the body cannot metabolize the essential amino acid phenylalanine. All infants born in hospitals in the United States and many other countries are required to be screened for PKU. If PKU is diagnosed early, an affected newborn can be managed through a combination of diet and medication and can grow up with essentially normal brain development. Before newborn screening for PKU became common, untreated PKU was known to be one of the most common causes of ASD symptoms and intellectual disability.

Mitochondrial Diseases

Mitochondrial diseases are rare conditions involving the mitochondria, an organelle responsible for energy metabolism, storage of calcium ions, and steroid synthesis. Recently, mitochondrial dysfunction was hypothesized to be associated with ASD. Possible mechanisms for such association include mitochondrial-induced oxidative stress, abnormal mitochondrial calcium handling, and mitochondrial activation of the immune system (Legido, Jethva, & Goldenthal, 2013). Similar to metabolic disorders, mitochondrial disorders often involve serious medical problems including neurologic symptoms. In one cohort study, 25 patients with a primary diagnosis of ASD and evidence of a disorder of mitochondrial energy metabolism were examined. Sixty-four percent of this cohort had significant deficits (median enzyme activity was 7% of normal; range, 0–20%) in complex I of the electron transport chain (ETC); 20% had deficiency (median enzyme activity was 20% of normal; range, 14–32%) in complex III of the ETC (Weissman et al., 2008).

SPECIFIC SYNDROMES

Specific genetic syndromes have been catalogued at the Genetics Home Reference administered by the U.S. National Library of Medicine (http://ghr.nlm.nih.gov) and the Online Mendelian Inheritance in Man (OMIM; http://omim.org) maintained by the National Human Genome Research Institute, Johns Hopkins University, and the Institute of Genetic Medicine. Here, eight syndromes have been selected for further discussion regarding their physical phenotypes, cognitive–behavioral phenotypes, genetics, as well as molecular biology. Figure 8.1 shows pictures of representative school-age children with each specific genetic syndrome.

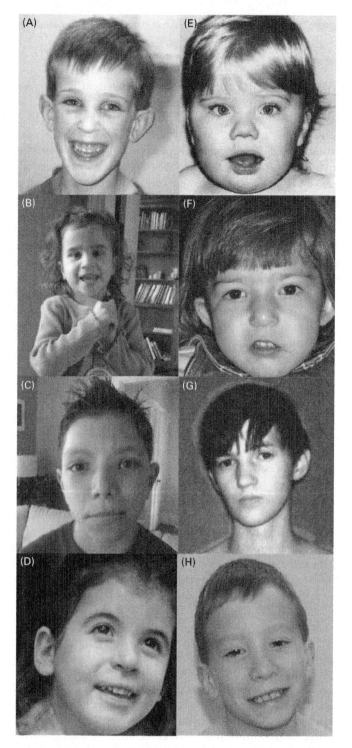

FIGURE 8.1 School-age children with (A) fragile X syndrome, (B) Rett syndrome, (C) neurofibromatosis type 1, (D) tuberous sclerosis, (E) Smith–Magenis syndrome, (F) velocardiofacial
syndrome, (G) XYY syndrome, and (H) Smith–Lemli–Opitz syndrome. *Sources: A, Jorde, L. B.,
Carey, J. C., Bamshad, M. J., & White, R. L. (2000). Medical Genetics (2nd ed.). St. Louis: Mosby (http://
medgen.genetics.utah.edu/photographs/pages/fragile_x.htm); B, The Eva Fini Fund (http://evafinifund.*

Fragile X Syndrome

Fragile X syndrome (FXS; aka Martin–Bell syndrome, marker X syndrome, or Escalante's syndrome) is the most common genetic cause of ASD (Reiss & Dant, 2003) and inherited cause of intellectual disability (Freund & Reiss, 1991). FXS was first described as a particular form of X-linked mental retardation by Purdon Martin and Julia Bell in London in 1943. In 1969, Herbert Lubs at Yale University showed that the X chromosome of a would-be FXS patient contained a marked secondary constriction. A derivation of this karyotype test for FXS became gradually used for diagnostic purposes in the 1970s. In 1991, researchers identified the *FMR1* gene that causes FXS (Verkerk et al., 1991). The society at large is clearly impacted by this neuropsychiatric–neurodevelopmental disease. The general prevalence of males with a full mutation of the affected gene *FMR1* is estimated as 1 in 4000, whereas the female prevalence is approximately 1 in 5000–8000 (Hill, Archibald, Cohen, & Metcalfe, 2010). Families of children with FXS experience substantial financial burden.

Physical Phenotypes

Individuals with *FMR1* full mutations can have mild dysmorphic features (long face with large mandible, large everted ears, and high-arched palate), as well as mild to severe cognitive deficits and behavioral abnormalities.

Cognitive–Behavioral Phenotypes

These individuals particularly exhibit deficits in executive function (Van der Molen et al., 2010), including attention, inhibition, working memory, and impulse control. Children and adults with FXS often exhibit gaze aversion, increased social anxiety, and social avoidance (Feinstein & Singh, 2007). Furthermore, impairments in visuospatial processing are common. Collectively, these factors may contribute to profound difficulties in maintaining appropriate social interactions with others.

Because FXS is a condition due to mutations within a specific gene on the X chromosome, males with this disease tend to have more severe symptoms than their female counterparts. Among females with FXS, the range in severity of symptoms is large; it is thought to be mainly due to the genetic variation in the form of X-inactivation, a process by which one of the two copies of the X chromosome present in females is inactivated. Whereas females with *FMR1* full mutation demonstrate intellectual abilities ranging from average function to moderate disability, males with full mutation can suffer from severe to

---

FIGURE 8.1 Continued

org/?page_id=57); C, The New England Genetics Collaborative (http://www.gemssforschools.org/conditions/ nf1/default.aspx); D, Tuberous Sclerosis Australia (https://www.atss.org.au); E, Smith, A. C., McGavran, L., Robinson, J., Waldstein, G., Macfarlane, J., Zonona, J., et al. (1986). Interstitial deletion of (17)(p11.2p11.2) in nine patients. American Journal of Medical Genetics, 24(3), 393–414; F, Tewfik TL, Manoukian JJ. The Syndromal Child. In: Bailey BJ, Johnson JT, Newlands SD, eds. Head & Neck Surgery - Otolaryngology. Vol 1. Philadelphia, PA: Lippincott Williams & Wilkins; 2006; G, geneticdisease2 (http://geneticdisease2.wiki-spaces.com/XYY+Syndrome+(an+extra+Y+chromosome+in+each+cell+of+a+male)); H, Nowaczyk, J. M., & Irons, M. B. (2012). Smith–Lemli–Opitz syndrome: Phenotype, natural history, and epidemiology. American Journal of Medical Genetics Part C: Seminars in Medical Genetics, 160C(4), 250–262.

profound intellectual disability. Most boys and approximately one-third of girls with FXS satisfy the criteria for attention deficit hyperactivity disorder (ADHD) per the *Diagnostic and Statistical Manual of Mental Disorders* (DSM), with the hyperactivity subtype more common in boys and inattentiveness more common in girls (Mazzocco, Baumgardner, Freund, & Reiss, 1998).

Genetics and Molecular Biology

The mutation responsible for FXS consists of large expansions of trinucleotide CGG repeats within the 5′ untranslated region of the *FMR1* gene on the long arm of the X chromosome. Typically developing individuals have approximately 30 CGG repeats, whereas those with the *FMR1* premutation have repeat lengths ranging between 50 and 200 copies. Individuals with the *FMR1* full mutation (and hence the diagnosis of FXS) typically have more than 200 CGG repeats. This expansion leads to DNA hypermethylation within *FMR1*, resulting in its transcriptional silencing, and therefore the absence or attenuation of the gene product, *FMR1* protein (FMRP).

Individuals with FXS have absent or reduced levels of FMRP, a protein that plays a prominent role in regulating the translation of a subset of mRNAs associated with synaptic plasticity, dendritic pruning, and axonal development (Santoro, Bray, & Warren, 2012). One of the most influential theories of FXS involves the glutamatergic pathways. In particular, long-term depression (LTD), a form of synaptic plasticity, is known to be regulated by the group 5 metabotropic glutamate receptor (mGluR5) (Huber, Gallagher, Warren, & Bear, 2002). Activation of mGluR5 leads to cascades of signaling events driving the activation of protein synthesis involved in the internalization of α-amino-3-hydroxy-5-methyl-4-isoxazolepropionic acid receptors (AMPARs). In the absence or substantial attenuation of FMRP, some of the proteins important for AMPAR trafficking become too abundant, thus increasing the internalization of AMPARs and resulting in exaggerated mGluR5-dependent LTD (Chowdhury et al., 2006). In addition to the glutamatergic system, many components of the GABAergic system are known to be dysfunctional in FXS. For example, the mRNA for the δ subunit of the $GABA_A R$ is a known target of FMRP. Abnormal levels of the α, β, and γ subunits of the $GABA_A R$, $GABA_A R$'s scaffolding protein, and enzymes involved in the metabolism of GABA, as well as the cellular transport of GABA, were found in *Fmr1* knockout mice (Paluszkiewicz, Martin, & Huntsman, 2011). FMRP was also shown to have a role in synaptic plasticity and signaling that involves retinoic acid (RA) (Soden & Chen, 2010). In normal mice, synaptic RA signaling was found to regulate inhibitory synaptic transmission in response to reduced synaptic excitation (Sarti, Zhang, Schroeder, & Chen, 2013). Different from RA's action at excitatory synapses, RA at inhibitory synapses was shown to cause a loss of $GABA_A Rs$. Interestingly, in the absence of FMRP (as in *Fmr1* knockout mice), RA fails to regulate inhibitory synaptic strength, resulting in an imbalance between synaptic excitation and inhibition that may contribute to the pathogenesis of FXS and ASD symptoms (Sarti et al., 2013).

Rett Syndrome

In the early 1960s, Austrian pediatrician Andreas Rett described two female patients who were wringing their hands in an unusual manner and rocking with autistic-like movements. After years of clinical and basic investigations, it was discovered in 1999 that mutations in the gene encoding methyl-CpG-binding protein 2 (MeCP2) are associated with both familial and sporadic forms of Rett syndrome (RTT). RTT affects an estimated 1 in 8500 females.

Physical Phenotypes

Although affected girls have normal head circumference at birth, microcephaly is frequently noted after the regression period. Phenotypic features of RTT are listed under the most current diagnostic criteria (Neul et al., 2010). There are two types of RTT diagnoses: (1) typical or classic RTT and (2) atypical or variant RTT. Both diagnoses require the identification of a period of regression followed by recovery or stabilization. In the case of *typical* or *classic RTT*, all main criteria and exclusion criteria (presented next) are met. In contrast, *atypical* or *variant RTT* can be diagnosed when two or more main criteria and five or more supportive criteria are met. The main criteria include the following: (1) partial or complete loss of acquired purposeful hand skills; (2) partial or complete loss of acquired spoken language; (3) gait abnormalities; and (4) stereotypic hand movements such as hand wringing/squeezing, mouthing, clapping/tapping, and washing/rubbing automatisms. Exclusionary criteria consist of (1) brain injury secondary to trauma, neurometabolic disease, or severe infection that causes neurological problems; and (2) grossly abnormal psychomotor development in the first 6 months of life. Supportive criteria comprise the following: (1) breathing disturbances when awake; (2) bruxism when awake; (3) impaired sleep pattern; (4) abnormal muscle tone; (5) peripheral vasomotor disturbances; (6) scoliosis/kyphosis; (7) growth retardation; (8) small, cold hands and feet; (9) inappropriate laughing/screaming spells; (10) diminished response to pain; and (11) intense eye communication—"eye pointing."

Cognitive–Behavioral Phenotypes

Most girls with RTT develop relatively normally for the first 6 months of life, followed by a period of developmental regression. Regression starts between the ages of 6 and 18 months, and the girls do not reach normal developmental milestones thereafter. During the period of developmental regression, stereotyped movements replace purposeful hand movements. These stereotyped hand movements are accompanied by abnormal gait and sometimes an inability to walk (Berger-Sweeney, 2011). Individuals with RTT often have communication deficits. In contrast to the findings of pervasive impairments in cognition, there are reports that girls with RTT develop increased social interaction with caregivers over time, suggesting that elements of social memory are intact.

Genetics and Molecular Biology

RTT is caused by mutations in the gene coding for MeCP2. Although MeCP2 has diverse functions, examination of MeCP2 mutant mice supports the hypothesis that MeCP2 deficiency leads to aberrant maturation and maintenance of synapses and circuits in multiple brain systems. Some of the deficits arise from alterations in specific intracellular pathways, such as the PI3K/Akt signaling pathway. These abnormalities can be at least partially rescued in MeCP2 mutant mice by treatment with targeted therapeutic agents.

Neurofibromatosis Type 1

The earliest description of neurofibromatosis type 1 (NF1) dates back to the 16th century. In the late 19th century, Friedrich von Recklinghausen provided the first clinical and pathological description of NF1. The *NF1* gene was cloned in 1990, and its gene product, neurofibromin, was identified. NF1 is one of the most common single-gene disorders to affect the human nervous system, with a frequency of approximately 1 in 3500. Population-based prevalence rates range from approximately 1 in 1000 in Israel to 1 in 7000 in Italy. NF1 has been identified in all ethnic groups; it occurs with equal frequency in males and females, and an estimated 2–3 million individuals are affected worldwide.

Physical Phenotypes

An NF1 diagnosis is usually first considered from a clinical examination, using diagnostic criteria developed by the National Institutes of Health. These criteria include two or more of the following manifestations: (1) six or more café au lait macules, (2) two or more neurofibromas or one plexiform neurofibroma, (3) axillary or inguinal freckling, (4) optic glioma, (5) two or more Lisch nodules, (6) sphenoid dysplasia or tibial pseudarthrosis, and (7) first-degree relative (parent or sibling) with confirmed NF1.

Cognitive–Behavioral Phenotypes

One of the most common complications of NF1 in childhood is cognitive dysfunction. Approximately 80% of children with NF1 experience significant impairment in one or more areas of cognitive functioning (Hyman, Shores, & North, 2005). Overall, intellectual disability is not a typical manifestation of NF1 (Hyman et al., 2005). However, children with NF1 experience impairments of executive function, including attention, working memory, spatial planning, and organization (Hyman, Arthur Shores, & North, 2006). Concerns regarding social skills and peer interaction are often reported for individuals with NF1. Parent and teacher questionnaires reveal that children with NF1 experience greater levels of anxiety, withdrawal, depression, and somatic complaints compared to their unaffected siblings (Barton & North, 2004). In a recent study, it was estimated that as many of 47% of patients with NF1 are likely to have significant symptoms within the autism spectrum (Garg et al., 2013).

Genetics and Molecular Biology

NF1 is caused by mutations in *NF1*, the gene coding for neurofibromin. Neurofibromin regulates the activity of the rat sarcoma protein (Ras)-bound intracellular signaling pathway, which in turn regulates complex cellular processes, including cell differentiation, growth, and apoptosis.

Tuberous Sclerosis Complex

Skin manifestations of tuberous sclerosis complex (TSC) were first illustrated in Pierre Francois Olive Rayer's *Treatise on Skin Diseases* in 1835. It was not until 1862 that Frederich von Recklinghausen reported the first pathological description of the lesions found in TSC. More than a century later, two genes responsible for TSC were identified. *TSC1* was found by Fryer and colleagues at the Royal United Hospital in Bath, United Kingdom, in 1987. *TSC2* was identified and cloned by the European Chromosome 16 Tuberous Sclerosis Consortium in 1993. The prevalence of TSC is approximately 1 in 6000 live births.

Physical Phenotypes

TSC is a genetic disorder that causes nonmalignant tumors to form in multiple organs, primarily in the brain, eyes, heart, kidney, and skin. TSC is also commonly associated with seizures, developmental delay, intellectual disability, and ASD. The diagnostic criteria for TSC, which largely depend on physical characterization, were updated in 2012 (Northrup et al., 2013). Major features of TSC include (1) hypomelanotic macules (≥3, at least 5-mm diameter), (2) angiofibromas (≥3) or fibrous cephalic plaque, (3) ungual fibromas (≥2), (4) shagreen patch, (5) multiple retinal hamartomas, (6) cortical dysplasias, (7) subependymal nodules, (8) subependymal giant cell astrocytoma, (9) cardiac rhabdomyoma, (10) lymphangioleiomyomatosis, and (11) angiomyolipomas (≥2). Minor features of TSC consist of the following: (1) "confetti" skin lesions, (2) dental enamel pits (>3), (3) intra-oral fibromas (≥2), (4) retinal achromic patch, (5) multiple renal cysts, and (6) nonrenal hamartomas. *Definite diagnosis* is defined as having two major features or one major feature with two or more minor features, whereas *possible diagnosis* is defined as having either one major feature or more than two minor features.

Cognitive–Behavioral Phenotypes

Children with TSC and cognitive impairment are more likely to have autistic features (Curatolo et al., 2010). Hyperactive behavior in children with TSC is also common. Stereotypies and purposeless movements are observed in approximately one-third of children with TSC. Individuals with *TSC2* mutations are significantly more likely to have a history of infantile spasms, a low intelligent quotient, and autistic disorder compared to those with *TSC1* mutations.

Genetics and Molecular Biology

Tuberous sclerosis is caused by the silencing of a single gene (*TSC1* at 9q34 or *TSC2* at 16p13) that codes for hamartin and tuberin, respectively. Hamartin and tuberin form a biochemical complex that inhibits the signal transduction pathway that controls translation, proliferation, and cell growth.

Smith–Magenis Syndrome

Smith–Magenis syndrome (SMS or 17p deletion syndrome) was first described in 1986 in a case series by Ann C. M. Smith, a genetics counselor at the National Institutes of Health, and Ruth Ellen Magenis, a pediatrician and geneticist at the Oregon Health Sciences University (Smith et al., 1986). They reported that eight patients with deletion of a portion of 17p11.2 had similar phenotype, including "brachycephaly, midface hypoplasia, prognathism, hoarse voice, and speech delay with or without hearing loss, psychomotor and growth retardation, and behavior problems." SMS affects an estimated 1 in 15,000 individuals.

Physical Phenotypes

Children with SMS are often described to have a broad, square-shaped face with deep-set eyes, flat nose bridge, full cheeks, a prominent lower jaw, and a full, outward-curving upper lip.

Cognitive–Behavioral Phenotypes

Variable levels of cognitive impairment, most frequently in the moderate range of intellectual disability, are universal in individuals with SMS. Language development delays are present in most cases, with receptive skills generally better than expressive skills. Learning abilities are characterized by strength in visual reasoning tasks and weakness in sequential processing. Short-term memory is poor, but long-term memory is considered a relative strength. Autistic-like behaviors and symptoms start to emerge between 18 and 36 months of age. A study of individuals with SMS with a confirmed deletion (del 17p11.2) found that 90% of the sample had symptoms on the autism spectrum (Laje et al., 2010). Symptoms of ADHD are also common in individuals with SMS.

Irritability and aggressive behaviors toward both self and others are common in SMS. In particular, onychotillomania (i.e., pulling out nails/nail yanking) and polyembolokoilamania (the insertion of foreign bodies into one's body orifices) are self-injurious behaviors (SIB) relatively unique to SMS as a genetic condition. Other manifestations of SIB in children with SMS include skin picking, wrist biting, head banging, and hitting self or objects. The SIB can be so severe that in some cases, parents have been reported to social services for suspicion of child abuse.

An additional characteristic feature of SMS is an involuntary upper body squeeze or "self-hug." Two types of self-hugging are described as (1) self-hugging and tensing the upper body and (2) hand clasping at chest level or under the chin while squeezing one's arms against one's sides and chests. These movements have a tic-like quality and appear as an expression of excitement.

Genetics and Molecular Biology
The majority of cases of SMS are due to a common deletion in chromosome 17p11.2 that includes the *RAI1* gene (Laje et al., 2010). Approximately 10% of cases of SMS are due to heterozygous mutations of the *RAI1* gene. The mechanisms by which the deletion or mutation of *RAI1* and contiguous genes cause psychopathology are unknown.

47,XYY Syndrome

The first published case of 47,XYY syndrome was reported by Avery Sandberg and colleagues at Roswell Park Memorial Institute in Buffalo, New York, in 1961. The patient was described as a 44-year-old obese white man of average intelligence with large facial features. 47,XYY syndrome is among the most common of human genetic disorders, occurring in approximately 1 in 1000 live male births.

Physical Phenotypes
The addition of the extra Y chromosome leads to tall stature and long legs. Clinodactyly and pes planus (flat feet) are commonly described in individuals with 47,XYY syndrome. There is no distinct set of dysmorphic facial features among males with this syndrome. Testicular size, pubertal progression, and testosterone levels are usually normal in affected individuals.

Cognitive–Behavioral Phenotypes
Cognitive abilities are typically in the average to low average range. Whereas visual–perceptual skills are considered a relative strength in persons with XYY trisomy, verbal skills are often a relative weakness. Social difficulties and social withdrawal were reported in a case series of 47,XYY syndrome. In the largest cohort of 52 individuals with

47,XYY syndrome, approximately 20% of the participants fulfilled the criteria for an ASD diagnosis (Bishop et al., 2011).

Genetics and Molecular Biology

47,XYY occurs as a result of a random event during the formation of sperm cells. This event, called nondysjunction, occurs when two copies of the Y chromosome fail to separate during anaphase II of meiosis II. When a sperm with such genetic defect contributes to the genetic makeup of a child, the child will have an extra Y chromosome in some or all of the body's cells.

Velocardiofacial Syndrome (DiGeorge Syndrome)

Velocardiofacial syndrome (VCFS) is also known as DiGeorge syndrome, Shprintzen syndrome, and 22q11 deletion syndrome (22q11DS). This syndrome was first described by Angelo DiGeorge and John Kirkpatrick in 1968 and later by speech pathologist Robert Shprintzen and colleagues at Montefiore Hospital in New York in 1978. The prevalence of VCFS is estimated as 1 in 4000 live births (Jonas et al., 2014).

Physical Phenotypes

Physical characteristics of patients with VCFS can be summarized by the mnemonic CATCH-22, which refers to *c*ardiac anomaly (especially tetralogy of Fallot), *a*bnormal facies, *t*hymic aplasia, *c*left palate, and *h*ypocalcemia/*h*ypoparathyroidism, with the *22* referring to the genetic abnormality found in chromosome 22. Shprintzen first described the faces of VCFS patients as characterized by "a large, fleshy nose with a broad nasal bridge, flattened malar region, narrow palpebral fissures with a downward obliquity, deep overbite with a class II malocclusion and retruded mandible, mild synophrys, abundant scalp hair, and a vertically long face" (Shprintzen et al., 1978, p. 57).

Cognitive–Behavioral Phenotypes

One of the most intriguing aspects of the syndrome is the variability in clinical and cognitive presentation. Children with 22q11.2 microdeletion have a high prevalence of ASD, ADHD, anxiety disorders (most commonly specific and social phobia), mood disorder, and psychotic disorder. Generally, however, as a group, they often have deficits in receptive language development and abstract reasoning. Younger children with VCFS often manifest social withdrawal, awkwardness, and shyness; they also frequently exhibit inattention, as well as hyperactivity. Visual–spatial deficits are common. Approximately 30% of individuals with VCFS are diagnosed with a psychotic disorder (schizophrenia or schizoaffective disorder) by adolescence or young adulthood.

Genetics and Molecular Biology

VCFS is caused by a hemizygous microdeletion of approximately 1.5–3 Mb on the long arm of chromosome 22. This syndrome represents one of the most common known recurrent CNVs. The 3-Mb region contains approximately 60 genes, some of which are expressed primarily in the brain. *COMT* and *PRODH* are two candidate genes that have been hypothesized to contribute to the behavioral phenotype of VCFS. The gene product of *COMT* is catechol-*O*-methyltransferase, a postsynaptic enzyme that modulates the clearance of dopamine. *PRODH* encodes for proline dehydrogenase, an enzyme that converts proline to glutamate in mitochondria.

Smith–Lemli–Opitz Syndrome

Smith–Lemli–Opitz syndrome (SLOS) was first described in 1964 by pediatricians David Smith, Luc Lemli, and John Opitz at the University of Wisconsin at Madison. SLOS was the first human multiple malformation syndrome attributed to an inborn error of sterol synthesis. The prevalence of SLOS is approximately 1 in 10,000–60,000 births.

Physical Phenotypes

In their first report, Smith et al. (1964) described three male patients with distinctive facial features, intellectual disability, microcephaly, developmental delay, and hypospadias. The severity of physical defects correlates with the severity of the cholesterol deficiency.

Cognitive–Behavioral Phenotypes

Behavioral abnormalities occur commonly in individuals with SLOS. Hyperactivity, SIB, sensory hypersensitivity, affect dysregulation, aggressiveness, stereotypic behaviors, persistence to sameness, and severe sleep cycle disturbances occur, even in the least physically affected individuals (Diaz-Stransky & Tierney, 2012). Approximately 75% of individuals with SLOS fulfill the criteria for ASD (Diaz-Stransky & Tierney, 2012).

Genetics and Molecular Biology

SLOS is caused by a mutation of the *DHCR7* gene on chromosome 11. This genetic insult results in elevated levels of the enzyme 7-dehydrocholesterol (7-DHC) reductase, which is responsible for the last step of cholesterol synthesis. Low levels of cholesterol are seen in 90% of patients.

EVALUATION OF INDIVIDUALS WITH AUTISM SPECTRUM DISORDER

The American Academy of Child and Adolescent Psychiatry (AACAP; Volkmar et al., 2014), American Association of Pediatrics (AAP; Johnson et al., 2007), American Association of Neurology (AAN; Filipek et al., 2000), and American College of Medical Genetics (ACMG; Schaefer & Mendelsohn, 2013) have published guidelines in the workup for ASD. The most updated versions of these guidelines have all included strategies to detect familial and genetic factors of ASD. Next, a systematic approach for detecting signs of syndromic ASD in a nongeneticist's clinic setting is presented.

History and Physical

Just like any medical and psychiatric evaluation, a diagnostic evaluation for ASD begins with the chief complaint and history of present illness. Although core symptoms (i.e., social communication impediment and repetitive behaviors/restricted interests) are important in establishing the diagnosis of ASD, other comorbid symptoms, such as inattention, hyperactivity, impulsivity, obsessions, compulsions, maladaptive eating habits, disruptive behaviors, aggression, and SIB, are also important. Many children with syndromic ASD (e.g., FXS and VCFS) often manifest ADHD symptoms. Young children who are obese (as a result of extreme and insatiable appetite) and have ASD should be considered for genetic evaluation to rule out Prader–Willi syndrome. Specific SIBs such as onychotillomania and polyembolo-koilamania should trigger the clinician to evaluate for genetic causes such as SMS.

Past psychiatric history may include the usual information of past psychiatric diagnoses, history of hospitalizations, medication history, and history of aggression toward self and others. As mentioned previously, many syndromic ASDs have comorbid conditions. Intellectual disability is very common in most syndromic ASDs. Impulse control disorders are sometimes diagnosed in individuals with FXS.

Medical problems are highly prevalent in syndromic ASD. Past medical history(PMH) should capture specific medical problems. Seizures are common in individuals with RTT, TSC, Phelan–McDermid syndrome, FXS, and metabolic disorders. Individuals with metabolic or mitochondrial diseases often have other severe neurologic symptoms. Individuals with VCFS often have congenital malformations of the cardiovascular system. In addition to cardiovascular problems, individuals with VCFS may have recurrent infections due to thymic dysfunction, and they may have convulsions due to hypocalcemia secondary to malfunctioning parathyroid glands. Due to the frequent occurrence of brain tumors in NF1, TSC, and PTEN-related conditions, focal neurologic deficits may be reported in PMH. Extremely low cholesterol level may be related to a mutation of the *DHCR7* gene (i.e., SLOS).

Developmental history may include an account of any problems during pregnancy and labor, as well as a thorough history of developmental milestones. Environmental contributions due to hypoxia during pregnancy and labor should be noted. Regression of gained developmental milestones should also prompt the clinician to include RTT and mitochondrial diseases as differential diagnoses and to consider referral for genetic workup. In taking the family history, a three-generation family history with pedigree analysis is recommended. This analysis will help the clinician determine patterns of inheritance. For example, a boy with a maternal uncle with FXS (or symptoms common in FXS) and/or a mother with a mild learning disability should be considered for referral for genetic evaluation and specific genetic testing for FXS. Social history may include the usual information on the patient's living environment, along with the parents' occupations and ages. Increased paternal age is associated with de novo mutations of ASD-related genes.

Physical examination may include heart auscultation; examination of the face, head, skin, hands, and feet; as well as determination of height, weight, and head circumference. Facial fibrous angiomatous lesions (adenoma sebaceum), hypopigmented macules (ash leaf spots and confetti hypopigmentation), shagreen patches, and periungual fibromas (determined with Wood's lamp) are classic findings of TSC. Submucosal cleft palate and nasal speech are sometimes found in patients with VCFS. Finger syndactyly can be found in individuals with Timothy syndrome. Macrocephaly can be found in patients with PTEN mutations, FXS, and Sotos syndrome. Microcephaly is a common feature of individuals with RTT (especially when the head size is normal in the first few months of life), MeCP2 duplication, and certain metabolic syndromes (e.g., methylene tetrahydrofolate reductase deficiency). Readers interested in advanced examination of dysmorphic features are referred to the Autism Dysmorphology Measure (Miles et al., 2008).

The mental status examination is dependent on developmental age, and it may consist mainly of behavioral observations. Hand wringing in a girl with ASD symptoms may remind the clinician of RTT. Frequent inappropriate laughter is sometimes found in individuals with Pitt–Hopkins syndrome, Angelman syndrome, Christianson syndrome, Mowat–Wilson syndrome, and adenylosuccinate lyase deficiency.

Decision on Referral for Further Workup and Consultations of Other Specialists

As of March 2015, there were 706 genes associated with ASD. (The Simons Foundation Autism Research Initiative (https://gene.sfari.org/autdb/HG_Home.do) maintains a comprehensive, up-to-date database for all known human genes associated with ASD.) In a community sample of children with ASD, the diagnostic yield for chromosomal microarray was 24% (McGrew, Peters, Crittendon, & Veenstra-Vanderweele, 2012). Due to the importance of the genetic component of ASD, the 2014 practice parameter for the assessment and treatment of individuals with ASD published by AACAP recommended routine genetic testing of children with a diagnosis of ASD (Volkmar et al., 2014). As a first tier, in addition to microarray, the ACMG practice guidelines recommend the inclusion of DNA testing for FXS. DNA testing for FXS (Johnson et al., 2007; Schaefer & Mendelsohn, 2013) should be performed routinely for male or female patients with ASD; it should also be ordered for male or female patients with unexplained intellectual disability. For patients with symptoms of seizures, extrapyramidal signs, failure to thrive, or regression, metabolic and/or mitochondrial testing are recommended. The AAP, AAN, and ACMG all recommended audiogram as part of the evaluation occurring early in the workup for ASD. Electroencephalogram is also recommended if there is a history or suspicion of seizures.

Referral to geneticists will be obtained when physical examination suggests dysmorphology and/or history indicates unusual features (as described in the previous section). According to the ACMG practice guidelines, geneticists' second-tier workup may include MeCP2 sequencing (to be performed for all females with ASDs), MeCP2 duplication testing (in males, if phenotype is suggestive), PTEN testing (only if the head circumference is greater than 2.5 SD above the mean), and fibroblast karyotype (if pigmentary anomaly is evident). For patients with microcephaly, regression, seizures, suspected diagnosis of TSC, and history of stupor/coma, magnetic resonance imaging of the brain is recommended.

CLINICAL CASES

CASE STUDY #1

A 23-year-old woman is referred to you for long-standing symptoms of anxiety and social avoidance and recent onset of depression. In the process of conducting your history and mental status examination, you discover that she lives at home and has a history of learning and attentional problems with below-average grades throughout school. She also has a brother with significant intellectual disability and ASD and a (maternal) grandfather with a progressive tremor–ataxia syndrome. Diagnostically, she might meet current or past criteria for social or generalized anxiety disorder, ADHD, specific learning disorder or intellectual disability, and a depressive disorder. Indeed, based on the DSM, she might receive two or more "comorbid" diagnoses. In the best of circumstances, you might offer this patient individual and/or group therapy, perhaps an antidepressant, and work with the patient and her family to determine how to optimize her social supports and vocational potential given her cognitive and psychiatric disabilities. This approach is *symptom-focused* and (it is hoped) based on the clinician's knowledge of evidence-based clinical trial results. Alternatively, the clinician conducting the initial evaluation might be aware that the patient's personal and family history, as well as current symptoms, is consistent with a diagnosis of FXS, a relatively common genetic condition associated with mutations of the *FMR1* gene on the X chromosome.

You send this young woman for genetic testing, and she is confirmed to be heterozygous for the fragile X full mutation. You then refer this patient (and her family) to a genetic counselor. Based on the recommendations of the National Society of Genetic Counselors (McConkie-Rosell et al., 2005), your patient and her family are counseled on reproductive issues, medical issues (e.g., premature ovarian insufficiency in female carriers of the premutation and fragile X-associated tremor–ataxia syndrome in older male carriers of the premutation), and family planning, and they are given resources to consult with knowledgeable health care providers in the patient's area and support groups.

CASE STUDY #2

A 17-year-old male teenager with mild developmental disability, poor social motivation, history of mild obsessive–compulsive symptoms, and possible paranoia is brought to the emergency room by police after he threw a DVD case at his father and pushed his mother. After a psychiatric evaluation, he is diagnosed with impulse control disorder and is admitted to an inpatient psychiatric unit, where you are one of the attending psychiatrists.

As you enter the interview room, you see that the patient has mildly dysmorphic facial features (narrow palpebral fissures and a broad nasal bridge). You further note that he has nasal speech. After you speak with him and his parents, you come to the preliminary conclusion that past and present aggressive behaviors are likely associated with parents' limit-setting and noncompliance with parental instructions. The teenager also discloses to you that his classmates have been ganging up on him. His parents endorse that he has been a victim of bullying for years, and he has no friends at school. The patient has a long history of problems with anxiety, including mild obsessive–compulsive symptoms, and has been taking citalopram for 8 years. Past medical history is significant for early surgery to repair a congenital cardiac defect.

As you formulate this case, you wonder if the aggressive behaviors, developmental disability, dysmorphic facial features, and medical history could be explained by a single genetic diagnosis. You order chromosomal microarray analysis, which shows a hemizygous microdeletion of 2 Mb on the long arm of chromosome 22. This patient is diagnosed with 22q11 deletion syndrome (or VCFS), which is often associated with ASD and a variety of psychiatric problems, including psychosis.

KEY POINTS

- The combination of ASD phenotype and specific characteristics (physical phenotypes, other cognitive–behavioral phenotypes, medical history, and family history) may be used to support testing for genetic abnormalities and confirming diagnosis of genetic disorders.
- The major classes of genetic disorders are monogenic diseases, chromosomal diseases, metabolic diseases, and mitochondrial diseases.
- The most salient cognitive–behavioral and physical features as well as genetics and molecular biology of eight syndromes (fragile X syndrome, Rett syndrome, neurofibromatosis type 1, tuberous sclerosis, Smith–Magenis syndrome, velocardiofacial syndrome, XYY syndrome, and Smith–Lemli–Opitz syndrome) are discussed.
- Due to the importance of the genetic contribution to ASD, the American Academy of Child and Adolescent Psychiatry recommends routine genetic testing of children with a diagnosis of ASD. A systematic approach for considering genetic evaluation of individuals with ASD diagnosis is presented in this chapter to guide clinicians to make decisions on ordering genetic testing and further referrals to medical geneticists.
- Recognition of genetic syndromes is not only helpful in understanding psychiatric symptoms but also critical in triggering support for medical problems associated with the genetic abnormalities.

DISCLOSURE STATEMENT

Dr. Lawrence K. Fung has nothing to disclose.

Dr. Allan L. Reiss was a consultant for Novartis and Genentech.

REFERENCES

Alvarez Retuerto, A. I., Cantor, R. M., Gleeson, J. G., Ustaszewska, A., Schackwitz, W. S., Pennacchio, L. A., et al. (2008). Association of common variants in the Joubert syndrome gene (*AHI1*) with autism. *Human Molecular Genetics, 17*(24), 3887–3896.

Baieli, S., Pavone, L., Meli, C., Fiumara, A., & Coleman, M. (2003). Autism and phenylketonuria. *Journal of Autism and Developmental Disorders,* 2003;33(2):201–204.

Barber, J. C., Hall, V., Maloney, V. K., Huang, S., Roberts, A. M., Brady, A. F., et al. (2013). 16p11.2–p12.2 duplication syndrome; A genomic condition differentiated from euchromatic variation of 16p11.2. *European Journal of Human Genetics, 21*(2), 182–189.

Barton, B., & North, K. (2004). Social skills of children with neurofibromatosis type 1. *Developmental Medicine & Child Neurology, 46*(8), 553–563.

Beal, J. C. (2014). Case report: Neuronal migration disorder associated with chromosome 15q13.3 duplication in a boy with autism and seizures. *Journal of Child Neurology, 29*(12), 186–188.

Berger-Sweeney, J. (2011). Cognitive deficits in Rett syndrome: What we know and what we need to know to treat them. *Neurobiology of Learning and Memory, 96*(4), 637–646.

Bergman, J. E., Janssen, N., Hoefsloot, L. H., Jongmans, M. C., Hofstra, R. M., & van Ravenswaaij-Arts, C. M. (2011). CHD7 mutations and CHARGE syndrome: The clinical implications of an expanding phenotype. *Journal of Medical Genetics, 48*(5), 334–342.

Bishop, D. V., Jacobs, P. A., Lachlan, K., Wellesley, D., Barnicoat, A., Boyd, P. A., et al. (2011). Autism, language and communication in children with sex chromosome trisomies. *Archives of Disease in Childhood, 96*(10), 954–959.

Buxbaum, J. D., Cai, G., Nygren, G., Chaste, P., Delorme, R., Goldsmith, J., et al. (2007). Mutation analysis of the *NSD1* gene in patients with autism spectrum disorders and macrocephaly. *BMC Medical Genetics, 8,* 68.

Carter, J. C., Capone, G. T., Gray, R. M., Cox, C. S., & Kaufmann, W. E. (2007). Autistic-spectrum disorders in Down syndrome: Further delineation and distinction from other behavioral abnormalities. *American Journal of Medical Genetics Part B: Neuropsychiatric Genetics, 144B*(1), 87–94.

Castro, J., Mellios, N., & Sur, M. (2013). Mechanisms and therapeutic challenges in autism spectrum disorders: Insights from Rett syndrome. *Current Opinion in Neurology, 26*(2), 154–159.

Celestino-Soper, P. B., Violante, S., Crawford, E. L., Luo, R., Lionel, A. C., Delaby, E., et al. (2012). A common X-linked inborn error of carnitine biosynthesis may be a risk factor for nondysmorphic autism. *Proceedings of the National Academy of Sciences of the USA, 109*(21), 7974–7981.

Chowdhury, S., Shepherd, J. D., Okuno, H., Lyford, G., Petralia, R. S., Plath, N., et al. (2006). Arc/Arg3.1 interacts with the endocytic machinery to regulate AMPA receptor trafficking. *Neuron, 52*(3), 445–459.

Conti, S., Condo, M., Posar, A., Mari, F., Resta, N., Renieri, A., et al. (2012). Phosphatase and tensin homolog (PTEN) gene mutations and autism: Literature review and a case report of a patient with Cowden syndrome, autistic disorder, and epilepsy. *Journal of Child Neurology, 27*(3), 392–397.

Curatolo, P., Napolioni, V., & Moavero, R. (2010). Autism spectrum disorders in tuberous sclerosis: Pathogenetic pathways and implications for treatment. *Journal of Child Neurology, 25*(7), 873–880.

Diaz-Stransky, A., & Tierney, E. (2012). Cognitive and behavioral aspects of Smith–Lemli–Opitz syndrome. *American Journal of Medical Genetics Part C: Seminars in Medical Genetics, 160C*(4), 295–300.

Douzgou, S., & Petersen, M. B. (2011). Clinical variability of genetic isolates of Cohen syndrome. *Clinical Genetics, 79*(6), 501–506.

Dykens, E. M., Lee, E., & Roof, E. (2011). Prader–Willi syndrome and autism spectrum disorders: An evolving story. *Journal of Neurodevelopmental Disorders, 3*(3), 225–237.

Feinstein, C., & Singh, S. (2007). Social phenotypes in neurogenetic syndromes. *Child & Adolescent Psychiatry Clinics of North America, 16*(3), 631–647.

Filipek, P. A., Accardo, P. J., Ashwal, S., Baranek, G. T., Cook, E. H., Jr., Dawson, G., et al. (2000). Practice parameter: Screening and diagnosis of autism; Report of the Quality Standards Subcommittee of the American Academy of Neurology and the Child Neurology Society. *Neurology, 55*(4), 468–479.

Freund, L. S., & Reiss, A. L. (1991). Cognitive profiles associated with the fra(X) syndrome in males and females. *American Journal of Medical Genetics, 38*(4), 542–547.

Frye, R. E. (2012). Mitochondrial disease in 22q13 duplication syndrome. *Journal of Child Neurology, 27*(7), 942–949.

Fung, L. K., Quintin, E. M., Haas, B. W., & Reiss, A. L. (2012). Conceptualizing neurodevelopmental disorders through a mechanistic understanding of fragile X syndrome and Williams syndrome. *Current Opinion in Neurology, 25*(2), 112–124.

Garg, S., Green, J., Leadbitter, K., Emsley, R., Lehtonen, A., Evans, D. G., et al. (2013). Neurofibromatosis type 1 and autism spectrum disorder. *Pediatrics, 132*(6), e1642–e1648.

Hill, M. K., Archibald, A. D., Cohen, J., & Metcalfe, S. A. (2010). A systematic review of population screening for fragile X syndrome. *Genetics in Medicine, 12*(7), 396–410.

Hoppman-Chaney, N., Wain, K., Seger, P. R., Superneau, D. W., & Hodge, J. C. (2013). Identification of single gene deletions at 15q13.3: Further evidence that CHRNA7 causes the 15q13.3 microdeletion syndrome phenotype. *Clinical Genetics, 83*(4), 345–351.

Huber, K. M., Gallagher, S. M., Warren, S. T., & Bear, M. F. (2002). Altered synaptic plasticity in a mouse model of fragile X mental retardation. *Proceedings of the National Academy of Sciences of the USA, 99*(11), 7746–7750.

Hyman, S. L., Shores, A., & North, K. N. (2005). The nature and frequency of cognitive deficits in children with neurofibromatosis type 1. *Neurology, 65*(7), 1037–1044.

Hyman, S. L., Arthur Shores, E., & North, K. N. (2006). Learning disabilities in children with neurofibromatosis type 1: Subtypes, cognitive profile, and attention-deficit-hyperactivity disorder. *Developmental Medicine & Child Neurology, 48*(12), 973–977.

Johnson, C. P., Myers, S. M., and the American Academy of Pediatrics Council on Children With Disabilities. (2007). Identification and evaluation of children with autism spectrum disorders. *Pediatrics, 120*(5), 1183–1215.

Jonas, R. K., Montojo, C. A., & Bearden, C. E. (2014). The 22q11.2 deletion syndrome as a window into complex neuropsychiatric disorders over the lifespan. *Biological Psychiatry, 75*(5), 351–360.

Kirkpatrick, J. A., Jr., & DiGeorge, A. M. (1968). Congenital absence of the thymus. *American Journal of Roentgenology Radium Therapy and Nuclear Medicine, 103*(1), 32–37.

Knerr, I., Gibson, K. M., Jakobs, C., & Pearl, P. L. (2008). Neuropsychiatric morbidity in adolescent and adult succinic semialdehyde dehydrogenase deficiency patients. *CNS Spectrums, 13*(7), 598–605.

Laje, G., Morse, R., Richter, W., Ball, J., Pao, M., & Smith, A. C. (2010). Autism spectrum features in Smith–Magenis syndrome. *American Journal of Medical Genetics Part C: Seminars in Medical Genetics, 154C*(4), 456–462.

Legido, A., Jethva, R., & Goldenthal, M. J. (2013). Mitochondrial dysfunction in autism. *Seminars in Pediatric Neurology, 20*(3), 163–175.

Lerma-Carrillo, I., Molina, J. D., Cuevas-Duran, T., Julve-Correcher, C., Espejo-Saavedra, J. M., Andrade-Rosa, C., et al. (2006). Psychopathology in the Lujan–Fryns syndrome: Report of two patients and review. *American Journal of Medical Genetics Part A, 140*(24), 2807–2811.

Lu, A. T., Dai, X., Martinez-Agosto, J. A., & Cantor, R. M. (2012). Support for calcium channel gene defects in autism spectrum disorders. *Molecular Autism, 3*(1), 3–18.

Lynch, N. E., Lynch, S. A., McMenamin, J., & Webb, D. (2009). Bannayan–Riley–Ruvalcaba syndrome: A cause of extreme macrocephaly and neurodevelopmental delay. *Archives of Disease in Childhood, 94*(7), 553–554.

Margari, L., Lamanna, A. L., Craig, F., Simone, M., & Gentile, M. (2014). Autism spectrum disorders in XYY syndrome: Two new cases and systematic review of the literature. *European Journal of Pediatrics, 173*(3), 277–283.

Mazzocco, M. M., Baumgardner, T., Freund, L. S., & Reiss, A. L. (1998). Social functioning among girls with fragile X or Turner syndrome and their sisters. *Journal of Autism and Developmental Disorders, 28*(6), 509–517.

McConkie-Rosell, A., Finucane, B., Cronister, A., Abrams, L., Bennett, R. L., & Pettersen, B. J. (2005). Genetic counseling for fragile X syndrome: Updated recommendations of the National Society of Genetic Counselors. *Journal of Genetic Counseling, 14*(4), 249–270.

McGrew, S. G., Peters, B. R., Crittendon, J. A., & Veenstra-Vanderweele, J. (2012). Diagnostic yield of chromosomal microarray analysis in an autism primary care practice: Which guidelines to implement? *Journal of Autism and Developmental Disorders, 42*(8), 1582–1591.

Miles, J. H., Takahashi, T. N., Hong, J., Munden, N., Flournoy, N., Braddock, S. R., et al. (2008). Development and validation of a measure of dysmorphology: Useful for autism subgroup classification. *American Journal of Medical Genetics Part A, 146A*(9), 1101–1116.

Neul, J. L., Kaufmann, W. E., Glaze, D. G., Christodoulou, J., Clarke, A. J., Bahi-Buisson, N., et al. (2010). Rett syndrome: Revised diagnostic criteria and nomenclature. *Annals of Neurology, 68*(6), 944–950.

Northrup, H., Krueger, D. A., and the International Tuberous Sclerosis Complex Consensus Group. (2013). Tuberous sclerosis complex diagnostic criteria update: Recommendations of the 2012 International Tuberous Sclerosis Complex Consensus Conference. *Pediatric Neurology, 49*(4), 243–254.

Nowaczyk, M. J., & Irons, M. B. (2012). Smith–Lemli–Opitz syndrome: Phenotype, natural history, and epidemiology. *American Journal of Medical Genetics Part C: Seminars in Medical Genetics, 160C*(4), 250–262.

Page, T., Yu, A., Fontanesi, J., & Nyhan, W. L. (1997). Developmental disorder associated with increased cellular nucleotidase activity. *Proceedings of the National Academy of Sciences of the USA, 94*(21), 11601–11606.

Paluszkiewicz, S. M., Martin, B. S., & Huntsman, M. M. (2011). Fragile X syndrome: The GABAergic system and circuit dysfunction. *Developmental Neuroscience, 33*(5), 349–364.

Ramaekers, V. T., Blau, N., Sequeira, J. M., Nassogne, M. C., & Quadros, E. V. (2007). Folate receptor autoimmunity and cerebral folate deficiency in low-functioning autism with neurological deficits. *Neuropediatrics, 38*(6), 276–281.

Reiss, A. L., & Dant, C. C. (2003). The behavioral neurogenetics of fragile X syndrome: Analyzing gene–brain–behavior relationships in child developmental psychopathologies. *Development and Psychopathology, 15*(4):927–968.

Ross, J. L., Roeltgen, D. P., Kushner, H., Zinn, A. R., Reiss, A., Bardsley, M. Z., et al. (2012). Behavioral and social phenotypes in boys with 47,XYY syndrome or 47,XXY Klinefelter syndrome. *Pediatrics, 129*(4), 769–778.

Sanders, S. J., Ercan-Sencicek, A. G., Hus, V., Luo, R., Murtha, M. T., Moreno-De-Luca, D., et al. (2011). Multiple recurrent de novo CNVs, including duplications of the 7q11.23 Williams syndrome region, are strongly associated with autism. *Neuron, 70*(5), 863–885.

Santoro, M. R., Bray, S. M., & Warren, S. T. (2012). Molecular mechanisms of fragile X syndrome: A twenty-year perspective. *Annual Review of Pathology, 7,* 219–245.

Sarasua, S. M., Boccuto, L., Sharp, J. L., Dwivedi, A., Chen, C. F., Rollins, J. D., et al. (2014). Clinical and genomic evaluation of 201 patients with Phelan–McDermid syndrome. *Human Genetics, 133*(7), 847–859.

Sarti, F., Zhang, Z., Schroeder, J., & Chen, L. (2013). Rapid suppression of inhibitory synaptic transmission by retinoic acid. *Journal of Neuroscience, 33*(28), 11440–11450.

Schaefer, G. B., & Mendelsohn, N. J. (2013). Clinical genetics evaluation in identifying the etiology of autism spectrum disorders: 2013 guideline revisions. *Genetics in Medicine, 15*(5), 399–407.

Schrier, S. A., Sherer, I., Deardorff, M. A., Clark, D., Audette, L., Gillis, L., et al. (2011). Causes of death and autopsy findings in a large study cohort of individuals with Cornelia de Lange syndrome and review of the literature. *American Journal of Medical Genetics Part A, 155A*(12), 3007–3024.

Shprintzen, R. J., Goldberg, R. B., Lewin, M. L., Sidoti, E. J., Berkman, M. D., Argamaso, R. V., et al. (1978). A new syndrome involving cleft palate, cardiac anomalies, typical facies, and learning disabilities: Velo-cardio-facial syndrome. *Cleft Palate Journal, 15*(1), 56–62.

Smith, A. C., McGavran, L., Robinson, J., Waldstein, G., Macfarlane, J., Zonona, J., et al. (1986). Interstitial deletion of (17)(p11.2p11.2) in nine patients. *American Journal of Medical Genetics, 24*(3), 393–414.

Smith, D. W., Lemli, L., & Opitz, J. M. (1964). A newly recognized syndrome of multiple congenital anomalies. *Journal of Pediatrics, 64,* 210–217.

Soden, M. E., & Chen, L. (2010). Fragile X protein FMRP is required for homeostatic plasticity and regulation of synaptic strength by retinoic acid. *Journal of Neuroscience, 30*(50), 16910–16921.

Thibert, R. L., Larson, A. M., Hsieh, D. T., Raby, A. R., & Thiele, E. A. (2013). Neurologic manifestations of Angelman syndrome. *Pediatric Neurology, 48*(4), 271–279.

Tordjman, S., Anderson, G. M., Cohen, D., Kermarrec, S., Carlier, M., Touitou, Y., et al. (2013). Presence of autism, hyperserotonemia, and severe expressive language impairment in Williams–Beuren syndrome. *Molecular Autism, 4*(1), 4–29.

Treadwell-Deering, D. E., Powell, M. P., & Potocki, L. (2010). Cognitive and behavioral characterization of the Potocki–Lupski syndrome (duplication 17p11.2). *Journal of Developmental and Behavioral Pediatrics, 31*(2), 137–143.

Van der Molen, M. J., Huizinga, M., Huizenga, H. M., Ridderinkhof, K. R., Van der Molen, M. W., Hamel, B. J., et al. (2010). Profiling fragile X syndrome in males: Strengths and weaknesses in cognitive abilities. *Research in Developmental Disabilities, 31*(2), 426–439.

Verkerk, A. J., Pieretti, M., Sutcliffe, J. S., Fu, Y. H., Kuhl, D. P., Pizzuti, A., et al. (1991). Identification of a gene (*FMR-1*) containing a CGG repeat coincident with a breakpoint cluster region exhibiting length variation in fragile X syndrome. *Cell, 65*(5), 905–914.

Volkmar, F., Siegel, M., Woodbury-Smith, M., King, B., McCracken, J., & State, M. (2014). Practice parameter for the assessment and treatment of children and adolescents with autism spectrum disorder. *Journal of the American Academy of Child & Adolescent Psychiatry, 53*(2), 237–257.

Weissman, J. R., Kelley, R. I., Bauman, M. L., Cohen, B. H., Murray, K. F., Mitchell, R. L., et al. (2008). Mitochondrial disease in autism spectrum disorder patients: A cohort analysis. *PLoS One, 3*(11), e3815.

Zufferey, F., Sherr, E. H., Beckmann, N. D., Hanson, E., Maillard, A. M., Hippolyte, L., et al. (2012). A 600 kb deletion syndrome at 16p11.2 leads to energy imbalance and neuropsychiatric disorders. *Journal of Medical Genetics, 49*(10), 660–668.

/// 9 /// AUTISM SPECTRUM DISORDER IN THE ELDERLY

PETER V. RABINS

INTRODUCTION

A perusal of geriatric psychiatry textbooks published in English reveals nothing written about the care of elderly individuals with autism spectrum disorder (ASD). It is only in recent years, with the increasing recognition of ASD as a prevalent disorder of children (Boyce et al., 2011; Fombonne, 2003), that questions about the life course and prognosis of childhood ASD have begun to emerge (Howlin & Moss, 2012; Piven & Rabins, 2011; Smith, Maenner, & Selzer, 2012). This chapter initially uses the terms "autism" and "Asperger syndrome" to examine autism in the elderly because those were the terms in use before publication of the fifth edition of the *Diagnostic and Statistical Manual of Mental Disorders* (DSM-5; American Psychiatric Association, 2013), when currently elderly individuals would have been initially diagnosed and treated. The term "autism spectrum disorder" (ASD) is used when appropriate.

There are several possible explanations for the paucity of information about ASD in older persons. One plausible reason is that Leo Kanner's initial 1943 description of 11 cases of "autistic disturbances of affective contact" (p. 250) as a syndrome characterized by a "combination of extreme autism, obsessiveness, stereotypy, and echolalia" (Kanner, 1943, p. 248) described children who would now be in their 70s and 80s. Because there were so few child psychiatrists at that time, it is plausible that the condition was significantly underdiagnosed in the 1940s and 1950s, when the current cohort of elders was born.

Although Kanner (1943) believed that the "pathognomonic" feature was "the children's' inability to relate themselves in the ordinary way to people and to situations from the beginning of life" (p. 242) and distinguished this illness from schizophrenia because of its lack of hallucinations and delusions and by its onset very early in life, other American psychiatrists disagreed and included the disorder within the construct of childhood schizophrenia. This is illustrated in the DSM-I and DSM-II criteria used in the 1950s–1970s. Thus, misdiagnosis early in life followed by lack of reconsideration once individuals achieved adulthood is another possible explanation for the dearth of elderly cases seen in clinical settings and research.

A third possible explanation for the paucity of elderly persons identified as having ASD is that the disorder changes over time. This would require that the symptoms completely (or mostly) resolve (it is "outgrown") or that they evolve into a different set of symptoms (e.g., dementia).

A fourth possibility to explain the seeming rarity of autism in the elderly is differential mortality or "survival bias." This would include early death from autism compared to the general population, early death from medical or social conditions associated with autism, or both.

Kanner was very focused on using outcome as a measure of both prognosis and validity of the syndrome. In 1971, he reported the 28-year follow-up of some of the first 11 cases he had diagnosed. He described 4 as having a poor outcome, 1 "a state of limited but positive usefulness," and 2 "real success stories." This suggests that, at least into early and mid-adulthood, the syndrome does not dramatically change for many individuals, but Kanner emphasized the improvement in several of his cases and attributed that improvement to supportive care. A similar conclusion was reached by Kanner in 1973 when he reported on the long-term follow-up of 96 individuals followed for 15–30 years. He reported that 7% lived independently, 11% were working, and that intelligence quotient (IQ) was the best predictor of a positive outcome.

Howlin, Goode, Hutton, and Rutter (2004) reported similar outcomes in a cohort from Britain followed for a mean of 28 years. Twenty-two percent of the individuals they followed had a good or very good outcome, 4% were living independently, and 18% had a poor or very poor outcome. They too found that outcome was better if IQ was greater than 70 but that a "normal IQ" was not necessarily associated with positive outcome.

Hans Asperger, a Viennese pediatrician, first described what he called "autistic psychopaths" in 1944. His work did not come to the attention of the English-speaking world until the early 1980s when renowned British child psychiatrist Lorna Wing identified it as a neglected but important childhood syndrome. Hippler and Klicpera (2003) were able to identify 74 cases seen by either Asperger or his major assistants between 1950 and 1986. All had an IQ greater than 84. They described 95% as having language "deviancies," 82% as having "special narrow interests," and 35% as having "deviant eye contact." Twenty-five percent met DSM criteria for autism.

Taken together, these follow-up studies suggest that many individuals with ASD continue to be symptomatic at least through mid-life, but they also show that a minority of individuals have improved. They do not eliminate the possibility that improved early treatment would alter the course of ASD. Neither do they eliminate the possibility of higher mortality rates in persons with ASD, but they indicate that this is unlikely to be the primary reason for the very low rate of diagnosed ASD in older adults.

EPIDEMIOLOGY

The best population-based data for examining the prevalence of autism in later life are from the British epidemiologic study of Brugha et al. (2011). They reported an overall prevalence in *adults* of 9.8/1000 or approximately 1%, similar to the rate reported by the Centers for Disease Control and Prevention of 1/110 births in the United States at the time the British study was being carried out. More relevant to the current discussion, Brugha et al. also found a non-statistically significant decline in prevalence across the adult age span. This is in contrast to US epidemiological studies that report no cases after age 60 years. The Brugha et al. study was specifically designed to identify persons with autism, suggesting that epidemiologic studies designed to detect psychiatric disorders in adults, broadly defined, either do not identify autism in the elderly or systematically exclude them based on method, instrumentation, or sampling frame.

The non-statistically significant decline in autism prevalence reported by Brugha et al. does not eliminate differential mortality or an evolution of symptoms because the small number of older cases lacks statistical power to detect such a change, but it does demonstrate that the use of current criteria can identify elderly individuals with the disorder. However, as Brugha et al. noted, their results are strongly influenced by their use of the standard Autism Diagnostic Observation Schedule-4 (ADOS-4) cutoff of 10 to determine prevalence. A higher or lower cutoff on this continuous scale would yield very different results, and it is plausible that a different cutoff would better balance sensitivity and specificity across the adult age span. In univariable analyses, male sex, not owning one's own home, having lower education, and having a lower verbal IQ all correlated with the presence of ASD. In a multivariable model, however, only male sex, low education, and lack of home ownership correlated with ASD.

CHANGES IN DIAGNOSTIC CRITERIA

From the perspective of persons currently older than age 60 or 65 years, autism was first identified when they were children or adolescents, and Asperger syndrome was not recognized in the English-speaking world until they were adults. Disagreements over classification when they were young are likely to have contributed to underrecognition because some individuals would have been diagnosed with childhood schizophrenia, whereas individuals with Asperger syndrome would not have been diagnosed because the diagnosis was not known in the English-speaking world during their youth.

Diagnostic practices have undoubtedly improved during the past two decades and led to enhanced recognition of ASD in children. However, this cannot be said with any confidence about adults who were not recognized when they were children. These changes in diagnostic practice are well illustrated by the widely cited study of Croen, Grether, and Selvin (2002), which demonstrated that between 1987 and 1994, the diagnosis of mental retardation declined by 9/10,000 and the diagnosis of autism increased by 9/10,000. Another change in diagnostic practice that would lead to underrecognition of ASD in now elderly individuals is the recognition that it can be comorbid with other disorders. For example, 30-50% of children with fragile X syndrome and 15-30% of children with Down syndrome are now identified as also having features of ASD. (It is worth noting that fragile X syndrome had not been identified when the current cohort of elders was young.) Hence, older individuals with ASD and lifelong intellectual disability would likely carry a diagnosis of only intellectual disability.

Strong support for the claim that misdiagnosis significantly contributes to low reported rates of ASD in American elders is provided by the intriguing study of Mandel and coworkers (2012), who found that 9.9% of elderly adults in one state hospital in Pennsylvania met criteria for lifelong autism but had all been diagnosed in adulthood as having schizophrenia even though their records documented that they had not experienced hallucinations or delusions at any time during their many years of hospitalization. A small British case series suggests that misdiagnosis and nonrecognition similarly occur in older adults with Asperger syndrome (James, Mukaetova-Ladinska, Reichelt, Briel, & Scully, 2006).

PROGNOSIS OF AUTISM SPECTRUM DISORDER ACROSS THE LIFESPAN

As noted previously, Kanner examined the prognosis in cases he had diagnosed with childhood autism and found improvement over time in some individuals but a persistence of symptoms and sustained impairment in many. Subsequent studies (Smith et al., 2012) have borne out this finding.

However, excess mortality in persons with autism has long been known and appears to continue to the present. For example, studies by Shavelle, Strauss, and Pickett (2001) and Mouridsen, Brønnum-Hansen, Rich, and Isager (2008) demonstrate two or three times higher rates of mortality in children with autism. Seizures and accidents appear to be the primary causes. In addition, intellectual disability is associated with a 13-year shorter life expectancy (Heslop et al., 2014), and this is likely true of persons with both intellectual disability and ASD. Thus, the possible decline in prevalence found by Brugha et al. (2011) across adulthood might, in part, reflect differential mortality. This is likely to be less of an issue in the future for two reasons. First, medical care has improved over time so that cohorts of persons with ASD born in recent years are likely to survive medically comorbid disorders that they might have succumbed to in the past. However, seizure disorder still carries an elevated risk of early mortality (Sillanpää, Jalava, Kaleva, & Shinnar, 1998), so this increased mortality risk will persist until this issue is resolved. Second, the provision of services in the community might avoid some of the mortality that would have been associated with institutionalization in the past. Third, the broadening of the concept of autism to ASD includes more individuals without the medical comorbidity associated with the more severe phenotype.

Longitudinal studies demonstrate that daily function abilities decline as persons with ASD age (Smith et al., 2012). Whether such decline is different than that experienced by those without ASD as they age is unknown, but persons with intellectual disability have more significant impairments (Smith et al., 2012).

CURRENT PERSPECTIVES

The question posed at the beginning of this chapter concerning why so few elders are diagnosed with ASD seems to have multiple answers. Lack of recognition when they were young, misdiagnosis, shorter life expectancy, and a failure to consider the diagnosis in an older person with lifelong psychiatric symptoms all contribute. Heightened awareness might bring needed services to elders who meet criteria for ASD, although this has not been demonstrated empirically.

As reviewed elsewhere in this text, the incidence and prevalence of ASD have been increasing dramatically. Although some of this change is likely due to evolving diagnostic practice, this does not appear to explain the entire phenomena. As the current cohort of individuals with ASD moves through adulthood into older age, several challenges will need to be addressed and should begin to be studied now.

First, what is the prognosis and course of autism into old age? For example, are there cognitive (Guerts & Vissers, 2012) and functional (Smith et al., 2012) changes that are specific or more likely to occur in persons with ASD than in age-matched individuals without ASD? Second, are there specific therapeutic, psychosocial, and environmental issues that occur with age that will affect persons with ASD differentially than those aging without ASD? For example, effective therapies have been developed to help persons with ASD address developmental transitions such as starting school, graduating from high school, and moving into the workforce. Are there similar transitions experienced in older age—for example, death of a parent, the development of new-onset health conditions, or the need to move to a new living setting—that would benefit from specific intervention? Are there specific medical conditions that persons with ASD are prone to develop as they age, or might medical care need to be provided in a specific way that would address the impairments with which ASD is associated? As more effective therapies are developed for children and young adults with ASD, will they need to continue in their present or an altered form as individuals move into older age? This possibility is highlighted by the finding of Kats, Payne, Parlier, and Piven (2013) that 40–60% of adults identified as having ASD required services to manage destructive, disruptive, or self-injurious behaviors. Although the individuals identified in this study are likely to represent those with more severe ASD, the increasing prevalence of ASD suggests that more such services will be required unless methods for preventing such outcomes are developed.

Clinical experience suggests that individuals with more severe ASD fare poorly when faced with the many changes in social support, medical care, and living arrangements that are common in later life. Descriptive studies and intervention trials are needed to determine whether this is the case; whether people with ASD are at higher risk of developing specific psychiatric, neurologic, or medical comorbidities, including dementia, than older individuals without ASD; and whether specific interventions can moderate or eliminate any increased risk of adverse outcome. The case described next illustrates the potential benefits of such research. This individual had a lifelong disorder that impaired his ability to function socially. However, the lack of recognition that he had features of ASD led to chronic institutionalization, chronic exposure to high-dose neuroleptics, tardive dyskinesia, and the lack of access to an environment that could meet his needs. Improved recognition of ASD and the development of services to meet the needs of people with ASD across the lifespan should mitigate such unnecessary and inappropriate outcomes.

CASE STUDY #1

A 62-year-old man was referred to a geriatric psychiatry outpatient clinic by the nursing home where he had resided for 3 years. It was requesting assessment of intermittent, physically aggressive behavior. He had been on high-dose neuroleptic medications for years because of these "outbursts," and the facility was concerned that there might not be justification for continuing neuroleptic medications under CMS (Medicare) guidelines. There was a paucity of history. His parents had died many years before, and other family had not been identified. As a result, he was a ward of the state. He had resided in a state psychiatric hospital for much of his adult life, but these records were not available at the time of the initial consultation. The accompanying note described the episodes of "aggression" as occurring once or twice a month; being very upsetting to other residents and staff; and consisting of yelling out, shaking his fists at people, and hitting furniture or walls very hard. The referring facility was concerned that he would harm himself or others during the episodes and wanted to continue the quetiapine 250 mg QHS that he had been on since admission. When asked, the staff reported no behavior suggesting hallucinations or delusions. Except for hypertension, he was in good health. His only other medications were lisinopril and docusate sodium. Mental status examination revealed a round-faced, well-nourished man who sat throughout the examination. He looked at the examiner only fleetingly; most of the time, he looked laterally to the right of the examiner but occasionally made very brief eye contact when asked a question. He was able to move his eyes in all directions when asked to do so. He had dyskinetic movements of his lips, jaw, and fingers. In addition, he would tap his fingers in a stereotyped manner for 30- to 60-second stretches throughout the examination. Spontaneous speech was sparse. He did not answer many questions. The answers he did give consisted of very few words. He usually repeated the phrase, "You bet your life," when a "yes" answer was indicated. No language errors were noted, and when he did speak, his answers were congruent with the situation. When asked if he liked where he was living, he replied, "It's ok." He had limited range of emotional expression but denied sadness. He answered "no" when asked about hallucinations. No suspiciousness or delusions were elicited. He did not answer questions about suicide. On cognitive examination, he was oriented to city, month, and year but not day, date, or place. He knew the name of the president. He recalled one of three objects in 2 minutes, but he did not attempt to do math or spell a five-letter word backwards. He was able to follow a three-step command, name common and uncommon objects, and copy interlocking pentagons. He did not answer questions about insight or his illness. A screening neurological examination was normal except for the dyskinetic mouth and hand movements.

A working diagnosis of ASD was made based on a many-year (probably lifelong) history of social isolation, poor eye contact, stereotyped finger tapping, sparse and stereotyped but grammatically correct language, lack of any history of hallucinations and delusions, intact activities of daily living, and stable cognition during the several-year period that he had lived in the facility. The "outbursts" were interpreted as occurring when routines were changed or when staff "insisted" that he do an activity.

A treatment plan was devised that emphasized avoidance of confrontation and ultimatums by the staff. They could recognize when he was becoming frustrated or upset and were instructed to "back off" rather than persist. A gradual tapering schedule for the quetiapine was initiated.

The state hospital records were received 3 months later. He had entered the state hospital system at age 18 years, 6 weeks after starting a job as a firefighter, the occupation of his father. He had gotten into an altercation with an instructor and had been remanded to the state hospital by the judge who oversaw the initial arraignment. A diagnosis of chronic undifferentiated schizophrenia had been made based on his social isolation, "uncooperativeness," seeming inability to adapt to social expectations, and lack of hallucinations and delusions. Numerous attempts at placement throughout his adult life had failed; his records attributed this to an "inability to adapt" to the demands and routine of the placements and his development of "violent" behavior for that reason. The records confirmed that he had not declined functionally or cognitively throughout adulthood.

At 6-month follow-up, the quetiapine had been discontinued. The staff reported that he still became "upset" once or twice a month but that they could quickly "de-escalate" the situation by early recognition, avoidance of pressure on him, and "apologizing" for "stressing him."

KEY POINTS

- The life course of ASD is poorly studied, but variable outcome is likely.
- Broad epidemiologic studies have not been adequately designed to detect autism in older individuals, but focused studies in England suggest a prevalence after age 60 years of approximately 1%.
- Older adults with ASD likely have unique medical, occupational, and social needs, but these are yet to be explicated.
- Whether early intervention will change the life course of ASD is unknown, but many individuals born before the current era were not recognized or diagnosed when young and therefore did not have early treatment.
- It is unknown if individuals with ASD are more or less likely to develop comorbid dementing illness compared to neurotypical individuals.

DISCLOSURE STATEMENT

Dr. Peter V. Rabins has provided legal testimony for Janssen Pharmaceutica.

REFERENCES

American Psychiatric Association. (2013). *Diagnostic and statistical manual of mental disorders* (5th ed.). Arlington, VA: American Psychiatric Publishing.

Asperger, H. (1944). Die "Autistischen Psychopathen" im Kindesalter. *Arch fur Psychiatrie und Nervenkrankheiten, 117,* 76–136.

Boyce, C. A., Boulet, S., Schieve, L. A., Cohen, R. A., Blumberg, S. J., Teargin-Allsopp, M., . . . Kogan, M. D. (2011). Trends in the prevalence of developmental disabilities in US children 1997–2008. *Pediatrics, 127,* 1034–1042.

Brugha, T. S., McManus, S., Bankart, J., Scott, F., Purdon, S., Smith, J., . . . Meltzer, H. (2011). Epidemiology of autism spectrum disorders in adults in the community in England. *Archives of General Psychiatry, 68,* 459–466.

Croen, L. A., Grether, J., & Selvin, S. (2002). The changing prevalence of autism in California. *Journal of Autism and Developmental Disorders, 32,* 207–215.

Fombonne, E. (2003). Epidemiologic surveys of autism and other pervasive developmental disorders: An update. *Journal of Autism and Developmental Disorders, 33,* 365–381.

Guerts, H. M., & Vissers, M. E. (2012). Elderly with autism: Executive functions and memory. *Journal of Autism and Developmental Disorders, 42,* 666–675.

Heslop, P., Blair, P. S., Fleming, P., Houghton, M., Marriott, A., & Russ, L. (2014). The confidential inquiry into premature deaths of people with intellectual disabilities in the UK: A population-based study. *Lancet, 383,* 889–895.

Hippler, K., & Klicpera, C. (2003). A retrospective analysis of the records of "autistic psychopaths" diagnosed by Hans Asperger and his team at the University Children's Hospital, Vienna. *Philosophical Transactions of the Royal Society of London Series B: Biological Sciences, 358,* 291–301.

Howlin, P., Goode, S., Hutton, J., & Rutter, M. (2004). Adult outcomes for children with autism. *Journal of Child Psychology and Psychiatry, 45,* 212–229.

Howlin, P., & Moss, P. (2012). Adults with autism spectrum disorders. *Canadian Journal of Psychiatry, 57,* 275–283.

James, I. A., Mukaetova-Ladinska, E., Reichelt, F. K., Briel, R., & Scully, A. (2006). Diagnosing Asperger's syndrome in the elderly: A series of case presentations. *International Journal of Geriatric Psychiatry, 21,* 951–960.

Kanner, L. (1943). Autistic disturbances of affective contact. *Nervous Child, 2,* 217–250.

Kanner, L. (1971). Follow-up study of eleven autistic children originally reported in 1943. *Journal of Autism and Child Schizophrenia, 1,* 119–145.

Kanner, L. (1973). How far can autistic children go in matters of social adaptation. In *Childhood psychosis: Initial studies and new insights* (pp. 189–213). New York, NY: Wiley.

Kats, D., Payne, L., Parlier, M., & Piven, J. (2013). Prevalence of selected clinical problems in older adults with autism and intellectual disability. *Journal of Neurodevelopmental Disorders, 5,* 27–39.

Mandel, D. S., Lawer, L. J., Branch, K., Brodkin, E. S., Healey, K., Eitalec, R., ... Gur, R. E. (2012). Prevalence and correlates of autism in a state psychiatric hospital. *Autism, 16,* 557–567.

Mouridsen, S., Brønnum-Hansen, H., Rich, B., & Isager, T. (2008). Mortality and causes of death in autism spectrum disorders: An update. *Autism, 12,* 403–414.

Piven, J., & Rabins, P. (2011). Autism spectrum disorders in older adults: Toward defining a research agenda. *Journal of the American Geriatrics Society, 59,* 2151–2155.

Shavelle, R. M., Strauss, D. J., & Pickett, J. (2001). Causes of death in autism. *Journal of Autism and Developmental Disorders, 31,* 569–576.

Sillanpää, M., Jalava, M., Kaleva, O., & Shinnar, S. (1998). Long-term prognosis of seizures with onset in childhood. *New England Journal of Medicine, 338,* 1715–1722.

Smith, L. E., Maenner, M. J., & Selzer, M. M. (2012). Developmental trajectories in adolescents and adults with autism: The case of daily living skills. *Journal of the American Academy of Child and Adolescent Psychiatry, 51,* 622–631.

ETIOLOGY

NEUROIMAGING OF AUTISM SPECTRUM DISORDER

NICOLE R. ZÜRCHER AND JACOB M. HOOKER

MAGNETIC RESONANCE IMAGING

Anatomical/Structural Magnetic Resonance Imaging

Anatomical magnetic resonance imaging (aMRI), also known as structural MRI (sMRI), refers to magnetic resonance imaging that allows in vivo investigation of brain anatomy. MRI is a noninvasive technique that provides high spatial resolution (state of the art is at ~1 mm and routine clinical is at ~2 or 3 mm), excellent soft tissue contrast, and is generally considered safe. See the top left panel of Figure 10.1 for an example of an anatomical scan image obtained using MRI.

Although numerous studies have reported neuroanatomical abnormalities in individuals with autism spectrum disorder (ASD), there is no consensus on which brain regions are the most affected. According to findings from sMRI experiments, the frontal and temporal lobes, cerebellum, corpus callosum, as well as the limbic system (including the amygdala) are the brain regions most often implicated in ASD.

Early sMRI reports described abnormalities in the cerebellum (reviewed in Courchesne et al., 2007). Developmental differences in cerebellar volume indicate that the normal time course of neural development is disturbed in ASD compared to typically developing controls. Current findings suggest that although individuals with ASD exhibit early brain overgrowth during infancy and toddlerhood, they show a faster rate of decline in cerebellum size later in life (Courchesne, Campbell, & Solso, 2011). Interestingly, abnormalities in the cerebellum were among the earliest reported neuroanatomical findings from *postmortem* histological studies in ASD (Bauman & Kemper, 1985) and have been replicated numerous times. In addition, histological studies have shown loss of Purkinje cells in the cerebellum (e.g., Kemper & Bauman, 1998), leading researchers to suggest that this decrease in cerebellar size could be due, at least in part, to a loss of Purkinje cells.

Another brain region for which neuroanatomical abnormalities have been reported in ASD are limbic structures, for which both increases and decreases in volume have been reported (for a review, see Palmen, van Engeland, Hof, & Schmitz, 2004). Differences in amygdala size observed between individuals with ASD and typically developing individuals seem to result from abnormal growth trajectory in ASD (reviewed in Amaral,

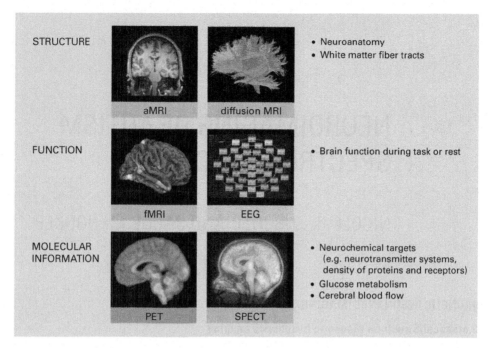

STRUCTURE
- Neuroanatomy
- White matter fiber tracts

aMRI   diffusion MRI

FUNCTION
- Brain function during task or rest

fMRI   EEG

MOLECULAR INFORMATION
- Neurochemical targets (e.g. neurotransmitter systems, density of proteins and receptors)
- Glucose metabolism
- Cerebral blood flow

PET   SPECT

FIGURE 10.1 Illustration of the different neuroimaging techniques discussed. Top panels show an anatomical MRI scan (left) and tractography from a diffusion scan (right). Middle panels show a statistical map of a functional MRI scan projected onto the surface of the brain (left) and EEG spectrograms at different electrode sites. Bottom panels illustrate a color scale representation of PET (left) and SPECT (right) radiotracer binding overlaid on an anatomical MRI image.

Schumann, & Nordahl, 2008). In accordance with sMRI studies, histological studies have also reported abnormalities in the amygdala, such as decreased neuron number (Schumann & Amaral, 2006).

To address the effect of age on ASD neuroanatomy, longitudinal studies will need to be performed. To date, most sMRI studies have been based on cross-sectional study designs, which compare individuals with ASD to healthy controls at one point in time. In the first longitudinal sMRI study of ASD, children were scanned multiple times between the ages of 1½ and 5 years in order to investigate differences in growth trajectory. This study found an abnormal growth rate in cerebral white matter and the gray matter of all lobes except the occipital lobe—that is, the frontal, temporal, and parietal lobes, as well as the cingulate (Schumann et al., 2010).

In addition to abnormalities in volume of anatomical structures such as the cerebellum and the amygdala, changes in cortical thickness have also been observed in ASD. In cross-sectional studies, both increases and decreases in cortical thickness have been reported in brain regions across all lobes in ASD (for a review, see Chen, Jiao, & Herskovits, 2011). The first longitudinal study investigating developmental changes in cortical thickness in children with ASD (8–12 years at baseline, subsequent follow-up ~2 years later) showed that the decrease in cortical thickness over time across frontal, temporal, and occipital lobes was greater in ASD compared to controls (Hardan, Libove, Keshavan, Melhem, & Minshew, 2009). Recently, a large longitudinal study that included individuals with ASD from early childhood (3 years) to adulthood (up to 36 years), scanned at an average inter-scan interval of 2.6 years, showed that group differences in cortical thickness were region specific, changed depending on developmental age, and were influenced by intelligence quotient (Zielinski et al., 2014). In this study, Zielinski and colleagues showed increased cortical thickness in childhood and decreased cortical thickness in adulthood, suggesting that in individuals with ASD, regional volume and cortical thickness measurements follow a similar path of early overgrowth followed by accelerated decline.

Diffusion Magnetic Resonance Imaging

Diffusion imaging allows assessment of the structural organization of white matter. See the top right panel of Figure 10.1 for an example of white matter fiber tract data obtained using a diffusion scan. The technique relies on the principle that water is more likely to diffuse along white matter fiber tracts than to diffuse across them. Fractional anisotropy (FA) is a measurement used to assess the spatial symmetry of the diffusion. If water can diffuse in all directions equally, the diffusion is referred to as isotropic, whereas diffusion restricted in a specific direction, thereby resulting in higher FA values, is referred to as anisotropic.

Diffusion experiments have shown that individuals with ASD exhibit altered diffusivity in the corpus callosum, cingulum, and areas of the temporal lobe (for a review of diffusion studies in ASD, see Travers et al., 2012). However, diffusion experiments are highly sensitive to motion artifacts and must be interpreted with caution unless specific measures have been taken to control for between-group differences in motion. A recent study that controlled for differences in motion between children with ASD and controls found that children with ASD showed abnormalities in the right inferior longitudinal fasciculus that connects the temporal lobe to the occipital lobe. The abnormalities included reduced FA, suggesting reduced tract integrity in this particular brain region in children with ASD (Koldewyn et al., 2014).

MRI technology is still being optimized, and the latest generation scanners, such as the Connectome scanner (Setsompop et al., 2013), now allow more detailed investigation of neuroanatomy in ASD.

Functional Magnetic Resonance Imaging

The vast majority of functional MRI (fMRI) experiments use blood oxygen level-dependent (BOLD) contrast to investigate brain activity while participants perform a specific task or are at rest (resting state fMRI). The BOLD contrast arises from the fact that the quantity of oxygen in the blood—that is, the concentration of oxyhemoglobin versus deoxyhemoglobin—will affect the magnetic susceptibility of blood. The combined effects of increases in the cerebral metabolic rate for oxygen, cerebral blood volume (CBV), and cerebral blood flow (CBF) lead to an increase in BOLD signal, which is used as a proxy for an increase in neural activity. BOLD therefore does not directly measure neural activity but instead represents a hemodynamic signal that depends on changes in the blood supply. Although BOLD is the most widely used contrast, others, such as CBF or CBV, can be used. Compared to CBF measurements assessed using arterial spin labeling, BOLD has a higher spatial resolution and a higher signal-to-noise ratio. This chapter focuses on BOLD contrast experiments. For an example of a BOLD fMRI map, see the middle left panel of Figure 10.1.

Not surprisingly, a large number of fMRI studies of ASD have focused on social cognition, given that social deficits lie at the core of the disorder. A meta-analysis of fMRI studies of ASD conducted by Philip and colleagues (2012) concluded that abnormalities in social brain regions are the most replicated findings. Numerous abnormalities have been observed in individuals with ASD during sociocognitive tasks, including face processing, eye gaze, and emotion processing. Earlier studies reported decreased fusiform face area (FFA) activation when individuals with ASD passively view faces (Schultz et al., 2000). However, more recent studies have shown that when participants with ASD are cued to the eye region, they display FFA activation to the same extent as controls (Hadjikhani et al., 2004). In addition, whereas individuals with ASD show reduced activation in the FFA for unfamiliar faces, they show normal activation for familiar faces (Pierce & Redcay, 2008). These studies suggest that attentional and motivational processes likely play a key role in face processing in ASD.

Theory of mind (ToM), which refers to the ability to attribute intentions, feelings, and beliefs to others, is impaired in most individuals with ASD. The brain regions involved in ToM include the medial prefrontal cortex, superior temporal sulcus, inferior frontal regions, and the temporal pole (Frith & Frith, 2003; Gallagher & Frith, 2003). Studies using fMRI have started to investigate the neural underpinnings of deficits in mentalizing (ToM) abilities in ASD and have found decreased activation in the brain regions associated with ToM in individuals with ASD (reviewed in Philip et al., 2012). Some fMRI studies have also suggested involvement of the mirror neuron system in ASD (e.g., Dapretto et al., 2006).

Atypical neural activation has also been observed in tasks assessing motor function, visual processing, audition, language processing, communication, and executive functioning in individuals with ASD (reviewed in Philip et al., 2012; Stigler, McDonald, Anand, Saykin, & McDougle, 2011).

Functional Connectivity

Studies involving task-based and resting state functional connectivity MRI (fcMRI) experiments are used to investigate functional connectivity between brain regions. Functional connectivity examines how activity in one brain region correlates with the activity of another brain region, thereby allowing investigation of functional nodes within a network (Stevenson, 2012). Whereas diffusion imaging investigates structural connectivity between brain regions (i.e., the presence of white matter fiber tracts connecting one part of the brain to another), functional connectivity assesses the temporal correlation in BOLD signal between brain regions.

In ASD, underconnectivity of brain areas has most often been observed, but overconnectivity has also been reported (for a review, see Muller et al., 2011). Network dysfunction leading to deficits in interregional information exchange may be related to ASD symptoms because large-scale brain circuits are likely essential for intact social and communication skills (Courchesne et al., 2007).

ELECTROENCEPHALOGRAPHY

Electroencephalography (EEG) is a noninvasive neuroimaging technique that involves recording electrical signals through electrodes placed on the surface of the scalp. A major advantage of using EEG is that it provides high temporal resolution, in the millisecond range, which currently cannot be achieved with MRI. Another advantage of EEG is that experiments can be designed without requiring participants to have language skills or the ability to perform a task, which gives researchers the option of enrolling infants or non-verbal individuals with ASD. However, compared to MRI, EEG has a much lower spatial resolution. In addition, the EEG signal is strongly dominated by cortical activity and has rather poor sensitivity for subcortical structures, such as the amygdala and hippocampus.

EEG activity is the ensemble of ionic currents generated by neurons in the range of the electrode. It is characterized by the power of oscillations in specific frequency bands (EEG power spectrum). These different frequency ranges are referred to as delta (1–3 Hz), theta (4–7 Hz), alpha (8–12 Hz), beta (13–35 Hz), and gamma (>35 Hz) bands. Different pro-cesses, such as sleep, attention, memory, and motor function, are characterized by a specific pattern of activity in these frequency bands. In addition, the electrical activity of the brain in response to a specific stimulus (e.g., a sensory or motor stimulus or cognitive task) can be detected as event-related potentials (ERPs). These ERPs are considered "time-locked" in response to an external stimulus and are composed of positive or negative peaks (indicated by a P or N, respectively), which occur at a specific time (measured in milliseconds) follow-ing stimulus presentation. Neural activation in response to sensory processing is observed in the earlier components of the ERP signal, whereas later components reflect cognitive processing. In addition to frequency bands and ERPs, recent studies have focused on coher-ence, in which functional relationships are assessed between brain regions based on phase correlation. See the middle right panel of Figure 10.1.

EEG was one of the first methods used in research to examine the underlying pathology of ASD, and it has a long history in ASD research, with numerous studies reporting abnor-mal EEG patterns in individuals with ASD. Another reason for the discussion of EEG mea-sures in ASD research is the usefulness of EEG in diagnosing epileptic seizures. Given that epilepsy is a common comorbidity with ASD, many individuals with ASD may undergo an EEG procedure at some point to test for epilepsy, either as part of a clinical assessment or as part of a research study.

Instead of EEG, magnetoencephalography (MEG) is sometimes used. Although MEG also has high temporal resolution, those systems are currently less available than EEG.

Task-Based Studies

Numerous task-based studies have focused on perception and cognitive tasks especially in the auditory and visual domains. Among others, experiments have included face and eye gaze processing, attention, and language.

A number of ERP studies have focused on selective attention and attentional novelty detection of auditory stimuli in ASD. The key component of those studies is the P300 ERP (P3), which can be subdivided into P3a and P3b components. The P3a, with maximum amplitude over frontal and central brain regions, is an index of attentional orienting, whereas the late visual evoked parietal component P3b reflects higher-level processing. An ERP study investigating sound processing found that individuals with ASD showed normal sen-sory response to different sounds, including speech sounds (vowel changes), but reduced P3a amplitudes, specifically in response to speech sounds (Ceponiene et al., 2003). Given that the P3a component reflects attentional orienting, the authors concluded that audi-tory orienting deficits in ASD might be speech–sound specific. Attention to novelty ERP studies repeatedly found that auditory P3b response amplitudes are smaller for individuals with ASD compared to the control group (reviewed in Jeste & Nelson, 2009). Courchesne and colleagues reported decreased auditory P3b amplitude in high-functioning individuals with ASD, although the target detection task was performed as accurately and rapidly as in controls, suggesting that individuals with ASD may be using alternative mechanisms for target detection (Courchesne, Lincoln, Yeung-Courchesne, Elmasian, & Grillon, 1989). Additional evidence suggesting that attention processing is atypical in ASD derives from studies showing that in attentional tasks, individuals with ASD display increased connectivity and synchronization and greater gamma activity compared to healthy individuals (reviewed in Gepner & Feron, 2009).

Given its noninvasive nature and that it simply requires the participant to wear an electrode cap, EEG can be used in young infants to search for the presence of abnormalities in perceptual or cognitive processes early in life (Banaschewski & Brandeis, 2007). In an interesting study, Elsabbagh and colleagues (2009) used EEG to investigate the broader ASD phenotype by examining the response to direct eye gaze by infants with siblings with autism compared to that of infants with unaffected siblings. For the P400 ERP, infants at higher risk for developing ASD took longer to respond to the direct gaze stimuli compared to infants with unaffected siblings. In infants, the P400 ERP is important for face processing and has been suggested to be a precursor to the N170 ERP. N170 is associated with face processing in adults and referred to as a face-sensitive component, which is localized over the occipital/temporal electrodes—consistent with face processing areas including the fusiform gyrus.

Resting State Studies

As is the case for fMRI, EEG can also be done in the absence of a specific stimulus presentation or task to be performed and is referred to as resting state EEG. Resting state EEG studies in individuals with ASD have often reported increased power in both low-frequency (delta and theta) and high-frequency (beta and gamma) bands but decreased power in the middle-range frequency (alpha) band (for a review, see Wang et al., 2013). In addition, some resting state studies have found evidence of atypical lateralization, with increased power observed in one hemisphere versus the other (reviewed in Wang et al., 2013).

For both task and resting state EEG, researchers have started searching for abnormalities in coherence, the correlation between signals measured at different electrodes. Abnormalities in signal correlation across brain regions would suggest altered functional integration between different areas. Whether deficits in functional connectivity of spontaneous EEG measures may underlie some of the core difficulties experienced by individuals with ASD is currently the source of active investigation.

POSITRON EMISSION TOMOGRAPHY AND SINGLE PHOTON EMISSION COMPUTED TOMOGRAPHY

The key strength of positron emission tomography (PET) and single photon emission computed tomography (SPECT) is that each technique has high sensitivity and allows for visualization and in many cases quantification of molecular events, such as the density of proteins and receptors. PET and SPECT can also be used to measure neurotransmitter release and occupancy. In addition, PET can be used to investigate cerebral blood flow and glucose metabolism, which have so far generated the highest number of studies in the field of ASD. In a typical PET or SPECT imaging experiment, a radioactive contrast agent (known as a radiotracer) is administered intravenously to a research participant or patient. Radioactivity (measured indirectly through positron annihilation in PET or directly through gamma rays in SPECT) is detected in a scanner. The radiotracer is administered at a very low mass dose and is intended to measure, but not perturb, the biological state. Many study designs exist, but for rigorously quantitative data, PET is preferred over SPECT with the disadvantage being that PET quantification can often require arterial blood sampling, which can be potentially challenging for studies including patients with ASD. For images of PET and SPECT scans, see the bottom panels of Figure 10.1.

By far the most common techniques used in PET for ASD have been blood flow (typically with oxygen-15 radiotracers such as [^{15}O]-water) and glucose metabolism, which relies on the uptake and retention of the glucose analog 2-deoxy-2-(^{18}F)fluoro-D-glucose (often simply referred to as FDG).

One of the most interesting findings of CBF studies in ASD is the observation of decreased blood flow toward the temporal lobe in children with ASD (Zilbovicius et al., 2000). In addition, when listening to speech-like sounds, both children and adults with ASD exhibit decreased blood flow toward the left temporal cortex and associated speech areas, highlighting abnormal auditory cortical processing (Boddaert et al., 2003, 2004).

There is currently no consensus concerning glucose metabolism in individuals with ASD because studies have reported hypometabolism, hypermetabolism, or no difference when comparing individuals with ASD to controls (Buchsbaum et al., 1992; De Volder, Bol, Michel, Congneau, & Goffinet, 1987; Haznedar et al., 2006; Herold, Frackowiak, Le Couteur, Rutter, & Howlin, 1988; Rumsey et al., 1985; Siegel et al., 1992).

The most-studied neurotransmitter in ASD is serotonin. Abnormalities in serotonin synthesis have been observed using the tracer α-[^{11}C]methyl-L-tryptophan (AMT) in the dentatothalamocortical pathway in individuals with ASD compared to their siblings (Chugani et al., 1997). In addition, developmental abnormalities and an atypical trajectory between 5 and 14 years have also been reported (Chugani et al., 1999). In children with ASD, abnormalities in the dentatothalamocortical pathway, which consisted of local increases or decreases in serotonin synthesis, were reported to be related to language function (Chandana et al., 2005). Two studies investigating the serotonin transporter (SERT) found decreased levels of SERT in brain regions that included the medial frontal cortex (Makkonen, Riikonen, Kokki, Airaksinen, & Kuikka, 2008), anterior cingulate, posterior cingulate, and precuneus (Nakamura et al., 2010). Studies using tracers to target the serotonin receptor have so far yielded mixed results, with one study reporting decreases and the other reporting no difference compared to the control group (Girgis et al., 2011; Murphy et al., 2006).

Although some studies have investigated neurotransmitters other than serotonin in ASD (including dopamine, γ-aminobutyric acid, glutamate, and acetylcholine), more studies using radiotracers are needed to obtain a more clear understanding of the respective neurotransmitter function/dysfunction in ASD.

SUMMARY

Key contributions from MRI, EEG, and PET/SPECT have furthered our understanding of ASD because all these neuroimaging techniques allow the study of brain structure and function in vivo. Differences in the underlying neuroanatomy have been observed in individuals with ASD using aMRI (especially in the cerebellum and limbic system), whereas fMRI experiments have shed light on social cognition deficits in individuals with ASD. EEG experiments have highlighted abnormalities in auditory processing of language, perception, and processing of social stimuli as well as attention in individuals with ASD of all ages, including infants. PET studies have investigated a number of neurotransmitter systems and revealed abnormalities in the serotonergic system and others.

Aims of ongoing and future neuroimaging studies in ASD include early endophenotype identification (preceding behavioral diagnosis), an improved understanding of developmental trajectory using longitudinal study designs, and stratification of the autism spectrum into subtypes based on biological signatures.

KEY POINTS

- Structural MRI allows investigation of neuroanatomy, and although differences have been observed in individuals with ASD, they seem to be mostly based on differences in developmental trajectory.
- Functional MRI experiments have shown that brain regions involved in social cognition (including face processing, emotion processing, and nonverbal as well as verbal communication) are abnormally activated in ASD.
- EEG is the method that can most easily be used in young infants and therefore holds promise for early endophenotype identification, potentially leading to earlier diagnosis.
- PET/SPECT studies have shown abnormalities in neurotransmitter systems, particularly in serotonin. Other neurochemical targets are being investigated.
- Future neuroimaging studies may be able to help in uncovering the pathophysiology underlying different subtypes of ASD and may promote the development of more targeted pharmacological or behavioral interventions.

DISCLOSURE STATEMENT

Dr. Nicole Zürcher has no conflicts of interest to disclose. She is funded by an Autism Speaks Meixner Translational Postdoctoral Fellowship (No. 9258).

Dr. Jacob M. Hooker's research interests and program relate to the content of this chapter. He receives funding from several government funding agencies (e.g., National Institutes of Health and the U.S. Department of Energy), pharmaceutical companies, and philanthropic donations. None of the support he receives creates a conflict of interest with the material presented in this chapter.

REFERENCES

Amaral, D. G., Schumann, C. M., & Nordahl, C. W. (2008). Neuroanatomy of autism. *Trends in Neurosciences, 31*(3), 137–145. doi:10.1016/j.tins.2007.12.005

Banaschewski, T., & Brandeis, D. (2007). Annotation: What electrical brain activity tells us about brain function that other techniques cannot tell us—A child psychiatric perspective. *Journal of Child Psychology and Psychiatry, 48*(5), 415–435. doi:10.1111/j.1469-7610.2006.01681.x

Bauman, M., & Kemper, T. L. (1985). Histoanatomic observations of the brain in early infantile autism. *Neurology, 35*(6), 866–874.

Boddaert, N., Belin, P., Chabane, N., Poline, J. B., Barthelemy, C., Mouren-Simeoni, M. C., . . . Zilbovicius, M. (2003). Perception of complex sounds: Abnormal pattern of cortical activation in autism. *American Journal of Psychiatry, 160*(11), 2057–2060.

Boddaert, N., Chabane, N., Belin, P., Bourgeois, M., Royer, V., Barthelemy, C., . . . Zilbovicius, M. (2004). Perception of complex sounds in autism: Abnormal auditory cortical processing in children. *American Journal of Psychiatry, 161*(11), 2117–2120. doi:10.1176/appi.ajp.161.11.2117

Buchsbaum, M. S., Siegel, B. V., Jr., Wu, J. C., Hazlett, E., Sicotte, N., Haier, R., et al. (1992). Brief report: Attention performance in autism and regional brain metabolic rate assessed by positron emission tomography. *Journal of Autism and Developmental Disorders, 22*(1), 115–125.

Ceponiene, R., Lepisto, T., Shestakova, A., Vanhala, R., Alku, P., Naatanen, R., & Yaguchi, K. (2003). Speech–sound-selective auditory impairment in children with autism: They can perceive but do not attend. *Proceedings of the National Academy of Sciences of the USA, 100*(9), 5567–5572. doi:10.1073/pnas.0835631100

Chandana, S. R., Behen, M. E., Juhasz, C., Muzik, O., Rothermel, R. D., Mangner, T. J., . . . Chugani, D. C. (2005). Significance of abnormalities in developmental trajectory and asymmetry of cortical serotonin synthesis in autism. *International Journal of Developmental Neuroscience23*(2–3), 171–182. doi:10.1016/j.ijdevneu.2004.08.002

Chen, R., Jiao, Y., & Herskovits, E. H. (2011). Structural MRI in autism spectrum disorder. *Pediatric Research, 69*(5 Pt. 2), 63R–68R. doi:10.1203/PDR.0b013e318212c2b3

Chugani, D. C., Muzik, O., Behen, M., Rothermel, R., Janisse, J. J., Lee, J., & Chugani, H. T. (1999). Developmental changes in brain serotonin synthesis capacity in autistic and non-autistic children. *Annals of Neurology, 45*(3), 287–295.

Chugani, D. C., Muzik, O., Rothermel, R., Behen, M., Chakraborty, P., Mangner, T., . . . Chugani, H. T. (1997). Altered serotonin synthesis in the dentatothalamocortical pathway in autistic boys. *Annals of Neurology, 42*(4), 666–669. doi:10.1002/ana.410420420

Courchesne, E., Campbell, K., & Solso, S. (2011). Brain growth across the life span in autism: Age-specific changes in anatomical pathology. *Brain Research, 1380,* 138–145. doi:10.1016/j.brainres.2010.09.101

Courchesne, E., Lincoln, A. J., Yeung-Courchesne, R., Elmasian, R., & Grillon, C. (1989). Pathophysiologic findings in nonretarded autism and receptive developmental language disorder. *Journal of Autism and Developmental Disorders, 19*(1), 1–17.

Courchesne, E., Pierce, K., Schumann, C. M., Redcay, E., Buckwalter, J. A., Kennedy, D. P., & Morgan, J. (2007). Mapping early brain development in autism. *Neuron, 56*(2), 399–413. doi:10.1016/j.neuron.2007.10.016

Dapretto, M., Davies, M. S., Pfeifer, J. H., Scott, A. A., Sigman, M., Bookheimer, S. Y., & Iacoboni, M. (2006). Understanding emotions in others: Mirror neuron dysfunction in children with autism spectrum disorders. *Nature Neuroscience, 9*(1), 28–30. doi:10.1038/nn1611

De Volder, A., Bol, A., Michel, C., Congneau, M., & Goffinet, A. M. (1987). Brain glucose metabolism in children with the autistic syndrome: Positron tomography analysis. *Brain & Development, 9*(6), 581–587.

Elsabbagh, M., Volein, A., Csibra, G., Holmboe, K., Garwood, H., Tucker, L., . . . Johnson, M. H. (2009). Neural correlates of eye gaze processing in the infant broader autism phenotype. *Biological Psychiatry, 65*(1), 31–38. doi:10.1016/j.biopsych.2008.09.034

Frith, U., & Frith, C. D. (2003). Development and neurophysiology of mentalizing. *Philosophical Transactions of the Royal Society of London Series B: Biological Sciences, 358*(1431), 459–473. doi:10.1098/rstb.2002.1218

Gallagher, H. L., & Frith, C. D. (2003). Functional imaging of "theory of mind." *Trends in Cognitive Sciences, 7*(2), 77–83.

Gepner, B., & Feron, F. (2009). Autism: A world changing too fast for a mis-wired brain? *Neuroscience and Biobehavioral Reviews, 33*(8), 1227–1242. doi:10.1016/j.neubiorev.2009.06.006

Girgis, R. R., Slifstein, M., Xu, X., Frankle, W. G., Anagnostou, E., Wasserman, S., . . . Hollander, E. (2011). The 5-HT(2A) receptor and serotonin transporter in Asperger's disorder: A PET study with [(1)

(1)C]MDL 100907 and [(1)(1)C]DASB. *Psychiatry Research, 194*(3), 230–234. doi:10.1016/j.
pscychresns.2011.04.007

Hadjikhani, N., Joseph, R. M., Snyder, J., Chabris, C. F., Clark, J., Steele, S., . . . Tager-Flusberg, H. (2004).
Activation of the fusiform gyrus when individuals with autism spectrum disorder view faces. *NeuroImage,
22*(3), 1141–1150. doi:10.1016/j.neuroimage.2004.03.025

Hardan, A. Y., Libove, R. A., Keshavan, M. S., Melhem, N. M., & Minshew, N. J. (2009). A preliminary longitudinal magnetic resonance imaging study of brain volume and cortical thickness in autism. *Biological
Psychiatry, 66*(4), 320–326. doi:10.1016/j.biopsych.2009.04.024

Haznedar, M. M., Buchsbaum, M. S., Hazlett, E. A., LiCalzi, E. M., Cartwright, C., & Hollander, E. (2006).
Volumetric analysis and three-dimensional glucose metabolic mapping of the striatum and thalamus in patients with autism spectrum disorders. *American Journal of Psychiatry, 163*(7), 1252–1263.
doi:10.1176/appi.ajp.163.7.1252

Herold, S., Frackowiak, R. S., Le Couteur, A., Rutter, M., & Howlin, P. (1988). Cerebral blood flow and
metabolism of oxygen and glucose in young autistic adults. *Psychological Medicine, 18*(4), 823–831.

Jeste, S. S., & Nelson, C. A., 3rd. (2009). Event related potentials in the understanding of autism spectrum disorders: An analytical review. *Journal of Autism and Developmental Disorders, 39*(3), 495–510.
doi:10.1007/s10803-008-0652-9

Kemper, T. L., & Bauman, M. (1998). Neuropathology of infantile autism. *Journal of Neuropathology and
Experimental Neurology, 57*(7), 645–652.

Koldewyn, K., Yendiki, A., Weigelt, S., Gweon, H., Julian, J., Richardson, H., . . . Kanwisher, N. (2014).
Differences in the right inferior longitudinal fasciculus but no general disruption of white matter tracts
in children with autism spectrum disorder. *Proceedings of the National Academy of Sciences of the USA,
111*(5), 1981–1986. doi:10.1073/pnas.1324037111

Makkonen, I., Riikonen, R., Kokki, H., Airaksinen, M. M., & Kuikka, J. T. (2008). Serotonin and dopamine
transporter binding in children with autism determined by SPECT. *Developmental Medicine and Child
Neurology, 50*(8), 593–597. doi:10.1111/j.1469-8749.2008.03027.x

Muller, R. A., Shih, P., Keehn, B., Deyoe, J. R., Leyden, K. M., & Shukla, D. K. (2011). Underconnected, but
how? A survey of functional connectivity MRI studies in autism spectrum disorders. *Cerebral Cortex,
21*(10), 2233–2243. doi:10.1093/cercor/bhq296

Murphy, D. G., Daly, E., Schmitz, N., Toal, F., Murphy, K., Curran, S., . . . Travis, M. (2006). Cortical
serotonin 5-HT2A receptor binding and social communication in adults with Asperger's syndrome: An in vivo SPECT study. *American Journal of Psychiatry, 163*(5), 934–936. doi:10.1176/
appi.ajp.163.5.934

Nakamura, K., Sekine, Y., Ouchi, Y., Tsujii, M., Yoshikawa, E., Futatsubashi, M., . . . Mori, N. (2010). Brain
serotonin and dopamine transporter bindings in adults with high-functioning autism. *Archives of General
Psychiatry, 67*(1), 59–68. doi:10.1001/archgenpsychiatry.2009.137

Palmen, S. J., van Engeland, H., Hof, P. R., & Schmitz, C. (2004). Neuropathological findings in autism. *Brain,
127*(Pt. 12), 2572–2583. doi:10.1093/brain/awh287

Philip, R. C., Dauvermann, M. R., Whalley, H. C., Baynham, K., Lawrie, S. M., & Stanfield, A. C. (2012). A
systematic review and meta-analysis of the fMRI investigation of autism spectrum disorders. *Neuroscience
and Biobehavioral Reviews, 36*(2), 901–942. doi:10.1016/j.neubiorev.2011.10.008

Pierce, K., & Redcay, E. (2008). Fusiform function in children with an autism spectrum disorder is a matter
of "who." *Biological Psychiatry, 64*(7), 552–560. doi:10.1016/j.biopsych.2008.05.013

Rumsey, J. M., Duara, R., Grady, C., Rapoport, J. L., Margolin, R. A., Rapoport, S. I., & Cutler, N. R. (1985).
Brain metabolism in autism: Resting cerebral glucose utilization rates as measured with positron emission tomography. *Archives of General Psychiatry, 42*(5), 448–455.

Schultz, R. T., Gauthier, I., Klin, A., Fulbright, R. K., Anderson, A. W., Volkmar, F., . . . Gore, J. C. (2000).
Abnormal ventral temporal cortical activity during face discrimination among individuals with autism
and Asperger syndrome. *Archives of General Psychiatry, 57*(4), 331–340.

Schumann, C. M., & Amaral, D. G. (2006). Stereological analysis of amygdala neuron number in autism.
Journal of Neuroscience, 26(29), 7674–7679. doi:10.1523/JNEUROSCI.1285-06.2006

Schumann, C. M., Bloss, C. S., Barnes, C. C., Wideman, G. M., Carper, R. A., Akshoomoff, N., . . . Courchesne, E. (2010). Longitudinal magnetic resonance imaging study of cortical development through early childhood in autism. *Journal of Neuroscience, 30*(12), 4419–4427. doi:10.1523/JNEUROSCI.5714-09.2010

Setsompop, K., Kimmlingen, R., Eberlein, E., Witzel, T., Cohen-Adad, J., McNab, J. A., . . . Wald, L. L. (2013). Pushing the limits of in vivo diffusion MRI for the Human Connectome Project. *NeuroImage, 80*, 220–233. doi:10.1016/j.neuroimage.2013.05.078

Siegel, B. V., Jr., Asarnow, R., Tanguay, P., Call, J. D., Abel, L., Ho, A., . . . Buchsbaum, M. S. (1992). Regional cerebral glucose metabolism and attention in adults with a history of childhood autism. *Journal of Neuropsychiatry and Clinical Neurosciences, 4*(4), 406–414.

Stevenson, R. A. (2012). Using functional connectivity analyses to investigate the bases of autism spectrum disorders and other clinical populations. *Journal of Neuroscience, 32*(50), 17933–17934. doi:10.1523/JNEUROSCI.4515-12.2012

Stigler, K. A., McDonald, B. C., Anand, A., Saykin, A. J., & McDougle, C. J. (2011). Structural and functional magnetic resonance imaging of autism spectrum disorders. *Brain Research, 1380*, 146–161. doi:10.1016/j.brainres.2010.11.076

Travers, B. G., Adluru, N., Ennis, C., Tromp do, P. M., Destiche, D., Doran, S., . . . Alexander, A. L. (2012). Diffusion tensor imaging in autism spectrum disorder: A review. *Autism Research, 5*(5), 289–313. doi:10.1002/aur.1243

Wang, J., Barstein, J., Ethridge, L. E., Mosconi, M. W., Takarae, Y., & Sweeney, J. A. (2013). Resting state EEG abnormalities in autism spectrum disorders. *Journal of Neurodevelopmental Disorders, 5*(1), 24. doi:10.1186/1866-1955-5-24

Zielinski, B. A., Prigge, M. B., Nielsen, J. A., Froehlich, A. L., Abildskov, T. J., Anderson, J. S., . . . Lainhart, J. E. (2014). Longitudinal changes in cortical thickness in autism and typical development. *Brain, 137*(Pt. 6), 1799–1812. doi:10.1093/brain/awu083

Zilbovicius, M., Boddaert, N., Belin, P., Poline, J. B., Remy, P., Mangin, J. F., . . . Samson, Y. (2000). Temporal lobe dysfunction in childhood autism: A PET study. *American Journal of Psychiatry, 157*(12), 1988–1993.

/// 11 /// GENETICS OF AUTISM SPECTRUM DISORDER

YAMINI J. HOWE, HARRISON BRAND, AND MICHAEL E. TALKOWSKI

INTRODUCTION

Autism spectrum disorder (ASD) is a complex neurodevelopmental condition character-ized by impairments in social interactions and communication, as well as by repetitive pat-terns of behavior (American Psychiatric Association, 2013). The estimated prevalence of ASD has been steadily rising based on changes in diagnostic classification, public awareness, and treatment availability. The most recent Centers for Disease Control and Prevention prevalence data estimate that 1 in 68 children have been diagnosed with ASD as of 2010 (Centers for Disease Control and Prevention, 2014). This is in stark contrast with early esti-mates of approximately 4 in 10,000 noted by studies in the 1960s and 1970s (Fombonne, 2003). The high prevalence of ASD highlights the importance of identifying the biological mechanisms that drive the disorder. Although the etiology of ASD is likely to also be influ-enced by environmental factors (e.g., prenatal maternal stress (Walder et al., 2014) or zinc deficiency (Yasuda, Yoshida, Yasuda, & Tsutsui, 2011)), the heritability of the disorder is high and there is substantial evidence to indicate a strong genetic component to its etiology.

Autism Spectrum Disorder Heritability

Twin studies from as early as the 1970s have demonstrated the importance of genetic fac-tors in the development of ASD. An early meta-analysis of twin studies and case reports found that identical twins with ASD had an average concordance of 64% and an average fraternal twin concordance of 9%, compared to population prevalence estimated to be 0.05% at the time of the study (Smalley, Asarnow, & Spence, 1988). More recent stud-ies have shown that in families that have one child with ASD, subsequent children are more likely to also develop ASD, with a recurrence risk reported to be as high as 10–18% (Constantino, Zhang, Frazier, Abbacchi, & Law, 2010; Ozonoff et al., 2011). Researchers who conducted a large-scale study in Sweden suggested that heritability for ASD is approximately 50% (Sandin et al., 2014), whereas another study estimated heritability to be as high as 90% (Bailey et al., 1995), suggesting that at least half, if not most, of ASD risk is due to genetics.

Recent technological advances in genomics have yielded seminal findings that have dramatically advanced our understanding of ASD (Talkowski, Minikel, & Gusella, 2014). First, a variety of different mutation classes, including rare single nucleotide variants (Iossifov et al., 2012; Lim et al., 2013; Neale et al., 2012; O'Roak et al., 2012a; Sanders et al., 2012; Yu et al., 2013), copy number variants (CNVs) (Beunders et al., 2013; Girirajan, Johnson, et al., 2013; Handrigan et al., 2013; Lionel et al., 2013; Michaelson et al., 2012; Pinto et al., 2010; Sebat et al., 2007; Talkowski et al., 2012), chromosomal abnormalities (Marshall et al., 2008; Talkowski et al., 2012), and common polymorphic variations, have been shown to contribute to the etiology of the disorder (Anney et al., 2010; Klei et al., 2012; Wang et al., 2009; Weiss, Arking, Daly, & Chakravarti, 2009). Second, new mutations that are not inherited from parents (de novo mutations) have been found to be dramatically increased in individuals with ASD compared to their unaffected siblings or general expectations under the null hypothesis; and the penetrance of de novo loss-of-function (LOF) mutations in individuals with ASD is substantial (Beunders et al., 2013; Girirajan, Johnson, et al., 2013; Handrigan et al., 2013; Lionel et al., 2013; Neale et al., 2012; O'Roak et al., 2012a; Sanders et al., 2012; Sebat et al., 2007; Talkowski et al., 2012). Third, regions of recurrent microdeletions and duplications mediated by non-allelic homologous recombination (NAHR; e.g., 16.p11.2,15q11–13) occur in a significant proportion of individuals with ASD (Cooper et al., 2011), whereas frequent CNV regions that are not mediated by NAHR have led to the identification of individual necessary and sufficient strong effect loci within microdeletion/duplication syndrome regions (e.g., MBD5 in 2q23.1 or SATB2 in 2q33.1) (Rosenfeld et al., 2010; Talkowski, Mullegama, et al., 2011; Talkowski et al., 2012; Williams et al., 2010). Fourth, genes that contribute to ASD represent diverse biological pathways, including synaptic function (Ben-David & Shifman, 2012; Iossifov et al., 2012), chromatin modification, and transcriptional regulation (Ben-David & Shifman, 2012; Iossifov et al., 2014; O'Roak et al., 2012a; Talkowski et al., 2012). Finally, many genes associated with ASD confer shared risk to a range of neurodevelopmental abnormalities and psychopathology (Cross-Disorder Group of the Psychiatric Genomics Consortium, 2013; Talkowski et al., 2012). Taken together, these studies demonstrate that a highly heterogeneous collection of genes can lead to a similar clinical presentation, and conversely, highly specific genetic lesions can be associated with widely variable clinical outcomes.

Recent Technological Advances

Early research into the genetics of ASD, prior to the availability of unbiased genome-wide surveys, focused on syndromic forms of the disorder and its comorbidity with known Mendelian syndromes such as fragile X syndrome, Rett syndrome, tuberous sclerosis, neurofibromatosis, Angelman syndrome, and macrocephaly associated with PTEN (phosphatase and tensin homolog) mutations (Betancur, 2011; Bolton & Griffiths, 1997; Brown et al., 1982; Butler et al., 2005; Gillberg & Forsell, 1984; Lam et al., 2000; Miles, 2011; Steffenburg, Gillberg, Steffenburg, & Kyllerman, 1996). With the completion of the Human Genome Project, studies investigating variation in select candidate genes were used to compare common polymorphisms between cases and controls to identify genetic risk for ASD (for an overview of historical milestones in genetic research in ASD, see Table 11.1). These studies were almost universally underpowered to detect modest effect sizes (e.g., odds ratios of 2

TABLE 11.1 Timeline of Milestones in Genetic Research as It Relates to Autism Spectrum Disorder

1953	Crick and Watson propose model for structure of DNA.
1959	Lejeune, Gautier, and Turpin identify trisomy 21 as the cause of Down syndrome.
1969	Development of Southern blot technique by Edwin Southern allowed detection of specific DNA sequences.
1977	Fred Sanger develops technique for DNA sequencing.
1982	Autism is associated with fragile X syndrome (Brown et al., 1982).
1983	PCR technique is developed.
1990s	Array techniques began to be developed; further sequencing technologies are developed.
1995–2000	Syndromes such as Angelman syndrome, neurofibromatosis, and tuberous sclerosis are noted to be associated with ASD (Bolton & Griffiths, 1997; Lam et al., 2000; Steffenburg et al., 1996).
1997	Autism Genetics Resource Exchange (AGRE) is founded (Lajonchere, 2010).
2003	Human Genome Project is completed.
2000–2010	PTEN is associated with autism (Butler et al., 2005); autism also associated with neuroligin and SHANK genes (Jamain et al., 2003; Leblond et al., 2014; Strauss et al., 2006).
2005–Present	Next-generation sequencing techniques are further developed.
2006	Autism Consortium–Boston is founded.
2008	Simons Simplex Collection (SSC) starts recruiting participants (Fischbach & Lord, 2010).

or less), but they did identify associations with several biological candidate genes and gene families that are still considered in neurobiological studies of ASD (e.g., neuroligins (Jamain et al., 2003), SHANK genes (Leblond et al., 2014), and neurexins (Strauss et al., 2006)).

In approximately the past decade, the development of array-based technologies to detect small DNA dosage changes (array comparative genomics hybridization (aCGH)) (Manning & Hudgins, 2007) as well as technology capable of simultaneously genotyping hundreds of thousands to millions of single nucleotide polymorphisms (SNPs) has allowed the unbiased genome-wide assessment of loci conferring risk to ASD. In the past several years, the advent of massively parallel sequencing (also called next-generation sequencing (NGS)) and targeted DNA-capture technology has allowed researchers to focus on either all 3.1 billion bases that comprise the human genome or the approximately 1% of the genome that is known to code for proteins through a technique referred to as whole-exome sequencing (WES). An overview of several of the most significant findings from these studies is provided next, although there are many others that are not reviewed here that have also helped to shape the emerging view of ASD etiology. For an overview of genes and loci implicated in ASD etiology, see Figure 11.4.

Single Nucleotide Variants

The effects of both common and rare single base mutations have provided significant insight into ASD etiology (Figure 11.1). Common variants have been studied using

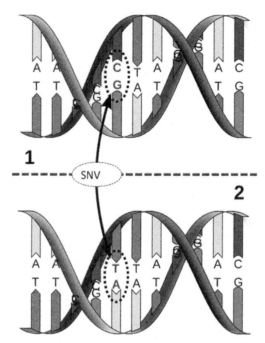

FIGURE 11.1 Single nucleotide variant. This drawing depicts a change in a single base pair.
Source: Adapted from David Eccles (http://commons.wikimedia.org/wiki/File:Dna-SNP.svg#file).

genome-wide association studies (GWAS), and rare variants have been studied predominantly using WES.

Genome-Wide Association Studies

The development of SNP-based microarrays has enabled researchers to investigate common variants across the entire genome using an association study design through analyses of both cases and controls as well as transmission from parents to affected offspring. Thus far, 2,111 GWAS studies have been published, identifying 15,396 trait-associated SNPs at the empirical threshold of statistical significance (www.genome.gov/gwastudies; accessed August 3, 2015). This approach has yielded remarkable new insights into several neuropsychiatric disorders, most notably schizophrenia, through a series of large-scale studies suggesting a strong polygenic risk of this disorder (Schizophrenia Psychiatric Genome-Wide Association Study (GWAS) Consortium, 2014). Ongoing large-scale studies across psychiatric disorders have also suggested a significant degree of shared genetic risk among multiple neurodevelopmental and psychiatric disorders (Cross-Disorder Group, 2013).

In ASD, however, progress from GWAS studies has been slower because power has been significantly limited compared to that of studies of schizophrenia. GWAS and family linkage analyses from SNP microarrays in three studies of ASD identified independent genome-wide significant associations (Anney et al., 2010; Wang et al., 2009; Weiss et al., 2009), but a meta-analysis of these studies did not support consistent effects of any loci (Devlin, Melhem, & Roeder, 2011). Recently, Devlin and colleagues have shown that common variants exerting weak additive effects collectively represent a major component of ASD risk (Gaugler et al., 2014). Thus, although none of the existing ASD GWAS studies have approached the yield that has been achieved in other psychiatric disorders, there is a growing consensus that a significant increase in sample size will produce substantially stronger effects of common variation in the population, which is likely to account for a meaningful portion of the heritability estimates for this disorder.

Whole Exome Sequencing

Whole exome sequencing (WES) is a powerful new technique for exploring the role of rare and de novo coding variations in ASD. The banking of genetic material and phenotypic data from individuals with ASD and their families has played a major role in the availability of well-characterized subjects for research. Large-scale consortia such as the Simons Simplex Collection (SSC; Fischbach & Lord, 2010), the Autism Genetic Resource Exchange (AGRE; Lajonchere, 2010), the Autism Consortium of Boston (http://autismconsortium. org), and the Autism Simplex Collection (Buxbaum et al., 2014) have all accumulated substantial sample resources for genetic studies. WES studies using data sets have confirmed advanced parental age as a significant risk factor for increased de novo mutation rates and have elucidated particular biological pathways as potential causal mechanisms. Several hypotheses-driven approaches have been used to uncover rare variations, including analysis of homozygous LOF mutations, or "complete knockouts" in the general ASD population and in individuals with ASD whose parents have shared ancestry, as well as gene-burden analysis of de novo LOF mutations among individuals with ASD and unrelated parents.

Loss-of-Function Mutations

Healthy individuals are estimated to carry approximately 100 mutations per genome that confer loss of function of the gene involved (Macarthur et al., 2012). A hypothesis for a recessive model of ASD inheritance would suggest that some individuals with ASD have by chance developed combinations of LOF alleles in critical genes, such that they have a complete knockout of the function of a particular gene. The possible mechanisms that could result in this mode of inheritance could be inheriting two copies of the same LOF allele (a homozygous state) or inheriting two different LOF alleles (a compound heterozygous state), or only having one copy of an allele that has the LOF mutation on the X chromosome in males. Among individuals with ASD, the chance of occurrence of such rare complete knockouts has been shown in case–control WES studies to be twofold greater than for typically developing controls, with a trend toward brain-expressed genes being overrepresented (Lim et al., 2013). In one study, complete knockouts were rare in both cases and controls, and a recessive LOF mode of inheritance is thought to explain up to approximately 5% of ASD cases (3% by autosomes and 2% by the X chromosome) (Nava et al., 2012).

An individual is more likely to inherit two copies of a complete knockout LOF mutation in instances in which parents are more closely related. In cases in which parents share ancestry, large regions of the genome may be identical between maternally inherited and paternally inherited DNA. These areas are called runs of homozygosity (ROH), and they represent the individual having inherited two copies of the same ancestral chromosomes. ROH have been studied in consanguineous families, isolated populations, and also in a small number of individuals whose parents are not known to be related in order to identify the role that homozygous LOF mutations may play in ASD risk. One such study specifically targeted consanguineous families that have multiple family members with ASD (Yu et al., 2013). In this study, the investigators implicated two genes, *AMT* and *PEX7*, for which partial LOF was found and total LOF was associated with more severe developmental phenotypes. The fraction of the genome covered by ROH is highly variable because even in families not known to be consanguineous, some common ancestry may exist. One study selected the 16 patients with the highest degree of homozygosity from the 1000 AGRE families and performed WES, finding candidate missense mutations in four genes (Chahrour et al., 2012).

Dominant De Novo Coding Variations

Much work has been done recently in elucidating the role of de novo coding variations in ASD risk. In families in which a child with ASD is born to unrelated parents, and no other relatives are affected, de novo mutations are more likely to occur in that child (Levy et al., 2011; Sanders et al., 2012; Sebat et al., 2007). Although de novo mutations may not be inherited or may arise from germline mosaics, they do contribute to some methodological approaches to estimating ASD heritability because they are usually shared between monozygotic twins. WES studies of parent–child trios have been very fruitful in recent years in identifying heterozygous de novo coding mutations in affected children (Iossifov et al., 2012, 2014; Neal et al., 2012; O'Roak et al., 2012a; Poultney et al., 2014; Sanders et al., 2012). These studies have shown that advanced parental age is associated with a higher total number of de novo coding variations in siblings, both affected (those with ASD) and unaffected (those without ASD) (Neal et al., 2012; O'Roak et al., 2012a; Sanders et al., 2012). Mutations found in affected siblings were more likely to be variants of functional importance than were those found in unaffected siblings. Affected siblings were more likely to have de novo nonsense and missense mutations (Iossifov et al., 2014; Neale et al., 2012; O'Roak et al., 2012a; Sanders et al., 2012). Using novel statistical methods, Poultney et al. (2014) found that 22 genes were implicated in autism cases, as well as a set of 107 genes likely to affect risk in greater than 5% of individuals with ASD in their study. The genes identified encode proteins for synapse formation, regulation of transcription, and remodeling of chromatin, and many were implicated in other conditions, such as epilepsy, schizophrenia, and intellectual disability. Another study in SSC conducted by Iossifov et al. (2014) examined affected children, unaffected siblings, and parents and similarly found chromatin modifiers to be affected, as well as fragile X mental retardation protein (FMRP)-associated genes and genes that had been previously implicated in intellectual disability and schizophrenia.

Structural Variants

Perhaps the most productive approach to understanding the genetic architecture of ASD has thus far come from studies investigating variations in genome structure. Structural variants (SVs) can be broadly subdivided into two categories: balanced and unbalanced. Balanced chromosomal rearrangements (BCRs) involve changing structure but without significant gain or loss of genetic material. Unbalanced SVs result in dosage changes of genome segments (i.e., CNVs). Conventional analysis of structural alterations to the chromosomes was reliant on karyotyping, a microscopic technique that enables visualization of chromosome number and structure at approximately 5–10 Mb resolution, depending on banding patterns. In an initial study of SVs at microscopic resolution, Scherer and colleagues reported a rate of karyotypically visible SVs (aneuploidies, translocations, inversions, deletions, and duplications) to be 5.8% in independent ASD cases (Marshall et al., 2008) (Figure 11.2).

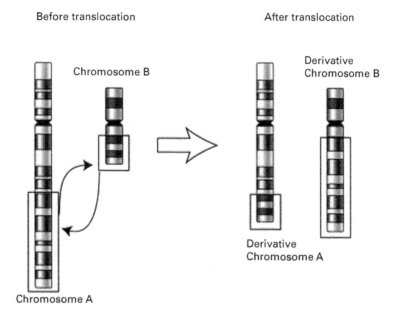

FIGURE 11.2 Translocation is an example of a chromosomal unbalanced structural variation. This drawing depicts an unbalanced translocation between two chromosomes. *Source: Adapted from the National Human Genome Research Institute (http://commons.wikimedia.org/wiki/File:Translocation-4-20.png).*

The availability of higher resolution aCGH and SNP microarray technologies has now made submicroscopic CNVs routinely accessible in basic research and clinical diagnostics; CNVs have been the predominant SV mutational class investigated in ASD to date. Early studies using array-based technologies were able to establish CNVs as a major source of genomic variation (Iafrate et al., 2004; Redon et al., 2006; Sebat et al., 2004), and as reviewed later, such structural chromosomal changes have been robustly established as major contributors to the genetic etiology of ASD. The evaluation of BCRs has been more challenging due to the fact that they are not detected by array technology because the absolute quantity of genetic material is preserved even though structure is not. Thus, karyotyping and labor-intensive serial positional cloning techniques have traditionally been necessary to find genes disrupted by BCRs. However, recent innovations in massively parallel sequencing have rapidly increased the resolution over conventional methods and have opened ready access to such rearrangements for basic research (Korbel et al., 2007; Talkowski, Ernst, et al., 2011).

Copy Number Variations

Reports of the impact of large, de novo CNVs in ASD have been remarkably consistent (Cook & Scherer, 2008), and this has been replicated in virtually every study conducted (Marshall et al., 2008; Pinto et al., 2010; Sanders et al., 2011) (Figure 11.3). These genomic imbalances associated with ASD can be recurrent or non-recurrent events. Recurrent events are usually caused by NAHR between regions of the genome with high homology (or similarity). Rearrangements and copy errors occur in these regions during replication in gametes (during meiosis), leading to development of chromosomes with reciprocal dosage imbalances (deletion and duplication) that are subsequently divided between the resulting

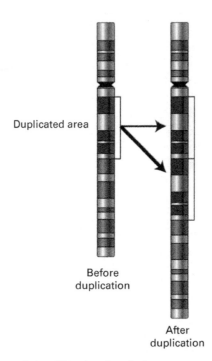

Duplicated area

Before
duplication

After
duplication

FIGURE 11.3 Copy number variation. This drawing depicts a copy number variation in which a region of a chromosome has been duplicated. *Source: Adapted from the National Human Genome Research Institute (http://en.wikipedia.org/wiki/File:Gene-duplication.png).*

ova or spermatozoa. This excess or depletion of genetic material occurs at a significantly increased frequency in individuals with ASD, as well as in those with other disorders, compared to developmentally normal controls. A classic example is the 16p11.2 microdeletion/microduplication syndrome, which confers susceptibility to ASD (Weiss et al., 2008). Other regions of recurrent CNV that have met significant statistical thresholds for association with ASD include 15q11–13 (Van Bon et al., 2009), 22q11.2 (Vorstman et al., 2006), and 1q21.1 (Girirajan, Dennis, et al., 2013).

Studies of recurrent CNVs have also provided insight into the impact of gene dosage on developing ASD. In many ASD-associated loci, risk for similar phenotypes is conferred by reciprocal copy number changes, suggesting the presence of genes whose normal function requires tight dosage control. For example, although associated with a broad spectrum of psychiatric and developmental phenotypes, as well as anthropometric traits (Jacquemont et al., 2011; McCarthy et al., 2009; Walters et al., 2010), both reciprocal gains and losses of 16p11.2 are associated with increased risk of ASD (Kumar et al., 2008; Weiss et al., 2008). Similar findings have been reported for other loci, including 22q11.2, 15q11–13, 1q21.1, and 2q23.1 (Cooper et al., 2011; Pinto et al., 2010; Schneider et al., 2014; Talkowski et al., 2012). The mechanisms by which these reciprocal alterations confer similar phenotypes are unknown and are a focus of ongoing research.

There are other CNVs that commonly disrupt specific genomic regions but are non-recurrent (e.g., not mediated by NAHR due to flanking repetitive sequences). The CNVs from these disruptions are of different sizes and include microdeletion/duplication regions such as 9q34.3 (Smalley, 1998), 2q23.1 (Talkowski, Mullegama, et al., 2011), 1q21 (Mefford et al., 2008), 2q33.1 (Balasubramanian et al., 2011; de Ravel, Balikova, Thiry,

Vermeesch, & Frijns, 2009; Rosenfeld, Ballif, et al., 2009; Talkowski, Ernst, et al., 2011), and 16q24.2 (Handrigan et al., 2013).

Initial research into CNVs revealed association with large genomic segments that included many genes and regulatory elements. However, much like linkage-based approaches, these studies rarely pointed directly to individual genes. Recently, the establishment of large patient cohorts has enabled the identification of critical regions that represent the minimal genomic segment in which non-recurrent CNVs overlap across many cases. Using this strategy, single genes have been identified as contributing to pathology in particular microdeletion or microduplication syndromes; these include *MBD5* in 2q23.1 (Hodge et al., 2014; Talkowski, Mullegama, et al., 2011; Williams et al., 2010), *SATB2* in 2q33.1 (Rosenfeld, Ballif, et al., 2009), *EHMT1* in 9q34.3 (Kleefstra et al., 2012), *CHD1L* in 1q21.1, and *ACACA* in 17p21 (Girirajan, Dennis, et al., 2013). Overall, these discoveries have led to a hypothesis that many of the recurrent changes to genomic segments associated with human disease are attributable to one or a few strong effect genes in the regions affected. It is hoped that these genes may serve as targets for therapeutic intervention.

Unfortunately, this method of using large patient cohorts to identify affected regions is not applicable to recurrent NAHR-mediated imbalances because they are localized to repeated sequences. In one study, researchers performed a series of individual gene knockdowns and overexpression in zebrafish in order to implicate a single contributory locus, *KCTD13*, in neuroanatomical phenotypes of the recurrent 16p11.2 microdeletion/duplication syndrome (Golzio et al., 2012). Similar approaches in other model organisms could provide a feasible approach to dissecting NAHR-mediated recurrent rearrangements, although direct association to the ASD phenotype in animals such as zebrafish is more difficult. In these settings, researchers rely instead on finding a measurable morphological trait or biomarker.

Balanced Chromosomal Rearrangements

In contrast to the large number of studies on the role of CNVs in ASD, few studies have evaluated the impact of BCRs. BCRs can involve balanced translocations, inversions, or excision/insertion events, and in each instance one or more genes can be disrupted at the breakpoints in a relatively balanced manner. Karyotyping at microscopic resolution has traditionally been used to identify BCRs, which has significantly limited the capacity to define individual loci disrupted at the breakpoints without labor- and cost-intensive positional cloning studies. Despite these challenges, positional cloning studies have uncovered a number of highly penetrant gene defects contributing to ASD, including those in *AUTS2* (Sultana et al., 2002), *NRXN1* (Kim et al., 2008), and *EHMT1* (Golzio et al., 2012). Recently, innovations in massively parallel sequencing have enabled detection of BCRs at sequence-based resolution (Chen et al., 2008, 2010; Chiang et al., 2012; Korbel et al., 2007; Talkowski, Ernst, et al., 2011; Talkowski et al., 2012). Snyder and colleagues initially demonstrated the feasibility of the detection of all classes of SV by using NGS methods (Korbel et al., 2007). Talkowski and colleagues performed the first large-scale sequencing study of constitutional BCRs, which revealed a highly complex chromosomal architecture associated with some BCRs in ASD (Chiang et al., 2012), including clustered rearrangements that have been recently dubbed in cancer studies as "chromothripsis"—once thought to be catastrophic chromosomal events that were exclusively somatic in origin (Stephens et al., 2011). Subsequent sequencing of de novo BCRs associated with ASD and related neurodevelopmental phenotypes has revealed a large number of genes whose disruption potentially contributes to these disorders. In these studies, as in exome sequencing studies, it is a challenge to distinguish among the LOF mutations that are benign and well tolerated, that represent highly penetrant pathogenic variations, or that represent moderately penetrant oligogenic/polygenic risk factors.

In one study of 38 subjects, 33 independent genes were found to be disrupted by BCR breakpoints, many of which were novel loci not previously associated with ASD, such as *CHD8, KIRREL3, METTL2B,* and many others (Talkowski et al., 2012). This study used a "convergent genomics" approach to interpret the significance of each gene disrupted by the BCR from the integration of gene expression data, CNVs, and GWAS. For many of the 33 genes, the approach identified a significantly increased CNV burden among more than 33,000 independent cases compared to almost 14,000 independent controls. Importantly, the study also found a significant association of ASD with common SNP alleles from the GWAS approach when considering these 33 genes, suggesting that outright inactivation in some persons and polymorphic variation of the same gene in many more individuals can both contribute to risk of neurodevelopmental abnormality. The study also found that these same genes were enriched for polygenic risk loci for schizophrenia GWAS studies, suggesting that these loci, many of which were involved in chromatin modification and transcriptional regulation, could confer pleiotropic effects across formal diagnostic boundaries. These data firmly support the hypothesis that many ASD-associated SVs disrupt genes that are under tight dosage regulation and that perturbations of their normal dosage of expression can affect the risk of developing a spectrum of neurodevelopmental phenotypes, including ASD.

FUNCTIONAL AND CLINICAL IMPLICATIONS

The initial fundamental hypothesis about ASD is that it is a clinical phenotype with a neurobiological cause distinct from other genetic or neurodevelopmental disorders, related to pathological processes that affect the development and function of neuronal synapses. This hypothesis has been partially supported by genetic research. For example, mutations in genes encoding members of protein families involved in cell signaling, cell adhesion, synaptic function, or plasticity have been strongly aligned with this hypothesis, including SHANK (Berkel et al., 2012; Gauthier et al., 2009; Leblond et al., 2012, 2014; Moessner et al., 2007; Pinto et al., 2010; Sato et al., 2012), neurexins (Gauthier et al., 2011; Kim et al., 2008; Vaags et al., 2012), neuroligin proteins (Glessner et al., 2009; Jamain et al., 2003), glutamate receptors (Talkowski et al., 2012), brain-derived neurotrophic factor (Ernst et al., 2012), KIRREL3 (Talkowski et al., 2012), and TSC1–TSC2 and mTOR and FMRP signaling pathways (Auerbach, Osterwell, & Bear, 2011). All of these proteins play a role in the interconnected network of proteins related to synaptic function, and many have been specifically implicated in ASD (Ebert & Greenberg, 2013).

However, a significant number of genetic discoveries in ASD suggest that diverse biological pathways contribute to this disorder and that these ASD-related genes have an etiological role in a spectrum of human developmental abnormalities and psychopathology rather than ASD alone. Gene network and gene set enrichment analyses have implicated a variety of networks and pathways associated with ASD (Ben-David & Shifman, 2012, 2013; Pinto et al., 2010; Voineagu et al., 2011). One such risk factor is CHD8, a chromodomain helicase involved in chromatin remodeling and transcriptional repression that was discovered to be disrupted by translocation in an individual with ASD (Talkowski et al., 2012), as well as by de novo LOF mutations in multiple exome sequencing studies (Neale et al., 2012; O'Roak et al., 2012b; Sanders et al., 2012). The *CHD8* gene was also associated with an increased CNV burden from both deletion and duplication in individuals with ASD or with macrocephaly and various developmental outcomes (O'Roak et al., 2012b; Talkowski et al., 2012). Follow-up studies of patients with CHD8 mutations and functional genomic analyses of neuronal cells with suppression of CHD8 have both suggested that CHD8 alterations may define a subtype of ASD early in development (Bernier et al., 2014; Sugathan et al., 2014). Point mutations in TCF4, which encodes a transcriptional regulator, have been shown to result in Pitt–Hopkins syndrome (Pitt & Hopkins, 1978; Rosenfeld, Leppig, et al., 2009), and disruption by a balanced translocation has been associated with ASD and other neurodevelopmental outcomes (Rosenfeld, Leppig, et al., 2009; Talkowski et al., 2012). Common variants in TCF4 have also been among the most significant genome-wide risk factors for schizophrenia and other psychiatric disorders (Cross-Disorder Group, 2013; Ripke et al., 2013). Disruption of *MBD5* by multiple independent BCRs has also been shown in patients with ASD, intellectual disability, epilepsy, and even later onset neurobehavioral regression (Chung et al., 2011; Hodge et al., 2014; Mullegama et al., 2014; Talkowski, Mullegama, et al., 2011; Talkowski et al., 2012; Williams et al., 2010). *MBD5* encodes a member of the methyl CpG-binding domain family of proteins that includes MeCP2, a known causal locus in Rett syndrome. Numerous other genes encoding transcriptional regulators and chromatin modifiers have emerged from SV and exome sequencing studies that have strongly implicated these global regulators of gene expression in ASD, as well as other diverse developmental and psychiatric phenotypes.

The heterogeneity in ASD is commonly thought to be related to a "final common pathway" model, relating ultimately to synaptic dysfunction. However, it is unclear how the genes and proteins presented previously would fit within this model, given that they are not limited to synapses. Thus, this is an active area of research. The links between ASD and other developmental phenotypes, as well psychiatric traits, are now well recognized from numerous CNV, BCR, and GWAS studies, as reviewed previously. Future research on the complex biological pathways involved in developing ASD will include determining whether there are definable endophenotypes with distinct genetic etiologies embedded among broader disease phenotypes. Furthermore, elucidating the genetic modifiers or environmental effects that may predispose an individual to a specific phenotypic outcome will be fundamental to understanding the etiology of ASD (Figure 11.4).

In all of the large studies reviewed previously, each individual genetic alteration identified explains a meaningful, but still small, proportion of the overall disease variance, with the most common risk factors, such as 16p11.2 alterations, accounting for approximately 1% of all ASD cases. However, it is important to recognize that all approaches discussed (GWAS, WES, and SV) have been applied in studies that were underpowered and therefore could detect only the strongest, most frequent contributors. The evidence from many other neuropsychiatric disorders, such as schizophrenia, indicates that polygenic effects are relatively weak but are increasingly detectable with adequate statistical power. To date, researchers studying rare exome variants have been able to investigate only the risk associated with de novo LOF mutations and have not been able to perform tests adequately powered for the full mutational spectrum, including synonymous, non-synonymous, and inherited variants, although such studies are ongoing. Similarly, studies of SVs have generally not accounted for small or multiallelic CNVs or for recurrent BCRs. Finally, submicroscopic balanced

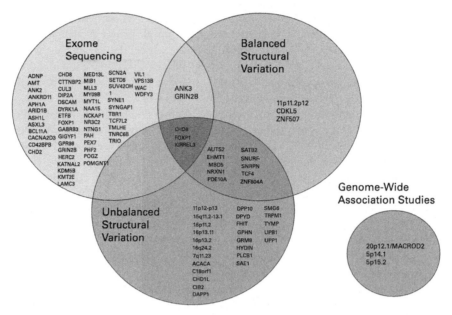

FIGURE 11.4 Autism risk is affected by overlapping sets of genes and loci. Exome sequencing has identified single nucleotide variants and small insertions/deletions. Unbalanced structural variations (whole-gene or chromosomal region deletions and duplications) and balanced structural variations (translocation, inversions, and chromothripsis) are shown. Genes and loci implicated are listed (specific studies are cited in the chapter). Also listed are signals reported in genome-wide association studies. *Source: Updated from Talkowski et al. (2014).*

events and small CNVs have not been studied in any capacity to date due to methodological limitations, although such studies are also ongoing.

The discoveries to date in the genetics of ASD show great promise, and we anticipate further contributions from future studies, especially those that address the interaction of genetic background and environmental factors that drive phenotypic outcomes. The discovery of a strong association between ASD and genes involved in epigenetic regulation opens at least one route to exploring potential environmental influences on such regulation. These studies could then potentially lead to identifying modifiable risk factors, as well as identifying targets for potential therapeutics.

SUMMARY

As reviewed in this chapter, the discovery of novel genetic factors contributing to ASD etiology has yielded remarkable insight in the past several years. There remains much debate in the field regarding the precise genetic architecture of ASD, with models ranging from those with common variation explaining the largest proportion of disease risk to those implicating rare but relatively penetrant risk factors that, although collectively important, individually explain very little of the overall disease risk of an individual. However, the advancement of genomic technologies and the capacity to perform unbiased genome-wide surveys for genomic variants that contribute risk to ASD have definitively proven a major genetic basis for ASD etiology.

KEY POINTS

- Identical twins with ASD have an average concordance rate of 64%, and fraternal twins have a concordance rate of 9% for ASD.
- Whole-exome sequencing studies of parent–child trios have shown that advanced paternal age is associated with a higher total number of de novo coding variants in siblings, both affected and unaffected.
- One hypothesis states that mutations in genes encoding members of protein families involved in cell signaling, cell adhesion, synaptic function, or plasticity result in a clinical phenotype with a neurobiological cause distinct from other genetic or neurodevelopmental disorders.
- Another hypothesis states the diverse biological pathways may contribute to ASD and that underlying ASD-related genes have an etiological role in a spectrum of human developmental abnormalities and psychopathology, rather than ASD alone.
- Future studies will address the interaction of genetic background and environmental factors that drive phenotypic outcomes.

DISCLOSURE STATEMENT

Dr. Yamini J. Howe has received funding from Autism Consortium for a research study in biomarkers in autism.

Dr. Harrison Brand has no conflicts to disclose. He is funded by the National Institutes of Health (T32HD007396).

Dr. Michael E. Talkowski has no conflicts to disclose. He is funded by the National Institutes of Health (R00MH095867 and R01HD081256), the Simons Foundation for Autism Research, the Nancy Lurie Marks Family Foundation, the March of Dimes, the Charles Hood Foundation, NARSAD, the Collaborative Center for X-Linked Dystonia Parkinsonism, and the CHARGE syndrome foundation.

REFERENCES

American Psychiatric Association. (2013). *Diagnostic and statistical manual of mental disorders* (5th ed.). Arlington, VA: American Psychiatric Publishing.

Anney, R., Klei, L., Pinto, D., Regan, R., Conroy, J., Magalhaes, T. R., et al. (2010). A genome-wide scan for common alleles affecting risk for autism. *Human Molecular Genetics, 19*(20), 4072–4082. doi:10.1093/hmg/ddq307

Auerbach, B. D., Osterweil, E. K., & Bear, M. F. (2011). Mutations causing syndromic autism define an axis of synaptic pathophysiology. *Nature, 480*(7375), 63–68. doi:10.1038/nature10658

Bailey, A., Le Couteur, A., Gottesman, I., Bolton, P., Simonoff, E., Yuzda, E., & Rutter, M. (1995). Autism as a strongly genetic disorder: Evidence from a British twin study. *Psychological Medicine, 25*(1), 63–77.

Balasubramanian, M., Smith, K., Basel-Vanagaite, L., Feingold, M. F., Brock, P., Gowans, G. C., . . . Parker, M. J. (2011). Case series: 2q33.1 microdeletion syndrome—Further delineation of the phenotype. *Journal of Medical Genetics, 48*(5), 290–298. doi:10.1136/jmg.2010.084491

Ben-David, E., & Shifman, S. (2012). Networks of neuronal genes affected by common and rare variants in autism spectrum disorders. *PLoS Genetics, 8*(3), e1002556. doi:10.1371/journal.pgen.1002556

Ben-David, E., & Shifman, S. (2013). Combined analysis of exome sequencing points toward a major role for transcription regulation during brain development in autism *Molecular Psychiatry, 18*, 1054–1056.

Bernier, R., Golzio, C., Xiong, B., Stessman, H. A., Coe, B. P., Penn, O., . . . Eichler, E. E. (2014). Disruptive CHD8 mutations define a subtype of autism early in development. *Cell, 158*(2), 263–276. doi:10.1016/j. cell.2014.06.017

Betancur, C. (2011). Etiological heterogeneity in autism spectrum disorders: More than 100 genetic and genomic disorders and still counting. *Brain Research, 1380*, 42–77. doi:10.1016/j.brainres.2010.11.078

Beunders, G., Voorhoeve, E., Golzio, C., Pardo, L. M., Rosenfeld, J. A., Talkowski, M. E., . . . Sistermans, E. A. (2013). Exonic deletions in AUTS2 cause a syndromic form of intellectual disability and suggest a critical role for the C terminus. *American Journal of Human Genetics, 92*(2), 210–220. doi:10.1016/j. ajhg.2012.12.011

Bolton, P. F., & Griffiths, P. D. (1997). Association of tuberous sclerosis of temporal lobes with autism and atypical autism. *Lancet, 349*(9049), 392–395. doi:10.1016/s0140-6736(97)80012-8

Brown, W. T., Jenkins, E. C., Friedman, E., Brooks, J., Wisniewski, K., Raguthu, S., & French, J. (1982). Autism is associated with the fragile-X syndrome. *Journal of Autism and Developmental Disorders, 12*(3), 303–308.

Butler, M. G., Dasouki, M. J., Zhou, X. P., Talebizadeh, Z., Brown, M., Takahashi, T. N., . . . Eng, C. (2005). Subset of individuals with autism spectrum disorders and extreme macrocephaly associated with germline PTEN tumour suppressor gene mutations. *Journal of Medical Genetics, 42*(4), 318–321. doi:10.1136/jmg.2004.024646

Buxbaum, J. D., Bolshakova, N., Brownfeld, J. M., Anney, R. J., Bender, P., Bernier, R., . . . Gallagher, L. (2014). The Autism Simplex Collection: An international, expertly phenotyped autism sample for genetic and phenotypic analyses. *Molecular Autism, 5*, 34. doi:10.1186/2040-2392-5-34

Centers for Disease Control and Prevention. (2014). Prevalence of autism spectrum disorder among children aged 8 years—Autism and Developmental Disabilities Monitoring Network, United States, 2010. *MMWR Surveillance Summaries, 63*(No. SS2), 1–20. doi:ss5810a1 [pii]

Chahrour, M. H., Yu, T. W., Lim, E. T., Ataman, B., Coulter, M. E., Hill, R. S., . . . Walsh, C. A. (2012). Whole-exome sequencing and homozygosity analysis implicate depolarization-regulated neuronal genes in autism. *PLoS Genetics, 8*(4), e1002635. doi:10.1371/journal.pgen.1002635

Chen, W., Kalscheuer, V., Tzschach, A., Menzel, C., Ullmann, R., Schulz, M. H., . . . Ropers, H. H. (2008). Mapping translocation breakpoints by next-generation sequencing. *Genome Research, 18*(7), 1143–1149. doi:10.1101/gr.076166.108

Chen, W., Ullmann, R., Langnick, C., Menzel, C., Wotschofsky, Z., Hu, H., . . . Ropers, H. H. (2010). Breakpoint analysis of balanced chromosome rearrangements by next-generation paired-end sequencing. *European Journal of Human Genetics, 18*(5), 539–543. doi:10.1038/ejhg.2009.211

Chiang, C., Jacobsen, J. C., Ernst, C., Hanscom, C., Heilbut, A., Blumenthal, I., . . . Talkowski, M. E. (2012). Complex reorganization and predominant non-homologous repair following chromosomal breakage in karyotypically balanced germline rearrangements and transgenic integration. *Nature Genetics, 44*(4), 390–397, s391. doi:10.1038/ng.2202

Chung, B. H., Stavropoulos, J., Marshall, C. R., Weksberg, R., Scherer, S. W., & Yoon, G. (2011). 2q23 de novo microdeletion involving the *MBD5* gene in a patient with developmental delay, postnatal microcephaly and distinct facial features. *American Journal of Medical Genetics Part A, 155A*(2), 424–429. doi:10.1002/ajmg.a.33821

Constantino, J. N., Zhang, Y., Frazier, T., Abbacchi, A. M., & Law, P. (2010). Sibling recurrence and the genetic epidemiology of autism. *American Journal of Psychiatry, 167*(11), 1349–1356. doi:10.1176/appi. ajp.2010.09101470

Cook, E. H., Jr., & Scherer, S. W. (2008). Copy-number variations associated with neuropsychiatric conditions. *Nature, 455*(7215), 919–923. doi:10.1038/nature07458

Cooper, G. M., Coe, B. P., Girirajan, S., Rosenfeld, J. A., Vu, T. H., Baker, C., . . . Eichler, E. E. (2011). A copy number variation morbidity map of developmental delay. *Nature Genetics, 43*(9), 838–846. doi:10.1038/ng.909

Cross-Disorder Group of the Psychiatric Genomics Consortium. (2013). Identification of risk loci with shared effects on five major psychiatric disorders: A genome-wide analysis. *Lancet, 381*(9875), 1371–1379. doi:10.1016/s0140-6736(12)62129-1

de Ravel, T. J., Balikova, I., Thiry, P., Vermeesch, J. R., & Frijns, J. P. (2009). Another patient with a de novo deletion further delineates the 2q33.1 microdeletion syndrome. *European Journal of Medical Genetics, 52*(2–3), 120–122. doi:10.1016/j.ejmg.2009.01.002

Devlin, B., Melhem, N., & Roeder, K. (2011). Do common variants play a role in risk for autism? Evidence and theoretical musings. *Brain Research, 1380*, 78–84. doi:10.1016/j.brainres.2010.11.026

Ebert, D. H., & Greenberg, M. E. (2013). Activity-dependent neuronal signalling and autism spectrum disorder. *Nature, 493*(7432), 327–337. doi:10.1038/nature11860

Ernst, C., Marshall, C. R., Shen, Y., Metcalfe, K., Rosenfeld, J., Hodge, J. C., . . . Talkowski, M. E. (2012). Highly penetrant alterations of a critical region including BDNF in human psychopathology and obesity. *Archives of General Psychiatry, 69*(12), 1238–1246. doi:10.1001/archgenpsychiatry.2012.660

Fischbach, G. D., & Lord, C. (2010). The Simons Simplex Collection: A resource for identification of autism genetic risk factors. *Neuron, 68*(2), 192–195. doi:10.1016/j.neuron.2010.10.006

Fombonne, E. (2003). Epidemiological surveys of autism and other pervasive developmental disorders: An update. *Journal of Autism and Developmental Disorders, 33*(4), 365–382.

Gaugler, T., Klei, L., Sanders, S. J., Bodea, C. A., Goldberg, A. P., Lee, A. B., . . . Buxbaum, J. D. (2014). Most genetic risk for autism resides with common variation. *Nature Genetics, 46*(8), 881–885. doi:10.1038/ng.3039

Gauthier, J., Siddiqui, T. J., Huashan, P., Yokomaku, D., Hamdan, F. F., Champagne, N., . . . Rouleau, G. A. (2011). Truncating mutations in NRXN2 and NRXN1 in autism spectrum disorders and schizophrenia. *Human Genetics, 130*(4), 563–573. doi:10.1007/s00439-011-0975-z

Gauthier, J., Spiegelman, D., Piton, A., Lafreniere, R. G., Laurent, S., St-Onge, J., . . . Rouleau, G. A. (2009). Novel de novo SHANK3 mutation in autistic patients. *American Journal of Medical Genetics Part B: Neuropsychiatrics Genetics, 150B*(3), 421–424. doi:10.1002/ajmg.b.30822

Gillberg, C., & Forsell, C. (1984). Childhood psychosis and neurofibromatosis—More than a coincidence? *Journal of Autism and Developmental Disorders, 14*(1), 1–8.

Girirajan, S., Dennis, M. Y., Baker, C., Malig, M., Coe, B. P., Campbell, C. D., . . . Eichler, E. E. (2013). Refinement and discovery of new hotspots of copy-number variation associated with autism spectrum disorder. *American Journal of Human Genetics, 92*(2), 221–237. doi:10.1016/j.ajhg.2012.12.016

Girirajan, S., Johnson, R. L., Tassone, F., Balciuniene, J., Katiyar, N., Fox, K., . . . Selleck, S. B. (2013). Global increases in both common and rare copy number load associated with autism. *Human Molecular Genetics, 22*(14), 2870–2880. doi:10.1093/hmg/ddt136

Glessner, J. T., Wang, K., Cai, G., Korvatska, O., Kim, C. E., Wood, S., . . . Hakonarson, H. (2009). Autism genome-wide copy number variation reveals ubiquitin and neuronal genes. *Nature, 459*(7246), 569–573. doi:10.1038/nature07953

Golzio, C., Willer, J., Talkowski, M. E., Oh, E. C., Taniguchi, Y., Jacquemont, S., . . . Katsanis, N. (2012). KCTD13 is a major driver of mirrored neuroanatomical phenotypes of the 16p11.2 copy number variant. *Nature, 485*(7398), 363–367. doi:10.1038/nature11091

Handrigan, G. R., Chitayat, D., Lionel, A. C., Pinsk, M., Vaags, A. K., Marshall, C. R., . . . Rosenblum, N. D. (2013). Deletions in 16q24.2 are associated with autism spectrum disorder, intellectual disability and congenital renal malformation. *Journal of Medical Genetics, 50*(3), 163–173. doi:10.1136/jmedgenet-2012-101288

Hodge, J. C., Mitchell, E., Pillalamarri, V., Toler, T. L., Bartel, F., Kearney, H. M., . . . Talkowski, M. E. (2014). Disruption of MBD5 contributes to a spectrum of psychopathology and neurodevelopmental abnormalities. *Molecular Psychiatry, 19*(3), 368–379. doi:10.1038/mp.2013.42

Iafrate, A. J., Feuk, L., Rivera, M. N., Listewnik, M. L., Donahoe, P. K., Qi, Y., . . . Lee, C. (2004). Detection of large-scale variation in the human genome. *Nature Genetics, 36*(9), 949–951. doi:10.1038/ng1416

Iossifov, I., O'Roak, B. J., Sanders, S. J., Ronemus, M., Krumm, N., Levy, D., . . . Wigler, M. (2014). The contribution of de novo coding mutations to autism spectrum disorder. *Nature, 515*(7526), 216–221. doi:10.1038/nature13908

Iossifov, I., Ronemus, M., Levy, D., Wang, Z., Hakker, I., Rosenbaum, J., . . . Wigler, M. (2012). De novo gene disruptions in children on the autistic spectrum. *Neuron, 74*(2), 285–299. doi:10.1016/j. neuron.2012.04.009

Jacquemont, S., Reymond, A., Zufferey, F., Harewood, L., Walters, R. G., Kutalik, Z., . . . Froguel, P. (2011). Mirror extreme BMI phenotypes associated with gene dosage at the chromosome 16p11.2 locus. *Nature, 478*(7367), 97–102. doi:10.1038/nature10406

Jamain, S., Quach, H., Betancur, C., Rastam, M., Colineaux, C., Gillberg, I. C., . . . Bourgeron, T. (2003). Mutations of the X-linked genes encoding neuroligins NLGN3 and NLGN4 are associated with autism. *Nature Genetics, 34*(1), 27–29. doi:10.1038/ng1136

Kim, H. G., Kishikawa, S., Higgins, A. W., Seong, I. S., Donovan, D. J., Shen, Y., . . . Gusella, J. F. (2008). Disruption of neurexin 1 associated with autism spectrum disorder. *American Journal of Human Genetics, 82*(1), 199–207. doi:10.1016/j.ajhg.2007.09.011

Kleefstra, T., Kramer, J. M., Neveling, K., Willemsen, M. H., Koemans, T. S., Vissers, L. E., . . . van Bokhoven, H. (2012). Disruption of an EHMT1-associated chromatin-modification module causes intellectual disability. *American Journal of Human Genetics, 91*(1), 73–82. doi:10.1016/j.ajhg.2012.05.003

Klei, L., Sanders, S. J., Murtha, M. T., Hus, V., Lowe, J. K., Willsey, A. J., . . . Devlin, B. (2012). Common genetic variants, acting additively, are a major source of risk for autism. *Molecular Autism, 3*(1), 9. doi:10.1186/2040-2392-3-9

Korbel, J. O., Urban, A. E., Affourtit, J. P., Godwin, B., Grubert, F., Simons, J. F., . . . Snyder, M. (2007). Paired-end mapping reveals extensive structural variation in the human genome. *Science, 318*(5849), 420–426. doi:10.1126/science.1149504

Kumar, R. A., KaraMohamed, S., Sudi, J., Conrad, D. F., Brune, C., Badner, J. A., . . . Christian, S. L. (2008). Recurrent 16p11.2 microdeletions in autism. *Human Molecular Genetics, 17*(4), 628–638. doi:10.1093/ hmg/ddm376

Lajonchere, C. M. (2010). Changing the landscape of autism research: The autism genetic resource exchange. *Neuron, 68*(2), 187–191. doi:10.1016/j.neuron.2010.10.009

Lam, C. W., Yeung, W. L., Ko, C. H., Poon, P. M., Tong, S. F., Chan, K. Y., . . . Fok, T. F. (2000). Spectrum of mutations in the *MECP2* gene in patients with infantile autism and Rett syndrome. *Journal of Medical Genetics, 37*(12), E41.

Leblond, C. S., Heinrich, J., Delorme, R., Proepper, C., Betancur, C., Huguet, G., . . . Bourgeron, T. (2012). Genetic and functional analyses of SHANK2 mutations suggest a multiple hit model of autism spectrum disorders. *PLoS Genetics, 8*(2), e1002521. doi:10.1371/journal.pgen.1002521

Leblond, C. S., Nava, C., Polge, A., Gauthier, J., Huguet, G., Lumbroso, S., . . . Bourgeron, T. (2014). Meta-analysis of SHANK mutations in autism spectrum disorders: A gradient of severity in cognitive impairments. *PLoS Genetics, 10*(9), e1004580. doi:10.1371/journal.pgen.1004580

Levy, D., Ronemus, M., Yamrom, B., Lee, Y. H., Leotta, A., Kendall, J., . . . Wigler, M. (2011). Rare de novo and transmitted copy-number variation in autistic spectrum disorders. *Neuron, 70*(5), 886–897. doi:10.1016/j.neuron.2011.05.015

Lim, E. T., Raychaudhuri, S., Sanders, S. J., Stevens, C., Sabo, A., MacArthur, D. G., . . . Daly, M. J. (2013). Rare complete knockouts in humans: Population distribution and significant role in autism spectrum disorders. *Neuron, 77*(2), 235–242. doi:10.1016/j.neuron.2012.12.029

Lionel, A. C., Vaags, A. K., Sato, D., Gazzellone, M. J., Mitchell, E. B., Chen, H. Y., . . . Scherer, S. W. (2013). Rare exonic deletions implicate the synaptic organizer Gephyrin (GPHN) in risk for autism, schizophrenia and seizures. *Human Molecular Genetics, 22*(10), 2055–2066. doi:10.1093/hmg/ddt056

MacArthur, D. G., Balasubramanian, S., Frankish, A., Huang, N., Morris, J., Walter, K., . . . Tyler-Smith, C. (2012). A systematic survey of loss-of-function variants in human protein-coding genes. *Science, 335*(6070), 823–828. doi:10.1126/science.1215040

Manning, M., & Hudgins, L. (2007). Use of array-based technology in the practice of medical genetics. *Genetics in Medicine, 9*(9), 650–653. doi:10.1097GIM.0b013e31814cec3a

Marshall, C. R., Noor, A., Vincent, J. B., Lionel, A. C., Feuk, L., Skaug, J., ... Scherer, S. W. (2008). Structural variation of chromosomes in autism spectrum disorder. *American Journal of Human Genetics, 82*(2), 477–488. doi:10.1016/j.ajhg.2007.12.009

Mefford, H. C., Sharp, A. J., Baker, C., Itsara, A., Jiang, Z., Buysse, K., ... Eichler, E. E. (2008). Recurrent rearrangements of chromosome 1q21.1 and variable pediatric phenotypes. *New England Journal of Medicine, 359*(16), 1685–1699. doi:10.1056/NEJMoa0805384

Michaelson, J. J., Shi, Y., Gujral, M., Zheng, H., Malhotra, D., Jin, X., ... Sebat, J. (2012). Whole-genome sequencing in autism identifies hot spots for de novo germline mutation. *Cell, 151*(7), 1431–1442. doi:10.1016/j.cell.2012.11.019

Miles, J. H. (2011). Autism spectrum disorders—A genetics review. *Genetics in Medicine, 13*(4), 278–294. doi:10.1097/GIM.0b013e3181ff67ba

Moessner, R., Marshall, C. R., Sutcliffe, J. S., Skaug, J., Pinto, D., Vincent, J., ... Scherer, S. W. (2007). Contribution of SHANK3 mutations to autism spectrum disorder. *American Journal of Human Genetics, 81*(6), 1289–1297. doi:10.1086/522590

Mullegama, S. V., Rosenfeld, J. A., Orellana, C., van Bon, B. W., Halbach, S., Repnikova, E. A., ... Elsea, S. H. (2014). Reciprocal deletion and duplication at 2q23.1 indicates a role for MBD5 in autism spectrum disorder. *European Journal of Human Genetics, 22*(1), 57–63. doi:10.1038/ejhg.2013.67

Nava, C., Lamari, F., Heron, D., Mignot, C., Rastetter, A., Keren, B., ... Depienne, C. (2012). Analysis of the chromosome X exome in patients with autism spectrum disorders identified novel candidate genes, including TMLHE. *Translational Psychiatry, 2*, e179. doi:10.1038/tp.2012.102

Neale, B. M., Kou, Y., Liu, L., Ma'ayan, A., Samocha, K. E., Sabo, A., ... Daly, M. J. (2012). Patterns and rates of exonic de novo mutations in autism spectrum disorders. *Nature, 485*(7397), 242–245. doi:10.1038/nature11011

O'Roak, B. J., Vives, L., Girirajan, S., Karakoc, E., Krumm, N., Coe, B. P., ... Eicher, E. E. (2012a). Sporadic autism exomes reveal a highly interconnected protein network of de novo mutations. *Nature, 485*(7397), 246–250. doi:10.1038/nature10989.

O'Roak, B. J., Vives, L., Fu, W., Egertson, J. D., Stanaway, I. B., Phelps, I. G., ... Shendure, J. (2012b). Multiplex targeted sequencing identifies recurrently mutated genes in autism spectrum disorders. *Science, 338*(6114), 1619–1622. doi:10.1126/science.1227764

Ozonoff, S., Young, G. S., Carter, A., Messinger, D., Yirmiya, N., Zwaigenbaum, L., ... Stone, W. L. (2011). Recurrence risk for autism spectrum disorders: A Baby Siblings Research Consortium study. *Pediatrics, 128*(3), e488–e495. doi:10.1542/peds.2010-2825

Pinto, D., Pagnamenta, A. T., Klei, L., Anney, R., Merico, D., Regan, R., ... Betancur, C. (2010). Functional impact of global rare copy number variation in autism spectrum disorders. *Nature, 466*(7304), 368–372. doi:10.1038/nature09146

Pitt, D., & Hopkins, I. (1978). A syndrome of mental retardation, wide mouth and intermittent overbreathing. *Australian Paediatric Journal, 14*(3), 182–184.

Poultney, C. S., Samocha, K., Kou, Y., Liu, L., Walker, S., Singh, T., ... Roeder, K. (2014). Synaptic, transcriptional and chromatin genes disrupted in autism. *Nature, 515*(7526), 209–215. doi:10.1038/nature13772

Redon, R., Ishikawa, S., Fitch, K. R., Feuk, L., Perry, G. H., Andrews, T. D., ... Hurles, M. E. (2006). Global variation in copy number in the human genome. *Nature, 444*(7118), 444–454. doi:10.1038/nature05329

Ripke, S., Wray, N. R., Lewis, C. M., Hamilton, S. P., Weissman, M. M., Breen, G., ... Sullivan, P. F. (2013). A mega-analysis of genome-wide association studies for major depressive disorder. *Molecular Psychiatry, 18*(4), 497–511. doi:10.1038/mp.2012.21

Rosenfeld, J. A., Ballif, B. C., Lucas, A., Spence, E. J., Powell, C., Aylsworth, A. S., ... Shaffer, L. G. (2009). Small deletions of SATB2 cause some of the clinical features of the 2q33.1 microdeletion syndrome. *PLoS One, 4*(8), e6568. doi:10.1371/journal.pone.0006568

Rosenfeld, J. A., Ballif, B. C., Torchia, B. S., Sahoo, T., Ravnan, J. B., Schultz, R., . . . Shaffer, L. G. (2010). Copy number variations associated with autism spectrum disorders contribute to a spectrum of neurodevelopmental disorders. *Genetics in Medicine, 12*(11), 694–702. doi:10.1097/GIM.0b013e3181f0c5f3

Rosenfeld, J. A., Leppig, K., Ballif, B. C., Thiese, H., Erdie-Lalena, C., Bawle, E., . . . Shaffer, L. G. (2009). Genotype–phenotype analysis of TCF4 mutations causing Pitt–Hopkins syndrome shows increased seizure activity with missense mutations. *Genetics in Medicine, 11*(11), 797–805. doi:10.1097/GIM.0b013e3181bd38a9

Sanders, S. J., Ercan-Sencicek, A. G., Hus, V., Luo, R., Murtha, M. T., Moreno-De-Luca, D., . . . State, M. W. (2011). Multiple recurrent de novo CNVs, including duplications of the 7q11.23 Williams syndrome region, are strongly associated with autism. *Neuron, 70*(5), 863–885. doi:10.1016/j.neuron.2011.05.002

Sanders, S. J., Murtha, M. T., Gupta, A. R., Murdoch, J. D., Raubeson, M. J., Willsey, A. J., . . . State, M. W. (2012). De novo mutations revealed by whole-exome sequencing are strongly associated with autism. *Nature, 485*(7397), 237–241. doi:10.1038/nature10945

Sandin, S., Lichtenstein, P., Kuja-Halkola, R., Larsson, H., Hultman, C. M., & Reichenberg, A. (2014). The familial risk of autism. *JAMA, 311*(17), 1770–1777. doi:10.1001/jama.2014.4144

Sato, D., Lionel, A. C., Leblond, C. S., Prasad, A., Pinto, D., Walker, S., . . . Scherer, S. W. (2012). SHANK1 deletions in males with autism spectrum disorder. *American Journal of Human Genetics, 90*(5), 879–887. doi:10.1016/j.ajhg.2012.03.017

Schizophrenia Psychiatric Genome-Wide Association Study (GWAS) Consortium. (2014). Biological insights from 108 schizophrenia-associated genetic loci. *Nature, 511*(7510), 421–427. doi:10.1038/nature13595

Schneider, M., Debbane, M., Bassett, A. S., Chow, E. W., Fung, W. L., van den Bree, M., . . . Eliez, S. (2014). Psychiatric disorders from childhood to adulthood in 22q11.2 deletion syndrome: Results from the International Consortium on Brain and Behavior in 22q11.2 Deletion Syndrome. *American Journal of Psychiatry, 171*(6), 627–639. doi:10.1176/appi.ajp.2013.13070864

Sebat, J., Lakshmi, B., Malhotra, D., Troge, J., Lese-Martin, C., Walsh, T., . . . Wigler, M. (2007). Strong association of de novo copy number mutations with autism. *Science, 316*(5823), 445–449. doi:10.1126/science.1138659

Sebat, J., Lakshmi, B., Troge, J., Alexander, J., Young, J., Lundin, P., . . . Wigler, M. (2004). Large-scale copy number polymorphism in the human genome. *Science, 305*(5683), 525–528. doi:10.1126/science.1098918

Smalley, S. L. (1998). Autism and tuberous sclerosis. *Journal of Autism and Developmental Disorders, 28*(5), 407–414.

Smalley, S. L., Asarnow, R. F., & Spence, M. A. (1988). Autism and genetics: A decade of research. *Archives of General Psychiatry, 45*(10), 953–961.

Steffenburg, S., Gillberg, C. L., Steffenburg, U., & Kyllerman, M. (1996). Autism in Angelman syndrome: A population-based study. *Pediatric Neurology, 14*(2), 131–136.

Stephens, P. J., Greenman, C. D., Fu, B., Yang, F., Bignell, G. R., Mudie, L. J., . . . Campbell, P. J. (2011). Massive genomic rearrangement acquired in a single catastrophic event during cancer development. *Cell, 144*(1), 27–40. doi:10.1016/j.cell.2010.11.055

Strauss, K. A., Puffenberger, E. G., Huentelman, M. J., Gottlieb, S., Dobrin, S. E., Parod, J. M., . . . Morton, D. H. (2006). Recessive symptomatic focal epilepsy and mutant contactin-associated protein-like 2. *New England Journal of Medicine, 354*(13), 1370–1377. doi:10.1056/NEJMoa052773

Sugathan, A., Biagioli, M., Golzio, C., Erdin, S., Blumenthal, I., Manavalan, P., . . . Talkowski, M. E. (2014). CHD8 regulates neurodevelopmental pathways associated with autism spectrum disorder in neural progenitors. *Proceedings of the National Academy of Sciences of the USA, 111*(42), E4468–E4477. doi:10.1073/pnas.1405266111

Sultana, R., Yu, C. E., Yu, J., Munson, J., Chen, D., Hua, W., . . . Villacres, E. C. (2002). Identification of a novel gene on chromosome 7q11.2 interrupted by a translocation breakpoint in a pair of autistic twins. *Genomics, 80*(2), 129–134.

Talkowski, M. E., Ernst, C., Heilbut, A., Chiang, C., Hanscom, C., Lindgren, A., . . . Gusella, J. F. (2011). Next-generation sequencing strategies enable routine detection of balanced chromosome rearrangements for clinical diagnostics and genetic research. *American Journal of Human Genetics*, *88*(4), 469–481. doi:10.1016/j.ajhg.2011.03.013

Talkowski, M. E., Minikel, E. V., & Gusella, J. F. (2014). Autism spectrum disorder genetics: Diverse genes with diverse clinical outcomes. *Harvard Review of Psychiatry*, *22*(2), 65–75. doi:10.1097/hrp.0000000000000002

Talkowski, M. E., Mullegama, S. V., Rosenfeld, J. A., van Bon, B. W., Shen, Y., Repnikova, E. A., . . . Elsea, S. H. (2011). Assessment of 2q23.1 microdeletion syndrome implicates MBD5 as a single causal locus of intellectual disability, epilepsy, and autism spectrum disorder. *American Journal of Human Genetics*, *89*(4), 551–563. doi:10.1016/j.ajhg.2011.09.011

Talkowski, M. E., Rosenfeld, J. A., Blumenthal, I., Pillalamarri, V., Chiang, C., Heilbut, A., . . . Gusella, J. F. (2012). Sequencing chromosomal abnormalities reveals neurodevelopmental loci that confer risk across diagnostic boundaries. *Cell*, *149*(3), 525–537. doi:10.1016/j.cell.2012.03.028

Vaags, A. K., Lionel, A. C., Sato, D., Goodenberger, M., Stein, Q. P., Curran, S., . . . Scherer, S. W. (2012). Rare deletions at the neurexin 3 locus in autism spectrum disorder. *American Journal of Human Genetics*, *90*(1), 133–141. doi:10.1016/j.ajhg.2011.11.025

van Bon, B. W., Mefford, H. C., Menten, B., Koolen, D. A., Sharp, A. J., Nillesen, W. M., . . . de Vries, B. B. (2009). Further delineation of the 15q13 microdeletion and duplication syndromes: A clinical spectrum varying from non-pathogenic to a severe outcome. *Journal of Medical Genetics*, *46*(8), 511–523. doi:10.1136/jmg.2008.063412

Voineagu, I., Wang, X., Johnston, P., Lowe, J. K., Tian, Y., Horvath, S., . . . Geschwind, D. H. (2011). Transcriptomic analysis of autistic brain reveals convergent molecular pathology. *Nature*, *474*(7351), 380–384. doi:10.1038/nature10110

Walder, D. J., Laplante, D. P., Sousa-Pires, A., Veru, F., Brunet, A., & King, S. (2014). Prenatal maternal stress predicts autism traits in 6(1/2) year-old children: Project Ice Storm. *Psychiatry Research*, *219*(2), 353–360. doi:10.1016/j.psychres.2014.04.034

Walters, R. G., Jacquemont, S., Valsesia, A., de Smith, A. J., Martinet, D., Andersson, J., . . . Beckmann, J. S. (2010). A new highly penetrant form of obesity due to deletions on chromosome 16p11.2. *Nature*, *463*(7281), 671–675. doi:10.1038/nature08727

Wang, K., Zhang, H., Ma, D., Bucan, M., Glessner, J. T., Abrahams, B. S., . . . Hakonarson, H. (2009). Common genetic variants on 5p14.1 associate with autism spectrum disorders. *Nature*, *459*(7246), 528–533. doi:10.1038/nature07999

Weiss, L. A., Arking, D. E., Daly, M. J., & Chakravarti, A. (2009). A genome-wide linkage and association scan reveals novel loci for autism. *Nature*, *461*(7265), 802–808. doi:10.1038/nature08490

Weiss, L. A., Shen, Y., Korn, J. M., Arking, D. E., Miller, D. T., Fossdal, R., . . . Daly, M. J. (2008). Association between microdeletion and microduplication at 16p11.2 and autism. *New England Journal of Medicine*, *358*(7), 667–675. doi:10.1056/NEJMoa075974

Williams, S. R., Mullegama, S. V., Rosenfeld, J. A., Dagli, A. I., Hatchwell, E., Allen, W. P., . . . Elsea, S. H. (2010). Haploinsufficiency of MBD5 associated with a syndrome involving microcephaly, intellectual disabilities, severe speech impairment, and seizures. *European Journal of Human Genetics*, *18*(4), 436–441. doi:10.1038/ejhg.2009.199

Yasuda, H., Yoshida, K., Yasuda, Y., & Tsutsui, T. (2011). Infantile zinc deficiency: Association with autism spectrum disorders. *Scientific Reports*, *1*, 129. doi:10.1038/srep00129

Yu, T. W., Chahrour, M. H., Coulter, M. E., Jiralerspong, S., Okamura-Ikeda, K., Ataman, B., . . . Walsh, C. A. (2013). Using whole-exome sequencing to identify inherited causes of autism. *Neuron*, *77*(2), 259–273. doi:10.1016/j.neuron.2012.11.002

/// 12 /// EPIDEMIOLOGY OF AUTISM SPECTRUM DISORDER

ALLISON PRESMANES HILL, KATHARINE ZUCKERMAN, AND ERIC FOMBONNE

INTRODUCTION

Epidemiological surveys of autism were first initiated in the mid-1960s in England (Lotter, 1966, 1967) and have since been conducted in more than 20 countries. This chapter provides a comprehensive review of the findings and methodological features of many published epidemiological surveys about the prevalence of autism spectrum disorder (ASD).[1] This chapter builds on previous reviews (Fombonne, 2003, 2005; Hill, Zuckerman, & Fombonne, 2014). The following are the specific questions addressed: (1) What is the range of prevalence estimates for ASD? and (2) How should the time trends observed in the current prevalence rates of ASD be interpreted?

Study Design and Methodological Issues

Epidemiologists use several measures of disease occurrence, including incidence, cumulative incidence, and prevalence. Prevalence is a measure used in cross-sectional surveys (in which there is no passage of time) and reflects the proportion of subjects in a given population who suffer from the disease at that point in time. Most epidemiological studies of ASD have assessed prevalence (point prevalence or period prevalence) as a cross-sectional approach that is more appropriate for disorders for which timing of diagnosis lags behind onset of symptoms and is likely to be influenced by a range of factors unrelated to risk. In designing a prevalence study, three elements are critical: case definition, case identification (or case ascertainment), and case evaluation methods (Fombonne, 2007).

Case Definition
The definition and diagnostic criteria of autism have changed over time. Starting with Kanner's (1943) description of autism, case definitions have progressively broadened to

---

[1] Autism spectrum disorder (ASD) is the modern term that replaces the former pervasive developmental disorder (PDD).

include criteria proposed by Rutter (1970) and subsequently the International Classification of Diseases, ninth revision (ICD-9; World Health Organization, 1977), and the *Diagnostic and Statistical Manual of Mental Disorders*, third edition (DSM-III; American Psychiatric Association(APA), 1980). Eventually, two more recent nosographies were adopted worldwide, the ICD-10 (World Health Organization, 1992) and the *Diagnostic and Statistical Manual of Mental Disorders*, fourth edition and text revision (DSM-IV and DSM-IV-TR, respectively; APA, 1994, 2000).

Early diagnostic criteria reflected the more qualitatively severe behavioral phenotypes, usually associated with severe delays in language and cognitive skills. In the 1980s, less severe forms of autism were recognized, either as a qualifier for autism occurring without intellectual disability (ID) (i.e., high-functioning autism) or as separate diagnostic categories (e.g., Pervasive Developmental Disorder Not Otherwise Specified (PDD-NOS) or ASD). Asperger's disorder appeared in the 1990s, with unclear validity, particularly with respect to its differentiation from high-functioning autism. Some ASD subtypes that were described in DSM-III subsequently disappeared (e.g., Autism-Residual State); however, other nomenclatures have since added new diagnostic categories, such as "atypical autism" and "PDD unspecified" (ICD-10).

The changes occurring with the introduction of the *Diagnostic and Statistical Manual of Mental Disorders*, fifth edition (DSM-5; APA, 2013), may impact prevalence estimates in the future. DSM-5 proposes a single new category of Autism Spectrum Disorder, conceptually equivalent to the previous diagnostic class of PDDs. However, fewer diagnostic criteria have been retained that are combined in two clusters of social communication deficits and restricted patterns of behavior and interests. The removal of the loosely defined PDD-NOS that was in DSM-IV-TR will likely increase the specificity of the ASD diagnostic category, and the removal of Asperger's disorder as a separate category is consistent with research that has generally failed to provide evidence for the discriminant validity of this diagnostic concept vis-à-vis forms of autistic disorder that are not associated with severe language impairments or intellectual deficits.

The impact of DSM-5 changes remains to be fully assessed in the context of epidemiological surveys. Two recent population-based surveys have addressed this issue. Maenner and colleagues (2014) retrospectively applied the new diagnostic criteria to a previously obtained population-based sample from the Centers for Disease Control and Prevention (CDC) 2006 and 2008 surveillance years. They found that 81.2% of children classified as having the equivalent of ASD according to DSM-IV-TR also met DSM-5 criteria, resulting in a DSM-5-based prevalence of 100/10,000—an estimate lower than the 2006 and 2008 estimates. In addition, 304 children met DSM-5 but not DSM-IV-TR criteria. In a similar study, Kim and colleagues (2014) reported that 92% of children with ASD according to DSM-IV-TR also met DSM-5 criteria. However, when DSM-5 ASD and Social Communication Disorder (a new diagnostic category in DSM-5) were considered together, there was no significant change in the prevalence estimate (Kim et al., 2014). It is important to note that new diagnostic information required in DSM-5 (e.g., emphasis on sensory processing deficits) is generally not available in prior studies, leading to potentially biased estimates. In addition, previous studies are often constrained in sampling children with a DSM-IV PDD diagnosis and cannot therefore accurately estimate the proportion of children who did not meet criteria for DSM-IV but would have met those for DSM-5.

Although there is currently high inter-rater reliability overall regarding diagnosis of ASD and commonality of concepts across experts, differences still persist between nomenclatures about the terminology and operationalized criteria of ASD. It is unclear to what extent the changing nomenclature of ASD plays a role in prevalence estimates described in epidemiological studies. Studies are currently under way that will provide further examination of the impact on prevalence estimates of narrowing the ASD definition in DSM-5.

Case Identification/Ascertainment

When a population is identified for a survey, different strategies are employed to find individuals matching the study's case definition. Some studies rely solely on service provider databases (Croen, Grether, Hoogstrate, & Selvin, 2002; Davidovitch, Hemo, Manning-Courtney, & Fombonne, 2013), special education databases (Fombonne, Zakarian, Bennett, Meng, & McLean-Heywood, 2006; Gurney et al., 2003; Maenner & Durkin, 2010), or national registers (Al-Farsi et al., 2011; Samadi, Mahmoodizadeh, & McConkey, 2011) for case identification. These studies have the common limitation of relying on a population group that was readily accessible rather than sampling from the population at large. As a result, individuals with the disorder who are not in contact with services are not included as cases, leading to an underestimation of prevalence. This limitation is particularly problematic in communities with recognized limitations in available services.

Other investigations have relied on a multistage approach to identify cases in underlying populations (e.g., CDC, 2014; Idring et al., 2012; Kim et al., 2011). In these studies' first screening stage, a wide net is cast to identify subjects possibly affected with ASD, with the final diagnostic status being determined at subsequent stages. This process often consists of sending letters or screeners to school and health professionals, searching for possible cases of autism. Few such investigations rely on systematic sampling techniques that would ensure a near complete coverage of the target population, and screening often varies substantially in ascertainment of all relevant data sources. In addition, surveyed areas often differ in terms of specific educational or health care systems available, and inclusion information sent often varies in reliability and validity. Finally, uneven participation rates in the screening stage can lead to variation in the screening efficiency of surveys.

To illustrate how differential participation in the screening stage affects prevalence estimates, two hypothetical scenarios are illustrated in Figure 12.1, both of which are based on a true ASD prevalence of 150/10,000 and a sensitivity of 100% for the screening process and total accuracy in the diagnostic confirmation. In scenario A, we assume 60% participation for ASD and non-ASD cases in the first screening stage, resulting in 90 participating ASD cases that screen positive. With 70% participation for both ASD and non-ASD cases in the diagnostic stage, we would identify and confirm 63 ASD cases in the second phase. Weighting back phase 2 data, we would obtain an unbiased prevalence estimate of 1.5% (or 150/10,000) in this scenario. In scenario B, we also assume 60% overall participation, but with an 80% participation rate for ASD cases, reflecting a scenario in which individuals with ASD are more likely to participate in the first screening stage than non-ASD cases. Thus, with the same participation rates in the first screening (60%) and final diagnostic stages (70%), we identify 84 ASD cases and calculate a biased prevalence estimate of 2% (200/10,000), an estimate that is 0.5% higher than true prevalence. The bias arises for two reasons: (1) Participation in screening is associated with case status (here, with ASD cases more likely to participate than non-cases); and (2) because investigators typically have no such information, weights used for prevalence estimation were not adjusted correspondingly, resulting in the upward bias.

It is also possible that individuals with ASD participate less than non-cases, which would result in underestimates of prevalence. For example, Posserud, Lundervold, Lie, and Gillberg (2010) reported ASD prevalence of 72/10,000 in their identified sample and estimated a prevalence of 128/10,000 in nonresponders (based on teacher ratings during the

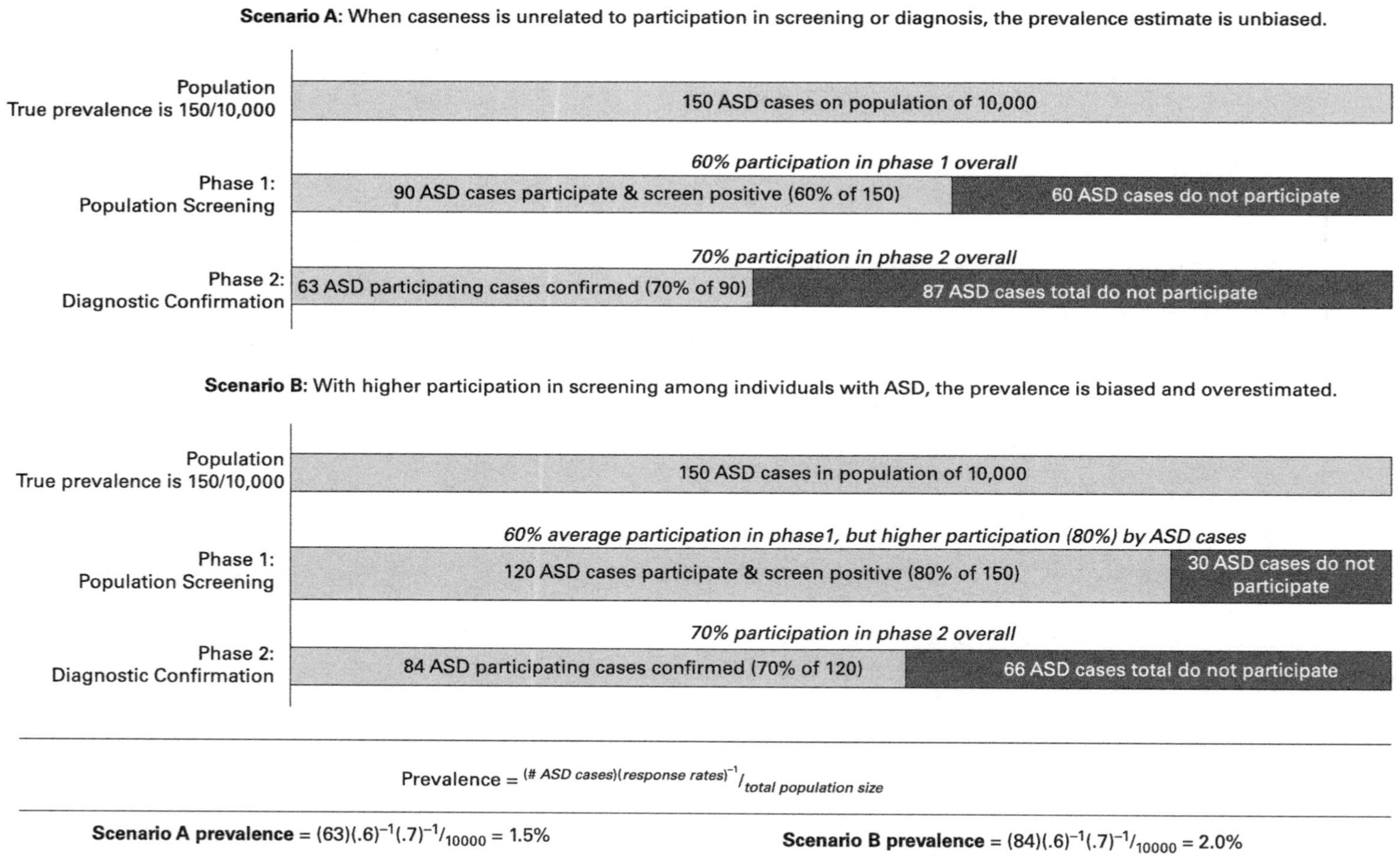

Scenario A: When caseness is unrelated to participation in screening or diagnosis, the prevalence estimate is unbiased.

Population
True prevalence is 150/10,000

150 ASD cases on population of 10,000

60% participation in phase 1 overall

Phase 1:
Population Screening

90 ASD cases participate & screen positive (60% of 150)

60 ASD cases do not participate

70% participation in phase 2 overall

Phase 2:
Diagnostic Confirmation

63 ASD participating cases confirmed (70% of 90)

87 ASD cases total do not participate

Scenario B: With higher participation in screening among individuals with ASD, the prevalence is biased and overestimated.

Population
True prevalence is 150/10,000

150 ASD cases in population of 10,000

60% average participation in phase1, but higher participation (80%) by ASD cases

Phase 1:
Population Screening

120 ASD cases participate & screen positive (80% of 150)

30 ASD cases do not participate

70% participation in phase 2 overall

Phase 2:
Diagnostic Confirmation

84 ASD participating cases confirmed (70% of 120)

66 ASD cases total do not participate

$$\text{Prevalence} = (\#\ ASD\ cases)(response\ rates)^{-1} \big/ _{total\ population\ size}$$

Scenario A prevalence = $(63)(.6)^{-1}(.7)^{-1}/_{10000} = 1.5\%$

Scenario B prevalence = $(84)(.6)^{-1}(.7)^{-1}/_{10000} = 2.0\%$

FIGURE 12.1 Assuming a true autism spectrum disorder prevalence of 150/10,000 and a sensitivity of 100% for the screening process and total accuracy in the diagnostic confirmation, weighting back phase 2 data results in an unbiased prevalence estimate when caseness is unrelated to participation in screening (Scenario A), but when participation in screening is more likely for autism spectrum disorder cases than for non-cases (Scenario B), prevalence will be overestimated (see discussion in text).

screening phase), indicating increased refusal rates among those with more ASD symptoms. Unfortunately, few studies have been able to estimate the extent to which willingness or refusal to participate is associated with final caseness, so it is not known what effect differential participation rates at different phases in population surveys may have on prevalence estimates.

The sensitivity of the screening methodology is difficult to gauge in autism surveys because the proportion of children truly affected with the disorder but not identified in the screening stage (false negatives) remains generally unmeasured. Few studies have provided an estimate of the reliability of the screening procedure. The usual approach, which consists of randomly sampling screen-negative subjects to adjust estimates, has not been generally used, mainly due to the relatively low frequency of ASD, which makes such a strategy both imprecise and costly.

As an example, the surveys conducted by the CDC (2007a, 2007b, 2009, 2012, 2014) rely, for case ascertainment, on scrutinizing educational and medical records. Children not accessing such services cannot be identified. Although some recent surveys that systematically screen the normal school population might detect a large pool of unidentified cases (Kim et al., 2011), it remains to be determined if this applies to most populations and requires change in sampling approaches for surveying autism. Of note, the CDC methodology identifies ASD cases without prior official ASD diagnosis (21% of identified cases in 2008; CDC, 2012), suggesting that underidentification is a widespread phenomenon.

Because more recent prevalence studies suggest that autism can no longer be regarded as rare, screening for false negatives may become a more common strategy. Currently, however, prevalence estimates must be understood as underestimates of "true" prevalence rates, with the magnitude of this underestimation unknown in each survey.

Case Evaluation

When the screening phase is completed, subjects identified as positive go through a more in-depth diagnostic evaluation to confirm case status. Similar considerations about methodological variability across studies apply in more intensive assessment phases. The information used to determine diagnosis usually involves a combination of data from informants (parents, teachers, pediatricians, other health professionals, etc.) and data sources (medical records and educational sources), with a direct assessment of the person with autism being offered in some but not all studies. When subjects are directly examined, assessments typically use various diagnostic instruments, ranging from a typical unstructured examination by a clinical expert (but without demonstrated psychometric properties) to the use of batteries of standardized measures by trained research staff. The Autism Diagnostic Interview–Revised (ADI-R; Lord, Rutter, & Couteur, 1994) and/or the Autism Diagnostic Observation Schedule (ADOS; Lord et al., 2000) have been increasingly used in the most recent surveys.

Obviously, surveys of large populations, such as those conducted in the United States' CDC Autism and Developmental Disabilities Monitoring (ADDM) Network (2007a, 2007b, 2009, 2012, 2014) or in national registers (Idring et al., 2012), cannot include direct diagnostic assessment of all subjects by researchers. However, investigators generally improve the accuracy of caseness determinations by undertaking, on a randomly selected subsample, a more complete diagnostic workup (Rice et al., 2007). The CDC surveys have established a methodology for surveys of large populations based on screening of the population using multiple data sources, standardized records abstraction, and systematic review and scoring of the data gathered in the screening phase. In the less obvious cases, this information is combined with input from experienced clinicians with known reliability and validity. This methodology is adequate for large samples, and it is likely to be used in the future for surveillance efforts.

SYSTEMATIC REVIEW OF PREVALENCE ESTIMATES

Unspecified Autism Spectrum Disorder in Earlier Surveys

A new objective of recent epidemiological surveys has been to estimate the prevalence of all disorders falling onto the autism spectrum, thereby prompting important changes in the conceptualization and design of surveys. However, in previous reviews, we documented that several studies performed in the 1960s and 1970s provided useful information on rates of syndromes similar to autism but not meeting the strict diagnostic criteria for autistic disorder then in use (Fombonne, 2003, 2005). At the time, different labels were used by authors to characterize these clinical pictures, such as the *triad of impairments* involving deficits in reciprocal social interaction, communication, and imagination (Wing & Gould, 1979); autistic mental retardation (Hoshino, Kumashiro, Yashima, Tachibana, & Watanabe, 1982); borderline childhood psychoses (Brask, 1970); or autistic-like syndromes (Burd, Fisher, & Kerbeshian, 1987). These syndromes would fall within our currently defined autistic spectrum, probably with diagnostic labels such as atypical autism and/or PDD-NOS. In 8 of 12 surveys providing separate estimates of the prevalence of these developmental disorders, higher rates for the atypical forms were actually found compared to those for more narrowly defined autistic disorder (Fombonne, 2003). However, this atypical group received little attention in previous epidemiological studies; these subjects were not defined as "cases" and were not included in the numerators of prevalence calculations, thereby underestimating systematically the prevalence of what would be defined today as the spectrum of autistic disorders.

For example, in the first survey by Lotter (1966), the prevalence would increase from 4.1 to 7.8/10,000 if these atypical forms of autism had been included in the case definition. Similarly, in Wing, Yeates, Brierly, and Gould's study (1976), the prevalence was 4.9/10,000 for autistic disorder, but the prevalence for the whole ASD spectrum was in fact 21.1/10,000 after the figure of 16.3/10,000 (Wing & Gould, 1979), corresponding to the triad of impairments, was added. The progressive recognition of the importance and relevance of these less typical clinical presentations has led to changes in the design of more recent epidemiological surveys that use case definitions that incorporate a priori these milder phenotypes.

Prevalence Estimates for Combined Autism Spectrum Disorder Since 2000

There have been 53 surveys that estimated the prevalence of the entire spectrum of ASD published since 2000, with the majority (55%) published in 2009 or later. The studies were performed in 18 different countries (including 14 studies in the United Kingdom and 12 in the United States, of which 5 were conducted by the CDC). Sample sizes ranged from 5007 to 4.5 million (median, 58,654; mean, 346,776). Ages of the surveyed populations ranged from 0 to 98 years (median, 8 years; mean, 9 years). One study was specifically conducted on adults and provided the only estimate (98.2/10,000) thus far available for adults (Brugha et al., 2011). Two surveys focusing on toddlers (Nygren et al., 2012) and preschoolers (Nicholas, Carpenter, King, Jenner, & Charles, 2009) provided estimates of approximately 80 per 10,000. In the 50 remaining surveys, the average median age was 8.23 years (standard deviation = 2.8).

The diagnostic criteria used in the 53 studies reflected the reliance on modern diagnostic schemes (11 studies used ICD-10, and 25 used the DSM-III, DSM-IV, or DSM-IV-TR; both schemes were used simultaneously in 9 studies). Assessments were often performed with standardized diagnostic measures (i.e., ADI-R and ADOS). In 26 studies in which IQ measures were reported, the proportion of subjects within the normal IQ range varied from 0% to 100% (median, 55.4%; mean, 53.9%)—a proportion that reflects the lesser association, or lack thereof, between intellectual impairment and milder forms of ASD. Overrepresentation of males was seen in the 47 studies reporting gender ratios, with male:female ratio ranging from 1.8:1 to 15.7:1 (median, 4.5:1; mean, 4.9:1).

There was a 189-fold variation in ASD prevalence, ranging from 1.4/10,000 to 264/10,000 (Figure 12.2). There was also substantial variation in confidence interval width, reflecting variation in sample sizes and consequently in each study's precision (range, 0.5–146; mean interval width, 22.4). However, some consistency in ASD prevalence is found in the center of this distribution, with a median rate of 61.9/10,000 and a mean rate of 68.9/10,000 (interquartile range, 44.2–84.0/10,000). Prevalence was negatively associated with sample size (Kendall's tau, −.23; $p = .01$), with small-scale studies reporting higher prevalence.

There was also a significant positive correlation between ASD prevalence estimates and publication year (Kendall's tau, .26; $p = .007$), with higher rates in more recent surveys. Since 2000, a number of studies have reported ASD prevalence estimates higher than 100/10,000 (Baird et al., 2006; CDC, 2012, 2014; Idring et al., 2012; Kawamura, Takahashi, & Ishii, 2008; Kim et al., 2011; Ouellette-Kuntz et al., 2006). Baird et al. (2006) and Kim et al. (2011) both employed proactive case finding techniques, relying on multiple and repeated screening phases, involving both different informants at each phase and surveying the same cohorts at different ages, which certainly enhanced the sensitivity of case identification. Multisource active surveillance techniques, as employed in the Stockholm Youth Cohort (Idring et al., 2012) and by the CDC's ADDM Network (2007a, 2007b, 2009, 2012, 2014), also improve identification of individuals with ASD. The most recent CDC prevalence estimate of 147 per 10,000 reflects the highest estimate to date across all of the previous ADDM Network reports (CDC, 2014).

Overall, results of recent surveys are in agreement that an average figure of 69/10,000 can be used as the current estimate for the spectrum of ASD. The convergence of estimates around 60 to 90 per 10,000 for all ASD combined, conducted in different regions and countries by different teams, is striking, especially when derived from studies with improved methodology. The prevalence figure of 69/10,000 (equivalent to 6.9/1,000 or .69%) translates into 1 child out of 145 with an ASD diagnosis. This estimate is now the best current estimate for the ASD prevalence. However, it represents an average and conservative figure, and substantial variability exists between studies and within studies, across sites or areas.

TIME TRENDS IN PREVALENCE AND THEIR INTERPRETATION

The debate on the hypothesis of a secular increase in rates of ASD has been obscured by a lack of clarity in the measures of disease occurrence. As noted previously, it is crucial to differentiate prevalence from incidence because only incidence rates can be used for causal research, and prevalence and incidence will increase when case definition is

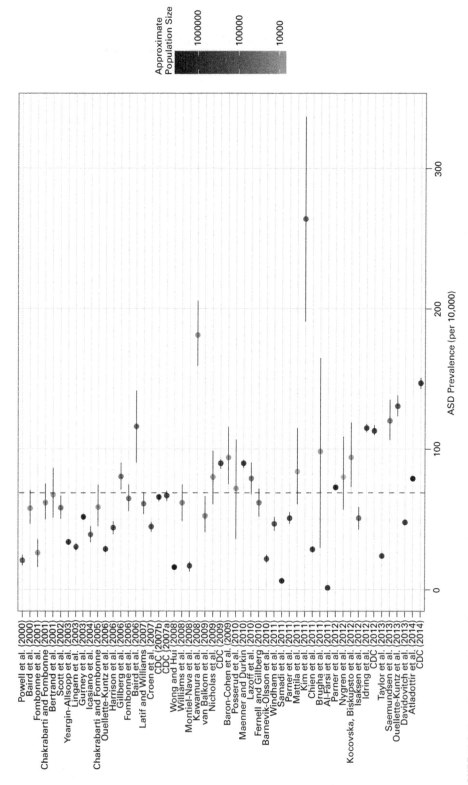

FIGURE 12.2 Prevalence estimates for autism spectrum disorder since 2000 (per 10,000 with 95% confidence intervals; also see Figure 12.4). The dashed vertical line denotes the mean prevalence of 69/10,000 across all 53 surveys.

broadened or case ascertainment is improved. Moreover, epidemiological surveys of ASD possess unique design features that could account almost entirely for between-study variation in prevalence estimates, making time trends even more difficult to gauge. Time trends in prevalence estimates can therefore only be evaluated in investigations that hold methodological parameters under strict control over time. Such requirements must be considered when reviewing evidence for a secular increase in rates of ASD or testing for the "epidemic" hypothesis.

The epidemic hypothesis emerged in the 1990s when, in most countries, increasing numbers were diagnosed with ASD leading to an upward trend in children registered in service providers' databases that was paralleled by higher prevalence rates in epidemiological surveys. These trends were interpreted as evidence that the actual population incidence of ASD was increasing. However, because methodological factors contribute to variability in prevalence estimates, these must be considered before concluding that there is a true increase in the number of children diagnosed with ASD. These factors are discussed here.

Use of Referral Statistics

Increasing numbers of children referred to specialist services or known to special education registers have been taken as evidence for increased ASD incidence. Such upward trends have been seen in many different countries (Gurney et al., 2003; Lotter, 1966; Shattuck, 2006), all occurring in the late 1980s and early 1990s. However, trends over time in *referred* samples are confounded by referral patterns, availability of services, heightened public awareness, decreasing age at diagnosis, and changes over time in diagnostic concepts and practices.

As an illustration, Figure 12.3 contrasts two methods for surveying ASD using hypothetical data—one based on sampling from the total population and the other relying solely on service access counts. Here, assuming a constant incidence and prevalence of 100/10,000 between Time 1 and Time 2 (meaning there is no epidemic), population surveys at two time points result in prevalence estimates that are not only accurate but also stable over time, showing no prevalence change in the target population. However, if prevalence is estimated based only on service access counts where the number of ASD individuals accessing services increases from 20% to 60% over time, prevalence would be underestimated at both time points but would appear to rise 200% while the underlying true incidence and prevalence remained stable. Such a pattern of results was reported based on special education data in Wisconsin (Maenner & Durkin, 2010), in which ASD prevalence rates were stable between 2002 and 2008 in school districts with initially high baseline prevalence rates ($\approx$120/10,000), whereas school districts with low baseline rates experienced significant increases in prevalence (e.g., in one district, rates increased from 5 to 70/10,000, corresponding to a 1300% increase in 6 years). Failure to control for these confounding factors was obvious in previous reports (Fombonne, 2001), including widely quoted reports from the California Developmental Database Services (CDDS, 2003).

In addition, the decreasing age at diagnosis results in increasing numbers of young children being identified in official statistics (Wazana, Bresnahan, & Kline, 2007) or referred to specialist medical and educational services. Earlier identification of children from the prevalence pool may therefore result in increased service activity that may lead to a misperception by professionals of an epidemic.

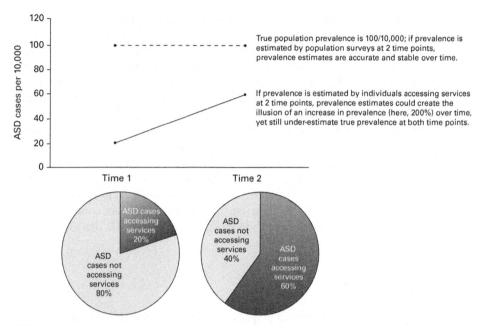

FIGURE 12.3 Assuming a constant incidence and prevalence of 100/10,000 between Time 1 and Time 2 (meaning there is no "epidemic"), prevalence estimates that rely solely on service access counts not only underestimate the true prevalence but may also create the illusion of rising prevalence over time (see discussion in text).

Diagnostic Substitution

Another possible explanation for increased prevalence in a diagnostic category is that children presenting with the same developmental disability may receive one particular diagnosis initially and another diagnosis subsequently. Such diagnostic substitution (or switching) may occur when diagnostic categories become increasingly familiar to health professionals and/or when access to better services is ensured by using a new diagnostic category.

The strongest evidence of diagnostic substitution contributing to ASD prevalence increase was shown in a complex analysis of US Department of Education data in 50 US states (Shattuck, 2006), indicating that a relatively high proportion of children previously diagnosed with mental retardation (MR) were subsequently identified as having ASD. Shattuck showed that the odds of having ASD increased by 1.21 during 1994–2003, whereas the odds of having learning disability (LD) (odds ratio (OR) = 0.98) and MR (OR = 0.97) decreased. Shattuck further demonstrated that the growing ASD prevalence was directly associated with decreasing prevalence of LD and MR within states and that a significant downward deflection in the historical trajectories of LD and MR occurred when ASD became reported in the United States as an independent category in 1993–1994.

Using individual-level data, a more recent study re-examined the hypothesis of diagnostic substitution in the California DDS data set (King & Bearman, 2009) and showed that 24% of the increase in caseload was attributable to diagnostic substitution (from MR to ASD). It is important to keep in mind that other types of diagnostic substitution are likely to have occurred as well for milder forms of ASD. For example, children currently diagnosed with Asperger's disorder may have been previously diagnosed with other psychiatric diagnoses (i.e., obsessive–compulsive disorder, school phobia, social anxiety, etc.)

in clinical settings before the developmental nature of their condition was fully recognized (Fombonne, 2009).

Cross-Sectional Variability in Epidemiological Surveys

Evidence that method factors could account for most of the variability in published prevalence estimates derives from a direct comparison of eight recent surveys conducted in the United Kingdom and the United States (Fombonne, 2005). In each country, four surveys were conducted during approximately the same year and with similar age groups. Because there is no reason to expect large variations in between-area differences in rates, prevalence estimates should be comparable within each country. However, there was a 6-fold variation in rates for UK surveys and a 14-fold variation in US rates. In each set of studies, high rates were found when intensive population-based screening techniques were employed, whereas lower rates were found in studies relying on passive administrative methods for case finding. Because no passage of time was involved, the magnitude of these gradients in rates is likely to reflect methodological differences.

Even more convincing evidence derives from the most recent survey by the CDC on 363,749 children aged 8 years in 2010, in which an average prevalence of 147/10,000 was reported across 11 US states (CDC, 2014). One striking finding in this report is the almost fourfold variation in prevalence rates by state (range, 57–219 per 10,000; see Figure 12.4). Across individual states, Alabama had the lowest rate of 57/10,000, whereas New Jersey had the highest rate of 219/10,000 (CDC, 2014). Estimated ASD prevalence was significantly lower in states that had access to health data sources only compared to that of states where educational data were also available (97.7 vs. 149 out

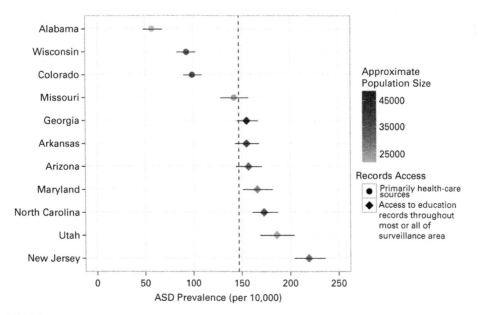

FIGURE 12.4 Estimated prevalence of autism spectrum disorders (with 95% confidence intervals) among children aged 8 years in the United States by ADDM site and type of records access in the 2010 surveillance year (CDC, 2014). The dashed vertical line denotes the average prevalence estimate of 147/10,000 across all sites.

of 10,000, respectively), a factor that is consistently associated with higher prevalence rates in the ADDM Network. It would be surprising if there were truly this much inherent state-to-state variability in the number of children with autism in the United States. Thus, these differences likely reflect ascertainment variability across sites in a study that was otherwise performed with the same methods, at the same time, on children of the same age, and within the same country.

Repeated Surveys in Defined Geographical Areas

Repeated surveys, using the same methodology and conducted in the same geographical area at different time points, can potentially yield useful information on time trends if methods are kept relatively constant. The Göteborg studies (Gillberg, 1984; Gillberg, Steffenburg, & Schaumann, 1991) provided three prevalence estimates that increased during a short period of time from 4.0 (1980) to 6.6 (1984) to 9.5/10,000 (1988), with the gradient being even steeper in urban areas only (Gillberg et al., 1991). However, comparison of these rates is not straightforward because different age groups were included in each survey. Furthermore, increased prevalence was associated with improved detection among those with intellectual delays in the second survey and with improved detection of cases born to immigrant parents in the third survey, suggesting that migration into the area could be a key explanation. Taken in conjunction with a change in local services and a progressive broadening of the autism definition over time (Gillberg et al., 1991), findings provide weak evidence for increased autism incidence. Similarly, studies conducted in Japan at different points in time in Toyota (Kawamura et al., 2008) and Yokohama (Honda, Shimizu, Misumi, Niimi, & Ohashi, 1996; Honda, Shimizu, & Rutter, 2005) showed increases in prevalence rates that their authors interpreted as reflecting the effect of both improved population screening of preschoolers and a broadening of diagnostic concepts and criteria.

Two separate surveys of children born between 1992 and 1995 and between 1996 and 1998 in Staffordshire, United Kingdom (Chakrabarti & Fombonne, 2001, 2005), were performed with rigorously identical methods for case definition and case identification. The prevalence for combined ASD was comparable and not statistically different in the two surveys (Chakrabarti & Fombonne, 2005), suggesting no upward trend in overall rates of ASD, at least during the short time interval between studies.

Birth Cohorts

In large surveys encompassing wide age ranges, increasing prevalence among most recent birth cohorts could be interpreted as indicating a secular increase in ASD incidence, provided that alternative explanations can be confidently eliminated. This analysis was used in two large French surveys (Fombonne & Du Mazaubrun, 1992; Fombonne, Du Mazaubrun, Cans, & Grandjean, 1997). The surveys included birth cohorts from 1972 to 1985 (735,000 children, 389 of whom had autism). When pooling the data of both surveys, age-specific rates showed no upward trend (Fombonne et al., 1997).

However, data assessing birth cohorts can be problematic, as illustrated in Figure 12.5, which shows an increase in the prevalence of ASD by year of birth across three hypothetical successive birth cohorts (a cohort effect; Figure 12.5, left). Within each birth cohort, followed longitudinally, prevalence increases as children age (Figure 12.5, right): For children in the 2000 birth cohort, based on previous ASD prevalence estimates, age 6 years prevalence is 20/10,000, whereas at age 12 years, we may expect prevalence of 80/10,000 for

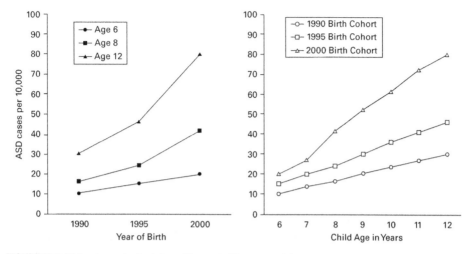

FIGURE 12.5 Using hypothetical data, Figure 5a illustrates rising prevalence rates among 6-, 8-, and 12-year-old children across three different birth cohorts. Prevalence rates also increase within birth cohorts as they age (Figure 5b), potentially coinciding with changes in patterns of referral, service availability, public awareness, and diagnostic concepts and practices (see discussion in text).

the same birth cohort. Increasing prevalence rates with age within birth cohorts is unlikely to reflect the onset of ASD in later childhood and early adolescence. It is more likely that observed increases in prevalence reflect underdiagnosis in the preschool years as well as changes in public awareness, service availability, and diagnostic concepts and practices.

For example, an analysis of special educational data from Minnesota showed a 16-fold increase in children identified with ASD from 1991–1992 to 2001–2002 (Gurney et al., 2003). However, during the same time period, an increase of 50% was observed for all disability categories (except severe ID), especially for the category including attention deficit hyperactivity disorder. The large sample size allowed the authors to assess age, period, and cohort effects. Prevalence increased regularly in successive birth cohorts; for example, among 7-year-olds, prevalence increased from 18/10,000 among those born in 1989 to 29/10,000 among those born in 1991 and 55/10,000 in those born in 1993. Within the *same* birth cohorts, age effects were also apparent because for children born in 1989, the prevalence increased with age from 13/10,000 at age 6 years to 21/10,000 at age 9 years and 33/10,000 at age 11 years. As argued by Gurney et al., this pattern is not consistent with the natural etiology of ASD, which first manifests in early childhood. Gurney et al.'s analysis also showed a marked period effect, where rates started to increase in all ages and birth cohorts in the 1990s. The authors noted that this phenomenon coincided closely with the inclusion of ASD in the federal Individuals with Disabilities Educational Act in the United States. A similar interpretation of upward trends had been put forward by Croen and colleagues (2002) in their analysis of the CDDS data and also by Shattuck (2006) in his analysis of trends in US Department of Education data.

CORRELATES OF AUTISM SPECTRUM DISORDER IN EPIDEMIOLOGICAL SURVEYS

Studies of associations between ASD and socioeconomic status (SES), race/ethnicity, and immigrant status have shown variable results and face numerous technical challenges.

In general, studies that base diagnosis rates on developmental service utilization may undercount minority and low SES children. Underprivileged children have less health services access overall (Shi & Stevens, 2005) and particularly low mental health services access (Kataoka, Zhang, & Wells, 2002), which can lead to underidentification of ASD. In contrast, children with more educated, wealthier, or more health-literate parents may have resources to make their way to ASD diagnostic services and, therefore, an ASD diagnosis (Tsai, Stewart, Faust, & Shook, 1982). Cross-sectional studies based on parent report of ASD are problematic for the same reason, as parent report of ASD is more likely among families who have adequate access to ASD-related services. Undercounting of minorities may additionally occur in the context of multistage, population-based research. Minority and low SES families may participate in such research studies at disproportionately low rates due to higher rates of distrust of scientific researchers (Rajakumar, Thomas, Musa, Almario, & Garza, 2009) or less access to research opportunities. They also may be excluded from studies or incorrectly assessed if forms are not available in appropriate languages or if a language-congruent assessor is not available (Laing & Kamhi, 2003). Finally, because ASD is a relatively rare event, population-based studies of ASD prevalence may have relatively small numbers of low SES, minority, or immigrant children meeting case criteria, making data difficult to interpret (Powell et al., 2000).

Socioeconomic Status

Socioeconomic status can be defined variously, with the most common methods being parental education, income, parental occupation, or some combination of these factors. More than 20 studies have investigated associations between these factors and ASD prevalence.

Many recent US-based studies suggest an association between higher SES (as assessed by one of the previously mentioned factors) and higher ASD prevalence. Several studies have used CDC ADDM data combined with imputed sociodemographic data from US Census tracts to show a link between parental income/education and ASD diagnosis. Using 2007 data from New Jersey, Thomas et al. (2012) showed that the ASD prevalence ratio between the highest income tract (>$90,000) and the lowest income tract (<$30,000) was 2.2. In addition, children in the higher income tracts were more likely to have a higher number of professional evaluations and a lower age of diagnosis, suggesting a referral bias or an underdiagnosis of children at the lower end of the SES spectrum. Using CDC ADDM data from all 14 participating states, Durkin et al. (2010) developed a composite SES indicator that took into account both parental education and household income. This study found a dose–response relationship between SES and ASD prevalence, regardless of gender and data source. SES-based differences in prevalence were significantly weaker when children with a previous ASD diagnosis (as opposed to a new diagnosis in the context of the study) were excluded—a finding that suggests that prior access to ASD diagnostic services may explain some of the difference. Both of these studies benefit from a population-based data collection framework; however, they are limited in that no individual-level SES data were available.

Similarly, Bhasin and Schendel (2007) conducted a population-based case–control study, directly measuring maternal education and imputing household income from census tract data in Atlanta, Georgia. Higher median family income was significantly associated with autism overall. Both markers of higher SES (higher maternal education and higher median family income) were significantly associated with autism without ID but not autism with ID, suggesting that, in addition to biases based on service access, diagnostic substitution may be occurring more frequently among children with higher SES. Leonard et al. (2011) observed a similar finding in Western Australian children born from 1984 to 1999. The prevalence of ASD without ID was significantly increased among children whose mothers had more economic resources.

One criticism of these recent studies, particularly the studies based in the United States, is that SES has been confounded by inequitable health services access and that in a setting where health services access is more equitable, the effects of SES might be lessened or even reversed. In a Denmark population-based case–control study, Larsson et al. (2005) found that the risk of ASD was actually higher among children with less parental wealth in bivariate analyses but that after adjusting for other demographic factors, there was no association of either parental education or wealth with ASD. In a Swedish case–control study by Rai, Lewis, and colleagues (2012), children in families with lower income and whose parents had manual occupations were at higher risk for ASD diagnosis after multivariate adjustment. In England, which also has national health insurance, Brugha et al. (2011) found that ASD adults with higher educational attainment had lower rates of autism after multivariate adjustment; however, it is likely that an ASD diagnosis may have reduced the subjects' educational attainment. In contrast, in a study performed in Israel, where access to and coverage of ASD-related services was reported to be excellent, Davidovitch et al. (2013) found lower prevalence of ASD in children who lived in low-income versus higher-income communities or whose families did not purchase supplemental private insurance.

Overall, many recent large-scale studies have shown an association between ASD prevalence and SES, although it appears that these differences were due to decreased access to diagnostic services among children with lower SES or diagnostic substitution between ID and ASD among children with higher SES. In settings where health care is more accessible, these effects seem to lessen or even reverse. To date, no plausible biological mechanism has been proposed or supported that might explain SES-related differences in ASD prevalence. The fact that older studies either did not show SES associations (Gillberg & Schaumann, 1982; Tsai et al., 1982) or showed variability based on referral source (Wing, 1980) or autism subtype (Sanua, 1987) also supports the fact that SES differences are due to differences in ASD ascertainment as opposed to an underlying biological or psychosocial mechanism.

Race and Ethnicity

Many studies of racial/ethnic minorities show lower rates of ASD compared to white or European populations, although these differences appear to be narrowing in more current studies. The evidence is strongest for African American and Hispanic populations in the United States. Several recent studies are highlighted here, although other recent studies show similar findings (Liptak et al., 2008; Mandell et al., 2009). Because minority race and ethnic status often correlates with lower SES and worse health care access, studies attempting to assess the effects of race/ethnicity on ASD diagnosis should control for SES and health care accessibility factors in their analyses.

Using administrative data from Texas school districts, Palmer, Walker, Mandell, Bayles, and Miller (2010) showed that the number of autism diagnoses in a school district was inversely proportional to the number of Hispanic schoolchildren in that district, after adjusting for number of pediatricians, child psychologists, and neurologists by county, as well as county median household income. One strength of this approach is that it did attempt to adjust for SES and differential services availability, as well as comorbid ID and LDs on a population level. Interestingly, these factors better explained variability in ASD diagnoses among white non-Hispanic children than Hispanic children, suggesting that SES and access factors alone do not explain lower diagnosis rates in Hispanics, at least on a population level. However, this ecological study did not measure individual-level access factors (e.g., insurance adequacy) or factors such as provider bias that may also impact ASD diagnostic rates.

The most recent CDC ADDM data (CDC, 2014) also suggest an overall lower rate of ASD among non-Hispanic black (123/10,000) and Hispanic children (108/10,000) compared to white children (158/10,000) in the United States. Although there was considerable variability among the states, all 11 sites reported higher rates of ASD among whites than among black and Hispanic children. However, the prevalence of ASD without ID among white children was nearly double the prevalence among either black or Hispanic children (OR = 1.8; $p < .01$), indicating that underdiagnosis of ASD in minority populations in the United States may be magnified in those children without comorbid ID. Pedersen et al. (2012) examined racial/ethnic differences more thoroughly using several waves of ADDM data in Arizona, which has a large Hispanic population. That study also found a lower rate of ASD in Hispanic children compared to non-Hispanic white children. ASD prevalence increased in both populations during the study years, and the gap in prevalence between racial/ethnic groups decreased. The authors speculated that much of this difference might be attributable to underutilization and lack of access to ASD services by Hispanic families. They also speculated that these differences might reflect the "Hispanic paradox" or "healthy immigrant" effect, in which Hispanic immigrants to the United States have lower rates of multiple adverse health outcomes despite multiple SES and health care access risk factors (Franzini, Ribble, & Keddie, 2001). However, the fact that differences in diagnostic rates are narrowing rather rapidly suggests that changes in awareness and utilization of services may be more likely than inherent genetic or developmental differences by race/ethnicity.

Windham et al. (2011) used a large administrative sample from multiple sources in northern California to show a lower prevalence of ASD among children of Hispanic and black mothers compared to children of white non-Hispanic mothers, after adjusting for maternal education and age, with similar decreases in racial differences during the study years. However, the observed racial variation was attenuated by adjustment for SES and varied significantly by data source, suggesting that variable health services utilization may have affected ASD rates.

Finally, in a US population-based study using parent report of ASD diagnosis, Kogan et al. (2009) found lower rates of ASD diagnosis in non-Hispanic black and multiracial children compared to white children, after adjusting for parental education and income. This study also noted a disproportionately high number of black children whose parents reported a past diagnosis of ASD that subsequently resolved, which runs contrary to most epidemiologic data about ASD lifetime trajectories. This finding suggests that low rates of ASD among black children may be due to racial differences in parent health beliefs about ASD. This study found no significant difference in ASD diagnoses by Hispanic versus non-Hispanic ethnicity; however, follow-up analysis of the same data set by Schieve et al. (2012) showed that there were significantly lower rates of ASD among Hispanic children with foreign-born parents compared to white children. Schieve et al. concluded that by failing to take into account the heterogeneity of Hispanic children with ASD, previous studies that grouped all Hispanics together might have been biased toward a null result. The authors believed that the findings were likely related to differences in parental awareness and access to care stemming from a lower level of acculturation for this subgroup. They also speculated that the findings might reflect the healthy immigrant effect.

In studies outside of the United States, reports about racial/ethnic differences in ASD prevalence have been more mixed, and most studies are not adjusted for SES, which makes it difficult to assess the unique effect of race/ethnicity from other confounders. In addition, these studies are difficult to interpret because what constitutes a minority race or ethnicity is quite variable by country. In Israel, Davidovitch et al. (2013) found a lower prevalence of ASD among Arab Israelis in rural settlements and in ultra-Orthodox Jews than in the general Israeli population, although prevalence was not adjusted for SES differences. Findings from a 1999–2003 census report in Stockholm, Sweden (Barnevik-Olsson, Gillberg, & Fernell, 2010), revealed that the prevalence rate of autism (autism and PDD-NOS/autistic-like condition) with LD was higher in Somali- versus non-Somali Swedish children. The study did not adjust for SES differences between these mothers and other Swedish mothers. The authors hypothesized that lower levels of vitamin D in immigrant Somali mothers may have affected fetal brain development and possibly led to autism and other concerning behavioral characteristics; however, the study did not measure vitamin D in any of the participants (see Kočovská, Fernell, Billstedt, Minnis, & Gillberg, 2012). Several older, unadjusted studies also suggest a higher prevalence of ASD among recent Swedish immigrants, although these immigrants' countries of origins were so mixed that it is difficult to interpret this information in terms of ethnic or racial differences (Gillberg, Steffenburg, Börjesson, & Andersson, 1987; Gillberg et al., 1991).

Overall, most recent studies on racial/ethnic differences in ASD diagnosis do suggest that race/ethnicity affects diagnostic rates above and beyond SES alone, at least in US-based populations. However, given that the racial/ethnic effects are present in several traditionally underserved racial/ethnic groups, are quite variable by data source and study type, and have narrowed over time, they are most likely explained by differential health services utilization, parental health beliefs, and acculturation. Little high-quality data are available on the effects of race/ethnicity in non-US settings.

Migration and Prenatal Exposure to Stressful Events

Migration has historically been implicated as a possible risk factor for autism, based on observed higher rates of autism among immigrant populations in some epidemiological surveys (Barnevik-Olsson et al., 2010; Gillberg et al., 1987, 1991; Wing, 1980). However, evidence for an association between migration and ASD has been inconsistent, with some studies reporting increased ASD risk among immigrant populations (Keen, Reid, & Arnone, 2010; Lauritsen, Pedersen, & Mortensen, 2005) and others reporting equivalent and even decreased ASD risk in some populations (Gillberg et al., 1987; Lauritsen et al., 2005). Most of the early claims about migration as a possible correlate of autism derived from post hoc observations of very small samples and were not subjected to rigorous statistical testing. However, recent studies have attempted to re-examine the association between migration and ASD. For example, in a study using a population-based Swedish cohort, Magnusson et al. (2012) found that children of migrant parents were at increased risk for ASD with ID compared to children of Swedish-born parents. However, the reverse was true for ASD without ID: Children of Swedish-born parents were at significantly higher risk than children of migrant parents, particularly those from countries with low human development indices. The authors suggest that the most plausible explanation for this pattern of findings is the underdiagnosis of ASD in migrant children with high cognitive abilities; for these children, the more subtle social deficits associated with ASD may be overlooked or misattributed to language or cultural differences. In addition, because case ascertainment was based on service use, migrant families may have been less aware of or less likely to seek services in the community in the absence of clear developmental or cognitive delays. However, the researchers also suggest that the possibility of environmental factors associated with migration and acting in utero that may contribute to ASD cannot be dismissed.

One environmental factor associated with migration that has been posited to contribute to ASD risk is prenatal exposure to stressful life events due to the fact that migration itself is likely to be a stressful event because it may occur when families flee armed conflict or other extreme conditions in their home country (Magnusson et al., 2012). Using a population-based cohort of approximately 1.5 million singleton children in Denmark, Li et al. (2009) examined whether prenatal exposure to maternal bereavement, defined by the loss of a child, spouse, parent, or sibling during or up to 1 year prior to pregnancy, was associated with increased risk of ASD. Li et al. found no evidence of an effect of maternal bereavement on autism risk, even after accounting for the timing, nature, and severity of the exposure, although maternal bereavement was rare even in the total population (experienced by 2.5%). Similarly, in a study utilizing population-based cohorts in Sweden and England, Rai, Golding, et al. (2012) also found no evidence for an association between ASD risk and prenatal exposure to stressful life events such as deaths, serious accidents, and diagnosis of serious illnesses in first-degree relatives, although again these events were extremely rare (experienced by 1% of the population). Thus, the hypothesis of an association between migration, as well as exposure to other prenatal stressful events, and ASD remains largely unsupported by the empirical results. However, note that even with large-scale population-based cohorts, these events were extremely rare.

Implications and Unmet Research Needs

Overall, the research findings related to low SES, minority, and immigrant populations primarily point to problems of underdiagnosis due to problems in access to health care services and health literacy. Evidence for a biological difference based on SES, race/ethnicity, or immigration is weak, as is the case for multiple other chronic health conditions among children and adults (Pearce, Foliaki, Sporle, & Cunningham, 2004). In order to obtain an accurate depiction of ASD prevalence in underserved populations, investigators will need to specifically reach out to these populations to ensure equal participation and also oversample these groups so that sample sizes are adequate. In addition, there is a need for validated screening and diagnostic tools in multiple languages to ensure that diagnoses, when they occur, are accurate. Finally, key variables in these analyses, such as parental education, income, and race/ethnicity, need to be directly measured as opposed to imputed from census tract data.

SUMMARY

Epidemiological surveys of ASD pose substantial challenges to researchers seeking to measure rates of ASD, particularly given the range of case definition, case identification, and case evaluation methods employed across surveys. However, from recent studies, a best estimate of 69/10,000 (equivalences = 6.9/1000 or .69% or 1 child in approximately 145 children) can be derived for the prevalence of ASD. Currently, the recent upward trend in rates of *prevalence* cannot be directly attributed to an increase in the *incidence* of the disorder or to an epidemic of autism. Although power to detect time trends is seriously limited in existing data sets, there is good evidence that changes in diagnostic criteria and practices, policies for special education, service availability, and awareness of ASD in both the lay and the professional public may be responsible for increasing prevalence over time. It is also noteworthy that the increase in the number of children diagnosed occurred concurrently in many countries in the 1990s, when services for children with ASD also expanded significantly. Statistical power may also be a significant limitation in most investigations; thus, variations of small magnitude in ASD incidence may be undetected or should be interpreted with caution.

Nonetheless, the possibility that a true increase in the incidence of ASD has also partially contributed to the upward trend in prevalence rates cannot, and should not, be completely eliminated based on available data. To assess whether the incidence has increased, methodological factors that account for an important proportion of the variability in rates must be stringently controlled for. New survey methods have been developed for use in multinational comparisons; ongoing surveillance programs are currently underway and will soon provide more meaningful data to evaluate this hypothesis. In addition, it remains to be determined how changes to diagnostic criteria introduced in the DSM-5 will impact ASD prevalence estimates going forward. Meanwhile, the available prevalence data carry straightforward implications for current and future needs in services and early educational intervention programs.

KEY POINTS

- Based on recent studies, a best estimate of 69/10,000 (equivalences = 6.9/1000 or .69% or 1 child in approximately 145 children) can be derived for the prevalence of ASD.
- Although prevalence estimates for ASD have been steadily increasing, epidemiological surveys of ASD possess unique design features that could account almost entirely for between-study variation in prevalence estimates, making time trends difficult to gauge.
- There is good evidence that changes in diagnostic criteria and practices, policies for special education, service availability, and awareness of ASD in both the lay and the professional public may be responsible for increasing prevalence over time.
- Research findings related to low socioeconomic status, minority, and immigrant populations primarily point to problems of underdetection and underdiagnosis due to problems in access to health care services and health literacy.
- It remains to be determined how changes to diagnostic criteria introduced in the DSM-5 will impact ASD prevalence estimates going forward.

DISCLOSURE STATEMENT

Dr. Alison Presmanes Hill, Dr. Katharine Zuckerman, and Dr. Eric Fombonne have nothing to disclose.

REFERENCES

Al-Farsi, Y. M., Al-Sharbati, M. M., Al-Farsi, O. A., Al-Shafaee, M. S., Brooks, D. R., & Waly, M. I. (2011). Brief report: Prevalence of autistic spectrum disorders in the Sultanate of Oman. *Journal of Autism and Developmental Disorders, 41*(6), 821–825. doi:10.1007/s10803-010-1094-8

American Psychiatric Association. (1980). *Diagnostic and statistical manual of mental disorders* (3rd ed.). Washington, DC: Author.

American Psychiatric Association. (1994). *Diagnostic and statistical manual of mental disorders* (4th ed.). Washington, DC: Author.

American Psychiatric Association. (2000). *Diagnostic and statistical manual of mental disorders* (4th ed., text revision). Washington, DC: Author.

American Psychiatric Association. (2013). *Diagnostic and statistical manual of mental disorders* (5th ed.). Arlington, VA: American Psychiatric Publishing.

Baird, G., Simonoff, E., Pickles, A., Chandler, S., Loucas, T., Meldrum, D., & Charman, T. (2006). Prevalence of disorders of the autism spectrum in a population cohort of children in South Thames: The Special Needs and Autism Project (SNAP). *Lancet, 368*(9531), 210–215. doi:10.1016/S0140-6736(06)69041-7

Barnevik-Olsson, M., Gillberg, C., & Fernell, E. (2010). Prevalence of autism in children of Somali origin living in Stockholm: Brief report of an at-risk population. *Developmental Medicine & Child Neurology, 52*(12), 1167–1168. doi:10.1111/j.1469-8749.2010.03812.x

Bhasin, T. K., & Schendel, D. (2007). Sociodemographic risk factors for autism in a US metropolitan area. *Journal of Autism and Developmental Disorders, 37*(4), 667–677. doi:10.1007/s10803-006-0194-y

Brask, B. H. (1970). *A prevalence investigation of childhood psychoses* (pp. 145–153). Presented at the Nordic Symposium on the Comprehensive Care of the Psychotic Children, Oslo, Norway.

Brugha, T. S., McManus, S., Bankart, J., Scott, F., Purdon, S., Smith, J., . . . Meltzer, H. (2011). Epidemiology of autism spectrum disorders in adults in the community in England. *Archives of General Psychiatry, 68*(5), 459–465. doi:10.1001/archgenpsychiatry.2011.38

Burd, L., Fisher, W., & Kerbeshian, J. (1987). A prevalence study of pervasive developmental disorders in North Dakota. *Journal of the American Academy of Child & Adolescent Psychiatry, 26*(5), 700–703. doi:10.1097/00004583-198709000-00014

California Department of Developmental Services. (2003). *Autistic spectrum disorders: Changes in the California caseload—An update 1999 through 2002.* Retrieved from http://www.dds.ca.gov/Autism/docs/AutismReport2003.pdf

Centers for Disease Control and Prevention. (2007a). Prevalence of autism spectrum disorders—Autism and Developmental Disabilities Monitoring Network, 14 sites, United States, 2002. *Centers for Disease Control and Prevention, 56*(SS01), 12–28.

Centers for Disease Control and Prevention. (2007b). Prevalence of autism spectrum disorders—Autism and Developmental Disabilities Monitoring Network, six sites, United States, 2000. *Centers for Disease Control and Prevention, 56*(SS01), 1–11.

Centers for Disease Control and Prevention. (2009). Prevalence of autism spectrum disorders—Autism and Developmental Disabilities Monitoring Network, United States, 2006. *Centers for Disease Control and Prevention, 58*(SS10), 1–20.

Centers for Disease Control and Prevention. (2012). Prevalence of autism spectrum disorders—Autism and Developmental Disabilities Monitoring Network, 14 sites, United States, 2008. *Centers for Disease Control and Prevention, 61*(3), 1–19.

Centers for Disease Control and Prevention. (2014). Prevalence of autism spectrum disorders among children aged 8 years—Autism and Developmental Disabilities Monitoring Network, 11 sites, United States, 2010. *Centers for Disease Control and Prevention, 63*(2), 1–22.

Chakrabarti, S., & Fombonne, É. (2001). Pervasive developmental disorders in preschool children. *Journal of the American Medical Association, 285*(24), 3093–3099. doi:10.1001/jama.285.24.3093

Chakrabarti, S., & Fombonne, É. (2005). Pervasive developmental disorders in preschool children: Confirmation of high prevalence. *American Journal of Psychiatry, 162*(6), 1133–1141. doi:10.1176/appi.ajp.162.6.1133

Croen, L. A., Grether, J. K., Hoogstrate, J., & Selvin, S. (2002). The changing prevalence of autism in California. *Journal of Autism and Developmental Disorders, 32*(3), 207–215.

Davidovitch, M., Hemo, B., Manning-Courtney, P., & Fombonne, É. (2013). Prevalence and incidence of autism spectrum disorder in an Israeli population. *Journal of Autism and Developmental Disorders, 43*(4), 785–793. doi:10.1007/s10803-012-1611-z

Durkin, M. S., Maenner, M. J., Meaney, F. J., Levy, S. E., DiGuiseppi, C., Nicholas, J. S., . . . Schieve, L. A. (2010). Socioeconomic inequality in the prevalence of autism spectrum disorder: Evidence from a US cross-sectional study. *PLoS ONE, 5*(7), e11551. doi:10.1371/journal.pone.0011551

Fombonne, É. (2001). Is there an epidemic of autism? *Pediatrics, 107*(2), 411–412.

Fombonne, É. (2003). Epidemiological surveys of autism and other pervasive developmental disorders: An update. *Journal of Autism and Developmental Disorders, 33*(4), 365–382.

Fombonne, É. (2005). Epidemiology of autistic disorder and other pervasive developmental disorders. *Journal of Clinical Psychiatry, 66*(Suppl. 10), 3–8.

Fombonne, É. (2007). Epidemiology. In A. Martin & F. Volkmar (Eds.), *Lewis's child and adolescent psychiatry: A comprehensive textbook* (4th ed., pp. 150–171). Philadelphia: Lippincott Williams & Wilkins.

Fombonne, É. (2009). Commentary: On King and Bearman. *International Journal of Epidemiology, 38*(5), 1241–1242. doi:10.1093/ije/dyp259

Fombonne, É., & Du Mazaubrun, Du, C. (1992). Prevalence of infantile autism in four French regions. *Social Psychiatry and Psychiatric Epidemiology, 27*(4), 203–210. doi:10.1016/S0890-8567(09)66566-7

Fombonne, É., Du Mazaubrun, C., Cans, C., & Grandjean, H. (1997). Autism and associated medical disorders in a French epidemiological survey. *Journal of the American Academy of Child & Adolescent Psychiatry, 36*(11), 1561–1569. doi:10.1016/S0890-8567(09)66566-7

Fombonne, É., Zakarian, R., Bennett, A., Meng, L., & McLean-Heywood, D. (2006). Pervasive developmental disorders in Montreal, Quebec, Canada: Prevalence and links with immunizations. *Pediatrics, 118*(1), e139–e150. doi:10.1542/peds.2005-2993

Franzini, L., Ribble, J. C., & Keddie, A. M. (2001). Understanding the Hispanic paradox. *Ethnicity & Disease, 11*(3), 496–518.

Gillberg, C. (1984). Infantile autism and other childhood psychoses in a Swedish urban region: Epidemiological aspects. *Journal of Child Psychology and Psychiatry and Allied Disciplines, 25*(1), 35–43. doi:10.1111/j.1469-7610.1984.tb01717.x

Gillberg, C., & Schaumann, H. (1982). Social class and infantile autism. *Journal of Autism and Developmental Disorders, 12*(3), 223–228.

Gillberg, C., Steffenburg, S., Börjesson, B., & Andersson, L. (1987). Infantile autism in children of immigrant parents: A population-based study from Göteborg, Sweden. *British Journal of Psychiatry, 150*, 856–858.

Gillberg, C., Steffenburg, S., & Schaumann, H. (1991). Is autism more common now than ten years ago? *British Journal of Psychiatry, 158*, 403–409.

Gurney, J. G., Fritz, M. S., Ness, K. K., Sievers, P., Newschaffer, C. J., & Shapiro, E. G. (2003). Analysis of prevalence trends of autism spectrum disorder in Minnesota. *Archives of Pediatrics & Adolescent Medicine, 157*(7), 622–627. doi:10.1001/archpedi.157.7.622

Hill, A. P., Zuckerman, K. E., & Fombonne, É. (2014). Epidemiology of autism spectrum disorders. In Volkmar, F.R., Paul, R., Rogers, S.J., Pelphrey, K.A., (Eds.), *Handbook of Autism and Pervasive Developmental Disorders* (pp. 57–96). John Wiley & Sons, Inc. Hoboken, NJ.

Honda, H., Shimizu, Y., Misumi, K., Niimi, M., & Ohashi, Y. (1996). Cumulative incidence and prevalence of childhood autism in children in Japan. *British Journal of Psychiatry, 169*(2), 228–235.

Honda, H., Shimizu, Y., & Rutter, M. (2005). No effect of MMR withdrawal on the incidence of autism: A total population study. *Journal of Child Psychology and Psychiatry and Allied Disciplines, 46*(6), 572–579. doi:10.1111/j.1469-7610.2005.01425.x

Hoshino, Y., Kumashiro, H., Yashima, Y., Tachibana, R., & Watanabe, M. (1982). The epidemiological study of autism in Fukushima-ken. *Psychiatry and Clinical Neurosciences, 36*(2), 115–124.

Idring, S., Rai, D., Dal, H., Dalman, C., Sturm, H., Zander, E., . . . Magnusson, C. (2012). Autism spectrum disorders in the Stockholm Youth Cohort: Design, prevalence and validity. *PLoS ONE, 7*(7), e41280. doi:10.1371/journal.pone.0041280

Kanner, L. (1943). Autistic disturbances of affective contact. *Nervous Child, 2*(3), 217–250.

Kataoka, S. H., Zhang, L., & Wells, K. B. (2002). Unmet need for mental health care among US children: Variation by ethnicity and insurance status. *American Journal of Psychiatry, 159*(9), 1548–1555.

Kawamura, Y., Takahashi, O., & Ishii, T. (2008). Reevaluating the incidence of pervasive develop-mental disorders: Impact of elevated rates of detection through implementation of an integrated system of screening in Toyota, Japan. *Psychiatry and Clinical Neurosciences, 62*(2), 152–159. doi:10.1111/j.1440-1819.2008.01748.x

Keen, D. V., Reid, F. D., & Arnone, D. (2010). Autism, ethnicity and maternal immigration. *British Journal of Psychiatry, 196*(4), 274–281. doi:10.1192/bjp.bp.109.065490

Kim, Y. S., Fombonne, É., Koh, Y.-J., Kim, S.-J., Cheon, K.-A., & Leventhal, B. L. (2014). A comparison of DSM-IV pervasive developmental disorder and DSM-5 autism spectrum disorder prevalence in an epi-demiologic sample. *Journal of the American Academy of Child & Adolescent Psychiatry, 53*(5), 500–508. doi:10.1016/j.jaac.2013.12.021

Kim, Y. S., Leventhal, B. L., Koh, Y.-J., Fombonne, É., Laska, E., Lim, E.-C., . . . Grinkler, R. R. (2011). Prevalence of autism spectrum disorders in a total population sample. *American Journal of Psychiatry, 168*(9), 904–912. doi:10.1176/appi.ajp.2011.10101532

King, M., & Bearman, P. (2009). Diagnostic change and the increased prevalence of autism. *International Journal of Epidemiology, 38*(5), 1224–1234. doi:10.1093/ije/dyp261

Kočovská, E., Fernell, E., Billstedt, E., Minnis, H., & Gillberg, C. (2012). Vitamin D and autism: Clinical review. *Research in Developmental Disabilities, 33*(5), 1541–1550. doi:10.1016/j.ridd.2012.02.015

Kogan, M. D., Blumberg, S. J., Schieve, L. A., Boyle, C. A., Perrin, J. M., Ghandour, R. M., . . . van Dyck, P. C. (2009). Prevalence of parent-reported diagnosis of autism spectrum disorder among children in the US, 2007. *Pediatrics, 124*(5), 1395–1403. doi:10.1542/peds.2009-1522

Laing, S. P., & Kamhi, A. (2003). Alternative assessment of language and literacy in culturally and linguistically diverse populations. *Language, Speech, and Hearing Services in Schools, 34*, 44–55. doi:10.1044/0161-1461(2003/005)

Larsson, H. J., Eaton, W. W., Madsen, K. M., Vestergaard, M., Olesen, A. V., Agerbo, E., . . . Mortensen, P. B. (2005). Risk factors for autism: Perinatal factors, parental psychiatric history, and socioeconomic status. *American Journal of Epidemiology, 161*(10), 916–925. doi:10.1093/aje/kwi123

Lauritsen, M. B., Pedersen, C. B., & Mortensen, P. B. (2005). Effects of familial risk factors and place of birth on the risk of autism: A nationwide register-based study. *Journal of Child Psychology and Psychiatry and Allied Disciplines, 46*(9), 963–971. doi:10.1111/j.1469-7610.2004.00391.x

Leonard, H., Glasson, E., Nassar, N., Whitehouse, A., Bebbington, A., Bourke, J., . . . Stanley, F. (2011). Autism and intellectual disability are differentially related to sociodemographic background at birth. *PLoS ONE, 6*(3), e17875. doi:10.1371/journal.pone.0017875

Li, J., Vestergaard, M., Obel, C., Christensen, J., Precht, D. H., Lu, M., . . . Olsen, J. (2009). A nationwide study on the risk of autism after prenatal stress exposure to maternal bereavement. *Pediatrics, 123*(4), 1102–1107. doi:10.1542/peds.2008-1734

Liptak, G. S., Benzoni, L. B., Mruzek, D. W., Nolan, K. W., Thingvoll, M. A., Wade, C. M., & Fryer, G. E. (2008). Disparities in diagnosis and access to health services for children with autism: Data from the National Survey of Children's Health. *Journal of Developmental & Behavioral Pediatrics, 29*(3), 152–160. doi:10.1097/DBP.0b013e318165c7a0

Lord, C., Risi, S., Lambrecht, L., Cook, E. H., Jr., Leventhal, B. L., DiLavore, P. C., . . . Rutter, M. (2000). The Autism Diagnostic Observation Schedule—Generic: A standard measure of social and communication deficits associated with the spectrum of autism. *Journal of Autism and Developmental Disorders, 30*(3), 205–223. doi:10.1023/A:1005592401947

Lord, C., Rutter, M., & Couteur, A. (1994). Autism Diagnostic Interview–Revised: A revised version of a diagnostic interview for caregivers of individuals with possible pervasive developmental disorders. *Journal of Autism and Developmental Disorders, 24*(5), 659–685. doi:10.1007/BF02172145

Lotter, V. (1966). Epidemiology of autistic conditions in young children. *Social Psychiatry, 1*(3), 124–135. doi:10.1007/bf00584048

Lotter, V. (1967). Epidemiology of autistic conditions in young children. *Social Psychiatry, 1*(4), 163–173. doi:10.1007/BF00578950

Maenner, M. J., & Durkin, M. S. (2010). Trends in the prevalence of autism on the basis of special education data. *Pediatrics, 126*(5), e1018–e1025. doi:10.1542/peds.2010-1023

Maenner, M. J., Rice, C. E., Arneson, C. L., Cunniff, C., Schieve, L. A., Carpenter, L. A., . . . Durkin, M. S. (2014). Potential impact of DSM-5 criteria on autism spectrum disorder prevalence estimates. *JAMA Psychiatry, 71*(3), 292–300. doi:10.1001/jamapsychiatry.2013.3893

Magnusson, C., Rai, D., Goodman, A., Lundberg, M., Idring, S., Svensson, A., . . . Dalman, C. (2012). Migration and autism spectrum disorder: Population-based study. *British Journal of Psychiatry, 201*, 109–115. doi:10.1192/bjp.bp.111.095125

Mandell, D. S., Wiggins, L. D., Carpenter, L. A., Daniels, J., DiGuiseppi, C., Durkin, M. S., . . . Kirby, R. S. (2009). Racial/ethnic disparities in the identification of children with autism spectrum disorders. *American Journal of Public Health, 99*(3), 493–498. doi:10.2105/AJPH.2007.131243

Nicholas, J. S., Carpenter, L. A., King, L. B., Jenner, W., & Charles, J. M. (2009). Autism spectrum disorders in preschool-aged children: Prevalence and comparison to a school-aged population. *Annals of Epidemiology, 19*(11), 808–814. doi:10.1016/j.annepidem.2009.04.005

Nygren, G., Cederlund, M., Sandberg, E., Gillstedt, F., Arvidsson, T., Carina Gillberg, I., . . . Gillberg, C. (2012). The prevalence of autism spectrum disorders in toddlers: A population study of 2-year-old Swedish children. *Journal of Autism and Developmental Disorders, 42*(7), 1491–1497. doi:10.1007/s10803-011-1391-x

Ouellette-Kuntz, H., Coo, H., Yu, C. T., Chudley, A. E., Noonan, A., Breitenbach, M., . . . Holden, J. J. (2006). Prevalence of pervasive developmental disorders in two Canadian providences. *Journal of Policy and Practice in Intellectual Disabilities, 3*(3), 164–172.

Palmer, R. F., Walker, T., Mandell, D., Bayles, B., & Miller, C.S. (2010). Explaining low rates of autism among Hispanic schoolchildren in Texas. *American Journal of Public Health, 100*(2), 270–272. doi:10.2105/AJPH.2008.150565

Pearce, N., Foliaki, S., Sporle, A., & Cunningham, C. (2004). Genetics, race, ethnicity, and health. *British Medical Journal, 328*(7447), 1070–1072. doi:10.1136/bmj.328.7447.1070

Pedersen, A., Pettygrove, S., Meaney, F. J., Mancilla, K., Gotschall, K., Kessler, D. B., . . . Cunniff, C. (2012). Prevalence of autism spectrum disorders in Hispanic and non-Hispanic white children. *Pediatrics, 129*(3), e629–e635. doi:10.1542/peds.2011-1145

Posserud, M., Lundervold, A. J., Lie, S. A., & Gillberg, C. (2010). The prevalence of autism spectrum disorders: Impact of diagnostic instrument and non-response bias. *Social Psychiatry and Psychiatric Epidemiology, 45*(3), 319–327. doi:10.1007/s00127-009-0087-4

Powell, J. E., Edwards, A., Edwards, M., Pandit, B. S., Sungum Paliwal, S. R., & Whitehouse, W. (2000). Changes in the incidence of childhood autism and other autistic spectrum disorders in preschool children from two areas of the West Midlands, UK. *Developmental Medicine & Child Neurology, 42*(9), 624–628.

Rai, D., Golding, J., Magnusson, C., Steer, C., Lewis, G., & Dalman, C. (2012). Prenatal and early life exposure to stressful life events and risk of autism spectrum disorders: Population-based studies in Sweden and England. *PLoS ONE, 7*(6), e38893. doi:10.1371/journal.pone.0038893

Rai, D., Lewis, G., Lundberg, M., Araya, R., Svensson, A., Dalman, C., . . . Magnusson, C. (2012). Parental socioeconomic status and risk of offspring autism spectrum disorders in a Swedish population-based study. *Journal of the American Academy of Child & Adolescent Psychiatry, 51*(5), 467–476. doi:10.1016/j.jaac.2012.02.012

Rajakumar, K., Thomas, S. B., Musa, D., Almario, D., & Garza, M. A. (2009). Racial differences in parents' distrust of medicine and research. *Archives of Pediatrics & Adolescent Medicine, 163*(2), 108–114. doi:10.1001/archpediatrics.2008.521

Rice, C. E., Baio, J., Van Naarden Braun, K., Doernberg, N., Meaney, F. J., Kirby, R. S.; ADDM Network. (2007). A public health collaboration for the surveillance of autism spectrum disorders. *Paediatric and Perinatal Epidemiology, 21*(2), 179–190. doi:10.1111/j.1365-3016.2007.00801.x

Rutter, M. (1970). Autistic children: Infancy to adulthood. *Seminars in Psychiatry, 2*(4), 435–450.

Samadi, S. A., Mahmoodizadeh, A., & McConkey, R. (2011). A national study of the prevalence of autism among five-year-old children in Iran. *Autism, 16*(1), 5–14. doi:10.1177/1362361311407091

Sanua, V. D. (1987). Infantile autism and parental socioeconomic status: A case of bimodal distribution. *Child Psychiatry & Human Development, 17*(3), 189–198. doi:10.1007/BF00706229

Schieve, L. A., Boulet, S. L., Blumberg, S. J., Kogan, M. D., Yeargin-Allsopp, M., Boyle, C. A., . . . Rice, C. (2012). Association between parental nativity and autism spectrum disorder among US-born non-Hispanic white and Hispanic children, 2007 National Survey of Children's Health. *Disability and Health Journal, 5*(1), 18–25. doi:10.1016/j.dhjo.2011.09.001

Shattuck, P. T. (2006). The contribution of diagnostic substitution to the growing administrative prevalence of autism in US special education. *Pediatrics, 117*(4), 1028–1037. doi:10.1542/peds.2005-1516

Shi, L., & Stevens, G. D. (2005). Disparities in access to care and satisfaction among US children: The roles of race/ethnicity and poverty status. *Public Health Reports, 120*(4), 431–441.

Thomas, P., Zahorodny, W., Peng, B., Kim, S., Jani, N., Halperin, W., & Brimacombe, M. (2012). The association of autism diagnosis with socioeconomic status. *Autism, 16*(2), 201–213. doi:10.1177/1362361311413397

Tsai, L., Stewart, M. A., Faust, M., & Shook, S. (1982). Social class distribution of fathers of children enrolled in the Iowa Autism program. *Journal of Autism and Developmental Disorders, 12*(3), 211–221. doi:10.1007/BF01531367

Wazana, A., Bresnahan, M., & Kline, J. (2007). The autism epidemic: Fact or artifact? *Journal of the American Academy of Child & Adolescent Psychiatry, 46*(6), 721–730.

Windham, G. C., Anderson, M. C., Croen, L. A., Smith, K. S., Collins, J., & Grether, J. K. (2011). Birth prevalence of autism spectrum disorders in the San Francisco Bay area by demographic and ascertainment source characteristics. *Journal of Autism and Developmental Disorders, 41*(10), 1362–1372. doi:10.1007/s10803-010-1160-2

Wing, L. (1980). Childhood autism and social class: A question of selection? *British Journal of Psychiatry, 137*(5), 410–417.

Wing, L., & Gould, J. (1979). Severe impairments of social interaction and associated abnormalities in children: Epidemiology and classification. *Journal of Autism and Developmental Disorders, 9*(1), 11–29.

Wing, L., Yeates, S. R., Brierley, L. M., & Gould, J. (1976). The prevalence of early childhood autism: Comparison of administrative and epidemiological studies. *Psychological Medicine, 6*(1), 89–100.

World Health Organization. (1977). *The ICD-9 classification of mental and behavioural disorders: Clinical descriptions and diagnostic guidelines.* Geneva: Author.

World Health Organization. (1992). *The ICD-10 classification of mental and behavioural disorders: Clinical descriptions and diagnostic guidelines.* Geneva: Author.

/// 13 /// NEUROPATHOLOGY OF AUTISM SPECTRUM DISORDER

MATTHEW P. ANDERSON

INTRODUCTION

Recent studies indicate that genetic defects, sometimes inherited but often de novo, underlie a large proportion of autism spectrum disorder (ASD) cases. The findings indicate that ASD is extremely heterogeneous, with each genetic abnormality accounting for less than 1% of cases. Heterogeneity was already evident clinically by the variable severity of each of the core behavioral domains and the variable comorbidities.

In light of the known genetic and clinical heterogeneity of ASD, one might expect heterogeneity in the neuropathological findings of postmortem brains as well; indeed, this is the case. Future studies of the postmortem brain in ASD would be strengthened by focusing on cases with the same genetic defect. A study focused on brains with the shared maternal 15q11–13 duplication is included later in this chapter as a representative example of this approach. There is also evidence for nongenetic causes in some cases of ASD. Defining these distinct nongenetic etiologies of ASD will be important to create a homogenous case series for studies of the postmortem brain.

Many neuropathologic studies of ASD have focused on the cerebral cortex, hippocampus, or cerebellum. Only a few have focused on the amygdala or brain stem. However, the behavioral deficits of ASD, whether core diagnostic components or frequent comorbidities, will each arise from distinct neuronal circuitries within the brain. Each subtype of ASD will have a distinctive set of behavioral deficits that will demand studies aimed at a distinct neuronal circuitry. These issues must also be considered when interpreting the significance of the current postmortem brain literature in ASD and deciding on the direction of future studies.

Technical and Other Issues in Postmortem Brain Analysis

Matching the brains of control subjects for age, sex, and postmortem interval will be very important in postmortem brain studies in ASD. Brain weight is affected by sex (male brains are larger than female brains) and age. There are a large number of sexually dimorphic properties of neuronal circuits that include differences in neuron numbers, dendritic arbor branching and spine densities, and regional and cellular gene and protein expression (for examples, see Yang & Shah, 2014).

Even more significant are the clinical conditions preceding death. Individuals experiencing cardiopulmonary insufficiency and support for prolonged periods of time will display the effects of episodic hypoxia (low oxygen supply to the brain) and/or ischemia (low blood flow to the brain) that can alter morphology, cause inflammatory cell reactions and infiltrates, and affect mRNA and protein expression levels. Similarly, if a patient died in status epilepticus (prolonged unremitting discharges of neuronal circuits), there will be changes due to excitotoxic cell death, innate immune responses, changes related to neural circuit plasticity, and anti-epileptic (homeostatic) and pro-epileptic changes in mRNA and protein expression; depending on the seizure type, these changes will be variable across many brain regions. The structural, transcriptional, and protein changes caused by a seizure can last for weeks. The hippocampus, thalamus, cerebellum, and cortex are just a few of the well-described sites that are strongly affected by generalized seizures. As described next, a number of ASD cases are associated with mutations in known epilepsy genes, and epilepsy is a frequent comorbidity in ASD; therefore, a large proportion of these postmortem brains will have changes related to recent or remote seizures.

Genetic and Postmortem Brain Studies of a Genetically Defined Type of Autism Spectrum Disorder: Idic15

In 1997, Cook et al. reported a family with a mother who transmitted supernumerary inverted duplicated chromosome15 (isodicentric chromosome 15, or Idic15, with two extra copies of the genomic region) to two children with ASD but not to one unaffected sibling. Significantly, the mother, who had inherited the Idic15 chromosome from her father, was unaffected, suggesting an imprinted gene was important. In 2010, Hogart, Wu, LaSalle, and Schanen reported that of 54 Idic15 subjects studied, 81% met strict criteria for ASD using the Autism Diagnostic Interview–Revised. In recent genome-wide transcriptional profiling studies, brain tissue from Idic15 ASD was compared to that of controls and undefined ASD cases, and similar transcriptional disturbances were reported in Idic15 and idiopathic ASD (Belgard & Geschwind, 2014, unpublished results). A neuropathologic comparison found Idic15 ASD brains (7 of 9 with epilepsy) to be microcephalic (1177 g), being significantly smaller than those of the idiopathic ASD cohort (1477 g; 4 of 10 with epilepsy) (Wegiel et al., 2012). Another difference was the finding of hippocampal granule neuron heterotopias (in CA4 alveus or dentate molecular layer) in 8 of 9 Idic15 cases but only 1 of the idiopathic ASD cases (Wegiel et al., 2012). Other types of hippocampal dysplasia were also more frequent in Idic15 than undefined ASD. Heterotopias in cerebellar white matter were found at an equivalent frequency (50% of cases for both Idic15 and idiopathic ASD). Similarly, three types of dysplastic changes were found in the cerebellum of the Idic15 and idiopathic ASD cases. These included dysplasia in parts of the nodulus and flocculus, vermis dysplasia, and focal polymicrogyria. By contrast, 50% of idiopathic ASD cases had dysplasia of the cerebral cortex (focal polymicrogyria, multifocal cortical dysplasia, and bottom-of-a-sulcus dysplasia), whereas cortical dysplasia was not found in any of the Idic15 ASD cases. Premorbid clinical electrophysiological studies to map the seizure foci can sometimes localize to regions of cortical dysplasia, but these were not presented in the study. Focal cortical and hippocampal dysplasia is often found in neurosurgical resections where the region was removed as a treatment for partial epilepsy clinically mapped to those sites. One can only speculate on whether any of these regions of dysplasia

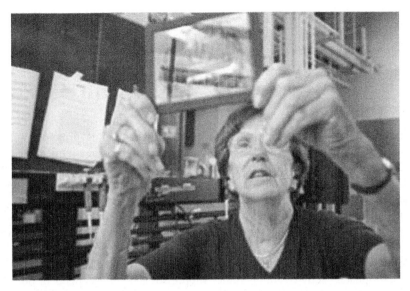

FIGURE 13.1 Some of the earliest studies of the neuropathology of autism were pioneered in the mid 1980's by Dr. Margaret L. Bauman (shown) and Dr. Thomas L. Kemper.

were epileptic foci and whether they had any role in producing the behavioral symptoms related to ASD or any of their associated comorbidities. Importantly, a correlation between the severity of the behavioral deficits and the seizure disorder has been noted in the literature for Idic15 (Dennis et al., 2006), and seizure-associated regression has been observed (http://www.dup15q.org). Knowing that heterogeneous genetic forms of ASD could account for as many as one-third of cases, one would anticipate heterogeneity in the neuropathology of ASD. This was illustrated previously when comparing the neuropathology of Idic15 and idiopathic ASD.

A common feature across published postmortem studies in ASD is the varied neuropathologies: (1) brain size: megalencephaly to microencephaly; (2) developmental malformations: cortical, hippocampal, or cerebellar dysplasia to absent brain stem nuclei; (3) cerebellar Purkinje neuron loss: severe to none; and (4) innate immune activation: severe, moderate, mild, or none.

Additional neuropathological findings in ASD can also be found in the following reviews: Blatt (2012); Amaral, Schumann, and Nordahl (2008); Bauman and Kemper (2005); and Palmen, van Engeland, Hof, and Schmitz (2004) (Figure 13.1).

MEGALENCEPHALY AND MICROCEPHALY IN AUTISM SPECTRUM DISORDER

Brains from individuals with ASD have been found in some cases to be larger (megalencephaly) or smaller (microcephaly) than those of control cohorts. Brain size could serve as a biomarker for ASD subtypes when trying to achieve efficacy in therapeutic trials and could cluster genetic subtypes into specific cellular and molecular pathways. Because ASD begins at an early age while the brain is still growing, it is important to compare brain size to that of age- and sex-matched controls. It is also important to monitor the brain growth trajectory. Seizures can have a delayed onset in ASD, and in some severe epilepsy disorders, regression in brain size and behavior are correlated with the onset and severity of seizures.

Severe epileptiform discharges are known to cause gross brain atrophy, excitotoxic neuronal cell death, and behavioral regression. Other ASD subtypes that begin with a normal brain size and behavior will regress in both domains in a pattern that appears to be independent of seizures (e.g., Rett's disorder).

Megalencephaly

Heterozygous mutations in chromodomain helicase DNA-binding protein 8 (CHD8) were originally discovered as rare missense mutations in whole exome sequencing studies of ASD cohorts (Neale et al., 2012; O'Roak et al., 2012), and CHD8 was disrupted in a rare balanced chromosome rearrangement (Talkowski et al., 2012). Subsequent sequencing of larger ASD and control cohorts identified 15 truncating mutations in 3730 cases (0.4%) while finding no mutations in 8792 unaffected siblings (Bernier et al., 2014). ASD was diagnosed in 13 of the 15 mutation-carrying individuals, indicating strong penetrance of the core behavioral deficits. Macrocephaly was also strongly penetrant (80%).

Phosphatase and tensin homolog deleted in chromosome 10 (PTEN) has dual protein and lipid phosphatase activity, and its tumor suppressor activity is dependent on its lipid phosphatase activity, which negatively regulates the phosphatidylinositol 3-kinase/Akt pathway. Mutations in the *PTEN* gene are associated with a broad spectrum of disorders, including Cowden disease-1 (CWD1; OMIM 158350), Bannayan–Riley–Ruvalcaba syndrome (OMIM 153480), and Lhermitte–Duclos disease. In a case series of 33 patients with ASD and macrocephaly, Klein, Sharifi-Hannauer, and Martinez-Agosto (2013) found that 22% harbored heterozygous mutations in *PTEN* in association with extreme macrocephaly (standard deviation >3; 99.7th percentile). O'Roak et al. (2012) identified three de novo mutations (two missense and one frameshift, all with macrocephaly) in the *PTEN* gene while sequencing 44 candidate genes among 2446 ASD probands, indicating the overall incidence among ASD cases is relatively low at 0.1%. Proteus syndrome (OMIM 176920), which is associated with gigantism of hands and feet, nevi, hemihypertrophy, and macrocephaly, is due to somatic activating mutations in the *AKT1* gene.

Amaral et al. (2008) reviewed the magnetic resonance imaging (MRI) evidence for an abnormal brain size and found that there may be a 5–10% enlargement (with a slightly greater increase of white matter volume) that may not persist into later childhood and adolescence. Neuropathological studies have reported increased brain weight in individual cases within cohorts of ASD (Bailey et al., 1998; Casanova, Buxhoeveden, Switala, & Roy, 2002a; Courchesne, Müller, & Saitoh, 1999; Kemper & Bauman, 1998; Williams, Hauser, Purpura, DeLong, & Swisher, 1980) (Figure 13.2).

Microcephaly

A subset of ASD cases present with brains that are small relative to those of controls. Cohen syndrome (ASD with mild facial dysmorphism and joint laxity) is one example (Hennies et al., 2004); Idic15 is another example (Wegiel et al., 2012). Heterozygous loss-of-function mutations in *DYRK1A*, another ASD gene, produce microcephaly in humans (van Bon et al., 2011). Christianson syndrome, a condition that presents as ASD or Angelman syndrome with mutism, intellectual disability, and generalized tonic–clonic epilepsy, is due to loss-of-function mutations in the X-linked gene *NHE6*, a sodium–proton exchange protein, and is characterized by a delayed onset postnatal microcephaly and cerebellar and brain stem atrophy (Pescosolido et al., 2014).

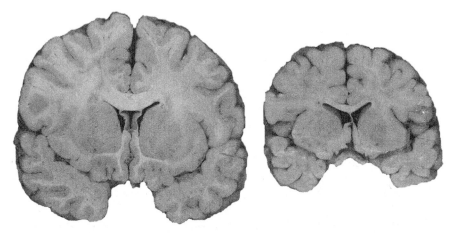

FIGURE 13.2 An example of human megalencephalic brain (left) as compared to a control (right), found in a subset of cases of autism spectrum disorder.

CEREBRAL CORTEX IN THE POSTMORTEM BRAIN IN AUTISM SPECTRUM DISORDER

Altered Cortical Thickness and Cortical Dysplasia

Increased cortical thickness and heterotopic and mal-oriented pyramidal neurons were reported in cases by Bailey et al. (1998). Polymicrogyria has been seen in two postmortem cases (Kemper & Bauman, 1998; Ritvo et al., 1986), and several MRI studies have observed developmental cortical abnormalities in a small proportion of subjects (Gaffney & Tsai, 1987; Piven et al., 1990). Bailey et al. (1998) reported cortical dysgenesis in four of six autistic cases, with thickened cortices, high neuronal density, the presence of neurons in the molecular layer, irregular laminar patterns, and poor gray–white matter boundaries. White matter abnormalities were also found in four cases, including ectopic gray matter in three cases and an increased number of white matter neurons in one case.

Cortical Tubers and Hemimegalencephaly

Somatic mutations in early progenitor cells that contribute to normal brain development underlie a subset of children and adults with drug-refractory epilepsy and comorbid intellectual disability and ASD. Somatic mutations within genes controlling cellular growth (tumor suppressor genes) are well-known to occur in cancer. A similar mechanism is thought to occur in the brains of individuals with the neurodevelopmental disorder tuberous sclerosis (TSc), in which individuals carry a germline mutation in either the *TSC1* or the *TSC2* gene. These individuals can often develop severe drug-refractory epilepsy disorders that are driven by a cortical tuber—an abnormally large cerebral cortex region (gyrus) that contains disorganized, often heterotopic, and abnormally large astroglia and neurons. The regions of cortical dysplasia are thought to arise from a second hit to the remaining normal *TSC1* or *TSC2* gene in the progenitor cell pool during cerebral cortical development. Some individuals without TSc can also present with drug-refractory focal seizures that on brain imaging show abnormal cerebral cortex gyri which are then treated through neurosurgery. These abnormal regions of cortex are removed surgically and are found histologically to be regions of cortical dysplasia. Again, the normal layered pattern of the cerebral cortex is often disorganized, sometimes with neurons of abnormal size, location, and numbers. Studies have shown that these abnormal cells often have constitutive activation of the same pathways affected by TSc mutations that promote aberrant growth, again suggesting somatic mutations of growth control genes as occurs in cancer. In some cases of refractory seizures, a very large proportion of one of the two hemispheres is expanded, called hemimegalencephaly. Recent studies identified somatic mutations in these brain overgrowth disorders of hemimegalencephaly associated with epilepsy and often intellectual disability (Lee et al., 2012; Poduri et al., 2012). For example, somatic mutations in several genes (*PIK3CA, AKT3*, and *mTOR*) were found in the neurons of these enlargements of just one hemisphere of the brain. The regions of dysplasia described previously in the neuropathological comparison between Idic15 and idiopathic ASD are likely to have resulted through similar somatic mutations in neural progenitor cell pools early during brain development.

Cortical Minicolumns

The configuration of so-called minicolumns was investigated in ASD and Asperger's disorder (Casanova, Buxhoeveden, Switala, & Roy, 2002b). More numerous, smaller, and less compact minicolumns were reported in 9 ASD subjects (7 with intellectual disability, 5 with epilepsy, and 4 with macroencephaly) compared with 9 control cases (Casanova et al., 2002b) and in 2 adults with Asperger's disorder compared with 18 control subjects (Casanova et al., 2002b).

Cortical Neuron Density Changes

Courchesne et al. (2011) reported an increase in the density of neurons in dorsolateral (78%) and mesial (28%) prefrontal cortex that statistically correlated with the increase in brain weight relative to an age-matched reference control weight. The ages of the male ASD cohort were 2, 3, 3, 4, 7, 8, and 16 years, with only one ASD case with known epilepsy.

Cortical Patches: Focal Loss of Molecular Markers

In a subsequent study by the Courchesne group (Stoner et al., 2014), in situ hybridization was performed using neuron layer-specific mRNAs. Based on the overgrowth pattern previously reported, one might have expected a poor demarcation of cortical layers with vertical dispersion of layer-specific mRNA markers. Instead, they found patches of morphologically normal cortex in which there was reduced or lost mRNA expression in the prefrontal or temporal cortex in 10 of 11 cases of ASD but in only 1 of 11 control cases. Interneuron markers (e.g., *PVALB* and *CALB1*) showed mild abnormalities, which were inconsistently present within patches across case samples, with a few exceptions (e.g., *GAD1* and *VIP*) that appeared to be relatively unaffected. Similarly, the glial markers were also unaffected with rare exceptions. The foci of reduced mRNA staining did not correspond to decreases in cell number. Foci of mRNA loss were not observed in occipital cortex. The significance of the finding remains undefined.

Cortical Neuron Spine Density Increases

Hutsler and Zhang (2010) reported increased spine density in cortical layer II pyramidal neurons. Tang et al. (2014) reported that in a small cohort of postmortem brains, the developmental decrease (pruning) in temporal lobe layer V pyramidal neuron basal dendrite spine density that normally occurs between childhood (2–8 years old) and adolescence (13–18 years old) failed to occur in age-matched ASD cases. However, when comparing the childhood age groups, there were no preexisting differences between ASD and control subjects. They also observed that during the period of childhood to adolescence, mTOR and S6 protein phosphorylation decreased in controls and that no significant decrease could be observed when averaged across the ASD cases. The postsynaptic density protein PSD95 also decreased across this developmental time period in controls, but it failed to decrease in ASD. They also found that LC3-II, a biomarker of autophagosomes, was reduced in ASD.

CEREBELLUM CHANGES IN POSTMORTEM BRAIN IN AUTISM SPECTRUM DISORDER

Purkinje Neuron Depletion

Williams et al. (1980) were the first to perform a detailed neuropathological analysis on four individuals with autistic behavior (three males, 12, 27, and 33 years of age; one female, 3 years of age; all presented with intellectual disability and two with seizures). Reduced Purkinje cell density was seen in one case, with concomitant epilepsy and profound intellectual disability. Ritvo et al. (1986) counted Purkinje cells in the cerebellum of four autistic cases (all males, three with intellectual disability and none with seizures) and three male controls. Autistic cases showed a decreased number of Purkinje cells in the cerebellar hemisphere and vermis. Kemper and Bauman (1998) also reported alterations in the cerebellum. All six autistic cases showed decreased numbers of Purkinje cells. Bailey et al. (1998), in their study of six ASD cases (all with intellectual disability and three with epilepsy) and seven age- and sex-matched controls, reported low Purkinje cell counts in all five adult ASD cases. Lee et al. (2002) examined two ASD cases (both with intellectual disability and one with epilepsy) and observed a decreased number of Purkinje cells in both cases. Fatemi, Halt, Realmuto, et al. (2002) were the first to examine the size of the cerebellar Purkinje cells. A 24% decrease in mean Purkinje cell size was reported in the ASD group.

NEUROTRANSMITTER SYSTEM CHANGES IN POSTMORTEM BRAIN IN AUTISM SPECTRUM DISORDER

GABAergic Neurons and Neurotransmission

Blatt (2012) reported on the GABAergic, serotonergic, cholinergic, and glutamatergic receptor binding sites in the postmortem ASD brain. They used radiolabeled muscimol and flunitrazepam binding to assess the $GABA_A$ receptor density. In 2007, Guptill et al. reported a 20% decrease in $GABA_A$ receptor binding sites in the hippocampus of ASD subjects compared to controls. In 2009 and 2011, Oblak, Gibbs, and Blatt found reduced $GABA_A$ receptor binding sites in superficial layers of anterior cingulate cortex (47%), posterior cingulate cortex (49%), and fusiform gyrus (31%) of subjects with ASD relative to control brains. In 2010, Oblak et al. also reported reduced GABA$_B$ receptor binding sites in anterior and posterior cingulate cortex, again most prominent in superficial layers (35% decrease). In the cases reported in 2009, four of the seven cases had known epilepsy, and three were on antiseizure medications. Fatemi, Halt, Stary, et al. (2002) showed that glutamic acid decarboxylase (GAD), the rate-limiting enzyme responsible for the conversion of glutamate to GABA in the brain, is reduced in ASD (five ASD and eight controls). GAD65 protein was reduced by 50% in the cerebellum and by 48% in the parietal cortex of ASD cases. GAD67 protein was reduced by 51% in the cerebellum and by 61% in the parietal cortex of ASD cases. Yip, Soghomonian, and Blatt (2007) demonstrated a 40% decrease in GAD67 mRNA in Purkinje neurons of posterolateral cerebellar cortex in ASD. Yip et al. (2008) also reported a 28% increase in GAD67 mRNA staining of cerebellar basket cells.

Serotonergic Neurons and Receptors

Azmitia, Singh, and Whitaker-Azmitia (2011) reported increased numbers of serotonergic axon terminals in the cortex of individuals with ASD. Oblak et al. (2013) reported reduced 5HT$_{1A}$ and 5HT$_{2A}$ receptor binding sites in the posterior cingulate cortex and fusiform gyrus in the brains of subjects with ASD relative to those of controls.

NEURODEGENERATIVE-TYPE CHANGES IN POSTMORTEM BRAIN IN AUTISM SPECTRUM DISORDER

Tauopathy in ASD-Related Neurodevelopmental Disorders

Christianson syndrome due to X-linked *NHE6* mutations shows tau-positive and Bielchowsky-positive neuronal and glial inclusions, as well as phosphorylated neurofilament inclusions particularly prominent in brain stem and subcortical regions (Garbern et al., 2010). Heterozygous deletion of *ADNP* in mice causes a tauopathy, neuronal cell death, and abnormalities in social behavior and cognitive functioning (Vulih-Shultzman et al., 2007), suggesting a similar change may be found in the brain of ASD cases with haploinsufficiency of *ADNP* (Helsmoortel et al., 2014). Interestingly, numerous neurofibrillary tangles were found in layers II and III of the cerebral cortex, especially in the temporal region, of a 24-year-old woman with ASD and intellectual disability attributed in this case to severe self-injurious behavior (Hof, Knabe, Bovier, & Bouras, 1991).

COMORBIDITY OF AUTISM SPECTRUM DISORDER AND EPILEPSY

De novo mutations in *SCN2A* and *SCN1A* are found in cases of ASD (reviewed in Krumm, O'Roak, Shendure, & Eichler, 2014). Interestingly, heterozygous missense mutations of these same genes are known to underlie forms of infantile epilepsy. Two of the genes are voltage-gated sodium channels *SCN2A* (*Nav1.2*) and *SCN1A* (*Nav1.1*). In Idic15, one of the more frequent strongly penetrant cytogenetic causes of ASD, seizures were reported in 63% of the 83 cases surveyed (Conant et al., 2014). In the postmortem neuropathology study described by Wegiel et al. (2012), the majority of Idic15 cases had epilepsy, and this was frequently the cause of premature death (sudden unexpected death in epilepsy). In a study of the clinical features of 65 individuals with 2q23.1 microdeletion syndrome in which microdeletion overlaps and balanced chromosomal rearrangements point to the *MBD5* gene, ASD and intellectual disability were comorbid with epilepsy in 85% of cases (Talkowski et al., 2011). These findings indicate that the neuropathology of ASD could variably include changes secondary to prolonged repetitive seizures such as hippocampal sclerosis, cerebral atrophy with astrogliosis and microgliosis, and cerebellar atrophy with loss of Purkinje cells and secondary Bergmann gliosis. A clinical clue is that these cases will also often have a history of regression sometimes coincident with seizures.

Seizure-Associated Neuropathology in Autism Spectrum Disorder

A subset of ASD cases present with hippocampal sclerosis, as recently reported in two cases of Idic15 (Boronat, Mehan, Shaaya, Thibert, & Caruso, 2014). In the *SCN2A* case reported by Kamiya et al. (2004), there was moderate diffuse atrophy by MRI, associated epilepsy, intellectual disability, psychomotor retardation, and ASD features. Cases of *SCN1A* mutation-associated migrating partial epilepsy of infancy, an epileptic encephalopathy, have been reported to show regression and an acquired progressive microcephaly (Carranza Rojo et al., 2011). Thus, some cases of microcephaly might result from the ongoing epileptiform discharge of circuits. Genetic forms of generalized epilepsy such as *SCN1A* (Mantegazza et al., 2005) develop a delayed mesial temporal sclerosis that then evolves into mesial temporal lobe epilepsy (focal seizures arising from the hippocampal formation and medial temporal lobe). Evidence suggests that repeated forebrain discharges travel to the hippocampal formation, where they cause excitotoxic cell death. Hyperexcitability then arises in the damaged local hippocampal circuits, which then become a new source of spontaneous epileptiform discharge. In studies of adult epilepsy patients, it is well documented that unilateral cortical status epilepticus (prolonged uncontrolled seizures, independent of medications) can cause a crossed cerebellar diaschisis with Purkinje cell and internal granule neuron depletion and associated cerebellar atrophy (Samaniego, Stuckert, Fischbein, & Wijman, 2010). Crossed cerebellar diaschisis is thought to represent cerebellar circuit injury caused by excessive neuronal transmission from prolonged excitatory synaptic activity via the corticopontine–cerebellar pathways. Based on the high incidence of epilepsy and the frequent Purkinje cell and granule neuron depletion and cerebellar atrophy in ASD, it is plausible that these types of changes in the cerebellum that have been reported in ASD postmortem brain studies result from chronic seizures. The behavioral significance of these histopathological defects in cerebellar circuits remains a subject of speculation but could in principle underlie some of the cognitive and/or social deficits present in ASD (for review, see Wang, Kloth, & Badura, 2014). Evidence supporting this notion is the finding that homozygous deletions of the *TSC1* or *TSC2* gene targeted to Purkinje neurons impair social behavior in mice (Reith et al., 2013; Tsai et al., 2012). Future conditional genetics approaches should facilitate mapping of the social behavior deficits and other comorbidities of the nonsyndromic genetic forms of ASD to specific neuronal circuits. Such studies are critical to helping focus the neuropathological studies of the ASD postmortem brain to specific behaviorally relevant neuronal circuitries, particularly when examining genetically defined subtypes of the condition.

Seizure Discharges During Sleep

In a number of the genetic ASD–epilepsy comorbidity disorders, seizures are prominent during sleep. This suggests that much of the epileptiform discharge could be clinically hidden. In the *SCN2A* case reported by Kamiya et al. (2004), the electroencephalogram showed frequent bilateral sharp waves or spike waves with maximum amplitude over the centroparietotemporal region that were semicontinuous during sleep. Similar bilateral sharp waves or spike waves during sleep are prominent in Idic15 (R. L. Thibert, personal communication).

INNATE IMMUNE SYSTEM IN POSTMORTEM BRAIN IN AUTISM SPECTRUM DISORDER

Molecular Markers of the Innate Immune System in Autism Spectrum Disorder Brain

Increased cytokines, chemokines, and growth factors have been identified in ASD brain tissue (anterior cingulate and cerebellum) and cerebrospinal fluid (Vargas, Nascimbene, Krishnan, Zimmerman, & Pardo, 2005) in some studies. Using an enzyme-linked immunosorbent assay approach focused on specific cytokines and chemokines, Li et al. (2009) confirmed an increase of tumor necrosis factor-α, interleukin-6 (IL-6), granulocyte–macrophage colony-stimulating factor, interferon-γ, and IL-8 in ASD compared to control brains. An increase of immune system-related mRNAs was also found in ASD postmortem brain tissue analyzed using unbiased genome-wide studies of transcripts (Garbett et al., 2008; Voineagu et al., 2011).

Activated Microglia in the Autism Spectrum Disorder Brain

In samples of postmortem prefrontal cortex, microglia-specific transcripts that are involved in their cellular responses were elevated in ASD relative to controls (Edmonson, Ziats, & Rennert, 2014): *TREM2* (1.75-fold), *DAP12* (1.5-fold), and *CX3CR1* (1.34-fold). However, another marker of activated microglia, *IBA1*, was not significantly elevated in ASD. Microglia play a critical role in synaptic pruning during postnatal brain development. In mice lacking *CX3CR1*, a chemokine receptor expressed by microglia in the brain, microglial cell numbers were transiently decreased and synaptic pruning was concurrently temporarily delayed (Paolicelli et al., 2011). The transient deficit in microglial numbers and increase in spine density were associated with a persistent deficit of prefrontal cortex–hippocampus connectivity as assessed by local field potential oscillatory coherence and functional MRI measurements, as well as some deficits in social behavior (Zhan et al., 2014). These model organism studies indicate that defects in microglial function could result in an increase in spine density as recently reported in ASD.

Activated Astroglia in the Autism Spectrum Disorder Brain

In samples of postmortem prefrontal cortex, the marker of activated astroglia, *GFAP* mRNA, was elevated 1.7-fold in ASD relative to controls. *GFAP* mRNA was even more strongly increased in cerebellum (2.63-fold) in ASD, but surprisingly, the microglial markers were instead slightly decreased in this brain region (Edmonson et al., 2014). In a separate study, GFAP protein was also increased 45–75% in frontal, parietal, and cerebellar cortex of ASD relative to control (Laurence & Fatemi, 2005). Another study found that the astroglia density was increased, whereas the number of branching processes and the branch lengths were reduced, in postmortem frontal cortex of ASD brains relative to those of controls, but these structural properties of astroglia were not altered in cerebellum (Cao et al., 2012). Aquaporin 4 protein, which localizes to the astroglia perivascular foot processes and functions as a water channel for fluid homeostasis, was reduced in ASD cerebellum relative to controls (Fatemi, Folsom, Reutiman, & Lee, 2008). Interestingly, the decrease of aquaporin 4 is opposite the change found in other neuropathologic conditions such as hypoxia/ischemia and trauma of the central nervous system, in which aquaporin 4 is increased (Benarroch, 2007).

Innate Immune Activity Indicates Neuropathology, Not Etiology

The fine delicate branches of the astrocyte become thickened and fewer and the quantity of somatic cytoplasm next to the nucleus increases with increased GFAP staining in a wide variety of neuropathological states. Astroglia and microglia become activated adjacent to regions of ischemic infarction in which early in the process, there are eosinophilic neurons, and later in the process there is loss of neurons with replacement foamy macrophages. In excitotoxic neuronal cell death due to a toxin, drug, or severe seizure, the distribution of neuronal death is scattered rather than in a vascular territory, but the same process of individual neuron degeneration with reactive microglia, foamy macrophages, and reactive astrocytes is seen. In areas of white matter demyelination, as in immune-mediated multiple sclerosis or progressive multifocal leukoencephalopathy due to polyoma JC virus infection, there is a microglial and macrophage infiltrate within the white matter with loss of myelin by luxol fast blue staining but relative preservation of axons by neurofilament or Bodian staining and many perivascular lymphocytic cuffs. There are also reactive microglia and astrocytes in brain regions infiltrated by tumor cells, whether an infiltrating glioma, a lymphoma, or a metastatic tumor. In addition, there are reactive astroglia and microglia in neurodegenerative diseases such as Alzheimer's disease, often prominent adjacent to neuritic plaques containing deposits of amyloid. A small subset of Alzheimer's cases result from genetic mutations or copy number variants within amyloid or amyloid processing proteins. In these situations, there are extracellular deposits of amyloid visible with β-amyloid staining and intracellular deposits visible with Bielshowski silver stain but more readily seen using antibodies to ubiquitin or τ- or α-synuclein. Interestingly, there appear to be rare subsets of ASD that have intraneuronal τ inclusions. ASD due to *NHE6* mutations (Christianson syndrome) display τ-positive inclusions (Garbern et al., 2010) and may progress as a neurodegenerative disease with age (E. Morrow, personal communication). Similarly, ASD due to haploinsufficiency of *ADNP* (Helsmoortel et al., 2014) is associated with τ inclusions in animal models of this condition. There are also reactive astrocytes and microglia in some genetic neuronal storage disorders, but there are no reports of increased intracellular storage material (glycogen, lipid, and lipofuscin) in the ASD neuropathology literature. Reactive astrocytes and microglia are found within regions of autoimmune encephalitis, such as Rasmussen's (antibodies to glutamate receptor type 3, α_7-acetylcholine receptor, and NMDA-type GluRϵ_2 receptor); however, in these conditions there are also concurrent T lymphocytes cuffing vessels and within the parenchyma and microglial nodules are found "attacking" cortical pyramidal neurons. These features have not yet been reported in any ASD postmortem brain cases. Astroglial and microglial activation is also observed within regions of viral encephalitis, but again, there are typically T lympho-cyte cuffs and microglial nodules surrounding infected neurons. In some cases of viral encephalitis, the intraneuronal inclusions contain dense collections of viral particles on electron microscopy. The lymphocytic and microglial reactions typical of a viral infec-tion of neurons or of an autoimmune disease have not been reported in the ASD neu-ropathology literature. Therefore, although these quantitative measures of microglial and astrocytic changes in ASD are helpful in establishing the presence of a pathological condition and the magnitude of this change might someday become a biomarker that correlates with the severity of clinical signs and symptoms in ASD, the findings alone are not sufficient to implicate a specific etiology. Again, one must also keep in mind that the neuropathology of ASD will be as heterogeneous as we are finding for the genet-ics of ASD. If ASD is anything like epilepsy, there will be genetic, autoimmune, viral, toxic–metabolic, and focal lesional causes. In the nongenetic epilepsies, there is often a distinctive neuropathology that can implicate one specific class of etiologies (e.g., corti-cal dysplasia). The same might be expected to be true for ASD.

Developmental Circuit Pruning Defects: Speculations on a Neuropathology Unique to Autism Spectrum Disorder

Chung et al. (2013) demonstrated that the genetic loss of two phagocytic receptors, Megf10 and Mertk, expressed on astroglia, impairs the ability of astroglia to phagocy-tize synapses and causes a failure to developmentally prune connections in the neuro-nal circuits that relay visual signals from the retina to the thalamus. The implication is that impaired astroglial function might arrest axonal pruning in all neuronal cir-cuits that normally must undergo postnatal developmental remodeling. Interestingly, the combined dominant negative and haploid insufficient loss of *LGI1* function in a human partial epilepsy (Kalachikov et al., 2002) also partially arrests developmen-tal pruning of hippocampal dentate gyrus synapses (Zhou et al., 2009) and retino-geniculate axons (Zhou et al., 2012) and leads to a severe epilepsy with premature early death when fully deleted only in glutamatergic neurons (Boillot et al., 2014). The retinogeniculate circuit is convenient for such studies because it undergoes quite dramatic changes—initially the axons of 6–10 retinal ganglion cells innervate each tha-lamic relay neuron, but then they prune to only a single or pair (with the second much weaker) of retinogeniculate axonal inputs to each relay neuron. This pruning occurs at approximately age 16–20 days in mice, probably equivalent to approximately age 1 or 2 years in the humans. Concurrent with this pruning, the strength of single axonal inputs is dramatically increased as the dendritic arbor of a single retinal ganglion cell's axon reoccupies the sites on the thalamic relay neuron dendrite that become exposed as the other retinal ganglion neuron axonal synapses are removed. The pruning process is sensory experience/neuronal activity-dependent and enables sensory experiences and features of the sensory organ to sculpt the sensory topographic map. The surpris-ing finding is that astrocytes play a critical role in this process. The implication is that genetic or other insults that impair astrocyte function during this critical period of circuit remodeling could partially block developmental circuit pruning to impair the fidelity and efficacy of transmission across sensory pathways. Far less is known about developmental pruning in other important neural systems that might underlie the non-sensory behavioral problems found in ASD.

ETIOLOGIES OF THE ACTIVATED INNATE IMMUNE SYSTEM IN THE BRAIN IN AUTISM SPECTRUM DISORDER

Maternal–Fetal Autoantibodies

Goines et al. (2011) reported the presence of antibodies to cerebellum proteins in individuals with ASD, but the same antibodies were also variably found in controls. Piras et al. (2014) correlated more severe ASD behavioral symptoms with increased anti-brain antibodies. Nordhal et al. (2013) correlated maternal–fetal autoantibodies to brain enlargement in ASD. As an approach to establish causal relationships between these antibodies and the autism-associated behavioral deficits, the Amaral group introduced the ASD-associated maternal autoantibodies into monkeys during pregnancy and found that progeny displayed aberrant social behaviors and an enlarged brain (Bauman et al., 2013).

Infections

A number of ASD cases have been associated with congenital cytomegalovirus infection (Yamashita, Fujimoto, Nakajima, Isagai, & Matsuishi, 2003). Cases of ASD and enterovirus encephalitis have also been reported (Marques, Brito, Conde, Pinto, & Moreira, 2014). As a step toward establishing causality between viral infection and some of the ASD brain postmortem findings, it was reported that in utero exposure to maternal influenza virus infection (Fatemi, Earle, et al., 2002) or viral analogs (Smith, Elliott, & Anderson, 2012) in pregnant mice resulted in an excessive number of neurons in the cerebral cortex at birth. The increased cell density was most prominent at birth and then partially receded with age. The changes triggered by the in utero viral infection/analog resemble those found in ASD postmortem brain, including the recently confirmed reduced neuronal soma size (Wegiel et al., 2014), the increased frontal lobe neuronal densities (Courchesne et al., 2011), and the early increased brain growth reported by many MRI studies in vivo (reviewed in Amaral et al., 2008). Activation of the maternal immune system during pregnancy is also sufficient to cause behavioral deficits of reduced social interaction (Smith, Li, Garbett, Mirnics, & Patterson, 2007) and increased fetal and early postnatal brain cytokines (Garay, Hsiao, Patterson, & McAllister, 2013) resembling those changes found in human ASD. Social deficits and increased repetitive behavior were also produced in monkeys when the mother was exposed to a viral analog during the first trimester (Bauman et al., 2014).

Seizures/Epileptiform Discharge

Dysplastic changes in cerebral cortex (a known source of epileptiform discharge; e.g., focal cortical dysplasia or cortical tubers of TSc) or cerebellum appear to be found in a higher proportion of ASD cases than controls (Weigel et al., 2012). As described previously, many of the recently identified rare single gene loss-of-function mutations found in ASD are also known to occur in cases of infantile epileptic encephalopathy. There is a very high incidence of epilepsy in ASD, and it is well documented that seizures activate the innate immune system.

Molecular Changes

Studies of the mRNAs in postmortem brain in ASD found increases in immune system-related gene expression (Garbett et al., 2008; Voineagu et al., 2011). Voineagu et al. identified a large increase of S100a8 mRNA, a native toll-like receptor 4 (TLR4) agonist in ASD. Systemic or direct brain inoculation with the TLR4 agonist lipopolysaccharide has been shown to be a robust stimulant of the brain's innate immune system. TLR4 receptors were recently shown to be important as an acute and chronic pro-epilepsy pathway (Maroso et al., 2010). TLR4 is increased in neurons and astroglia (not in microglia) of human mesial temporal lobe resection specimens removed for temporal lobe epilepsy, and the levels correlate with the frequency of seizures per month prior to removal (Pernhorst et al., 2013). However, in the same study, IL-8 expression was inversely related to seizure frequency in the human samples, but it is elevated in ASD postmortem brain (Garbett et al., 2008).

SUMMARY

This chapter reviewed results from studies of the postmortem brain in ASD. As with the clinical presentation and genetic causes in ASD, the heterogeneity of findings is apparent. Future studies in neuropathology will focus on cases with the same genetic defect. In addition, distinct nongenetic etiologies, such as immune, infectious, toxic–metabolic, and focal lesional causes, will be found to have a distinctive neuropathology.

KEY POINTS

- To date, the results from neuropathologic studies of ASD have yielded heterogeneous findings of brain abnormality.
- Cases of larger (megalencephaly) and smaller (microcephaly) brains in ASD have been identified in postmortem studies; some of these abnormalities have been linked to specific genetic defects.
- The areas of the brain that have most consistently been found to be abnormal in the postmortem brain in ASD are the cerebral cortex and the cerebellum.
- Seizures occur in 25–33% of individuals with ASD; as a result, changes in postmortem brain secondary to repetitive seizures will need to be considered in the findings.
- Evidence for activation of the innate immune system has been found in the postmortem brain of some individuals with ASD in some studies.

DISCLOSURE STATEMENT

Dr. Matthew P. Anderson has nothing to disclose.

REFERENCES

Amaral, D. G., Schumann, C. M., & Nordahl, C. W. (2008). Neuroanatomy of autism. *Trends in Neuroscience*, *31*(3), 137–145.

Azmitia, E. C., Singh, J. S., & Whitaker-Azmitia, P. M. (2011). Increased serotonin axons (immunoreactive to 5-HT transporter) in postmortem brains from young autism donors. *Neuropharmacology*, *60*(7–8), 1347–1354.

Bailey, A., Luthert, P., Dean, A., Harding, B., Janota, I., Montgomery, M., et al. (1998). A clinicopathological study of autism. *Brain, 121*(Pt. 5), 889–905.

Bauman, M. D., Iosif, A. M., Ashwood, P., Braunschweig, D., Lee, A., Schumann, C. M., et al. (2013). Maternal antibodies from mothers of children with autism alter brain growth and social behavior development in the rhesus monkey. *Translational Psychiatry, 3*:e278. doi:10.1038/tp.2013.47

Bauman, M. D., Iosif, A. M., Smith, S. E., Bregere, C., Amaral, D. G., & Patterson, P. H. (2014). Activation of the maternal immune system during pregnancy alters behavioral development of rhesus monkey offspring. *Biological Psychiatry, 75*(4), 332–341.

Bauman, M. L., & Kemper, T. L. (2005). Neuroanatomic observations of the brain in autism: A review and future directions. *International Journal of Developmental Neuroscience, 23*(2–3), 183–187.

Benarroch, E. E. (2007). Aquaporin-4, homeostasis, and neurologic disease. *Neurology, 69*(24), 2266–2268.

Bernier, R., Golzio, C., Xiong, B., Stessman, H. A., Coe, B. P., Penn, O., et al. (2014). Disruptive CHD8 mutations define a subtype of autism early in development. *Cell, 158*(2), 263–276.

Blatt, G. J. (2012). The neuropathology of autism. *Scientifica (Cairo), 2012*:703675. doi:10.6064/2012/703675

Boillot, M., Huneau, C., Marsan, E., Lehongre, K., Navarro, V., Ishida, S., et al. (2014). Glutamatergic neuron-targeted loss of *LGI1* epilepsy gene results in seizures. *Brain, 137*(Pt. 11), 2984–2996.

Boronat, S., Mehan, W. A., Shaaya, E. A., Thibert, R. L., & Caruso, P. (2014). Hippocampal abnormalities in magnetic resonance imaging (MRI) of 15q duplication syndromes. *Journal of Child Neurology, 30*(3), 333–338.

Cao, F., Yin, A., Wen, G., Sheikh, A. M., Tauqeer, Z., Malik, M., et al. (2012). Alteration of astrocytes and Wnt/β-catenin signaling in the frontal cortex of autistic subjects. *Journal of Neuroinflammation, 9*(1), 223.

Carranza Rojo, D., Hamiwka, L., McMahon, J. M., Dibbens, L. M., Arsov, T., Suls, A., et al. (2011). De novo SCN1A mutations in migrating partial seizures of infancy. *Neurology, 77*(4), 380–383.

Casanova, M. F., Buxhoeveden, D. P., Switala, A. E., & Roy, E. (2002a). Neuronal density and architecture (Gray Level Index) in the brains of autistic patients. *Journal of Child Neurology, 17*(7), 515–521.

Casanova, M. F., Buxhoeveden, D. P., Switala, A. E., & Roy, E. (2002b). Asperger's syndrome and cortical neuropathology. *Journal of Child Neurology, 17*(2), 142–145.

Chung, W. S., Clarke, L. E., Wang, G. X., Stafford, B. K., Sher, A., Chakraborty, C., et al. (2013). Astrocytes mediate synapse elimination through MEGF10 and MERTK pathways. *Nature, 504*(7480), 394–400.

Conant, K. D., Finucane, B., Cleary, N., Martin, A., Muss, C., Delany, M., et al. (2014). A survey of seizures and current treatments in 15q duplication syndrome. *Epilepsia, 55*(3), 396–402.

Cook, E. H., Jr., Lindgren, V., Leventhal, B. L., Courchesne, R., Lincoln, A., Shulman, C., et al. (1997). Autism or atypical autism in maternally but not paternally derived proximal 15q duplication. *American Journal of Human Genetics, 60*(4), 928–934.

Courchesne, E., Mouton, P. R., Calhoun, M. E., Semendeferi, K., Ahrens-Barbeau, C., Hallet, M. J., et al. (2011). Neuron number and size in prefrontal cortex of children with autism. *JAMA, 306*(18), 2001–2010.

Courchesne, E., Müller, R. A., & Saitoh, O. (1999). Brain weight in autism: Normal in the majority of cases, megalencephalic in rare cases. *Neurology, 52*(5), 1057–1059.

Dennis, N. R., Veltman, M. W., Thompson, R., Craig, E., Bolton, P. F., & Thomas, N. S. (2006). Clinical findings in 33 subjects with large supernumerary marker(15) chromosomes and 3 subjects with triplication of 15q11–q13. *American Journal of Medical Genetics A, 140*(5), 434–441.

Edmonson, C., Ziats, M. N., & Rennert, O. M. (2014). Altered glial marker expression in autistic post-mortem prefrontal cortex and cerebellum. *Molecular Autism, 5*(1), 3.

Fatemi, S. H., Earle, J., Kanodia, R., Kist, D., Emamian, E. S., Patterson, P. H., et al. (2002). Prenatal viral infection leads to pyramidal cell atrophy and macrocephaly in adulthood: Implications for genesis of autism and schizophrenia. *Cellular and Molecular Neurobiology, 22*(1), 25–33.

Fatemi, S. H., Folsom, T. D., Reutiman, T. J., & Lee, S. (2008). Expression of astrocytic markers aquaporin 4 and connexin 43 is altered in brains of subjects with autism. *Synapse, 62*(7), 501–507.

Fatemi, S. H., Halt, A. R., Realmuto, G., Earle, J., Kist, D. A., Thuras, P., et al. (2002). Purkinje cell size is reduced in cerebellum of patients with autism. *Cellular and Molecular Neurobiology, 22*(2), 171–175.

Fatemi, S. H., Halt, A. R., Stary, J. M., Kanodia, R., Schulz, S. C., & Realmuto, G. R. (2002). Glutamic acid decarboxylase 65 and 67 kDa proteins are reduced in autistic parietal and cerebellar cortices. *Biological Psychiatry*, 52(8), 805–810.

Gaffney, G. R., & Tsai, L. Y. (1987). Magnetic resonance imaging of high level autism. *Journal of Autism and Developmental Disorders*, 17(3), 433–438.

Garay, P. A., Hsiao, E. Y., Patterson, P. H., & McAllister, A. K. (2013). Maternal immune activation causes age- and region-specific changes in brain cytokines in offspring throughout development. *Brain, Behavior, and Immunity*, 31, 54–68.

Garbern, J. Y., Neumann, M., Trojanowski, J. Q., Lee, V. M., Feldman, G., Norris, J. W., et al. (2010). A mutation affecting the sodium/proton exchanger, SLC9A6, causes mental retardation with tau deposition. *Brain*, 133(Pt. 5), 1391–1402.

Garbett, K., Ebert, P. J., Mitchell, A., Lintas, C., Manzi, B., Mirnics, K., et al. (2008). Immune transcriptome alterations in the temporal cortex of subjects with autism. *Neurobiology of Disease*, 30(3), 303–311.

Goines, P., Haapanen, L., Boyce, R., Duncanson, P., Braunschweig, D., Delwiche, L., et al. (2011). Autoantibodies to cerebellum in children with autism associate with behavior. *Brain, Behavior, and Immunity*, 25(3), 514–523. doi:10.1016/j.bbi.2010.11.017

Guptill, J. T., Booker, A. B., Gibbs, T. T., Kemper, T. L., Bauman, M. L., & Blatt, G. J. (2007). [3H]-Flunitrazepam-labeled benzodiazepine binding sites in the hippocampal formation in autism: A multiple concentration autoradiographic study. *Journal of Autism and Developmental Disorders*, 37(5), 911–920.

Helsmoortel, C., Vulto-van Silfhout, A. T., Coe, B. P., Vandeweyer, G., Rooms, L., van den Ende, J., et al. (2014). A SWI/SNF-related autism syndrome caused by de novo mutations in ADNP. *Nature Genetics*, 46(4), 380–384.

Hennies, H. C., Rauch, A., Seifert, W., Schumi, C., Moser, E., Al-Taji, E., et al. (2004). Allelic heterogeneity in the *COH1* gene explains clinical variability in Cohen syndrome. *American Journal of Human Genetics*, 75(1), 138–145.

Hof, P. R., Knabe, R., Bovier, P., & Bouras, C. (1991). Neuropathological observations in a case of autism presenting with self-injury behavior. *Acta Neuropathologica*, 82(4), 321–326.

Hogart, A., Wu, D., LaSalle, J. M., & Schanen, N. C. (2010). The comorbidity of autism with the genomic disorders of chromosome 15q11.2–q13. *Neurobiology of Disease*, 38(2), 181–191.

Hutsler, J. J., & Zhang, H. (2010). Increased dendritic spine densities on cortical projection neurons in autism spectrum disorders. *Brain Research*, 1309, 83–94.

Kalachikov, S., Evgrafov, O., Ross, B., Winawer, M., Barker-Cummings, C., Martinelli Boneschi, F., et al. (2002). Mutations in LGI1 cause autosomal-dominant partial epilepsy with auditory features. *Nature Genetics*, 30(3), 335–341.

Kamiya, K., Kaneda, M., Sugawara, T., Mazaki, E., Okamura, N., Montal, M., et al. (2004). A nonsense mutation of the sodium channel gene *SCN2A* in a patient with intractable epilepsy and mental decline. *Journal of Neuroscience*, 24(11), 2690–2698.

Kemper, T. L., & Bauman, M. (1998). Neuropathology of infantile autism. *Journal of Neuropathology &Experimental Neurology*, 57(7), 645–652.

Klein, S., Sharifi-Hannauer, P., & Martinez-Agosto, J. A. (2013). Macrocephaly as a clinical indicator of genetic subtypes in autism. *Autism Research*, 6(1), 51–56.

Krumm, N., O'Roak, B. J., Shendure, J., & Eichler, E. E. (2014). A de novo convergence of autism genetics and molecular neuroscience. *Trends in Neuroscience*, 37(2), 95–105.

Laurence, J. A., & Fatemi, S. H. (2005). Glial fibrillary acidic protein is elevated in superior frontal, parietal and cerebellar cortices of autistic subjects. *Cerebellum*, 4(3), 206–210.

Lee, J. H., Huynh, M., Silhavy, J. L., Kim, S., Dixon-Salazar, T., Heiberg, A., et al. (2012). De novo somatic mutations in components of the PI3K–AKT3–mTOR pathway cause hemimegalencephaly. *Nature Genetics*, 44(8), 941–945.

Lee, M., Martin-Ruiz, C., Graham, A., Court, J., Jaros, E., Perry, R., et al. (2002). Nicotinic receptor abnormalities in the cerebellar cortex in autism. *Brain*, 125(Pt. 7), 1483–1495.

Li, X., Chauhan, A., Sheikh, A. M., Patil, S., Chauhan, V., Li, X. M., et al. (2009). Elevated immune response in the brain of autistic patients. *Journal of Neuroimmunology, 207*(1–2), 111–116.

Mantegazza, M., Gambardella, A., Rusconi, R., Schiavon, E., Annesi, F., Cassulini, R. R., et al. (2005). Identification of an Nav1.1 sodium channel (SCN1A) loss-of-function mutation associated with familial simple febrile seizures. *Proceedings of the National Academy of Sciences of the USA, 102*(50), 18177–18182.

Maroso, M., Balosso, S., Ravizza, T., Liu, J., Aronica, E., Iyer, A. M., et al. (2010). Toll-like receptor 4 and high-mobility group box-1 are involved in ictogenesis and can be targeted to reduce seizures. *Nature Medicine, 16*(4), 413–419.

Marques, F., Brito, M. J., Conde, M., Pinto, M., & Moreira, A. (2014). Autism spectrum disorder secondary to enterovirus encephalitis. *Journal of Child Neurology, 29*(5), 708–714. doi:10.1177/0883073813508314

Neale, B. M., Kou, Y., Liu, L., Ma'ayan, A., Samocha, K. E., Sabo, A., et al. (2012). Patterns and rates of exonic de novo mutations in autism spectrum disorders. *Nature, 485*(7397), 242–245.

Nordahl, C. W., Braunschweig, D., Iosif, A. M., Lee, A., Rogers, S., Ashwood, P., et al. (2013). Maternal autoantibodies are associated with abnormal brain enlargement in a subgroup of children with autism spectrum disorder. *Brain, Behavior, and Immunity, 30*, 61–65. doi:10.1016/j.bbi.2013.01.084

Oblak, A., Gibbs, T. T., & Blatt, G. J. (2009). Decreased GABAA receptors and benzodiazepine binding sites in the anterior cingulate cortex in autism. *Autism Research, 2*(4), 205–219.

Oblak, A., Gibbs, T. T., & Blatt, G. J. (2013). Reduced serotonin receptor subtypes in a limbic and a neocortical region in autism. *Autism Research, 6*(6), 571–583.

Oblak, A. L., Gibbs, T. T., & Blatt, G. J. (2010). Decreased GABA(B) receptors in the cingulate cortex and fusiform gyrus in autism. *Journal of Neurochemistry, 114*(5), 1414–1423.

Oblak, A. L., Gibbs, T. T., & Blatt, G. J. (2011). Reduced GABAA receptors and benzodiazepine binding sites in the posterior cingulate cortex and fusiform gyrus in autism. *Brain Research, 1380*, 218–228.

O'Roak, B. J., Vives, L., Fu, W., Egertson, J. D., Stanaway, I. B., Phelps, I. G., et al. (2012). Multiplex targeted sequencing identifies recurrently mutated genes in autism spectrum disorders. *Science, 338*(6114), 1619–1622.

Palmen, S. J., van Engeland, H., Hof, P. R., & Schmitz, C. (2004). Neuropathological findings in autism. *Brain, 127*(Pt. 12), 2572–2583.

Paolicelli, R. C., Bolasco, G., Pagani, F., Maggi, L., Scianni, M., Panzanelli, P., et al. (2011). Synaptic pruning by microglia is necessary for normal brain development. *Science, 333*(6048), 1456–1458.

Pernhorst, K., Herms, S., Hoffmann, P., Cichon, S., Schulz, H., Sander, T., et al. (2013). TLR4, ATF-3 and IL8 inflammation mediator expression correlates with seizure frequency in human epileptic brain tissue. *Seizure, 22*(8), 675–678.

Pescosolido, M. F., Stein, D. M., Schmidt, M., El Achkar, C. M., Sabbagh, M., Rogg, J. M., et al. (2014). Genetic and phenotypic diversity of *NHE6* mutations in Christianson syndrome. *Annals of Neurology, 76*(4), 581–593.

Piras, I. S., Haapanen, L., Napolioni, V., Sacco, R., Van de Water, J., & Persico, A. M. (2014). Anti-brain antibodies are associated with more severe cognitive and behavioral profiles in Italian children with Autism Spectrum Disorder. *Brain, Behavior, and Immunity, 38*, 91–99. doi:10.1016/j.bbi.2013.12.020

Piven, J., Berthier, M. L., Starkstein, S. E., Nehme, E., Pearlson, G., & Folstein, S. (1990). Magnetic resonance imaging evidence for a defect of cerebral cortical development in autism. *American Journal of Psychiatry, 147*(6), 734–739.

Poduri, A., Evrony, G. D., Cai, X., Elhosary, P. C., Beroukhim, R., Lehtinen, M. K., et al. (2012). Somatic activation of AKT3 causes hemispheric developmental brain malformations. *Neuron, 74*(1), 41–48.

Reith, R. M., McKenna, J., Wu, H., Hashmi, S. S., Cho, S. H., Dash, P. K., et al. (2013). Loss of Tsc2 in Purkinje cells is associated with autistic-like behavior in a mouse model of tuberous sclerosis complex. *Neurobiology of Disease, 51*, 93–103.

Ritvo, E. R., Freeman, B. J., Scheibel, A. B., Duong, T., Robinson, H., Guthrie, D., et al. (1986). Lower Purkinje cell counts in the cerebella of four autistic subjects: Initial findings of the UCLA–NSAC Autopsy Research Report. *American Journal of Psychiatry, 143*(7), 862–866.

Samaniego, E. A., Stuckert, E., Fischbein, N., & Wijman, C. A. (2010). Crossed cerebellar diaschisis in status epilepticus. *Neurocritical Care, 12*(1), 88–90.

Smith, S. E., Elliott, R. M., & Anderson, M. P. (2012). Maternal immune activation increases neonatal mouse cortex thickness and cell density. *Journal of Neuroimmune Pharmacology, 7*(3), 529–532.

Smith, S. E., Li, J., Garbett, K., Mirnics, K., & Patterson, P. H. (2007). Maternal immune activation alters fetal brain development through interleukin-6. *Journal of Neuroscience, 27*(40), 10695–10702.

Stoner, R., Chow, M. L., Boyle, M. P., Sunkin, S. M., Mouton, P. R., Roy, S., et al. (2014). Patches of disorganization in the neocortex of children with autism. *New England Journal of Medicine, 370*(13), 1209–1219.

Talkowski, M. E., Mullegama, S. V., Rosenfeld, J. A., van Bon, B. W., Shen, Y., Repnikova, E. A., et al. (2011). Assessment of 2q23.1 microdeletion syndrome implicates *MBD5* as a single causal locus of intellectual disability, epilepsy, and autism spectrum disorder. *American Journal of Human Genetics, 89*(4), 551–563.

Talkowski, M. E., Rosenfeld, J. A., Blumenthal, I., Pillalamarri, V., Chiang, C., Heilbut, A., et al. (2012). Sequencing chromosomal abnormalities reveals neurodevelopmental loci that confer risk across diagnostic boundaries. *Cell, 149*(3), 525–537.

Tang, G., Gudsnuk, K., Kuo, S. H., Cotrina, M. L., Rosoklija, G., Sosunov, A., et al. (2014). Loss of mTOR-dependent macroautophagy causes autistic-like synaptic pruning deficits. *Neuron, 83*(5), 1131–1143.

Tsai, P. T., Hull, C., Chu, Y., Greene-Colozzi, E., Sadowski, A. R., Leech, J. M., et al. (2012). Autistic-like behaviour and cerebellar dysfunction in Purkinje cell Tsc1 mutant mice. *Nature, 488*(7413), 647–651.

van Bon, B. W., Hoischen, A., Hehir-Kwa, J., de Brouwer, A. P., Ruivenkamp, C., Gijsbers, A. C., et al. (2011). Intragenic deletion in DYRK1A leads to mental retardation and primary microcephaly. *Clinical Genetics, 79*(3), 296–299.

Vargas, D. L., Nascimbene, C., Krishnan, C., Zimmerman, A. W., & Pardo, C. A. (2005). Neuroglial activation and neuroinflammation in the brain of patients with autism. *Annals of Neurology, 57*(1), 67–81.

Voineagu, I., Wang, X., Johnston, P., Lowe, J. K., Tian, Y., Horvath, S., et al. (2011). Transcriptomic analysis of autistic brain reveals convergent molecular pathology. *Nature, 474*(7351), 380–384.

Vulih-Shultzman, I., Pinhasov, A., Mandel, S., Grigoriadis, N., Touloumi, O., Pittel, Z., et al. (2007). Activity-dependent neuroprotective protein snippet NAP reduces tau hyperphosphorylation and enhances learning in a novel transgenic mouse model. *Journal of Pharmacology and Experimental Therapeutics, 323*(2), 438–449.

Wang, S. S., Kloth, A. D., & Badura, A. (2014). The cerebellum, sensitive periods, and autism. *Neuron, 83*(3), 518–532.

Wegiel, J., Flory, M., Kuchna, I., Nowicki, K., Ma, S., Imaki, H., et al. (2014). Stereological study of the neuronal number and volume of 38 brain subdivisions of subjects diagnosed with autism reveals significant alterations restricted to the striatum, amygdala and cerebellum. *Acta Neuropathologica Communications, 2*(1), 141.

Wegiel, J., Schanen, N. C., Cook, E. H., Sigman, M., Brown, W. T., Kuchna, I., et al. (2012). Differences between the pattern of developmental abnormalities in autism associated with duplications 15q11.2–q13 and idiopathic autism. *Journal of Neuropathology & Experimental Neurology, 71*(5), 382–397.

Williams, R. S., Hauser, S. L., Purpura, D. P., DeLong, G. R., & Swisher, C. N. (1980). Autism and mental retardation: Neuropathologic studies performed in four retarded persons with autistic behavior. *Archives of Neurology, 37*(12), 749–753.

Yamashita, Y., Fujimoto, C., Nakajima, E., Isagai, T., & Matsuishi, T. (2003). Possible association between congenital cytomegalovirus infection and autistic disorder. *Journal of Autism and Developmental Disorders, 33*(4), 455–459.

Yang, C. F., & Shah, N. M. (2014). Representing sex in the brain, one module at a time. *Neuron, 82*(2), 261–278.

Yip, J., Soghomonian, J. J., & Blatt, G. J. (2007). Decreased GAD67 mRNA levels in cerebellar Purkinje cells in autism: Pathophysiological implications. *Acta Neuropathologia, 113*(5), 559–568.

Yip, J., Soghomonian, J. J., & Blatt, G. J. (2008). Increased GAD67 mRNA levels in cerebellar inter-neurons in autism: Implications for Purkinje cell dysfunction. *Journal of Neuroscience Research, 86,* 525–530.

Zhan, Y., Paolicelli, R. C., Sforazzini, F., Weinhard, L., Bolasco, G., Pagani, F., et al. (2014). Deficient neuron–microglia signaling results in impaired functional brain connectivity and social behavior. *Nature Neuroscience, 17*(3), 400–406.

Zhou, Y. D., Lee, S., Jin, Z., Wright, M., Smith, S. E., & Anderson, M. P. (2009). Arrested maturation of excitatory synapses in autosomal dominant lateral temporal lobe epilepsy. *Nature Medicine, 15*(10), 1208–1214.

Zhou, Y. D., Zhang, D., Ozkaynak, E., Wang, X., Kasper, E. M., Leguern, E., et al. (2012). Epilepsy gene *LGI1* regulates postnatal developmental remodeling of retinogeniculate synapses. *Journal of Neuroscience, 32*(3), 903–910.

/// 14 /// IMMUNOLOGICAL ASPECTS OF AUTISM SPECTRUM DISORDER

THAYNE L. SWEETEN AND CHRISTOPHER J. MCDOUGLE

INTRODUCTION

Since the first description of autism spectrum disorder (ASD) by Leo Kanner (1943), clinicians and researchers have sought to understand the pathological mechanisms underlying these conditions. In the 1970s, twin and family studies revealed a strong genetic component to these developmental disorders (Folstein & Rutter, 1977). During the same decade, evidence emerged implicating infection and/or a possible role for immune factors in some cases (Chess, 1971; Money, Bobrow, & Clarke, 1971). Initially, immune-related studies were few and far between and of uncertain contribution; however, throughout the decades, research using increasingly powerful designs and innovative methods continued to detect immunological abnormalities in subjects with ASD and their families. These findings included abnormal immune cell responses, along with altered production of cytokines and antibodies (Stigler, Sweeten, Posey, & McDougle, 2009). Immune genes in the major histocompatibility complex region of chromosome 6 were also implicated (Warren et al., 1991), and family histories revealed an increased frequency of immune-mediated diseases (i.e., autoimmune) in relatives of probands with ASD (Comi, Zimmerman, Frye, Law, & Peeden, 1999). Taken together, these studies suggested that infectious or immune-mediated mechanisms might contribute to the pathophysiology of at least a subtype of ASD; however, more definitive neuroimmune studies were lacking. Prior to the turn of the century, postmortem histological investigations revealed that approximately one out of six brains from individuals with ASD showed signs of immune cell infiltration (reviewed in Stigler et al., 2009), but research specifically investigating immune parameters in postmortem brain tissue was not published until 2005 (Vargas, Nascimbene, Krishnan, Zimmerman, & Pardo, 2005).

Theories and supporting data implicating the immune system and infection in the pathophysiology of a subtype of those with ASD are explored in this chapter. Results from preliminary drug treatment studies targeting dysregulated immune mechanisms are also discussed.

NEUROINFLAMMATION

The brain is considered an immunologically privileged organ. Under normal conditions, the blood–brain barrier limits the movement of most immune cell types and proteins from the capillaries into brain tissue. Therefore, the brain relies heavily on its own resident immune cells, the microglia, to provide innate immune surveillance and protection. Making up approximately 10% of the glial cells in the brain, microglia are derived from monocyte lineage. In the adult, new microglia can be generated from hematogenous monocytes/macrophages (Lawson, Perry, & Gordon, 1992; Zhang et al., 2007). Microglia contain cellular processes that continually probe their immediate surrounding area. They become activated when their processes encounter damaged tissue, metabolic waste products such as oxidized lipoproteins, or invading microorganisms. Upon activation, they undergo morphological changes to engulf materials and secrete immunomodulatory chemicals such as cytokines and chemokines (Wake, Moorhouse, Jinno, Kohsaka, & Nabekura, 2009). Acting as the brain's "electricians," it appears that microglial processes can strip axon terminals away from dendrites, thereby modifying neuronal synapses in development and plasticity (Graeber, Bise, & Mehraein, 1993). Postnatal synaptic pruning by microglia utilizes complement-dependent mechanisms (Schafer et al., 2012).

A seminal case–control study examined postmortem brain tissue from 11 individuals with ASD along with cerebrospinal fluid (CSF) from six living subjects. Results revealed active neuroinflammation in the cerebral cortex, white matter, and cerebellum, including marked activation of microglia and astroglia. CSF and immunocytochemical studies showed a proinflammatory profile of cytokines, including a substantial increase in macrophage chemoattractant protein-1 and tumor growth factor (TGF)-β1 (Vargas et al., 2005). Subsequent neuropathological studies have confirmed and built upon these findings, showing activated microglia in a majority of postmortem brains observed among individuals with ASD, independent of age, in various cortical regions and in white matter (Li et al., 2009; Morgan et al., 2010, 2012; Tetreault et al., 2012). Activated microglia are more frequently present near neurons, indicating a neuron-directed microglial response (Morgan et al., 2012). A positron emission tomography study measuring microglial activation in living young adults found excessive microglial activation in multiple brain regions, most prominently the cerebellum, in subjects with ASD compared to controls (Suzuki et al., 2013).

Gene expression profiling of brain tissue from individuals with ASD shows increased messenger RNA transcription levels of many immune system-related genes among the transcript levels that are abnormal (Garbett et al., 2008). Similar results have been seen in subsequent genome and transcriptome analysis studies (Saxena et al., 2012; Voineagu et al., 2011). Summarizing their data, Garbett et al. (2008) state, "Overall, these expression patterns appear to be more associated with the late recovery phase of autoimmune brain disorders, than with the innate immune response characteristic of neurodegenerative diseases." (p. 303)

In studying and treating individuals with ASD, it is important to note that the relatively consistent behavioral phenotype likely contains multiple etiologic subtypes. Approximately 10% of cases of ASD are linked to disorders of genetic etiology, such as fragile X syndrome, tuberous sclerosis, and Rett's disorder, whereas environmental factors are believed to play a role in some cases. However, the majority of cases remain idiopathic. It now appears that immune activation in the brain is also associated with a subset of cases. Yet, many questions remain regarding this subset, such as what triggers immune activation and what influence it has, if any, on neurodevelopment and behavior.

INFECTION

One etiological theory is that either a congenital infection or an infection early in life could alter brain development and lead to ASD. Evidence to support this theory emerged after the rubella viral epidemic of 1964. Congenital rubella or German measles is caused by first-trimester infection with rubella virus. A resultant syndrome in some infected infants may include deafness, developmental delay, intellectual disability (ID), and seizures. The epidemic of 1964 resulted in the birth of approximately 20,000 infants with congenital rubella syndrome in the United States. Investigation of this population discovered a larger than expected subset of children who developed ASD as an additional sequela (Chess, 1971).

Rubella is included in the group of infectious agents most commonly causing congenital anomalies represented by TORCH, an acronym for *t*oxoplasmosis, *o*ther (syphilis, varicella-zoster, and parvovirus B19), *r*ubella, *c*ytomegalovirus (CMV), and *h*erpes infections. CMV infection, the most common cause of congenital and perinatal viral infection, can develop into clinically apparent cytomegalic inclusion disease in a minority of cases. Sequelae of CMV inclusion disease can include hepatosplenomegaly, microcephaly, ID, petechiae, motor disability, jaundice, cerebral calcifications, hearing loss, seizures, chorioretinitis, and death.

CMV and other viruses of the Herpesviridae family, such as herpes simplex virus (HSV), are of much interest in ASD because they are known to cause encephalitis (HSV) or congenital infection of the brain (CMV). At least 15 cases of ASD diagnosed following intrauterine CMV infection have been described in the literature (Stubbs, 1978; Sweeten, Posey, & McDougle, 2004), and other case studies have described the development of autistic symptoms in association with HSV encephalitis (Delong, Bean, & Brown, 1981; Ghaziuddin, Al-Khouri, & Ghaziuddin, 2002). Most of these HSV-associated cases are unique in that the infections were acquired after the age of 5 years and in some patients the autistic symptoms were transient. For instance, DeLong et al. described two children, ages 5 and 7½ years of age, respectively, with acute HSV encephalitis leading to an autistic syndrome. The cases were described as examples of "acquired and reversible autistic syndrome" because both children fully recovered.

An estimate of the incidence of cases of ASD associated with rubella or herpes family virus infection was inferred from a medical record review of 233 patients with ASD born in Utah. Ritvo, Mason-Brothers, Freeman, and Pingree (1990) found that 6 of the 233 subjects had congenital viral infection or suspected viral infection from rubella virus ($n = 2$), CMV ($n = 1$), and HSV ($n = 3$). Vaccination efforts have protected the public against rubella-associated ASD in many countries, including the United States; vaccination resulted in the elimination of endemic rubella in 2004. It is important to note that the "autistic" behavior seen in these infection-associated cases is typically seen in conjunction with other physical sequelae as part of a particular viral syndrome. Individuals with idiopathic ASD do not generally have these associated medical conditions.

Infection with a specific pathogen typically results in a long-term increase in blood antibody levels against the pathogen. Therefore, case–control studies have measured sera antibody titers in subjects with ASD and controls to help determine the association between ASD and previous infection with specific pathogens. These studies have found no replicable results implicating a particular pathogen (Libbey, Sweeten, McMahon, & Fujinami, 2005). Studies using molecular techniques to detect viral nucleic acids in tissue from subjects with ASD compared to controls are few in number and also have yielded no conclusive results implicating a particular pathogen.

Some retrospective epidemiological studies investigating rates of infection in individuals with ASD as children have found little to no difference compared with controls (Atladóttir et al., 2012a; Rosen, Yoshida, & Croen, 2007). A more recent publication suggested that children with ASD have an increased risk of hospital admission due to infection (Abdallah et al., 2012). Some, but not all, studies have shown that individuals with ASD experience more frequent otitis media than control comparisons (Comi et al., 1999; Konstantareas & Homatidis, 1987; Tanoue & Oda, 1989).

Two Danish studies found little evidence for an association between various types of mild common infectious diseases in mothers during pregnancy and ASD (Abdallah et al., 2012; Atladóttir, Henriksen, Schendel, & Parner, 2012b). Maternal influenza infection was associated with a twofold increased risk of ASD in one study, but this was not reported by others (Atladóttir et al., 2012b; Zerbo et al., 2013a). An investigation of all children born in Denmark from 1980 through 2005 revealed no association between maternal infection and ASD considering the entire period of gestation. However, admission to the hospital due to maternal viral infection in the first trimester and maternal bacterial infection in the second trimester were found to be associated with the diagnosis of ASD in the offspring (Atladóttir et al., 2010). Similarly, Zerbo et al. (2013b) found no overall association between maternal infection during pregnancy and ASD. However, women with infections diagnosed during a hospital admission, particularly bacterial infections, were at increased risk of delivering a child with ASD. Maternal fever during pregnancy has also been associated with an increased risk of ASD or developmental delay (Atladóttir et al., 2012b; Zerbo et al., 2013a).

ALLOIMMUNITY

It is still not well understood why a fetus is not rejected by the maternal immune system. Because half of the fetal genes are derived from the father, the developing embryo and placenta must be considered a "semi-allograft." If an organ donation were mismatched in a similar way, powerful immunosuppressant drugs would be required to prevent rejection. However, the mother's immune system typically recognizes the fetus as "temporary self" and does not attack it. There are exceptions, such as when IgG autoantibodies from mothers with systemic lupus erythematosus, Graves' disease, or Hashimoto's thyroiditis cross the placenta and cause disease in newborns. Likewise, maternal antibodies can target paternal antigens, such as in the disease erythroblastosis fetalis, in which paternally derived Rh determinants on fetal red blood cells can be attacked by maternal antibodies, leading to hemolytic anemia in the fetus.

Alloimmunity is an immune response to foreign antigens (alloantigens) from members of the same species. It has been hypothesized that a subset of ASD could be the result of an alloimmune-type reaction in which maternal antibodies and/or other maternal immune responses against the fetus disrupt normal neurodevelopment in utero. In evaluating this theory, three criteria should be met with reasonable certainty pertaining to both alloimmune and autoimmune disorders: direct evidence, indirect evidence, and circumstantial evidence (Rose & Bona, 1993).

Direct Evidence

Direct evidence requires that pathogenic antibodies or T cells transferred from a diseased individual will cause similar disease in a healthy recipient. Data in this category are limited to models in which maternal antibodies are transferred to pregnant animals and the resultant offspring are observed. The antibodies do not cause disease in the mothers but can produce abnormal behavior and pathology in offspring by disrupting in utero development, presumably prior to full development of the blood–brain barrier.

The first study to test this pathological mechanism injected serum from the mother of a child with ASD into pregnant mice. This mother was of interest because immunohistochemistry and flow cytometry showed that antibodies in her blood bound to mice cerebellar Purkinje cells, as well as to other brain cells. Mice exposed in utero to the blood of the mother showed altered exploratory behavior and reduced motor coordination compared to controls (Dalton et al., 2003).

A second investigation using a similar pregnant dam mouse model pooled purified IgG antibody from 63 mothers of children with ASD. IgG antibodies are the only class of antibodies that cross the placenta. Purified antibody from 63 mothers of unaffected children served as the control. Offspring of damns injected with antibody from mothers of children with ASD demonstrated differences in motor activity, anxiety, startle response, and sociability. Evidence of cytokine and glial activation was observed in the embryonic brains of the offspring exposed to IgG from mothers of children with ASD. Of interest, no gross anatomical abnormalities were seen in brain sections, and alterations in behavior persisted in adolescent and adult offspring (Singer et al., 2009). These findings are consistent with ASD and the lifelong nature of the disorder. In a subsequent study, Braunschweig et al. (2012b) demonstrated that even a single gestational exposure of IgG derived from individual mothers of children with ASD caused alterations in early growth trajectories, significantly impaired motor and sensory development, and increased anxiety in mice offspring.

Although rodent models of disease can provide valuable information, they are limited in their ability to mirror complex behaviors present in neurobehavioral disorders of humans. The use of more advanced species, such as nonhuman primates, can be more revealing. For example, Martin et al. (2008) injected four pregnant rhesus monkeys with purified IgG antibody pooled from the sera of 12 mothers who had at least one child with ASD or purified IgG antibody pooled from the sera of mothers of children without ASD. The monkeys born to the mothers that were injected with IgG from mothers with at least one child with ASD consistently demonstrated increased whole-body stereotypies across multiple testing paradigms and also displayed more hyperactivity compared to controls. Stereotypies are considered one of the defining features of ASD, whereas approximately 50% of children with ASD display symptoms of attention deficit hyperactivity disorder (Gadow & DeVincent, 2005; Gadow, DeVincent, Pomeroy, & Azizian, 2004). A subsequent study utilizing a similar design observed abnormal social behavior and enlarged brain volumes in offspring of monkeys that had been injected with IgG isolated from mothers of children with ASD compared to controls (Bauman et al., 2013). Enlarged brain volumes are frequently seen in individuals with ASD (Courchesne et al., 2001; Piven et al., 1995).

Indirect Evidence

The most common type of indirect evidence requires the isolation and characterization of the pathogenic antibodies or T cells. Numerous studies have investigated mothers of children with ASD for the presence of antibodies that react against fetal brain antigens.

Using immunoblotting, Zimmerman et al. (2007) screened serum from mothers of children with ASD and found specific patterns of antibody reactivity to rat prenatal brain, but not to postnatal or adult rat brain proteins, in each of the 11 mothers tested. Similar antibody binding patterns were seen in 12 of 12 children with ASD, as well as in many children with other neurodevelopmental disorders. Subsequent research found that IgG from 7 of 61 (11.5%) mothers of children with ASD, but none of 62 mothers of typically developing children or 40 mothers of children with non-ASD developmental delay, demonstrated IgG reactivity against human fetal brain proteins at approximately 37 and 73 kDa (Braunschweig et al., 2008). Similar results have been found by other researchers, including one group using mid-pregnancy blood specimens from mothers of children with ASD and another utilizing subjects from Spain (Croen et al., 2008; Rossi, Fuentes, Van de Water, & Amaral, 2014; Singer et al., 2008) (Table 14.1).

Further characterization of the maternal antibodies that recognize fetal brain has revealed specificity for seven primary antigens: lactate dehydrogenase A and B, cypin, stress-induced phosphoprotein 1, collapsing response mediator proteins 1 and 2, and Y-box-binding protein. These proteins are highly expressed in developing brain, and most are involved in neurodevelopment. Exclusive reactivity to specific antigen combinations was noted in 23% of mothers of children with ASD and only 1% of controls (Braunschweig et al., 2013). A number of investigators have expressed caution regarding any proposed antibody test until these results have been replicated by independent laboratories (Underwood, 2013).

Circumstantial Evidence

Genetic alleles associated with autoimmune disease in family members of children with ASD, especially mothers, can provide circumstantial evidence for alloimmunity, assuming that immune regulatory genes that contribute to autoimmune disease would also

TABLE 14.1 Maternal Antibodies Against Fetal Brain in Autism Spectrum Disorder

Reference	Reacts Against	No. of Subjects (% positive)
Dalton et al. (2003)	Purkinje cells; brain stem neurons	1 case (100%); 4 controls (0%)
Zimmerman et al. (2007)	Protein > 250 kDa; protein bands between 20 and 30 kDa	11 cases (100%); 10 controls (0%)
Braunschweig et al. (2008)	Both 37- and 73-kDa protein bands	84 cases (11.5%); 152 controls (0%)
Croen et al. (2008)	Both 39- and 73-kDa protein bands	84 cases (3.6%); 200 controls (0%)
Singer et al. (2008)	36-kDa protein band	100 cases (10%); 100 controls (2%)
Goines et al. (2011)	Both 37- and 73-kDa protein bands Both 39- and 73-kDa protein bands	259 cases (9.3%); 180 controls (0%) 259 cases (8.9%); 180 controls (1.7%)
Braunschweig et al. (2012a)	Both 37- and 73-kDa protein bands	143 cases (7%); 183 controls (0%)
Nordahl et al. (2013)	Both 37- and 73-kDa protein bands	131 cases (7.6%); 50 controls (0%)
Brimberg, Sadiq, Gregersen, and Diamond (2013)	Neurons in frontal cortex, hippocampus, and cerebellum	2431 cases (10.5%); 653 controls (2.6%); 318 cases (8.8%), 2nd cohort
Rossi et al. (2014)	Both 37- and 73-kDa protein bands Both 39- and 73-kDa protein bands	37 cases (5%); 37 controls (0%) 37 cases (3%); 37 controls (0%)

predispose to alloimmunity. Family members often share autoimmune susceptibility genes; therefore, if a child has a specific autoimmune disease, then family members are more likely to have the same or another type of autoimmune disease (Broadley, Dean, Sawcer, Clayton, & Compston, 2000; Prahalad, Shear, Thompson, Giannini, & Glass, 2002). Thus, knowing if families with children with ASD have an increased prevalence of autoimmune diseases compared to a control population can provide meaningful etiological clues.

A case report published more than 40 years ago described an unusually high number of autoimmune disorders in family members of a child with ASD (Money et al., 1971). It was not until 1999, however, that this observation was followed up on a larger scale by surveying families with children with ASD and families with healthy children regarding the occurrence of autoimmune disease in first- and second-degree relatives. The frequency of autoimmune disorders in the families with children with ASD was found to be higher than that in controls, particularly among parents—and especially mothers—of children with ASD (Comi et al., 1999). Other researchers replicated this finding, noting a numerical increase of autoimmune diseases in grandmothers and uncles, as well as mothers and brothers, of probands with ASD, suggesting a possible mother-to-son transmission of susceptibility to autoimmune disease in relatives of a proband with ASD (Sweeten, Bowyer, Posey, Halberstadt, & McDougle, 2003). Most studies, many using large populations and medical record verification, have replicated the finding of increased autoimmune diseases in family members of subjects with autism (Table 14.2). A wide variety of autoimmune diseases, including rheumatoid arthritis, type 1 diabetes mellitus, and autoimmune thyroid disease, have been found in family members. As circumstantial evidence, these findings do not specifically implicate ASD as an alloimmune or autoimmune disease, but they do suggest that genes involved in immune regulation could play a role.

One such gene of interest, the null allele of C4B, has been shown to be associated with ASD and to be increased in children with ASD with a family history of autoimmune disease (Mostafa & Shehab, 2010; Warren et al., 1991). The C4B gene codes for a complement protein involved in innate immunity. It is found on chromosome 6 in the human leukocyte antigen (HLA) region—a region containing many important genes for immune function. The null allele is a deficient allele that does not produce protein. Complement C4 proteins are involved in numerous immune functions, including lysing pathogens and marking pathogens for clearance by immune cells. A deficiency in C4 protein is among the strongest genetic risk factors for the development of the autoimmune disease systemic lupus erythematosus (Yang et al., 2004).

Although much of the research investigating immunoregulatory genes in ASD has focused solely on affected children, recent interest has turned toward maternal genetics. Certain alleles of important immunoregulatory genes have been associated with mothers of children with ASD. For instance, the frequency of HLA-DR4 appears to be increased in mothers, as well as individuals with ASD (Lee et al., 2006; Warren et al., 1996). Mothers of children with ASD are more likely to inherit HLA-DR4 alleles from their parents who have this gene (Johnson et al., 2009). HLA-DR4 is a class II HLA gene that codes for a protein important in antigen presentation to T cells. The DR4 allele has been identified as one of the susceptibility markers for certain autoimmune diseases, such as rheumatoid arthritis, and is strongly associated with others such as hypothyroidism and type 1 diabetes mellitus (Levin et al., 2004; Wordsworth et al., 1989). Some studies indicate that these disorders are increased in family members of children with ASD, especially in mothers of children with ASD (Comi et al., 1999; Malloy et al., 2006; Sweeten et al., 2003).

Natural killer (NK) cells are of pivotal importance in innate immune reactions. Upon activation, they produce inflammatory cytokines such as interferon (IFN)-γ and tumor

TABLE 14.2 Epidemiological Studies of Autoimmune Disease and Related Conditions in Families
of Children With Autism Spectrum Disorder

Reference	No. of Subjects	Assessment	Associated With ASD	Associated Autoimmune Disease or Immune Condition
Comi et al. (1999)	61 cases; 46 controls	Self-report	Yes	General autoimmunity, rheumatoid arthritis
Sweeten et al. (2003)	101 cases; 202 controls	Self-report	Yes	General autoimmunity, hypothyroidism and Hashimoto's thyroiditis, rheumatic fever
Micali, Chakrabarti, and Fombonne (2004)	79 cases; 61 controls	Self-report	No	None
Croen et al. (2005)	420 cases; 2,100 controls	Medical records	Yes	Psoriasis, asthma, allergies
Molloy et al. (2006)	308 cases	Self-report	Yes	General autoimmunity, autoimmune thyroid disease
Mouridsen, Rich, Isager, and Nedergaard (2007)	111 cases; 330 controls	Medical records	Yes	Ulcerative colitis, type 1 diabetes
Valicenti-McDermott, McVicar, Cohen, Wershil, and Shinnar (2008)	100 cases	Self-report	Yes	Rheumatoid arthritis, celiac disease, inflammatory bowel disease
Atladóttir et al. (2009)	3,325 cases; 685,871 controls	Medical records	Yes	Rheumatoid arthritis, celiac disease, type 1 diabetes
Keil et al. (2010)	1227 cases; 30,693 controls	Medical records	Yes	General parental autoimmune disease, idiopathic thrombocytopenia purpura, myasthenia gravis, rheumatic fever

necrosis factor (TNF)-α, generating an inflammatory environment helpful in controlling
infections but potentially pathological in autoimmune conditions. Decreased killing by NK
cells (Vojdani et al., 2008; Warren, Foster, & Margaretten, 1987) and increased numbers
of circulating NK cells have been observed in ASD (Ashwood et al., 2011a). On a genetic
level, two groups have shown a genetic milieu that favors NK cell activation in children with
ASD (Guerini et al., 2014; Torres, Westover, Gibbons, Johnson, & Ward, 2012). An even
stronger skewing toward NK cell activating genotypes is observed in mothers of children
with ASD (Guerini et al., 2014). This may be of importance in ASD because the uterus is
known to host a large number of NK cells at the fetal–maternal interface. There is evidence
from animal models that maternal immune activation at the placenta, involving inflammatory cytokines such as interleukin (IL)-6, can cause neuroimmune abnormalities in the

fetus, as well as behavioral abnormalities reminiscent of ASD (Hsiao & Patterson, 2011; Parker-Athill & Tan, 2010).

AUTOIMMUNITY

Autoimmunity is a long-standing theory in the etiology of ASD with speculation that an aberrant response from the child's own immune system disrupts normal brain function. Autoimmune diseases typically occur in females and increase in prevalence with age. In contrast, ASD has a male-to-female ratio of approximately 4:1. However, a substantial subset of autoimmune disorders occurring predominately in males does exist, including amyotrophic lateral sclerosis, ankylosing spondylitis, and type 1 diabetes mellitus (Beeson, 1994). The onset of type 1 diabetes mellitus typically occurs in childhood and, similar to ASD, its incidence has been on the rise (Craig, Howard, Silink, & Chan, 2000).

There is no direct evidence to indicate that ASD is an autoimmune disease. Support for this theory derives from indirect and circumstantial evidence. Many studies have identified increased levels of autoantibodies to adult brain antigens in the blood of a small fraction of children with ASD. Antibody targets vary between studies, and many of the results have not been replicated (Stigler et al., 2009). Antigens of interest have included myelin basic protein, neuron–axon acidic protein, brain-derived neurotrophic factor, glial filament protein, cerebellar proteins, and other brain tissue proteins that have not yet been identified. Autoantibodies have also been found against neuronal progenitor cell proteins by some researchers (Mazur-Kolecka et al., 2014), but others did not find abnormal reactivity to fetal brain in individuals with ASD (Morris, Zimmerman, & Singer, 2009; Rossi et al., 2014). Although autoantibodies are more frequently seen in subjects with ASD, they are also frequently seen in control subjects and are not unique to ASD. It is unclear whether these antibodies have direct pathologic significance.

There is a wide variety of circumstantial evidence to implicate autoimmunity in ASD, some of which has been described previously. Many studies report an increase or decrease in the frequency of various immune-related genes such as HLA alleles or haplotypes in ASD. These genes could play a role in autoimmunity or other immune abnormalities in ASD (Table 14.3). Also, peripheral immune abnormalities commonly found in ASD (discussed next) could result from autoimmune mechanisms.

PERIPHERAL IMMUNE ACTIVATION

Although many peripheral immune parameters appear to be abnormal in ASD, the cause of these abnormalities is unknown. Factors that could contribute to these often inconsistent findings include autoimmunity, infection, allergies, tissue damage, inflammation, or perhaps other unknown genetic or neurological factors related to ASD.

Some peripheral evidence suggests increased immune activity in those with ASD. For instance, neopterin, a chemical produced by monocytes and macrophages during periods of immune activation, has been found to be elevated in blood samples of individuals with ASD (Sweeten, Posey, & McDougle, 2003). An upregulation of the CD95 marker on circulating monocytes is indicative of activation of these cells in ASD subjects (Ashwood et al., 2011a). These finding could be relevant to the brain because an increased infiltration of monocytes and perivascular macrophages is observed in postmortem brain samples of individuals with ASD (Vargas et al., 2005). Multiple studies have reported abnormalities in

TABLE 14.3 Immune Genes, Alleles, and Haplotypes Repeatedly
Associated With Autism Spectrum disorder

Gene/Allele/Haplotype	Reference
HLA-DR4	Torres et al. (2002)
	Lee et al. (2006)
	Johnson et al. (2009)
	Chien et al. (2012)
C4B null allele	Warren et al. (1991)
	Odell et al. (2005)
	Mostafa and Shehab (2010)
HLA-A2	Stubbs and Magenis (1980)
	Torres et al. (2006)
B44-SC30-DR4	Warren et al. (1992)
	Daniels et al. (1995)
	Odell et al. (2005)
KIR/HLA complexes	Torres et al. (2012)
	Guerini et al. (2014)

T cell ratios and increased T, B, or NK cell numbers, including evidence for increased T and B cell activity in subjects with ASD compared to controls (Ashwood et al., 2011a; Denney, Frei, & Gaffney, 1996; Plioplys, Greaves, Kazemi, & Silverman, 1994). Some measures show that children with ASD have reductions in certain immune parameters, such as low NK cell cytotoxicity (Vojdani et al., 2008; Warren et al., 1987) or decreased levels of IgM and IgG classes of immunoglobulin (Heuer et al., 2008).

Complement protein irregularities have also been reported in ASD. A proteomic study quantifying 6348 peptide components derived from serum samples of children with ASD found elevated complement protein C1q among the few implicated proteins (Corbett et al., 2007). C1q is part of the first component of the classical complement pathway. It is involved in synaptic pruning and opsonizing synapses to prepare them for removal by macrophages (Stevens et al., 2007). Uncontrolled complement biosynthesis and activation in the central nervous system is thought to contribute to neurodegenerative disorders (Gasque, Dean, McGreal, VanBeek, & Morgan, 2000). Complement can bind to antibodies to trigger cell death or damage through the formation of membrane attack complexes, providing a possible mechanism whereby autoreactive antibodies could produce pathology and alter behavior in some persons with ASD (Goines et al., 2011).

Many peripheral immune findings have been associated with ASD-related behaviors (reviewed in Onore, Careaga, & Ashwood, 2012). For instance, lower levels of the soluble adhesion molecule P-selectin have been associated with greater impairment in social skills (Iwata et al., 2008), and children with ASD appear to show transient improvement in certain aberrant behaviors during periods of fever (Curran et al., 2007).

CYTOKINES

The term *cytokine* derives from the Greek roots *cyto* for cell and *kinos* for movement. Cytokines are either peptides, proteins, or glycoproteins that are released from one cell to regulate activity of other cells by binding to specific cell membrane receptors and triggering signal transduction pathways that ultimately alter gene expression in the target cells. Cytokines have pronounced effects on many cellular functions in all branches of the immune system. Many cytokines can alter brain chemistry and profoundly affect neuronal development, migration, differentiation, and synapse formation (Deverman & Patterson, 2009). Abnormal cytokine levels have been implicated by many researchers to play a role in the pathophysiology of ASD (Onore et al., 2012).

Elevated plasma levels of proinflammatory cytokines and macrophage migration inhibitory factor have been detected in plasma of individuals with ASD (Ashwood et al., 2011b; Grigorenko et al., 2008). In contrast, the anti-inflammatory cytokine, transforming growth factor-β, appears to be low in adults and neonatal blood samples from individuals with ASD (Abdallah et al., 2013; Okada et al., 2007). Others have not seen different plasma cytokine levels between children with ASD and their typically developing siblings, although correlations between cytokine levels and quantitative clinical traits have been reported (Napolioni et al., 2013).

Analysis of postmortem brain samples from subjects with ASD has revealed an active neuroinflammatory process in the cerebral cortex, white matter, and cerebellum. The production of many cytokines was increased, with macrophage chemoattractant protein-1 and TGF-β1 being the most prevalent. Macrophage chemoattractant protein-1 and IFN-γ, among others, have been found to be markedly increased in the CSF of individuals with ASD (Vargas et al., 2005). The cause of this neuroinflammation is unknown, but it could represent an autoinflammatory condition, perhaps resulting from a maternal alloimmune attack, autoimmune disease, or reaction to a pathogen or an inflammatory response to another unknown pathological process (Doria et al., 2012).

IFN-γ provides a hypothetical example for cytokine involvement in ASD pathology. IFN-γ levels have been found to be elevated in brain tissue of individuals with ASD, as well as in their CSF, by 232.5-fold (Li et al., 2009; Vargas et al., 2005). IFN-γ can upregulate production of the enzyme inducible nitric oxide synthase in astrocytes and microglia, thereby enabling increased production of nitric oxide (NO) in the brain. The free radical NO is secreted by activated immune cells such as macrophages, and it is toxic to pathogens (Seguin et al., 1994). In the brain, NO is typically produced by neurons and it acts as an intercellular messenger modulating synaptogenesis, dendrite and axonal growth, and neuronal release of various neurotransmitters (Hess, Patterson, Smith, & Skene, 1993; Lizasoain, Weiner, Knowles, & Moncada, 1996; Lonart, Wang, & Johnson, 1992). Increased NO production by IFN-γ responsive immune cells in the brain would likely alter these processes that are important for synaptic plasticity and function. Problems with synaptic development and plasticity are implicated in the neuropathology of ASD (Ebert & Greenberg, 2013). In some studies, blood samples showed evidence of elevated NO production in subjects with ASD, which was positively correlated with plasma IFN-γ concentration (Sweeten, Posey, Shankar, & McDougle, 2004; Tostes, Teixeira, Gattaz, Brandão, & Raposo, 2012).

OTHER IMMUNE CONSIDERATIONS: GASTROINTESTINAL INFLAMMATION AND THE MEASLES, MUMPS, AND RUBELLA VACCINE

Clinicians treating children with ASD will encounter patients with gastrointestinal (GI) conditions that are similar to those seen in individuals without ASD. These conditions can be challenging to evaluate in minimally verbal or nonverbal persons with ASD. Possible associated conditions include food allergies or other adverse reactions to foods, inflammation, and immunological dysfunction in the GI tract. The prevalence of GI abnormalities in individuals with ASD is not well understood, ranging from 9% (equal to the typical population) to 70% or higher (Buie et al., 2010). After reviewing prevalence studies, a multidisciplinary panel of experts summarized, "The preponderance of data were consistent with the likelihood of a high prevalence of GI symptoms and associated disorders associated with ASDs" (Buie et al., 2010, p. S4). Overall, however, there is an absence of high-quality clinical research data in this area.

The GI tract serves as a barrier to many harmful materials and pathogens; accordingly, it is also the largest immune organ in the body. Some researchers have suggested a relationship between inflammation in the GI tract and the GI symptoms seen in ASD. Pan-enteric infiltration of lymphocytes and eosinophils in the gut mucosa has consistently been shown in children with ASD (Torrente et al., 2004). One group reported IgG and complement deposition on the surface epithelium of the GI tract that is characteristic of autoimmune pathology (Torrente et al., 2002). Because GI pathology is a relatively understudied area in ASD, more research is needed to better understand the GI/immune relationship and how this contributes to the pathophysiology of a subtype of individuals with ASD.

Some researchers and health care providers have proposed the existence of a specific "autistic enterocolitis" ostensibly triggered by the measles, mumps, and rubella (MMR) vaccine in a setting of abnormal immune function or increased gut permeability (Wakefield et al., 1998). Based on correlational observations published in *The Lancet*, these researchers set off a firestorm in the general public by claiming that the MMR vaccine led to not only enterocolitis but also regressive ASD.

Since this claim, more than 20 studies of thousands of children from multiple countries have been published to investigate the possible association of the MMR vaccine and ASD. No connection between the MMR vaccine and ASD has been verified (Allan & Ivers, 2010; DeStefano, 2007; Libbey et al., 2007). In 2004, 10 of the 13 authors of the Wakefield et al. (1998) article retracted the interpretation of their results, followed by the editors of *The Lancet* retracting the entire article (*The Lancet* Editors, 2010; Murch et al., 2004). Not only did the Wakefield et al. study have limitations in the study design, including inadequate control groups, lack of validated and standardized definitions, and speculative interpretation, but also Britain's General Medical Council and others exposed multiple ethical breeches committed by the lead author and others involved (Allen & Ivers, 2010; Deer, 2011; Dyer, 2010).

DRUG TREATMENT STUDIES

There have been a number of reports on the use of anti-inflammatory and immunomodulatory drugs in individuals with ASDs. These have consisted of case reports, case series, open-label trials, and a limited number of double-blind, placebo-controlled studies. The results of these preliminary investigations are summarized here.

Corticosteroids

Corticosteroids are anti-inflammatory and immunosuppressive agents that inhibit pro-inflammatory cytokine production, alter T lymphocyte activity, and may also modulate microglial activation (Ros-Bernal et al., 2011; Schweingruber, Reichardt, Lühder, &

Reichardt, 2012). There have been a number of reports of improvement in symptoms of ASD in individuals treated with corticosteroids.

An almost 3-year-old boy with regressive ASD and an autoimmune lymphoproliferative condition showed improved social interaction and vocalization with chronic oral prednisolone treatment (Shenoy, Arnold, & Chatila, 2000). To treat the autoimmune condition, the patient initially received prednisolone at a dose of 2 mg/kg/day for a period of 10 weeks. During the first month of treatment, the boy was described as having increased social interaction. Eventually, a dose of 0.5 mg/kg every other day was found to be an effective maintenance dose for treatment of the autoimmune condition, as well as the ASD symptoms. Continuing improvement in speech was noted during the subsequent 12 months of treatment, with the emergence of a vocabulary of more than 200 words. Improvement was also seen in gesturing, nonverbal communication, and language expression and comprehension.

A 6-year-old boy with ASD also showed improved symptoms with prednisolone treatment (Stefanatos, Grover, & Geller, 1995). The patient was diagnosed with ASD based on prominent language and behavioral regression at the age of 22 months, with persistent impaired social interactions, motor stereotypies, and echolalia. A 28-week course of prednisolone at a dose of 2 mg/kg/day was initiated, followed by a gradual reduction in dose during the treatment period. Within a few weeks of beginning treatment, significant improvement in social communication was noted. By the end of treatment, the boy had made relative gains of 26–36 months in expressive and receptive vocabulary in less than 18 months.

A report of two children with ASD, seizures, and motor deficits treated with corticosteroids has also been published (Mordekar, Prendergast, Chattopadhyay, & Baxter, 2009). The children, one male and one female (both aged 4.5 years), were given a course of prednisolone (initial dose 2 mg/kg/day) for 10 and 3 weeks, respectively. Both patients demonstrated a return of previously lost spoken language and a reduction in psychomotor agitation. They reportedly maintained this improvement following discontinuation of the drug.

An open-label study was used to investigate high-dose corticosteroid treatment in 44 children with ASD and evidence of abnormal epileptiform activity on electroencephalogram (EEG) (mean age, 5.6 years) (Chez et al., 1998). Prednisolone or methylprednisolone at a dose of 10 mg/kg/week was added to ongoing treatment with divalproex sodium for 18 months. Among the 25 children that had clinical and EEG outcomes reported after addition of a corticosteroid, clinical improvement in speech and EEG was noted in 82 and 60% of cases, respectively. No significant adverse effects were observed, even after 18 months of treatment.

A retrospective study of open-label prednisolone (2 mg/kg) treatment (mean duration, 9.125 ± 3.26 months) of 20 children with ASD (aged 3–5 years) compared the effects on the 4-Hz frequency modulated evoked response (FMAER) arising from language cortex of the superior temporal gyrus, and on EEG background activity, language, and behavior, to measures obtained in an untreated clinical convenience sample of age-matched children with ASD (Duffy et al., 2014). None of the children had Landau–Kleffner syndrome. The prednisolone-treated group showed a significant increase in the 4-Hz FMAER spectral response and a significant reduction in response distortion compared to the untreated group (Figure 14.1). The treated group's language ratings were significantly improved, and more subjects who received prednisolone compared to those who were untreated showed significant language improvement. Most treated subjects also showed significant behavioral improvement, based on diagnostic criteria of the fourth edition of the *Diagnostic and Statistical Manual of Mental Disorders* (American Psychiatric Association, 1994).

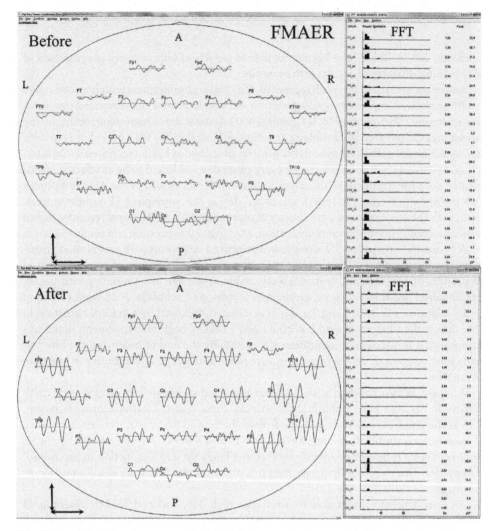

FIGURE 14.1 FMAER and corresponding FFT, before and after steroids in regressive autism. 4 Hz FMAER waveform data are shown within schematic ovals in vertex view with nose up, and left side of scalp to image left. The corresponding power spectra are shown to the immediate right. The top waveform and FFT displays were obtained prior to steroid administration. The bottom, corresponding displays were obtained after steroid administration. The vertical arrow to the lower left of each image represents 10 μV and the horizontal arrow beneath represents one second waveform length. The labels adjacent to the FMAER waveforms correspond to the standard EEG electrode 10–10 naming convention. Twenty-four electrodes' waveforms are shown. The FFT power spectral data horizontal axis covers the 0–30 Hz range. Note the near absent 4 Hz FMAER waveform response before and excellent 4 Hz waveform response after steroid administration. Note the spread of spectral power over many frequencies in the FFT display before (above) which represents a distorted response. This contrasts to the nearly perfect 4 Hz response after steroid treatment (below) which shows little spectral spread (little distortion). For the vertex view display, waveforms are shown overlying their standard '10-10' locations. For the FFT graphs, channel order from top to bottom is: F3, F4, C3, C4, P3, P4, O1, O2, Fp1, Fp2, F7, F8, T7, T8, P7, P8, FT9, FT10, TP9, TP10, Fz, Cz, Pz, Oz. The common average reference is utilized for the displayed data (a reference free or 'rfr' technique) [10]. Abbreviations: A = anterior, P = posterior, L-left, R = right, FMAER = 4 Hz frequency modulated auditory evoked response, FFT = fast Fourier transform -power spectrum analysis shown as μV2/Hz, μV =microvolt, Hz = Hertz or cycles per second. *This figure is made available by Biomedical Central under its Open Access policy.*

Language and behavioral improvement persisted for 1 year after prednisolone discontinuation. The two groups did not differ in terms of minor EEG abnormalities. Almost all prednisolone-treated subjects demonstrated Cushingoid appearance and weight gain associated with increased appetite. For all subjects, however, weight and appearance returned to normal within several months of discontinuation of prednisolone. Half of the treated subjects initially experienced behavioral worsening, typically irritability, that was usually managed by a slight reduction of steroid medication.

Pregnenolone

Pregnenolone is a naturally occurring neurosteroid directly metabolized from cholesterol and the precursor of many neurosteroids. Pregnenolone is converted to multiple metabolites when given orally to humans, including the most abundant of the metabolites, allopregnanolone. Allopregnanolone regulates and positively modulates $GABA_A$ receptors. Fung, Libove, Phillips, Haddad, and Hardan (2014) conducted a 12-week open-label pilot trial of pregnenolone in 12 adults with ASD. Pregnenolone resulted in a statistically significant improvement in the primary outcome measure, the Aberrant Behavior Checklist (ABC)–Irritability subscale score (from 17.4 ± 7.4 to 11.2 ± 7.0). Statistically significant improvement was also found on the ABC–Lethargy/Social Withdrawal subscale and the total Short Sensory Profile score; no significant change occurred on the Social Responsiveness Scale. Pregnenolone was well tolerated other than single reports of tiredness, diarrhea, and depressive affect.

Adrenocorticotropic Hormone

Adrenocorticotropic hormone (ACTH) is a hormone produced by the anterior pituitary gland that stimulates the release of corticosteroids from the adrenal cells. Children with ASD have been reported to have both abnormal circulating levels and physiologic responses to ACTH (Hamza, Hewedi, & Ismail, 2010; Marinović-Curin et al., 2008).

An 8-week controlled crossover trial investigated the use of synthetic ACTH (40 mg/day) in 21 children (aged 5–15 years) with ASD (Buitelaar et al., 1992a). Significant improvement was seen in overall ASD symptom severity alongside improvements in social interaction. Although use of ACTH was generally well tolerated, 6 children had an increase in mood lability and "inner tension" by parent or teacher report compared to only 2 children on placebo. These findings supported the results of a previous double-blind, placebo-controlled crossover trial involving 14 children with ASD (aged 5–13 years). In that study, treatment with ACTH (20 mg/day) was noted to improve stereotypic behaviors and enhance social interaction in the subjects (Buitelaar, van Engeland, van Ree, & de Wied, 1990; Buitelaar et al., 1992b).

Lenalidomide

Lenalidomide, an immunomodulatory agent and an analog of thalidomide, is commonly used to treat hematologic and solid malignancies. Lenalidomide inhibits release of the proinflammatory cytokines IL-1, IL-6, IL-12, and in particular TNF-α, while also increasing release of the anti-inflammatory cytokine IL-10 (Kotla et al., 2009).

In a 12-week, open-label study of lenalidomide (2.5 mg/day) in seven children with ASD (aged 7–12 years), participants had improvement in symptoms of autism and expressive language, although statistical significance was not achieved (Chez, Low, Parise, & Donnel, 2012). The subjects also had elevated levels of TNF-α in their CSF. Biochemical outcomes included CSF and serum levels of TNF-α. Serum TNF-α was significantly reduced by 57%, and although CSF TNF-α was also reduced by 57%, this reduction did not reach statistical significance. There was a significant improvement in expressive and receptive language after 6 weeks of treatment, although at 12 weeks, only improvement in expressive language remained statistically significant. Three children had to be removed from the study—two due to the development of a rash and one due to a marked drop in neutrophil count. The rashes and reduced neutrophil count resolved with the discontinuation of lenalidomide.

Celecoxib

Celecoxib, a cyclooxygenase-2 inhibitor with anti-inflammatory effects, in combination with risperidone, was studied in a 10-week randomized double-blind, placebo-controlled trial involving 40 children with ASD (aged 5–11 years) (Asadabadi et al., 2013). Subjects were assigned to risperidone plus celecoxib or risperidone plus placebo. Celecoxib was initiated at 100 mg/day and titrated to either 200 or 300 mg/day depending on body weight (limited to 200 mg/day if the child weighed less than 30 kg). Risperidone was started at a dose of 0.5 mg/day with an increase of 0.5 mg/week to 2 or 3 mg/day depending on body weight.

Outcomes were measured using the subscales of the ABC at 2, 4, 6, and 10 weeks. By the end of the study, the risperidone plus celecoxib arm demonstrated significant improvement in irritability, social withdrawal, and stereotypic behavior compared to risperidone plus placebo. In addition, whereas risperidone plus placebo resulted in a treatment response in 20% of subjects, a significantly higher percentage (55%) responded to risperidone plus celecoxib. Response was defined as a 50% reduction in the ABC–Irritability subscale score. Adverse effects were similar between treatment groups, with extrapyramidal symptoms, likely due to risperidone, reported in half of participants (50% celecoxib group and 45% placebo group). Abdominal pain was reported in three patients receiving risperidone plus celecoxib compared to only one patient given risperidone plus placebo.

Pentoxifylline

Pentoxifylline has also been studied as a treatment for ASD (reviewed in Gupta, Rimland, & Schilling, 1996). Pentoxifylline is a compound that exhibits immunomodulatory effects, including inhibition of proinflammatory cytokines. A 10-week randomized double-blind, placebo-controlled study investigated pentoxifylline as an adjunctive treatment to risperidone in the treatment of irritability in ASD (Akhondzadeh et al., 2010). Forty children with ASD (aged 4–12 years) were randomly assigned to risperidone plus pentoxifylline or risperidone plus placebo. Initial dosing and dose limits for pentoxifylline were dependent on body weight, with children less than 40 kg receiving an initial dose of 200 mg/day with a dose limit of 400 mg/day compared to those more than 40 kg who received an initial dose of 300 mg/day with a dose limit of 600 mg/day. Risperidone was started at a dose of 0.5 mg for all participants, with the final dose dependent on body weight (2 mg/day for those less than 40 kg and 3 mg/day for those more than 40 kg). Compared to risperidone plus placebo, risperidone plus pentoxifylline was associated with significantly greater improvement in the five ABC subscales, namely Irritability, Lethargy/Social Withdrawal, Stereotypic Behavior, Hyperactivity, and Inappropriate Speech.

Pioglitazone

Pioglitazone, a member of the thiazolidinedione class of medication, is commonly used to treat diabetes mellitus. Thiazolidinediones have also demonstrated anti-inflammatory effects that may well extend to glial cells in the brain. They are useful in a range of autoimmune conditions and have been investigated for the treatment of ASD in one open-label pilot study. Twenty-five children with ASD received pioglitazone for up to 4 months (30 mg/day for 3- to 5-year-olds and 60 mg/day for 6- to 17-year-olds) (Boris et al., 2007). Outcomes were measured with the ABC, with significant improvement seen in the Irritability, Social Withdrawal, Stereotypy, and Hyperactivity subscales.

Oral Human Immunoglobulin

One 8-week open-label trial of oral human immunoglobulin (IGOH) (420 mg/day) in 12 male children (aged 3–7 years) with ASD and GI disturbances found that 50% of those treated had symptomatic improvement of both conditions (Schneider et al., 2006). GI outcomes were measured using the Gastrointestinal Severity Index, whereas symptoms of ASD were measured with the Clinical Global Impression–Improvement (CGI-I) and –Severity scales and the ABC. Significant improvement in ASD symptoms, as measured by the ABC, were seen not only at 8 weeks but also at 30 days after discontinuation of medication. Three of the children withdrew from the study while receiving IGOH following the development of vomiting and fever, vomiting and nausea, and rash, respectively.

There has been one double-blind, placebo-controlled, randomized trial of IGOH in the treatment of ASD (Handen et al., 2009). This study involved 125 children with ASD and chronic GI symptoms. The treatment phase was of 12 weeks' duration with four treatment arms, including placebo and three different dosages of IGOH (140, 420, and 840 mg/day). In contrast to the open-label study, IGOH was not found to be beneficial in reducing ASD or GI symptoms in this controlled trial.

Intravenous Immunoglobulin

Several open-label studies examining the effects of intravenous immunoglobulin (IVIG) in ASD have yielded mixed results. One study involving seven children with ASD, aged 3½–6 years, reported on the effects of IVIG given at monthly intervals for 6 months (400 mg/kg/month) (DelGiudice-Asch, Simon, Schmeidler, Cunningham-Rundles, & Hollander, 1999). Two children did not finish the study: In one case, a diagnosis of Landau–Kleffner syndrome was suspected, and in the other case the family received the last 2 months of IVIG outside of the study. There was no significant improvement in behaviors or ASD severity as measured by several scales, including the Childrens Yale–Brown Obsessive Compulsive Scale, the Ritvo–Freeman Real Life Rating Scale, and the CGI-I.

In a study involving 10 children with ASD (aged 4–17 years) and documented immunologic abnormalities, IVIG was administered every 6 weeks for a total of four infusions (dose, 200–400 mg/kg). Eight of the 10 children had been noted to have had ASD diagnosed following regression in early life. In this study, 5 children did not have any change in symptoms, 4 children had minor improvements that the authors suggested could have been due to placebo effect, and 1 child had an "almost total amelioration" of ASD symptoms with treatment (Plioplys, 1998). The improvements were temporary, with symptoms returning to their baseline levels 5 months after treatment cessation. The authors concluded that the response rate of 10% was too low to justify the high economic costs associated with immunologic testing and IVIG administration.

However, there have been more favorable reports of IVIG, including one involving 10 children with ASD and immunological abnormalities (Gupta, Aggarwal, & Heads, 1996). The children were given IVIG on a monthly basis for 6 months (dose, 400 mg/kg). Following treatment, half of the children ($n = 5$) were deemed to have had a marked ($n = 4$) or striking ($n = 1$) clinical improvement. Enhanced language use, eye contact, and a reduction in agitation were specifically identified.

In addition, favorable reports were obtained from one open-label retrospective study involving 26 children with ASD who were treated with IVIG for 6 months (dose, 400 mg/kg/month) (Fudenberg, 1996). Treatment resulted in a significant decrease in the total ABC score alongside each of the ABC subscales (Irritability, Social Withdrawal, Stereotypy, Hyperactivity, and Inappropriate Speech). Biochemical investigations on the participants revealed evidence of substantial immunological and inflammatory abnormalities, including 54% as having an elevated erythrocyte sedimentation rate, 65% having antibodies to myelin, and 31% having thyroid antibodies.

SUMMARY

This chapter discussed neuroinflammatory processes in ASD; reviewed evidence for potential causes of neuroinflammation, including infection, alloimmunity, and autoimmunity; described results from studies of peripheral immune activation in humans; and summarized the literature on drug treatment studies with anti-inflammatory and immune modulating drugs in ASD. In this context, this chapter provided evidence for central nervous system microglia activation and inflammation from postmortem and neuroimaging studies in individuals with ASD. The chapter presented findings from animal models that antibodies from mothers of children with ASD injected into laboratory animals during gestation can produce offspring with a behavioral syndrome similar to that seen in ASD. It also described results from small, pilot treatment studies of drugs with effects on immune function that have provided benefit to some individuals with ASD, including core disturbances of social and communication ability. Although significantly more research is necessary, evidence to date suggests there may be an identifiable subtype of ASD associated with primary or secondary immune dysregulation.

KEY POINTS

- Examination of postmortem brain tissue from subjects with ASD has revealed evidence of neuroinflammation.
- Injection of blood from mothers of children with ASD into pregnant rodents and nonhuman primates can result in ASD-like behavior in the progeny.
- An increased prevalence of autoimmune disorders has been found in first- and second-degree relatives of probands with ASD compared to control probands in some studies.

- In addition to neuroinflammation, inflammation in the gastrointestinal tract has been found in a subgroup of subjects with ASD.
- Small open-label studies have found that some drugs with anti-inflammatory or immune modulating properties can improve some symptoms associated with ASD.

ACKNOWLEDGMENT

This work was supported in part by the Robert and Donna Landreth Fund.

DISCLOSURE STATEMENT

Dr. Thayne L. Sweeten and Dr. Christopher J. McDougle have no conflicts of interest to disclose.

REFERENCES

Abdallah, M. W., Hougaard, D. M., Nørgaard-Pedersen, B., Grove, J., Bonefeld-Jørgensen, E. C., & Mortensen, E. L. (2012). Infections during pregnancy and after birth, and the risk of autism spectrum disorders: A register-based study utilizing a Danish historic birth cohort. *Turkish Journal of Psychiatry, 23*(4), 229–235.

Abdallah, M. W., Mortensen, E. L., Greaves-Lord, K., Larsen, N., Bonefeld-Jørgensen, E. C., Nørgaard-Pedersen, B., . . . Grove, J. (2013). Neonatal levels of neurotrophic factors and risk of autism spectrum disorders. *Acta Psychiatrica Scandinavica, 128*(1), 61–69.

Akhondzadeh, S., Fallah, J., Mohammadi, M. R., Imani, R., Mohammadi, M., Salehi, B., . . . Forghani, S. (2010). Double-blind placebo-controlled trial of pentoxifylline added to risperidone: Effects on aberrant behavior in children with autism. *Progress in Neuro-Psychopharmacology and Biological Psychiatry, 34*(1), 32–36.

Allan, G. M., & Ivers, H. (2010). The autism-vaccine story: Fiction and deception? *Canadian Family Physician, 56*, 1013.

American Psychiatric Association. (1994). *Diagnostic and statistical manual of mental disorders* (4th ed.). Washington, DC: Author.

Asadabadi, M., Mohammadi, M. R., Ghanizadeh, A., Modabbernia, A., Ashrafi, M., Hassanzadeh, E., . . . Akhondzadeh, S. (2013). Celecoxib as adjunctive treatment to risperidone in children with autistic disorder: A randomized, double-blind, placebo-controlled trial. *Psychopharmacology, 225*(1), 51–59.

Ashwood, P., Corbett, B. A., Kantor, A., Schulman, H., Van de Water, J., & Amaral, D. G. (2011a). In search of cellular immunophenotypes in the blood of children with autism. *PloS One, 6*(5), e19299.

Ashwood, P., Krakowiak, P., Hertz-Picciotto, I., Hansen, R., Pessah, I., & Van de Water, J. (2011b). Elevated plasma cytokines in autism spectrum disorders provide evidence of immune dysfunction and are associated with impaired behavioral outcome. *Brain, Behavior, and Immunity, 25*(1), 40–45.

Atladóttir, H. Ó., Henriksen, T. B., Schendel, D. E., & Parner, E. T. (2012a). Using maternally reported data to investigate the association between early childhood infection and autism spectrum disorder: The importance of data source. *Paediatric and Perinatal Epidemiology, 26*(4), 373–385.

Atladóttir, H. Ó., Henriksen, T. B., Schendel, D. E., & Parner, E. T. (2012b). Autism after infection, febrile episodes, and antibiotic use during pregnancy: An exploratory study. *Pediatrics, 130*(6), e1447–e1454.

Atladóttir, H. O., Pedersen, M. G., Thorsen, P., Mortensen, P. B., Deleuran, B., Eaton, W. W., & Parner, E. T. (2009). Association of family history of autoimmune diseases and autism spectrum disorders. *Pediatrics, 124*(2), 687–694.

Atladóttir, H. O., Thorsen, P., Østergaard, L., Schendel, D. E., Lemcke, S., Abdallah, M., & Parner, E. T. (2010). Maternal infection requiring hospitalization during pregnancy and autism spectrum disorders. *Journal of Autism and Developmental Disorders, 40*(12), 1423–1430.

Bauman, M. D., Iosif, A. M., Ashwood, P., Braunschweig, D., Lee, A., Schumann, C. M., . . . Amaral, D. G. (2013). Maternal antibodies from mothers of children with autism alter brain growth and social behavior development in the rhesus monkey. *Translational Psychiatry, 3*(7), e278.

Beeson, P. B. (1994). Age and sex associations of 40 autoimmune diseases. *American Journal of Medicine, 96,* 457–462.

Boris, M., Kaiser, C. C., Goldblatt, A., Elice, M. W., Edelson, S. M., Adams, J. B., & Feinstein, D. L. (2007). Effect of pioglitazone treatment on behavioral symptoms in autistic children. *Journal of Neuroinflammation, 4*(3). doi:10.1186/1742-2094-4-3

Braunschweig, D., Ashwood, P., Krakowiak, P., Hertz-Picciotto, I., Hansen, R., Croen, L. A., . . . Van de Water, J. (2008). Autism: Maternally derived antibodies specific for fetal brain proteins. *Neurotoxicology, 29*(2), 226–231.

Braunschweig, D., Duncanson, P., Boyce, R., Hansen, R., Ashwood, P., Pessah, I. N., . . . Van de Water, J. (2012a). Behavioral correlates of maternal antibody status among children with autism. *Journal of Autism and Developmental Disorders, 42*(7), 1435–1445.

Braunschweig, D., Golub, M. S., Koenig, C. M., Qi, L., Pessah, I. N., Van de Water, J., & Berman, R. F. (2012b). Maternal autism-associated IgG antibodies delay development and produce anxiety in a mouse gestational transfer model. *Journal of Neuroimmunology, 252*(1–2), 56–65.

Braunschweig, D., Krakowiak, P., Duncanson, P., Boyce, R., Hansen, R. L., Ashwood, P., . . . Van de Water, J. (2013). Autism-specific maternal autoantibodies recognize critical proteins in developing brain. *Translational Psychiatry, 3,* e277.

Brimberg, L., Sadiq, A., Gregersen, P. K., & Diamond, B. (2013). Brain-reactive IgG correlates with autoimmunity in mothers of a child with an autism spectrum disorder. *Molecular Psychiatry, 18*(11), 1171–1177.

Broadley, S. A., Dean, J., Sawcer, S. J., Clayton, D., & Compston, D. A. S. (2000). Autoimmune disease in first-degree relatives of patients with multiple sclerosis. *Brain, 123,* 1102–1111.

Buie, T., Campbell, D. B., Fuchs, G. J., Furuta, G. T., Levy, J., VandeWater, J., . . . Winter, H. (2010). Evaluation, diagnosis, and treatment of gastrointestinal disorders in individuals with ASDs: A consensus report. *Pediatrics, 125*(Suppl. 1), S1–S18.

Buitelaar, J. K., van Engeland, H., de Kogel, K., de Vries, H., van Hooff, J., & van Ree, J. (1992a). The adrenocorticotrophic hormone (4–9) analog ORG 2766 benefits autistic children: Report on a second controlled clinical trial. *Journal of the American Academy of Child & Adolescent Psychiatry, 31*(6), 1149–1156.

Buitelaar, J. K.,van Engeland, H., de Kogel, K. H., de Vries, H., van Hooff, J. A., van Ree, J. M. (1992b). The use of adrenocorticotrophic hormone (4–9) analog ORG 2766 in autistic children: Effects on the organization of behavior. *Biological Psychiatry, 31*(11), 1119–1129.

Buitelaar, J. K., van Engeland, H., van Ree, J. M., & de Wied, D. (1990). Behavioral effects of Org 2766, a synthetic analog of the adrenocorticotrophic hormone (4–9), in 14 outpatient autistic children. *Journal of Autism and Developmental Disorders, 20*(4), 467–478.

Chess, S. (1971). Autism in children with congenital rubella. *Journal of Autism and Childhood Schizophrenia, 1,* 33–47.

Chez, M., Low, R., Parise, C., & Donnel, T. (2012). Safety and observations in a pilot study of lenalidomide for treatment in autism. *Autism Research and Treatment, 2012,* 291601. doi:10.1155/2012/291601

Chez, M. G., Loeffel, M., Buchanan, C. P., & Field-Chez, M. (1998). Pulse high-dose steroids as combination therapy with valproic acid in epileptic aphasia patients with pervasive developmental delay or autism. *Annals of Neurology, 44*(3), 539–539.

Chien, Y. L., Wu, Y. Y., Chen, C. H., Gau, S. S. F., Huang, Y. S., Chien, W. H., . . . Chao, Y. L. (2012). Association of HLA-DRB1 alleles and neuropsychological function in autism. *Psychiatric Genetics, 22*(1), 46–49.

Comi, A. M., Zimmerman, A. W., Frye, V. H., Law, P. A., & Peeden, J. N. (1999). Familial clustering of autoimmune disorders and evaluation of medical risk factors in autism. *Journal of Child Neurology, 14*(6), 388–394.

Corbett, B. A., Kantor, A. B., Schulman, H., Walker, W. L., Lit, L., Ashwood, P., . . . Sharp, F. R. (2007). A proteomic study of serum from children with autism showing differential expression of apolipoproteins and complement proteins. *Molecular Psychiatry, 12*(3), 292–306.

Courchesne, E., Karns, C. M., Davis, H. R., Ziccardi, R., Carper, R. A., Tigue, Z. D., ... Courchesne, R. Y. (2001). Unusual brain growth patterns in early life in patients with autistic disorder an MRI study. *Neurology, 57*(2), 245–254.

Craig, M. E., Howard, N. J., Silink, M., & Chan, A. (2000). The rising incidence of childhood type 1 diabetes in New South Wales, Australia. *Journal of Pediatric Endocrinology and Metabolism, 13*(4), 363–373.

Croen, L. A., Braunschweig, D., Haapanen, L., Yoshida, C. K., Fireman, B., Grether, J. K., ... Van de Water, J. (2008). Maternal mid-pregnancy autoantibodies to fetal brain protein: The early markers for autism study. *Biological Psychiatry, 64*(7), 583–588.

Croen, L. A., Grether, J. K., Yoshida, C. K., Odouli, R., & Van de Water, J. (2005). Maternal autoimmune diseases, asthma and allergies, and childhood autism spectrum disorders: A case–control study. *Archives of Pediatrics & Adolescent Medicine, 159*(2), 151–157.

Curran, L. K., Newschaffer, C. J., Lee, L. C., Crawford, S. O., Johnston, M. V., & Zimmerman, A. W. (2007). Behaviors associated with fever in children with autism spectrum disorders. *Pediatrics, 120*(6), e1386–e1392.

Dalton, P., Deacon, R., Blamire, A., Pike, M., McKinlay, I., Stein, J., ... Vincent, A. (2003). Maternal neuronal antibodies associated with autism and a language disorder. *Annals of Neurology, 53*(4), 533–537.

Daniels, W. W., Warren, R. P., Odell, J. D., Maciulis, A., Burger, R. A., Warren, W. L., & Torres, A. R. (1995). Increased frequency of the extended or ancestral haplotype B44-SC3O-DR4 in autism. *Neuropsychobiology, 32*(3), 120–123.

Deer, B. (2011). How the case against the MMR vaccine was fixed. *BMJ, 342*, c5347.

DelGiudice-Asch, G., Simon, L., Schmeidler, J., Cunningham-Rundles, C., & Hollander, E. (1999). Brief report: A pilot open clinical trial of intravenous immunoglobulin in childhood autism. *Journal of Autism and Developmental Disorders, 29*(2), 157–160.

DeLong, R., Bean, S. C., & Brown, F. R. (1981). Acquired reversible autistic syndrome in acute encephalopathic illness in children. *Archives of Neurology, 38*(3), 191–194.

Denney, D. R., Frei, B. W., & Gaffney, G. R. (1996). Lymphocyte subsets and interleukin-2 receptors in autistic children. *Journal of Autism and Developmental Disorders, 26*(1), 87–97.

DeStefano, F. (2007). Vaccines and autism: Evidence does not support a causal association. *Clinical Pharmacology and Therapeutics, 82*(6), 756–759.

Deverman, B. E., & Patterson, P. H. (2009). Cytokines and CNS development. *Neuron, 64*(1), 61–78.

Doria, A., Zen, M., Bettio, S., Gatto, M., Bassi, N., Nalotto, L., ... Punzi, L. (2012). Autoinflammation and autoimmunity: Bridging the divide. *Autoimmunity Reviews, 12*(1), 22–30.

Duffy, F. H., Shankardass, A., McAnulty, G. B., Eksioglu, Y. Z., Coulter, D., Rotenberg, A., & Als, H. (2014). Corticosteroid therapy in regressive autism: A retrospective study of effects on the Frequency Modulated Auditory Evoked Response (FMAER), language, and behavior. *BMC Neurology, 14*(1), 70.

Dyer, C. (2010). Wakefield was dishonest and irresponsible over MMR research, says GMC. *BMJ, 340*, c593.

Ebert, D. H., & Greenberg, M. E. (2013). Activity-dependent neuronal signaling and autism spectrum disorder. *Nature, 493*(7432), 327–337.

Folstein, S., & Rutter, M. (1977). Infantile autism: A genetic study of 21 twin pairs. *Journal of Child Psychology and Psychiatry, 18*(4), 297–321.

Fudenberg, H. H. (1996). Dialysable lymphocyte extract (DLyE) in infantile onset autism: A pilot study. *Biotherapy, 9*(1–3), 143–147.

Fung, L. K., Libove, R. A., Phillips, J., Haddad, F., & Hardan, A. Y. (2014). Brief report: An open-label study of the neurosteroid pregnenolone in adults with autism spectrum disorder. *Journal of Autism and Developmental Disorders, 44*(11), 2971–2977.

Gadow, K. D., & DeVincent, C. J. (2005). Clinical significance of tics and attention-deficit hyperactivity disorder (ADHD) in children with pervasive developmental disorder. *Journal of Child Neurology, 20*(6), 481–488.

Gadow, K. D., DeVincent, C. J., Pomeroy, J., & Azizian, A. (2004). Psychiatric symptoms in preschool children with PDD and clinic and comparison samples. *Journal of Autism and Developmental Disorders, 34*(4), 379–393.

Garbett, K., Ebert, P. J., Mitchell, A., Lintas, C., Manzi, B., Mirnics, K., & Persico, A. M. (2008). Immune transcriptome alterations in the temporal cortex of subjects with autism. *Neurobiology of Disease, 30*(3), 303–311.

Gasque, P., Dean, Y. D., McGreal, E. P., VanBeek, J., & Morgan, B. P. (2000). Complement components of the innate immune system in health and disease in the CNS. *Immunopharmacology, 49*(1), 171–186.

Ghaziuddin, M., Al-Khouri, I., & Ghaziuddin, N. (2002). Autistic symptoms following herpes encephalitis. *European Child & Adolescent Psychiatry, 11*(3), 142–146.

Goines, P., Haapanen, L., Boyce, R., Duncanson, P., Braunschweig, D., Delwiche, L., . . . Van de Water, J. (2011). Autoantibodies to cerebellum in children with autism associate with behavior. *Brain, Behavior, and Immunity, 25*(3), 514–523.

Graeber, M. B., Bise, K., & Mehraein, P. (1993). Synaptic stripping in the human facial nucleus. *Acta Neuropathologica, 86*(2), 179–181.

Grigorenko, E. L., Han, S. S., Yrigollen, C. M., Leng, L., Mizue, Y., Anderson, G. M., . . . Bucala, R. (2008). Macrophage migration inhibitory factor and autism spectrum disorders. *Pediatrics, 122*(2), e438–e445.

Guerini, F. R., Bolognesi, E., Chiappedi, M., Manca, S., Ghezzo, A., Agliardi, C., . . . Clerici, M. (2014). Activating KIR molecules and their cognate ligands prevail in children with a diagnosis of ASD and in their mothers. *Brain, Behavior, and Immunity, 36*, 54–60.

Gupta, S., Aggarwal, S., & Heads, C. (1996). Brief report: Dysregulated immune system in children with autism: Beneficial effects of intravenous immune globulin on autistic characteristics. *Journal of Autism and Developmental Disorders, 26*(4), 439–452.

Gupta, S., Rimland, B., & Shilling, P. D. (1996). Pentoxifylline: Brief review and rationale for its possible use in the treatment of autism. *Journal of Child Neurology, 11*(6), 501–504.

Hamza, R. T., Hewedi, D. H., & Ismail, M. A. (2010). Basal and adrenocorticotropic hormone stimulated plasma cortisol levels among Egyptian autistic children: Relation to disease severity. *Italian Journal of Pediatrics, 36*, 71.

Handen, B. L., Melmed, R. D., Hansen, R. L., Aman, M. G., Burnham, D. L., Bruss, J. B., & McDougle, C. J. (2009). A double-blind, placebo-controlled trial of oral human immunoglobulin for gastrointestinal dysfunction in children with autistic disorder. *Journal of Autism and Developmental Disorders, 39*(5), 796–805.

Hess, D. T., Patterson, S. I., Smith, D. S., & Skene, J. P. (1993). Neuronal growth cone collapse and inhibition of protein fatty acylation by nitric oxide. *Nature, 366*(6455), 562–565.

Heuer, L., Ashwood, P., Schauer, J., Goines, P., Krakowiak, P., Hertz-Picciotto, I., . . . Van de Water, J. (2008). Reduced levels of immunoglobulin in children with autism correlates with behavioral symptoms. *Autism Research, 1*(5), 275–283.

Hsiao, E. Y., & Patterson, P. H. (2011). Activation of the maternal immune system induces endocrine changes in the placenta via IL-6. *Brain, Behavior, and Immunity, 25*(4), 604–615.

Iwata, Y., Tsuchiya, K. J., Mikawa, S., Nakamura, K., Takai, Y., Suda, S., . . . Mori, N. (2008). Serum levels of P-selectin in men with high-functioning autism. *British Journal of Psychiatry, 193*(4), 338–339.

Johnson, W. G., Buyske, S., Mars, A. E., Sreenath, M., Stenroos, E. S., Williams, T. A., . . . Lambert, G. H. (2009). HLA-DR4 as a risk allele for autism acting in mothers of probands possibly during pregnancy. *Archives of Pediatrics & Adolescent Medicine, 163*(6), 542–546.

Kanner, L. (1943). Autistic disturbances of affective contact. *Nervous Child, 2*(3), 217–250.

Keil, A., Daniels, J. L., Forssen, U., Hultman, C., Cnattingius, S., Söderberg, K. C., . . . Sparen, P. (2010). Parental autoimmune diseases associated with autism spectrum disorders in offspring. *Epidemiology, 21*(6), 805–808.

Konstantareas, M. M., & Homatidis, S. (1987). Brief report: Ear infections in autistic and normal children. *Journal of Autism and Developmental Disorders, 17*(4), 585–594.

Kotla, V., Goel, S., Nischal, S., Heuck, C., Vivek, K., Das, B., & Verma, A. (2009). Mechanism of action of lenalidomide in hematological malignancies. *Journal of Hematology & Oncology, 2*(36), 36.

Lawson, L. J., Perry, V. H., & Gordon, S. (1992). Turnover of resident microglia in the normal adult mouse brain. *Neuroscience, 48*(2), 405–415.

Lee, L. C., Zachary, A. A., Leffell, M. S., Newschaffer, C. J., Matteson, K. J., Tyler, J. D., & Zimmerman, A. W. (2006). HLA-DR4 in families with autism. *Pediatric Neurology, 35*(5), 303–307.

Levin, L., Ban, Y., Concepcion, E., Davies, T. F., Greenberg, D. A., & Tomer, Y. (2004). Analysis of HLA genes in families with autoimmune diabetes and thyroiditis. *Human Immunology, 65*(6), 640–647.

Li, X., Chauhan, A., Sheikh, A. M., Patil, S., Chauhan, V., Li, X. M., . . . Malik, M. (2009). Elevated immune response in the brain of autistic patients. *Journal of Neuroimmunology, 207*(1), 111–116.

Libbey, J. E., Coon, H. H., Kirkman, N. J., Sweeten, T. L., Miller, J. N., Lainhart, J. E., . . . Fujinami, R. S. (2007). Are there altered antibody responses to measles, mumps, or rubella viruses in autism? *Journal of Neurovirology, 13*(3), 252–259.

Libbey, J. E., Sweeten, T. L., McMahon, W. M., & Fujinami, R. S. (2005). Autistic disorder and viral infections. *Journal of Neurovirology, 11*(1), 1–10.

Lizasoain, I., Weiner, C. P., Knowles, R. G., & Moncada, S. (1996). The ontogeny of cerebral and cerebellar nitric oxide synthase in the guinea pig and rat. *Pediatric Research, 39*(5), 779–783.

Lonart, G., Wang, J., & Johnson, K. M. (1992). Nitric oxide induces neurotransmitter release from hippocampal slices. *European Journal of Pharmacology, 220*(2), 271–272.

Marinović-Ćurin, J., Marinović-Terzić, I., Bujas-Petković, Z., Zekan, L., Škrabić, V., Đogaš, Z., & Terzić, J. (2008). Slower cortisol response during ACTH stimulation test in autistic children. *European Child & Adolescent Psychiatry, 17*(1), 39–43.

Martin, L. A., Ashwood, P., Braunschweig, D., Cabanlit, M., Van de Water, J., & Amaral, D. G. (2008). Stereotypies and hyperactivity in rhesus monkeys exposed to IgG from mothers of children with autism. *Brain, Behavior, and Immunity, 22*(6), 806–816.

Mazur-Kolecka, B., Cohen, I. L., Gonzalez, M., Jenkins, E. C., Kaczmarski, W., Brown, W. T., . . . Frackowiak, J. (2014). Autoantibodies against neuronal progenitors in sera from children with autism. *Brain and Development. 36*, 322–329.

Micali, N., Chakrabarti, S., & Fombonne, E. (2004). The broad autism phenotype findings from an epidemiological survey. *Autism, 8*(1), 21–37.

Molloy, C. A., Morrow, A. L., Meinzen-Derr, J., Dawson, G., Bernier, R., Dunn, M., . . . Lord, C. (2006). Familial autoimmune thyroid disease as a risk factor for regression in children with autism spectrum disorder: A CPEA study. *Journal of Autism and Developmental Disorders, 36*(3), 317–324.

Money, J., Bobrow, N. A., & Clarke, F. C. (1971). Autism and autoimmune disease: A family study. *Journal of Autism and Childhood Schizophrenia, 1*(2), 146–160.

Mordekar, S. R., Prendergast, M., Chattopadhyay, A. K., & Baxter, P. S. (2009). Corticosteroid treatment of behaviour, language and motor regression in childhood disintegrative disorder. *European Journal of Paediatric Neurology, 13*(4), 367–369.

Morgan, J. T., Chana, G., Abramson, I., Semendeferi, K., Courchesne, E., & Everall, I. P. (2012). Abnormal microglial–neuronal spatial organization in the dorsolateral prefrontal cortex in autism. *Brain Research, 1456*, 72–81.

Morgan, J. T., Chana, G., Pardo, C. A., Achim, C., Semendeferi, K., Buckwalter, J., . . . Everall, I. P. (2010). Microglial activation and increased microglial density observed in the dorsolateral prefrontal cortex in autism. *Biological Psychiatry, 68*(4), 368–376.

Morris, C. M., Zimmerman, A. W., & Singer, H. S. (2009). Childhood serum anti-fetal brain antibodies do not predict autism. *Pediatric Neurology, 41*(4), 288–290.

Mostafa, G. A., & Shehab, A. A. (2010). The link of C4B null allele to autism and to a family history of autoimmunity in Egyptian autistic children. *Journal of Neuroimmunology, 223*(1), 115–119.

Mouridsen, S. E., Rich, B., Isager, T., & Nedergaard, N. J. (2007). Autoimmune diseases in parents of children with infantile autism: A case–control study. *Developmental Medicine & Child Neurology, 49*(6), 429–432.

Murch, S. H., Anthony, A., Casson, D. H., Malik, M., Berelowitz, M., Dhillon, A. P., . . . Walker-Smith, J. A. (2004). Retraction of an interpretation. *Lancet, 363*(9411), 750.

Napolioni, V., Ober-Reynolds, B., Szelinger, S., Corneveaux, J. J., Pawlowski, T., Ober-Reynolds, S., . . . Huentelman, M. J. (2013). Plasma cytokine profiling in sibling pairs discordant for autism spectrum disorder. *Journal of Neuroinflammation, 10*(1), 38.

Nordahl, C. W., Braunschweig, D., Iosif, A. M., Lee, A., Rogers, S., Ashwood, P., . . . Van de Water, J. (2013). Maternal autoantibodies are associated with abnormal brain enlargement in a subgroup of children with autism spectrum disorder. *Brain, Behavior, and Immunity, 30*, 61–65.

Odell, D., Maciulis, A., Cutler, A., Warren, L., McMahon, W. M., Coon, H., . . . Torres, A. (2005). Confirmation of the association of the C4B null allele in autism. *Human Immunology, 66*(2), 140–145.

Okada, K., Hashimoto, K., Iwata, Y., Nakamura, K., Tsujii, M., Tsuchiya, K. J., . . . Mori, N. (2007). Decreased serum levels of transforming growth factor-β1 in patients with autism. *Progress in Neuro-Psychopharmacology and Biological Psychiatry, 31*(1), 187–190.

Onore, C., Careaga, M., & Ashwood, P. (2012). The role of immune dysfunction in the pathophysiology of autism. *Brain, Behavior, and Immunity, 26*(3), 383–392.

Parker-Athill, E. C., & Tan, J. (2010). Maternal immune activation and autism spectrum disorder: Interleukin-6 signaling as a key mechanistic pathway. *Neurosignals, 18*(2), 113–128.

Piven, J., Arndt, S., Bailey, J., Havercamp, S., Andreasen, N. C., & Palmer, P. (1995). An MRI study of brain size in autism. *American Journal of Psychiatry, 152*(8), 1145–1149.

Plioplys, A. V. (1998). Intravenous immunoglobulin treatment of children with autism. *Journal of Child Neurology, 13*(2), 79–82.

Plioplys, A. V., Greaves, A., Kazemi, K., & Silverman, E. (1994). Lymphocyte function in autism and Rett syndrome. *Neuropsychobiology, 29*(1), 12–16.

Prahalad, S., Shear, E. S., Thompson, S. D., Giannini, E. H., & Glass, D. N. (2002). Increased prevalence of familial autoimmunity in simplex and multiplex families with juvenile rheumatoid arthritis. *Arthritis & Rheumatism, 46*(7), 1851–1856.

Ritvo, E. R., Mason-Brothers, A., Freeman, B. J., & Pingree, C. (1990). The UCLA–University of Utah epidemiologic survey of autism: The etiologic role of rare diseases. *American Journal of Psychiatry, 147*(12), 1614–1621.

Ros-Bernal, F., Hunot, S., Herrero, M. T., Parnadeau, S., Corvol, J. C., Lu, L., . . . Vyas, S. (2011). Microglial glucocorticoid receptors play a pivotal role in regulating dopaminergic neurodegeneration in parkinsonism. *Proceedings of the National Academy of Sciences of the USA, 108*(16), 6632–6637.

Rose, N. R., & Bona, C. (1993). Defining criteria for autoimmune diseases (Witebsky's postulates revisited). *Immunology Today, 14*(9), 426–430.

Rosen, N. J., Yoshida, C. K., & Croen, L. A. (2007). Infection in the first 2 years of life and autism spectrum disorders. *Pediatrics, 119*(1), e61–e69.

Rossi, C. C., Fuentes, J., Van de Water, J., & Amaral, D. G. (2014). Brief report: Antibodies reacting to brain tissue in Basque Spanish children with autism spectrum disorder and their mothers. *Journal of Autism and Developmental Disorders, 44*(2), 459–465.

Saxena, V., Ramdas, S., Ochoa, C. R., Wallace, D., Bhide, P., & Kohane, I. (2012). Structural, genetic, and functional signatures of disordered neuro-immunological development in autism spectrum disorder. *PloS One, 7*(12), e48835.

Schafer, D. P., Lehrman, E. K., Kautzman, A. G., Koyama, R., Mardinly, A. R., Yamasaki, R., . . . Stevens, B. (2012). Microglia sculpt postnatal neural circuits in an activity and complement-dependent manner. *Neuron, 74*(4), 691–705.

Schneider, C. K., Melmed, R. D., Barstow, L. E., Enriquez, F. J., Ranger-Moore, J., & Ostrem, J. A. (2006). Oral human immunoglobulin for children with autism and gastrointestinal dysfunction: A prospective, open-label study. *Journal of Autism and Developmental Disorders, 36*(8), 1053–1064.

Schweingruber, N., Reichardt, S. D., Lühder, F., & Reichardt, H. M. (2012). Mechanisms of glucocorticoids in the control of neuroinflammation. *Journal of Neuroendocrinology, 24*(1), 174–182.

Seguin, M. C., Klotz, F. W., Schneider, I., Weir, J. P., Goodbary, M., Slayter, M., . . . Green, S. J. (1994). Induction of nitric oxide synthase protects against malaria in mice exposed to irradiated *Plasmodium berghei* infected mosquitoes: Involvement of interferon gamma and CD8+ T cells. *Journal of Experimental Medicine, 180*(1), 353–358.

Shenoy, S., Arnold, S., & Chatila, T. (2000). Response to steroid therapy in autism secondary to autoimmune lymphoproliferative syndrome. *Journal of Pediatrics, 136*(5), 682–687.

Singer, H. S., Morris, C. M., Gause, C. D., Gillin, P. K., Crawford, S., & Zimmerman, A. W. (2008). Antibodies against fetal brain in sera of mothers with autistic children. *Journal of Neuroimmunology, 194*(1), 165–172.

Singer, H. S., Morris, C., Gause, C., Pollard, M., Zimmerman, A. W., & Pletnikov, M. (2009). Prenatal exposure to antibodies from mothers of children with autism produces neurobehavioral alterations: A pregnant dam mouse model. *Journal of Neuroimmunology, 211*(1), 39–48.

Stefanatos, G. A., Grover, W., & Geller, E. (1995). Case study: Corticosteroid treatment of language regression in pervasive developmental disorder. *Journal of the American Academy of Child & Adolescent Psychiatry, 34*(8), 1107–1111.

Stevens, B., Allen, N. J., Vazquez, L. E., Howell, G. R., Christopherson, K. S., Nouri, N., . . . Barres, B. A. (2007). The classical complement cascade mediates CNS synapse elimination. *Cell, 131*(6), 1164–1178.

Stigler, K. A., Sweeten, T. L., Posey, D. J., & McDougle, C. J. (2009). Autism and immune factors: A comprehensive review. *Research in Autism Spectrum Disorders, 3*(4), 840–860.

Stubbs, E. G. (1978). Autistic symptoms in a child with congenital cytomegalovirus infection. *Journal of Autism and Childhood Schizophrenia, 8*(1), 37–43.

Stubbs, E. G., & Magenis, R. E. (1980). HLA and autism. *Journal of Autism and Developmental Disorders, 10*(1), 15–19.

Suzuki, K., Sugihara, G., Ouchi, Y., Nakamura, K., Futatsubashi, M., Takebayashi, K., . . . Mori, N. (2013). Microglial activation in young adults with autism spectrum disorder. *JAMA Psychiatry, 70*(1), 49–58.

Sweeten, T. L., Bowyer, S. L., Posey, D. J., Halberstadt, G. M., & McDougle, C. J. (2003). Increased prevalence of familial autoimmunity in probands with pervasive developmental disorders. *Pediatrics, 112*(5), e420–e420.

Sweeten, T. L., Posey, D. J., & McDougle, C. J. (2003). High blood monocyte counts and neopterin levels in children with autistic disorder. *American Journal of Psychiatry, 160*(9), 1691–1693.

Sweeten, T. L., Posey, D. J., & McDougle, C. J. (2004). Brief report: Autistic disorder in three children with cytomegalovirus infection. *Journal of Autism and Developmental Disorders, 34*(5), 583–586.

Sweeten, T. L., Posey, D. J., Shankar, S., & McDougle, C. J. (2004). High nitric oxide production in autistic disorder: A possible role for interferon-γ. *Biological Psychiatry, 55*(4), 434–437.

Tanoue, Y., & Oda, S. (1989). Weaning time of children with infantile autism. *Journal of Autism and Developmental Disorders, 19*(3), 425–434.

Tetreault, N. A., Hakeem, A. Y., Jiang, S., Williams, B. A., Allman, E., Wold, B. J., & Allman, J. M. (2012). Microglia in the cerebral cortex in autism. *Journal of Autism and Developmental Disorders, 42*(12), 2569–2584.

The Lancet Editors. (2010). Retraction—Ileal–lymphoid–nodular hyperplasia, non-specific colitis, and pervasive developmental disorder in children. *Lancet, 375,* 445.

Torrente, F., Anthony, A., Heuschkel, R. B., Thomson, M. A., Ashwood, P., & Murch, S. H. (2004). Focal-enhanced gastritis in regressive autism with features distinct from Crohn's and *Helicobacter pylori* gastritis. *American Journal of Gastroenterology, 99*(4), 598–605.

Torrente, F., Ashwood, P., Day, R., Machado, N., Furlano, R. I., Anthony, A., . . . Murch, S. H. (2002). Small intestinal enteropathy with epithelial IgG and complement deposition in children with regressive autism. *Molecular Psychiatry, 7*(4), 375–382.

Torres, A. R., Maciulis, A., Stubbs, E., Cutler, A., & Odell, D. (2002). The transmission disequilibrium test suggests that HLA-DR4 and DR13 are linked to autism spectrum disorder. *Human Immunology, 63*(4), 311–316.

Torres, A. R., Sweeten, T. L., Cutler, A., Bedke, B. J., Fillmore, M., Stubbs, E., & Odell, D. (2006). The association and linkage of the HLA-A2 class I allele with autism. *Human Immunology, 67*(4), 346–351.

Torres, A. R., Westover, J. B., Gibbons, C., Johnson, R. C., & Ward, D. C. (2012). Activating killer-cell immunoglobulin-like receptors (KIR) and their cognate HLA ligands are significantly increased in autism. *Brain, Behavior, and Immunity, 26*(7), 1122–1127.

Tostes, M. H. F. S., Teixeira, H. C., Gattaz, W. F., Brandão, M. A. F., & Raposo, N. R. B. (2012). Altered neurotrophin, neuropeptide, cytokines and nitric oxide levels in autism. *Pharmacopsychiatry, 45*(6), 241–243.

Underwood, E. (2013). Alarm over autism test. *Science, 341*(6151), 1164–1167.

Valicenti-McDermott, M. D., McVicar, K., Cohen, H. J., Wershil, B. K., & Shinnar, S. (2008). Gastrointestinal symptoms in children with an autism spectrum disorder and language regression. *Pediatric Neurology*, *39*(6), 392–398.

Vargas, D. L., Nascimbene, C., Krishnan, C., Zimmerman, A. W., & Pardo, C. A. (2005). Neuroglial activation and neuroinflammation in the brain of patients with autism. *Annals of Neurology*, *57*(1), 67–81.

Voineagu, I., Wang, X., Johnston, P., Lowe, J. K., Tian, Y., Horvath, S., . . . Geschwind, D. H. (2011). Transcriptomic analysis of autistic brain reveals convergent molecular pathology. *Nature*, *474*(7351), 380–384.

Vojdani, A., Mumper, E., Granpeesheh, D., Mielke, L., Traver, D., Bock, K., . . . McCandless, J. (2008). Low natural killer cell cytotoxic activity in autism: The role of glutathione, IL-2 and IL-15. *Journal of Neuroimmunology*, *205*(1), 148–154.

Wake, H., Moorhouse, A. J., Jinno, S., Kohsaka, S., & Nabekura, J. (2009). Resting microglia directly monitor the functional state of synapses in vivo and determine the fate of ischemic terminals. *Journal of Neuroscience*, *29*(13), 3974–3980.

Wakefield, A. J., Murch, S. H., Anthony, A., Linnell, J., Casson, D. M., Malik, M., . . . Walker-Smith, J. A. (1998). Retracted: Ileal–lymphoid–nodular hyperplasia, non-specific colitis, and pervasive developmental disorder in children. *Lancet*, *351*(9103), 637–641.

Warren, R. P., Foster, A., & Margaretten, N. C. (1987). Reduced natural killer cell activity in autism. *Journal of the American Academy of Child & Adolescent Psychiatry*, *26*(3), 333–335.

Warren, R. P., Odell, J. D., Warren, W. L., Burger, R. A., Maciulis, A., Daniels, W. W., & Torres, A. R. (1996). Strong association of the third hypervariable region of HLA-DRβ1 with autism. *Journal of Neuroimmunology*, *67*(2), 97–102.

Warren, R. P., Singh, V. K., Cole, P., Odell, J. D., Pingree, C. B., Warren, W. L., & White, E. (1991). Increased frequency of the null allele at the complement C4b locus in autism. *Clinical & Experimental Immunology*, *83*(3), 438–440.

Warren, R. P., Singh, V. K., Cole, P., Odell, J. D., Pingree, C. B., Warren, W. L., . . . McCullough, M. (1992). Possible association of the extended MHC haplotype B44-SC30-DR4 with autism. *Immunogenetics*, *36*(4), 203–207.

Wordsworth, B. P., Lanchbury, J. S., Sakkas, L. I., Welsh, K. I., Panayi, G. S., & Bell, J. I. (1989). HLA-DR4 subtype frequencies in rheumatoid arthritis indicate that DRB1 is the major susceptibility locus within the HLA class II region. *Proceedings of the National Academy of Sciences*, *86*(24), 10049–10053.

Yang, Y., Chung, E. K., Zhou, B., Lhotta, K., Hebert, L. A., Birmingham, D. J., . . . Yu, Y. (2004). The intricate role of complement component C4 in human systemic lupus erythematosus. *Current Directions in Autoimmunity*, *7*, 98–132.

Zerbo, O., Iosif, A. M., Walker, C., Ozonoff, S., Hansen, R. L., & Hertz-Picciotto, I. (2013a). Is maternal influenza or fever during pregnancy associated with autism or developmental delays? Results from the CHARGE (Childhood Autism Risks from Genetics and Environment) study. *Journal of Autism and Developmental Disorders*, *43*(1), 25–33.

Zerbo, O., Qian, Y., Yoshida, C., Grether, J. K., Van de Water, J., & Croen, L. A. (2013b). Maternal infection during pregnancy and autism spectrum disorders. *Journal of Autism and Developmental Disorders*, advanced online publication. doi:10.1007/s10803-013-2016-3

Zhang, J., Shi, X. Q., Echeverry, S., Mogil, J. S., De Koninck, Y., & Rivest, S. (2007). Expression of CCR2 in both resident and bone marrow-derived microglia plays a critical role in neuropathic pain. *Journal of Neuroscience*, *27*(45), 12396–12406.

Zimmerman, A. W., Connors, S. L., Matteson, K. J., Lee, L. C., Singer, H. S., Castaneda, J. A., & Pearce, D. A. (2007). Maternal antibrain antibodies in autism. *Brain, Behavior, and Immunity*, *21*(3), 351–357.

TREATMENT

/// 15 /// BEHAVIORAL TREATMENT OF AUTISM SPECTRUM DISORDER

SUZANNAH IADAROLA AND TRISTRAM SMITH

INTRODUCTION

CASE STUDY #1: "SAMUEL"

The Reyes family has presented for an initial consultation with you. Their son Samuel is almost 3 years old and has been recently diagnosed with autism spectrum disorder (ASD). For the past 18 months, Samuel has been receiving home-based early intervention (EI) services, including speech therapy, occupational therapy, and physical therapy. Although he has made some progress, his language is still very limited. Samuel will soon transition out of EI, and his parents are wondering what the best placement for him will be. They have considered preschool, but because Samuel has difficulty communicating, they are concerned he will "get lost" among his classmates. In addition, Samuel sometimes hits and kicks others when he is frustrated. The Reyes family would like to know where Samuel's next placement should be and what supports they should ask for.

How would you advise the Reyes family? What information is necessary to adequately counsel them on next steps? For families of newly diagnosed children with ASD, a pivotal decision is whether to continue with EI and preschool services as usual or seek specialized behavioral treatment. Often, another pressing concern is how to deal with problem behaviors that occur at home or in the community. As children with ASD grow up and become adults, families (and eventually the children themselves) face many additional decisions about whether and how to obtain behavioral treatment. What guidance or direct help can you offer?

Although ASD is a neurodevelopmental disorder, psychosocial and educational interventions are currently the primary treatments (Odom, Collet-Klingenberg, Rogers, & Hatton, 2010). Of these, treatments described as "behavioral" have been studied extensively and are potentially useful for individuals with ASD at all ages and stages of development.

Therefore, a working knowledge of behavioral treatment is indispensible for clinicians who serve this population. This chapter gives an overview of the defining features of behavioral treatment and some of the many and varied applications of this treatment available to meet the particular needs of individuals with ASD. The chapter also presents considerations to guide decision-making and resources to facilitate access to treatment.

APPLIED BEHAVIOR ANALYSIS AND OTHER BEHAVIORAL TREATMENTS

One form of "practical" behaviorism that is particularly relevant to ASD is applied behavior analysis (ABA). ABA focuses on interpreting and changing the behavior of individuals through systematic environmental manipulations. Like many other behavioral approaches, ABA is based on what is called the three-term contingency of antecedent–behavior–consequence. Specifically, ABA aims to understand behavior through systematic evaluation of what comes before a behavior (antecedents) and what comes after (consequences). Both antecedents and consequences are essential for maintaining or changing behavior. Although commonly associated with ASD and related disorders, ABA is certainly not specific to this population. Rather, the principles of ABA are generally applicable to all individuals, including children, students, parents, colleagues, and significant others (Cooper, Heron, & Heward, 2007). As human beings, we have a remarkable innate capacity for subtly, and sometimes overtly, influencing the behavior of those with whom we interact. The study and practice of ABA represents a more systematic approach to strategies we already use.

Much behavioral treatment for ASD is based on ABA. Furthermore, of the numerous intervention approaches for treatment of ASD symptoms, ABA has by far the longest history of research, dating back to the early 1960s (Smith, 2010), and now has a large evidence base (Reichow, Doehring, Cicchetti, & Volkmar, 2011). However, other behavioral interventions such as outpatient therapy for social skills (see Chapter 20) and developmental approaches, which emphasize continuous back-and-forth social communication in the context of playful interactions (Dawson et al., 2010), have been increasingly studied since the mid-2000s (Maglione, Gans, Das, Timbie, & Kasari, 2012).

PROVIDERS OF BEHAVIORAL SERVICES AND SETTINGS

To review programs and recommend services for individuals with ASD, it is important to be aware that a variety of professionals provide behavioral services. These providers represent a complicated network of services with sometimes overlapping roles and responsibilities that can vary by state, region, and school. Moreover, providers can have quite different titles, despite having similar backgrounds and expertise. Professionals who work with individuals with ASD often seek specialized training in ABA skills, such as systematically assessing and tracking behavior; designing, implementing, and evaluating behavior intervention plans; and teaching functional skills. Those with a degree in an educational, medical, or mental health-related field can complete additional coursework and clinical internships to become a Board Certified Behavior Analyst (BCBA) or Board Certified Assistant Behavior Analyst (BCaBA). BCBAs should ideally be incorporated into ABA treatment planning for individuals with ASD. They may supervise or consult with other professionals (outlined in Table 15.1) with experience in behavioral interventions who fulfill important roles on the treatment team.

TABLE 15.1 Providers of Behavioral Services

Provider Title	Education and Training	Instructional Setting	Role
Board Certified Behavior Analysts (BCBAs)	Bachelor's degree: Assistant Level (BCaBA) Master's degree: BCBA Doctoral degree: BCBA-D National certification exam Supervised practicum hours	Classrooms, home, community, vocational, outpatient	Systematically assess and track behavior; design, implement, and evaluate behavior intervention plans; teach functional skills through individual instruction; coordinate classroom-wide behavioral supports; develop and implement educational interventions
Special education teachers	Bachelor's/master's degree in special education or related field State-issued license or certification	Self-contained or inclusion classrooms	Implement curricular modifications, instructional/environmental adaptations, behavior intervention plans, social supports; coordinate support staff
Direct service providers (behavioral therapists, paraprofessionals, special education itinerant teachers, therapeutic support staff, aides)	Varied	Classrooms, home, community, vocational	Provide individualized behavioral support for the learner in his or her daily environment (e.g., implement behavior plans, promote attention, provide academic assistance, facilitate social interactions)
School psychologists	Master's/doctoral degree State and sometimes national certification	Public and private schools	Support the academic and social–emotional development of students; educational consultation; liaise with families; conduct psychoeducational testing; facilitate social interactions; provide direct instruction/counseling in socioemotional skills
Clinical psychologists	Doctoral degree National and sometimes state licensure	Outpatient clinic, home, school	Conduct diagnostic evaluations; provide psychoeducational testing; provide behavioral intervention to children and families (e.g., decrease challenging behavior, improve attention, cope with anxiety and depression, social skills training, family therapy, parent training)
Job coaches	Varied	Home, vocational	Facilitate vocational success through conducting vocational assessments, finding a good job match, teaching job-related skills, helping the individual maintain effective interpersonal relationships with coworkers and supervisors

The makeup of the team usually depends on the setting and type of services provided. The following are common examples:

- *Private, ABA agencies.* Many children younger than age 5 years participate in ABA programs run by private, nonprofit ABA agencies that are supported through public funding or insurance reimbursement. These programs are usually led by a BCBA and may also employ special education teachers, speech and language pathologists (SLPs), occupational therapists (OTs), and other professionals. Specialized ABA schools are less common for older children, although they do exist in some areas.

- *Public early intervention programs.* Young children may receive behavioral treatments in developmental or early childhood special education classes funded through the state or local school district. These classes usually have a special education teacher and specialized providers such as SLPs and OTs. Alternatively, children and families may receive behavioral treatment in their homes or through a combination of center- and home-based services.

- *School-based services.* Children and youth with ASD who attend public school may be included in the general education setting. Alternatively, they may be placed in a self-contained classroom (i.e., a classroom in which all students have special education needs), which is taught by a special education teacher with assistance from paraprofessionals and preferably supported by an ASD specialist or outside behavioral consultant. Behavioral treatment can take place within the classroom, or students may be pulled out for therapy sessions. Often, SLPs and OTs implement behavioral strategies for teaching new skills. School psychologists frequently help develop behavior intervention plans to address challenging behavior when necessary and provide counseling on issues such as improving peer interactions or reducing anxiety.

- *Wraparound services.* In some regions, ABA wraparound services are available to support children and families before and after school. Goals often relate to socialization, self-help, safety, and community skills.

- *Adult services.* Adults who require a high level of care may live at residential facilities that include staff members with behavioral training. ABA-based vocational training can also be provided through a job coach or supported employment programs.

- *Outpatient clinics.* Outpatient, clinic-based ABA services are available in some locations. Service providers are usually licensed mental health professionals with training in behavioral strategies. They may provide ongoing care or targeted, time-limited behavioral interventions such as cognitive–behavioral therapy (CBT), and social skills instruction.

- *Inpatient programs.* Partial day treatment centers and inpatient programs exist at a few centers nationally, where expert ABA providers support individuals with severe problems such as dangerous self-injury or aggression.

APPLIED BEHAVIOR ANALYSIS STRATEGIES

Rather than representing one specific teaching approach, ABA provides the overarching framework for implementing a large assortment of strategies. Core characteristics of ABA across the range of strategies include the following:

- A focus on observable and measureable behaviors that are important for the individual's functioning

- Individualization of instruction to the learner's abilities, needs, and interests
- Systematic manipulation of antecedents and consequences (i.e., reliance on behavioral principles)
- The use of data collection to evaluate progress

While maintaining these core features, ABA programs may differ markedly from one another. This reflects the importance placed on designing programming to best meet the learner's particular needs and capitalize on his or her strengths.

Intervention programs vary along several dimensions, including the teaching format, techniques, and provider of the treatment. Intervention can occur one-to-one (in a teacher–student dyad), in small groups, or in a large group setting (e.g., classroom-wide). Generally, one-to-one instruction best suits very young learners, with the goal of progressing to group instruction over time. ABA teaching techniques extend from highly structured and adult-led to incidental and child-led. For example, *discrete trial teaching* (DTT) is a carefully prearranged, didactic approach to teaching skills that is fast-paced, breaks skills down into small units of instruction, provides ample learning opportunities per session, and is highly individualized. These characteristics make DTT a good instructional match for new learners and new skills (Smith, 2001). *Incidental approaches* differ from DTT in that they take advantage of natural learning opportunities that arise throughout an individual's day, as opposed to the more contrived format associated with DTT. Although incidental teaching strategies are intended to be integrated into the learner's daily routine, the environment can be modified somewhat to create teaching moments. For example, providers can encourage a learner to make requests by placing favorite objects in sight but out of reach. Incidental strategies also utilize naturally occurring reinforcers and focus on learner motivation (e.g., helping the learner communicate in the context of preferred materials and activities). Because the teaching environment closely mirrors the daily routine, incidental teaching is often associated with long-term maintenance and skill *generalization* (the transfer of skills across contexts, settings, and people; Ingersoll & Schreibman, 2006). To promote generalization, it can also be helpful to augment adult-facilitated treatment by guiding typically developing peers or family members to act as models and coaches to teach skills. Some teaching approaches represent a blend between structured and incidental techniques. For example, activity schedules (McClannahan & Krantz, 2010) involve visual supports, such as pictures or checklists to help learners complete daily routines (e.g., classroom schedule and getting dressed). Although schedules are frequently created and taught in a structured way by adults, they become more akin to incidental teaching as the individual learns to complete each step independently.

APPLIED BEHAVIOR ANALYSIS INTERVENTION MODELS

ABA intervention models exist for individuals with ASD at all ages and stages of development. Some models are comprehensive, designed to address all areas of need, whereas others are directed toward a more circumscribed set of goals (Odom, Boyd, Hall, & Hume, 2010). Table 15.2 summarizes some of these models.

Early Intensive Behavioral Intervention

Early intensive behavioral intervention (EIBI) consists of 20–40 hours per week of treatment for 2 or 3 years, beginning prior to age 5 years. EIBI involves individualized intervention

TABLE 15.2 Behavioral Intervention Across the Lifespan

Stage of Development	Setting	Overarching Goals	Language	Social–Emotional	Adaptive	Family Interventions
Toddler/preschooler	EIBI Specialized or developmental preschool Center-based program	Catch up in skills and development	Functional communication (e.g., PECS, sign, words) Requesting Labeling	Functional play Parallel play with peers Orienting to a speaker Eye contact	Feeding Toileting Dressing	Psychoeducation Family support Parent management training
Young school age (K–5th grade)	School-based Outpatient services (e.g., speech, occupational, and physical therapy; counseling)	Academics Daily living skills	Increasing language complexity Vocabulary Increasing spontaneity of language Conversation with adults and peers	Creative play Group games Cooperative play with peers	Personal care routines Visual schedules to increase independence Safety	Educational consultation Parent management training
Older school age (6–12th grade)	School-based Outpatient Community	Academics Daily living skills Community skills Transition planning Social skills	Written communication Jokes/sarcasm	Cooperative play Friendships Frustration tolerance and emotional regulation	Chores Self-care	
Transition age	Community Worksite	Job readiness Community-based skills Daily living skills Increasing independence		Friendships Romantic relationships	Cooking Cleaning Independent self-care	Transition planning Decision-making for long-term placement
Adult	Community Worksite Independent living	Increase independence Vocational skills		Coworker relationships Romantic relationships	Financial responsibility Leisure activities	Transfer of medical care Ongoing placement decisions

based on a broad curriculum that addresses communication; social skills; self-management; cognition; and pre-academic skills such as imitation, matching, and letter and number concepts (Smith, 2011). Many EIBI models exist (Handleman & Harris, 2001), of which the best known was developed by Lovaas and colleagues at UCLA (Smith, 2010). Intervention in this approach begins in children's homes, with a focus on highly structured one-to-one instruction, especially DTT. The initial goal is to help children learn foundational skills that are considered prerequisites for learning other, more advanced skills. Examples of such skills are cooperation with simple instructions, imitation of others, and discriminating among objects and pictures. Once a child has learned these foundational skills, the priority shifts to teaching skills that will improve the child's everyday functioning. Of particular importance are communication skills such as requesting or labeling objects, daily living skills such as dressing, and play skills such as completing puzzles. The later stages of intervention use naturalistic strategies to promote peer interaction and support children's entry into community settings such as schools.

Many other EIBI models resemble the UCLA/Lovaas model in that they rely extensively on structured, one-to-one instruction (Handleman & Harris, 2001; Maurice, Green, & Foxx, 2001; Maurice, Green, & Luce, 1996). Still other early intervention programs place a greater emphasis on incidental ABA teaching procedures. Notably, Learning Experiences: An Alternative Program for Preschoolers and Parents (LEAP) integrates children with ASD with typically developing peers in early childhood education and focuses extensively on improving peer interaction. However, evidence on the efficacy of this program is mixed (Boyd et al., 2014; Strain & Bovey, 2011). Another prominent early intervention approach, which can be adapted for use with older children, is Pivotal Response Treatment (PRT). This intervention aims to teach "pivotal" responses that, when acquired, have the potential to improve performance across many other skill areas (Koegel & Kern Koegel, 2006). A number of studies document short-term benefits from PRT, but data on long-term outcomes are unavailable. The Early Start Denver Model (ESDM) is another example of a comprehensive intervention that blends ABA strategies with developmental approaches that emphasize child preference and play-based interactions (Rogers & Dawson, 2010). Initial studies (Dawson et al., 2010) on ESDM indicate that it is a promising intervention that merits additional research.

Overall, despite some important studies failing to show gains from EIBI (Boyd et al., 2014), most experts consider EIBI to be efficacious and regard the UCLA/Lovaas model as having the strongest support (Reichow, 2012). Nevertheless, EIBI has important limitations. Notably, outcomes vary greatly across children. Some catch up to their typically developing peers on IQ tests and other standardized measures, whereas others learn much more slowly. Moreover, little is known about optimal delivery of EIBI (e.g., how many hours a week are needed and for how long), the relative efficacy of different EIBI approaches, mechanisms of change, or the durability of improvements over time.

CASE STUDY #1 CONTINUED

Given the current state of the science, Samuel's pediatrician, Dr. Nolan, strongly encouraged the Reyes family to investigate the EIBI program offered by the school district. She said it could give Samuel the push he needs to start speaking communicatively and increase his overall readiness for school. In addition, the program's service providers would also be able to consistently address Samuel's mild aggression. Dr. Nolan noted that there is considerable evidence that EIBI produces these benefits for many children with ASD. She added that most professionals believe that intervening early and intensively, as occurs in EIBI, is quite important for children with ASD. However, she was careful to make clear that improvements vary greatly across children and that it was difficult to predict how much Samuel might gain. She also emphasized that EIBI would demand a high level of commitment from Samuel, the family, and the EIBI providers, even above what would be entailed in a less intensive program. However, the extra commitment should be time-limited (no more than 2 or 3 years).

Essentially, Dr. Nolan is recommending that the Reyes family consider an empirical trial of EIBI for Samuel during his preschool years. If the parents choose to enroll him in EIBI, they may then have additional questions about the quality of the program and the progress Samuel is making. Although characteristics of a high-quality treatment program are specific to each learner, some general indicators are listed here (see Behavior Analysis Certification Board (BACB), 2012):

- The program is supervised by a BCBA, although treatment may be carried out by other professionals.
- The program is sufficiently intensive, such as fulfilling the number of hours per week outlined by the BACB practice guidelines.
- The program involves shared decision-making among the interdisciplinary team and caregivers.
- Data collection is regularly used to develop intervention plans (e.g., through curriculum-based assessment or goal benchmarking) and to monitor progress (e.g., skill acquisition and reduction in challenging behavior).
- The program incorporates caregiver training and consultation.

Although Samuel's parents have some difficult choices to make, they are fortunate to have options that include placing Samuel in an evidence-based program. What if the family was not offered different options? What if, as often happens, the parents had already learned about EIBI from other families or from their own research and had decided to seek EIBI for Samuel, but this intervention was not available from the school? Clinicians are usually not in a position to recommend any particular EIBI provider, but they can identify some consensus "best practices" for early intervention and preschool services. An authoritative statement on best practices was issued by a National Academy of Sciences working group (National Research Council, 2001). These practices included 25 or more hours per week of intervention, with curriculum specifically targeting the social–communication deficits characteristic of ASD, ongoing data collection to monitor a child's progress, and use of these data to customize the child's intervention. Clinicians also can direct families to online information (see Table 15.3).

Other Comprehensive Applied Behavior Analysis Models

Although EIBI was developed for toddlers and preschoolers with ASD and thus is appropriate for that age group, comprehensive ABA models have also been developed for older children and adults with ASD throughout the lifespan. These programs take place in specialized

TABLE 15.3 Resources for Parents and Professionals

Online Resources

Resource	Website	Description
Association for Science in Autism Treatment (ASAT)	http://www.asatonline.org	Evidence-based practice and dissemination of findings from the scientific literature to practitioners and consumers
Autism Speaks Tool Kits	https://www.autismspeaks.org/family-services/tool-kits	Review common behavioral strategies to address a wide variety of issues for individuals with ASD (e.g., new diagnosis, accessing behavioral services, sleep, feeding, toileting, medication, constipation, blood draws)
Autism Wandering Awareness Alerts Response and Education (AWAARE) Collaboration	http://awaare.nationalautismassociation.org	Caregiver and first responder toolkits from the National Autism Association to improve safety for children who are at-risk for wandering
Devereux	http://www. autismhandbook.org	Transition planning guide
Ohio Center for Autism and Low Incidence (OCALI)	http://www.ocali.org/media/videos	Webcasts and videos on ABA techniques, antibullying, assistive technology, community support programs, vocational issues, guardianship, school placement, and social skills interventions
Organization for Autism Research	http://www.researchautism.org	Transition to adulthood guide
Parent Center Network	http://www.parentcenternetwork.org	Information on locating services, coordinators, and advocates by state

Manuals and Books

Autism Resource Toolkits from the American Academy of Pediatrics (https://www.aap.org)

Building Social Relationships: A Systematic Approach to Teaching Social Interaction Skills to Children and Adolescents With Autism Spectrum Disorders and Other Social Difficulties, by Scott Bellini (2006)

Behavioral intervention for Young Children With Autism: A Manual for Parents and Professionals, by Catherine Maurice, Gina Green, and Stephen Luce (1996)

Early Start Denver Model for Young Children With Autism: Promoting Language, Learning, and Engagement, by Sally Rogers and Geraldine Dawson (2010)

Handbook of Adolescent Transition Education for Youth With Disabilities, by Michael Wehmeyer and Kristine Webb (2012)

Making a Difference: Behavioral Intervention for Autism, by Catherine Maurice, Gina Green, and Richard Foxx (2001)

Making Inclusion Work for Students With Autism Spectrum Disorders, edited by Tristram Smith (2012)

(continued)

TABLE 15.3 Continued

Manuals and Books

Making Sense of Autism, by Travis Thompson (2007)

Prevent, Teach, Reinforce: The School-Based Model of Individualized Positive Behavior Support, by Glen Dunlap, Rose Iovannone, Donald Kincaid, Kelly Wilson, Kathy Christiansen, Phillip Strain, and Carie English (2010)

Sleep Better! A Guide to Improving Sleep for Children With Special Needs, by V. Mark Durand (2014)

Social Thinking Curriculum, by Michelle Garcia Winner (http://www.socialthinking.com)

Taking Care of Myself: A Hygiene, Puberty and Personal Curriculum for Young Persons With Autism, by Mary Wrobel (2003)

Toilet Training for Individuals With Autism or Other Developmental Issues (2nd ed.), by Maria Wheeler and Carol Kranowitz (2007)

Topics in Autism book series (Woodbine House)

Treating Eating Problems of Children With Autism Spectrum Disorders and Developmental Disabilities: Interventions for Professionals and Parents, by Keith Williams and Richard Foxx (2007) classrooms, residences, or occupational settings. They differ from EIBI in that they provide less one-to-one, structured teaching and focus instead on participation in group activities and promoting independence (i.e., without direct supervision). The goals of intervention also differ based on the age and functioning level of the individual with ASD. For example, children with ASD in elementary school might receive ABA instruction on playing with peers, taking care of personal hygiene, and mastering early academic skills. Youth with ASD in middle or high school might receive ABA instruction related to puberty and sexuality, household chores, and participation in peer groups. As they approach adulthood, instruction might focus on independent living skills (e.g., using public transportation or managing finances), job readiness, and comprehension of romantic relationships. Adults might take part in vocational training, as well as social skills training on how to interact effectively with coworkers and with friends or family at home. Research shows that persons with ASD in these comprehensive programs learn many new skills (McClannahan, MacDuff, & Krantz, 2002). Still, little information is available on long-term outcomes such as whether graduates of the programs succeed afterward in less specialized settings.

Skills-Focused Techniques

Intervention strategies that target specific skills (e.g., communication and social interactions) can be used as part of, in conjunction with, or separately from more comprehensive treatment packages. These more focused interventions may involve individual instruction with the learner with ASD, as well as teaching others (e.g., parents, siblings, peers, and providers) to use behavioral strategies. Empirical support for engaging these individuals to deliver ABA interventions under professional supervision is well documented in the literature (Sarokoff & Sturmey, 2004), and doing so increases dissemination of these important treatments. Because skill-based interventions can be mediated through various teachers or "coaches," instruction can occur in structured programs (e.g., classroom and vocational placement) and everyday settings (e.g., home and community). Training typically involves psychoeducation (e.g., the relevance of ASD symptomatology to the target skills), assessment of learner strengths and needs within the skill area, instruction and in vivo feedback on implementing ABA strategies, data collection, and a collaborative team-based approach (e.g., high communication and shared goal-setting and decision-making). Specific intervention strategies are usually introduced in a workshop or other intensive training format. Program implementation is then monitored via ongoing consultation, first on an intensive basis (e.g., 1 or 2 hours per week) and then faded over time.

Communication

Because deficits in communication are a defining feature of ASD, many individuals with ASD receive ABA interventions to increase functional communication skills. Enhancing an individual's communication skills helps him or her more successfully interact with the world and concurrently may decrease problem behavior (Tiger, Hanley, & Bruzek, 2008). Vocal communication goals range from producing word approximations and first words (for minimally verbal learners) to using complete sentences (for learners with phrase speech), improving articulation, syntax, and grammar (for learners with complex speech), and engaging in conversation (for more fluent speakers; Koegel & Kern Koegel, 2006; Maurice et al., 1996).

Augmentative and alternative communication (AAC) systems such as sign language, gestures, or pictures are used to increase communication in minimally verbal learners. One of the most common ABA-based systems for AAC is the Picture Exchange Communication System (PECS), in which children with ASD are taught to select a picture symbol and hand it to another person in order to make requests or comments (Bondy & Frost, 2001). Alternatively, voice output communication aides, which incorporate technology into this process by translating pictorial or textual icons into spoken words, may be a useful advance for those with limited spoken language (Shane et al., 2012). Because individuals with ASD often struggle with natural motivation to communicate, spontaneous language remains a concern, even after initial skills have been learned (Smith, 2001). Thus, a key component of intervention is to promote initiation of communication and generalization across a variety of people and situations (Yoder & Warren, 1999).

CASE STUDY #1 CONTINUED

Samuel's parents have been pleased with their son's progress in his new EIBI program. However, early on they shared concerns with the speech therapist that Samuel did not seem to be progressing in his language. Through his EI services, he had started vocalizing but was not yet using single words or gestures to communicate. This was especially frustrating for Mrs. Reyes because she spent the most time with Samuel and felt that she never knew what he wanted. When the speech therapist suggested starting the PECS program with Samuel, Mrs. Reyes was reluctant. She worried that if Samuel could use pictures to communicate, he would never want to speak. The speech therapist explained that the initial goal of PECS is to teach children *how to communicate* (not just how to talk) because young children with ASD do not always learn this naturally. She talked about the high success rate of increasing communication with PECS and shared research findings suggesting that using PECS may actually help children learn spoken language. Reassured, Mr. and Mrs. Reyes agreed to start using PECS with Samuel at home to supplement what he learns during speech therapy sessions.

Social Skills

The social interaction difficulties associated with ASD necessitate structured intervention to increase social skills. Although the quality of the empirical literature in this area is uneven, a number of well-designed studies support ABA social skills interventions. For young children, common intervention targets include early socialization skills such as joint attention, play, and imitation (Ingersoll & Dvortcsak, 2010; Maurice et al., 1996, 2001). Involving peers in intervention is often helpful because peers may be less intrusive and stigmatizing than service providers in settings such as play groups, and skills that are learned from peers may be more likely to generalize to typical social situations outside of treatment (Weiss & Harris, 2001). Strategies that may improve generalization and maintenance include teaching individuals with ASD to self-monitor their responses to others, implementing classwide interventions, providing scripts or cues of social interactions that the child can use across a variety of peers or situations, and using strategies to expand on social initiations that some individuals with ASD spontaneously direct toward peers (Bellini, 2006). For school-age children, social interventions more directly target peer-related social interaction skills and expanding the individual's social network. Examples include the use of "peer buddies" and video modeling techniques (Bellini, 2006).

CASE STUDY #2: "JACKSON"

Jackson Williams is a 10-year-old boy with ASD who is currently placed in a general education classroom, with support from an aide. Although Jackson is doing well academically, he struggles to form friendships with his classmates. Often, he prefers to sit alone reading rather than joining in with peers during recess. Jackson's teachers have also noticed that he sometimes approaches other students in an awkward way. For example, he loves planets and will frequently share facts about them with his peers, even when they are not interested.

Based on a recommendation from Jackson's therapist, he will soon be starting social skills instruction at school. In addition to working individually with the school psychologist, Jackson will work with Shawn, another boy in his class. Shawn's role will be to help Jackson interact with his classmates by asking him to join group games and ensuring he is included in conversations. Jackson will also participate in the school's "Lunch Bunch" program, which provides adult-mediated opportunities for interaction among children with various social needs. In order to ensure that these changes are implemented consistently, Jackson's therapist recommended that this social treatment program be incorporated into Jackson's Individualized Education Program, the document that outlines the school-based services that Jackson receives.

Given that social demands change across the lifespan, it is unclear how effective these approaches are for adolescents and adults with ASD. Research on social interventions in this group has been fairly limited, although some encouraging findings have been reported (McClannahan et al., 2002).

Daily Living, Community, and Vocational Skills

Adaptive behavior represents an individual's ability to demonstrate skills as part of his or her daily functioning, and these skills allow an individual to be as independent as possible. Individuals with ASD may have limited skills across self-help domains, such as dressing, maintaining personal hygiene, engaging in community activities, preparing food, and developing vocational skills (Anderson, Jablonski, Thomeer, & Knapp, 2007), as well as community skills such as purchasing (McClannahan et al., 2002).

Techniques such as task analysis, which involves breaking down a complex behavior into small steps, and the use of visual schedules, in which steps of an activity are displayed in separate pictures or photographs, appear especially useful. In addition, ABA curricula have been developed to teach academic and vocational skills; these curricula are based on task analyses of the skills and involve developing the skills in a series of carefully planned, small steps (Engelmann, Becker, Carnine, & Gersten, 1988). However, because evaluations of the effectiveness of these curricula for individuals with ASD are sparse, this is an area that merits further research (Wehman et al., 2013).

CASE STUDY #2 CONTINUED

During a parent–teacher conference, Jackson's father mentions that Jackson has difficulty independently caring for himself at home. He still requires frequent reminders and assistance for getting dressed in the morning, brushing his teeth, and cleaning up after himself. Because the teacher reports that visual checklists have helped Jackson organize his assignments at school, Jackson's father decides to try using them at home as well. He posts a checklist of Jackson's routine for getting dressed (e.g., put on shirt, pull up pants, button pants, pull on socks) on the wall in his room and a picture schedule of Jackson's teeth-brushing routine in the bathroom. As Jackson completes each step, he checks them off with a marker. After 2 weeks, Jackson's father notices that it is taking Jackson less time to get ready in the morning.

Decreasing Problem Behavior

Some individuals with ASD engage in problem behaviors that impede learning or interfere with daily living skills. These behaviors range from mild (e.g., noncompliance) to moderate (e.g., disruption and tantrums) and severe (e.g., dangerous aggression, self-injury, and property destruction; Matson & Rivet, 2008). Related to the limited social awareness and circumscribed interests that are characteristic of ASD, the behavior may take unusual or unsettling forms, such as undressing in public or becoming excessively preoccupied with a particular person. Intervention is informed by a *functional behavioral assessment* (FBA). An FBA involves systematic data collection on multiple aspects of the problem behavior, including what it looks like, how frequently it happens, how long it lasts, and what are the antecedents and consequences (O'Neill et al., 1997). Data are then analyzed to identify patterns in behavior and to generate a hypothesis regarding the *function* (or maintaining variables) of the behavior. In the ASD literature, the functions of challenging behavior most commonly include access to attention; access to a tangible, desired item or activity; escape from an unwanted demand; and automatic reinforcement (e.g., sensory feedback produced by the behavior itself).

Information gathered from an FBA should be used to develop a behavior intervention plan to break associations among antecedents, consequences, and the behavior (O'Neill et al., 1997; see Table 15.4). Antecedent manipulations are prevention strategies that reduce the likelihood that the behavior will occur in the first place. Consequence-based strategies involve changing the environmental response such as how others react to the behavior. Problem behavior can also occur when an individual does not have the skills to complete a presented task. To alleviate frustration in this situation, instructional supports are indicated, such as teaching prerequisite skills and matching goals to the individual's developmental level or cognitive functioning. Finally, teaching skills to "replace" a challenging behavior (e.g., saying "I'm hungry" instead of having a tantrum) is often associated with positive behavioral outcomes (Tiger et al., 2008).

CASE STUDY #2 CONTINUED

Although Jackson has generally been adjusting well to his new classroom this school year, he occasionally has outbursts that include yelling, throwing classroom materials, and hitting his teacher. These tantrums usually occur when Jackson is asked to work on a difficult assignment. The school team meets to discuss how to address these tantrums because they are disruptive to the rest of the class. The team's BCBA suggests an intervention plan that addresses both the antecedents and the consequences of Jackson's behavior. In

TABLE 15.4 Function-Based Intervention for Challenging Behavior

Function	Change Antecedents	Teach Appropriate Behavior	Consequences
Attention	Provide ample attention at regularly scheduled times Provide attention for appropriate behavior Increase opportunities for appropriate interactions Move desk away from other students	Teach appropriate ways to get attention (e.g., "Excuse me," "tapping someone's shoulder)	Withhold attention in response to inappropriate behavior Provide time-out from attention for a brief period (e.g., 1 minute) Loss of privileges
Escape/avoidance	Provide regular breaks throughout the learner's day Provide a mixture of easy and difficult tasks Minimize the number of non-preferred activities Use motivating materials during non-preferred activities Provide the learner with choices about which task to do next Provide instruction through visual supports (e.g., pictures, checklists) Use a timer to signal the amount of time left until tasks are complete	Teach the learner to ask for a break (either with words or use of a "break" card) Teach the learner to ask for help during difficult tasks	Ignore the problem behavior, but calmly redirect the student every few seconds to complete the task or an alternate task Loss of tokens (if the student has an established reinforcement system for earning breaks from instruction)
Tangible items	Provide access to the item throughout the learner's day Increase opportunities to appropriately request and earn items Use visual supports (e.g., timer) to show how long the learner can use the item	Teach the learner a variety of ways to request the item appropriately Gradually teach the learner to wait before receiving an item	Do not provide access to the item in response to problem behavior
Automatic/sensory	Provide limited access to the behavior at appropriate times (i.e., when it will not interfere with learning), if the behavior is not dangerous Reinforce the learner for engaging in other, appropriate behavior Provide the learner with an object that can "compete" with the behavior Provide regular access to activities that the learner enjoys Limit access to items that may contribute to the problem behavior	Teach the learner to follow class/job/house rules Teach the learner to engage in a behavior that is incompatible with the problem behavior (e.g., hands in pockets versus hand flapping)	Do not provide attention in response to the problem behavior Use gentle physical guidance to redirect the learner

collaboration with Jackson's teacher, he develops several strategies to help Jackson seek assistance when he encounters difficult material, including placing a visual "ask for help" cue on Jackson's desk and reminding the class as a whole that they can ask the teacher questions. The teacher will also implement a "token" reward system, wherein Jackson earns checkmarks each time he completes an academic activity without having a tantrum. At the end of the day, Jackson can exchange his checkmarks for a small treat or privilege (e.g., first choice of games at recess or being the line leader). Finally, the team will monitor Jackson's behavior and will pursue a formal FBA if his tantrums get worse or more frequent over time.

Addressing Anxiety and Rigidity

Anxiety can be a substantial source of distress for individuals with ASD and their caregivers. CBT is one of the most empirically supported treatments for anxiety disorders, and with some adaptations, its success has been replicated in the ASD population (Wood et al., 2009). Inflexibly adhering to the daily schedule, feeling compelled to complete repetitive sequences of behavior, or insisting on others acting in a certain way can also be distressing. Although pharmacological management is often used to address rigidity, behavioral interventions also can be considered (Cotugno, 2009).

CASE STUDY #1 CONTINUED

Samuel's parents are seeking home-based support because lately he has been unlocking the front door and running out into the street. This poses a serious risk because the family lives on a main road. Because this behavior happens at unpredictable times, Mr. and Mrs. Reyes believe they have to be with Samuel constantly. They would like to know more about what they can do to keep Samuel safe. The behavioral team recommends that the Reyes family make some environmental changes (e.g., installing childproof covers on the door handles) to make it more difficult for Samuel to leave the house. Samuel should also be taught safety skills, such as stopping when directed by an adult and following visual cues (e.g., a large STOP sign on the front door). Additional supports should be put in place in case Samuel does make it out of his house. For instance, he should carry a card with his name and address on it, and the neighbors and local businesses should be educated on how to help Samuel return home safely.

Biobehavioral Problems

Individuals with ASD often have physiological symptoms or co-occurring medical conditions. Although pharmacological intervention is sometimes the best approach to treating these difficulties, if there is not a clear medical etiology, behavioral strategies can also be indicated, either as the primary intervention or in combination with medication.

Sleep

Difficulties falling asleep and sleeping through the night are extremely common in ASD, and they are linked to daytime problem behavior, ASD symptomatology, and family stress (Malow et al., 2012). Although medical interventions such as administration of melatonin can be considered, behavioral treatment is also an option (Malow et al., 2012). Common behavioral strategies include establishing good sleep hygiene—for example, implementing a consistent bedtime routine, providing a relaxing bedtime environment, reducing opportunities for daytime sleep, limiting electronics prior to bedtime, fading out sleep associations (e.g., with a parent in the room or the television on), and using visual supports (e.g., picture schedules, sticker charts, and nightlights that turn off when it is time to get up) (Durand, 2014).

Feeding

The most commonly reported feeding problems in ASD are behavioral in nature (e.g., food refusal, food selectivity, gagging, and disruptive mealtime behavior) and related to sensory sensitivity (e.g., avoiding food with specific textures or appearances; Schwarz, 2003). These problems are often associated with elimination problems such as constipation or diarrhea, and they can lead to nutritional deficiencies, although, fortunately, medically urgent malnutrition appears to be rare (Hyman et al., 2012). Behavioral approaches to feeding problems include graduated exposure to non-preferred foods, escape extinction (not removing the food until the individual consumes it), shaping procedures (reinforcing gradual food tolerance), texture fading, and establishing good mealtime habits (instituting a consistent schedule and standard location to eat, limiting grazing at other times, and turning off electronics; Williams & Foxx, 2007). It is often prudent to collaborate with a dietitian to evaluate the nutritional adequacy of the individual's diet and recommend foods to introduce, as well as an SLP or OT to determine whether the individual has impairments in chewing or swallowing (Volkmar & Weisner, 2004).

Some individuals with ASD engage in pica (ingesting non-food substances; McAdam, Sherman, Sheldon, & Napolitano, 2004). This behavior may warrant a medical evaluation because it can reflect nutritional deficiencies and can lead individuals to consume toxic, infectious, or unsafe items, such as large or sharp objects. Behavioral strategies for pica include teaching individuals to distinguish between food and non-food items, identifying the function of the behavior, and implementing function-based interventions (McAdam et al., 2004).

Toilet Training

Many individuals with ASD are delayed in developing daytime and nighttime bladder control, and they often do not achieve bowel control until much later. In addition, they may resist giving up habits such as defecating in a pull-up (Dalrymple & Ruble, 1992). Behavioral techniques for toilet training include gradual exposure to the toilet, frequent practice of toileting skills (sometimes encouraged by increasing the child's fluid intake), systematic reinforcement for sitting on the toilet and for successfully urinating in it, and helping the child overcome barriers such as fears of sights and sounds in the bathroom (Wheeler & Kranowitz, 2007). Other strategies include scheduling regular times for children to sit on the toilet, video modeling, and the use of moisture alarms (e.g., bell and pad alarms; Wheeler & Kranowitz, 2007).

CASE STUDY #1 CONTINUED

Mr. and Mrs. Reyes schedule a visit with Dr. Nolan because during the past few months, Samuel has been refusing to stay in bed. As soon as his parents are gone, he cries and tries to leave his room. Mr. and Mrs. Reyes struggle to keep Samuel in his room until he finally falls asleep in their bed at approximately 10:30 p.m. This is problematic for both parents, who wake up early to go to work. The Reyes family is exhausted and wants to know how they can help Samuel sleep in his own bed.

In talking more about the bedtime routine, Dr. Nolan learns that Samuel is put in bed anytime between 7:00 and 8:00 p.m., depending on when the family finishes dinner, whether Samuel gets a bath, and whether they decide to let him watch an episode of his favorite television show. She suggests that his parents consider a more structured routine that includes a predictable sequence of evening activities, such as dinner, bath time, and a consistent bedtime at 7:30 p.m. Dr. Nolan also counsels Mr. and Mrs. Reyes on how exposure to the artificial light in televisions and computers can interfere with falling asleep. Instead of watching a television show, she asks if Samuel's parents could read him his favorite books. She also compliments them on their persistence in taking Samuel back to his room so many times. If they can consistently keep it up until he falls asleep in his own bed, he will likely begin staying in his room at bedtime. Dr. Nolan warns the Reyes' that learning new sleep habits can sometimes take a while, and she tells them not to get discouraged if Samuel's sleep does not improve for several weeks.

Combining Behavioral Interventions With Medication

Although not effective in treating the core features of ASD, psychotropic medication (discussed in Chapter 16) can be used in concert with behavioral interventions to maximize outcomes in treatment for aggression and other disruptive behavior (Aman et al., 2009). Although little research is available, many clinicians believe that combined medication and behavioral treatment also may be helpful for other symptoms associated with ASD, such as sleep problems, anxiety, mood disruption, aggression, and inattention or impulsivity. Behavioral strategies such as systematic, data-based monitoring on and off medication are also informative for comprehensively evaluating potential benefits and adverse reactions (LaRue et al., 2008).

WHEN TO REFER TO A SPECIALIST

With a solid understanding of behavioral strategies, it is often straightforward and efficient to counsel families on implementing behavioral interventions to address their concerns about the individual with ASD. For medical providers, this counseling is generally accomplished within the confines of a relatively brief office visit (Malow et al., 2014). Providers who deliver ongoing therapeutic services can implement behaviorally based treatment in their sessions, offer parent training, and consult with other providers. If the problem persists or becomes exacerbated over time, referral to a specialist may be indicated. Initially, providers should review the usual considerations, especially the severity of the behavior (e.g., How long has it lasted? Is the individual's functioning impaired? Is there a safety risk?). However, additional factors also may be relevant, including the following:

- Is the intervention developmentally appropriate? Ensuring a good match between the intervention and the individual's strengths and weaknesses will maximize the likelihood of improvement. Programming may be too remedial (e.g., EIBI services that extend beyond early elementary school) or too challenging (e.g., school placement in which the student does not have the skills necessary to meet expectations).

- Have strategies been implemented consistently for an adequate amount of time? Behavioral treatment usually requires weeks or months to yield practical benefit, although signs of incremental improvement should be apparent from data on the individual's progress. Rates of learning vary greatly across individuals (Reichow, 2012). Consistent use of techniques across people, settings, and time is necessary for promoting communication or resolving behavior problems.
- Has the individual experienced a recent life transition? Physical changes such as puberty and psychosocial events such as moving, divorce, or school placement transitions can be disruptive to individuals with ASD, who may be more sensitive to these changes than their peers. Increases in problem behavior, biobehavioral issues, and rigidity may be associated with such changes. However, these problems are often temporary and are likely to respond well to brief behavioral intervention or resolve on their own. If they persist or begin to significantly interfere with the individual's functioning, the behavior may warrant specialized intervention.

KEY POINTS

- Behavioral interventions teach skills and decrease challenging behavior by changing what comes before (i.e., antecedents) and what comes after (i.e., consequences) the behavior.
- ABA-based interventions take many forms and can be relevant for individuals with ASD at all ages and developmental stages and for a variety of skills.
- Although behavioral intervention plans should be highly individualized, there are several quality indicators, such as supervision by a BCBA, service intensity that adheres to published practice guidelines, shared decision-making among team members and families, and systematic data collection.
- Comprehensive approaches such as early intensive behavioral intervention address skill-building across all areas of development in young children with ASD.
- Problem behavior is most effectively addressed through functional behavioral assessment and function-based intervention procedures.

DISCLOSURE STATEMENT

Dr. Tristram Smith and Dr. Suzannah Iadarola receive research funding from the National Institutes of Health. Dr. Smith also receives research funding from the Institute of Education Sciences, Autism Speaks, and the Maternal Child Health Bureau of the Health Resources and Services Administration.

REFERENCES

Aman, M. G., McDougle, C. J., Scahill, L., Handen, B., Arnold, L. E., Johnson, C., . . . Wagner, A. (2009). Medication and parent training in children with pervasive developmental disorders and serious behavior problems: Results from a randomized clinical trial. *Journal of the American Academy of Child & Adolescent Psychiatry*, 48(12), 1143–1154.

Anderson, S. R., Jablonski, A. L., Thomeer, M. L., & Knapp, V. M. (2007). *Self-help skills for people with autism: A systematic teaching approach*. Bethesda, MD: Woodbine House.

Behavior Analyst Certification Board. (2012). *Health plan coverage of applied behavior analysis treatment for autism spectrum disorder.* Retrieved from http://bacb.com/Downloadfiles/ABA_Guidelines_for_ASD.pdf

Bellini, S. (2006). *Building social relationships textbook edition: A systematic approach to teaching social interaction skills to children and adolescents with autism spectrum disorders and other social difficulties.* Shawnee Mission, KS: AAPC Publishing.

Bondy, A., & Frost, L. (2001). The picture exchange communication system. *Behavior Modification, 25*(5), 725–744.

Boyd, B. A., Hume, K., McBee, M. T., Alessandri, M., Gutierrez, A., Johnson, L., . . . Odom, S. L. (2014). Comparative efficacy of LEAP, TEACCH and non-model-specific special education programs for preschoolers with autism spectrum disorders. *Journal of Autism and Developmental Disorders, 44*(2), 366–380.

Cooper, J. O., Heron, T. E., & Heward, W. L. (2007). *Applied behavior analysis* (2nd ed.). Upper Saddle River, NJ: Pearson Prentice Hall.

Cotugno, A. J. (2009). Social competence and social skills training and intervention for children with autism spectrum disorders. *Journal of Autism and Developmental Disorders, 39*(9), 1268–1277.

Dalrymple, N. J., & Ruble, L. A. (1992). Toilet training and behaviors of people with autism: Parent views. *Journal of Autism and Developmental Disorders, 22*(2), 265–275.

Dawson, G., Rogers, S., Munson, J., Smith, M., Winter, J., Greenson, J., . . . Varley, J. (2010). Randomized, controlled trial of an intervention for toddlers with autism: The Early Start Denver Model. *Pediatrics, 125*(1), e17–e23.

Dunlap, G., Iovannone, R., Kincaid, D., Wilson, K., Christiansen, K., Strain, P., & English, C. (2010). *Prevent–teach–reinforce: The school-based model of individualized positive behavior support.* Baltimore, MD: Brookes.

Durand, V. M. (2014). *Sleep better! A guide to improving sleep for children with special needs.* Baltimore, MD: Brookes.

Engelmann, S., Becker, W. C., Carnine, D. W., & Gersten, R. (1988). The Direct Instruction Follow Through model: Design and outcomes. *Education & Treatment of Children, 11*(4), 303–317.

Handleman, J. S., & Harris, S. L. (2001). *Preschool education programs for children with autism.* Austin, TX: Pro-Ed.

Hyman, S. L., Stewart, P. A., Schmidt, B., Lemcke, N., Foley, J. T., Peck, R., . . . Ng, P. K. (2012). Nutrient intake from food in children with autism. *Pediatrics, 130*(Suppl. 2), S145–S153.

Ingersoll, B., & Dvortcsak, A. (2010). *Teaching social communication to children with autism: A manual for parents.* New York, NY: Guilford.

Ingersoll, B., & Schreibman, L. (2006). Teaching reciprocal imitation skills to young children with autism using a naturalistic behavioral approach: Effects on language, pretend play, and joint attention. *Journal of Autism and Developmental Disorders, 36*(4), 487–505.

Koegel, R. L., & Kern Koegel, L. (2006). *Pivotal response treatments for autism: Communication, social, and academic development.* Baltimore, MD: Brookes.

LaRue, R. H., Northup, J., Baumeister, A. A., Hawkins, M. F., Seale, L., Williams, T., & Ridgway, A. (2008). An evaluation of stimulant medication on the reinforcing effects of play. *Journal of Applied Behavior Analysis, 41*(1), 143–147.

Maglione, M. A., Gans, D., Das, L., Timbie, J., & Kasari, C. (2012). Nonmedical interventions for children with ASD: Recommended guidelines and further research needs. *Pediatrics, 130*(Suppl. 2), S169–S178.

Malow, B. A., Adkins, K. W., Reynolds, A., Weiss, S. K., Loh, A., Fawkes, D., . . . Clemons, T. (2014). Parent-based sleep education for children with autism spectrum disorders. *Journal of Autism and Developmental Disorders, 44*(1), 216–228.

Malow, B. A., Byars, K., Johnson, K., Weiss, S., Bernal, P., Goldman, S., . . . Glaze, D. G. (2012). A practice pathway for the identification, evaluation, and management of insomnia in children and adolescents with autism spectrum disorders. *Pediatrics, 130*(Suppl. 2), S106–S124.

Matson, J. L., & Rivet, T. T. (2008). Characteristics of challenging behaviours in adults with autistic disorder, PDD-NOS, and intellectual disability. *Journal of Intellectual and Developmental Disability, 33*(4), 323–329.

Maurice, C., Green, G., & Foxx, R. M. (2001). *Making a difference: Behavioral intervention for autism.* Austin, TX: Pro-Ed.

Maurice, C. E., Green, G. E., & Luce, S. C. (1996). *Behavioral intervention for young children with autism: A manual for parents and professionals.* Austin, TX: Pro-Ed.

McAdam, D. B., Sherman, J. A., Sheldon, J. B., & Napolitano, D. A. (2004). Behavioral interventions to reduce the pica of persons with developmental disabilities. *Behavior Modification, 28,* 45–72.

McClannahan, L. E., & Krantz, P. (2010). *Activity schedules for children with autism: Teaching independent behavior (Topics in Autism).* Bethesda, MD: Woodbine House.

McClannahan, L. E., MacDuff, G. S., & Krantz, P. J. (2002). Behavior analysis and intervention for adults with autism. *Behavior Modification, 26*(1), 9–26.

National Research Council. (2001). *Educating children with autism.* Washington, DC: National Academic Press.

Odom, S. L., Boyd, B. A., Hall, L. J., & Hume, K. (2010). Evaluation of comprehensive treatment models for individuals with autism spectrum disorders. *Journal of Autism and Developmental Disorders, 40*(4), 425–436.

Odom, S. L., Collet-Klingenberg, L., Rogers, S. J., & Hatton, D. D. (2010). Evidence-based practices in interventions for children and youth with autism spectrum disorders. *Preventing School Failure: Alternative Education for Children and Youth, 54*(4), 275–282.

O'Neill, R. E., Horner, R. H., Albin, R. W., Sprague, J. R., Storey, K., & Newton, J. S. (1997). *Functional assessment and program development for problem behavior: A practical handbook* (2nd ed.). Pacific Grove, CA: Brooks/Cole.

Reichow, B. (2012). Overview of meta-analyses on early intensive behavioral intervention for young children with autism spectrum disorders. *Journal of Autism and Developmental Disorders, 42*(4), 512–520.

Reichow, B., Doehring, P., Cicchetti, D. V., & Volkmar, F. R. (Eds.). (2011). *Evidence-based practices and treatments for children with autism.* New York, NY: Springer.

Rogers, S. J., & Dawson, G. (2010). *Early Start Denver Model for young children with autism: Promoting language, learning, and engagement.* New York, NY: Guilford.

Sarokoff, R. A., & Sturmey, P. (2004). The effects of behavioral skills training on staff implementation of discrete-trial teaching. *Journal of Applied Behavior Analysis, 37*(4), 535–538.

Schwarz, S. M. (2003). Feeding disorders in children with developmental disabilities. *Infants & Young Children, 16*(4), 317–330.

Shane, H. C., Laubscher, E. H., Schlosser, R. W., Flynn, S., Sorce, J. F., & Abramson, J. (2012). Applying technology to visually support language and communication in individuals with autism spectrum disorders. *Journal of Autism and Developmental Disorders, 42*(6), 1228–1235.

Smith, T. (2001). Discrete trial training in the treatment of autism. *Focus on Autism and Other Developmental Disabilities, 16*(2), 86–92.

Smith, T. (2010). Early and intensive behavioral intervention in autism. In J. R. Weisz & A. E. Kazdin (Eds.), *Evidence-based psychotherapies for children and adolescents* (2nd ed.). New York, NY: Guilford.

Smith, T. (2011). Applied behavior analysis and early intensive intervention. In D. G. Amaral, G. Dawson, & D. H. Geschwind (Eds.), *Autism spectrum disorders.* New York, NY: Oxford University.

Smith, T. (Ed.). (2012). *Making inclusion work for students with autism spectrum disorders.* New York, NY: Guilford.

Strain, P. S., & Bovey, E. H. (2011). Randomized, controlled trial of the LEAP model of early intervention for young children with autism spectrum disorders. *Topics in Early Childhood Special Education, 31*(3), 133–154.

Thompson, T. (2007). *Making sense of autism.* Baltimore, MD: Brookes.

Tiger, J. H., Hanley, G. P., & Bruzek, J. (2008). Functional communication training: A review and practical guide. *Behavior Analysis in Practice, 1,* 16–23.

Volkmar, F. R., & Wiesner, L. A. (2004). *Healthcare for children on the autism spectrum: A guide to medical, nutritional, and behavioral issues.* Bethesda, MD: Woodbine House.

Wehman, P., Schall, C., McDonough, J., Molinelli, A., Riehle, E., Ham, W., . . . Thiss, W. (2013). Project SEARCH for youth with autism spectrum disorders increasing competitive employment on transition from high school. *Journal of Positive Behavior Interventions, 15*(3), 144–155.

Wehmeyer, M. L., & Webb, K. W. (2012). *Handbook of adolescent transition education for youth with disabilities.* New York, NY: Routledge.

Weiss, M. J., & Harris, S. L. (2001). Teaching social skills to people with autism. *Behavior Modification, 25*(5), 785–802.

Wheeler, M., & Kranowitz, C. S. (2007). *Toilet training for individuals with autism or other developmental issues* (2Snd ed.). Arlington, TX: Future Horizons.

Williams, K. E., & Foxx, R. M. (2007). *Treating eating problems of children with autism spectrum disorders and developmental disabilities: Interventions for professionals and parents.* Austin, TX: Pro-Ed.

Wood, J. J., Drahota, A., Sze, K., Har, K., Chiu, A., & Langer, D. A. (2009). Cognitive behavioral therapy for anxiety in children with autism spectrum disorders: A randomized, controlled trial. *Journal of Child Psychology and Psychiatry, 50*(3), 224–234.

Wrobel, M. (2003). *Taking care of myself: A hygiene, puberty and personal curriculum for young persons with autism.* Arlington, TX: Future Horizons.

Yoder, P. J., & Warren, S. F. (1999). Facilitating self-initiated proto-declaratives and proto-imperatives in pre-linguistic children with developmental disabilities. *Journal of Early Intervention, 22*(4), 337–354.

PSYCHOPHARMACOLOGY OF AUTISM SPECTRUM DISORDER

JAMES T. MCCRACKEN
AND MICHAEL GANDAL

INTRODUCTION

The use of a broad range of medications as a component of treatment for children and adults with autism spectrum disorder (ASD) has become common clinical practice. Most surveys report that by 8 years of age, as many as 60–70% of individuals with ASD will receive a medication for management of behavioral or emotional problems within 12 months (Esbensen, Greenberg, Seltzer, & Aman, 2009; Oswald & Sonenklar, 2007). The use of medications in ASD climbs with increasing age, as does combination pharmacotherapy. In part, this practice pattern reflects a growing body of evidence demonstrating the safety and benefits of psychotropic medications in this population. However, it is not without concern, given the continued large gaps in appropriate studies needed to establish a more comprehensive base of knowledge of medication efficacy and safety in ASD. In this light, note that most psychotropic use in ASD is "off-label" because there are currently only two medications approved by the US Food and Drug Administration (FDA) for individuals with ASD, both of which are approved only for the treatment of associated behaviors. Moreover, in efforts to find treatments that reduce disability and improve outcomes, the history of ASD treatments is rife with examples of purported "cures" rapidly taken up in community settings, which ultimately failed when subjected to rigorous study (e.g., secretin and hyperbaric oxygen). No current psychotropics have definitively shown major benefits on the core deficits of ASD—social communication deficits and delays and the intense preoccupations, repetitive behaviors, and marked sensory sensitivities that make up the syndrome—although this is a subject of intensive research efforts (see Emerging Therapies). Therefore, it behooves professionals to maintain the same standards for evidence for any ASD therapy that would be required for any other medical intervention. However, many treatments are now accepted as indicated or possibly indicated to treat a range of commonly associated and impairing behavioral targets in individuals with ASD. This chapter helps orient the clinician in identifying those targets for possible intervention with pharmacotherapy in ASD; indicates what choices are best supported by their known efficacy and safety; and provides suggested approaches to initiate, evaluate, and monitor safety of these treatments. The emphasis in this review relies on empirical evidence and usual standards used to evaluate medical treatments. After reviewing the currently best-supported treatments, the chapter reviews current practice patterns against the state of the science of psychopharmacology in ASD in order to highlight areas of concern. Finally, emerging research efforts to identify possible medications for core deficits of ASD are briefly described.

TARGETING PSYCHOPHARMACOLOGIC TREATMENT IN AUTISM SPECTRUM DISORDER: WHAT'S TO TREAT?

Individuals with ASD present with a wide array of challenges, behaviors, and impairments that may merit intervention. It is well-known that individuals with any developmental or intellectual disability are at markedly increased risk for co-occurring problems, especially all forms of psychiatric disorders. At the broadest level, rates of psychopathology are often reported to be two- or threefold greater among samples of children and adults with intellectual disabilities compared to non-intellectually disabled comparison groups. The same increased risk certainly holds for ASD. Depending on the age range studied, 33–41% of individuals with intellectual disabilities meet definite criteria for psychiatric diagnoses (Einfeld & Tonge, 1996). In one representative study of children with ASD, 81% of the children were described as impaired by symptoms of a psychiatric disorder based on parent and teacher report of diagnostic symptoms listed in the fourth edition of the *Diagnostic and Statistical Manual of Mental Disorders* (American Psychiatric Association, 2004). Although establishing categorical diagnoses is challenging in a population in which communication of emotional symptoms and disordered thinking is often difficult, rates of co-occurring psychopathology show solid agreement from study to study. The patterns of reported impairing behaviors and symptoms appear to hold true across reports, with inattentive, hyperactive, and impulsive behaviors, oppositional–defiant behaviors, anxious/withdrawal symptoms, aggression, and self-injurious behaviors being most commonly identified by parents and teachers (Figure 16.1). Other efforts to characterize the behavioral problems commonly brought to clinician attention highlight the high rates of parent and individual complaints of sleep–wake disruptions. Taken together, these constellations of symptoms are often so impairing as to interfere with learning, ability to be retained in a more inclusive classroom or school setting, or even threaten the safety and well-being of the individual with ASD and/or his or her family members, despite the individual's access to behavioral or other therapies. Such symptoms form the majority of the behavioral targets considered for psychopharmacologic treatment. Because treatment goals are currently symptom-based, this chapter later reviews clinically useful tools to assess and monitor treatment outcomes. In the next section, the best-studied behavioral targets that possess evidence for pharmacotherapeutic management are reviewed.

PSYCHOPHARMACOLOGIC TREATMENT OF TARGETED BEHAVIORS IN AUTISM SPECTRUM DISORDER

Irritability, Aggression, and Self-Injury

Aggression and related symptoms such as agitation, severe tantrumming, and mood lability, often referred to collectively as "irritability," are associated problems that often elicit concern

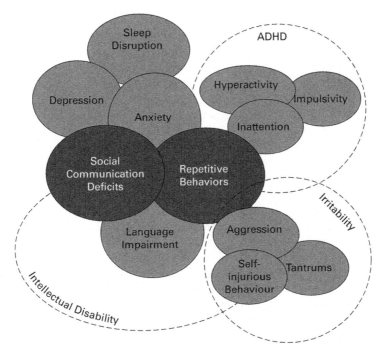

FIGURE 16.1 Common co-occurring maladaptive behaviors and medication targets in autism spectrum disorder.

in ASD. Although the term "aggression" can encompass different subtypes of symptoms with varying behavioral and functional mechanisms, taken together this is a very common accompanying complaint in ASD. Analysis of data on 1584 children aged 2–17 years in clinics comprising the Autism Treatment Network estimated a prevalence of aggression of 53.7% based on a "yes" or "no" response from parents on a single question about aggression. Another prevalence study involving 1380 subjects with ASD showed that 68% demonstrated aggression to a caregiver and 49% to non-caregivers (Einfeld & Tonge, 1996). The "subtype" of self-aggression, or self-injurious behavior (SIB), is also a common and frequently severe challenge: More than 50% of children with autism show SIB, and as many as 15% suffer from severe levels of SIB. Overall, aggression may lead to hospitalization, family disruption, institutionalization, removal from less restrictive school settings, and a worse prognosis (Baghdadli, Pascal, Grisi, & Aussilloux, 2003; Nazeer, 2011). The causes of irritability and aggression are multifactorial: comprehension difficulties; decreased ability to communicate and express needs and desires; reduced confrontation skills; conflict with teachers, supervisors, and authority figures; psychosocial dysfunction; and undiagnosed pain and mood and anxiety disorders (Nazeer, 2011). The first step to address the aggressive behavior is to perform a "functional analysis" of the behavior, carefully delineating the contexts, antecedents, environmental responses or consequences, and other causative or maintaining influences. The deeper understanding of the behavior generally guides clinicians to the most appropriate therapeutic approach (behavioral management and/or medication). Although behavioral and environmental approaches are recommended as the initial treatment, persistent, severe, or even dangerous behaviors are complaints that lead to consideration of pharmacological intervention. The following classes of medications have empirical support for the management of irritability and its aggressive, agitated, and self-injurious behaviors.

Antipsychotics

First- and second-generation antipsychotics have shown moderate to large benefits in controlling aggressive symptoms in autism (Nazeer, 2011), beginning with early controlled trials of haloperidol, a conventional dopamine 2 receptor subtype antagonist (Campbell et al., 1978). Antipsychotics, predominately second-generation agents, have become commonly used medications in ASD for the treatment of irritability (Mandell et al., 2008), perhaps influenced by observations of possible additional benefits for a variety of other associated behaviors and the fact that two of these agents, risperidone and aripiprazole, represent the only FDA-approved medications for ASD.

In 2002, the National Institute of Mental Health's Research Units on Pediatric Psychopharmacology (RUPP) Autism Network reported on a multicenter randomized clinical trial (RCT) that evaluated the efficacy and safety of short- and intermediate-term risperidone in children and adolescents aged 5–17 years with autistic disorder accompanied by severe tantrums, aggression, and SIB (McCracken et al., 2002). The results showed that short-term, low-dose risperidone treatment was markedly superior to placebo (positive responders, 75% vs. 12%, respectively). In addition to major decreases in irritability (aggression, SIB, and severe temper outbursts) associated with risperidone, broader benefits on other maladaptive behaviors were also documented versus placebo, including decreased hyperactivity and reductions in stereotypies. Risperidone treatment has been shown to be well tolerated for up to 6 months. Importantly, common extrapyramidal side effects seen with haloperidol in earlier studies were comparatively lower with risperidone. Sedation, drowsiness, weight gain, and hyperprolactinemia were the most commonly reported side effects, with reductions in these adverse effects over time noted. From a total of eight randomized clinical trials with risperidone, two meta-analyses and two association studies demonstrated consistent efficacy over placebo for irritability for risperidone (Aman, Hollway, et al., 2008; Canitano & Scandurra, 2011; Gencer et al., 2008; Kent, Hough, Singh, Karcher, & Pandina, 2013; Kent, Kushner, et al., 2013; Luby et al., 2006; McDougle, Stigler, Erickson, & Posey, 2008; Nagaraj, Singhi, & Malhi, 2006; Pandina, Bossie, Youssef, Zhu, & Dunbar, 2007; Shea et al., 2004; Troost et al., 2005). Effective doses were low, averaging 2 mg/day, although lower doses (0.125–0.175 mg/day) were not effective compared to placebo (Kent, Kushner, et al., 2013). No evidence of tolerance or need for dose escalation over time have been reported for subjects followed for up to 6 months of treatment. Paliperidone, the active 9-hydroxy metabolite of risperidone, showed similar effectiveness in an 8-week open-label clinical trial involving adolescents and young adults with ASD (Stigler, Mullett, Erickson, Posey, & McDougle, 2012).

The FDA has also approved aripiprazole for treatment of severe irritability in children with autistic disorder aged 6–17 years. Two double-blind, placebo-controlled RCTs showed that aripiprazole is effective in treating irritability in ASD (Marcus et al., 2009; Owen et al., 2009; Siegel & Beaulieu, 2012), with secondary improvements also noted for hyperactivity and stereotypies. Aripiprazole is well tolerated in dose ranges of 5–15 mg/day, and it is associated with lower mean weight gain compared to several other atypical antipsychotics, as measured during the initial 8 weeks of exposure. The efficacy and side effect profile of aripiprazole and risperidone were similar when compared head-to-head in a recent prospective, double-blind 8-week clinical trial (Ghanizadeh, Sahraeizadeh, & Berk, 2014), although overall clinical positive responder rates were modestly lower for aripiprazole versus risperidone (55% vs. 75%, respectively).

Two RCTs with children with ASD using haloperidol showed significant positive effects on behavioral symptoms and global functioning (Anderson et al., 1984, 1989). Comparing broad-based measures of maladaptive behaviors and ASD symptoms, a small, head-to-head, 12-week, randomized double-blind comparator trial of haloperidol versus risperidone found risperidone to be superior to haloperidol across most measures and to be associated with lower side effect ratings (including rigidity) versus haloperidol at equal doses (mean, 2 mg/day) (Miral et al., 2008). In summary, although haloperidol has shown consistent behavioral benefits versus placebo in reducing aggressive and disruptive behaviors in children with autism accompanied by severe and challenging behaviors (Canitano & Scandurra, 2011), the high rates of extrapyramidal side effects, including withdrawal dyskinesias, have led to its infrequent use.

Other atypical antipsychotics need further clinical evaluation. Olanzapine has not been studied in randomized placebo-controlled trials of adequate sample size in children or adults with ASD. However, some case studies and an open-label trial reported positive results (Heimann, 1999; Horrigan, Barnhill, & Courvoisie, 1997; Potenza, Holmes, Kanes, & McDougle, 1999). In addition, a randomized trial with a parallel control group treated with haloperidol reported positive results, although patients had significant weight gain (Malone, Cater, Sheikh, Choudhury, & Delaney, 2001). The prolonged use of olanzapine may induce significant metabolic changes, which can restrict its long-term use in ASD (Bonanno, Davydov, & Botts, 2001). Ziprasidone was investigated in one open-label study that included 12 adolescents with ASD treated with doses ranging from 20 to 160 mg/day. A 75% response rate to ziprasidone was observed according to Clinical Global Impression–Improvement (CGI-I) scale ratings. In addition, improvements in the Aberrant Behavior Checklist (ABC) subscales of irritability and hyperactivity were noted. Ziprasidone did not cause weight gain, but a regular increase in the QTc interval of 14.7 msec in the sample was described (Malone, Delaney, Hyman, & Cater, 2007), implying the need for special monitoring. Another open-label clinical study and a retrospective review of clinical records showed promising results for ziprasidone in patients with ASD (Cohen, Fitzgerald, Khan, & Khan, 2004; McDougle, Kem, & Posey, 2002). Double-blind, placebo-controlled studies are needed to validate the use of ziprasidone in this population. Three small, open-label trials have failed to demonstrate efficacy for quetiapine in ASD, with mixed reports on its tolerability (Findling et al., 2004; Golubchik, Sever, & Weizman, 2011; Martin, Koenig, Scahill, & Bregman, 1999). Given the risk of potentially serious side effects of seizures and agranulocytosis, there is no evidence to substantiate clozapine as an ASD treatment, with only case reports available (Chen, Bedair, McKay, Bowers, & Mazure, 2001). No data are available for lurasidone or asenapine in ASD. Thus, comparatively speaking, only risperidone and aripiprazole possess sufficient evidence for firm support for treating the target behaviors of irritability in ASD, with paliperidone possibly indicated, whereas the other antipsychotics lack data to support use as first- or second-line therapies. Haloperidol has been shown to be more efficacious than placebo for irritability in children with ASD, but its short- and longer-term side effect profiles often limit treatment.

Adverse Effects of Antipsychotics

All antipsychotics in children carry the risk of potentially serious side effects, such as neuroleptic malignant syndrome, hyperprolactinemia with associated galactorrhea (except for aripiprazole), dyskinesias, cardiovascular changes, and allergic reactions. Fortunately, these serious adverse events are estimated to be rare or uncommon; a review estimated the annualized risk for tardive dyskinesia to be less than 0.5%, and remission of the disorder after drug discontinuation is a common observation (Correll & Kane, 2007). Nevertheless, it is of obvious importance to systematically monitor for the appearance of such untoward effects and develop strategies to minimize them. Although a comprehensive discussion of this topic is beyond the scope of this chapter, an excellent review is available (Correll, 2008).

Other Agents

There is evidence that agents other than antipsychotics may be effective for irritability and agitated behaviors in ASD. The anticonvulsant and mood stabilizer valproic acid has shown some efficacy for these target symptoms, although results are mixed. A randomized, double-blind, placebo-controlled trial of valproic acid in 55 children and adolescents with ASD found a significantly higher response rate in the treatment group (62.5%) compared with placebo (9%), as measured by CGI-I ratings focused on irritability (Hollander et al., 2010). However, a smaller trial of 30 subjects aged 6–20 years with pervasive developmental disorders failed to find an effect (Hellings et al., 2005). An early open-label study of valproic acid in 14 subjects with autism found a significant response rate (70%) with improvements in affective instability, impulsivity, and aggression (Hollander, Dolgoff-Kaspar, Cartwright, Rawitt, & Novotny, 2001). Valproic acid's less robust benefits coupled with its requirement for added monitoring of hematologic and liver functions, and the need for therapeutic drug-level testing, relegate it to lesser status as a third- or fourth-line treatment option for irritability in ASD.

Emerging evidence suggests that the glutamatergic modulator and antioxidant N-acetylcysteine (NAC) may also be effective for disruptive behaviors in autism. A 12-week double-blind, placebo-controlled trial involving 33 subjects with autism (aged 3–11 years) demonstrated significant reduction in the ABC-Irritability subscale (primary outcome), with treatment response of 78% for NAC versus 50% for placebo (Hardan et al., 2012). Likewise, an 8-week double-blind, placebo-controlled add-on trial of NAC to ongoing risperidone in 40 children and adolescents with autism showed a significant benefit of NAC compared with risperidone plus placebo on irritability (Ghanizadeh & Moghimi-Sarani, 2013). At least two other studies of NAC in patients with autism have been performed but not published (NCT00453180 and NCT00889538). NAC deserves additional exploration as a treatment, and it is potentially appealing given its relatively benign side effect profile.

Limited evidence, mostly from uncontrolled case series, on possible benefits of escitalopram, mirtazapine, clonidine, and methylphenidate for the treatment of aggression and irritability in ASD have also been reported. Depending on the constellation of presenting symptoms in the individual, these agents are often considered, although none have achieved sufficient evidence to support their routine use as first-line treatments for irritability in ASD.

Self-Injurious Behavior

The literature is mixed with respect to drug effects on the irritability subtype of SIB. Naltrexone, an opioid receptor antagonist, has received the greatest amount of research attention on its effects in samples of individuals, mostly adults, with ASD and other intellectual disabilities, with some summaries finding support for its benefits. However, a Cochrane meta-analytic review did not find evidence to support naltrexone's efficacy for managing SIB in adults, nor for any other medication (Rana, Gormez, & Varghese, 2013). Clinically, assessing for other treatable comorbidities commonly associated with SIB, such as depression, anxiety, or an underlying medical illness, may provide the best guidance for empirical treatment selection.

Clinical Implications

Aggressive behaviors toward self and others displayed by many children with ASD represent an important and often seriously impairing target for treatment. The clinical challenge of evaluating aggressive behaviors is to identify any other potentially treatable "primary" or contributing psychiatric symptoms, such as anxiety, depression, or hyperactivity/impulsivity, as well as comorbid medical conditions. If no such conditions are evident, or treatment of these other targets is ineffective at reducing aggression, the atypical antipsychotics risperidone and aripiprazole represent the most studied agents in ASD, are FDA-approved for treating irritability (not ASD per se), and have shown solid evidence of efficacy. Paliperidone, the risperidone metabolite, and older haloperidol studies also provide favorable evidence for their off-label use. However, the evidence is also high for the risk of developing clinically limiting side effects for all antipsychotics, such as the extrapyramidal effects of conventional agents or the metabolic changes of atypical neuroleptics (Campbell et al., 1978; McCracken et al., 2002; Owen et al., 2009). Close monitoring of patients on these agents is essential. Divalproex and NAC are off-label options with modest evidence of effectiveness. The decision to initiate pharmacological treatment should be based on severity of symptomatology, degree of impairment, risk to self or others, and prevention of hospitalization. Although no clinical treatment algorithms for treatment choice for aggression have been widely endorsed, clinicians generally attempt initial treatment with lower-risk alternatives to antipsychotics. However, in the context of poor response or tolerability, or severe and dangerous symptoms, clinicians often turn to one of the two FDA-approved antipsychotics for rapid management and stabilization. Length of recommended treatment is difficult to derive from published evidence, but treatment benefits appear durable for up to 6–12 months. Efforts to gradually reduce and possibly discontinue such treatment at the end of this period should be strongly considered.

Hyperactivity, Impulsivity, and Inattention

Symptoms of attention deficit hyperactivity disorder (ADHD) are very common in individuals with ASD, affecting between 28% and 74% of children (Aman, Lam, & Collier-Crespin, 2003; Goldstein & Schwebach, 2004). Inattention has been described in 50% of children with autism, with hyperactivity in 49% and 21% according to parents and teachers, respectively (Aman, Farmer, Hollway, & Arnold, 2008). To date, RCT for this set of symptoms have only been conducted with methylphenidate and atomoxetine in ASD. Three RCTs have investigated the effects of methylphenidate in children with ASD (Handen, Johnson, & Lubetsky, 2000; Quintana et al., 1995; Research Units on Pediatric Psychopharmacology Autism Network, 2005). In the largest of these, low to moderate doses of methylphenidate were compared to placebo in a study of 66 participants with ASD in a crossover design (Research Units on Pediatric Psychopharmacology Autism Network, 2005). This study was classified as showing strong clinical evidence of benefit, with 49% of subjects rated to be positive responders to methylphenidate versus 18% on placebo by virtue of showing a 25% decrease in ADHD symptoms from baseline and a CGI-I rating of "much improved" or "very much improved." However, 18% dropped out of the trial due to inability to tolerate the medication, most commonly due to irritability (Siegel & Beaulieu, 2012). Two other small studies with 10 and 13 children, respectively, have been judged to be solidly designed, leading to the determination of a promising level of evidence for treatment with methylphenidate for hyperactivity in children with ASD (Reichow, Volkmar, & Bloch,

2013). Importantly, best or "optimal" methylphenidate doses in the RUPP study were often found to be moderate (0.25 mg/kg) or even low (0.125 mg/kg) administered three times daily, suggesting that initiating stimulant treatment in children with ASD should begin at low doses and increase more gradually compared to usual titration in typically developing children with ADHD. Children with ASD and comorbid ADHD also have higher but acceptable risks of adverse effects from stimulant treatment compared to typically developing children with ADHD (Nikolov, Jonker, & Scahill, 2006).

Atomoxetine is a selective norepinephrine reuptake inhibitor that is FDA-approved for treatment of ADHD in typically developing children and adults. A small RCT was conducted with atomoxetine in 16 children aged 5–15 years with autism and ADHD. The treatment resulted in a response rate of 43%, defined as a 25% improvement on the ABC-Hyperactivity subscale and a CGI-I rating of "much improved" or "very much improved." A significant improvement over placebo in hyperactive/impulsive symptoms was also observed (Arnold et al., 2006). Adverse effects were relatively mild. A recent, large ($N = 97$) European RCT found evidence for superiority of atomoxetine versus placebo on ADHD symptom measures but no difference in response rates, which were low (21% vs. 9%, respectively) (Harfterkamp et al., 2012). In a 20-week open-label extension period after the initial 8-week trial, there was continued improvement in ADHD symptoms, in both inattention and hyperactivity domains, with a concomitant decrease in adverse events, although response rates were not reported (Harfterkamp et al., 2013).

The alpha-$_2$ (α_2) agonists clonidine (0.004–0.01 mg/kg/day) and guanfacine (1–3 mg/day immediate release) have inconclusive but suggestive evidence for benefit for the target of hyperactive–impulsive behaviors in ASD from small controlled or open-label trials. In general, these agents are well tolerated, with expected side effects of drowsiness, sedation, fatigue, mood changes, and mild hypotension and bradycardia. Only sparse data are available on the cognitive effects of the stimulants, atomoxetine, and α_2 agonists from studies of subjects with ASD.

Atypical Antipsychotics
Secondary analyses of the ABC-Hyperactivity subscale from large RCTs demonstrated that risperidone and aripiprazole are associated with major reductions in hyperactivity in children with ASD (McCracken et al., 2002; Owen et al., 2009).

Clinical Implications
Hyperactive, inattentive, and impulsive behaviors are among the most common co-occurring maladaptive behaviors in ASD. Greater efforts are needed to identify individuals with this often unrecognized but treatable behavioral target. Stimulants, especially methylphenidate, have data supporting their use for this target, and atomoxetine and the α_2 agonists are possibly indicated as off-label interventions for those individuals who are refractory or intolerant of stimulants. Because of the identified increase in risk of adverse effects, dosing of stimulants should be conservative, starting with low milligram per kilogram initial doses and proceeding to titrate slowly with small increments while carefully monitoring symptoms and adverse effects. α_2 agonists represent promising therapies for hyperactivity in ASD, and they often form a solid second-line treatment choice. Although antipsychotics have also shown effectiveness for marked hyperactivity, their side effect risk with long-term exposure should temper their use for this behavioral target.

Repetitive Behaviors

Behavioral therapies are the first-line treatment for restricted, repetitive behaviors (RRBs) in ASD, but these behaviors can be quite difficult to manage with psychosocial interventions alone. RRBs, when severe and frequent, can greatly interfere with educational and social performance; as a result, pharmacological treatment is often considered. The medications discussed next have been evaluated and are often prescribed for the target of RRBs.

Selective Serotonin Reuptake Inhibitors

Because of the superficial similarity of RRBs with the phenomenology of selective serotonin reuptake inhibitor (SSRI)-responsive obsessions and compulsions, and modest evidence of serotoninergic dysfunction in ASD, SSRIs have been examined for management of RRBs.

Meta-analysis of available studies of SSRIs has shown lack of clinically significant efficacy in the treatment of repetitive behaviors and restricted interests in pediatric subjects with ASD (Williams, Brignell, Randall, Silove, & Hazell, 2013). Only one methodologically sound study showed modest positive results of an SSRI (fluoxetine) compared to placebo in children with ASD, but improvements were minor (Hollander et al., 2005). In the largest RCT of the treatment of repetitive behaviors in ASD comparing citalopram to placebo, no benefits were found for citalopram, and side effects such as hyperactivity, insomnia, and behavioral deterioration were common (King et al., 2009). Interestingly, in contrast to studies in children, two rigorous RCTs showed benefits for fluvoxamine and fluoxetine on measures of repetitive behaviors for adults; however, again the benefits in the fluoxetine study were minor relative to placebo (Hollander et al., 2012; McDougle et al., 1996). Taken together, there is limited evidence to support the use of SSRIs as treatment for repetitive behaviors in ASD, especially in youth. No large-scale controlled trials have examined their effects for the treatment of anxiety or depressive symptoms in individuals with ASD.

Atypical Antipsychotics

Although not designed to test benefits for RRBs, secondary analyses of pivotal trials for risperidone and aripiprazole both showed significant reductions in RRBs versus placebo. In the RUPP risperidone study of irritability, risperidone achieved significantly greater reduction of repetitive behavior than did placebo (35% vs. 15% reductions from baseline, respectively), as reflected in clinician ratings of compulsions on the Childrens Yale–Brown Obsessive Compulsive Scale modified for ASD (McDougle et al., 2005). Pivotal trials of aripiprazole showed twofold greater reductions in RRBs in aripiprazole- versus placebo-treated subjects in secondary analyses (Marcus et al., 2009; Owen et al., 2009).

Divalproex

A small 8-week RCT of divalproex sodium (mean dose, 823 mg/day) versus placebo in 13 individuals with ASD showed a significant group difference for divalproex on improvement in repetitive behaviors. However, reductions were small and clinically insignificant (decrease of 6% in divalproex group) (Hollander et al., 2006).

Clinical Implications

RRBs are a core and impairing behavior in many individuals with ASD, but treatment options are limited. Few medications have any consistent evidence to support their use for treating RRBs, and those that do—primarily the atypical antipsychotics—carry significant risks of side effects. Identifying contributing symptoms such as anxiety or mood symptoms temporally associated with increasing RRBs can be useful in treatment selection.

Depression and Anxiety

Despite the common features of mood lability, apparent dysphoria, and anxiety in many individuals with ASD, there are no controlled trials of available agents to form a solid evidence base to guide clinical treatment of these targets in this population. Acknowledging that there is strong empirical support for the efficacy of SSRIs as treatments for typically developing children, adolescents, and adults with anxiety disorders, it is reasonable though unproven whether benefits seen in typical individuals can be extrapolated to children with ASD. The consistent finding of increased sensitivity to SSRI side effects in children with ASD should increase caution for their use. However, the two controlled studies in adults with fluvoxamine and fluoxetine do suggest possible benefit for the treatment of anxiety and depression in ASD, although neither study selected subjects on the basis of impairing anxiety or depression. Clinicians need to evaluate the options on a case-by-case basis and attempt to discern medication effects by careful monitoring.

Sleep Disorders

ASD patients show much higher rates of insomnia and circadian rhythm disorders than typically developing children (Richdale, 1999). Behavioral approaches to managing sleep problems in ASD have been developed and are recommended as the first step in treatment. However, these measures often fail, and physicians are faced with impairing sleep disruptions and insufficiency that can have a wide negative impact on functioning. Although there are no FDA-approved treatments for this problem in ASD, a significant number of RCTs have consistently shown benefits for melatonin in doses from 3 to 15 mg 1 or 2 hours before desired bedtime. These doses of melatonin are very well tolerated, and they yield advancements in sleep onset time of up to 1 hour and lengthening of sleep duration by a similar amount. The effects of long-term melatonin treatment in ASD have not been examined. Because a number of other psychotropics used in the treatment of ASD can have sedative side effects, they are often given at bedtime in an effort to promote sleep onset. α_2 agonists, atypical antipsychotics, and atypical antidepressants such as trazodone and mirtazapine may aid sleep onset, but they lack studies to document their benefit and safety for this purpose.

COMMUNITY PRACTICE PATTERNS IN AUTISM SPECTRUM DISORDER

A number of recent reports have examined the prevalence of psychotropic use in different samples of youth with ASD. The frequency of psychotropic use by drug class is included in Table 16.1. Overall, these reports are in agreement that psychotropic use in children with ASD is very common; more than half of all children with ASD who are older than age 6 years have histories of receiving at least one psychotropic, and polypharmacology (receiving two or more psychotropics concurrently) is seen in nearly 20% or more of 6- to 17-year-olds. Although increasing age is clearly associated with higher rates of psychotropic usage, psychotropic treatment is not uncommon in children with ASD who are 3–5 years old. In addition to age, absolute rates of psychotropic use are also influenced by practice setting, region, comorbidity,

TABLE 16.1 Selected Surveys of Psychotropic Use in Children With Autism Spectrum Disorder

Reference	Sample Size Age Range Mean Age	Medication Usage Overall Drug Class		Factors Associated With Higher Psychotropic Use
Langworthy-Lam, Aman, and Van Bourgondien (2002)	1,538 3–56 years 16 years		46%	Age, autism severity, ID severity, restricted housing
		PPh[a]	14%	
		AD	22%	
		AP	17%	
		STM	14%	
		AED	17%	
		AAG	10%	
		SED	7%	
Oswald and Sonenklar (2007)	1,942 0–20 years 9 years		83%	Age
		AD	40%	
		STM	33%	
		AP	29%	
		AED	18%	
		AAG	15%	
Mandell et al. (2008)	60,641 Medicaid 0–21 years		56%	Age, male, white race, foster care, comorbidity, urban density
		PPh[b]	11%	
		AD	25%	
		AP	31%	
		STM	22%	
		AED	21%	
Coury et al. (2012)	2,843 2–17 years 53% <6 years		27%	Age, private insurance, white race, comorbidity
		PPh[a]	7%	
Frazier et al. (2011)	890 13–17 years 15 years		42%	ADHD, white race
		AD	58%	
		AP	42%	
		STM	31%	
		AED	21%	
Rosenberg et al. (2010)	5,181 IAN Registry 0–17 years 49% 6–11 years		35%	Age, ID, comorbidity, poor county, region (South, Midwest)
		PPh[b]	9%	
		AD	14%	
		AP	15%	
		AED	7%	
		AAG	8%	

(continued)

TABLE 16.1 Continued

Reference	Sample Size Age Range Mean Age	Medication Usage Overall Drug Class		Factors Associated With Higher Psychotropic Use
Schubart, Camacho, and Leslie (2013)	12,843–18,562 Medicaid 2000–2003 3–17 years 50% 6–11 years	PPh[a] AD AP STM AED SED ANX	65% 26% 29% 39% 25% 16% 14% 11%	Age, secular trend, poverty, foster care, white race
Spencer et al. (2013)	33,565 0–20 years 60% 2–10 years	PPh[a]	64% 35%	Age, psychiatrist visit, comorbidity, white race

[a]Two or more concurrent medications between drug classes.
[b]Three or more concurrent medications between drug classes.
AAG, α_2 agonists; AD, antidepressants; ADHD, attention deficit hyperactivity disorder; AED, anticonvulsants + mood stabilizers; ANX, anxiolytics; AP, antipsychotics; IAN, Interactive Autism Network; ID, intellectual disability; PPh, polypharmacy; SED, sedative/hypnotics; STM, stimulants.

degree of intellectual disability, and ethnicity and race. Trends in prescribing practices appear more variable; however, studies that have examined multiyear periods tend to report increasing usage of antidepressants and antipsychotics, although not necessarily at as great a rate of increase as seen in comparison to children without ASD from the same cohorts.

What conclusions about community use of psychotropics can be drawn from the extant data? As described previously, maladaptive, sometimes severe, co-occurring behaviors are common in ASD and may well merit pharmacological intervention. However, some deviations from the available evidence base are notable. First, the common use of psychotropics of all types in children with ASD younger than 5 years of age, despite the almost complete absence of data on safety and efficacy of psychotropics in this age group, is a cause for concern. The risk of harm in most cases would seem unacceptably high. Second, the continued high rate of antidepressant use, especially the SSRIs, in children and adolescents—in some samples approaching 50%—stands in the face of the limited support for efficacy and sensitivity to adverse events reviewed previously. Clinicians should develop strong evidence for the presence of an anxiety or depressive disorder comorbidity before instituting SSRIs. Another concern is the not uncommon rate of polypharmacy within the same drug class noted in some studies, despite this practice being summarily disapproved of in psychiatric practice. Lastly, atypical antipsychotic usage is common. Although several members of this class of drugs have solid support for their efficacy, long-term use has not been well studied with regard to safety, especially concerning tardive dyskinesia risk, as well as metabolic and growth effects. It is reassuring that rates of tardive dyskinesia in children treated with antipsychotics for 1 year are approximately half those seen in adults (0.4% vs. 0.8%, respectively) (Correll & Kane, 2007). However, early antipsychotic use portends possible longer exposures over the lifetime, and cross-sectional rates of tardive dyskinesia in children have been reportedly as high as 38%, in contrast to results from the prospective studies. Therefore, clinicians must continually re-evaluate the need for and benefits of antipsychotic treatment against the ever-increasing risks associated with long-term exposure. They also need to consider cautious tapering or discontinuation periods along with the possible substitution of safer alternatives, if necessary.

CASE STUDY #1: "FRED"

Fred is a 7-year-old boy with a prior diagnosis of autistic disorder who was brought to the psychiatrist by his parents for evaluation and possible treatment of his difficult classroom behavior and peer problems. His prior history was notable for initial concerns about speech delay, lack of interest in peers, and limited play skills that first became evident by his limited word use and lack of development of phrase speech by 24 months of age. A comprehensive developmental assessment at 30 months of age led to a diagnosis of autistic disorder, and Fred was subsequently placed in a 20-hour/week early intervention program. By parent report, Fred made excellent progress during the next 3 years, especially in his impressive increase of receptive and expressive language, so much so that he was able to enter a mainstream kindergarten class 1 year prior to this evaluation. During his kindergarten year, Fred received the support of a classroom aide. Academically, Fred reportedly did well, and he stayed at grade level. Behaviorally, he required frequent prompting from his aide to stay in his seat or with his group to persist with the classroom activities. Socially, Fred was well accepted by his peers, but he often preferred more solitary activities on the playground during recess. Even when joining play with other classmates was supported by the aide, eventually Fred would drift away from the group. At other times, he would become easily upset or frustrated, and he would tantrum, which would alarm his peers. This year, his school district no longer provided an aide, believing that Fred had become overly reliant on external support and needed to develop better self-control. During the past 3 months, teachers had begun to express concern that Fred's learning was not keeping pace with the class and that his frequent off-task behavior, self-stimming, and occasional tantrums were impairing his overall progress. His parents are also worried about his social behavior: When they observe him at school, he rarely seems to be included in play with others, and Fred has said that he has been teased following some of his angry and tearful outbursts. Overall, especially at home when he is allowed to play freely, his parents see Fred as usually happy, although minor frustrations or deviations from some routines can provoke angry, brief protests. Teacher reports on the Child Behavior Checklist show elevations on subscales of externalizing behaviors, withdrawn/depressed, attention problems, social problems, and rule-breaking behavior. Parent report on the Child Behavior Checklist showed elevations on subscales of social problems and attention problems. Parent report on the Social Responsiveness Scale-2 was elevated, consistent with ASD. On exam, Fred showed little eye contact, moved about the exam room without exploring toys, and needed frequent repetition of questions. Repetitive movements of his hands were observed. Mood appeared euthymic. The psychiatrist noted the long-standing history of disruptive behaviors in addition to Fred's prior diagnosis of ASD, and she suspected that the removal of the school aide had unmasked Fred's difficulties in regulating his behavior in a more structured environment compared to his home. She requested parents and teacher complete the SNAP scale and the Aberrant Behavior Checklist. Both parent and teacher SNAP ratings of ADHD symptoms were elevated compared to norms, and the ABC-Hyperactivity subscale score was similarly increased. The diagnosis of ADHD was made, and a trial of a stimulant, methylphenidate long-acting (methylphenidate-LA), was prescribed at an initial dose of 10 mg each morning. After 1 week, the teacher reported no change as based on SNAP ratings, but his parents noted some improvement at home with sitting longer during meals and rated a 15% decrease on SNAP scores. An increase to 20 mg each morning was tried, with both teacher and parents endorsing improvement. An additional week of 30 mg of methylphenidate-LA each morning was associated with markedly reduced appetite, initial insomnia, and Fred seeming withdrawn at home. After Fred's dosage was reduced to 20 mg daily and monitored for the next 3 weeks, both teacher and parent SNAP ratings showed declines from initial ratings of more than 50%, and Fred's schoolwork and cooperation were noticeably improved. Fred was also observed to be more able to persist with play activities with peers during recess, and he began to describe his interactions with particular students as friendly. He showed fewer emotional outbursts at school. At home, Fred for the first time showed interest in exploring books and playing games with his older brother. After 3 months, he remained improved. Blood pressure and heart rate showed minor increases, and his weight had not changed.

CASE STUDY #2: FRED (CONTINUED)

Six years after his initial evaluation and institution of stimulant treatment, Fred's parents contacted the psychiatrist and requested an urgent appointment. Fred's parents explained that he had continued to do well overall while continuing the stimulant, enjoyed school and was learning at grade level, and had made two friends that he had maintained for some time. However, they reported that Fred entered middle school this year. In their view, the transition had been extremely challenging for him. The new school was much larger, and Fred was no longer among as many children that he knew from elementary school. The requirement of multiple classrooms and teachers was also stressful for Fred to manage because he had difficulty tracking classroom assignments and a heavier workload. Most concerning to the parents was the emergence of emotional outbursts, occurring both at home and at school. In response to minor upsets or frustrations, Fred was described as becoming loud, screaming, and difficult to calm down. Sometimes if approached during an outburst, Fred would lash out physically to push away or possibly strike out, and twice at school he had been accused of knocking down another student. At home, his parents tried to manage the behavior by ignoring and withdrawing themselves or Fred from the situation, but frequently if Fred was left alone in his room to calm down, he would throw things or hit the wall with his fists, and he had knocked three holes in his bedroom wall. The parents stated that these outbursts initially occurred once or twice per week, but in the past month, they had escalated to daily explosions of a significant degree. Parents had sought out an outpatient therapist who had been advising them on strategies to manage these behaviors, but to no avail. Additional history was pertinent for Fred's refusal to maintain a regular sleep pattern. He was staying up late at night. Although his parents noted that at times Fred could be engaged in other activities and seem happy, they emphasized his volatile moods and quick temper. Appetite was normal. Fred continued to show his interest in a particular video game and two friends that shared his interest in the same game, but he had had several outbursts while spending time with them. In interview, Fred acknowledged often feeling "mad" and being easily upset. He did not express any remorse or guilt over the effects of his behaviors. He said he disliked school and hoped he would be suspended. Activity level was normal, occasional repetitive speech was noted, and he often returned to discussing his favored video game. The parents completed an ABC scale, and Fred completed a Child Depression Inventory with the psychiatrist. Parent ratings showed an elevated ABC-Irritability subscale score =22; several depressive symptoms were endorsed by Fred but below clinical cut-offs. Although several symptoms of major depressive disorder were noted, they lacked the persistence and overall number to meet criteria for the disorder. The diagnosis of Mood Disorder, Not Otherwise Specified was made, and the psychiatrist recommended treatment with risperidone, starting at 0.5 mg each evening. After 1 week, some improvements with increased sleep and reduced irritability were noted, but Fred reportedly had three major outbursts. An increase in risperidone to 0.5 mg twice daily was made; then after 1 more week, due to complaints of daytime drowsiness and continued mood lability, this was changed to 1.5 mg at bedtime. His parents noted much improvement overall, with temper outbursts occurring much less frequently and with less intensity. They were often able to avert outbursts by redirecting Fred or encouraging him to distract himself with a quiet activity. The ABC-Irritability subscale score dropped to 10—a 55% decrease. The psychiatrist assisted the parents in obtaining an Individualized Education Plan in order to implement accommodations at school to assist Fred's acclimation and need for academic and social support. After 6 months, the ABC-Irritability subscale score was 6, the AIMS score was 0, fasting blood glucose was 90, and a lipid panel was normal except for elevated triglycerides, but Fred had gained 10 pounds. The parents were instructed in dietary changes to reduce high-caloric foods and drinks, to increase activity, and consider dose decreases of risperidone during the upcoming summer school break.

ASSESSMENTS FOR TREATMENT PLANNING AND MONITORING

A positive development in the field of ASD treatment is the emerging consensus for appropriate measures of behaviors often considered as possible treatment targets. The standard of care has evolved to now mandate careful attempts to document need for treatment and treatment outcomes. Fortunately, a number of readily available and easily obtained measures can be applied in clinical settings. Several of these are "broad-band," meaning that they capture a wide range of possible and common behaviors; others are "narrow-band" assessments of particular dimensions of behavior, such as disruptive or ADHD-like symptoms. Those most commonly employed measures in clinical treatment studies are shown in Table 16.2.

TABLE 16.2 Assessment and Monitoring Measures for Pharmacotherapy in Autism Spectrum Disorder

Measure	Type	Domain(s)	Content Administration	Scoring	Reference	Strengths/weaknesses
	Broad					
Clinical Global Impression–Severity (CGI-S)		Overall severity of core + associated behaviors	Clinician (using all available information)	1–7 (not ill—extremely ill)	Guy (1976)	Widely used, ease of use, treatment sensitive
Clinical Global Impression–Improvement (CGI-I)		Overall change observed with treatment	Clinician (using all available information)	1–7 (very much improved—very much worse)	Guy (1976)	Widely used, ease of use, treatment sensitive
Aberrant Behavior Checklist–Community Version (ABC-CV)		Measures core and associated behaviors across five factors	Parent, caregiver, and teacher report; 58 items	Items scored 0–3	Aman, Singh, Stewart, and Field (1985)	Widely used in clinical trials, drug sensitive, ease of use and scoring, norms and comparative data, multiple translations
Child Behavior Checklist (CBCL)		Broad measure of psychopathology; subscales relate to diagnostic groups + social competence	Parent, teacher, and self-report (high functioning adolescents + adults)	Items scored 0–2	Achenbach and Edelbrock (1983)	Widely used in child mental health, not developed for intellectually disabled populations, not commonly used as a treatment measure
Behavior Problems Inventory–Short Form (BPI-S)		Measure of common maladaptive behaviors in intellectual disability	Parent, caregiver, and teacher report on 30 items; three subscales of SIB, Stereotypy, Aggressive/Destructive behaviors	Frequency 0–4 (never—hourly); Severity 0–3 (no problem—severe)	Rojahn et al. (2012)	Ease of use, appropriate for population, few tests of treatment sensitivity

Measure	Behaviors	Informant	Scoring	Citation	Comments
Pervasive Developmental Disorder Behavior Inventory (PDDBI)	Broad measure of core and associated maladaptive behaviors in ASD	Parent (188 items), teacher (180 items); nine domains	Scored 0–4 (never—often)	Cohen and Sudhalter (2005)	Breadth of symptoms, age norms, limited use in intervention studies, lengthy
Child and Adolescent Symptom Inventory–4R (CASI-4R)	Multiple DSM cardinal symptoms	Parent and teacher report	Scored 0–3 (never—very often)	Gadow and Sprafkin (2005)	Utility and validity in assessing categories of behavior, subscales may be suitable for monitoring (e.g., anxiety)
Narrow					
Anxiety Depression and Mood Scale (ADAMS)	Mood and anxiety symptoms	Parent, teacher, and clinician report on 28 items	Scored 0–3 (not a problem—very much)	Esbensen, Rojahn, Aman, and Ruedrich (2003)	Evidence for validity
Swanson, Nolan, and Pelham, version IV (SNAP-IV)	Disruptive behaviors	Parent and teacher report (40 items) keyed to DSM ADHD, Oppositional Defiant Disorder	Scored 0–3 (not at all—very much)	Swanson et al. (2001)	Ease of use and scoring, drug sensitive, norms
Pervasive Developmental Disorder Children's Yale–Brown Obsessive Compulsive Scale (PDD CYBOCS)	Compulsive, repetitive behaviors	Clinician rated	Compulsion items rated 0–4 on severity	Scahill et al. (2006)	Demonstrated reliability
Repetitive Behavior Scale–Revised (RBSR)	Repetitive, stereotypic behaviors	Parent and caregiver report	Scored 0–3 (does not occur—severe problem)	Bodfish, Symons, and Lewis (1999)	Reliable, may be treatment sensitive

ADHD, attention deficit hyperactivity disorder; ASD, autism spectrum disorder; DSM, *Diagnostic and Statistical Manual of Mental Disorders*; SIB, self-injurious behavior.

EMERGING THERAPIES

Significant efforts are underway to identify pharmacologic treatments that target core symptoms of autism. Preclinical investigation in rodent models of autism and fragile X syndrome (FXS), a monogenic disorder with considerable overlap with ASDs, has identified abnormal balance of synaptic inhibitory and excitatory signaling in brain circuits as a key target for therapeutic intervention (Delorme et al., 2013). This work prompted a recent randomized, double-blind, placebo-controlled crossover trial of the $GABA_B$ receptor agonist arbaclofen in 63 subjects with FXS, aged 6–39 years, with mixed results (Berry-Kravis et al., 2012). Although the drug showed no difference from placebo on the trial's primary endpoint, the ABC-Irritability subscale, secondary analyses indicated a significant treatment effect on the ABC-Social withdrawal subscale. In an 8-week open-label study of 32 children and adolescents with ASD, arbaclofen was well tolerated and significantly reduced irritability (primary endpoint), as well as measures of social withdrawal, hyperactivity, and repetitive behaviors, among others. The loop diuretic and chloride antagonist bumetanide is another GABA-activating agent that has been recently investigated in autism (Lemonnier et al., 2012). In a 3-month, randomized, double-blind, placebo-controlled trial of 60 children with ASD, the treatment group showed significant improvement on the Childhood Autism Rating Scale (primary endpoint), as well as clinical impression (77% response to drug vs. 33% response to placebo). Replication and extension of these studies of GABAergic agents in autism are warranted and, in some cases, are currently underway (NCT01966679).

Recent work has identified excessive glutamatergic signaling as a potential target for therapeutic intervention in autism (Delorme et al., 2013). Extensive preclinical evidence has demonstrated that blockade of metabotropic glutamate receptor 5 (mGluR5)-mediated signaling can reverse neural abnormalities in animal models of FXS and autism. However, a randomized, double-blind, placebo-controlled crossover trial of the mGluR5 antagonist AFQ056 in 30 adults with FXS found no treatment effect on the ABC scale (primary endpoint) (Jacquemont et al., 2011). Studies of other glutamatergic antagonists in autism have included memantine, an NMDA receptor antagonist FDA-approved for Alzheimer's dementia, which has shown promise in several open-label studies and case reports and has been generally well tolerated (Doyle & McDougle, 2012). An open-label, add-on study of memantine addition to ongoing psychotropic treatments in 151 subjects with ASD aged 2–26 years showed significant improvement in language, behavior, and self-stimulatory behaviors with 82% of subjects continuing the medication during a 21-month follow-up period (Chez et al., 2007). The only published randomized, double-blind, placebo-controlled clinical trial showed that memantine addition to risperidone was superior to risperidone plus placebo for irritability, hyperactivity, and stereotypic behavior in 40 children with autism during a 10-week period (Ghaleiha et al., 2013). However, an unpublished randomized, placebo-controlled clinical trial of memantine in 104 children and adolescents with autism failed to show a treatment effect on the Social Responsiveness Scale (SRS; primary endpoint) during 12 weeks (NCT00872898). Based on these results, several additional clinical trials are currently underway.

Finally, there has been considerable recent interest in the use of oxytocin and vasopressin as potential therapeutic interventions for ASD. Oxytocin and vasopressin are highly evolutionarily conserved endogenous neuropeptides integrally involved in the development of social affiliative behaviors and the regulation of social cognition (Meyer-Lindenberg, Domes, Kirsch, & Heinrichs, 2011). Genetic variation in the neural receptors for oxytocin and vasopressin has been linked to autism, and decreased levels of these hormones have been reported in patients (Meyer-Lindenberg et al., 2011). Studies of oxytocin in autism are limited by the drug's short half-life and difficulty crossing the blood–brain barrier, requiring frequent intranasal dosing to maintain therapeutic levels. Several small, randomized, double-blind, placebo-controlled studies involving single intravenous infusions of oxytocin have been conducted on subjects with autism, with demonstrated efficacy on repetitive behaviors (Hollander et al., 2003), emotion recognition (Guastella et al., 2010), and affective speech comprehension (Hollander et al., 2007). However, two recent trials with repeated intranasal dosing schedules have shown mixed results. In a randomized, double-blind, placebo-controlled trial of 38 adolescents with ASD, daily dosing of oxytocin for 4 consecutive days failed to show an effect compared with placebo on a range of measures, including emotional recognition, social interaction skills, and general behavioral adjustment (Dadds et al., 2014). In a 6-week randomized, double-blind, placebo-controlled trial involving 19 adults with ASD, twice-daily dosing of intranasal oxytocin did not differ from placebo on primary outcome measures of social cognition, social function (30% responders in treatment group vs. 10% placebo), or repetitive behaviors. However, oxytocin was well tolerated and did show efficacy on some secondary measures, including social perception and quality of life (Anagnostou et al., 2012).

SUMMARY

An evidence base to guide the safe and effective use of medications as adjunctive treatments in ASD has been growing rapidly. For several targeted behaviors, especially irritability and aggression, hyperactive–impulsive symptoms, and sleep problems, clinicians can rely on several treatment approaches that have been well-established through positive controlled studies. When faced with other common ASD-associated behaviors such as RRBs, social and communication impairments, and anxiety/depression, clinicians lack solid evidence on which medication to choose as the most appropriate and effective intervention. As emphasized previously, careful assessment is crucial to accurately identifying the underlying nature of the presenting behavioral problems. Clinicians need to be prepared to discuss these challenging clinical situations openly with parents and patients and to resist the common community practice of "adding on" multiple medications in the face of inadequate responses. A careful stepwise empirical approach with extensive monitoring of targeted symptoms is key to the evaluation of ongoing treatment response and to minimize untoward effects of pharmacotherapy. Pharmacological treatment should always be viewed as one component of a broader, comprehensive treatment plan that augments other educational, behavioral, and social interventions. Substantial gaps in information still exist for ASD, especially for effectively treating mood and anxiety symptoms. Emerging medication treatments hold the promise of addressing the core symptoms of ASD, based on a growing appreciation of disrupted molecular pathways that may be causative. The use of widely available clinical tools for monitoring response and side effects should be considered a part of standard practice.

KEY POINTS

- Although the use of medications in the management of ASD is becoming increasingly common, available therapeutics are symptom-based and do not modify disease trajectory.
- No current medications have consistently shown major benefits on the core social and communication deficits of ASD.

- The only FDA-approved medications for ASD are the antipsychotics risperidone and aripiprazole, which are effective for irritability, hyperactivity, and possibly repetitive behaviors; the use of all other psychotropics is considered "off-label."
- Stimulants, especially methylphenidate, and α_2 agonists, especially guanfacine, are effective for co-occurring hyperactive, inattentive, and impulsive symptoms in ASD.
- The use of widely available clinical tools for monitoring response to medication and side effects should be considered a part of standard practice.

ACKNOWLEDGMENTS

Support for preparation of this chapter was provided by grant UA3 MC 11055 AIR-B from the Maternal and Child Health Research Program, Maternal and Child Health Bureau (Combating Autism Act Initiative), Health Resources and Services Administration, US Department of Health and Human Services, grant 2P50 HD055784-06 from the National Institute of Child Health and Human Development, and grant 1R01MH083747-01A2 from the National Institute of Mental Health.

DISCLOSURE STATEMENT

Dr. James T. McCracken has received consultant income from Roche and DART Neuroscience, and research contract support from Roche.

Dr. Michael Gandal has no financial interests to disclose.

REFERENCES

Achenbach, T. M., & Edelbrock, C. S. (1983) *Manual for the child behavior checklist and revised child behavior profile*. Burlington, VT: University of Vermont.

Aman, M. G., Farmer, C. A., Hollway, J., & Arnold, L. E. (2008). Treatment of inattention, overactivity, and impulsiveness in autism spectrum disorders. *Child and Adolescent Psychiatric Clinics of North America, 17*, 713–738.

Aman, M. G., Hollway, J. A., McDougle, C. J., Scahill, L., Tierney, E., McCracken, J. T., . . . Posey, D. J. (2008). Cognitive effects of risperidone in children with autism and irritable behavior. *Journal of Child and Adolescent Psychopharmacology, 18*, 227–236.

Aman, M. G., Lam, K. S., & Collier-Crespin, A. (2003). Prevalence and patterns of use of psychoactive medicines among individuals with autism in the Autism Society of Ohio. *Journal of Autism and Developmental Disorders, 33*, 527–534.

Aman, M. G., Singh, N. N., Stewart, A. W., & Field, C. J. (1985). The Aberrant Behavior Checklist: A behavior rating scale for the assessment of treatment effects. *American Journal of Mental Deficiency, 89*, 485–491.

American Psychiatric Association. (1994). *Diagnostic and statistical manual of mental disorders* (4th ed.). Washington, DC: Author.

Anagnostou, E., Soorya, L., Chaplin, W., Bartz, J., Halpern, D., Wasserman, S., . . . Hollander, E. (2012). Intranasal oxytocin versus placebo in the treatment of adults with autism spectrum disorders: A randomized controlled trial. *Molecular Autism, 3*, 16.

Anderson, L. T., Campbell, M., Adams, P., Small, A. M., Perry, R., & Shell, J. (1989). The effects of haloperidol on discrimination learning and behavioral symptoms in autistic children. *Journal of Autism and Developmental Disorders, 19*, 227–239.

Anderson, L.T., Campbell, M., Grega, D. M., Perry, R., Small, A. M., & Green, W. H. (1984). Haloperidol in the treatment of infantile autism: Effects on learning and behavioral symptoms. *American Journal of Psychiatry, 141*, 1195–1202.

Arnold, L. E., Aman, M. G., Cook, A. M., Witwer, A. N., Hall, K. L., Thompson, S., & Ramadan, Y. (2006). Atomoxetine for hyperactivity in autism spectrum disorders: Placebo-controlled crossover pilot trial. *Journal of the American Academy of Child and Adolescent Psychiatry, 45*, 1196–1205.

Baghdadli, A., Pascal, C., Grisi, S., & Aussilloux, C. (2003). Risk factors for self-injurious behaviours among 222 young children with autistic disorders. *Journal of Intellectual Disability Research, 47*, 622–627.

Berry-Kravis, E. M., Hessl, D., Rathmell, B., Zarevics, P., Cherubini, M., Walton-Bowen, K., . . . Hagerman, R. J. (2012). Effects of STX209 (arbaclofen) on neurobehavioral function in children and adults with fragile X syndrome: A randomized, controlled, phase 2 trial. *Science Translational Medicine, 4*, 152ra127.

Bodfish, J. W., Symons, F. J., & Lewis, M. H. (1999). *The Repetitive Behavior Scales (RBS)*. Western Carolina Center Research Reports.

Bonanno, D. G., Davydov, L., & Botts, S. R. (2001). Olanzapine-induced diabetes mellitus. *Annals of Pharmacotherapy, 35*, 563–565.

Campbell, M., Anderson, L. T., Meier, M., Cohen, I. L., Small, A. M., Samit, C., & Sachar, E. J. (1978). A comparison of haloperidol and behavior therapy and their interaction in autistic children. *Journal of the American Academy of Child Psychiatry, 17*, 640–655.

Canitano, R., & Scandurra, V. (2011). Psychopharmacology in autism: An update. *Progress in Neuro-Psychopharmacology & Biological Psychiatry, 35*, 18–28.

Chen, N. C., Bedair, H. S., McKay, B., Bowers, M. B., Jr., & Mazure, C. (2001). Clozapine in the treatment of aggression in an adolescent with autistic disorder. *Journal of Clinical Psychiatry, 62*, 479–480.

Chez, M. G., Burton, Q., Dowling, T., Chang, M., Khanna, P., & Kramer, C. (2007). Memantine as adjunctive therapy in children diagnosed with autistic spectrum disorders: An observation of initial clinical response and maintenance tolerability. *Journal of Child Neurology, 22*, 574–579.

Cohen, I. L., & Sudhalter, V. (2005). *The PDD Behavior Inventory*. Lutz, FL: Psychological Assessment Resources.

Cohen, S. A., Fitzgerald, B. J., Khan, S. R., & Khan, A. (2004). The effect of a switch to ziprasidone in an adult population with autistic disorder: Chart review of naturalistic, open-label treatment. *Journal of Clinical Psychiatry, 65*, 110–113.

Correll, C. U. (2008). Antipsychotic use in children and adolescents: Minimizing adverse effects to maximize outcomes. *Journal of the American Academy of Child and Adolescent Psychiatry, 47*, 9–20.

Correll, C. U., & Kane, J. M. (2007). One-year incidence rates of tardive dyskinesia in children and adolescents treated with second-generation antipsychotics: A systematic review. *Journal of Child and Adolescent Psychopharmacology, 17*, 647–656.

Coury, D. L., Anagnostou, E., Manning-Courtney, P., Reynolds, A., Cole, L., McCoy, R., . . . Perrin, J. M. (2012). Use of psychotropic medication in children and adolescents with autism spectrum disorders. *Pediatrics, 130*(Suppl. 2), S69–S76.

Dadds, M. R., Macdonald, E., Cauchi, A., Williams, K., Levy, F., & Brennan, J. (2014). Nasal oxytocin for social deficits in childhood autism: A randomized controlled trial. *Journal of Autism and Developmental Disorders, 44*(3), 521–531.

Delorme, R., Ey, E., Toro, R., Leboyer, M., Gillberg, C., & Bourgeron, T. (2013). Progress toward treatments for synaptic defects in autism. *Nature Medicine, 19*, 685–694.

Doyle, C. A., & McDougle, C. J. (2012). Pharmacotherapy to control behavioral symptoms in children with autism. *Expert Opinion on Pharmacotherapy, 13*, 1615–1629.

Einfeld, S. L., & Tonge, B. J. (1996). Population prevalence of psychopathology in children and adolescents with intellectual disability: I. Rationale and methods. *Journal of Intellectual Disability Research, 40*(Pt. 2), 91–98.

Esbensen, A. J., Greenberg, J. S., Seltzer, M. M., & Aman, M. G. (2009). A longitudinal investigation of psychotropic and non-psychotropic medication use among adolescents and adults with autism spectrum disorders. *Journal of Autism and Developmental Disorders, 39*, 1339–1349.

Esbensen, A. J., Rojahn, J., Aman, M. G., & Ruedrich, S. (2003). Reliability and validity of an assessment instrument for anxiety, depression, and mood among individuals with mental retardation. *Journal of Autism and Developmental Disorders, 33*, 617–629.

Findling, R. L., McNamara, N. K., Gracious, B. L., O'Riordan, M. A., Reed, M. D., Demeter, C., & Blumer, J. L. (2004). Quetiapine in nine youths with autistic disorder. *Journal of Child and Adolescent Psychopharmacology, 14,* 287–294.

Frazier, T. W., Shattuck, P. T., Narendorf, S. C., Cooper, B. P., Wagner, M., & Spitznagel, E. L. (2011). Prevalence and correlates of psychotropic medication use in adolescents with an autism spectrum disorder with and without caregiver-reported attention-deficit/hyperactivity disorder. *Journal of Child and Adolescent Psychopharmacology, 21,* 571–579.

Gadow, K. D., & Sprafkin, J. (2005). *Child and Adolescent Symptom Inventory.* Stony Brook, NY: Checkmate Plus.

Gencer, O., Emiroglu, F. N., Miral, S., Baykara, B., Baykara, A., & Dirik, E. (2008). Comparison of long-term efficacy and safety of risperidone and haloperidol in children and adolescents with autistic disorder: An open label maintenance study. *European Child & Adolescent Psychiatry, 17,* 217–225.

Ghaleiha, A., Asadabadi, M., Mohammadi, M. R., Shahei, M., Tabrizi, M., Hajiaghaee, R., . . . Akhondzadeh, S. (2013). Memantine as adjunctive treatment to risperidone in children with autistic disorder: A randomized, double-blind, placebo-controlled trial. *International Journal of Neuropsychopharmacology, 16,* 783–789.

Ghanizadeh, A., & Moghimi-Sarani, E. (2013). A randomized double blind placebo controlled clinical trial of *N*-acetylcysteine added to risperidone for treating autistic disorders. *BMC Psychiatry, 13,* 196.

Ghanizadeh, A., Sahraeizadeh, A., & Berk, M. (2014). A head-to-head comparison of aripiprazole and risperidone for safety and treating autistic disorders, a randomized double blind clinical trial. *Child Psychiatry and Human Development, 45*(2), 185–192.

Goldstein, S., & Schwebach, A. J. (2004). The comorbidity of pervasive developmental disorder and attention deficit hyperactivity disorder: Results of a retrospective chart review. *Journal of Autism and Developmental Disorders, 34,* 329–339.

Golubchik, P., Sever, J., & Weizman, A. (2011). Low-dose quetiapine for adolescents with autistic spectrum disorder and aggressive behavior: Open-label trial. *Clinical Neuropharmacology, 34,* 216–219.

Guastella, A. J., Einfeld, S. L., Gray, K. M., Rinehart, N. J., Tonge, B. J., Lambert, T. J., & Hickie, I. B. (2010). Intranasal oxytocin improves emotion recognition for youth with autism spectrum disorders. *Biological Psychiatry, 67,* 692–694.

Guy, W.; National Institute of Mental Health, Psychopharmacology Research Branch, Division of Extramural Research Programs. (1976). *ECDEU assessment manual for psychopharmacology.* Rockville, MD: U.S. Department of Health, Education, and Welfare, Public Health Service, Alcohol, Drug Abuse, and Mental Health Administration, National Institute of Mental Health, Psychopharmacology Research Branch, Division of Extramural Research Programs.

Handen, B. L., Johnson, C. R., & Lubetsky, M. (2000). Efficacy of methylphenidate among children with autism and symptoms of attention-deficit hyperactivity disorder. *Journal of Autism and Developmental Disorders, 30,* 245–255.

Hardan, A. Y., Fung, L. K., Libove, R. A., Obukhanych, T. V., Nair, S., Herzenberg, L. A., . . . Tirouvanziam, R. (2012). A randomized controlled pilot trial of oral N-acetylcysteine in children with autism. *Biological Psychiatry, 71,* 956–961.

Harfterkamp, M., Buitelaar, J. K., Minderaa, R. B., van de Loo-Neus, G., van der Gaag, R. J., & Hoekstra, P. J. (2013). Long-term treatment with atomoxetine for attention-deficit/hyperactivity disorder symptoms in children and adolescents with autism spectrum disorder: An open-label extension study. *Journal of Child and Adolescent Psychopharmacology, 23,* 194–199.

Harfterkamp, M., van de Loo-Neus, G., Minderaa, R. B., van der Gaag, R. J., Escobar, R., Schacht, A., . . . Hoekstra, P. J. (2012). A randomized double-blind study of atomoxetine versus placebo for attention-deficit/hyperactivity disorder symptoms in children with autism spectrum disorder. *Journal of the American Academy of Child and Adolescent Psychiatry, 51,* 733–741.

Heimann, S. W. (1999). High-dose olanzapine in an adolescent. *Journal of the American Academy of Child and Adolescent Psychiatry, 38,* 496–498.

Hellings, J. A., Weckbaugh, M., Nickel, E. J., Cain, S. E., Zarcone, J. R., Reese, R. M., . . . Cook, E. H. (2005). A double-blind, placebo-controlled study of valproate for aggression in youth with pervasive developmental disorders. *Journal of Child and Adolescent Psychopharmacology, 15*, 682–692.

Hollander, E., Bartz, J., Chaplin, W., Phillips, A., Sumner, J., Soorya, L., . . . Wasserman, S. (2007). Oxytocin increases retention of social cognition in autism. *Biological Psychiatry, 61*, 498–503.

Hollander, E., Chaplin, W., Soorya, L., Wasserman, S., Novotny, S., Rusoff, J., . . . Anagnostou, E. (2010). Divalproex sodium vs placebo for the treatment of irritability in children and adolescents with autism spectrum disorders. *Neuropsychopharmacology, 35*, 990–998.

Hollander, E., Dolgoff-Kaspar, R., Cartwright, C., Rawitt, R., & Novotny, S. (2001). An open trial of divalproex sodium in autism spectrum disorders. *Journal of Clinical Psychiatry, 62*, 530–534.

Hollander, E., Novotny, S., Hanratty, M., Yaffe, R., DeCaria, C. M., Aronowitz, B. R., & Mosovich, S. (2003). Oxytocin infusion reduces repetitive behaviors in adults with autistic and Asperger's disorders. *Neuropsychopharmacology, 28*, 193–198.

Hollander, E., Phillips, A., Chaplin, W., Zagursky, K., Novotny, S., Wasserman, S., & Iyengar, R. (2005). A placebo controlled crossover trial of liquid fluoxetine on repetitive behaviors in childhood and adolescent autism. *Neuropsychopharmacology, 30*, 582–589.

Hollander, E., Soorya, L., Chaplin, W., Anagnostou, E., Taylor, B. P., Ferretti, C. J., . . . Settipani, C. (2012). A double-blind placebo-controlled trial of fluoxetine for repetitive behaviors and global severity in adult autism spectrum disorders. *American Journal of Psychiatry, 169*, 292–299.

Hollander, E., Soorya, L., Wasserman, S., Esposito, K., Chaplin, W., & Anagnostou, E. (2006). Divalproex sodium vs. placebo in the treatment of repetitive behaviours in autism spectrum disorder. *International Journal of Neuropsychopharmacology, 9*, 209–213.

Horrigan, J. P., Barnhill, L. J., & Courvoisie, H. E. (1997). Olanzapine in PDD. *Journal of the American Academy of Child and Adolescent Psychiatry, 36*, 1166–1167.

Jacquemont, S., Curie, A., des Portes, V., Torrioli, M. G., Berry-Kravis, E., Hagerman, R. J., . . . Gomez-Mancilla, B. (2011). Epigenetic modification of the FMR1 gene in fragile X syndrome is associated with differential response to the mGluR5 antagonist AFQ056. *Science Translational Medicine, 3*, 64ra61.

Kent, J. M., Hough, D., Singh, J., Karcher, K., & Pandina, G. (2013). An open-label extension study of the safety and efficacy of risperidone in children and adolescents with autistic disorder. *Journal of Child and Adolescent Psychopharmacology, 23*, 676–686.

Kent, J. M., Kushner, S., Ning, X., Karcher, K., Ness, S., Aman, M., . . . Hough, D. (2013). Risperidone dosing in children and adolescents with autistic disorder: A double-blind, placebo-controlled study. *Journal of Autism and Developmental Disorders, 43*, 1773–1783.

King, B. H., Hollander, E., Sikich, L., McCracken, J. T., Scahill, L., Bregman, J. D., . . . Network, S. P. (2009). Lack of efficacy of citalopram in children with autism spectrum disorders and high levels of repetitive behavior: Citalopram ineffective in children with autism. *Archives of General Psychiatry, 66*, 583–590.

Langworthy-Lam, K. S., Aman, M. G., & Van Bourgondien, M. E. (2002). Prevalence and patterns of use of psychoactive medicines in individuals with autism in the Autism Society of North Carolina. *Journal of Child and Adolescent Psychopharmacology, 12*, 311–321.

Lemonnier, E., Degrez, C., Phelep, M., Tyzio, R., Josse, F., Grandgeorge, M., . . . Ben-Ari, Y. (2012). A randomised controlled trial of bumetanide in the treatment of autism in children. *Translational Psychiatry, 2*, e202.

Luby, J., Mrakotsky, C., Stalets, M. M., Belden, A., Heffelfinger, A., Williams, M., & Spitznagel, E. (2006). Risperidone in preschool children with autistic spectrum disorders: An investigation of safety and efficacy. *Journal of Child and Adolescent Psychopharmacology, 16*, 575–587.

Malone, R. P., Cater, J., Sheikh, R. M., Choudhury, M. S., & Delaney, M. A. (2001). Olanzapine versus haloperidol in children with autistic disorder: An open pilot study. *Journal of the American Academy of Child and Adolescent Psychiatry, 40*, 887–894.

Malone, R. P., Delaney, M. A., Hyman, S. B., & Cater, J. R. (2007). Ziprasidone in adolescents with autism: An open-label pilot study. *Journal of Child and Adolescent Psychopharmacology, 17*, 779–790.

Mandell, D. S., Morales, K. H., Marcus, S. C., Stahmer, A. C., Doshi, J., & Polsky, D. E. (2008). Psychotropic medication use among Medicaid-enrolled children with autism spectrum disorders. *Pediatrics, 121,* e441–e448.

Marcus, R. N., Owen, R., Kamen, L., Manos, G., McQuade, R. D., Carson, W. H., & Aman, M. G. (2009). A placebo-controlled, fixed-dose study of aripiprazole in children and adolescents with irritability associated with autistic disorder. *Journal of the American Academy of Child and Adolescent Psychiatry, 48,* 1110–1119.

Martin, A., Koenig, K., Scahill, L., & Bregman, J. (1999). Open-label quetiapine in the treatment of children and adolescents with autistic disorder. *Journal of Child and Adolescent Psychopharmacology, 9,* 99–107.

McCracken, J. T., McGough, J., Shah, B., Cronin, P., Hong, D., Aman, M. G., . . . McMahon, D.; Research Units on Pediatric Psychopharmacology Autism Network. (2002). Risperidone in children with autism and serious behavioral problems. *New England Journal of Medicine, 347,* 314–321.

McDougle, C. J., Kem, D. L., & Posey, D. J. (2002). Case series: Use of ziprasidone for maladaptive symptoms in youths with autism. *Journal of the American Academy of Child and Adolescent Psychiatry, 41,* 921–927.

McDougle, C. J., Naylor, S. T., Cohen, D. J., Volkmar, F. R., Heninger, G. R., & Price, L. H. (1996). A double-blind, placebo-controlled study of fluvoxamine in adults with autistic disorder. *Archives of General Psychiatry, 53,* 1001–1008.

McDougle, C. J., Scahill, L., Aman, M. G., McCracken, J. T., Tierney, E., Davies, M., . . . Vitiello, B. (2005). Risperidone for the core symptom domains of autism: Results from the study by the autism network of the research units on pediatric psychopharmacology. *American Journal of Psychiatry, 162,* 1142–1148.

McDougle, C. J., Stigler, K. A., Erickson, C. A., & Posey, D. J. (2008). Atypical antipsychotics in children and adolescents with autistic and other pervasive developmental disorders. *Journal of Clinical Psychiatry, 69*(Suppl. 4), 15–20.

Meyer-Lindenberg, A., Domes, G., Kirsch, P., & Heinrichs, M. (2011). Oxytocin and vasopressin in the human brain: Social neuropeptides for translational medicine. *Nature Reviews Neuroscience, 12,* 524–538.

Miral, S., Gencer, O., Inal-Emiroglu, F. N., Baykara, B., Baykara, A., & Dirik, E. (2008). Risperidone versus haloperidol in children and adolescents with AD: A randomized, controlled, double-blind trial. *European Child & Adolescent Psychiatry, 17,* 1–8.

Nagaraj, R., Singhi, P., & Malhi, P. (2006). Risperidone in children with autism: Randomized, placebo-controlled, double-blind study. *Journal of Child Neurology, 21,* 450–455.

Nazeer, A. (2011). Psychopharmacology of autistic spectrum disorders in children and adolescents. *Pediatric Clinics of North America, 58,* 85–97.

Nikolov, R., Jonker, J., & Scahill, L. (2006). Autistic disorder: Current psychopharmacological treatments and areas of interest for future developments. *Revista Brasileira de Psiquiatria, 28*(Suppl. 1), S39–S46.

Oswald, D. P., & Sonenklar, N. A. (2007). Medication use among children with autism spectrum disorders. *Journal of Child and Adolescent Psychopharmacology, 17,* 348–355.

Owen, R., Sikich, L., Marcus, R. N., Corey-Lisle, P., Manos, G., McQuade, R. D., . . . Findling, R. L. (2009). Aripiprazole in the treatment of irritability in children and adolescents with autistic disorder. *Pediatrics, 124,* 1533–1540.

Pandina, G. J., Bossie, C. A., Youssef, E., Zhu, Y., & Dunbar, F. (2007). Risperidone improves behavioral symptoms in children with autism in a randomized, double-blind, placebo-controlled trial. *Journal of Autism and Developmental Disorders, 37,* 367–373.

Potenza, M. N., Holmes, J. P., Kanes, S. J., & McDougle, C. J. (1999). Olanzapine treatment of children, adolescents, and adults with pervasive developmental disorders: An open-label pilot study. *Journal of Clinical Psychopharmacology, 19,* 37–44.

Quintana, H., Birmaher, B., Stedge, D., Lennon, S., Freed, J., Bridge, J., & Greenhill, L. (1995). Use of methylphenidate in the treatment of children with autistic disorder. *Journal of Autism and Developmental Disorders, 25,* 283–294.

Rana, F., Gormez, A., & Varghese, S. (2013). Pharmacological interventions for self-injurious behaviour in adults with intellectual disabilities. *Cochrane Database of Systematic Reviews, 4,* CD009084.

Reichow, B., Volkmar, F. R., & Bloch, M. H. (2013). Systematic review and meta-analysis of pharmacological treatment of the symptoms of attention-deficit/hyperactivity disorder in children with pervasive developmental disorders. *Journal of Autism and Developmental Disorders, 43,* 2435–2441.

Research Units on Pediatric Psychopharmacology Autism Network. (2005). Randomized, controlled, crossover trial of methylphenidate in pervasive developmental disorders with hyperactivity. *Archives of General Psychiatry, 62,* 1266–1274.

Richdale, A. L. (1999). Sleep problems in autism: Prevalence, cause, and intervention. *Developmental Medicine and Child Neurology, 41,* 60–66.

Rojahn, J., Rowe, E. W., Sharber, A. C., Hastings, R., Matson, J. L., Didden, R., . . . Dumont, E. L. (2012). The Behavior Problems Inventory–Short Form for individuals with intellectual disabilities. Part I: Development and provisional clinical reference data. *Journal of Intellectual Disability Research, 56,* 527–545.

Rosenberg, R. E., Mandell, D. S., Farmer, J. E., Law, J. K., Marvin, A. R., & Law, P. A. (2010). Psychotropic medication use among children with autism spectrum disorders enrolled in a national registry, 2007–2008. *Journal of Autism and Developmental Disorders, 40,* 342–351.

Scahill, L., McDougle, C. J., Williams, S. K., Dimitropoulos, A., Aman, M. G., McCracken, J. T., . . . Vitiello, B.; Research Units on Pediatric Psychopharmacology Autism Network. (2006). Children's Yale–Brown Obsessive Compulsive Scale modified for pervasive developmental disorders. *Journal of the American Academy of Child and Adolescent Psychiatry, 45,* 1114–1123.

Schubart, J. R., Camacho, F., & Leslie, D. (2014). Psychotropic medication trends among children and adolescents with autism spectrum disorder in the Medicaid program. *Autism, 18*(6), 631–637.

Shea, S., Turgay, A., Carroll, A., Schulz, M., Orlik, H., Smith, I., & Dunbar, F. (2004). Risperidone in the treatment of disruptive behavioral symptoms in children with autistic and other pervasive developmental disorders. *Pediatrics, 114,* e634–e641.

Siegel, M., & Beaulieu, A. A. (2012). Psychotropic medications in children with autism spectrum disorders: A systematic review and synthesis for evidence-based practice. *Journal of Autism and Developmental Disorders, 42,* 1592–1605.

Spencer, D., Marshall, J., Post, B., Kulakodlu, M., Newschaffer, C., Dennen, T., . . . Jain, A. (2013). Psychotropic medication use and polypharmacy in children with autism spectrum disorders. *Pediatrics, 132,* 833–840.

Stigler, K. A., Mullett, J. E., Erickson, C. A., Posey, D. J., & McDougle, C. J. (2012). Paliperidone for irritability in adolescents and young adults with autistic disorder. *Psychopharmacology, 223,* 237–245.

Swanson, J. M., Kraemer, H. C., Hinshaw, S. P., Arnold, L. E., Conners, C. K., Abikoff, H. B., . . . Wu, M. (2001). Clinical relevance of the primary findings of the MTA: Success rates based on severity of ADHD and ODD symptoms at the end of treatment. *Journal of the American Academy of Child and Adolescent Psychiatry, 40,* 168–179.

Troost, P. W., Lahuis, B. E., Steenhuis, M. P., Ketelaars, C. E., Buitelaar, J. K., van Engeland, H., . . . Hoekstra, P. J. (2005). Long-term effects of risperidone in children with autism spectrum disorders: A placebo discontinuation study. *Journal of the American Academy of Child and Adolescent Psychiatry, 44,* 1137–1144.

Williams, K., Brignell, A., Randall, M., Silove, N., & Hazell, P. (2013). Selective serotonin reuptake inhibitors (SSRIs) for autism spectrum disorders (ASD). *Cochrane Database of Systematic Reviews, 8,* CD004677.

/// 17 /// COMPLEMENTARY AND ALTERNATIVE (BIOMEDICAL) TREATMENTS FOR AUTISM SPECTRUM DISORDER

ROBERT L. HENDREN

INTRODUCTION

The National Center for Complementary and Alternative Medicine (NCCAM) has referred to complementary and alternative medicine (CAM) as a group of diverse medical and health care systems, practices, and products that are not generally considered to be part of conventional medicine. More recently, NCCAM refers to CAM as an array of health care approaches with a history of use or origins outside of mainstream medicine (NCCAM, 2008) and divides CAM into natural products and mind and body practices. However, NCCAM notes that some approaches, such as the practices of traditional healers, Ayurvedic medicine from India, traditional Chinese medicine, homeopathy, and naturopathy, may not fit neatly into either of these groups. This chapter focuses primarily on natural products but briefly reviews mind/body practices as potential therapeutic approaches in autism spectrum disorder (ASD).

The list of potential biomedical CAM treatments is long, and most have inadequate evidence to judge potential efficacy. See Box 17.1 for a list of most of the biomedical/CAM treatments for ASD. Three comprehensive reviews of these treatments with some efficacy data have been published (Cheng, Widjaja, Choi, & Hendren, 2013; Hendren, 2013; Lofthouse, Hendren, Hurt, Arnold, & Butter, 2012). In this chapter, the biomedical CAM treatments that have the most published evidence, that have generated the greatest interest, and/or that nonetheless have significant promise for treating ASD or ASD-associated symptoms are briefly discussed. These treatments include melatonin, omega-3 fatty acids, injectable methylcobalamin (methyl B_{12}), N-acetylcysteine (NAC), memantine, pancreatic digestive enzymes, probiotics, micronutrients, and immune therapies.

Twelve percent of children and adolescents in the United States use CAM (Birdee, Phillips, Davis, & Gardiner, 2010). Up to 70% of children with ASD are reported to be using some form of biological treatment (Wong & Smith, 2006). Twenty-eight to 82% of children recently diagnosed with ASD use CAM. The main reasons for choosing CAM

BOX 17.1
POTENTIAL CAM BIOMEDICAL TREATMENTS OF
AUTISM SPECTRUM DISORDER

Acupuncture

Amino acids

Animal-assisted therapy

Antibiotics

Antifungals (fluconazole (Diflucan), nystatin)

Antiviral (valacyclovir hydrochloride (Valtrex))

Auditory integration therapy (music therapy)

Chelation

Chiropractic

Cholestyramine

Coenzyme Q10

Craniosacral therapy

Curcumin

Cyproheptadine

Dehydroepiandrosterone (DHEA)

Digestive enzymes

Dimethylglycine (DMG), trimethylglycine (TMG)

Fatty acids (omega-3)

Folic/folinic acid

Glutathione (GSH)

Gluten-free casein-free (GFCF) diet

Food-allergy treatment

5-Hydroxytryptophan

Hyperbaric oxygen treatment

Infliximab (Remicade)

Immune therapies

Intravenous Immune Globulin (IVIG)

Iron

l-Carnosine

Magnesium

Melatonin

Methylcobalamin (methyl B_{12})

N-acetylcysteine (NAC)

Naltrexone

Neurofeedback

Oxalate (low) diet

Oxytocin

Pioglitazone hydrochloride (Actos)

Probiotics

Pyridoxal phosphate

Ribose and dehydroepiandrosterone

S-adenosyl-methionine

Secretin

Sensory integration therapy

Specific carbohydrate therapy

St. John's wort

Steroids

Transfer factor

Vitamin A

Vitamin B_3

Vitamin B_6 with magnesium

Vitamin C

Zinc

Source: Hendren (2013).

given by parents are related to concerns with the safety and side effects of prescribed medications (Hanson et al., 2007), but there is concern that traditional physicians are not familiar with CAM.

CAM might be better named as it is becoming less likely to refer to assessments and treatments that are complementary, alternative, or where there are not published studies to consider. Often, integrative medicine is placed in the CAM category, as are biomedical treatments, in large part because historically they have not been well studied and the evidence for their efficacy is limited. However, this is changing as medicine is increasingly studying nutritional or nutraceutical treatments for cancer, vascular disease, and, recently, central nervous system disorders. In part, the scientific basis for this shift is the increasing evidence for gene–environment interactions as key to understanding the endophenotype and phenotype of medical disorders.

ASD clearly has a genetic basis. Multiple genes have been identified, and a clear genetic etiology accounts for as many as 25% of cases of ASD. It also appears that for the majority, hundreds of genetic mutations, some de novo, lead to many ways to develop ASD (Iossifov et al., 2012; Levy et al., 2011; Miles, 2011; Murdoch & State, 2013). A number of recent studies have concluded that it is the gene–environment interaction that provides the best explanation for the etiology of ASD. Susceptibility to ASD has moderate genetic heritability and a substantial shared twin environmental component (Hallmayer et al., 2011). Polygenic models exist in which spontaneous coding mutations in any of a large number of genes increase risk for ASD by 5- to 20-fold (Neale et al., 2012). Among children born in Sweden, the individual risk of ASD increased with increasing genetic relatedness. Heritability of ASD and autistic disorder was estimated to be approximately 50% (Sandin et al., 2014).

What are these environmental contributors that add to genetic risk and lead to ASD? Documented environmental contributors to ASD include prenatal or early postnatal exposure to viral infections (rubella), valproic acid, and thalidomide (Herbert, 2010; Landrigan, 2010). There is increasing evidence for the contribution of parental age (Durkin et al., 2008; Frans et al., 2013; Herbert, 2010; Shelton, Tancredi, & Hertz-Picciotto, 2010), maternal metabolic conditions (Krakowiak et al., 2012), influenza or fever during pregnancy (Zerbo et al., 2013), environmental pollution (Schuler, 2013), and epigenetics (Hagerman & Hendren, 2014).

This epigenetic or gene expression approach is leading to a paradigm shift in thinking about disorders to the point where we are now considering whole body systems rather than a single organ in the etiology and treatment of disordered development. Epigenetics refers to the reversible regulation of various genomic functions, independent of DNA sequence, mediated principally through DNA methylation, chromatin sequence, and RNA-mediated gene expression (Jaenisch & Bird, 2003). The related endophenotypes (measurable components along the epigenetic pathway between the genotype and the distal symptom, personal characteristic, or phenotype) are simple biologic aspects of a disease that can be observed in people with a similar endophenotype at a higher rate than in the general population (Saresella et al., 2009) and that are potentially reversible through nutrition, social factors, behavioral interventions, and drugs (Rutten & Mill, 2009). Finding ways to improve this epigenetic interaction during the disease process using health-enhancing strategies found in CAM or biomedical approaches through interventions such as dietary supplements or nutraceuticals is increasingly attractive.

Assessment is based on understanding the elements of gene expression, not just DNA and symptoms. Treatment is based on targeting processes rather than a diagnosis, and there is increasing interest in studying biomarker targets (Hagerman & Hendren, 2014; Insel, 2014).

Significant subsets of children with ASD have an endophenotype of intestinal inflammation, digestive enzyme abnormalities, metabolic impairments, oxidative stress, mitochondrial dysfunction, and immune problems, which range from immune deficiency to hypersensitivity and autoimmunity (Box 17.2). In many cases, improvement of autistic symptoms is achieved by a combination of nutritional recommendations, prescription medications, and addressing the underlying medical conditions seen in these children (Frye & Rossignol, 2014; Hagerman & Hendren, 2014; Mumper, 2012). For instance, a

---

BOX 17.2
EPIGENETIC PROCESSES IN AUTISM SPECTRUM DISORDER

- Immune abnormalities/inflammation (Goines & Van de Water, 2010)
- Oxidative stress (James et al., 2009)
- Disturbed methylation (James et al., 2009)
- Mitochondrial dysfunction (Frye & Rossignol, 2011; Manji et al., 2012)
- Free fatty acid metabolism (Bell et al., 2010)
- Excitatory/inhibitory imbalance (Rubenstein, 2010)
- Hormonal effects (Harony & Wagner, 2010)
- Microglia (Cunningham, Martinez-Cerdeno, & Noctor, 2013)

subset of children with ASD have mitochondrial dysfunction, which can be inherited or acquired. Evidence links oxidative stress, mitochondrial dysfunction, and immune dysregulation/inflammation to brain regions involved in speech and auditory processing and social behavior (Rossignol, Genuis, & Frye, 2014). Treatments used for mitochondrial disease (L-carnitine, multivitamins with B vitamins, antioxidants, vitamin E, coenzyme Q10, vitamin C, methyl B_{12}, NAC, ubiquinol, and carnosine), all thought of as CAM treatments, have demonstrated significant improvements in ASD (Frye, Sequeira, Quadros, James, & Rossignol, 2013).

There are a number of reasons why CAM/biomedical treatments have not been well studied (Bent & Hendren, 2010), including the following:

1. Most treatments have a small effect requiring a large sample size.
2. The trials have been of relatively short duration.
3. ASD is a heterogeneous disorder.
4. Few biomarkers used for subject inclusion in studies have been validated.
5. The need to hold other treatments constant during the study period in order to show an effect may present ethical concerns.
6. Blinding is often a challenge.
7. There is formulation variability.
8. Institutional review boards typically have concerns about CAM treatments.
9. Funding is often challenging because many of these treatments would not be eligible for patents, making them less desirable to pharmaceutical companies.

Nevertheless, there are an increasing number of studies of potential biomarkers that might be used for assessment and outcome measures for treatment studies of compounds that have traditionally been thought of as CAM.

ASSESSMENT

The strongest evidence for biomarkers in the assessment of ASD continues to be routine laboratory tests, most of which have a low yield (Goldani, Downs, Widjaja, Lawton, & Hendren, 2015). These include a metabolic panel that includes glucose and liver function tests and a compete blood count with differential and platelet count. Increasingly, practitioners interested in taking more of an integrative medicine approach (especially when supported by the history and physical) will include magnesium, selenium, zinc/copper, vitamin C, vitamin D_3 (usually 1,25(OH)), fat-soluble vitamins, ferritin, total iron, total iron binding capacity, percentage iron saturation, lead screening, serum amino and urine organic acids, cholesterol (lipid panel if indicated), red blood cell folate, and vitamin B_{12} (Boxes 17.3–17.5).

CAM/BIOMEDICAL TREATMENTS

Melatonin

Melatonin is an endogenous neurohormone that causes drowsiness, establishes circadian rhythms and synchronization of peripheral oscillators, and is produced from serotonin (Tordjman et al., 2013). It has been suggested that melatonin may also benefit social

---

BOX 17.3

POSSIBLE OXIDATIVE STRESS BIOMARKERS

- Glutathione—reduced/oxidized
- Methionine
- Cysteine
- Organic acid test—α-hydroxybutyrate, pyroglutamate, and sulfate
- Plasma F2t-isoprostanes (F2-IsoPs)
- Urine 8-OHdG
- Transferrin
- Ceruloplasmin
- Plasma 3-chlortyrosine (3CT)
- 3-Nitrotyrosine (3NT)

BOX 17.4

POSSIBLE MITOCHONDRIAL FUNCTION BIOMARKERS

- Lactate
- Pyruvate
- Lactate:pyruvate ratio
- Carnitine (free and total)
- Alanine
- Quantitative plasma amino acids
- Ubiquinone
- Ammonia
- CD
  - AST/ALT
  - CO_2
  - Aspartate aminotransferase
  - Serum creatine kinase

---

communication impairments and stereotyped behaviors or interests (Tordjman et al., 2013). A review and meta-analysis of 35 studies reported that of 18 treatment studies, there were 5 randomized controlled trials (RCTs) ($N = 61$, 2–10 mg/day) in which sleep duration was increased (44 min, Effect size [ES] = 0.93), sleep onset latency was decreased (39 min, ES = 1.28), but nighttime awakenings were unchanged (Rossignol & Frye, 2011). The duration of the studies varied between 4 weeks and 4 years. One study indicated a loss of benefit at 4 weeks, whereas a study of 4 years reported continued benefits. Side effects were minimal to none (Table 17.1).

BOX 17.5
POSSIBLE IMMUNE/INFLAMMATORY BIOMARKERS

Subjects With Autism Spectrum Disorder

- TGF-β
- CCL2
- CCL5
- IGM
- IgG
- Th1/Th2
- Neopterin
- S110B protein
- Anti-ganglioside M1 antibodies
- Antineuronal antibodies
- Serum antinuclear antibodies
- BDNF
- C-reactive protein
- Cytokines

Mothers of Subjects With Autism Spectrum Disorder

- IFN-γ
- IL-4
- IL-5
- IL-6

Melatonin is one of the best studied CAM/biomedical treatments of ASD. Although small sample sizes, variability in sleep assessments, and lack of follow-up limit the value of these studies in supporting its use, treatment with melatonin has a clear physiologic rationale, and it is easy to use, inexpensive, and safe.

Vitamin D

The "ecological evidence" for the role of vitamin D in the etiology of ASD is mostly anecdotal and includes speculation that the incidence of ASD may be higher in northern latitudes, where there is more rainfall, and in those with greater skin pigment in low sunlight areas (Cannell, 2013). Low levels of vitamin D are reported in the pediatric population, but especially so among children with ASD (Cannell, 2013). Vitamin D activates a serotonin-synthesizing gene (Patrick & Ames, 2014) and is a "potent neurosteroid" (McGrath, Feron, Eyles, & Mackay-Sim, 2001). There are no published studies of vitamin D treatment of ASD, but therapeutic doses are commonly given, especially if the 25(OH) D level is at or below 30 ng/mL.

TABLE 17.1 Biomedical Therapeutic Strategies

Immune/Inflammation	Oxidative Stress
Melatonin	Glutathione[d]
IV/IG	Methyl B$_{12}$[e]
	Curcumin[f]—anti-inflammatory and antioxidant activity
Corticosteroids	**Neurotransmitter Production**
	Tetrahydrobiopterin[g]
Celecoxib: RCT for irritability, withdrawal, and stereotypy[a]	Rivastigmine[h]—parasympathomimetic or cholinergic agent
	Galantamine[i]—acetylcholinesterase inhibitor
Methylation	**GABA**
Folic/folinic acid[b]	Arbaclofen[j] (STX209)
Mitochondrial Function[c]	Bumetanide[k]—diuretic
Carnitine	**Glutamate**
Coenzyme Q10	Riluzole[l]—used to treat amyotrophic lateral sclerosis
Vitamin C	d-Cycloserine[m]—partial agonist of the neuronal NMDA receptor
Lipoic acid	
Pantothenate	
Vitamin E	
l-Carnosine	

[a]Asadabadi et al. (2013).
[b]Surenet al. (2013).
[c]Rossignol and Frye (2012).
[d]Kern et al. (2011).
[e]Bertoglio et al. (2010).
[f]Darvesh et al. (2012).
[g]Frye, Delatorre, et al. (2013).
[h]Chez et al. (2004).
[i]Nicolson, Craven-Thuss, and Smith (2006).
[j]Wang et al. (2011).
[k]Hadjikhani et al. (2015).
[l]Wink, Erickson, Stigler, and McDougle (2011).
[m]Posey et al. (2004).
IVIG, intravenous immunoglobulin; NMDA, N-methyl-d-aspartate; RCT, randomized controlled trial.

Hyperbaric Oxygen Treatment

Although some uncontrolled and controlled studies have suggested that hyperbaric oxygen treatment (HBOT) is effective for the treatment of ASD, these promising effects have not been replicated (Ghanizadeh, 2012). Two negative RCTs have been reported (Granpeesheh et al., 2010; Jepson et al., 2011).

One open-label study of change in cytokines as a possible mechanism for the benefit of HBOT included 10 children with ASD who underwent 80 sessions at 1.5 atmospheres absolute and 100% oxygen (Bent, Bertoglio, Ashwood, Nemeth, & Hendren, 2012). Nine of 10 parents reported that their child was "much improved" or "very much improved," and they reported improvements in irritability, lethargy, hyperactivity, aggressiveness, and learning and memory. However, enrolled children did not exhibit abnormal cytokine levels at baseline, and no significant changes in mean cytokine levels were observed. Study raters did not report improvements. The evidence at this point does not support the use of HBOT for the treatment of ASD.

Methylcobalamine

Methylcobalamine (Methyl B_{12}) is a vital cofactor for the regeneration of methionine from homocysteine by providing methyl groups for metabolic pathways involving trans-methylation and transsulfuration. Reduced activity in the transsulfuration pathway can lead to reduced levels of cysteine and glutathione (GSH), which are crucial antioxidants responsible for minimizing macromolecular damage produced by oxidative stress. Metabolic biomarkers of increased oxidative stress and impaired methylation capacity have been reported in children with ASD (James et al., 2004). One study that included 30 patients with ASD in a 12-week double-blind, crossover trial of methyl B_{12} administered subcutaneously (SubQ) in the buttocks at a dosage of 67.5 µg/kg every 3 days for 6 weeks found no statistically significant mean differences in behavioral outcome measures or in glutathione status between active and placebo groups. Minor trauma from SubQ injections and increased hyperactivity were the only side effects reported. Nine patients demonstrated clinically significant improvement on the Clinical Global Impression–Improvement scale (CGI-I) and at least two additional behavioral measures. Responders exhibited significantly increased plasma concentrations of GSH and significantly increased GSH:glutathione disulfide ratio (Bertoglio, James, Deprey, Brule, & Hendren, 2010).

In a study from the same group, 53 newly recruited children with ASD between the ages of 3 and 7 years were randomly assigned to 8 weeks of treatment with methyl B_{12} at 75 µg/kg or placebo given SubQ every 3 days. The mean CGI-I at 8 weeks showed significantly more improvement in the methyl B_{12} group compared to the placebo group. Improvement on the CGI-I was significantly correlated with methionine, decreases in S-adenosylhomocysteine (SAH), and an increase in the S-adenosylmethionine (SAM/SAH) ratio (Hendren et al., 2015). Although these initial studies are promising for a subgroup of children with ASD, and SubQ methyl B_{12} supplementation seems to be safe and well tolerated, additional study is needed to determine whether this will become a recommended treatment for ASD.

N-Acetylcysteine

N-Acetylcysteine (NAC) is a glutamatergic modulator and an antioxidant. In a 12-week randomized double-blind, placebo-controlled study of NAC in 33 children with ASD (3.2–10.7 years), the compound resulted in significant improvement compared to placebo on the Aberrant Behavior Checklist–Irritability subscale (ABC-I). NAC was initiated at 900 mg daily for 4 weeks, increased to 900 mg twice daily for 4 weeks, and then increased again to 900 mg three times daily for 4 weeks. Oral NAC was well tolerated with limited side effects (Hardan et al., 2012). The results are promising, especially because the supplement is well tolerated and many current treatments for irritability in ASD are associated with significant side effects. This study will need to be replicated before recommendations can be offered, however.

Omega-3 Fatty Acids

Omega-3 fatty acids are a type of polyunsaturated fatty acid (PUFA); they are long-chain orthomolecules that are essential for brain health and growth and that aide in synaptic plasticity and neuroprotection (Freeman et al., 2006). They are a critical component of neuronal membranes, essential for their optimal functioning. They also serve as substrates for the production of the eicosanoids, such as prostaglandins, which are necessary for cell communication and immune regulation. The two omega-3 fatty acids of primary interest are eicosapentaenoic acid (EPA) and docosahexaenoic acid (DHA). Based on data from studies of other disorders, these fatty acids might be expected to improve mood, attention, and activity level, as well as—conceivably—core symptoms of ASD. Low levels of omega-3 fatty acids have been reported in children with ASD (Bell et al., 2004; Meguid, Atta, Gouda, & Khalil, 2008; Vancassel et al., 2001). Published evidence in support of the clinical benefit for ASD is limited, however (Bent, Bertoglio, & Hendren, 2009).

In one study, children aged 3–8 years with ASD were randomly assigned to 12 weeks of omega-3 fatty acids (1.3 g/day) or placebo. Hyperactivity improved more in the omega-3 group compared to the placebo group, but not to a statistically significant level. Correlations were found between decreases in five fatty acid levels and decreases in hyperactivity (Bent, Bertoglio, Ashwood, Bostrom, & Hendren, 2011).

A recent study was conducted via the Internet and included 58 subjects with ASD and also teacher ratings. The results showed that omega-3 fatty acids led to a greater improvement on the ABC–Hyperactivity subscale score compared to placebo, but again, not to a statistically significant degree. The sample size of the study was not powered to determine the efficacy of omega-3 fatty acids with confidence (Bent et al., 2014).

In addition to the previously mentioned studies, there have been four open-label trials (Meguid et al., 2008; Meiri, Bichovsky, & Belmaker, 2009) and two randomized double-blind, placebo-controlled pilot trials of omega-3 fatty acids in children with ASD (Amminger et al., 2007; Johnson, Handen, Zimmer, & Sacco, 2010). Amminger and colleagues randomized 13 children with ASD (aged 5–17 years) to EPA 840 mg/day and DHA 700 mg/day ($n = 7$) or placebo ($n = 6$) for 6 weeks. There were no significant differences between groups on the ABC, possibly because of the small sample and insufficient power. Omega-3 fatty acids seemed nominally superior to placebo for the ABC subscales for stereotypy, hyperactivity, and inappropriate speech.

Despite the weak evidence and the modest effect, there is some rationale for the use of omega-3 fatty acids in ASD, and they are easy to use, inexpensive, and safe.

Cerebral Folate Deficiency

A high prevalence (75%) of folate receptor-α autoantibodies (FRAs) is found in subjects with ASD. FRAs are autoantibodies that prevent folic acid from entering the brain. Improvement in ASD symptoms with high-dose folinic acid (2 mg/kg/day; maximum 50 mg/day in two divided doses) was found in a 12-week trial in children with ASD. There is the possibility that this treatment improves mitochondria function, specifically the ability of the mitochondria to be resilient against oxidative stress in this population (Frye, Sequeira, et al., 2013; Ramaekers, Quadros, & Sequeira, 2013). Although promising, this study needs to be replicated for FRAs to become routinely considered.

Vitamin Mineral Supplement

Although multivitamin and mineral levels generally are not found to be abnormal in children with ASD, biomarkers of general nutritional status have been reported to be associated with the severity of ASD (Adams et al., 2011b). An RCT of an oral vitamin/mineral supplement was given for 3 months to 141 children and adults with ASD and was found to improve the nutritional and metabolic status of children with ASD, including improvements in methylation, glutathione, oxidative stress, sulfation, ATP, NADH, and NADPH. The supplement group had significantly greater improvements compared to the placebo group on the Parental Global Impression–Revised Average Change, Hyperactivity, and Tantrumming scale (Adams et al., 2011a).

Diet

Inconsistencies between parent reports and the results of clinical trials are reported for a gluten-free casein-free (GFCF) diet in children with ASD, with no RCT showing benefit (Cheng et al., 2013). Several studies suggest a relationship between non-celiac gluten sensitivity (NCGS) and ASD (Catassi et al., 2013). Detailed metabolic screening in a Greek cohort of ASD patients revealed biomarkers (urine 3-hydroxyisovaleric acid and serum β-hydroxybutyrate) in 7% (13/187) of patients with ASD for whom biotin supplementation or institution of a ketogenic diet resulted in mild to significant clinical improvement in autistic features (Spilioti et al., 2013). The Specific Carbohydrate Diet has been anecdotally shown to improve symptoms of ASD, and an RCT is underway (Autism Network for Dietary Intervention, 2014; Catassi et al., 2013; Cheng et al., 2013; Spilioti et al., 2013).

Other Vitamin and Mineral Treatments

A number of other vitamin and mineral treatments are thought by some to benefit ASD, but studies have been inconclusive or limited. These include B_6/magnesium, folic acid, iron, L-carnosine, ascorbic acid, zinc and copper, and inositol. Further discussion of these potential treatments can be found in more extensive reviews (Cheng et al., 2013; Lofthouse et al., 2012).

Microbiome

The human microbiome (or human microbiota) is the aggregate of the ecological community of commensal, symbiotic, and pathogenic microorganisms that reside on the surface and in deep layers of skin, in saliva and oral mucosa, in conjunctiva, and in the gastrointestinal (GI) tract. They include bacteria, fungi, and archaea. Some of these organisms perform tasks that are useful for the human host, but their functions are poorly understood.

Probiotics

Probiotics (consisting of microorganisms thought to improve digestive health by repopulating the GI tract with favorable flora) have also been proposed to improve digestion and gut–brain activity in children with ASD. Some proponents suggest that these agents may also help remove toxins and improve immune function (Critchfield, Van Hemert, Ash, Mulder, & Ashwood, 2011). A recent study, using the maternal immune activation (MIA) mouse model that displays features of ASD, demonstrated GI barrier defects and microbiota alterations. Oral treatment of MIA offspring with the human commensal *Bacteroides fragilis* (a probiotic) corrected gut permeability; altered microbial composition; and ameliorated defects in communicative, stereotypic, anxiety-like, and sensorimotor behaviors. This supports a gut–microbiome–brain connection in a mouse model of ASD and identifies a potential probiotic therapy for GI and particular behavioral symptoms (Hsiao et al., 2013). There are no reported trials of probiotics in persons with ASD, but use is common and safe.

Pancreatic Digestive Enzymes

Enzyme deficiencies in some children with ASD result in an inability to digest protein (Williams et al., 2011), which affects the production of amino acids, essential for brain function, and suggests a target for treatment (de Theije et al., 2011). This finding suggests a possible benefit from a comprehensive digestive enzyme supplement with meals to aid digestion of all proteins and peptides, especially for children with ASD who have GI disturbance.

A commercially developed product (CM-AT by Curemark) has been specifically developed to target enzyme deficiencies that affect the availability of amino acids in children with ASD, and a multisite clinical trial has been completed. Fecal chymotrypsin was used as a biomarker for study entry. Curemark notes that it has reached its targeted enrollment for a phase III study of a total of 170 children with ASD at 18 sites (Curemark, 2014). The results from the Curemark study are currently unpublished, and the U.S. Food and Drug Administration is reviewing the findings (ClinicalTrials.gov, 2009 April 13—Identifier: NCT00881452; 2009 June 2—Identifier NCT00912691).

Oxytocin

Genetic studies have shown that some patients with ASD have decreased expression in the gene that controls expression of the oxytocin receptor (Gregory et al., 2009). One RCT crossover study of intranasal oxytocin in 16 male participants with ASD, aged 12–19 years, found improvement in the ability to recognize others' emotions (Guastella et al., 2010). Long-term administration (7 months) of intranasal oxytocin was found to be a safe and promising therapy for early adolescents with ASD. Six of the 8 participants showed improved scores on Autism Diagnostic Observation Schedule communication and social interaction scores (Tachibana et al., 2013). All dose levels tested, including a 0.4 IU/kg/dose, were well tolerated over 12 weeks, and several measures of social cognition/function, repetitive behaviors, and anxiety improved (Anagnostou et al., 2014; Gregory et al., 2009; Guastella et al., 2010; Tachibana et al., 2013).

Immune Therapies

Evidence is accumulating that there are subgroups of patients with ASD who have immune deficiencies and signs of autoimmunity, such as atopy (Goines & Van de Water, 2010). Various approaches have been tried to boost immune function or block autoimmunity. One of the most obvious candidates has been intravenous immunoglobulin (IVIG) treatment, and there are now six published open-label trials of IVIG treatment in ASD.

In one open-label study, IVIG treatment improved eye contact, speech, behavior, echolalia, and other autistic features (Gupta, 1999). Others have claimed that IVIG treatment led to improvements in GI signs and symptoms, as well as behavior. Subsequent studies have shown questionable benefits and mixed results for language and behavior.

IVIG is a biomedical treatment whose overall results have been limited; it carries some significant risks. Other immune-boosting therapies may be of benefit but have not been adequately studied. For future studies, it is unclear if an underlying immunologic dysfunction is present in all individuals with ASD or if treatment trials should target the patients with demonstrable inflammatory/immune changes.

Prescribed Medications

A number of off-label uses of approved medications have demonstrated at least theoretical benefit for symptoms of ASD, but results have been limited by sample size and other factors. These include propranolol (Narayanan et al., 2010; Zamzow et al., 2014), amantadine (King et al., 2001), D-cycloserine (Posey et al., 2004), cholinesterase inhibitors (Chez, Aimonovitch, Buchanan, Mrazek, & Tremb, 2004), nicotinic agonists (Deutsch, Urbano, Neumann, Burket, & Katz, 2010), naltrexone (Brown & Panksepp, 2009), buspirone (Buitelaar, Van Der Gaag, & Van Der Hoeven, 1998), risperidone plus memantine (Ghaleiha et al., 2013), and amitriptyline (Bhatti et al., 2013).

Although memantine was thought to be of potential benefit for symptoms of ASD based on open-label studies (Chez et al., 2007) and a plausible theoretical foundation that aberrant functioning of N-methyl-D-aspartate (NMDA) receptors and/or altered glutamate may play a role in ASD, a recent multisite RCT did not show separation of active drug from placebo (Hendren, 2014). A high placebo response rate limited the ability of memantine to demonstrate significant benefit, but the longer term extension study and blinded taper-off of the drug also did not demonstrate separation from placebo (Hendren et al., 2014).

Mind and Body Practices

Mind and body practices include a large and diverse group of procedures or techniques administered or taught by a trained practitioner or teacher. These include acupuncture, massage therapy, meditation, movement therapies, music therapy, relaxation techniques, spinal manipulation, cranial manipulation, tai chi and qi gong, yoga, neurofeedback, and animal-assisted therapy (AAT). Acupuncture (Cheuk, Wong, & Chen, 2011), exercise, music therapy, and AAT have adequate evidence to warrant further RCTs (Lofthouse et al., 2012).

SUMMARY

Some CAM/biomedical therapies have a place in an integrated approach to the treatment of ASD. A first priority is the medical evaluation that includes the assessment of genetic, neurologic, GI, and other medical symptoms. Speech, language, and occupational therapy are an essential part of most treatment programs. Behavioral treatments have the most evidence for efficacy and should be part of all treatment plans. Associated symptoms causing significant distress might be treated with more traditional psychopharmacology. In addition to these, biomedical assessments and treatments should be considered even if only to help understand the family's point of view and desires and to help provide an informed plan of action. Based on the literature and safety profiles, it is reasonable to consider melatonin, omega-3 fatty acids, vitamin D_3, probiotics, and digestive enzymes as potential treatments for ASD (Hendren, 2013). As interest, expertise, and the scientific literature grows, consideration might be given to methyl B_{12}, folinic acid, magnesium, pycnogenol, zinc–copper, L-carnitine, coenzyme Q10, oxytocin nasal spray, naltrexone, and inositol.

CASE STUDY #1: "ERIC"

Eric is a 5-year-old boy with moderately impairing symptoms of ASD who is receiving applied behavioral analysis treatment at preschool and home and speech and language therapy at school. He has no significant behavioral problems, but he does not initiate social interaction with other children, is mildly anxious on occasion but does not "melt down," and is making slow but steady progress in his treatment programs. However, Eric has difficulty falling asleep at night, and his parents consult you to consider what they can do about his sleeping patterns and to determine if there are any medications that might help him with chronic constipation and to help him progress faster in treatment. You suggest the family consider a trial of melatonin starting at 2 or 3 mg and increasing up to 9 or 10 mg if needed, 30–60 minutes before his bedtime for his initial insomnia. You also suggest adding 1 g of omega-3 fatty acids per day and, considering the addition of a high-potency multiple vitamin, and probiotics two or three times a day. You state that there are no conventional medications with an indication for the social impairment experienced by Eric at this time, but there are several undergoing clinical trials that may be helpful in the future. If the melatonin is not successful, there are several conventional medications, with some side effects such as daytime sedation and weight gain, that can be considered if necessary for his sleep.

KEY POINTS

- The National Center for Complementary and Alternative Medicine refers to CAM as an array of healthcare approaches with a history of use or origins outside of mainstream medicine.
- Families commonly seek alternative and complementary biomedical treatments for their children with ASD.
- A rationale for CAM/biomedical treatments for ASD is their potentially beneficial effect on epigenetic processes, which are increasingly demonstrated to be part of the gene–environment interactions that underlie the development of ASD.
- Three agents with a rationale for use with ASD, and at least one RCT showing efficacy and safety data, are melatonin, omega-3 fatty acids, and micronutrients.
- Additional agents with promise include NAC, methyl B_{12}, and digestive enzymes.

DISCLOSURE STATEMENT

Dr. Robert L. Hendren has received research grants from Forest Pharmaceuticals, Inc., Curemark, BioMarin Pharmaceutical, Roche, Shire, Autism Speaks, Sunovion, and the

Vitamin D Council. He is on advisory boards for Curemark, BioMarin, Forest, Coronado Biosciences, and Janssen. He is on no speakers bureaus.

REFERENCES

Adams, J. B., Audhya, T., McDonough-Means, S., Rubin, R. A., Quig, D., Geis, E., . . . Lee, W. (2011a). Effect of a vitamin/mineral supplement on children and adults with autism. *BMC Pediatrics, 11,* 111. doi:10.1186/1471-2431-11-111

Adams, J. B., Audhya, T., McDonough-Means, S., Rubin, R. A., Quig, D., Geis, E., . . . Lee, W. (2011b). Nutritional and metabolic status of children with autism vs. neurotypical children, and the association with autism severity. *Nutrition & Metabolism, 8,* 34. doi:10.1186/1743-7075-8-34 1743-7075-8-34 [pii]

Amminger, G. P., Berger, G. E., Schafer, M. R., Klier, C., Friedrich, M. H., & Feucht, M. (2007). Omega-3 fatty acids supplementation in children with autism: A double-blind randomized, placebo-controlled pilot study. *Biological Psychiatry, 61,* 551–553. doi:10.1016/j.biopsych.2006.05.007

Anagnostou, E., Soorya, L., Brian, J., Dupuis, A., Mankad, D., Smile, S., & Jacob, S. (2014). Intranasal oxytocin in the treatment of autism spectrum disorders: A review of literature and early safety and efficacy data in youth. *Brain Research, 1580,* 180–198. doi:S0006-8993(14)00134-6 [pii] 10.1016/j.brainres.2014.01.049

Asadabadi, M., Mohammadi, M. R., Ghanizadeh, A., Modabbernia, A., Ashrafi, M., Hassanzadeh, E., . . . Akhondzadeh, S. (2013). Celecoxib as adjunctive treatment to risperidone in children with autistic disorder: A randomized, double-blind, placebo-controlled trial. *Psychopharmacology, 225,* 51–59. doi:10.1007/s00213-012-2796-8

Autism Network for Dietary Intervention. (2014). *The Specific Carbohydrate Diet (SCD)* [Online]. Retrieved from http://www.autismndi.com/news/advanced-dietary-interventions/the-specific-carbohydrate-d iet-scd.html#.VdoHbX2qvcs accessed June 9, 2014.

Bell, J. G., MacKinlay, E. E., Dick, J. R., MacDonald, D. J., Boyle, R. M., & Glen, A. C. (2004). Essential fatty acids and phospholipase A2 in autistic spectrum disorders. *Prostaglandins, Leukotrienes, and Essential Fatty Acids, 71,* 201–204. doi:10.1016/j.plefa.2004.03.008

Bell, J. G., Miller, D., MacDonald, D. J., MacKinlay, E. E., Dick, J. R., Cheseldine, S., . . . O'Hare, A. E. (2010). The fatty acid compositions of erythrocyte and plasma polar lipids in children with autism, developmental delay or typically developing controls and the effect of fish oil intake. *British Journal of Nutrition, 103,* 1160–1167. doi:10.1017/S0007114509992881

Bent, S., Bertoglio, K., Ashwood, P., Bostrom, A., & Hendren, R. L. (2011). A pilot randomized controlled trial of omega-3 fatty acids for autism spectrum disorder. *Journal of Autism and Developmental Disorders, 41,* 545–554. doi:10.1007/s10803-010-1078-8

Bent, S., Bertoglio, K., Ashwood, P., Nemeth, E., & Hendren, R. L. (2012). Brief report: Hyperbaric oxygen therapy (HBOT) in children with autism spectrum disorder: A clinical trial. *Journal of Autism and Developmental Disorders, 42,* 1127–1132. doi:10.1007/s10803-011-1337-3

Bent, S., Bertoglio, K., & Hendren, R. L. (2009). Omega-3 fatty acids for autistic spectrum disorder: A systematic review. *Journal of Autism and Developmental Disorders, 39,* 1145–1154. doi:10.1007/s10803-009-0724-5

Bent, S., & Hendren, R. L. (2010). Improving the prediction of response to therapy in autism. *Neurotherapeutics 7,* 232–240. doi:10.1016/j.nurt.2010.05.011

Bent, S., Hendren, R. L., Zandi, T., Law, K., Choi, J. E., Widjaja, F., . . . Law, P. (2014). Internet-based, randomized, controlled trial of omega-3 Fatty acids for hyperactivity in autism. *Journal of the American Academy of Child and Adolescent Psychiatry, 53,* 658–666. doi:10.1016/j.jaac.2014.01.018 S0890-8567(14)00162-2 [pii]

Bertoglio, K., James, S. J., Deprey, L., Brule, N., & Hendren, R. L. (2010). Pilot study of the effect of methyl B12 treatment on behavioral and biomarker measures in children with autism. *Journal of Alternative and Complementary Medicine, 16,* 555–560. doi:10.1089/acm.2009.0177

Bhatti, I., Thome, A., Smith, P. O., Cook-Wiens, G., Yeh, H. W., Gaffney, G. R., & Hellings, J. A. (2013). A retrospective study of amitriptyline in youth with autism spectrum disorders. *Journal of Autism and Developmental Disorders, 43,* 1017–1027. doi:10.1007/s10803-012-1647-0

Birdee, G. S., Phillips, R. S., Davis, R. B., & Gardiner, P. (2010). Factors associated with pediatric use of complementary and alternative medicine. *Pediatrics, 125*, 249–256. doi:10.1542/peds.2009-1406

Brown, N., & Panksepp, J. (2009). Low-dose naltrexone for disease prevention and quality of life. *Medical Hypotheses, 72*, 333–337. doi:10.1016/j.mehy.2008.06.048

Buitelaar, J. K., Van Der Gaag, R. J., & Van Der Hoeven, J. (1998). Buspirone in the management of anxiety and irritability in children with pervasive developmental disorders: Results of an open-label study. *Journal of Clinical Psychiatry, 59*, 56–59.

Cannell, J. J. (2013). Autism: Will vitamin D treat core symptoms? *Medical Hypotheses, 81*, 195–198. doi:10.1016/j.mehy.2013.05.004 S0306-9877(13)00233-8 [pii]

Catassi, C., Bai, J. C., Bonaz, B., Bouma, G., Calabro, A., Carroccio, A., . . . Fasano, A. (2013). Non-celiac gluten sensitivity: The new frontier of gluten related disorders. *Nutrients, 5*, 3839–3853. doi:10.3390/nu5103839 nu5103839 [pii]

Cheng, J., Widjaja, F., Choi, J., & Hendren, R. (2013). Considering biomedical/CAM treatments. *Adolescent Medicine, 24*, 446–464.

Cheuk, D. K., Wong, V., & Chen, W. X. (2011). Acupuncture for autism spectrum disorders (ASD). *Cochrane Database of Systematic Reviews*, CD007849. doi:10.1002/14651858.CD007849.pub2

Chez, M. G., Aimonovitch, M., Buchanan, T., Mrazek, S., & Tremb, R. J. (2004). Treating autistic spectrum disorders in children: Utility of the cholinesterase inhibitor rivastigmine tartrate. *Journal of Child Neurology, 19*, 165–169.

Chez, M. G., Burton, Q., Dowling, T., Chang, M., Khanna, P., & Kramer, C. (2007). Memantine as adjunctive therapy in children diagnosed with autistic spectrum disorders: An observation of initial clinical response and maintenance tolerability. *Journal of Child Neurology, 22*, 574–579. doi:10.1177/0883073807302611

Clinicaltrials.Gov. (2009, April 13–Identifier: NCT00881452). *A trial of CM-AT in children with autism* [Online]. Bethesda, MD: National Library of Medicine. Available at https://clinicaltrials.gov/ct2/show/NCT00881452?term=NCT00881452&rank=1; accessed June 9, 2014.

Clinicaltrials.Gov (2009, June 2–Identifier NCT00912691). *A trial of CM-AT in children with autism—Open label extension study* [Online]. Bethesda, MD: National Library of Medicine. Available at http://clinicaltrials.gov/ct2/show/NCT00912691?term=NCT00912691&rank=1; accessed June 9, 2014.

Critchfield, J. W., Van Hemert, S., Ash, M., Mulder, L., & Ashwood, P. (2011). The potential role of probiotics in the management of childhood autism spectrum disorders. *Gastroenterology Research & Practice, 2011*, 161358. doi:10.1155/2011/161358

Cunningham, C. L., Martinez-Cerdeno, V., & Noctor, S. C. (2013). Microglia regulate the number of neural precursor cells in the developing cerebral cortex. *Journal of Neuroscience, 33*, 4216–4233. doi:10.1523/JNEUROSCI.3441-12.2013

Curemark. (2014). *Curemark I novel approaches to the treatment of neurological diseases* [Online]. Available at http://curemark.com; accessed June 9, 2014.

Darvesh, A. S., Carroll, R. T., Bishayee, A., Novotny, N. A., Geldenhuys, W. J., & Van Der Schyf, C. J. (2012). Curcumin and neurodegenerative diseases: A perspective. *Expert Opinion on Investigational Drugs, 21*, 1123–1140. doi:10.1517/13543784.2012.693479

de Theije, C. G., Wu, J., Da Silva, S. L., Kamphuis, P. J., Garssen, J., Korte, S. M., & Kraneveld, A. D. (2011). Pathways underlying the gut-to-brain connection in autism spectrum disorders as future targets for disease management. *European Journal of Pharmacology, 668*(Suppl. 1), S70–S80. doi:10.1016/j.ejphar.2011.07.013 S0014-2999(11)00788-6 [pii]

Deutsch, S. I., Urbano, M. R., Neumann, S. A., Burket, J. A., & Katz, E. (2010). Cholinergic abnormalities in autism: Is there a rationale for selective nicotinic agonist interventions? *Clinical Neuropharmacology, 33*, 114–120. doi:10.1097/WNF.0b013e3181d6f7ad

Durkin, M. S., Maenner, M. J., Newschaffer, C. J., Lee, L. C., Cunniff, C. M., Daniels, J. L., . . . Schieve, L. A. (2008). Advanced parental age and the risk of autism spectrum disorder. *American Journal of Epidemiology, 168*, 1268–1276. doi:10.1093/aje/kwn250

Frans, E. M., Sandin, S., Reichenberg, A., Langstrom, N., Lichtenstein, P., McGrath, J. J., & Hultman, C. M. (2013). Autism risk across generations: A population-based study of advancing grandpaternal and paternal age. *JAMA Psychiatry, 70,* 516–521. doi:10.1001/jamapsychiatry.2013.1180

Freeman, M. P., Hibbeln, J. R., Wisner, K. L., Davis, J. M., Mischoulon, D., Peet, M., . . . Stoll, A. L. (2006). Omega-3 fatty acids: Evidence basis for treatment and future research in psychiatry. *Journal of Clinical Psychiatry, 67,* 1954–1967.

Frye, R., & Rossignol, D. (2014). Treatments for biomedical abnormalities associated with autism spectrum disorder. *Frontiers in Pediatrics, 2,* 66.

Frye, R. E., Delatorre, R., Taylor, H. B., Slattery, J., Melnyk, S., Chowdhury, N., & James, S. J. (2013). Metabolic effects of sapropterin treatment in autism spectrum disorder: A preliminary study. *Translational Psychiatry, 3,* e237. doi:10.1038/tp.2013.14 tp201314 [pii]

Frye, R. E., & Rossignol, D. A. (2011). Mitochondrial dysfunction can connect the diverse medical symptoms associated with autism spectrum disorders. *Pediatric Research, 69,* 41R–47R. doi:10.1203/PDR.0b013e318212f16b

Frye, R. E., Sequeira, J. M., Quadros, E. V., James, S. J., & Rossignol, D. A. (2013). Cerebral folate receptor autoantibodies in autism spectrum disorder. *Molecular Psychiatry, 18,* 369–381. doi:10.1038/mp.2011.175

Ghaleiha, A., Asadabadi, M., Mohammadi, M. R., Shahei, M., Tabrizi, M., Hajiaghaee, R., . . . Akhondzadeh, S. (2013). Memantine as adjunctive treatment to risperidone in children with autistic disorder: A randomized, double-blind, placebo-controlled trial. *International Journal of Neuropsychopharmacology, 16,* 783–789. doi:10.1017/S1461145712000880

Ghanizadeh, A. (2012). Hyperbaric oxygen therapy for treatment of children with autism: A systematic review of randomized trials. *Medical Gas Research, 2,* 13. doi:10.1186/2045-9912-2-13 2045-9912-2-13 [pii]

Goines, P., & Van de Water, J. (2010). The immune system's role in the biology of autism. *Current Opinion in Neurology, 23,* 111–117. doi:10.1097/WCO.0b013e3283373514

Goldani, A. S., Downs, S., Widjaja, F., Lawton, B., & Hendren, R. (2015). Biomarkers in autism. *Front Psychiatry, 5,* 100. doi:10.3389/fpsyt.2014.00100. eCollection 2014.

Granpeesheh, D., Tarbox, J., Dixon, D. R., Wilke, A. E., Allen, M. S., & Bradstreet, J. J. (2010). Randomized trial of hyperbaric oxygen therapy for children with autism. *Research in Autism Spectrum Disorders, 4,* 268–275.

Gregory, S. G., Connelly, J. J., Towers, A. J., Johnson, J., Biscocho, D., Markunas, C. A., . . . Pericak-Vance, M. A. (2009). Genomic and epigenetic evidence for oxytocin receptor deficiency in autism. *BMC Medicine, 7,* 62. doi:10.1186/1741-7015-7-62

Guastella, A. J., Einfeld, S. L., Gray, K. M., Rinehart, N. J., Tonge, B. J., Lambert, T. J., & Hickie, I. B. (2010). Intranasal oxytocin improves emotion recognition for youth with autism spectrum disorders. *Biological Psychiatry, 67,* 692–694. doi:10.1016/j.biopsych.2009.09.020

Gupta, S. (1999). Treatment of children with autism with intravenous immunoglobulin. *Journal of Child Neurology, 14,* 203–205.

Hadjikhani, N., Zurcher, N. R., Rogier, O., Ruest, T., Hippolyte, L., Ben-Ari, Y., & Lemonnier, E. (2015). Improving emotional face perception in autism with diuretic bumetanide: A proof-of-concept behavioral and functional brain imaging pilot study. *Autism, 19*(2), 149–157. doi:1362361313514141 [pii] 10.1177/1362361313514141

Hagerman, R., & Hendren, R. (Eds.). (2014). *Treatment of neurodevelopmental disorders: Targeting neurobiologic mechanisms.* New York: Oxford University Press.

Hallmayer, J., Cleveland, S., Torres, A., Phillips, J., Cohen, B., Torigoe, T., . . . Risch, N. (2011). Genetic heritability and shared environmental factors among twin pairs with autism. *Archives of General Psychiatry, 68,* 1095–1102. doi:10.1001/archgenpsychiatry.2011.76

Hanson, E., Kalish, L. A., Bunce, E., Curtis, C., McDaniel, S., Ware, J., & Petry, J. (2007). Use of complementary and alternative medicine among children diagnosed with autism spectrum disorder. *Journal of Autism and Developmental Disorders, 37,* 628–636. doi:10.1007/s10803-006-0192-0

Hardan, A. Y., Fung, L. K., Libove, R. A., Obukhanych, T. V., Nair, S., Herzenberg, L. A., . . . Tirouvanziam, R. (2012). A randomized controlled pilot trial of oral N-acetylcysteine in children with autism. *Biological Psychiatry, 71,* 956–961. PMID:22342106. doi:10.1016/j.biopsych.2012.01.014

Harony, H., & Wagner, S. (2010). The contribution of oxytocin and vasopressin to mammalian social behavior: Potential role in autism spectrum disorder. *Neuro-Signals, 18,* 82–97. doi:10.1159/000321035.

Hendren, R. (2013). Autism: Biomedical complementary treatment approaches. *Child and Adolescent Psychiatric Clinics of North America, 22,* 443–456.

Hendren, R., James, J., Widjaja, F., Lawton, B., Rosenblatt, A., & Bent, S. (2015). A randomized, placebo-controlled trial of methyl B12 for children with autism. Submitted for publication.

Hendren, R., Melmed, R., Findling, R., Hardan, A., Aman, M., Katz, E., . . . Graham, S. (2014). Memantine in children with autism: Results from a two-part, open-label/double-blind randomized, placebo-controlled trial and an open-label extension. Presented at the 167th annual meeting of the American Psychiatric Association, New York, NY.

Hendren, R. L. (2014). Poster Session 6: Memantine in children with autism: Results from a two-part, open-label/double-blind randomized, placebo-controlled trial and an open-label extension. Presented at the 167th annual meeting of the American Psychiatric Association, New York, NY.

Herbert, M. R. (2010). Contributions of the environment and environmentally vulnerable physiology to autism spectrum disorders. *Current Opinion in Neurology, 23,* 103–110. doi:10.1097/WCO.0b013e328336a01f

Hsiao, E. Y., McBride, S. W., Hsien, S., Sharon, G., Hyde, E. R., McCue, T., . . . Mazmanian, S. K. (2013). Microbiota modulate behavioral and physiological abnormalities associated with neurodevelopmental disorders. *Cell, 155,* 1451–1463. doi:10.1016/j.cell.2013.11.024 S0092-8674(13)01473-6 [pii]

Insel, T. R. (2014). The NIMH Research Domain Criteria (RDoC) Project: Precision medicine for psychiatry. *American Journal of Psychiatry, 171,* 395–397. doi:10.1176/appi.ajp.2014.14020138 1853442 [pii]

Iossifov, I., Ronemus, M., Levy, D., Wang, Z., Hakker, I., Rosenbaum, J., . . . Wigler, M. (2012). De novo gene disruptions in children on the autistic spectrum. *Neuron, 74,* 285–299. doi:10.1016/j.neuron.2012.04.009

Jaenisch, R., & Bird, A. (2003). Epigenetic regulation of gene expression: How the genome integrates intrinsic and environmental signals. *Nature Genetics, 33*(Suppl.), 245–254. doi:10.1038/ng1089

James, S. J., Cutler, P., Melnyk, S., Jernigan, S., Janak, L., Gaylor, D. W., & Neubrander, J. A. (2004). Metabolic biomarkers of increased oxidative stress and impaired methylation capacity in children with autism. *American Journal of Clinical Nutrition, 80,* 1611–1617.

James, S. J., Melnyk, S., Fuchs, G., Reid, T., Jernigan, S., Pavliv, O., . . . Gaylor, D. W. (2009). Efficacy of methylcobalamin and folinic acid treatment on glutathione redox status in children with autism. *American Journal of Clinical Nutrition, 89,* 425–430. doi:10.3945/ajcn.2008.26615

Jepson, B., Granpeesheh, D., Tarbox, J., Olive, M. L., Stott, C., Braud, S., . . . Allen, M. S. (2011). Controlled evaluation of the effects of hyperbaric oxygen therapy on the behavior of 16 children with autism spectrum disorders. *Journal of Autism and Developmental Disorders, 41,* 575–588. doi:10.1007/s10803-010-1075-y

Johnson, C. R., Handen, B. L., Zimmer, M., & Sacco, K. (2010). Polyunsaturated fatty acid supplementation in young children with autism. *Journal of Developmental and Physical Disabilities, 22,* 1–10.

Kern, J. K., Geier, D. A., Adams, J. B., Garver, C. R., Audhya, T., & Geier, M. R. (2011). A clinical trial of glutathione supplementation in autism spectrum disorders. *Medical Science Monitor, 17,* CR677–CR682. doi:882125 [pii]

King, B. H., Wright, D. M., Handen, B. L., Sikich, L., Zimmerman, A. W., McMahon, W., . . . Cook, E.H., Jr. (2001). Double-blind, placebo-controlled study of amantadine hydrochloride in the treatment of children with autistic disorder. *Journal of the American Academy of Child and Adolescent Psychiatry, 40,* 658–665. doi:10.1097/00004583-200106000-00010

Krakowiak, P., Walker, C. K., Bremer, A. A., Baker, A. S., Ozonoff, S., Hansen, R. L., & Hertz-Picciotto, I. (2012). Maternal metabolic conditions and risk for autism and other neurodevelopmental disorders. *Pediatrics, 129,* e1121–e1128. doi:10.1542/peds.2011-2583

Landrigan, P. J. (2010). What causes autism? Exploring the environmental contribution. *Current Opinion in Pediatrics, 22,* 219–225. doi:10.1097/MOP.0b013e328336eb9a

Levy, D., Ronemus, M., Yamrom, B., Lee, Y. H., Leotta, A., Kendall, J., ... Wigler, M. (2011). Rare de novo and transmitted copy-number variation in autistic spectrum disorders. *Neuron, 70,* 886–897. doi:10.1016/j. neuron.2011.05.015 S0896-6273(11)00396-5 [pii]

Lofthouse, N., Hendren, R., Hurt, E., Arnold, L. E., & Butter, E. (2012). A review of complementary and alternative treatments for autism spectrum disorders. *Autism Research and Treatment, 2012,* 870391. doi:10.1155/2012/870391

Manji, H., Kato, T., Di Prospero, N. A., Ness, S., Beal, M. F., Krams, M., & Chen, G. (2012). Impaired mitochondrial function in psychiatric disorders. *Nature Reviews Neuroscience, 13,* 293–307. doi:10.1038/nrn3229

McGrath, J., Feron, F., Eyles, D., & Mackay-Sim, A. (2001). Vitamin D: The neglected neurosteroid? *Trends in Neurosciences, 24,* 570–572. doi:S0166-2236(00)01949-4 [pii]

Meguid, N. A., Atta, H. M., Gouda, A. S., & Khalil, R. O. (2008). Role of polyunsaturated fatty acids in the management of Egyptian children with autism. *Clinical Biochemistry, 41,* 1044–1048. doi:10.1016/j. clinbiochem.2008.05.013.

Meiri, G., Bichovsky, Y., & Belmaker, R. H. (2009). Omega 3 fatty acid treatment in autism. *Journal of Child and Adolescent Psychopharmacology, 19,* 449–451. doi:10.1089/cap.2008.0123

Miles, J. H. (2011). Autism spectrum disorders—A genetics review. *Genetics in Medicine, 13,* 278–294. doi:10.1097/GIM.0b013e3181ff67ba

Mumper, E. (2012). A call for action: Recognizing and treating medical problems of children with autism. *North American Journal of Medicine and Science, 5*(3), 180–184.

Murdoch, J. D., & State, M. W. (2013). Recent developments in the genetics of autism spectrum disorders. *Current Opinion in Genetics & Development, 23,* 310–315. doi:10.1016/j.gde.2013.02.003

Narayanan, A., White, C. A., Saklayen, S., Scaduto, M. J., Carpenter, A. L., Abduljalil, A., ... Beversdorf, D. Q. (2010). Effect of propranolol on functional connectivity in autism spectrum disorder—A pilot study. *Brain Imaging and Behavior, 4,* 189–197. doi:10.1007/s11682-010-9098-8

National Center for Complementary and Alternative Medicine. (2008). *Complementary, alternative, or integrative health: What's in a name?* [Online]. Available at https://nccam.nih.gov/health/whatiscam; accessed June 9, 2014.

Neale, B. M., Kou, Y., Liu, L., Ma'ayan, A., Samocha, K. E., Sabo, A., ... Daly, M. J. (2012). Patterns and rates of exonic de novo mutations in autism spectrum disorders. *Nature, 485,* 242–245. doi:10.1038/ nature11011 nature11011 [pii]

Nicolson, R., Craven-Thuss, B., & Smith, J. (2006). A prospective, open-label trial of galantamine in autistic disorder. *Journal of Child and Adolescent Psychopharmacology, 16,* 621–629. doi:10.1089/cap.2006.16.621

Patrick, R. P., & Ames, B. N. (2014). Vitamin D hormone regulates serotonin synthesis. Part 1: Relevance for autism. *FASEB Journal, 28*(6), 2398–2413. doi:10.1096/fj.13-246546

Posey, D. J., Kem, D. L., Swiezy, N. B., Sweeten, T. L., Wiegand, R. E., & McDougle, C. J. (2004). A pilot study of d-cycloserine in subjects with autistic disorder. *American Journal of Psychiatry, 161,* 2115–2117. doi:10.1176/appi.ajp.161.11.2115

Ramaekers, V. T., Quadros, E. V., & Sequeira, J. M. (2013). Role of folate receptor autoantibodies in infantile autism. *Molecular Psychiatry, 18,* 270–271. doi:10.1038/mp.2012.22 mp201222 [pii]

Rossignol, D. A., & Frye, R. E. (2011). Melatonin in autism spectrum disorders: A systematic review and meta-analysis. *Developmental Medicine and Child Neurology, 53,* 783–792. doi:10.1111/ j.1469-8749.2011.03980.x

Rossignol, D. A., & Frye, R. E. (2012). A review of research trends in physiological abnormalities in autism spectrum disorders: Immune dysregulation, inflammation, oxidative stress, mitochondrial dysfunction and environmental toxicant exposures. *Molecular Psychiatry, 17,* 389–401. doi:10.1038/mp.2011.165

Rossignol, D. A., Genuis, S. J., & Frye, R. E. (2014). Environmental toxicants and autism spectrum disorders: A systematic review. *Translational Psychiatry, 4,* e360. doi:10.1038/tp.2014.4.

Rubenstein, J. L. (2010). Three hypotheses for developmental defects that may underlie some forms of autism spectrum disorder. *Current Opinion in Neurology, 23,* 118–123. doi:10.1097/WCO.0b013e328336eb13

Rutten, B. P., & Mill, J. (2009). Epigenetic mediation of environmental influences in major psychotic disorders. *Schizophrenia Bulletin, 35,* 1045–1056. doi:10.1093/schbul/sbp104

Sandin, S., Lichtenstein, P., Kuja-Halkola, R., Larsson, H., Hultman, C. M., & Reichenberg, A. (2014). The familial risk of autism. *JAMA*, *311*, 1770–1777. doi:10.1001/jama.2014.4144 1866100 [pii].

Saresella, M., Marventano, I., Guerini, F. R., Mancuso, R., Ceresa, L., Zanzottera, M., . . . Clerici, M. (2009). An autistic endophenotype results in complex immune dysfunction in healthy siblings of autistic children. *Biological Psychiatry*, *66*, 978–984. doi:10.1016/j.biopsych.2009.06.020

Schuler, K. (2013). *Autism: What do environment and diet have to do with it?* [Online]. Available at http://www.iatp.org/documents/autism-what-do-environment-and-diet-have-to-do-with-it. Accessed 8/2/15.

Shelton, J. F., Tancredi, D. J., & Hertz-Picciotto, I. (2010). Independent and dependent contributions of advanced maternal and paternal ages to autism risk. *Autism Research*, *3*, 30–39. doi:10.1002/aur.116

Spilioti, M., Evangeliou, A. E., Tramma, D., Theodoridou, Z., Metaxas, S., Michailidi, E., . . . Gibson, K. M. (2013). Evidence for treatable inborn errors of metabolism in a cohort of 187 Greek patients with autism spectrum disorder (ASD). *Frontiers in Human Neuroscience*, *7*, 858. doi:10.3389/fnhum.2013.00858

Suren, P., Roth, C., Bresnahan, M., Haugen, M., Hornig, M., Hirtz, D., . . . Stoltenberg, C. (2013). Association between maternal use of folic acid supplements and risk of autism spectrum disorders in children. *JAMA*, *309*, 570–577. doi:10.1001/jama.2012.155925 1570279 [pii]

Tachibana, M., Kagitani-Shimono, K., Mohri, I., Yamamoto, T., Sanefuji, W., Nakamura, A., . . . Taniike, M. (2013). Long-term administration of intranasal oxytocin is a safe and promising therapy for early adolescent boys with autism spectrum disorders. *Journal of Child and Adolescent Psychopharmacology*, *23*, 123–127. doi:10.1089/cap.2012.0048

Tordjman, S., Najjar, I., Bellissant, E., Anderson, G. M., Barburoth, M., Cohen, D., . . . Vernay-Leconte, J. (2013). Advances in the research of melatonin in autism spectrum disorders: Literature review and new perspectives. *International Journal of Molecular Sciences*, *14*, 20508–20542. doi:10.3390/ijms141020508 ijms141020508 [pii]

Vancassel, S., Durand, G., Barthelemy, C., Lejeune, B., Martineau, J., Guilloteau, D., . . . Chalon, S. (2001). Plasma fatty acid levels in autistic children. *Prostaglandins, Leukotrienes, and Essential Fatty Acids*, *65*, 1–7. doi:10.1054/plef.2001.0281

Wang, P., Erickson, C. A., Ginsberg, L, Rathmell, B., Cherubini, M., Zarevics, P., & King, B. (2011). *Effects of STX209 (arbaclofen) on social and communicative function in ASD: Results of an 8-week open-label trial* (Abstract 8281). Presented at the International Meeting for Autism Research, May 14, 2011, San Diego, CA.

Williams, B. L., Hornig, M., Buie, T., Bauman, M. L., Cho Paik, M., Wick, I., . . . Lipkin, W. I. (2011). Impaired carbohydrate digestion and transport and mucosal dysbiosis in the intestines of children with autism and gastrointestinal disturbances. *PLoS One*, *6*, e24585. doi:10.1371/journal.pone.0024585 PONE-D-11-08639 [pii]

Wink, L. K., Erickson, C. A., Stigler, K. A., & McDougle, C. J. (2011). Riluzole in autistic disorder. *Journal of Child and Adolescent Psychopharmacology*, *21*, 375–379. doi:10.1089/cap.2010.0154

Wong, H. H., & Smith, R. G. (2006). Patterns of complementary and alternative medical therapy use in children diagnosed with autism spectrum disorders. *Journal of Autism and Developmental Disorders*, *36*, 901–909. doi:10.1007/s10803-006-0131-0

Zamzow, R. M., Christ, S. E., Saklayen, S. S., Moffitt, A. J., Bodner, K. E., Higgins, K. F., & Beversdorf, D. Q. (2014). Effect of propranolol on facial scanning in autism spectrum disorder: A preliminary investigation. *Journal of Clinical and Experimental Neuropsychology*, *36*, 431–445. doi:10.1080/13803395.2014.904844

Zerbo, O., Iosif, A. M., Walker, C., Ozonoff, S., Hansen, R. L., & Hertz-Picciotto, I. (2013). Is maternal influenza or fever during pregnancy associated with autism or developmental delays? Results from the CHARGE (CHildhood Autism Risks from Genetics and Environment) study. *Journal of Autism and Developmental Disorders*, *43*, 25–33. doi:10.1007/s10803-012-1540-x

18

SPEECH AND LANGUAGE ASSESSMENT AND TREATMENT FOR AUTISM SPECTRUM DISORDER

KATELYN A. BRUNO, KRISTINA L. GULATI, AND MARIA MODY

INTRODUCTION

Autism spectrum disorder (ASD) comprises a wide array of symptoms and levels of impairment that negatively impact communication. Individuals with the disorder can range from being verbal to minimally verbal or nonverbal. The recent increase in prevalence rates of autism (1:68; Centers for Disease Control and Prevention, 2014) has led to an increase in the number of children with ASD on the caseload of speech–language pathologists (SLPs). As a specialist in the treatment of communication disorders, the SLP is an important member of the care team of the individual with ASD, which may include pediatricians, neurologists, psychiatrists, occupational therapists, behavioral therapists, neuropsychologists, teachers, social workers, and parents—all of whom contribute to treatment decisions.

The complex nature of ASD and the wide range of associated symptoms make it challenging to evaluate for the SLP. In addition, the role of the SLP in the treatment of the disorder has greatly expanded throughout the years with rapid developments in alternative and augmentative communication (AAC), a popular intervention tool used with individuals on the spectrum. As the terms implies, AAC refers to a set of procedures and strategies by which an individual's receptive and expressive language skills can be maximized for functional and effective communication. It entails supplementing or replacing natural speech and/or writing with aided symbols (i.e., involving the use of additional equipment) and/or unaided symbols (ASHA, 2002). Regardless of whether the approach is traditional speech–language therapy or involves AAC, it is critical to start intervention early—before 3 years of age or immediately following diagnosis—because it impacts communication outcomes in later years (Rutter, Mahwood, & Howlin, 1992).

CORE DEFICITS IN SPEECH AND LANGUAGE IN ASD

As mentioned previously, individuals with ASD have a wide range of speech and language deficits of varying severity. Most notable are their deficits in social communication and their struggles from early on with intentional communication (Paul, 2007). Here, the core speech and language deficits in ASD are summarized under the broad headings of receptive and expressive language.

Receptive Language

Receptive language refers to the comprehension of spoken language. It is known to develop at a quicker pace than expressive language during the early years of normal language acquisition (Hudry et al., 2010). Although children on the autism spectrum also start out understanding more words than they are able to produce, the gap between what they understand and what they say does not close. In contrast, this receptive–expressive gap reduces significantly in typically developing children as they start producing more words (Flusberg, Paul, & Lord, 2005). Furthermore, unlike other neurodevelopmental disorders involving language, children with ASD have a significantly greater receptive language deficit, resulting in substantially reduced development of receptive over expressive ability (Rutter et al., 1992).

Difficulties with spoken language comprehension are evident in nonverbal as well as higher functioning individuals with ASD, although as one can expect, it is more difficult to judge the true receptive language abilities of the former. Individuals with ASD may have difficulty comprehending simple directions (e.g., "Turn off the lights," "Put your shoes on," and "Raise your hand"), "wh-" questions (e.g., "Where is mom?"), figurative language (e.g., "You have ants in your pants!"), and inferences (e.g., "How do you think the boy felt?"), as well as understanding ordinary conversation (e.g., "Hi! How are you?"). These difficulties appear to extend to wide-ranging atypicalities in auditory perception, including (1) superior pitch perception, making them more inclined toward music; (2) heightened perception of loudness and sensitivity toward sounds in general; (3) abnormal orientation to auditory stimuli (i.e., they are less responsive toward speech or their name being called); (4) abnormal processing of prosody or intonation; and (5) difficulty understanding speech in background noise (for review, see O'Connor, 2012). However, difficulties with attention, lack of motivation, and failure to engage with unfamiliar test stimuli in individuals with ASD may also contribute to some of these findings.

Expressive Language

Expressive language refers to an individual's ability to verbally express wants, needs, and thoughts. Due to their limited speech and/or use of AAC, little is known about the verbal capacity of individuals on the spectrum who are nonverbal. Those who are verbal present with a unique expressive language profile. For the most part, articulation has been found to be within normal limits in individuals with ASD (Kjelgaard & Tager-Flusberg, 2001). However, difficulties with speech initiation and planning, especially in minimally verbal children with ASD, have led to speculations about childhood apraxia of speech as a basis for the disorder (Gernsbacher, Sauer, Geye, Schweigert, & Goldsmith, 2008; Page & Boucher, 1998), although the evidence appears to be lacking (Shriberg, Paul, Black, & van

Santen, 2011). The acquisition of morphology (i.e., the ability to meaningfully combine the smallest units of language called morphemes) and syntax in ASD has also been found to be comparable to that in typically developing children, although perhaps at a slightly slower rate (Rapin, Dunn, Allen, Stevens, & Fein, 2009). Interestingly, high-functioning children with ASD tend to have rich vocabularies but do not use their word knowledge in normal ways. Semantic deficits (e.g., atypical word associations, idiosyncratic word use, neologisms, and excessively literal interpretation of statements) are among the few consistent language findings in ASD (Vogindroukas, Papageorgiou, & Vostanis, 2003). Not surprisingly, these children also have difficulty interpreting and using social–emotional vocabulary (i.e., "sad," "mad," "feel," etc.) (Eskes, Bryson, & McCormick, 1990), in keeping with the impaired prosody (i.e., lexical stress and affective intonation) and pragmatics (i.e., contextually appropriate responses during social interactions) that have come to be accepted as hallmarks of their social communication impairment (Mundy & Markus, 1997; Shriberg et al., 2001).

In summary, individuals with ASD may vary widely in their language profiles (Tager-Flusberg, Lindgren, & Mody, 2008). For the SLP, the challenge is one of assessing and treating a communication system that is linguistically fragmented, socially disengaged, and frequently weighed down by sensory issues.

COMMUNICATION ASSESSMENT IN AUTISM SPECTRUM DISORDER

Speech–language assessment of individuals with ASD is a challenging task, mainly due to the fact that it is a very complex, heterogeneous population. Individuals who are higher functioning and verbal may perform well on standardized measures but have difficulty interacting with other children in everyday situations, such as on the playground (Ozonoff, Goodlin-Jones, & Solomon, 2005). Nonverbal individuals with ASD, on the other hand, are difficult to assess accurately during standardized testing due to attention issues, in addition to difficulties interacting with others and producing spoken responses. Taken together, these characteristics make it challenging to obtain a baseline test score in minimally verbal individuals with ASD.

Speech and language assessment of individuals with ASD is typically composed of both formal and informal measures based on a combination of parent report, standardized testing, and language sampling during informal or semistructured play activities (Tager-Flusberg, Paul, & Lord, 2005), which help provide a more complete picture of the individual's receptive, expressive, and social–pragmatic language skills. In addition, for individuals on the spectrum who do not speak or whose speech is difficult to understand, a full AAC assessment may be required. As mentioned previously, the term AAC is used to describe various methods of communication that help people who do not use speech to express their thoughts and needs. An AAC assessment resembles a standard speech–language evaluation in that the clinician must first examine the individual's current communicative capabilities. This is typically composed of informal measures such as parent report and observation. After a baseline is obtained, the clinician proceeds with "feature matching," a process used to assess and match the communication needs of the individual with ASD with an appropriate AAC system (Gosnell, Costello, & Shane, 2011; Lloyd, Fuller, & Arvidson, 1997). Regardless of whether we are speaking of a standard speech–language assessment or an AAC assessment, the final objective of the evaluation is to capture the true language abilities of the individual in order to develop an appropriate treatment plan tailored to his or her communication needs and potential.

COMPONENTS OF THE COMMUNICATION ASSESSMENT PROCESS

An important first step in any evaluation is to gather pertinent information regarding the individual with ASD, including the patient's diagnoses, age, family history, medical history, developmental milestones, educational history, and current services. This can be done through a combination of parent/caregiver interview, chart review, and completion of an intake form by the caregiver. Whereas the final speech and language report may vary widely among clinicians, a standard speech and language evaluation of a patient with ASD will include the following:

* Background and history: Medical, educational, and family
* Receptive language skills
* Expressive language skills
* Articulation and oral motor skills
* Pragmatic language skills
* Summary and recommendations
* Treatment objectives
* Treatment plan

Throughout the session, the clinician makes detailed notes and observations about the individual's energy level, ability to focus, mood, social disposition, and any maladaptive behaviors because these will help determine the treatment approach. For the individual who does not speak or is minimally verbal, the clinician completes an AAC evaluation. In the next two sections, a broad overview of the evaluation process is presented.

Speech and Language Evaluation

The assessment of speech and language is composed of formal and informal measures. Easy-to-administer standardized tests of receptive language such as the Peabody Picture Vocabulary Test–Fourth Edition (PPVT-4) and the Receptive One Word Picture Vocabulary Test (ROWPVT) may be used with a wide range of individuals with ASD, from those who speak to those who are nonverbal. Each of these tests involves listening to a spoken word and identifying the picture that best represents that word. However, individuals with comorbid attention difficulties and hyperactivity may have difficulty focusing and pointing to the appropriate picture. Furthermore, some individuals will have difficulty comprehending the directions of the test and may point to all the pictures or randomly point without looking. For high-functioning individuals on the spectrum, the clinician may administer language tests to assess the individuals' ability to make comparisons, understand cause–effect relationships, and process sentences of increasing length and complexity (e.g., subtests of the Clinical Evaluation of Language Fundamentals (CELFP-2, CELF-5) or the Comprehensive Assessment of Spoken Language (CASL)). Given the challenges of formal, structured testing with individuals on the spectrum, a clinician may also informally examine the patient's ability to follow familiar compared to novel directions and make simple inferences.

In contrast to receptive language measures, use of standardized expressive language tests (e.g., the Expressive One Word Picture Vocabulary Test (EOWPVT), the Expressive Vocabulary Test (EVT), or subtests of the CELF or CASL) is limited to those individuals who can respond verbally. For individuals with ASD who are primarily nonverbal, clinicians rely on parent report and language samples from informal play sessions or on some form of AAC (e.g., picture symbols, communication books, speech-generating devices, sign language, and gestures). Popular tests such as the Goldman–Fristoe Test of Articulation (GFTA-2), used to assess speech sound production, naturally pose a problem as well. All individuals with ASD, however, undergo an oral motor examination to assess more basic aspects of speech production, including the intactness of the speech structures (e.g., lips, teeth, tongue, velum, and jaw), their associated movements (e.g., oral agility as in producing sound sequences), and quality of phonation.

With regard to social pragmatics, there are few standardized tests designed to assess language use and interactions across different environments. For the most part, the field relies on checklists and observation scales (e.g., CELF-Descriptive Pragmatics Profile), but these tend to be subjective. Nevertheless, having communication partners from different environments (e.g., parent, teacher, and social worker) complete these scales can provide useful insight about the individual's daily struggles with communication.

Finally, care must be taken never to underestimate the current language skills of an individual with ASD because they may know more than they show at the time of evaluation. Speech and language assessment in these individuals should be an ongoing process as they acquire skills over time.

Augmentative and Alternative Communication Evaluation

One of the greatest challenges for SLPs is best serving individuals with ASD who are primarily nonverbal or limited in their verbal expression. Approximately one-third to one-half of individuals with ASD do not use speech functionally (Mirenda, 2003). That a certain percentage of these individuals with ASD will never or rarely speak their entire lives highlights the significance of AAC intervention to enable them to express themselves. First, various AAC methods are reviewed before the AAC evaluation process is discussed.

AAC can be divided into two major categories: unaided and aided. Unaided AAC includes methods of communication that do not require additional equipment, such as manual sign, body language, finger spelling, gesturing, and facial expressions. Aided AAC includes methods of communication that require additional equipment, aids, or tools, such as picture exchange, communication books, voice output communication aids, and/or speech-generating devices. Aided AAC can be further divided into three types: low–tech, mid-tech, and high-tech. "Lite" or "low- tech" AAC consists of a communication system that does not require a power source, such as picture communication books and boards. Among the more commonly used low-tech systems for individuals with ASD are the Picture Exchange Communication System (PECS; Bondy & Frost, 1998; see Figure 18.1) and the Pragmatic Organization Dynamic Display (PODD; Porter & Cafiero, 2009). Based on evidence from neuroimaging research that suggests that individuals with ASD often exhibit strengths in the ability to identify visual patterns and perceive visual objects (Samson, Mottron, Soulières, & Zeffiro, 2012; Sahyoun, Belliveau, Soulières, Schwartz, & Mody, 2010), these low-tech visual supports are a promising option for use with individuals with ASD. Low-tech AAC systems also offer the advantages of being relatively inexpensive, easy to replace, easy to customize, and portable. On the other hand, size limitations (e.g., the amount of vocabulary available to the individual), the manpower required to create these systems, and the lack of knowledge of how to systematically use and implement these systems are some of their most frequently cited disadvantages.

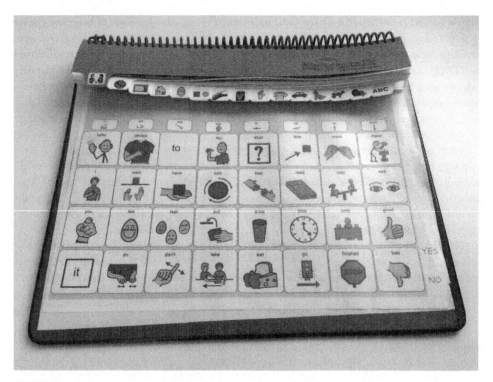

FIGURE 18.1 Sample low-tech AAC system: Flip'nTalk (2007 Inman Innovations, LLC).

"Mid-tech" AAC refers to any communication system that requires a source of power, uses recorded speech, and requires some level of training to program and maintain the device. It typically includes some combination of buttons and/or pictures with prerecorded or recordable messages. Common examples of mid-tech devices are Step by Step and Big Mack (recordable voice-output buttons), the GoTalk series of devices (Attainment, Verona, WI), and S32 (Tobii, Dedham, MA). The advantages of mid-tech devices are that they are less expensive than high-tech devices, messages are fairly easy to record and change as necessary, and they provide a helpful transition for individuals who are moving from a low-tech communication system to higher tech forms of AAC. However, one disadvantage of mid-tech devices is that they are limited in the number of messages that can be recorded, although the message limit varies greatly with the device.

Finally, a "high-tech" AAC device is a communication system that requires a power source and extensive training to competently program and maintain the device. These devices are often referred to as having a "dynamic display" because the display pages in these devices change when the user touches them (Figure 18.2). High-tech devices incorporate sophisticated electronics or computers. Examples of high-tech devices are the Accent series (Prentke Romich, Wooster, OH); Tobii's C8, C12, and P10 devices; NovaChat and ALT-Chat (Saltillo, Millersburg, OH); and the Maestro and T10 (DynaVox, Pittsburg, PA). In addition to dedicated communication devices, several AAC applications are available for the iPad, including Proloquo2Go, LAMP Words for Life, TouchChat HD, and Speak for Yourself. Among these, the Language Acquisition through Motor Planning (LAMP) approach is gaining significant popularity. It is based on neurological and motor learning principles, and it requires the user to learn the visuomotor plan corresponding to

FIGURE 18.2 Sample high-tech AAC device: Vantage Lite Speech Generating Device (Prentke Romich Company).

the physical locations of various target word categories on the device's display page. The placement of these categories in the display remains the same even when more vocabulary items are added, thereby leveraging the visual processing strengths of individuals with ASD for purposes of learning and recall. The advantages of high-tech devices are that they are dynamic, customizable, and, most important, their vocabulary can "grow" with the user. However, these devices are expensive; funding can be difficult; technical problems can occur; and their use requires training and support for families, caregivers, and school staff who regularly interact with the user.

In summary, AAC devices, including speech-generating devices that feature voice output, can enhance both receptive and expressive language in individuals with ASD by providing them audio and/or visual supports as a way to express themselves. Importantly, these devices are yielding positive results by motivating the nonverbal child to produce speech, as well as independently initiate communication (Binger, Berens, Kent-Walsh, & Hickman, 2008).

The main goal of an AAC evaluation in ASD is to match the individual to an appropriate device or method of communication based on his or her communication needs and abilities. This is a lengthy process and can occur over several sessions. The feature matching and final clinical decision process entails the consideration of several parameters:

- Access: Can the individual direct select—that is, physically isolate one finger to touch the screen or display? Is a keyboard keyguard, which is an overlay designed to help users with limited motor skills access the keys through corresponding holes, needed to aid the individual to more accurately select a specific key? Does the individual have motor impairments requiring the use of assistive technologies such as a button, switch, or a joystick or eye-operated communication and control? Where is the access point located (e.g., hand, chin, or cheek)?

- Symbol type: Does the individual do best with symbols or photograph representation?
- Symbol size and display type: How large do the symbols have to be and how many per page can the individual handle?
- Type of system needed: Does the individual require a high-, mid-, or low-tech system?
- Keyboard access: Can the user type and spell? Can he or she use word prediction, a software that incorporates user vocabularies to predict which word is being typed? By finishing typing the word for the user, the program reduces the number of keystrokes needed for typing, thereby saving the patient time and energy and facilitating language expression. What about the ability to sequence or combine? That is, can the individual access a board with one, two, three, or four hits? Regarding language capabilities, what kind of grammar does the individual use? Does the individual understand categories? Is a phrase-based or core word system needed? Or are visual scene displays more appropriate?
- Speech: Does the individual produce spoken words? What is the individual's mean length of utterance? Does the length of utterance increase when using AAC?
- Durability: Is the device likely to be thrown, dropped, handled roughly, etc.?
- Portability: Can the individual carry the device? Is a mount required to attach the device to a wheelchair or walker? Does the individual require a lightweight system?

Clearly, the success of an AAC evaluation in ASD depends on how best to select and tailor the individual's AAC device to match his or her strengths and weaknesses while keeping in mind the user's vision, hearing, and general cognitive skills. It is important to remember that a high-tech device is not necessarily better than a low-tech device. Some individuals with ASD have not been exposed to high-tech speech-generating devices, iPads, or other types of technology, and they have difficulty grasping the cause–effect relationship. In addition, some individuals perseverate on the voice-output and dynamic features of a high-tech device, and they may not be able to view the system as a way to communicate. Typically, the SLP will recommend a formal trial period with the selected AAC device across all settings before a purchase is made. Finally, whereas individuals with ASD may benefit from learning words and concepts, incorporating phrase-based representations can be useful to socially communicate with peers in real time during conversations and interactions.

In summary, a thorough and accurate assessment of the communication abilities of individuals with ASD is a challenge even for the experienced clinician. The sensory issues in this population (e.g., tactile and auditory sensitivities; Kern et al., 2006; Rogers, Hepburn, & Wehner, 2003) add to the challenge and serve to emphasize the importance of increased collaboration among professionals for a complete assessment of an individual's abilities and more accurate decision-making during the AAC evaluation process.

SPEECH AND LANGUAGE TREATMENT IN AUTISM SPECTRUM DISORDER

Speech–language treatment of individuals with ASD can vary widely due to the heterogeneous nature of the disorder, but the ultimate goal of treatment is to help the individual with ASD to successfully and spontaneously communicate across multiple environments. There are several different evidence-based approaches that SLPs can utilize during treatment sessions to optimize outcomes in the receptive, expressive, and pragmatic language domains. In addition, there are several evidence-based strategies and components of occupational therapy, physical therapy, and behavioral therapy programs that SLPs can draw on to help individuals with ASD achieve their communicative goals. With the boom in technology during the past decade, SLPs increasingly find themselves using AAC methods and strategies with individuals across the spectrum.

The National Research Council (2001) identified a number of aspects of effective treatment for individuals with ASD, including the following:

1. Children who received early intensive intervention by age 3 years had much better outcomes than children who began intervention after 5 years of age.
2. Active engagement in intensive instructional programming is very beneficial for children with ASD.
3. Repeated, planned teaching opportunities should be implemented in a series of short intervals and focus heavily on the individual objectives or goals.
4. Speech–language intervention for individuals with ASD should include parent training and family involvement. The treating SLP should focus heavily on teaching the caregivers strategies to help the child communicate in order to maximize the benefits of the extended time spent together.
5. A low student:teacher ratio is beneficial for the child with ASD to be able to receive adequate individualized instruction, as well as attain goals.
6. Treatment objectives should be measured on an ongoing basis and modified as needed.

Based on a review of the evidence, the New Hampshire Task Force on Autism (2001) concluded that there are numerous approaches to the treatment of ASD and strong opinions about the efficacy of each. It concluded that "there is no one treatment or intervention that works well for all people (with ASD). However, there are many approaches that are effective and work well for specific individuals." (p. 24)

Treatment Approaches

A number of different intervention approaches are used with individuals with ASD. These approaches fall along a continuum of naturalness and include child-centered, hybrid, and clinician-directed approaches (Fey, 1986). Child-centered treatment approaches are the most natural in that the child directs the session. The key component of this approach is for the clinician to both wait and then respond to the child's communicative behavior. Several techniques can be used by the clinician when responding to the child, including playing at the child's level, self-talk, parallel talk, and imitation, as well as expansions, extensions, build ups, break downs, and recasts, in which the clinician expands or adds information to the child's utterance or modifies and restates what the child initially says (Paul, 2007). Floor Time, a Developmental, Individual-differences, Relationship-based model (DIR; Greenspan & Weider, 2009), and SCERTS (Social Communication, Emotional Regulation, and Transactional Support; Prizant, Wetherby, Rubin, Laurent, & Rydell, 2006) are two well-known examples of child-centered approaches.

In the hybrid approach, the clinician controls a good portion of the therapy activity and materials selection but also allows the child to make spontaneous comments. Focused stimulation, which relies heavily on the clinician modeling target words, and vertical structuring, in which the clinician expands on a child's initial utterance and then asks a contingent question as a way of engaging the child in active listening and conversation, are examples of a hybrid approach.

At the other end of Fey's (1986) continuum of naturalness is the clinician-directed approach. Here, the clinician controls all aspects of the intervention from the therapy materials used to the type and frequency of reinforcement utilized and the order of activities. It is a much less naturalistic approach that maximizes the opportunities for the child to produce targeted words or skills. Clinician-directed approaches can be effective in helping children efficiently acquire new language forms and increase joint attention. A very common clinician-directed approach is applied behavioral analysis (ABA). Developed specifically for individuals with ASD, the primary emphasis in ABA is the use of intensive, direct instructional methods that alter behavior in systematic and measurable ways (Anderson, Taras, & O'Malley-Cannon, 1996). The main goal of ABA is to reduce inappropriate behavior and increase communication, learning, and appropriate social behavior. Thus, ABA uses instructional methods such as discrete trial training (DTT) and reinforcements. In general, students learn smaller, easier skills first and then progress toward larger, more complicated skills as each smaller one is mastered through structured drill procedures. Both reinforcement and prompting are used in DTT and are faded over time until the child is completely independent. Behavioral approaches such as ABA have been found to be effective in initially developing attention and understanding of language, in addition to aiding speech production in preverbal children with ASD (Goldstein, 2002; Rogers, 2006), although DTT, which is often used in ABA, can limit generalization outside of treatment sessions.

LANGUAGE AREAS AND TREATMENT STRATEGIES IN AUTISM SPECTRUM DISORDER

Speech and language treatment in ASD typically focuses on receptive, expressive, and pragmatic language deficits. Here, some of the common objectives and strategies to improve language in these areas are reviewed.

Receptive Language Treatment

The ability of individuals with ASD to comprehend language used around them is highly dependent on their mood, attention, and motivation. Thus, clinicians need to engage their patient while targeting receptive language. Active listening and aided language stimulation, during which a communication partner points to a graphic symbol while simultaneously producing the corresponding spoken word during natural communication, have proven to be useful strategies here. During treatment of receptive language, the clinician typically targets the following areas:

- Following directions: The focus here is on the ability of individuals with ASD to be able to follow directions ranging from functional, everyday directions (e.g., "Sit down" and "Turn on the lights") to novel directions (e.g., " Put the small blue ball in the box"). Embedded in these are basic language concepts such as temporal concepts (e.g., before, after, and then), location (e.g., next to, closest to, farthest, and top/bottom), dimension/size (e.g., tallest and big/little), sequence (e.g., first/last, second/third, and last), and inclusion/exclusion (e.g., both, all, except, and either/or). Typically, the therapist moves from highly familiar, functional one-step directions to less familiar, multiple-step directions with basic language concepts embedded within them.
- Receptive vocabulary: A major area of receptive language treatment is improving receptive vocabulary. One simple technique is through the creation of word webs,

which involves selecting a central "target" word (written or drawn) and then coming up with words that expand on its attributes (e.g., texture, shape, and category) in the form of strands of a web emanating from the center. Another common approach used to improve receptive vocabulary is the Lindamood–Bell Visualizing and Verbalizing (V–V) program, which helps to strengthen word associations and connections through concept imagery. It builds on the visual strengths of individuals with ASD by having them imagine what the word makes them think of, which in turn is used to stimulate new words and multiple sentences. Clinicians need training and certification to use the program, although similar strategies are informally used in therapy.

- Sequencing events: The ability to sequence a series of events is very important and often a part of speech–language treatment for individuals with ASD. This can be targeted in several ways, ranging from sequencing very basic, everyday events such as brushing one's teeth to sequencing a story. For individuals with ASD who are higher functioning and verbal, sequencing can be taught by presenting a series of photos corresponding to the progression of a story they have just heard and asking them to put the photos in the correct order. After they can put them in the correct order, they will then be asked to verbally state the sequence.

- Answering "wh-" questions: This is a very important, functional area of receptive language to address in individuals with ASD because they frequently encounter questions in their everyday interactions. Wh- questions can range from very basic questions such as the what, who, and where to more abstract wh- questions including when and why. Wh- questions should focus heavily on functional, common questions to which the child with ASD is most likely to be exposed. Therapy can address wh- questions through interactive play with activities such as bingo games.

- Comprehension of higher language and inferential skills: Individuals with ASD tend to be very concrete and have a difficult time comprehending abstract language, which can be a barrier in communicating with peers and adults on a daily basis. It can hinder their academic performance as well. One way to increase word flexibility is for the clinician to work with words that have multiple meanings. This, in turn, can help individuals with ASD better understand idioms, metaphors, and similes. Storyboards have also been found useful in training inference and reasoning skills, important not just for academic work but also for interpreting social situations.

Expressive Language Treatment

A common goal in speech and language treatment of high- and low-functioning individuals with ASD is to improve expressive vocabulary. For those who are higher functioning and verbal (see Case Study 1), expressive language treatment may involve objectives such as enhancing meaningful use of expressive vocabulary, speaking in grammatically sound sentences, expanding mean length of utterance, and being able to retell stories. Each of these areas addressed in treatment is briefly described next.

Case Study #1 Verbal Child With Autism Spectrum Disorder: "Jack"

Jack is an 8-year-old verbal child diagnosed with ASD. He lives with his mother and is an only child. He currently attends public school and is in an integrated classroom. He is pulled out of his classroom a few times a week to receive individual speech–language therapy, social skills group therapy, and occupational therapy. Jack's receptive and expressive language skills are mildly reduced for his chronological age; however, his pragmatic or social language skills are significantly weaker in comparison. Jack has a very difficult time interacting with peers and prefers to play on his own. He is also very concrete and inflexible in his thinking. He has difficulty dealing with any change to his routine and has frequent meltdowns over this. Jack's mother was concerned that he was not making enough progress in school and wanted him to be successful with his peers, as well as improve his overall language skills. Thus, Jack was referred for a speech–language evaluation, and individual speech–language therapy as well as a social skills group were recommended. Individual speech–language sessions focused on improving his comprehension of higher level language such as idioms, metaphors, and expressions. In addition, the clinician focused on improving his ability to make verbal inferences using visual supports. During the individual sessions, specific social skills were also explicitly taught and practiced for Jack to apply during social skills group therapy with age- and skills-matched peers. Jack made excellent progress and after 1 year was discharged from outpatient therapy.

A diverse expressive vocabulary is essential for an individual with ASD to succeed in multiple settings and contexts. In speech–language therapy, an important first step is to identify the target vocabulary items for the individual with ASD. This can be done through a variety of structured language activities in conjunction with receptive language activities such as word webs and the V–V program. The clinician may also use pictures to have the child with ASD retell a story he or she has just heard to hone in on specific vocabulary targets. Ample use of visuals with this population is crucial because they tend to be visual learners. Unlike vocabulary, syntax and grammar are most likely to be targeted in high-functioning individuals, although they may be addressed in nonverbal individuals later on in treatment with the help of AAC, depending on their cognitive level. Generally, the treatment of syntactic errors progresses from highly structured activities to less structured activities in which the child has to spontaneously use the correct targeted grammatical form. For individuals with ASD who use AAC, grammar is taught and targeted as they learn to communicate using their AAC system, with clinicians often using aided language stimulation to first model morphological and syntactical structures on an AAC device. Expanding the mean length of utterance (MLU) in both written and spoken language is yet another common speech–language goal for individuals with ASD. Again, this can be done through structured language activities, including story retelling with visual supports. In general, it is important to always model one step ahead of the child. For example, if the child has an MLU of 2—that is, on average the child produces two-word combinations—then the clinician should model three-word combinations.

Pragmatic Language Treatment

Difficulty with social skills and pragmatic language skills is one of the core defining features of ASD. Social skill deficits can affect both lower and higher functioning individuals with the disorder. Pragmatic language skills may be targeted within speech–language therapy in which the clinician explicitly teaches the skills and then role-plays with the child. However, a more effective treatment approach is to address social language deficits within the natural context of a group setting with peers. Social skills groups address the following areas:

- Improved interpersonal communication or conversational skills: The aim here is to improve the individual with ASD's ability to converse with both peers and adults. Common components of conversation typically addressed in treatment include improving ability to initiate conversation, turn-taking, staying on topic, asking relevant questions and making comments, and successfully terminating a conversation. Ideally, the individual with ASD will learn explicit skills at the beginning of a social skills group session, will practice the specific skill with peers, and will generalize the skill to everyday conversation.
- Interpreting nonverbal behavior and body language: Another important area commonly addressed within social skills training is the ability to correctly interpret nonverbal behavior or body language. Individuals with ASD often have a very difficult time interpreting emotions and do not know what to do. Again, interpreting body language or nonverbal behavior can be taught either individually or within a social skills group setting. Within a session, the clinician will work with the individual to pay attention to the clinician's emotions. The clinician can direct basic activities such as identifying and labeling facial expressions and emotions, as well as answering questions about how a person might feel in a given situation. Another way to work on interpreting body language is to role play, in which the clinician can turn his or her back to the individual or not look at the individual while he or she is talking. During these instances, the individual learns to identify when the clinician is not paying attention.
- Ability to problem solve and make social inferences: Training social skills in individuals with ASD also involves problem solving and making social inferences or guesses. This is a key area of struggle for many individuals with ASD and can be addressed during individual speech–language treatment sessions or social group settings. The clinician may have the individual look at various pictures and then answer several questions, moving from close-ended questions with answer choices to a more open-ended question format. In addition, the individual learns to make social inferences based on what he or she saw in the pictures.

Social Thinking (Winner, 2007) is one of the most commonly used programs to treat social pragmatic skills in ASD. Increasingly, video modeling techniques have also been effective in improving a number of skills in individuals with ASD, including social interactions, play, and daily living skills (Ganz, Earles-Vollrath, & Cook, 2011).

THE ROLE OF AAC IN SPEECH–LANGUAGE THERAPY IN AUTISM SPECTRUM DISORDER

Following the completion of a speech–language evaluation and/or AAC evaluation, the clinician is ready to make appropriate recommendations, which may or may not include the use of AAC. The implementation of AAC varies among individuals with lower functioning ASD and those with higher functioning ASD. For individuals with ASD who are nonverbal (see Case Study 2), important components in AAC treatment are feature matching the individual to a specific system; teaching core vocabulary; providing an ample amount of aided language modeling; communication partner training; and addressing the major language areas, including receptive, expressive, and pragmatic language skills, using the individual's AAC system.

Case Study #2 Nonverbal Adult With Autism Spectrum Disorder: "Steven"

Steven is a 31-year-old man with a diagnosis of ASD. He lives in a group home and attends a day program for adults with developmental disabilities during the week. Steven has a history of aggression and disruptive behaviors that have interfered with his ability to participate in therapy and in activities at his day program. Steven is nonverbal and communicates through sign, some vocalizations, a communication book, and a GoTalk 20 voice-output device. He can produce several clearly spoken words, such as "no" and "bye," but his primary means of communication are his communication book and GoTalk 20 device. These AAC systems were recommended 2 years ago following a complex AAC evaluation. When using these forms of AAC, Steven is able to produce greetings, answer questions, request items and activities, combine two to four words, respond yes/no, ask questions, and label. He can also communicate about feelings and medical needs by pointing to symbols in his communication book. Steven attends speech–language therapy sessions each week, in which he uses each AAC system to work on increasing his expressive and receptive language abilities. His parents are very supportive and attend each therapy session. They report one difficult issue is that of carryover of the use of AAC into Steven's group home and day program because staff are often unfamiliar with each AAC system and do not use them with Steven very often. This issue has been addressed during meetings at his day program and by inviting staff to attend speech–language therapy sessions. Sessions have also been videotaped in order to show Steven's success in communicating with his book and GoTalk device.

Higher functioning individuals with ASD who speak may also benefit from AAC strategies and visual supports that help improve general language comprehension, social communication, and expressive language.

The use of AAC techniques and strategies in teaching core language has made a significant contribution to the field of speech and language treatment in ASD. Core language consists of high-frequency, reusable words that comprise approximately 80% of words used on a daily basis (Banajee, Dicarlo, & Striclin, 2003) and that a child can combine in a number of ways to produce spontaneous utterances. The remaining 20% of words are referred to as "fringe vocabulary" because they are specific to the child (van Tatenhove, 2009). Prentke Romich Company, a well-known manufacturer in the field of AAC devices, has developed six stages (ranging from the emergent communicator with 85 one-word utterances to the full-blown communicator who uses all parts of language to form complete sentences spontaneously) for use by clinicians to guide their development of goals and objectives related to the teaching of core language. Overall, teaching core language gives the individual much more communicative power and allows the individual to produce an unlimited number of spontaneous novel utterances or word combinations. Core language can be taught in several ways, and there are numerous activities that can occur across multiple environments and natural contexts to help develop core language use. As such, some important considerations for the clinician when implementing core language intervention include using focused aided language stimulation, teaching new core words using highly structured language activities, engaging in practice activities, continuously providing repeated exposure to new core words, and periodically checking continued comprehension of core words (Zangari, 2012). Finally, it is important to constantly provide support to the individual and honor any attempt to use core language, even when words are used incorrectly; this provides an opportunity for the communication partner to model a correct response. Ultimately, the AAC user must learn to generalize his or her communication skills to situations outside of the treatment environment to be effective in all settings. Although families often have concerns about AAC negatively impacting the development of speech, as mentioned previously, there is no evidence to support this; rather, studies indicate gains in speech production following AAC intervention (Binger et al., 2008; Schlosser & Wendt, 2008).

SUMMARY

Communication deficits lie at the core of ASD. Although speech and language treatment of individuals with ASD may vary widely, the ultimate goal is to help individuals on the spectrum spontaneously and successfully communicate across multiple environments. Exciting new advances in the field of neuroimaging are paving the way for the development of robust biomarkers for use in speech–language intervention (Mody et al., 2013). These findings will help inform the work of the SLPs as they guide individuals with ASD in navigating a path to successful and independent communication.

KEY POINTS

- Consider how each area of sensory processing (e.g., auditory, visual, tactile, and motor) may impact a patient with ASD.
- Remember the importance of family support and counseling when working with this population.
- Collaboration and regular communication between all members of the care team, including parents and teachers, is critical for the individual with ASD to make progress.
- Do not underestimate what individuals with ASD understand or judge their abilities based on whether they are verbal or nonverbal.
- In selecting an AAC device, plan ahead so as to optimize its use based on the patient's needs and profile while maximizing potential for growth in communication skills.

DISCLOSURE STATEMENT

Katelyn A. Bruno, Kristina L. Gulati, and Dr. Maria Mody have nothing to disclose.

REFERENCES

American Speech-Language-Hearing Association (2002). Augmentative and alternative communication: Knowledge and skills for service delivery. *ASHA Leader, 7*(Suppl. 22), 97–106.

Anderson, S. R., Taras, M., & O'Malley Cannon, B. (1996). Teaching new skills to young children with autism. In C. Maurice, G. Green, & S. C. Luce (Eds.), *Behavioral intervention for young children with autism. A manual for parents and professionals* (pp. 181–194). Austin, TX: Pro-Ed.

Banajee, M., Dicarlo, C., & Striclin, S. B. (2003). Core vocabulary determination for toddlers. *Augmentative and Alternative Communication, 19*(2), 67–73.

Binger, C., Berens, J., Kent-Walsh, J., & Hickman, S. (2008). The effects of aided AAC interventions on AAC use, speech, and symbolic gestures. *Seminars in Speech and Language, 29*, 101–111.

Bondy, A. S., & Frost, L. A. (1998). The Picture Exchange Communication System. *Seminars in Speech and Language, 19*(4), 373–388.

Centers for Disease Control and Prevention. (2014). Morbidity and mortality weekly report: Prevalence of autism spectrum disorders among children aged 8 years—Autism and Developmental Disabilities Monitoring Network, 11 sites, United States, 2010. *Centers for Disease Control and Prevention, 63*(2), 1–22.

Eskes, G. A., Bryson, S. E., & McCormick, T. A. (1990). Comprehension of concrete and abstract words in autistic children. *Journal of Autism and Developmental Disorders, 20*, 61–73.

Fey, M. (1986). *Language disorders in children.* Boston, MA: Allyn & Bacon.

Ganz, J. B., Earles-Vollrath, T. L., & Cook, K. E. (2011). Video modeling: A visually based intervention for children with autism spectrum disorder. *Teaching Exceptional Children, 43*(6), 8–19.

Gernsbacher, M. A., Sauer, E. A., Geye, H. M., Schweigert, E. K., & Goldsmith, H. H. (2008). Infant and toddler oral and manual motor skills predict later speech fluency in autism. *Journal of Child Psychology and Psychiatry, 49*, 43–50.

Goldstein, H. (2002). Communication intervention for children with autism: A review of treatment efficacy. *Journal of Autism and Developmental Disorders, 32*, 373–396.

Gosnell, J., Costello, J., & Shane, H. (2011). *There isn't always an app for that: Perspectives on augmentative and alternative communication.* Rockland, MD: American Speech Language Hearing Association.

Greenspan, S., & Weider, S. (2009). *Engaging autism: Using the Floor Time approach to help children relate, communicate, and think.* Philadelphia, PA: Da Capo Lifelong Books.

Hudry, K., Leadbitter, K., Temple, K., Slonims, V., McConachie, H., Aldred, C., . . . Charman, T.; the PACT Consortium. (2010). Preschoolers with autism show greater impairment in receptive compared with expressive language abilities. *International Journal of Language & Communication Disorders, 45*(6), 681–690.

Kern, J. K., Trivedi, M. H., Garver, C.R., Grannemann, B. D., Andrews, A. A., Savla, J. S., . . . Schroeder, J. L. (2006). The pattern of sensory processing abnormalities in autism. *Autism, 10*(5), 480–494.

Kjelgaard, M., & Tager-Flusberg, H. (2001). An investigation of language impairment in autism: Implications for genetic subgroups. *Language and Cognitive Processes, 16*, 287–308.

Lloyd, L., Fuller, D. R., & Arvidson, H. (1997). Feature checklist. In L. Lloyd, D. R. Fuller, & H. Arvidson (Eds.), *Augmentative and alternative communication* (p. 494). Boston, MA: Allyn & Bacon.

Mirenda, P. (2003). Toward functional augmentative and alternative communication for students with autism: Manual signs, graphic symbols, and voice output communication aids. *Language, Speech, and Hearing Services in Schools, 34*(3), 203.

Mody, M., Manoach, D., Gunther, F., Kenet, T., Bruno, K., McDougle, C., & Stigler, K. A. (2013). Speech and language in autism spectrum disorder: Through the lens of behavior and brain imaging. *Neuropsychiatry, 3*(2), 1–10.

Mundy, P., & Markus, J. (1997). On the nature of communication and language impairment in autism. *Mental Retardation and Developmental Disabilities Research, 3*(4), 343–349.

National Research Council. (2001). *Educating children with autism.* Washington, DC: National Academy Press.

New Hampshire Task Force on Autism. (2001). *Part 1: Assessment and interventions.* Concord, NH: State of New Hampshire, Department of Health and Human Services.

O'Connor, K. (2012). Auditory processing in autism spectrum disorder: A review. *Neuroscience & Biobehavioral Reviews, 36*(2), 836–854.

Ozonoff, S., Goodlin-Jones, B. L., & Solomon, M. (2005). Evidence-based assessment of autism spectrum disorders in children and adolescents. *Journal of Clinical Child and Adolescent Psychology, 34*(3), 523–540.

Page, J., & Boucher, J. (1998). Motor impairments in children with autistic disorder. *Child Language Teaching and Therapy, 14,* 233–259.

Porter, G., & Cafiero, J. (2009). Pragmatic Organization Dynamic Display (PODD) communication books: A promising practice for individuals with autism spectrum disorder. *Perspectives on Augmentative & Alternative Communication, 18*(4), 121.

Paul, R. (2007). *Language disorders from infancy through adolescent: Intervention and assessment.* New York: Elsevier.

Prizant, B., Wetherby, A., Rubin, E., Laurent, A., & Rydell, P. (2006). *The SCERTS model: A comprehensive educational approach for children with autism spectrum disorders.* Baltimore, MD: Brookes.

Rapin, I., Dunn, M. A., Allen, D. A., Stevens, M. C., & Fein, D. (2009). Subtypes of language disorders in school-age children with autism. *Developmental Neuropsychology, 34*(1), 66–84.

Rogers, S. (2006). Evidence-based intervention for language development in young children with autism. In T. Charman & W. Stone (Eds.), *Social and communication development in autism spectrum disorders: Early identification, diagnosis, and intervention.* New York: Guildford.

Rogers, S. J., Hepburn, S., & Wehner, E. (2003). Parent reports of sensory symptoms in toddlers with autism and those with other developmental disorders. *Journal of Autism and Developmental Disorders, 33*(6), 631–642.

Rutter, M., Mawhood, L., & Howlin, P. (1992). Language delay and social development. In P. Fletcher & D. Hall (Eds.), *Specific speech and language disorders in children: Correlates, characteristics and outcomes* (pp. 63–78). London, England: Whurr.

Sahyoun, C. P., Belliveau, J. W., Soulières, I., Schwartz, S., & Mody, M. (2010). Neuroimaging of the functional and structural networks underlying visuospatial versus linguistic reasoning in high-functioning autism. *Neuropsychologia, 48,* 86–95.

Samson, F., Mottron, L., Soulières, I., & Zeffiro, T. A. (2012). Enhanced visual functioning in autism: An ALE meta-analysis. *Human Brain Mapping, 33,* 1553–1581.

Schlosser, R., & Wendt, O. (2008). Effects of augmentative and alternative communication intervention on speech production in children with autism: A systematic review. *American Journal of Speech–Language Pathology, 17*(3), 212–230.

Shriberg, L., Paul, R., Black, L., & van Santen, J. (2011). The hypothesis of apraxia of speech in children with autism spectrum disorder. *Journal of Autism Developmental Disorders, 41,* 405–426.

Shriberg, L., Paul, R., McSweeney, J., Klin, A., Cohen, D., & Volkmar, F. (2001). Speech and prosody characteristics of adolescents and adults with high-functioning autism and Asperger syndrome. *Journal of Speech, Language, and Hearing Research, 44,* 1097–1115.

Tager-Flusberg, H., Lindgren, K., & Mody, M. (2008). Structural and functional imaging research on language disorder: Specific language impairment and autism spectrum disorder. In L. Wolf, H. Schreiber, & J. Wasserstein (Eds.), *Adult learning disorders: Contemporary issues* (pp. 127–158, Neuropsychology Handbook Series) New York, NY: Taylor & Francis.

Tager-Flusberg, H., Paul, R., & Lord, C. L. (2005). Language and communication in autism. In F. Volkmar, R. Paul, & A. Klin (Eds.), *Handbook of autism and pervasive developmental disorder* (3rd ed., pp. 335–364). New York, NY: Wiley.

van Tatenhove, G. M. (2009). Building language competence with students using AAC devices: Six challenges. *Perspectives on Augmentative and Alternative Communication, 18*(2), 38–47.

Vogindroukas, I., Papageorgiou, V., & Vostanis, P. (2003). Pattern of semantic errors in autism: A brief research report. *Autism, 7*(2), 195–203.

Winner, M. G. (2007). *Thinking about YOU thinking about me* (2nd ed.). San Jose, CA: Think Social.

Zangari, C. (2012). Helping the general education team support students who use AAC. *Perspectives on Augmentative and Alternative Communication, 21,* 82–91.

19

OCCUPATIONAL THERAPY FOR AUTISM SPECTRUM DISORDER

JENNIFER L. STORNELLI

INTRODUCTION

Occupational therapy (OT) is a critical component of treatment for many individuals with autism spectrum disorder (ASD). There is strong evidence that treatment by a qualified occupational therapist can improve functioning and reduce impairing symptoms in both children and adults with ASD. This chapter describes the symptoms with which OT can be helpful, and it describes the approach that an occupational therapist may take in evaluating and treating an individual with ASD.

Goals of Occupational Therapy

The occupational therapist's primary focus is on supporting functional participation in daily life activities and routines. Engagement in meaningful and purposeful activity ("occupation") can lead to increased "health, well-being, and life satisfaction" (American Occupational Therapy Association (AOTA), 2002). The World Health Organization (2001) has recognized the impact that an inability to successfully perform daily tasks and participate in meaningful activities can have on one's overall health. Engaging in motivating and meaningful occupations not only serves as a medium for developing lost or absent skills but also is often, in itself, the desired outcome of intervention.

The domain of OT is broad but well-defined by the practice framework in terms of scope, function, and relevance to life roles and routines. Consideration of performance in areas of occupation is made, including activities of daily living (ADLs), instrumental activities of daily living (IADLs), education, work, play, leisure, and social participation (AOTA, 2002). An OT assessment examines an individual's ability to care for him- or herself (bathe, dress, groom, and feed), care for his or her home and family (do laundry, vacuum, and prepare a meal), access education, participate in leisure activities, and interact with others.

When considering these areas of occupation and how they are impacted by disability, the occupational therapist examines the performance skills and performance patterns relevant to the activity. Performance skills may include motor skills (posture, mobility, coordination, strength and effort, and energy/endurance), process skills (knowledge, temporal organization including initiation/sequencing/termination, and organizing space/objects), and communication/interaction skills. Impairments in one or many of these areas may contribute to the disability observed in the areas of occupation described previously. Performance patterns refer to the habits, routines, and roles that shape an individual's day-to-day life (Figure 19.1).

Evaluation

The evaluation process consists of two main parts: the occupational profile and the analysis of occupational performance. An "occupational profile" as defined by the OT practice framework (AOTA, 2002) is a collection of information that "describes the client's occupational history and experiences, patterns of daily living, interests, values, and needs" (p. 616). This information is generally gathered through patient or caregiver interview and provides an understanding of the priorities and desired outcomes of the patient and his or her family.

Once the patient's occupational profile has been pieced together, an analysis of occupational performance must occur. This starts with a close examination of the performance skills and patterns relevant to that occupation that may be impacting function, as discussed previously. Identifying factors that inhibit as well as support occupation is critical to this process. Patient priorities and goals identified in the occupational profile help guide the direction and focus of this analysis.

Performance Areas
Activities of Daily Living
Instrumental Activities of
   Daily Living
Work
Education
Play
Leisure
Social Participation

Performance Skills		Performance Patterns
Motor Skills		Habits
Process Skills		Routines
Communication/Interaction Skills		Roles
Context	Activity Demands	Client Factors
Cultural	Objects and Actions	Body Functions &
Physical	Space Demands	Structures
Social	Social Demands	
Temporal	Required Body Functions &	
	Structure	

FIGURE 19.1 Domain of occupational therapy. *Source: Adapted from American Occupational Therapy Association (2002).*

Intervention: Therapeutic Use of Occupations and Activities

Once the performance skills, patterns, contexts, activity demands, and patient factors that are compromising function have been identified, an intervention plan to address these factors is created and implemented in collaboration with the patient. Specific interventions are selected with the goal of engagement in meaningful activities to support greater independence and a better quality of life. Some interventions target performance skills directly (e.g., home exercise program to increase standing balance for lower body dressing), whereas others focus on retraining at the performance area level with adaptations and accommodations in place (e.g., using adaptive equipment to get dressed independently).

The therapeutic use of occupation or activity is central to the occupational therapist's intervention approach. Three types of intervention are identified in the practice framework as follows: (1) occupation-based activities (activities in context that hold meaning for the patient), (2) purposeful activity (goal-directed behavior that leads to participation in occupation), and (3) preparatory methods (methods that support or make one ready for engagement in meaningful activity) (Table 19.1).

Whether intervention addresses performance skills or habits, works directly on performance areas (ADLs, IADLs, etc.), or focuses on the impact of patient factors, activity demands, and context, all of these factors are interrelated and dynamic in nature. Assessment is an ongoing process that occurs throughout intervention, guiding the course of treatment and shaping the plan of care.

OCCUPATIONAL THERAPY IN AUTISM SPECTRUM DISORDER: TARGET SYMPTOMS

Many individuals with ASD have impairments that are amenable to the approach of OT. These symptoms include sensory dysfunction, disordered or maladaptive play behavior, impairments in ADLs, social impairments, behavioral problems, and, for adults, difficulties in learning skills for independent living. Any impairment that interferes with an individual's ability to safely and successfully participate in daily activities and routines falls within the realm of OT. This section discusses these impairments in more detail from the occupational therapist's perspective.

TABLE 19.1 Types of Occupational Therapy Intervention

Intervention	Purpose	Examples
Occupation-based activity	Engagement in the actual occupations that relate to client goals	Preparing a meal Making one's bed Getting dressed independently
Purposeful activity	Engagement in goal-directed activities that lead to an occupation	Practice slicing and spreading with a knife Practice fastening buttons on a button strip
Preparatory methods	Prepares the client for activity	Sensory input to achieve optimal arousal level Stretching/range-of-motion exercises

Source: Adapted from the American Occupational Therapy Association (2002).

Reasons for Seeking Referral

Individuals with ASD frequently suffer from functional impairments that can be addressed within the OT framework. According to a survey by the Interactive Autism Network (IAN, 2008), OT is the third most requested service by parents of children with ASD. According to IAN, the most common reasons why parents seek OT for their children are to address concerns with executive functioning (planning, organizational skills, and problem solving) and social interaction. Specifically, the two most common reasons for seeking sensory-integrative therapy in particular are to address maladaptive behaviors and stereotypic behaviors (e.g., hand flapping and spinning).

Cohn, Miller, and Tickle-Degnen (2000) examined parents' hopes prior to the start of OT and identified three main themes relating to their child's functioning: social participation, self-regulation, and perceived competence. Other common themes identified in the study included the parents' own need for support and the desire to support their child through learned strategies and personal validation of their own experience as a parent. Cohn et al. (2000) examined this question even further by asking parents directly why they sought OT for their child. All of the parents asked revealed that they sought OT because their child was not "fitting in" or "keeping up" with the other children (at school). They did not seek OT because of deficits in specific skills but, rather, to address the larger issue of social rejection.

Other studies examined parents' satisfaction following OT intervention and their perceptions of its effectiveness. Anderson (1993) found that parents reported progress in their children in several areas, including "willingness to try new play activities, socialization with other children, and the ability to express emotions and desires." Other parent testimonials have suggested that OT intervention (using a sensory integration approach) improves the overall quality of life for their family (Anderson & Emmons, 1995; Occupational Therapy Associates, 1995).

Sensory Symptoms

Disturbances in sensory processing and responsivity are among the most common symptoms that occupational therapists are asked to treat in individuals with ASD. As many as 94% of individuals with ASD have abnormalities in sensory processing compared to 65% of individuals with other developmental disabilities (Leekham, Nieto, Libby, Wing, & Gould, 2007). Furthermore, these symptoms often involve multiple sensory domains. Sensory symptoms widely reported in ASD include impairments in the modulation of sensory input, deficits in auditory processing (hypo- or hyperresponsivity), unusual visual behaviors (poor eye contact, gaze aversion, visual inspection of objects, and overreliance on peripheral vision), and tactile sensitivity (Tomcheck & Dunn, 2007). Individuals with ASD often experience a combination of over- and underresponsivity to various stimuli across sensory systems. Retrospective studies using videotape analysis have found evidence that some of these sensory symptoms may be evident in early infancy (Tomcheck & Dunn, 2007). Some of the common sensory processing difficulties in ASD are outlined in Table 19.2.

Specific examples of overresponsivity (or hyperresponsivity) may be a child who covers his ears when he hears a toilet flushing or screams when his parents try to dress him in the morning. Examples of underresponsivity (or hyporesponsivity) include a child who does not respond to his or her name or does not notice that his or her face or hands are messy.

TABLE 19.2 Common Sensory Processing Difficulties in Autism Spectrum Disorder

Factor	Related Behavioral Outcomes
Sensory Seeking	Seeks all kinds of movement that interferes with daily routines
	Twirls/spins self frequently throughout the day
	Takes excessive risks during play; takes movement or climbing risks that compromise personal safety
	Seeks opportunities to fall without regard for personal safety
	Frequently "on the go"
	Jumps from one activity to another
Emotional Reactivity	Anxiety or distress that interferes with daily routines
	Difficulty tolerating changes in routines
	Poor frustration tolerance
	Difficulty making friends
Inattention/Distractibility	Is distracted by or has trouble functioning with background noise
	Appears not to hear what you say; doesn't respond to name when called despite normal hearing
Poor Registration	Decreased awareness of pain and temperature
	Doesn't notice when people enter the room
	Does not seem to smell strong odors
	Does not notice when hands or face are messy
Sensory Sensitivity	Becomes anxious/distressed when feet leave the ground
	Difficulty tolerating various food textures
	Avoids certain tastes or food smells that are typically part of children's diets
	Difficulty tolerating tags on clothing, seams on socks
	Withdrawal from touch; signs of distress when touched

Source: From Dunn, W. (1999). *Sensory Profile: Caregiver Questionnaire.* Copyright © 1999 NCS Pearson, Inc. Reproduced with permission. All rights reserved. "Sensory Profile" is a trademark, in the US and/or other countries, of Pearson Education, Inc. or its affiliates(s).

Hyporesponsivity can be understood in more than one way. It may suggest a higher threshold for that particular sensation, whereas a stronger stimulus would be needed to elicit a response. However, it may also be the result of poor filtering or prioritizing of sensory input, which impacts the individual's ability to register the new stimulus effectively. In other cases, a lack of response to a stimulus can occur when a sensory system is "overloaded" and unable to process additional information. Individuals with ASD may require more sensory feedback from their environment than others due to higher neurological thresholds in certain systems. This may manifest in a pattern of sensory-seeking behaviors such as seeking out excessive movement, licking or mouthing nonfood items, or touching things/people in excess.

The ability to filter out background information (the sound of the clock ticking, the flicker of the fluorescent light bulb, etc.) is also often a challenge for those with ASD. Poor habituation to sensory stimuli can lead to increased arousal or anxiety and difficulty registering more relevant stimuli, such as someone calling one's name or the sight of a car approaching in a parking lot, in the immediate environment.

Difficulty regulating responses to sensations and environmental stimuli can manifest in a variety of ways and behavioral patterns. Each individual with ASD presents with a unique pattern of responses, which may include overresponsivity, underresponsivity, and sensory-craving across various sensory systems. Furthermore, these responses can vary depending on the contextual factors in which the sensory input is experienced.

Children with ASD often seek proprioceptive input through actions such as jumping off pieces of equipment or furniture, hanging from a jungle gym, or pushing their bodies into furniture or surfaces (Mailloux & Roley, 2010). Proprioceptive information can be alerting or calming, but it almost always has an organizing effect. It is a unique sensory system in this way in that too much information to this system does not tend to lead to overload or dysregulation.

The vestibular system, located in the inner ear, contributes to our sense of balance and spatial orientation. Various components of the inner ear detect linear or rotational movements as well as vertical or horizontal accelerations, providing us with a sense of body-in-space when stationary or in motion. Vestibular input can have dramatic effects on alertness, and it can quickly become disorganizing if one's system is overstimulated. Effects of overstimulation include dizziness, nausea, and sometimes vomiting. These symptoms are often transient, but at times they can have lasting effects (e.g., seasickness).

Different types of movement elicit different reactions in the inner ear, resulting in varied effects on arousal, posture, and sometimes emotional state. The type, speed, and rhythmicity of the movement can be altered to elicit different reactions. In general, slow, rhythmic, linear movement will have a calming effect, whereas fast, arrhythmical, or rotary movement will be alerting. Furthermore, positioning (upright, prone, etc.) is another variable that can be used to vary the movement experience and related postural challenges. Individuals vary significantly in their processing of vestibular sensation. Children often seek more vestibular input compared to adults, with vestibular systems becoming more sensitive as people age. In an OT sensory integration (SI) treatment session, equipment such as platform swings, tire swings, bolster swings, suspended hammocks and nets, and large exercise balls are used to create a variety of movement experiences and challenges in a variety of positions.

Outside of therapy sessions, children with ASD often seek out vestibular input by spinning themselves, running or pacing back and forth, jumping or bouncing up and down, or swinging for long periods of time. Other children with ASD may have a more sensitive vestibular system and may avoid movement activities, or they may demonstrate fear or distress during activities in which their head is not in an upright position relative to gravity. For these children, providing graded movement experiences in a controlled and supportive way with opportunities for adaptive responses is important.

The ability to process tactile sensations effectively is also of great significance to one's development of body scheme and, in conjunction with the proprioceptive system, one's awareness of body in the absence of vision. The tactile system has important functions that are both discriminatory and protective in nature. Tactile discrimination allows us to identify or manipulate an object within our grasp without relying on vision (e.g., reaching into a purse to get keys). It is very important for our ability to manipulate tools or objects and to adjust our grasp spontaneously on objects as needed. The tactile system also provides critical information about pain and temperature that serves a protective function (e.g., pulling hand from a hot stove).

Although tactile sensitivity is an issue for many individuals with ASD, poor discrimination of tactile information may also be present. Poor tactile discrimination can affect fine motor skills, and it may result in actions that appear clumsy, messy, and miscalculated. Ineffective processing of tactile information can also affect physical appearance, for instance, if a child does not feel his shirt twisted on his body or toothpaste or food on his face. This can in turn impact social participation and acceptance and also the development of self-esteem.

Behaviors such as hand flapping, spinning, aimless running, aggression, self-stimulatory behaviors, and sometimes self-injury have also been correlated with the sensory processing deficits seen in ASD (Watling & Dietz, 2007). Some individuals with ASD have explained the regulatory function that self-stimulatory behaviors serve, allowing the individual to better respond to the sensory stimuli around him or her and avoid sensory overload (Shoener, Kinnealey, & Koenig, 2008). The manifestation of these sensory behaviors in ASD can not only interfere with functional skills and daily routines but also have a significant impact on social participation and can lead to isolation and rejection by peer groups. Identifying environmental factors that support one's sensory needs while helping the individual learn strategies for self-regulation across contexts is a key component of the occupational therapist's role with this population and can greatly improve one's quality of life.

Motor Skills

Individuals with ASD have often been described as "clumsy" or "uncoordinated," having poor body awareness, bumping into things and people, and having difficulty with basic skills such as tying their shoes or buttoning their shirts. Although motor deficits were not traditionally included in the criteria for an ASD diagnosis, recent research suggests that differences in motor skills and praxis may in fact comprise an important feature of ASD.

Several researchers have described a range of gross and fine motor differences in ASD that have included measures of muscle tone, postural reactions, and dyspraxia (Bhat, Landa, & Galloway, 2011; Ming, Brimacombe, & Wagner, 2007). Differences in gait and impairments in anticipatory postural control are among these findings (Bhat et al., 2011). Furthermore, studies have shown that motor differences can be seen as early as infancy and may include delayed acquisition of gross motor milestones, abnormal muscle tone, decreased motor activity, and postural asymmetries (Bhat et al., 2011; Phagava et al., 2008). Poor motor and gestural imitation in infants later diagnosed with ASD has been linked to deficits in communication and social skills in the second and third years of life (Bhat et al., 2011). Deficits in praxis seen in ASD have been well documented during the past several years, with recent studies showing the presence of dyspraxia even in the absence of cognitive delay (Bhat et al., 2011). Some researchers have examined various areas of the brain related to praxis and have described impairments in individuals with ASD related to the formation of spatial representations (parietal regions), poor linking of sensory information with motor areas (premotor cortex), and deficits in motor execution (motor cortex) (Dowell, Mahone, & Mostofsky, 2009). Another key finding in motor research is the delayed or atypical cerebral lateralization and dominance (Escalante-Mead, Minshew, & Sweeney, 2003; Hauck & Dewey, 2001), which may contribute to the poor bilateral skills and sequencing observed in children with ASD. Furthermore, difficulty establishing cerebral dominance has been speculated to contribute to the disordered language development seen in this population (Escalante-Mead et al., 2003) (Table 19.3).

Play: The Occupation of Childhood

Play is as critical to a child's early development as learning to dress or feed oneself because it is through play that many of the other building blocks of development emerge. Engaging in play not only draws on the underlying skills of social engagement, imitation, and the

TABLE 19.3 Motor Differences in Autism Spectrum Disorder[a]

Motor Skill/Foundation	Presentation in Children With Autism Spectrum Disorder
Postural control	Differences in quality of muscle tone
	Use of feedback rather than feedforward mechanism to maintain postural stability
Praxis skills and motor coordination	Difficulty with initiation of motor sequences
	Poor timing of movements in space
	Poor bilateral integration and interlimb coordination
	Poor motor imitation (gestures, postures)
	Decrease in variability and complexity of movement repertoire
	Diminished ideation for novel actions/concepts
Gross motor skills	Poor force modulation; difficulty regulating speed/pace
	Delays and/or disordered learning of early developmental positions and sequential movement patterns (rolling, crawling)
Anticipatory motor control	Poor postural readiness in preparation for movement/action
	Overreliance on visual guidance to aid body awareness
Fine motor skills	Decreased quality in grasp patterns and manipulation
	Poor lateralization; delay or deficiency in differentiated hand use
Oral motor	Decreased quality of sucking, chewing, blowing
	Poorly coordinated breath support for both speech and feeding
Ocular motor	Poor functional use of vision to guide movements, anticipate actions

[a]This is not an exhaustive list of motor findings.
Source: Adapted from Stackhouse (2010).

generation of new ideas but also can be used as a platform for developing these same skills. Because play is often described as the primary occupation of childhood, an examination of play skills and behaviors is a relevant component of a pediatric OT evaluation. Because the play activities and behaviors of children with ASD are often strikingly different than those of typically developing children, interventions that address the components of play (e.g., imitation, body awareness, motor skills, and praxis) are often key elements of the occupational therapist's plan of care.

Play is a complex behavior, and there are multiple factors that may be involved in the play of a child with ASD. May-Benson (2010) notes that children with ASD often engage in stereotypic play that focuses on the sensorimotor properties afforded by an object rather than their assumed function. Caution should be used not to interpret the actions of a person with ASD through one's own lens of social or cultural expectations because the function of that behavior for them may be quite different. This is illustrated through the following example: A young child with ASD bangs one block against another that is positioned on the table. An onlooker might assume the child is trying to stack the blocks by placing one on top of the other and is either lacking the refined skill to do so or is demonstrating willfulness in refusing to meet the expectation. However, the child with ASD may simply find the noise created by the collusion of the two blocks to be a more salient reinforcer than the act of stacking.

Abnormalities in sensory processing, described previously, are often a strong contributor to the atypical play behavior in children with ASD. Bundy, Shia, Qi, and Miller (2007) found that children with sensory processing disorders scored significantly lower on the Test of Playfulness compared to typical peers. Children with ASD tend toward interactions with objects based on their *sensory* qualities (visual appeal, sound, texture, and temperature) rather than the affordances of objects for action (ability to bounce it, throw it, and catch it). They may engage in repetitive actions with the objects to meet a sensory need (e.g., banging an object to hear the sound that it makes or spinning the wheels on a toy car for the visual stimulation).

Play might also be affected by impairments in praxis. Praxis refers to the ability to conceptualize and formulate a plan for a motor act or sequence and then execute this plan. When discussing praxis, there are three different steps (Ayres, 1972): ideation (generating an idea for action: "I will climb into that tent"), motor planning (creation of a plan of action: "First I will bend down and pull back the flap at the door entrance. . ."), and execution of the plan. An impairment in any one of these steps may impact an individual's ability to play; however, for individuals with ASD, difficulties with ideation and planning tend to be the greatest challenges with praxis.

Effective ideation allows for the many affordances of objects to be recognizable, which fosters the generation of ideas for play (May-Benson, 2010). Furthermore, an inability to generate ideas for action can lead to play that is stereotypical and repetitive in nature rather than representational (Ozonoff, 1997). In turn, the engagement in repetitive actions with objects can further limit exploration. Effective motor planning relies on our ability to access our vast repertoire of sensorimotor experiences and apply this information to a novel situation and context. Early sensorimotor experiences provide the foundation for the development of one's own body "map" and body-in-space perception. When the ability to form this body map is hindered by a paucity of sensorimotor experience or poor integration of information from sensory systems, accurate planning of movements in space is affected. This can result in movements that appear clumsy, poorly timed, and sometimes dangerous (May-Benson, 2010).

Activities of Daily Living

Children and some adults with ASD often face challenges with even the most basic self-care activities and daily routines, such as getting dressed, brushing teeth, bathing, and preparing or eating a simple meal. Sensitivity to certain sensory inputs (touch, temperature, and sound), the craving and preoccupation with other sensations, difficulty with motor planning and sequencing, and a lack of intrinsic motivation to perform such tasks (due to limited concern for, or awareness of, the social relevance of personal hygiene) are all factors that may contribute to poor self-care skills. Jasmine et al. (2009) found that sensory overresponsivity and fine motor skills were highly correlated with daily living skills for young children with ASD, even when accounting for cognition. Using activity analysis, occupational therapists can help identify the specific sensory and motor impairments underlying these functional challenges. OT intervention often includes a combination of targeted skill remediation, paired with environmental and task modifications needed to support function.

Social Participation: Family, Community, and Peers

One of the core features of ASD is marked impairment in social functioning. This impairment often causes major disruption in family routines, participation in community activities, and social interactions. Occupational therapy has a role in mitigating the impact that symptoms of ASD can have in these domains and in bolstering the social functioning of the individual.

Family and Community

Anecdotal evidence suggests that having a child with ASD can add tremendous stress to a family and can result in a significant shift in family routines, roles, and lifestyle. Many compromises may be necessary to accommodate the special needs and functional limitations of the child. Basic daily routines such as getting dressed and ready for school, eating breakfast, and going to the bathroom can become very time-consuming and energy-demanding events that impact all members of the family unit. Children with ASD often require much more of their parents' resources with regard to time, energy, and financial investment than their siblings, which may have an impact on sibling relationships. Furthermore, family routines such as mealtime may be difficult to coordinate given the sensory needs, dietary restrictions, and busy schedule (including medical and therapy appointments) of the child with ASD.

The different sensory experiences of children with ASD can have a notable impact on family occupations, particularly with regard to activity selection and how the family prepares for those activities or events (Bagby, Dickie, & Baranek, 2012). Basic routines such as going to the grocery store, going to the park or library, or eating at a restaurant may present conflicts so significant that a withdrawal from these activities may occur. Bagby et al. (2012) interviewed parents of children with ASD and found that they choose family activities and outings based on what situations need to be avoided (e.g., bowling alleys may be too loud and movie theaters are too dark). Furthermore, these parents reported the need for much more time to prepare for such activities, as well as the need to have alternate plans in place just in case. Events that would otherwise be highly valued (e.g., birthday parties) are often avoided altogether.

Participation in family activities and meaningful events is an important aspect of an individual's overall functioning. Occupational therapists can help establish strategies to improve participation in these activities and help restore the ability to engage in meaningful activities as a family unit.

Social Skills

One of the key features of ASD is impaired social skills often characterized by poor or inconsistent eye contact, difficulty initiating or maintaining social interaction, difficulty interpreting nonverbal communication cues, and a poor understanding of social norms. Challenges with social interaction often result in difficulty developing close relationships with others, which can lead to alienation at school and within other peer groups. The ability to interact successfully with those around us is critical not just for getting basic needs met but also as a platform for participation in all of life's activities. Successful social participation does not hinge only on the ability to communicate verbally with another but also involves a much greater skill set that allows us to share space, time, and ideas with other people in a way that promotes participation in meaningful activities. Individuals with ASD have difficulty with these critical components of interaction and often do things that are not aligned with accepted social norms, often perpetuating a cycle of negative responses from those around them. Furthermore, behaviors associated with sensory-seeking and sensory overresponsivity, as well as the tendency toward repetitive or stereotypical behaviors, can further alienate these individuals. Difficulties with social interaction pose a significant barrier to occupational performance and can significantly affect an individual's ability to participate in work, leisure, and educational endeavors.

Addressing these social issues through social skills training, participation in small peer groups, and consistent opportunities for social modeling is an important piece of the intervention plan for a child with ASD. Social skill curricula often involve a multidisciplinary team that may include speech/language pathologists, child psychologists, teachers, developmental specialists, and occupational therapists. The occupational therapist's role in social skills training often focuses on how one uses and manages his or her body in social interactions, strategies for emotional regulation and the regulation of arousal level, managing self-stimulating or sensory-seeking behaviors that interfere with social participation, and environmental considerations.

The ability to have successful social interactions relies on the ability to share physical space with others, not only in a way that is safe but also in a way that promotes and supports that interaction. Things that become intuitive for typically developing children at a young age are not intuitive for those with ASD. For example, the concept of personal space is one that often needs to be taught overtly to children and adolescents with ASD. A certain proximity to our communication partner is necessary to indicate intent and to allow for successful interaction. However, when someone violates this space, it can feel very uncomfortable and sometimes threatening, and it can very easily result in an unsuccessful interaction. When someone stands too close, the person who is being approached may take a step back, and a typical individual would likely take that cue as a sign that he or she may have been too close. A person with ASD, however, may not notice or correctly interpret that nonverbal cue and may violate that personal space boundary once again. Understanding how personal space etiquette may differ from one situation to another (e.g., how close to a peer to sit during circle time and how close to stand to peers in line at school) poses an additional challenge for children and adolescents with ASD who are often very rule-based and concrete in their thinking.

Personal space is not the only consideration for how we use our body in social situations. Michelle Garcia Winner discusses the concept of keeping one's "body in the group" to communicate participation in a shared activity or idea (Winner & Crooke, 2008). In the book, *You Are a Social Detective! Explaining Social Thinking to Kids*, Winner and Crooke illustrate the importance of body position and posture in being part of a social group. Simple behaviors such as turning your body toward the others in the group, looking at the person who is talking, and staying in close proximity to the group can have a significant impact on how the others think about you and accept you. These nonverbal cues are difficult for individuals with ASD and often have to be taught as discrete skills and then implemented into practice across various settings.

Modulating the volume and tone of one's voice during social interaction is another challenge that can compromise social interaction for individuals with ASD and an area in which OT can be helpful. Some children with ASD speak very loudly and with an atypical prosody. Others may speak too softly, making it difficult for others to hear. The ability to modify voice volume in response to changes in the environment (e.g., a loud fire truck driving by or entering quiet library space) can present a challenge because it relies on an awareness of these environmental and social cues. Using a voice that is too loud for the context may relay anger or aggression, and it can shift the tone of the interaction. Likewise, a voice that is too soft can be difficult to hear and may not be sufficient to sustain the attention of the conversational partner.

Many social interactions involve some sort of physical contact, such as a handshake, a pat on the back, or a hug. Understanding the appropriate use of these gestures is critical to avoid awkward or potentially offensive situations. For individuals with ASD, differentiating what action is appropriate under a particular set of circumstances is often a struggle. It relies on an appreciation of different types of relationships (e.g., family member vs. acquaintance) and an awareness of social context. Using the appropriate amount of *force* during these physical interactions can also be a challenge for individuals with ASD. Squeezing someone too hard when hugging or hitting them on the back when attempting to pat them lightly are the types of behaviors that might result. These can be interpreted as intentional behaviors or aggressive acts, but often they are simply a result of poor proprioceptive awareness. They may not be able to anticipate the correct amount of force needed for the action, may have difficulty grading the force, and may not realize even after the event that too much force was applied.

The sensory-seeking behaviors observed with many children with ASD can also impact social interactions with peers and others. Behaviors such as seeking out constant movement (e.g., moving around the room when supposed to be seated or repositioning frequently in a chair), pushing feet against things/people, and fidgeting with everything in close proximity can interfere with social interaction in that they can be very distracting, can draw the person away from the social encounter, and can be confusing or concerning to the other party.

Teaching strategies to manage these sensory-seeking behaviors is an important role of the occupational therapist and often involves the implementation of sensory materials that will provide the desired input but in a more subtle or socially acceptable manner. For example, for children who have difficulty sitting in one place and have a tendency to frequently get up from their chair during school, a (textured) air cushion on their chair can sometimes be very effective in limiting their need for movement out of the chair. Likewise, for children who tend to reach out and touch everything in close proximity in such a manner that it interferes with participation and social interaction, attaching *fidgets* (items that are stretchy, textured, bendable, or plush) to the inside of their pants' pocket or to the underside of their desk is often effective.

In assessing social interaction skills, the occupational therapist must consider environmental factors that either support or hinder social participation. Assessing the need for adaptive materials and/or seating for participation in age-appropriate play and/or leisure skills may be necessary to allow for opportunities for more natural social interaction and engagement in similar activities. Adapting the environment to promote social participation may involve change to the physical space, reducing excessive auditory distractions, and/or limiting visual clutter that can lead to overstimulation. Creating defined space for activities (e.g., carpet squares during circle time) is important for some children with ASD.

Problems in School

Children spend a large part of their day in school; therefore, ensuring that the supports and environment that they need within this context to be successful are in place is critical to their overall well-being and progress. School brings with it many challenges for a child with ASD beyond the curriculum. Busy hallways, waiting in line, tolerating loud noises of crowds and bells, and frequent transitions are just some of the factors that can serve as barriers to success in this setting. An occupational therapist can help implement a variety of strategies (behavioral, environmental, and sensory) to support children with ASD within their school program.

Many school-based OT programs focus primarily on fine motor skills, the ability to use classroom tools, and handwriting. These are important skills. However, for children with ASD, an examination of their physical and sensory environment is also critical. Specifically, the use of visual supports to facilitate transitions, preferential seating to support attention, reduction of visual clutter, an organized and consistent physical environment, and the implementation of a "sensory diet" (Wilbarger, 1984) are key components of the OT intervention within the classroom/school. A sensory diet is a scheduled regimen of sensory-enhanced activities that is designed to meet an individual's unique sensory cravings and needs in a way that is safe, appropriate, and predictable. By building these sensorimotor experiences into one's schedule proactively, sensory-seeking behaviors that may be disruptive, unsafe, or inappropriate to context/place can often be avoided. For others, the right sensory diet can help with arousal regulation and mood. The occupational therapist's role here, ultimately, is to determine what strategies and/or modifications would be most effective in supporting the child's functioning within the given context. A list of common challenges faced by children with ASD within their school setting and suggested strategies are provided in Table 19.4.

Independent Living and the Transition to Adulthood

The transition to adulthood brings with it many changes and challenges for individuals with ASD. For some, this involves a transition to independent living, the branching out of one's

TABLE 19.4 Common School Challenges for Children With Autism Spectrum Disorder and Related Strategies

Challenge	Strategies
Difficulty navigating safely through crowded hallways—bumps into peers, too stimulating, etc.	Allow child to travel hallways at less busy times (e.g., 5 minutes before bell rings)
	Practice route to and from classroom(s), gym, library, and cafeteria during off hours to familiarize child with layout and routine
Difficulty standing in line	Allow child to be at end of line so that no one is in his or her "backspace"
	Reinforce "one arm's length" rule for personal space
Remaining at desk during seated work	Provide an air cushion for seat to create dynamic seating
	Allow child to shift position or stand at desk for brief periods as needed to regulate arousal level
	Provide brief movement breaks for whole class or engage child in movement through classroom activities (e.g., passing out materials and collecting papers)
Difficulty processing auditory instructions	Provide visual supports or written instructions at desk to supplement verbal instructions
Distractibility	Allow the use of noise-cancellation headphones in class
	Offer preferential seating (front row, away from door/window)

social network, and entrance into the workforce. The occupational therapist can play a critical role in preparing for this transition. Career planning can be a stressful and complicated process for anyone, let alone someone with a disability. Choosing a job that is a good fit involves exploring not only one's current skill set and capacity for growth and learning but also one's personal interests and vocational goals. It is also important to consider job environment, schedule, and the occupational demands of a given line of work. For example, some individuals with ASD may find more success in a job in which they have limited social contact and work more or less independently in a private workspace. Others may do better with a job that involves constant movement and being on one's feet, as opposed to a desk job, because sitting for long periods may be difficult. Many individuals with ASD thrive on concrete and consistent tasks and outcomes, for whom a job involving more rote activity may be the best fit. Others may succeed in a more creative capacity where adhering to a specific protocol is neither required nor encouraged. Occupational therapists can play a key role in this process for individuals with ASD given their unique ability to anticipate the occupational demands of various jobs through activity analysis, assess the unique skills and limitations of an individual, and make considerations for environmental and task modification to support vocational success.

The occupational therapist's role, however, extends beyond job selection and often involves training in related life skills needed to secure employment. For example, writing a resume and attending a job interview are necessary skills that are often very difficult for individuals with ASD. Job interviews arguably pose one of the major challenges due to the heavy focus on social interaction, the ability to respond to introspective questions on the spot, perspective taking (including the interpretation of nonverbal cues), and first impressions. Occupational therapists, in conjunction with other related professions, often play a key role in preparing individuals for these inevitable and challenging interactions. This often involves a discussion of anticipated scenarios; rehearsal of greeting, introductions, and responses to expected questions; and assistance with presentation (wardrobe, personal appearance, portfolio, etc.). Compensatory strategies such as providing or bringing written materials (e.g., cover letter and hard copies of resume), using notes (written list of key points for discussion), and implementing any of their own learned strategies for self-regulation or impulse control can be very helpful. In some cases, suggesting the interview take place in a less stimulating or distracting environment (private room, one interviewer) or opting for a phone interview versus face-to-face, if possible, may trigger less anxiety.

Once a job placement or career path has been determined, the occupational therapist in some cases may assist with job skill training (learning the specific skills needed for the job), including strategies for compensation. Establishing healthy work routines and habits to promote success is also important. Learning how to drive or successfully access public transportation may be necessary to secure employment. Furthermore, for some, the concepts of money management and financial planning come into play.

IADLs: The Skills for Independent Living

Many individuals with ASD live at home with their parents or other family members well into adulthood. A 2005 study by Wagner, Newman, Cameto, Garza, and Levine found that only 4% of adults with ASD live alone. A recent study found that young adults with ASD were more likely to live with their parents or other family members and least likely to have ever lived independently compared to adults with other developmental disabilities (Anderson, Liang, & Lord, 2014).

The skills needed to live alone greatly exceed the basic skills of self-care. Instrumental skills of living are the basic life skills needed to successfully manage one's life both at home and within the community. These skills include completing household chores, telephone use, managing finances, using or accessing transportation, caring for plants or pets, doing laundry, grocery shopping, and meal preparation. Many of the specific skills required to perform these tasks can be taught. However, overall safety and well-being may be compromised by poor executive functioning. Individuals with ASD may not anticipate or identify potential safety hazards or concerns. Furthermore, difficulty with social skills can impact their relationship with neighbors and their ability to use neighbors as a resource when needed. Time management can also be an issue affecting punctuality at work, as well as the timely completion of personal or household responsibilities.

OCCUPATIONAL THERAPY ASSESSMENT FOR INDIVIDUALS WITH AUTISM SPECTRUM DISORDER

The occupational therapist's assessment process, as outlined at the beginning of this chapter, begins with an examination of an individual's occupational profile and an analysis of occupational performance. This often begins with a patient and/or caregiver interview to determine how the patient's day-to-day life is impacted by his or her disability. A top-down approach such as this allows the occupational therapist to first consider the impact of the disability on function as it plays out in the course of one's actual day or week and then to break it down further to determine what impairments or skill deficits may be at the root. Methods of assessment often include a combination of interview, questionnaire, standardized testing, and skilled observation.

Parent/Caregiver Interview

When evaluating a child with ASD, an interview with the child's parent(s) or primary caregiver is essential in gaining a true perspective on the impact that the child's disability has on daily activities and family routines. Understanding how the child's challenges play out in a typical day provides a more complete perspective on the reason for referral than would review of the patient's medical record alone. Gathering information from the child's teacher, school-based therapists, and others who work with or interact with the child regularly can be another very valuable piece of the assessment process because it allows for a broad perspective of how the child behaves, performs, and interacts across contexts. Questions generally focus on daily routines, behavior, play, and specific age-level skills. An understanding of the impact that the child's disability has on his or her family and the degree to which it inhibits or compromises participation in community and school activities is essential.

Sensory Questionnaires

Sensory questionnaires are a common part of the OT evaluation for a child with ASD. These questionnaires are generally filled out by the child's parents or primary caregiver; however, some formats, such as the Adolescent Sensory Profile: Self Assessment (Brown & Dunn, 2002) and Sensory Processing Measure: School & Classroom forms (Kuhaneck, Henry, & Glennon, 2007), are created for completion by the patient or school staff/teacher, respectively. These questionnaires are composed of statements relating to the behavioral outcomes of sensory processing. Interpretation by the occupational therapist of not only individual responses but also, more important, the pattern of responses across sensory systems and related factors is critical to being able to use this information to create an appropriate and effective plan of care.

Standardized Testing

The inclusion of standardized test measures in a complex evaluation is useful not only for comparison to normative data to determine skill deficit and delay but also to show measurable, objective change over time. The ability to document quantifiable data such as this is often necessary to determine eligibility for services. A variety of standardized tests are utilized by occupational therapists when evaluating children with ASD and related disorders. For lower functioning or nonverbal patients, standardized testing may be difficult. Even if receptive language is poor, many test items can be taught through demonstration; however, basic imitation skills are often necessary.

Standardized tests used by occupational therapists to evaluate children with ASD focus on the assessment of skills in the following areas: (1) fine motor skills and upper extremity functioning, (2) gross motor coordination and planning, (3) visual–perceptual skills, (4) visual–motor integration, and (5) sensory discrimination and praxis. In many cases, adaptations to standardized administration may be necessary in order to engage the child and ensure comprehension of the requested task. Adaptations may include the need for additional verbal cues or prompting, rewording of the task instructions, the provision of visual supports to aid in comprehension, and/or demonstration of the task in cases in which performance on verbal instruction alone would be otherwise expected. These deviations from standardized protocol must be documented and can affect validity. A brief list of assessments commonly used by occupational therapists when evaluating children with ASD is provided in Table 19.5.

Skilled Observation

One of the most valuable methods of assessment that occupational therapists use when evaluating a child with ASD is observation. Observing children during both structured and unstructured tasks provides an array of information about how they interact with their environment, what motivates them, how they approach a task and engage in problem solving, and what barriers or limitations they face along the way. Observations can be formal or informal, and they may or may not require direct therapist intervention (Watling, 2010). Simply observing a child at play can provide rich information about his or her language ability, attention, interests, and motor skills. Therapist involvement may be necessary to set up opportunities for new challenges and experiences and also to grade or adapt the activities as needed along the way. For example, observing a child interacting with a puzzle can provide information about that child's visual perceptual skills and the ability to both visualize where the piece should be inserted and manipulate the piece effectively for placement. Furthermore, if the task appears challenging, observations can be made with regard to the child's frustration tolerance and ability to problem solve in order to successfully complete the task. Simultaneously, observations about the child's sitting posture, grasp, and bilateral coordination are made as the child attempts to complete the puzzle. Factors that should also be considered include the child's attention, distractibility, tendency to become preoccupied or to give up, and general affect during play. If in a social or group

TABLE 19.5 Assessments Used by Occupational Therapists to Assess Children/Adolescents With Autism Spectrum Disorder[a]

Type of Assessment	Examples of Assessment Tools	Areas Measured
Sensory questionnaires	Sensory Profile: Caregiver Questionnaire	Responses to various sensory input, body awareness and planning, behavioral/emotional outcomes to sensory processing
	Sensory Processing Measure	
Developmental motor assessments	Bruininks–Osertesky Test of Motor Proficiency, Second Edition	Measures fine motor skills, motor coordination, balance, etc.
	Peabody Developmental Motor Scales, Second Edition	Measures grasping and early visual motor skills
Perceptual–motor skills	Developmental Test of Visual Perception, Second Edition	Measures various aspects of visual perception and visual motor integration
	Motor-free Visual Perceptual Test, Third Edition	Measures various aspects of visual perception in the absence of motor demand
	Beery–Buktenica Test of Visual Motor Integration	Measures ability to copy shapes and line designs of increasing complexity
Tests of sensory discrimination	Miller Assessment of Preschoolers Sensory Integration & Praxis Tests	Measures tactile discrimination, visual discrimination and perception, postural/constructional/oral praxis, etc.

[a]This is not an exhaustive list of assessment measures.

situation, such as day care or school, then observations about social interaction and play skills in a peer setting can also be made as other children approach the child and attempt parallel or cooperative play.

Skilled observations are used by occupational therapists as a means not only to learn about specific skills and abilities but also to understand the big picture of how that child interacts with the world around him or her. These observations can be categorized into many areas, including posture and movement, ideation and planning, attention and arousal, sensory-seeking or -avoiding behaviors that interfere with play or functioning, communication ability, and general affect.

OCCUPATIONAL THERAPY INTERVENTION IN AUTISM SPECTRUM DISORDER

Once a thorough evaluation has been conducted and the effect of the child's impairments on occupational performance has been outlined, a plan of care can be created. The occupational therapist must determine if OT intervention is indicated or not and, if so, in what setting, at what frequency, and in what format the services should be delivered. For example, if a focus on fine motor skills, tool use, and handwriting is emphasized, then services delivered within the child's school program may be most appropriate. Alternatively, if working on increasing independence with self-care activities within the context of the child's morning routine is determined to be a priority, then services delivered within the child's home may be most beneficial.

Delivering services within a child's natural environment, such as at home or in school, limits the need to generalize a skill from one setting to another and allows the skills to be learned in real time in the space in which they would naturally occur. Simulated tasks in an outside setting, such as an outpatient clinic, can be beneficial but may not generalize well to other settings. Unfortunately, home-based services are not always feasible and sometimes require significant out-of-pocket expense. In addition, home services are limited by the space, physical layout, and the materials and equipment available within the child's home.

For many children with ASD who have profound sensory processing dysfunction, an outpatient center or private therapy clinic may offer a more optimal treatment venue in that it allows for access to a variety of therapy materials, equipment, and resources that may not be available within the child's natural environment. Treatment in these settings should include parent education through direct participation, observation, or discussion to ensure that carryover of therapeutic activities and implementation of strategies at home are successful.

Addressing Sensory Issues in Autism Spectrum Disorder

Given the significant impact of sensory processing challenges on daily occupations and performance, treatment strategies to ameliorate these symptoms and related issues are often a central focus of intervention. Watling, Dietz, Kanny, and McLaughlin (1999) surveyed 72 occupational therapists who worked extensively with children with ASD and found that the most common treatment approach utilized with this population was SI.

Ayres Sensory Integration

Ayres Sensory Integration (ASI) is both a theory and an intervention approach used commonly by occupational therapists working with children with ASD. Sensory integration theory was developed by Jean Ayres, an occupational therapist and researcher with a background in both educational psychology and neuroscience. The theory is based on the premise that effective processing and integrating of sensory information from one's environment is necessary for *adaptive behavior*. She theorized that poor *sensory integration* often resulted in behavior and learning challenges, and that the inability of higher centers to modulate and regulate lower brain centers (sensorimotor) is the cause (Ayres, 1972). Sensory integration theory is based on a few key postulates that include the following: (1) The nervous system is capable of change (plasticity), (2) interactions between an individual and the environment are critical for brain development, and (3) meaningful sensorimotor activity is an important substrate for learning and neural change (Schaaf & Miller, 2005). Sensory integration therapy is a child-directed approach that emphasizes active participation in sensory-rich activities that provide the "just right challenge" to stimulate problem solving and the scaffolding of new skills and ideas. The therapist, using a sensory integration approach, introduces sensorimotor activities that are rich in tactile, proprioceptive, and vestibular sensations and that provide the child with opportunities to build on her current abilities as she engages in new experiences with the environment. The therapist grades the activities to provide a meaningful challenge while taking care not to exceed the threshold of what is possible for that child. The four basic principles of the sensory integration approach are outlined in Table 19.6.

TABLE 19.6 The Four Principles of Sensory Integration Therapy

Principle	Description
The "just right challenge"	Creating a challenge that is not so much that it interferes with success.
Adaptive response	The creation of new useful strategies in response to novel challenges.
Active engagement	It is essential that the child is an active participant and not a passive recipient in the activities; active exploration of a sensory-rich environment that presents a myriad of novel motor experiences and challenges is key.
Child directed	The therapist follows the child's lead and reads his or her cues to modify the environment as needed.

Source: Adapted from Schaaf and Miller (2005).

Whereas interventions such as the implementation of a sensory diet can be used in a variety of settings (home, school, and community), ASI therapy is a treatment approach that requires a more structured environment. ASI is frequently provided in a clinic space equipped with floor mats, suspended equipment, balls, bolsters, and other materials to create the potential for a variety of sensorimotor challenges. The environment is designed to provide a variety of movement experiences in time and space, paired with various tactile and proprioceptive inputs to increase body perception through somatosensory awareness. Visual and auditory stimuli can be manipulated to reduce distractions or to heighten awareness, as needed. The therapist, in playful collaboration with the child, creates new situations that require motor planning and execution and then modifies or adapts the activities as needed to promote success (see Figure 19.2). The environment is structured to promote praxis and increase organization of behavior through carefully graded vestibular, proprioceptive, and tactile experiences (Mailloux & Roley, 2010).

Praxis relies on the underlying concept of body scheme, awareness of body movements in space, and the ability to anticipate and plan movements and actions seamlessly in a dynamic environment. Children with ASD often do not process body sensations effectively, nor do they integrate these sensations to get an overall sense of their body in space. ASI therapy provides a framework for building these skills by targeting the underlying foundations of sensory processing and the effective integration of information from different sensory systems to produce an adaptive response.

Currently, there is no consensus in the literature regarding the effectiveness of the ASI approach with children with ASD (May-Benson & Koomar, 2010), but the use of this treatment approach by occupational therapists working with this population is widespread. Watling et al. (1999) surveyed a group of pediatric occupational therapists and found that 99% of the occupational therapists working with children with ASD used a sensory integration frame of reference frequently or always and that this was the most frequently used treatment approach with this population. Other researchers have suggested that up to 90% of occupational therapists working in schools use an SI frame of reference when working with children with ASD and other disorders that may be associated with difficulties processing and organizing sensory information (Miller & Fuller, 2006).

Although further study regarding the efficacy of the ASI approach is needed, there is a great deal of evidence to support its use. A 2010 review by May-Benson and Koomar specifically examined 27 individual studies of the effectiveness of the ASI approach with children with sensory processing challenges using various outcome measures. With regard to motor performance, 10 of the 14 related studies found positive gains with ASI that were at least

FIGURE 19.2 Many children with autism spectrum disorder have difficulty with praxis; occupational therapists create sensorimotor challenges to work on the timing and sequencing of movements within a motivating and sensory-rich context.

equal to, if not greater than, those of alternative interventions. Furthermore, measurable gains were maintained over time even after direct intervention was discontinued. Earlier reviews of the effectiveness of SI treatment with children with learning disabilities found a pattern of findings suggesting that OT–SI with this population is at least as effective as alternative interventions, with the greatest gains reported in motor performance (Polatajko, Kaplan, & Wilson, 1992). Similarly, Humphries, Wright, McDougall, and Vertes (1990) and Humphries, Wright, Snider, and McDougall (1992) found that although OT intervention using ASI and treatment using a perceptual–motor approach both yielded more positive results than no treatment at all, the gains observed varied by treatment approach. Specifically, the SI approach had the greatest impact on improving gross motor skills, bilateral coordination, strength, and motor accuracy, whereas the perceptual–motor approach yielded the greatest gains in visual motor ability and balance.

Other researchers have compared the effectiveness of the OT–SI approach to that of non-OT intervention that was activity-based for children with sensory processing issues (Miller, Coll, & Schoen, 2007). These researchers found that the children receiving the SI treatment had more significant gains in attention, cognitive, and social skills compared to the alternative group. Furthermore, the SI group demonstrated significantly greater improvements in individual goals relating to daily living skills. Similarly, Pfeiffer, Koenig, Kinnealey, Sheppard, and Henderson (2011) compared the effectiveness of OT–SI for school-age children with ASD to OT treatment targeting fine motor skills (tabletop activities) and found a significant reduction in autistic mannerisms (stereotypical behaviors, highly restricted interests, etc.) in the SI group compared to the fine motor group. An earlier study by Smith, Press, Koenig, and Kinnealey (2005) found similar findings, including a reduction in self-stimulatory behaviors, following a course of treatment employing SI.

Interestingly, Miller et al. (2007) also examined a group of children with poor sensory modulation and, using electrodermal responses as an outcome measure, found decreased stress response (to repetitive sensory stimuli) following SI therapy. These findings are interesting in light of testimonials from individuals with ASD who have described self-stimulatory behaviors as modulators of stress, used to self-regulate with the function of effectively avoiding sensory overload (Shoener et al., 2008).

Other studies examined the effect of OT–SI specifically with children with ASD. A review by Baranek (2002) examined the effects of OT–SI on children with ASD and found a trend of positive outcomes particularly in social skills, play, and sensory overresponsivity. Recent research has reported similar findings. A case study by Schaaf, Hunt, and Benevides (2012) demonstrated improved sensory discrimination, regulation, motor skills, communication, and overall behavior of a child with ASD following a 10-week course of OT–SI. Parent report indicated significant positive change specifically with regard to activity level, safety and impulsivity, self-care tasks, and play skills. Specific parent observations included greater independence with dressing, better bedtime routine and sleep habits, and increased participation in family activities. School staff also reported observable differences, including improved play skills, an increase in social participation, improved attention to task, and more successful completion of schoolwork. Improvements in both standardized test measures, as well as parent and teacher report of changes in behavior and functioning, reflect positive outcomes with both proximal (sensory and motor) and distal (behavior and participation) factors. This provides further evidence that changes at the level of sensory and motor processes can lead to improvements in participation and overall occupational performance.

Recent investigation into brain plasticity and the impact of sensory processing on neuronal structure and function may provide further support for ASI, as well as a framework for understanding its effects. A review by Lane and Schaaf (2010) examined studies of the relationship between sensory input, brain function, and behavior. The findings indicated that direct sensory input or exposure to an enriched sensory environment resulted in changes in neuronal structure and function, which were sometimes reflected in behavioral outcomes. Furthermore, these changes were observed primarily in the areas of the brain related to learning and memory. Some effects observed were found to be long-lasting, although this was found to be highly dependent on personal and environmental factors. The review concluded that there is ample support for the postulate that rich sensory input provided in the context of meaningful activity facilitates neuroplasticity, with active engagement and interest in task being important factors.

Despite these findings that support the use of ASI as a viable treatment approach with children with ASD, many studies had reported inconclusive findings. Inconsistencies in research results, small sample sizes, and methodological weaknesses continue to compromise the integrity of this research and limit our ability to fully understand and demonstrate the effects of this treatment approach compared to other interventions. Further research is most certainly necessary.

Sensory Diets

As discussed previously, the sensory symptoms observed in ASD are widespread and highly variable. Regardless of variability in presentation, however, they frequently interfere with successful participation in daily activities, completion of important routines, and productive and meaningful interactions with others. It is important to examine how these behaviors interfere with occupational performance across contexts and determine how these sensory needs can be honored while simultaneously supporting successful engagement in occupation.

A sensory diet, as discussed previously, is a regimen of structured sensory-based activities provided at regular intervals throughout the day that provide the types of sensory input that the child craves and seeks. Embedding these activities into the child's daily routines helps with consistency and can facilitate better carryover across settings such as home, day care, or school. For example, for a child who is spinning herself, rocking, or in frequent motion, participating in certain activities at recess, including swinging on the swing set, sitting on the seesaw, or engaging in games such as Ring Around the Rosie or duck-duck-goose, can provide some of that extra input that she needs to stay regulated. Likewise, a child who is touching everything or everyone around her may benefit from a sensory diet rich in tactile sensation. Activities such as finger painting, playing in a sensory/tactile bin (e.g., a tub filled with dried beans and rice), or playing with clay or Play Doh can help meet the child's sensory needs in a more adaptive, less intrusive way (Figure 19.3).

In addition to activities that provide specific sensory input that the child is seeking, it is important to introduce strategies or accommodations to assist with attention and self-regulation during specific activities. Strategies might include adaptive or preferential seating, opportunities for breaks, reduction of distractions, and access to materials such as fidgets or weighted lap pads. Furthermore, children who tend to present with overresponsivity may need opportunities to retreat to a quiet space when overstimulated (e.g., indoor tent, ball pit, or cozy corner). Breaks such as this can often improve overall participation (Figure 19.4). A sample sensory diet is provided in Table 19.7.

For children who experience overresponsivity to certain sensations, providing opportunities for graded exposure to these stimuli throughout the day can foster a gradual desensitization. For example, a child who has tactile defensiveness may avoid playing in the sandbox at recess. In some cases, avoidance of the playground altogether may ensue.

FIGURE 19.3 A rice bin is an excellent medium for tactile play.

FIGURE 19.4 Many children with autism spectrum disorder (ASD) retreat to cozy spaces to self-regulate; burrowing in a ball pit (or under couch cushions, in a sleeping bag, etc.) can be calming and organizing for a child with ASD.

Providing graded exposure to the sandbox, for instance, in a way that is safe and controlled can help the child acclimate to this over time.

For some children, social stories (Gray, 2000) can be very helpful in introducing the event or situation through discussion and pictures only (e.g., a social story about playing in the sandbox during recess). A next step may be seeing the activity or stimulus from a distance (e.g., standing on the playground at recess several feet away from the sandbox). Seeing others interact with the stimulus in a positive way without negative consequence can minimize the aversion and be a starting point in building trust. Eventually, direct contact may be made (e.g., touching the sand with one finger, then with whole hand, then two hands, etc.), although not until success has been met at these prerequisite levels. If the child has a meltdown when he sees the sandbox, then forcing him to play in it will likely exacerbate this reaction and can lead to a more significant aversion and withdrawal.

It is the role of the occupational therapist to determine the appropriate type, frequency, and intensity of sensory input based on the individual needs of the patient and to monitor responses to the input over time in order to make the appropriate changes and modifications that are needed.

ENVIRONMENTAL CONSIDERATIONS

Providing selected sensory inputs via a structured sensory diet can have a significant impact on the regulatory abilities of a child with ASD. However, environmental factors can also play a major role in arousal and regulation. Visual factors such as lighting, visual clutter,

TABLE 19.7 Sample Sensory Diet

Time of Day/ Routine	Sensory Input/ Activity	Environmental Modification	Behavioral/ Organizational Techniques
Waking up	Bouncing on physioball to increase arousal as needed.	Lights on; gradual introduction of more sounds/music.	Allow child to wake up at his or her own pace with support as needed.
Breakfast	Provide air cushion on chair to increase sitting tolerance and help maintain awake/ alert state.	Reduce unnecessary distractions (background noise, TV, etc.).	Avoid offering too many choices
In classroom: desk work	Provide hand fidgets as needed to maintain attention during listening activities and seated work.	Offer preferential seating (front of class, away from windows); close windows to reduce excess noise.	Keep classroom materials well-organized and highly visual.
Lunchtime: cafeteria	If sound sensitivity is an issue, provide noise-cancellation headphones; allow child to move around as needed to self-regulate during lunch break (provide structured movement breaks if possible—access to gym/ outdoor playground).	Consider seating away from high-traffic area and farther from kitchen, particularly if overresponsive to food smells.	Make child aware of menu prior to lunchtime; encourage bag lunch from home if child has food sensitivities.
After school: transition home	Provide a sensory break for child upon arriving home; consider child's own sensory needs: quiet space versus movement and heavy work.	Keep demands and distractions low during transition, when possible, to allow child to regroup.	Provide visual supports as needed to review evening schedule (e.g. dinner, homework, book/TV, bedtime).
Dinner time	Same as breakfast.		
Bedtime	Offer child "quiet time" with dimmed lights, relaxing music, and books to look at (or audio books). Avoid video games or TV shows that are very visually stimulating; avoid tasks requiring high cognitive demand.	Keep materials and supplies for bedtime routine well-organized and stored in consistent locations (e.g., pajamas and toothpaste/ toothbrush).	Keep bedtime routine very consistent with regard to time and sequence of events. Provide visual supports for this as needed (e.g., visual timer to indicate bedtime and picture schedule to review nighttime routine).

crowds and movement, and visual distractions can set a very different mood and can over-load a visual system or hinder the processing of other, more relevant stimuli. Similarly, audi-tory factors such as background noise (humming of a fan or clock ticking), environmental sounds (traffic, beeping of the crosswalk signal, or rain on a rooftop), and the sound of people talking can be received in various ways by different individuals with ASD, and at times the cumulative nature of these sounds can be too much to process even when the individual sounds may be benign. These visual and auditory factors may be more rele-vant at certain times of day or during daily activities that require more concentration and effort. Suggestions for home might include the use of soft or natural light in place of fluo-rescent light or the reduction of background noise during mealtime or self-care routines. Considering the scheduling of certain tasks can be helpful as well. For instance, running the dishwasher or washing machine during the day when school is in session can help avoid a challenging situation later.

In the community, finding ways to alter the environment can be much more challeng-ing. In these cases, it may be necessary to implement strategies, as discussed previously, to make challenging environmental stimuli more tolerable. Examples of this include wearing noise-cancellation headphones at the airport or when walking through the grocery store or wearing sunglasses or a visor when outside at the park. These are simple strategies that, for some children with ASD, make a major difference in their ability to function in the world around them.

Improving Self-Regulation

Williams and Shellenberger (1996) define self-regulation as "the ability to attain, main-tain, and change arousal appropriately for a task or situation" (pp. 1–5). The ability to self-regulate begins in infancy and is driven mostly by processes in the autonomic nervous system, reticular formation, and limbic system relating to automatic body functions and state maintenance. As the child begins to interact more with his or her physical world, sen-sorimotor strategies for self-regulation are discovered. However, for young children, the ability to self-regulate is still not a conscious process, with changes in arousal level (or alert-ness) often being facilitated by parent/caregiver. As children grow older, however, they develop greater awareness of their own arousal state, as well as a greater capacity to regulate it. However, for many children, including children with ASD, the development of these higher level processes may be impaired. As a result, they may have more difficulty monitor-ing and affecting positive change on their state of arousal in a way that effectively matches and supports the current context and task demands.

The Alert Program ("How Does Your Engine Run?") was created by two occupa-tional therapists to teach strategies for self-regulation to school-age children and young adults who may struggle in this area (Williams & Shellenberger, 1996). The program is broken into stages that include recognizing one's own arousal level using visual supports and simple language and metaphors, observing changes in arousal level when various activities or inputs are introduced, and, finally, the spontaneous regulation of one's own arousal state.

Williams and Shellenberger (1996) emphasize the importance of using a bottom-up approach to inhibition (e.g., body sending messages to brain) through sensorimotor strat-egies rather than relying solely on the less efficient top-down approach involving mind over body. The concept of the "sensory diet" discussed previously is based on this premise as well.

When using The Alert Program, children are asked to think about their body as an engine. Different "engine speeds" (high, low, and just right) are discussed and illustrated through simple pictures. Using visual supports, children learn to identify their own arousal level at various times throughout the day. As strategies for regulation are introduced, connections are made between certain inputs/activities (as well as environmental factors) and corresponding changes in alertness. Parents can begin to understand how their child's state of arousal fluctuates over the course of the day and begin to better understand their child's sensory needs over time (see Table 19.2).

Interventions for Praxis

Praxis has historically been defined as the ability of the brain to conceptualize, plan out, and perform a series of unfamiliar actions (Ayres, 1972). Intervention strategies to address praxis issues depend on what component(s) of praxis is impaired. Furthermore, these deficits should be addressed through both remediation and compensation. Remediation often includes both addressing the underlying sensorimotor mechanisms relating to praxis and the direct teaching of specific skills within an occupational framework.

For children who have difficulty with ideation, strategies might include direct practice with idea generation in context. For example, during a play activity, a child might be provided with a simple item (e.g., a hula hoop) and asked to generate three ideas for action with this object. One action might be the obvious one involving spinning the hoop around one's torso. However, ideation would be needed to come up with additional ideas of how to interact with the hoop based on its basic attributes and affordances. If the child becomes stuck, simple clues could be provided either verbally ("Its round. I wonder if it rolls?") or visually (e.g., by placing the hoop flat on the ground to generate ideas of jumping into it or running around it or holding it up vertically to suggest that it may be used to throw things into).

Likewise, if a child is engaging in repetitive play with a toy (e.g., pushing a car back and forth repeatedly in one spot), demonstrating other actions with the toy (e.g., rolling the car down a ramp or moving the car along a drawn-out path) can help expand the play scheme and may lead to the exploration of other possibilities. Strategies such as this can help increase the child's play repertoire. The strategy chosen needs to match the language and cognitive abilities of the child. Compensatory strategies for a child with poor ideation might include providing the child with choices (either verbally or visually) for action given an object or scenario and/or demonstrating the action for the child to imitate. Demonstration can be used both to improve ideational abilities and to compensate for this deficit.

To address deficits specifically with motor *planning* that relate to the learning of new motor skills or engagement in a novel activity, the following strategies are often implemented: (1) Break tasks down into smaller components—teach the individual components and then begin to piece them back together one piece at a time; (2) allow more time to practice new skills—encourage repetition; (3) slow down the pace of an action or motor sequence—learn it in slow motion, and then build up pace as possible; and (4) provide visual feedback (mirror, video playback, etc.) when possible to foster self-correction and compensate for poor body awareness.

Compensatory strategies implemented by occupational therapists to address these motor planning deficits might include (1) providing physical assistance for the child during novel or challenging motor tasks; (2) avoiding situations that will likely present such challenges without available support; (3) allowing the child to perform certain actions in a modified manner; and/or (4) modifying the task, physical environment, or social context to support success.

Children with dyspraxia (with or without ASD) do not just have difficulty with the discrete learning of new motor skills. Dyspraxia can make any activity or situation that is open-ended, difficult to predict, or out of sight very distressing or anxiety-provoking. For instance, going to a place where the child has never been or transitioning away from a familiar routine or place without an understanding of what is happening next can cause much distress for a child with praxis issues. This may be one explanation for the consistent difficulties with transitions reported by parents of children with ASD.

Other strategies often used by occupational therapists include (1) providing a visual schedule (picture schedule) to outline daily activities in sequence, (2) using a visual timer (see http://www.timetimer.com) to create a visual endpoint for otherwise open-ended tasks, (3) using social stories (Gray, 2000) to introduce new places or situations that may occur (e.g., social story about going to the grocery store or riding the school bus), (4) educating parents on the importance of keeping living space well-organized with the child's personal belongings stored in consistent locations (toothbrush/paste, clothing, toys, etc.), and (5) providing verbal warnings when a change to the schedule or routine is anticipated. These strategies can help prevent distress and create an environment that is predictable and safe while simultaneously allowing for a more manageable way to approach unavoidable changes in routine or schedule that may arise.

Deficits specifically in *motor execution* are less common in individuals with ASD. However, if ideation and planning are impaired, then smooth execution of movements and actions in real time will be affected. Likewise, when support is provided for ideation and the motor planning process, improvements in motor output are often observed.

Using Ayres Sensory Integration to Improve Praxis

Ayres Sensory Integration is based on the premise that the nervous system is capable of change and that meaningful sensorimotor activity is a powerful mediator of this plasticity (Schaaf & Miller, 2005). As discussed previously, active participation by the child is critical in order to elicit these changes. Using an SI approach, occupational therapists can address the underlying praxis deficits of children with ASD by providing opportunities for ideation, motor planning, and execution of novel motor sequences within a controlled environment. By providing a rich sensory environment with graded motor challenges that match the child's ability, motor learning can occur.

SUMMARY

Individuals with ASD experience many sensory and motor impairments that impact their lives in a variety of ways. Occupational therapists play an important role in identifying how these deficits impact the individual's daily life skills including self-care, household chores, vocational skills, and the ability to fulfill meaningful roles within his or her family and community. Occupational therapists often work closely with physical therapists and speech/language pathologists in addressing functional limitations and improving safety and quality of life. Occupational therapists use a variety of assessment tools and intervention techniques in evaluating and treating individuals with ASD. A combination of skill remediation, task modification, and environmental adaptation is often implemented to improve functional outcomes. A referral to OT is indicated when functional limitations are interfering with an individual's ability to successfully and safely participate in daily life activities and/or fulfill basic life roles. Occupational therapists are an important component of the health care team for children and adults with ASDs.

KEY POINTS

- The focus of occupational therapy is on improving function, participation, and independence in daily activities and routines.
- Identifying an individual's values, interests, and life experiences is critical to the analysis of occupational performance and in determining appropriate and meaningful goals for intervention.
- Occupational therapy often involves a combination of skill remediation, task modification, and environmental adaptation to improve functional outcomes.
- Individuals with ASD experience the world differently than others; the way they take in, integrate, and interpret the sensory information from their immediate environment (through sight, touch, movement, hearing, etc.) leads to a unique way of responding to the things, people, and events that unfold around them.
- In ASD, we must caution ourselves not to interpret a single behavior as simply a deviation from the norm that must be corrected; instead, we must search for a pattern of behaviors that defines how that individual responds to the world around him or her. Through that understanding, we can mold the world around the individual and build the skills needed for success.

DISCLOSURE STATEMENT

Jennifer L. Stornelli is currently employed by Spaulding Rehabilitation Hospital, an entity of Partners HealthCare, as an occupational therapist and clinical supervisor, responsible for program development and the coordination of service delivery for the patient population, which is composed in large part of individuals with autism spectrum disorder.

REFERENCES

American Occupational Therapy Association. (2002). Occupational therapy practice framework: Domain and process. *American Journal of Occupational Therapy, 56*, 609–639.

Anderson, D. K., Liang, J. W., & Lord, C. (2014). Predicting young adult outcome among more and less cognitively able individuals with autism spectrum disorders. *Journal of Child Psychology and Psychiatry, 55*(5), 485–494.

Anderson, E., & Emmons, P. (1995). Sensory integration: The hidden disorder. *Sensory Integration Quarterly Newsletter, 23*(2–3), 8–9.

Anderson, E. L. (1993). *Parental perceptions of the influence of occupational therapy utilizing sensory integrative techniques on the daily living skills of children with autism.* Unpublished master's thesis, University of Southern California, Los Angeles.

Ayres, A. J. (1972). *Sensory integration and learning disorders.* Los Angeles, CA: Western Psychological Services.

Bagby, M. S., Dickie, V. A., & Baranek, G. T. (2012). How sensory experiences of children with and without autism affect family occupations. *American Journal of Occupational Therapy, 66*(1), 78–86.

Baranek, G. T. (2002). Efficacy of sensory and motor interventions for children with autism. *Journal of Autism and Developmental Disorders*, 32, 397–422.

Bhat, A. N., Landa, R. J., & Galloway, J. C. C. (2011). Current perspectives on motor functioning in infants, children, and adults with ASD. *Physical Therapy*, 91, 111–29.

Brown, C. E., & Dunn, W. (2002). *Adolescent/adult sensory profile*. San Antonio, TX: Pearson.

Bundy, A. C., Shia, S., Qi, L., & Miller, L. J. (2007). How does sensory processing dysfunction affect play? *American Journal of Occupational Therapy*, 61, 201–208.

Cohn, E. S., Miller, L. J., & Tickle-Degnen, L. (2000). Parental hopes for therapy outcomes: Children with sensory modulation disorders. *American Journal of Occupational Therapy*, 54, 36–43.

Dowell, L. R., Mahone, E. M., & Mostofsky, S. H. (2009). Associations of postural knowledge and basic motor skill with dyspraxia in autism: Implications for abnormalities in distributed connectivity and motor learning. *Neuropsychology*, 23(5), 563–570.

Dunn, W. (1999). *Sensory Profile: Caregiver Questionnaire*. Bloomington, MN: NCS Pearson.

Escalante-Mead, P., Minshew, N., & Sweeney, J. (2003). Abnormal brain lateralization in high-functioning autism. *Journal of Autism and Developmental Disorders*, 33(5), 539–543.

Gray, C. (2000). *The new social story book*. Arlington, TX: Future Horizons.

Hauck, J. A., & Dewey, D. (2001). Hand preference and motor functioning in children with autism. *Journal of Autism and Developmental Disorders*, 31(3), 265–277.

Humphries, T., Wright, M., McDougall, B., & Vertes, J. (1990). The efficacy of sensory integration therapy for children with learning disability. *Physical and Occupational Therapy in Pediatrics*, 10, 1–17.

Humphries, T., Wright, M., Snider, L., & McDougall, B. (1992). A comparison of the effectiveness of sensory integrative therapy and perceptual-motor training in treating children with learning disabilities. *Journal of Developmental and Behavioral Pediatrics*, 13, 31–40.

Interactive Autism Network. (2008). *IAN research findings: Occupational therapy*. Retrieved from https://www.autismspeaks.org/news/news-item/ian-research-findings-occupational-therapy.

Jasmine, E., Courture, M., McKinley, E. P., Reid, E. G., Fombonne, E., & Gisel, E. E. (2009). Sensori-motor and daily living skills of preschool children with autism spectrum disorders. *Journal of Autism and Developmental Disorders*, 39, 231–241.

Kuhaneck, H., Henry, D., & Glennon, T. (2007). *Sensory processing measure*. Los Angeles, CA: Western Psychological Services.

Lane, S. J., & Schaaf, R. C. (2010). Examining the neuroscience evidence for sensory-driven neuroplasticity: Implications for sensory-based occupational therapy for children and adolescents. *American Journal of Occupational Therapy*, 64, 375–390.

Leekham, S. R., Nieto, C., Libby, S. J., Wing, L., & Gould, J. (2007). Describing the sensory abnormalities of children and adults with autism. *Journal of Autism and Developmental Disorders*, 37, 894–910.

Mailloux, Z., & Roley, S. S. (2010). Sensory integration. In H. Miller Kuhaneck & R. Watling (Eds.), *Autism: A comprehensive occupational therapy approach* (pp. 469–507). Bethesda, MD: AOTA Press.

May-Benson, T. (2010). Play and praxis in children with an autism spectrum disorder. In H. Miller Kuhaneck & R. Watling (Eds.), *Autism: A comprehensive occupational therapy approach* (pp. 383–425). Bethesda, MD: AOTA Press.

May-Benson, T. A., & Koomar, J. A. (2010). Systematic review of the research evidence examining the effectiveness of interventions using a sensory integrative approach for children. *American Journal of Occupational Therapy*, 64, 403–414.

Miller, L., & Fuller, D. (2006). *Sensational kids: Hope and help for children with sensory processing disorder*. Denver, CO: Penguin.

Miller, L. J., Coll, J. R., & Schoen, S. A. (2007). A randomized controlled pilot study of the effectiveness of occupational therapy for children with sensory modulation disorder. *American Journal of Occupational Therapy*, 61, 228–238.

Ming, X., Brimacombe, M., & Wagner, G. C. (2007). Prevalence of motor impairment in autism spectrum disorders. *Brain and Development*, 29(9), 565–570.

Occupational Therapy Associates. (1995, Spring). *The sensory connection*. Watertown, MA: Author.

Ozonoff, S. (1997). Causal mechanisms of autism: Unifying perspective from an information-processing framework. In D. J. Cohen & F. R. Volkmar (Eds.), *Handbook of autism and pervasive developmental disorders* (2nd ed., pp. 868–879). New York, NY: Wiley.

Pfeiffer, B. A., Koenig, K., Kinnealey, M., Sheppard, M., & Henderson, L. (2011). Research scholars initiative-effectiveness of sensory integration interventions in children with autism spectrum disorders: A pilot study. *American Journal of Occupational Therapy, 65,* 76–85.

Phagava, H., Muratori, F., Einspieler, C., Maestro, S., Apicella, F., Guzzetta, A., . . . Cioni, G. (2008). General movements in infants with autism spectrum disorders. *Georgian Medical News, 156,* 100–105.

Polatajko, H. J., Kaplan, B. J., & Wilson, B. N. (1992). Sensory integration treatment for children with learning disabilities: Its status 20 years later. *Occupational Therapy Journal of Research, 12*(6), 323–341.

Schaaf, R. C., Hunt, J., & Benevides, T. (2012). Occupational therapy using sensory integration to improve participation of a child with autism: A case report. *American Journal of Occupational Therapy, 66,* 547–555.

Schaaf, R. C., & Miller, L. J. (2005). Occupational therapy using a sensory integrative approach for children with developmental disabilities. *Mental Retardation and Developmental Disabilities Research Reviews, 11,* 143–148.

Shoener, R. F., Kinnealey, M., & Koenig, K. P. (2008). You can know me if you listen: Sensory, motor and communication issues in a nonverbal person with autism. *American Journal of Occupational Therapy, 62,* 547–553.

Smith, S. A., Press, B., Koenig, K. P., & Kinnealey, M. (2005). Effects of sensory integration intervention on self-stimulating and self-injurious behaviors. *American Journal of Occupational Therapy, 59,* 418–425.

Stackhouse, T. M. (2010). Motor differences in autism spectrum disorders. In H. Miller Kuhaneck & R. Watling (Eds.), *Autism: A comprehensive occupational therapy approach* (pp. 163–200). Bethesda, MD: AOTA Press.

Tomcheck, S. D., & Dunn, W. (2007). Sensory processing in children with and without autism: A comparative study using the Short Sensory Profile. *American Journal of Occupational Therapy, 61,* 190–200.

Wagner, M., Newman, L., Cameto, R., Garza, N., & Levine, D. (2005). *After high school—A first look at the postschool experiences of youth with disabilities: A report from the National Longitudinal Transition Study-2 (NLTS-2).* Retrieved from http://www.nlts2.org/reports/2005_04/index.html.

Watling, R. (2010). Occupational therapy evaluation for individuals with an autism spectrum disorder. In H. Miller Kuhaneck & R. Watling (Eds.), *Autism: A comprehensive occupational therapy approach* (pp. 285–303). Bethesda, MD: AOTA Press.

Watling, R., Dietz, J., Kanny, E. M., & McLaughlin, J. F. (1999). Current practice of occupational therapy for children with autism. *American Journal of Occupational Therapy, 53,* 498–505.

Watling, R. L., & Dietz, J. (2007). Immediate effect of Ayres' sensory integration-based occupational therapy intervention on children with autism spectrum disorders. *American Journal of Occupational Therapy, 61,* 574–583.

Wilbarger, P. (1984). Planning a "sensory diet": Application of sensory processing theory during the first year of life. *Zero to Three, 5*(1), 7–12.

Williams, M., & Shellenberger, S. (1996). *How does your engine run? A leader's guide to the Alert Program for self-regulation.* Albuquerque, NM: Therapy Works.

Winner, M. G., & Crooke, P. (2008). *You are a social detective! Explaining social thinking to kids.* San Jose, CA: Think Social.

World Health Organization. (2001). *International classification of functioning, disability and health.* Geneva: Author.

/// 20 /// SOCIAL SKILLS TRAINING FOR AUTISM SPECTRUM DISORDER

D. SCOTT MCLEOD, KRISTIN W. MALATINO, AND DOROTHY LUCCI

SOCIAL SKILLS IN INDIVIDUALS WITH AUTISM SPECTRUM DISORDER

Social skills can be defined as interpersonal responses that allow an individual to adapt to the environment through verbal and nonverbal communication (Matson, Matson, & Rivet, 2007). Social skills are necessary for engaging appropriately with others, establishing relationships, and maintaining friendships. Throughout development, social behaviors are learned naturally through interactions with others in various contexts. Social skills are generally observable, and they can be both verbal and nonverbal. Typically, these skills can be learned by watching others and through trial and error. However, individuals diagnosed with autism spectrum disorder (ASD) or social communication disorder experience marked social challenges (American Psychiatric Association (APA), 2013).

A central component of ASD includes "persistent deficits in social communication and social interaction across multiple contexts" (APA, 2013, p. 50). Social problems may include deficits in (1) social–emotional reciprocity; (2) nonverbal communication behaviors; and/or (3) developing, maintaining, and understanding relationships (APA, 2013). Although the social impairments of ASD fall on a spectrum from "requiring very substantial support" to "requiring supports," this chapter focuses primarily on individuals with high-functioning ASD (HFA) or Asperger's disorder (Asperger's syndrome (AS)), as formerly classified in the *Diagnostic and Statistical Manual of Mental Disorders* (fourth edition, text revision) (APA, 2000). These classifications generally include individuals who have average to above average intelligence and do not experience a language delay. Within this classification, individuals may experience deficits in social interactions (e.g., initiating communication, negotiating personal space, and engaging in to-and-fro conversation), nonverbal communication (e.g., modulating eye contact, and reading facial expressions in others), perspective taking (e.g., understanding the thoughts and feelings of others), or emotional reciprocity (Baron-Cohen, Tager-Flusberg, & Lombardo, 2013). For example, these skills would be necessary in asking for help at school, initiating play on the playground, asking a peer out on a date, or interviewing for a job.

The negative consequences of social skill deficits can be quite profound. Poor social skills are related to significant social problems across the lifespan, including peer rejection, bullying, and difficulty establishing romantic relationships (Church, Alisanski, & Amanullah, 2000; Krasny, Williams, Provencal, & Ozonoff, 2003). Beyond the relational consequences, poor social skills have also been linked to increased mental health issues, such as anxiety and depression (Attwood, 2006; Sterling, Dawson, Estes, & Gleeson, 2008; White, Oswald, Ollendick, & Scahill, 2009). Social skill deficits can also impact academic achievement and performance evaluations at school and work (Church et al., 2000; Hendricks, 2010). In fact, adults with ASD have higher rates of unemployment and are frequently employed below their skill level (Hendricks, 2010).

A key element of social communication that often poses a challenge for persons with ASD is perspective taking, or theory of mind. Happé (1994) defines theory of mind as "the ability to attribute independent mental states to oneself and others, in order to explain behaviour" (p. 39). Figure 20.1 represents the classic Smarties task, which is an example of a theory of mind assessment tool. A child is shown a container, recognizes the label, and thinks that he or she knows what is in it (candy). However, prior to showing the child the container, the examiner placed a pencil in it. The examiner shows the child that the pencil, not the expected candy, is placed in the container. The child is asked to guess what another boy, who is not privy to what is in the container, will say is in it. Typically developing children will predict that the boy who is naive to the replacement will expect to see candy in a candy container. Some individuals with ASD will have weaker theory of mind and inaccurately think that the other will expect a pencil.

Winner (2007) stresses that social interaction requires the ability to consider the perspective of the other. The Smarties task is one method to test this ability. When a person exhibits the ability to integrate the perspective of the other within a social interaction, the person is said to be "thinking social" or using "social thinking" (Winner, 2007).

Social deficits create a vicious cycle for individuals with ASD because their poor social thinking and skills prevent them from creating social connections that could have offered prosocial modeling and feedback. Also, even when social skills are learned, individuals with ASD struggle to generalize the skills to novel situations. For example, an individual with ASD may learn an appropriate greeting for a teacher in school (e.g., eye contact and saying "good morning") but may not understand that a similar greeting would be appropriate with a doctor or on a job interview. These social challenges often lead to difficulties establishing relationships and functioning appropriately across contexts.

Although individuals with social challenges may lack self-awareness and appropriate behavior in social situations, they are often keenly aware of their social skill deficits. Given their average to above average intelligence, they often know what good social skills look like and who in their peer group has those skills, whether or not they are able to implement these skills themselves. For example, in a study by Knott, Dunlop, and MacKay (2006), children with HFA/AS rated themselves as having significantly lower social skills (e.g., temper management and joining groups) and social competence (e.g., development of close friendships) than typically developing children. Notably, in the same study, these children's parents rated them as having even lower skills than they rated themselves (Knott et al., 2006).

Given the profound and pervasive influence of social skills on healthy development and functioning, social skill development has become a critical area of focus for interventions with individuals with ASD. Interventions that address social skill development are of critical importance throughout the lifespan because "individuals with ASD do not 'outgrow'

FIGURE 20.1 Theory of mind—Smarties task.

social skill deficits, but they persist into adulthood" (Rao, Beidel, & Murray, 2008, p. 354). Social skill interventions seek to teach the skills that do not come naturally to individuals with ASD while also giving opportunities to apply these skills in real-world settings. These interventions move beyond a simple focus on social skills to address the needs of the whole person because social skills cannot be viewed in isolation.

Interventions have been developed to assist individuals with ASD to improve social skills and develop healthy and meaningful relationships. Historically, social skill interventions focused on direct remediation of skill deficits (National Autism Center, 2009). However, current approaches to treatment are more holistic and utilize a multidisciplinary approach. In fact, the best treatments include integrated delivery of multiple intervention modalities (e.g., education, communication, and sensorimotor; individual, family, and group therapy; and psychopharmacology) implemented across contexts (e.g., home, school, and community). These treatments address the myriad of symptoms that may be present (e.g., social skill deficits, executive dysfunction, sensory issues, anxiety, and allergies) and are tailored to the individual. Although a treatment plan would rarely view social skills in isolation, this chapter focuses on social skill interventions specifically while taking into account the strengths and weaknesses of the whole person. Other chapters in this book provide for more information on behavioral therapy (Chapter 15), psychopharmacology (Chapter 16), speech and language therapy (Chapter 18), and occupational therapy (Chapter 19).

SOCIAL SKILLS ASSESSMENT

Before a social skill intervention can be identified, a thorough assessment is necessary. ASD is a *spectrum* disorder. Individuals will have vastly different strengths and weaknesses, particularly with regard to their social skills. To plan for appropriate treatment, the following areas need to be considered during evaluation: perspective taking (e.g., theory of mind and understanding the thoughts of others), self-awareness (e.g., the level of knowledge about personal strengths/weaknesses), executive functioning skills (e.g., cognitive flexibility, problem solving, and processing speed), sensory processing, and comorbid mental health difficulties (e.g., anxiety and depression). Assessments should include formal and informal components as well as observations of the individual in a variety of settings. Observations are indicated because individuals with ASD may score well on standardized assessments and/or they may look higher functioning in the structured clinical assessment. The results of this evaluation are critical for providers to understand when determining the type of treatment indicated for each individual, which may vary based on Kasari and Locke's (2011) "active ingredients," which are defined later. For example, many individuals with ASD have comorbid anxiety disorders (White et al., 2009), which may interfere with their social relationships and need to be addressed in the course of their treatment. Moreover, even when not diagnosed with an anxiety disorder, individuals with ASD often experience subclinical levels of anxiety that will interfere with their social performance.

Regarding assessment of theory of mind, Michelle Garcia Winner offers a tool for classifying individuals by levels of social communication. The levels include significantly challenged, challenged, emerging, nuanced challenged, neurotypical, and resistant social communicators. Individuals are classified into one of these categories based on understanding one's own and others' minds, emotional coping, social problem solving, peer interaction, self-awareness, academic skills, and mental manipulation (Winner, Crooke, & Madrigal, 2011). In addition to Garcia Winner's evaluation model, clinical interview and structured group assessment have been utilized to determine one's social skill profile and pattern of strengths and weaknesses.

When assessing for group participation, assessment of social skills needs to go beyond individual evaluation and consider group composition and group formation (Cotugno, 2009). A structured, intentional, and clinically informed system for group formation is critical to facilitating the success of group interventions. Individuals may be matched within groups based on similar levels of perspective taking, previous exposure to social skill content, and developmental level, along with numerous other factors. Depending on the individuals' needs, group composition may also vary based on number of participants (e.g., dyads and small group), interests, comorbid diagnosis, processing speed, or attention. Groups should not be formed simply based on shared diagnostic label or convenience factors.

SOCIAL SKILLS INTERVENTION

Based on the results of the assessment process, interventions are determined that best fit with the unique needs of the individual and/or the group. The primary goal of social skill interventions is to teach the social behavior and social thinking necessary to build and foster relationships and socially adapt to different people in various contexts (Winner, 2013). Social skill interventions provide individuals with ASD social knowledge, including education in how to understand the mental and emotional states of others by interpreting the context and observable behaviors and using prior knowledge.

Social skill interventions can vary immensely. Kasari and Locke (2011) identify five "active ingredients" in social skill interventions: (1) the context of implementation (e.g., home, school, and community), (2) the method of implementation (e.g., applied behavior analysis and social scripts), (3) the agent of intervention (e.g., peer-, sibling-, and adult-mediated), (4) the content (e.g., peer engagement, social knowledge, and perspective taking), and (5) the dose (e.g., how often and how long). Based on the variability within these five factors, interventions can take many forms. For example, an intervention may provide direct instruction about skills and strategies for applying them. Other interventions may rely on peer or sibling modeling of social behavior. The content of interventions may also focus on skills that are related to social competence, such as a stress management curriculum for managing anxiety in social situations. Another type of intervention may focus on increasing self-awareness through self-assessment of strengths and weaknesses in order to facilitate an understanding of self in relation to others. Regardless of their variability, an important shared goal of social skill interventions should be to help individuals generalize the skills and knowledge to novel settings.

There are numerous existing social skill treatment models. These interventions include social stories (Grey, 2010); video modeling of appropriate skills (Bellini & Akullian, 2007; Mason, Rispoli, Ganz, Boles, & Orr, 2012); social skills group interventions (Cotugno, 2009); Relational Developmental Intervention (Gutstein & Sheeley, 2002), Social Communication, Emotional Regulation, and Transactional Analysis (Prizant, Wetherby, Rubin, Laurent, & Rydell, 2005); and the use of peers in integrated classroom settings (Strain, Kohler, & Goldstein, 1996). Mindfulness-based interventions, which help individuals increase their awareness of themselves and others, can facilitate increased attention to internal states. Singh et al. (2011a, 2011b) obtained promising results by teaching adolescents with ASD to shift their attention within a 9-week mindfulness-based stress reduction (MBSR) class. Participants in the MBSR group were able to shift their attention from their negative emotions to the soles of their feet. McLeod and Lucci (2009) and Lucci, Levine, Challen-Wittmer, and McLeod (2014) embrace an integrated approach to educating individuals with ASD and have shown promise in teaching self-awareness, mindfulness, and stress reduction techniques. Groden, Kantor, Woodard, and Lipsitt (2011) have implemented a positive psychology approach to educating students with ASD.

Case Study #1: "John"

John is an 8-year-old boy with high cognitive ASD. His verbal IQ is well above average, and his performance IQ is average. He has read all the Harry Potter books, plays jazz piano, and abhors sports and physical activity. In the parlance of Michelle Garcia Winner (2007), he is a weak interactive social communicator. John adheres to rules rigidly and expects others to do the same. His quirky style gathers the attention of peers who typically overestimate his social competency. He does well in small, structured, academically focused groups and often proves to be a leader in that context. At recess, he barges into the personal space of peers and initiates monologues about topics of his interest. Peers tend to listen inattentively for a moment and then walk away. John has received more than adequate social pragmatics instruction and scores very well on paper assessments of his social knowledge. His pediatrician has noted that John has an abnormally high heart rate, his sleep is limited, and he demonstrates restricted food interests. He denies experiencing anxiety. In fact, he has difficulty naming any emotion.

Assessment and Intervention

John's cognitive ability and history of social skill instruction have supported his excellent knowledge of age and context-appropriate social competence. Further direct instruction will likely lead him to feel patronized and misunderstood. Traditional individual therapy with an adult counselor or therapist will likely include in-depth conversations about social pragmatics with little transfer and generalization of what is learned to his social environment. John's alexithymia, the inability to identify emotion, requires immediate attention. He appears to struggle to identify emotions and may quite well be affected by, but not having a phenomenological experience of, anxiety.

Treatment should be brought into his personal living environment. In school, this would mean having the speech and language pathologist or school guidance counselor provide whole classroom instruction on a variety of topics, including the naming of emotions, nonverbal communication of emotional states, and social awareness strategies such as direct instruction about "reading" the emotional state of the group. Advice for "reading the room" can be communicated verbally or visually. The purpose is to have the student make a conscious effort to scan the environment to assess the tone, attitude, and intentions of others so that he can match his interactions to the context. At the Aspire summer camp, groups would engage in activities of interest and counselors would teach and support skill development in vivo. For example, in the activity of canoeing, social goals would be attended to. Navigation of a two-person canoe requires explicit communication regarding each person's intention: Prior to setting off, John would be coached by his counselor on how to determine the intention of his peer and to negotiate differences. Once on the water, the counselor could supportively intervene with comments such as, "Great job asking Mike about going fast! I like the way you listened when he said he wants to go slow!" Treatment foci would be shared with parents and other providers so they can reinforce progress across contexts. John would be taught less pragmatics and more on a metacognitive level: He would be taught the purpose of the skill rather than the skill itself. He would be supported to better know his own strengths, weaknesses, and preferred methods and styles of communication.

GROUP VERSUS INDIVIDUAL INTERVENTIONS

Interventions directed at improving social interactions take the form of individual or group treatments. Group training models are particularly effective and important because they offer opportunities for structured and facilitated peer interactions. The group context also provides opportunities to give and receive peer feedback. The norms of peer culture also emerge within the group setting. For example, individuals are exposed to age-appropriate topics of conversation and other individuals who may have shared interests. Furthermore, and notably, group interventions provide an environment for genuine application of learned social skills. As individuals with ASD learn the skills needed to compensate for their social deficits, they require opportunities to practice these skills and to generalize the skills to novel situations. In this way, group treatments provide a more "real-life" milieu than individual treatments. For example, in Aspire groups, handheld computers were employed to record real-time self and counselor assessments of factors that effected social success. Data were tracked and graphically represented to teach how factors such as sleep duration or anxiety might influence social engagement. Through a pilot study, McLeod and Lucci (2009) found that individuals with ASD were able to use this technology to improve their understanding of their personal components of social success.

In addition to group models, individual treatment for social skills can also be effective. Individual treatment, with one client and one therapist, can take many forms, but it is often grounded in cognitive–behavioral theory (CBT) and social learning theory (Attwood, 2008; Bauminger, 2002, 2007; Ho, Stephenson, & Carter, 2014; Matson et al., 2007). However, both individual and group treatments can be grounded in CBT (Ho et al., 2014). CBT is based on the theory that thoughts, feelings, and behaviors are interrelated, and by changing one of these three areas, typically thoughts or behaviors, the others are subsequently altered. CBT is often applied to maladaptive thought patterns (e.g., black-and-white thinking) and behavior patterns (e.g., social avoidance) that inhibit healthy social relationships. Cognitive–behavioral interventions have been found to be effective in improving social skills, social competence, and social cognition for individuals with HFA (Bauminger, 2002, 2007). Weiss and Lunsky (2010) found promising results for treating anxiety and depression in adults with ASD by using CBT. To obtain some of the previously stated benefits of group treatment, individual counseling may include opportunities for in vivo practice within community settings (e.g., practice with an assigned peer), assigned homework to practice skills, or role-play and videotaping within the session (Bauminger, 2002). Individual therapy may also provide a more appropriate context for addressing sensitive personal issues, such as comorbid mental health problems or family issues.

Case Study #2: "Samantha"

Samantha is a 15-year-old student with generally average cognitive abilities with the exception of a mild weakness in processing speed. Samantha has a difficult time with comprehension in situations in which there are more than one peer and/or when peers communicate with any rapidity. She enjoys the *Twilight* movie series but shows no other special interests. She exhibits and acknowledges a high level of generalized anxiety and occasional panic attacks. She expects to attain near perfect grades and works approximately triple the time of a typical student on homework. Her peer group finds her repeated worries about the same topics tiresome. She tends to be shy and expects peers to dislike her. She agrees to all treatment suggestions yet rarely follows through. Samantha acknowledges she has ASD but can only articulate a superficial understanding of its meaning for her. She would be considered an emerging social communicator according to Winner (2007). Samantha tends to share her worries in a manner that seems to expect everyone to know and care as deeply about them as she does.

Assessment and Intervention

Samantha, like John, has learned basic social pragmatics. Teaching to these skills will offer only modest improvement to her overall social success. Given her limited social awareness combined with her being generally pleasant and socially nonthreatening, Samantha should be given simple "scripts" to communicate her worries in a more socially acceptable manner. For example, she could state, "I know I worry too much. I really don't mean to burden you. Sometimes I just can't stop talking about it." Greater self-awareness can support more successful self-disclosure. In schools in which Aspire provides consultation, a general education curriculum called "Science of Me" has been created (Lucci et al., 2014). All students are taught about the brain, neuropsychology, stress, and relaxation; the effects on the brain due to sleep and nutrition are among the numerous topics covered. Samantha can be directly taught about stress, coping, and relaxation. She can learn that her brain is responding to the construct of "low grades" in a manner more similar to a person in a life-or-death/fight-or-flight response. Knowing this about herself, Samantha can learn to modulate her response. A simple intervention might include a picture of a thermometer with levels of anxiety on one side paired with the appropriate types of responses on the other.

Other modalities of instruction can be used as well. Sensors have been developed that can be worn on the wrist or ankle to measure psychophysiological correlates of stress, including galvanic skin response, heart rate, and movement. Data collected from the sensors can inform Samantha's counselors about her changing anxiety states but also triggers to her anxiety. Given Samantha's profile, she may not easily make the connection between triggers and responses. The data can be graphically presented to highlight, for example, that classes with frequent quizzes elicit the greatest amount of anxiety. Sample data collection screens and a single graph are shown in Figure 20.2. The upper portion depicts screens that staff and student use to concurrently record data. The lower portion depicts the collected data graphically. For example, staff and Samantha review the graphs to help her better understand how she perceives and responds to stress.

EVIDENCE-BASED TREATMENTS

A review of the research on the effectiveness of social skill interventions for individuals with ASD generally suggests positive effects of treatment with children and adolescents (Woods, Mahdavi, & Ryan, 2013). However, "despite their widespread clinical use, empirical support for social skill interventions for HFA/AS is minimal at this time" (Rao et al., 2008, p. 353). There are numerous empirical issues that make social skill interventions difficult to study, such as a lack of consistent definition of social skills; small sample sizes; variability in measurement tools; lack of generalization of treatment effects to contexts outside of the treatment environment; limited follow-up assessments to determine maintenance of treatment gains over time; and differences in the levels, intensity, duration, or context of implementation (Cappadocia & Weiss, 2011; Rao et al., 2008; Williams White, Keonig, & Scahill, 2007; Woods et al., 2013). Furthermore, of the existing research, many studies

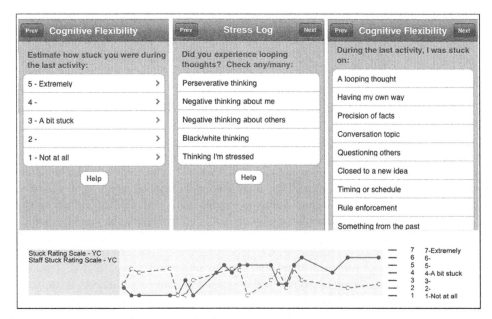

FIGURE 20.2 Data collection screens and a graph of student (solid dot) and staff (open dot) data points.

are not randomized controlled trials or do not utilize a comparison group (Cappadocia & Weiss, 2011). Despite these empirical challenges, comprehensive literature reviews and meta-analytic studies have been conducted and have found that there is empirical support for the use of social skills training for improving social skills among youth with ASD.

Cappadocia and Weiss (2011) conducted a review of group social skill interventions. They classified the group treatments into three categories: traditional (3 studies reviewed), cognitive–behavioral (3 studies reviewed), and parent inclusive (4 studies reviewed). Notwithstanding the empirical limitations noted by the authors, as a result of this review, they concluded that there is preliminary evidence for the efficacy of social skill interventions with children and youth diagnosed with ASD.

Rao and colleagues (2008) reviewed the literature for both group and individual social skill training programs in children diagnosed with HFA and AS. Their review consisted of 10 peer-reviewed journal articles meeting selection criteria (e.g., children and adolescents aged 18 years or younger and direct measurement of change in social skills). The authors classified the studies as including "traditional social skills training" in either a clinic or a classroom setting or "social skills training plus generalization," which included a community practice or homework to increase opportunities for generalization (p. 355). The results of this literature review revealed that 70% of the studies reported positive treatment effects.

Williams White and colleagues (2007) conducted a review of all published studies of group social skill interventions between 1985 and 2006 involving individuals with ASD. Based on 14 reviewed studies, the authors proposed the following promising intervention strategies for social skills training in ASD: (1) increased social motivation, (2) increased social initiation, (3) improvement in appropriate social responding, (4) reduction of interfering behaviors, and (5) promotion of skill generalization (Williams White et al., 2007).

This brief review of existing literature indicates that there is a growing research body to support the efficacy of social skill interventions for individuals with ASD. However, there is a clear need for more research in this area, including randomized controlled trials and studies of social skill interventions with adults. Future research should work to understand the mechanisms of change (i.e., mediators and moderators) through which social skill interventions are effective (Lerner, White, & McPartland, 2012).

THE ASPIRE PROGRAM

As discussed herein, many approaches address the social learning needs of individuals with ASD. Most of them focus on acquiring a series of skills and behaviors while decreasing aberrant behaviors. Individuals with ASD can and should learn more than how to exhibit prosocial behaviors. The Aspire model includes deeper assessment about the etiology of social challenges. For example, many individuals with ASD often have heightened levels of anxiety and/or depression. Pharmacologic intervention is often used to treat these symptoms. Symptom relief can also be found with other approaches. Especially for persons with ASD, these symptoms often stem from an individual's limited emotional understanding and regulation. Bellini (2004) and other researchers proposed models that teach individuals with ASD that there are different ways to label affective experiences (emotional reappraisal). The emotional responses that influence the amount of anxiety and depression experienced can be modified, which can lead to symptom reduction. Samson, Huber, and Gross (2012) found that individuals with ASD use emotional reappraisal less than typical peers. Individuals with ASD instead utilize emotional suppression when faced with negative emotions. By understanding how individuals with ASD process emotional information, targeted interventions may positively impact reduction in anxiety and depression and improved social performance. Symptom relief and social development can and should be enhanced through an integrated and systemic view.

The Aspire approach capitalizes on the strengths and interests of individuals with ASD. Aspire promotes this growth through our three pillars of instruction: social competence, self-awareness, and stress management. The Collaborative for Academic, Social, and Emotional Learning (2003) supports this more broad approach. It defines the following areas as core competencies of social–emotional learning that have positive outcomes on student development: self-management, self-awareness, responsible decision-making, relationship skills, and social awareness.

Case Study #3: "Eric"

Eric graduated high school with excellent grades in math and science and passing grades in all other courses. His superior collegiate aptitude scores landed him in a highly competitive engineering university. He acknowledged his diagnosis of ASD due to several years of social skill training as an adolescent. However, in college, he never sought help because his raw cognitive abilities rarely let him down in terms of academic achievement. After 3 weeks into his first year, he stopped attending classes and began to disregard his hygiene and spent more than 20 hours per day on Internet-based multiplayer games. Socially, Eric withdrew totally. He did not interact with his hallmates in the dormitory, and he did not return e-mails from his professors. He had been prescribed a benzodiazepine to be used as needed to prevent panic attacks. He stopped using it. His parents believed him when he told them that he was enjoying college and doing "fine." According to Winner (2007), Eric would be considered a socially anxious communicator. His, relatively speaking, higher level of perspective-taking ability would lead a clinician to infer that his communication with his parents was purposefully deceptive: He anticipated that his parents would be concerned about his school performance. He lied to avoid the overwhelming anxiety that would occur had his troubles come out in the open.

Assessment and Intervention

Eric's social isolation began with weak executive functioning skills that made it difficult for him to follow a schedule and plan ahead for long-term assignments. This led to challenges dealing with growing anxiety with the realization that he was quickly falling behind. Eric had little practice with disclosure and self-advocacy. When he started to experience trouble, he did not have a written or internal template to access support. Upon recognition of his impending challenges, he coped with his anxiety by dismissing it outright and engaging in pleasurable activities. This cycle was self-perpetuating.

As with the other two case studies, the etiology of Eric's social difficulties was not about social competence. Indeed, in his multiplayer games, he is viewed as a leader and helper: He organizes many of the games and counsels these peers on personal issues that are discussed while game playing. Telling him that he "should" be showering or that he "should" be attending class would lead to his agreement but not action. Given the level of dysfunction, it would be recommended that Eric leave school temporarily so that he can make a more firm connection in his thinking about school performance and work success.

Having work experience prior to immersion in college provides the purpose behind school success. At the Aspire Internship Program, young adults such as Eric experience the work environment and the specific components that support success (e.g., timeliness, reporting to a boss, and meeting deadlines). In group therapy that runs concurrently with the internship, peers are encouraged to talk with each other about the effects of tardiness, social faux pas, and poor planning. They also receive support with mapping out how college and work success may contribute to life satisfaction.

SOCIAL COMPETENCE

As discussed previously, direct instruction of social skills is necessary but not sufficient in maximizing social performance (Winner, 2014). It has been reported anecdotally that many children and adolescents with high cognitive skills score well on tests of social pragmatics such as the Test of Pragmatic Language (TOPL-2) but functionally perform at a lower level than the test would predict. Intellectual understanding of appropriate social behavior does not directly lead to good social performance. The transfer and generalization of social skills often requires instruction and support in their own right.

Many individuals with ASD learn new material in a context-dependent manner. Application of a skill in one context requires support to be enacted in another. Social competence involves social knowledge, social executive functioning, and dynamic intelligence that allows for fluid appraisal of ever-changing social feedback.

Aspire programming includes lessons on social skills across settings and then direct practice with using those skills in real-world contexts. For example, as cited in the adult case of Eric, he learns appropriate workplace behaviors in his Aspire group and then practices those skills in the workplace with the support of a job coach. Eric may also practice generalizing these skills to a lunchroom or break room setting where he interacts with coworkers.

SELF-AWARENESS

For social success, it is essential that individuals with ASD have a strong understanding of their particular strengths and weaknesses, their cognitive profile, their social impact on others, and their personal motive/intentions and social goals. As discussed previously, individuals with ASD often have compromised abilities in terms of theory of mind or perspective taking. Self-awareness instruction focuses on improving accurate understanding of one's issues and desires. Such instruction also focuses on improving the awareness of how one is perceived by others. Even on the level of psychophysiology, persons with ASD often are inaccurate reporters of physical pain, moods states, and arousal levels. The broad area of self-awareness includes recognizing one's emotions, intrinsic values, strengths, and challenges; knowing what brings one joy, anger, sadness, etc.; knowing how one perceives the world through one's personality and outlook (e.g., optimist or pessimist); and one's mindset (e.g., growth-oriented or fixed). Improvement in self-awareness allows individuals with ASD to become better at self-advocacy.

Aspire seeks to foster self-awareness. It may include identification of thoughts and feelings in younger children or completion and interpretation of self-assessment tools (e.g., personality inventories, career assessments, and executive function questionnaires) in adolescents and adults. In the child case of John, he would be challenged by counselors to learn about how to label feelings and where in his body he experiences emotions. In the case of Eric, he would be directly instructed about how he processes social information. Staff may review his neuropsychological assessments with him. He would be taught how to disclose this information judiciously with school, family, or employer.

STRESS MANAGEMENT

Individuals with ASD often experience heightened levels of anxiety and stress, and they have limited coping skills for managing them. Our autonomic nervous system (ANS) consists of the parasympathetic and sympathetic branches. The parasympathetic branch is responsible for "rest-and-digest" activities that occur when the body is calm. The sympathetic branch is responsible for stimulating activities related to the "fight-or-flight" response. Stressors can be external (being under attack) or internal (worried about a test). Porges (1992, 2011) proposes a three-stage response to stress and social engagement in his polyvagal theory. The first stage is the activation of the parasympathetic branch that immobilizes the system (fright). The second stage mobilizes the system for action (fight/flight). The third stage controls cardiac output, which can influence engagement or disengagement with the social world. Heart rate and heart rate variability measures provide information in vivo about the ANS (McCraty, 2005; Porges, 1992, 2011). This information can be communicated to the person experiencing stress so that he or she can implement stress management strategies and react in a healthier manner. Experiencing the world as persistently stressful, which many individuals with ASD do, can lead to a chronic stress response. This can have a serious negative impact on the body and produce symptoms, such as a lower stress response threshold and heightened anxiety, that can lead to chronic illness and disease and hinder social engagement (Seligman, 2006).

A frequent trigger for stress in individuals with ASD is their rigid thought patterns. In addition to frequently misperceiving relatively benign situations as anxiety provoking, they can retain negative inaccurate beliefs for inappropriately long periods of time. These inaccurate beliefs negatively impact social interactions, which inhibits social success. Repeated social failure weakens a sense of resiliency and competence. Improved emotional regulation can have long-lasting positive effects on social performance (Dickerson & Kemeny, 2004). Cognitive coping skills are also helpful for teaching skills to identify and address the inaccurate thought patterns that lead to stress.

Learning stress management skills is a critical component of fostering healthy development. In the adolescent case of Samantha, she attends classes in a program called Science of Me, which is facilitated through Aspire consultation. In these classes, Samantha learns about her nervous system, stress responses, physiological responses, and stress reduction techniques. The lessons include education and practice with recognizing that stressors are internal or external and linking stressors to thoughts, feelings, and behaviors. Samantha is exposed to a variety of stress reduction methods (e.g., progressive muscle relaxation, mindfulness, and relaxation breathing) that are coupled with the use of visual supports and technology to enhance her ability to regulate her responses. The stress management tools are generalized to other settings through homework practice and opportunities for reinforcement from teachers and parents.

THE ASPIRE PROGRAM

Grounded in the three S's (social competence, self-awareness, and stress management), Aspire helps individuals with ASD to better understand themselves and others to help foster healthy development across the lifespan.

Aspire's programs are developmentally focused, group based, and take place in natural settings (e.g., community and schools) to provide an authentic learning environment. Programs are tailored to individuals across the lifespan and help them learn about themselves and others as emotional, social, and mental beings. This includes learning about their own strengths and weaknesses to better understand themselves, similarities and differences with others, and how others perceive them. Aspire participants engage in some direct instruction using creative strategies and hands-on learning activities (e.g., verbal and nonverbal, theory of mind, and relational). They also learn to apply these skills within real-world settings (e.g., on the job, at the store, at school, and in restaurants), both as an individual and while attending to the needs of a larger group (e.g., budgeting and team projects).

By combining the three S's model into a lifespan program, individuals with ASD can be taught to embrace the traits and virtues that lead to a more fulfilling life. By helping individuals gain knowledge about the three S's, they can experience the rewards of mastery of the concepts and they are better able to be active participants in their own lives.

SUMMARY

This chapter highlights the complexity and the importance of social skill training in individuals with ASD. Understanding a person's social skill development entails close consideration of both the person and the environment because social interactions inherently involve more than just the individual. In addition, to understand one's social skills, there is a need for in-depth assessment and careful treatment planning. Social skills cannot be viewed in isolation but instead as interacting skills along with emotional, behavioral, academic, and cultural factors that influence development.

Social skill interventions must match this level of complexity by taking into account individual and contextual factors, a developmental perspective, and a comprehensive whole person approach. It is only through comprehensive assessment of an individual and the etiology of his or her social struggles that an appropriate treatment plan can be created. This chapter gives an overview of important components of social skill interventions for individuals with ASD, and it provides examples from the Aspire model, which is grounded in the three S's (social competence, self-awareness, and stress management).

Current research generally supports the effectiveness of social skill interventions for individuals with ASD. However, despite the widespread use of social skill interventions, there is a critical need for increased research. A primary challenge to effective evaluation and assessment of these interventions is the complexity of individual profiles and the equally complex nature of appropriate social skill interventions. Nonetheless, there is a need for more evidence-based support for social skill treatments.

In summary, social skills deficits can be quite profound for individuals with ASD, and comprehensive, integrated, and developmentally appropriate evidence-based treatments are necessary to remediate these areas of weakness. Social skills training, such as the programs described previously, can foster healthy social development and build satisfying reciprocal relationships for individuals with ASD.

KEY POINTS

- Social skills deficits are a primary and defining core symptom domain of ASD.
- To plan for appropriate social skills treatment, comprehensive assessment is necessary, and the following areas should be considered: perspective taking, self-awareness, executive functioning skills, sensory processing, and comorbid mental health difficulties.
- Group training models for social skills are particularly effective and important because they offer a more "real-life" milieu than individual treatments.
- A structured, intentional, and clinically informed system for group formation is critical to facilitating the success of group interventions.
- Effective social skills training programs should be developmentally focused, group based, and take place in natural settings (e.g., community and schools) to provide an authentic learning environment.

DISCLOSURE STATEMENT

Dr. D. Scott McLeod and Dr. Kristin W. Malatino have nothing to disclose.

Dorothy Lucci serves on the Clinical Scientific Leadership Board of SymTrend, Inc. She does not receive financial compensation or salary support for her participation as an advisor.

REFERENCES

American Psychiatric Association. (2000). *Diagnostic and statistical manual of mental disorders* (4th ed., text rev.). Washington, DC: Author.
American Psychiatric Association. (2013). *Diagnostic and statistical manual of mental disorders* (5th ed.). Arlington, VA: American Psychiatric Publishing.

Attwood, T. (2006). *The complete guide to Asperger's syndrome.* London, England: Kingsley.

Baron-Cohen, S., Tager-Flusberg, H., & Lombardo, M. (Eds.). (2013). *Understanding other minds: Perspectives from developmental social science.* New York, NY: Oxford University Press.

Bellini, S. (2004). Social skills deficits and anxiety in high-functioning adolescents with autism spectrum disorders. *Focus on Autism and Developmental Disabilities, 19*(2), 78–86.

Bellini, S., & Akullian, J. (2007). A meta-analysis of video modeling and video self-modeling interventions for children and adolescents. *Exceptional Children, 73,* 264. doi:10.1177/001440290707300301

Bauminger, N. (2002). The facilitation of social–emotional understanding and social interaction in high-functioning children with autism: Intervention outcomes. *Journal of Autism and Developmental Disorders, 32*(4), 283–298.

Bauminger, N. (2007). Brief report: Individual social–multi-modal intervention for HFASD. *Journal of Autism and Developmental Disorders, 37,* 1593–1604.

Cappadocia, M. C., & Weiss, J. A. (2011). Review of social skill training groups for youth with Asperger syndrome and high functioning autism. *Research in Autism Spectrum Disorders, 5,* 70–78. doi:10.1016/j.rasd.2010.04.001

Collaborative for Academic, Social, and Emotional Learning. (2003). *Safe and sound: An educational leader's guide to evidence-based social and emotional learning (SEL) programs.* Retrieved from http://www.communityschools.org/assets/1/AssetManager/1A_Safe_&_Sound.pdf

Church, C., Alisanski, S., & Amanullah, S. (2000). The social, behavioral and academic experiences of children with Asperger syndrome. *Focus on Autism and Other Developmental Disabilities, 15,* 12–20.

Cotugno, A. J. (2009). Social competence and social skills training and intervention for children with autism spectrum disorders (ASD). *Journal of Autism and Developmental Disorders, 39*(9), 1268–1277.

Dickerson, S. S., & Kemeny, M. E. (2004). Acute stressors and cortisol responses: A theoretical integration and synthesis of laboratory research. *Psychological Bulletin, 130*(3), 355–391.

Grey, C. (2010). *The new social story book* (10th ed.). Arlington, TX: Future Horizons.

Groden, J., Kantor, A., Woodard, C. R., & Lipsitt, L. (2011). *How everyone on the autism spectrum, young and old, can . . . become resilient, be more optimistic, enjoy humor, be kind, and increase self-efficacy: A positive psychology approach.* Philadelphia, PA: Kinsley.

Gutstein, S. E., & Sheely, R. K. (2002). *Relationship development intervention with children, adolescents and adults.* Philadelphia, PA: Kinsley.

Happé, F. (1994). Autism: An introduction psychological theory. Cambridge, MA. Harvard University Press.

Hendricks, D. (2010). Employment and adults with autism spectrum disorders: Challenges and strategies for success. *Journal of Vocational Rehabilitation, 32*(2), 125–134. doi:10.3233/JVR-2010-0502

Ho, B. P. V., Stephenson, J., & Carter, M. (2014). Cognitive–behavioral approach for children with autism spectrum disorders: A meta-analysis. *Review Journal of Autism and Developmental Disorders, 1,* 18–33. doi:10.1007/s40489-013-0002-5

Kasari, C., & Locke, J. (2011). Social skills interventions for children with autism spectrum disorders. In D. Amaral, D. Geschwind, & G. Dawson (Eds.), *Autism spectrum disorders* (pp. 1156–1166). New York, NY: Oxford University Press. doi:10.1093/med/9780195371826.003.0074

Knott, F., Dunlop, A.-W., & MacKay, T. (2006). Living with ASD: How do children and their parents assess their difficulties with social interaction and understanding? *Autism, 10*(6), 609–617.

Krasny, L., Williams, B. J., Provencal, S., & Ozonoff, S. (2003). Social skills interventions for the autism spectrum: Essential ingredients and a model curriculum. *Child and Adolescent Psychiatric Clinics of North America, 12*(1), 107–122.

Lerner, M. D., White, S. W., & McPartland, J. C. (2012). Mechanisms of change in psychosocial interventions for autism spectrum disorders. *Dialogues in Clinical Neuroscience, 14,* 307–318.

Lucci, D., Levine, M., Challen-Wittmer, K., & McLeod, D. S. (2014). Technologies to support intervention for social emotional intelligence, self-awareness or personal style and self-regulation. In K. I. Boser, M. S. Goodwin, & S. C. Wayland (Eds.), *Technology tools for students with autism: Innovations that enhance independence and learning* (pp. 201–226). Baltimore, MD: Brookes.

Lucci, D., & McLeod, D. S. (2008). *Pilot use of PDA technology to teach teens with ASD & NLD about flexibility, feelings, and sensory states at a therapeutic summer day camp.* Poster presented at the International Meeting for Autism Research, London, England.

Mason, R. A., Rispoli, M., Ganz, J. B., Boles, M. B., & Orr, K. (2012). Effects of video modeling on communicative social skills of college students with Asperger syndrome. *Developmental Neurorehabilitation, 15,* 425–434.

Matson, J. L., Matson, M. L., & Rivet, T. T. (2007). Social skills treatments for children with autism spectrum disorders: An overview. *Behavior Modification, 31,* 682.

McCraty, R. (2005). Enhancing emotional, social, and academic learning with heart rhythm coherence feedback. *Biofeeback, 33*(4), 130–134.

McLeod, S. D., & Lucci, D. (2009). *PDA technology to improve self-awareness in teens with ASD.* Poster presented at the International Meeting for Autism Research, Chicago, IL.

National Autism Center. (2009). National Autism Center report. Retrieved from. http://www.nationalautismcenter.org/reports/

Porges, S. W. (1992). Vagal tone: A physiological marker of stress vulnerability. *Pediatrics, 9*(3), 498–504.

Porges, S. W. (2011). *The polyvagal theory: Neurophysiological foundations of emotions, attachment, communication and self-regulation.* New York, NY: Norton.

Prizant, B., Wetherby, A., Rubin, E., Laurent, A., & Rydell, P. (2005). *The SCERTS model: A comprehensive educational approach for children with autism spectrum disorders.* Baltimore, MD: Brookes.

Rao, P. A., Beidel, D. C., & Murray, M. J. (2008). Social skills interventions for children with Asperger's syndrome or high-functioning autism: A review and recommendations. *Journal of Autism and Developmental Disorders, 38,* 353–361. doi:10.1007/s10803-007-0402-4

Samson, A. C., Huber, O., & Gross, J. (2012). Emotion regulation in Asperger's syndrome and high functioning autism. *Emotion, 12*(4), 659–665.

Seligman, M. (2006). *Learned optimism: How to change your mind and your life.* New York, NY: Vintage Books.

Singh, N. N., Lancioni, G. E., Manikam, R., Winton, A. S. W., Singh, A. N. A., Singh, J., & Singh, A. D. A. (2011a). A mindfulness-based strategy for self-management of aggressive behavior in adolescents with autism. *Research in Autism Spectrum Disorders, 5,* 1153–1158.

Singh, N. N., Lancioni, G. E., Singh, A. D. A., Winton, A. S. W., Singh, A. N. A., & Singh, J. (2011b). Adolescents with Asperger syndrome can use a mindfulness-based strategy to control their aggressive behavior. *Research in Autism Spectrum Disorders, 5,* 1103–1109.

Sterling, L., Dawson, G., Estes, A., & Greenson, J. (2008). Characteristics associated with presence of depressive symptoms in adults with autism spectrum disorder. *Journal of Autism and Developmental Disorders, 38,* 1011–1018.

Strain, P. S., Kohler, F. W., & Goldstein, H. (1996). Learning experiences . . . an alternative program: Peer-mediated interventions for young children with autism. In E. Hibbs & P. Jensen (Eds.), *Psychosocial treatments for child and adolescent disorders* (pp. 573–586). Washington, DC: American Psychological Association.

Weiss, J. A., & Lunsky, Y. (2010). Group cognitive behavior therapy for adults with Asperger syndrome and anxiety or mood disorder: A case series. *Clinical Psychology and Psychotherapy, 17,* 438–446.

White, S. W., Oswald, D., Ollendick, T., & Scahill, L. (2009). Anxiety in children and adolescents with autism spectrum disorders. *Child Psychology Review, 29*(3), 216–2229. doi:10.1016/j.cpr.2009.01.003

Williams White, S., Keonig, K., & Scahill, L. (2007). Social skills development in children with autism spectrum disorders: A review of the intervention research. *Journal of Autism and Developmental Disorders, 37,* 1858–1868.

Winner, M. G. (2007). *Thinking about you thinking about me* (2nd ed.). San Jose, CA: Think Social.

Winner, M. G. (2014). *Why teach social thinking?* San Jose, CA: Think Social.

Winner, M. G., Crooke, P., & Madrigal, S. (2011). The Social Thinking–Social Communication Profile (formerly known as the Perspective Taking Spectrum): A practice-informed theory. Retrieved from https://www.socialthinking.com/what-is-social-thinking/social-thinking-social-communication-profile.

Woods, A. G., Mahdavi, E., & Ryan, J. P. (2013). Treating clients with Asperger's syndrome and autism. *Child and Adolescent Psychiatry and Mental Health, 7,* 32–47. doi:10.1186/1753-2000-7-32

OTHER CARE DELIVERY SERVICES AND PERSPECTIVES

/// 21 /// EDUCATIONAL ISSUES IN AUTISM SPECTRUM DISORDER

SAMUEL L. ODOM, VERONICA P. FLEURY,
LESLIE C. FOX, SUSAN H. HEDGES, NIGEL
P. PIERCE, AND MELISSA A. SRECKOVIC

INTRODUCTION

At an international meeting for research on autism spectrum disorder (ASD), Peter Mundy, a prominent cognitive and developmental scientist, stated that school-based intervention, treatment, and instructional programs may be "the best hope" for children and youth with ASD (McIntyre et al., 2013). In the United States, children and youth with ASD are in schools for a significant period of their week, for the majority of the year, from childhood into early adulthood. Schools have the mandate to provide a free and appropriate public education for children with all types of disabilities, including ASD. Professionals should plan programs with parents and, at times, students should be involved. This chapter describes the educational process for children and youth with ASD in the United States and addresses current and future educational issues.

The primary focus of this chapter is on public educational programs, which can begin at age 3 years and continue up to age 22 years in many states. The early intervention system for infants and toddlers with ASD in the United States operates primarily outside of the public education system (i.e., often implemented through state health departments), but when issues arise that are pertinent for infants and toddlers and their families, they are addressed. This chapter begins with a brief review of diagnostic criteria and the parallel eligibility definitions that exist in US federal law. The continuum of educational services across childhood and adolescence, the unique learning needs of individuals with ASD during those years, the quality features of programs that address learning needs, and validated, evidence-based intervention practices are delineated. The chapter describes issues related to families in the educational process and concludes with a discussion of the use of technology in education for students with ASD.

DIAGNOSTIC AND EDUCATIONAL ELIGIBILITY DEFINITIONS OF AUTISM SPECTRUM DISORDER

Common agreement about ASD as a disorder is essential when discussing both science and services for students with ASD. Diagnostic criteria are situated in the psychiatric and medical communities. To qualify for educational services in the United States, however, children and youth with ASD must meet "eligibility" requirements, which have a parallel set of definitional criteria.

Diagnostic Criteria

The 5th edition of the *Diagnostic and Statistical Manual of Mental Disorders* (DSM-5; American Psychiatric Association, 2013) provides the diagnostic criteria primarily followed in the United States. The defining characteristics of ASD are deficits in social communication and the presence of restrictive and repetitive behavior, with characteristics being manifest before the age of 3 years. DSM-5 eliminated the classifications of autistic disorder, Asperger's disorder, Rett's disorder, childhood disintegrative disorder, and pervasive developmental disorder, not otherwise specified, which were in the previous edition. The international community often employs the 10th edition of the *International Classification of Diseases* (ICD-10; World Health Organization, 1992) for diagnosis of autism. Grouped with a superordinate category called Pervasive Developmental Disorders, there are diagnostic classifications termed childhood autism, atypical autism, Rett's syndrome, childhood disintegrative disorder, and Asperger's syndrome. These disorders share the common characteristics of having difficulties in forming social relationships, language delays/disorder, and/or repetitive or challenging behavior. The World Health Organization (2013) recently grouped these disorders under the ASD umbrella term, which makes it consistent with the US terminology. A more detailed discussion of psychiatric diagnosis and classification appears in Chapter 1 of this book.

Educational Eligibility Criteria

Children and youth with ASD, like all children in the United States, are entitled to a free and appropriate public education. The Individuals With Disabilities Education Act (IDEA; 34 C.F.R. §§ 300.1 et seq., 2009) stipulates that special education services be made available to children with disabilities who meet eligibility criteria. The eligibility definition for children with ASD, which is termed "autism" in the federal regulation, states the following:

> Autism means a developmental disability significantly affecting verbal and nonverbal communication and social interaction, generally evident before age three that adversely affects a child's educational performance. Other characteristics often associated with autism are engagement in repetitive activities and stereotyped movements, resistance to environmental change or change in daily routines, and unusual responses to sensory experiences. (IDEA, 300.8.c.1.i; http://idea.ed.gov/explore/view/p/,root,regs,300,A, 300%252E8)

A multidisciplinary team conducts a variety of assessments to determine a child's qualification for special education services under the autism definition.

THE CONTINUUM OF EDUCATIONAL SERVICES

IDEA separates services for children with special needs into two programs. Part B of IDEA delineates the timeline and minimum requirements for school-age children (i.e., 3–21 years). Part C of IDEA governs the early childhood intervention (ECI) programs for children birth to age 3 years. There are commonalities between Part B and Part C services. They each seek to identify children with special needs and use multidisciplinary teams to conduct developmental assessments and make service recommendations. However, there are several notable differences between the two processes related to referrals: location of services, degree of parent involvement, philosophical foundations, cost, and the referral-to-service implementation timeline.

ECI services in a given community may be sponsored by a school district, private/nonprofit organization, or county mental health program. Either parents or health care providers typically initiate referrals to ECI programs. Because primary care physicians routinely see children younger than the age of 5 years for well child appointments, they are often the first to field questions from parents regarding their child's developmental skills and abilities. It is not necessary for infants and toddlers to have a formal diagnosis in order for families to receive ECI services. If a child shows a significant delay in one or more areas of development (e.g., cognition, communication, physical–motor, social–emotional, and self-help/adaptive skills), then an assessment team can establish eligibility. Many children who later receive an ASD diagnosis initially qualify for ECI services based on developmental delays in communication, but they may also present with unusual motor patterns and social skills.

Early physician referrals and provision of information to parents on available services are associated not only with early access to intervention but also parent ratings of satisfaction with medical care (Liptak et al., 2006). In fact, early developmental as well as ASD-specific screenings are recommended practices for pediatricians (American Academy of Pediatrics, 2012). Once a referral is submitted to an ECI program, the program has up to 45 calendar days to complete an evaluation and develop an Individualized Family Service Plan (IFSP). The IFSP is a parent-driven document that reflects functional goals and outcomes relative to the child's skills and abilities. Services are provided year-round in the child's "natural environment," such as the child's home or day care, but may also take place in other settings identified by parents.

After a child's third birthday, the ECI will arrange a transition planning conference with the local education agency (LEA). If a child were not identified prior to age 3 years, the responsibility for evaluation and service provision would fall to the LEA. Parents frequently initiate referrals for children 3–5 years old often based on information provided by health care providers. Classroom teachers and related service providers typically initiate special education referrals for children kindergarten age or older. Once a referral is submitted to the special education program, schools must complete the evaluation, eligibility determination, and development of an Individualized Education Program (IEP) within 45 school days. The goals of the IEP are less parent-driven than the IFSP and more specific to academic objectives. These services are usually provided during the regular academic year and rarely extend over summer and holiday breaks.

The IEP services are provided in the "least restrictive environment" available to meet the child's educational goals. To the maximum extent appropriate, a child with ASD should be included in the general education classroom and provided access to the general curriculum. Inclusion of students with disabilities in the general education classroom with typically developing peers is dependent on the individual needs of the child and can be established by providing additional supports such as assistive technology, a special educator, a paraprofessional, or other specialist.

Parents participate in the development of the IEP and act as consenting authorities for school-based services. When appropriate, children with special needs are expected to attend IEP meetings, and as they grow and transition from childhood to adolescence they are encouraged to actively participate. By age 16 years, each child's IEP must include an Individual Transition Plan (IDEA; 34 C.F.R. §§ 300.1 et seq., 2009), and the student must be invited to attend the meeting. Transition plans are developed by the IEP team and outline specific measureable post-secondary goals related to education/training, employment, and independent living (if appropriate) along with specific transition activities to help achieve those goals. Most states have vocational rehabilitation agencies that may be invited to attend transition IEP meetings and assist with the transition out of high school for adolescents with disabilities.

Some individuals with disabilities graduate from high school and are accepted into post-secondary education settings. This transition can be difficult because many parents are unaware of the different laws that govern accommodations and access in post-secondary settings (US Department of Education, Office of Civil Rights, 2007). Families who are not knowledgeable of such differences may struggle to prepare their child to access accommodations when starting college. Even though a student may have had a diagnosis of ASD from a young age, additional diagnostic information or documentation may be required when transitioning into the post-secondary setting if the student has not recently been evaluated.

LEARNING NEEDS OF STUDENTS WITH AUTISM SPECTRUM DISORDER

Individuals with ASD may exhibit specific learning needs across the age range; however, those needs may vary by individual. In educational settings, student success is often measured by academic achievement. Research suggests that some individuals with ASD are behind their same-age peers in academic areas, and as children get older and enter secondary school, the gap often continues to widen. In addition to academics, individuals with ASD often struggle to keep up socially with their same-age peers, which may limit their participation in class and schoolwide activities. Children who enter formal schooling lacking social and emotional competence, a core feature of ASD, will likely have difficulty succeeding in school (National Center for Special Education Research, 2006). These difficulties begin early in life. Very young children with ASD may lack or lag behind in developing foundational social communication skills, such as joint attention and imitation. Without early intervention, these difficulties may persist, hindering children's performance in educational settings. For example, children with ASD may have trouble following a teacher's direction, staying on task, and/or participating in group activities. In addition, an intense focus or preoccupation with a restricted range of interests creates challenges for children with ASD and may limit their participation in classroom activities.

Individuals who are unresponsive to a teacher's direction, unable to independently complete tasks, or engage in stereotypic behaviors usually cannot fully participate in, and thereby benefit from, classroom activities without appropriate support. These behaviors may result in students being placed in more restrictive school settings (Machalicek, O'Reilly, Beretvas, Sigafoos, & Lancioni, 2007), which in turn limits access to the general education curriculum and typically developing peers. It is helpful for practitioners to understand how core behaviors characteristic of ASD can affect an individual's ability to learn in educational settings. The core features of ASD are described next in relation to how they may impact students regarding academics, social competence, and independence.

Academics

Federal legislative acts such as the No Child Left Behind Act (2002) and the Individuals With Disabilities Education Improvement Act (IDEA, 2004) hold schools accountable for student achievement in core curricular areas such as math, reading, and science. The IDEA specifically requires that students with disabilities have access to and make progress in the general education curriculum to the fullest extent appropriate. Students who are educated in inclusive settings have been found to spend more time engaged in curricular activities and demonstrate significant gains in academic achievement compared to students with ASD who are educated primarily in self-contained classrooms (Kurth & Mastergeorge, 2012). Most individuals with ASD who take courses in general education classrooms receive some type of academic accommodation (e.g., untimed testing). Two-thirds have the curriculum modified (e.g., simplifying the text in a reading passage), and roughly one-half take modified tests in which they work toward the same grade-level standards as their same-age peers who are nondisabled, but with alternate achievement targets (Newman, 2007).

Although the diagnostic criteria for ASD do not imply academic difficulties, impairments in the social communication domain, as well as engagement in restricted, repetitive, and stereotypic behaviors, may contribute to the challenges around academic performance and have proven to be predictive of future academic achievement (Estes, Rivera, Bryan, Cali, & Dawson, 2011). Understanding the academic profile of individuals with ASD is complex due to a high prevalence of comorbid intellectual disability (ID), a higher prevalence of learning disabilities than occurs in the general population, and splinter skills or uneven skill profiles that make accurate assessment difficult. Generally, individuals with ASD have an overall strength for rote or procedural skills. For an elementary-age student, this may be reflected in above average ability to decode words (e.g., letter–sound identification), spell, and memorize math facts. Conversely, this same student may have a weakness in abstract or inferential skills. This weakness may become more apparent during high school, when the same student may have difficulty comprehending complex texts and applied math problems and writing analytical essays (Kurth & Mastergeorge, 2010).

Social Competence

Schools are highly social contexts and success is often dependent on the relationships that develop between students with ASD, their teachers, and their peers. Across the age range, students are expected to work with peers in groups and contribute to group projects in a meaningful way. Starting as early as preschool, students are expected to interact with their peers by sharing classroom materials, taking turns, and participating in cooperative play and work. As students enter middle and high school, the social dynamic becomes more complex. They often place greater emphasis on friendships and become more selective in their peer groups. For students with ASD, developing and maintaining peer relationships can be difficult. In fact, elementary-age students with ASD have reported poorer friendship quality and fewer reciprocal friendships compared to their peers without ASD (Kasari, Locke, Gulsrud, & Rotheram-Fuller, 2011). Wagner, Cadwallader, Garza, and Cameto (2004) reported that adolescent students with ASD participating in a national longitudinal study were the least likely (in comparison with students having other disabilities) to frequently see friends outside of school, receive telephone calls from friends, and get invited to another student's social event. Unfortunately, not only do these students have difficulties making positive peer relationships but also they are bullied by their peers at alarmingly high rates across the elementary, middle, and high school years (Sreckovic, Brunsting, & Able, 2014).

The core diagnostic features of ASD imply difficulties developing social competence and establishing relationships. For instance, due to deficits in social interaction and communication, students may not understand how to join a conversation or may dominate a conversation by excessively talking about their special interests. For example, an elementary-age student with an intense interest in trains may dominate conversations and persist on talking about Thomas the Tank Engine. Similarly, a middle or high school student may have a special interest in US highways, which becomes the central theme of his conversations. Although some students may be impressed with the ASD student's vast knowledge of US highways, most students will find the obsessive interest odd, further isolating the student with ASD. In addition, students may have difficulty reading facial expressions, body language, and prosody, making comprehending conversations challenging. For students who engage in unusually restrictive and repetitive behaviors, their behaviors may hinder their ability to participate in school activities. The presence of unusual behaviors can make students with ASD stand out from their peers and make them vulnerable to being bullied. Students with ASD also often have difficulty understanding the intentions and thoughts of others (Baron-Cohen, Leslie, & Frith, 1985), making it difficult for them to discriminate when their peers have ill intentions. At the elementary, middle, and high school levels, peers may take advantage of the gullibility of students with ASD. For example, peers may tell the student with ASD to make inappropriate comments to the teacher or a student of the opposite sex. Students with ASD who may have difficulty recognizing these ill intentions are often compliant to their peers' requests, making them easy targets for bullying victimization (Sofronoff, Dark, & Stone, 2011). To develop social competence and establish peer relationships, individuals with ASD need explicit instruction as well as authentic opportunities to practice social skills and foster friendships (Carter et al., 2014).

Independence

In educational settings, independent functioning (i.e., "on-task engagement in an activity in the absence of adult prompting"; Hume & Odom, 2007, p. 1172) is a necessary skill in school and beyond. Starting as early as kindergarten, students are expected to complete classroom tasks independently without adult assistance. As students enter late elementary school and secondary school, autonomy increases; students are expected to manage not only in-class assignments but also homework and class projects independently. Independence is also necessary for post-school success. Unfortunately, research has found very poor post-school outcomes for students with ASD. In a national survey, less than 40% of young adults with ASD participated in some type of independent employment since leaving high school, and only 17% were living independently (Newman et al., 2011).

The diagnostic criteria and core features of ASD do not specifically include difficulties with independence. However, limited social interaction and social communication skills may contribute to challenges of independence. For example, many students learn skills necessary for independence by observing others. However, challenges within the social and communication domain often limit the ability of students with ASD to observe peers and learn necessary skills for independent functioning because these students often have difficulty discriminating among the multiple social cues in the environment (Plavnick & Hume, 2014). Asking questions and seeking clarification may also be difficult for students with ASD because they may not know what questions to ask or who to ask (Hurlbutt &

Chalmers, 2004). In addition, the preference for sameness and limited flexibility can make changes in daily routines extremely challenging and disruptive. Children and youth with ASD often become dependent on adult prompts, and withdrawing such prompts may be difficult for students who prefer sameness (Hume, Loftin, & Lantz, 2009).

Difficulties with independence can appear similar across grade levels. For example, an elementary student who does not understand a writing assignment may sit at his or her desk, staring at the paper, rather than asking a peer or the teacher for help. This same student might express similar difficulties in middle and high school. However, at the middle and high school level, students may demonstrate more difficulties around independence because they are expected to navigate several classes a day, which can entail managing multiple materials, assignments, projects, and teacher expectations. For students with ASD and ID, the challenges of achieving independence are even greater because research suggests they have lower levels of daily living skills and gain skills at a slower rate compared to their counterparts with ASD without ID (Smith, Maenner, & Seltzer, 2012). The heightened importance of independence starting in preschool and extending to post-school highlights the need for interventions focused on building independence across the age range. Given the multifaceted needs of children and youth with ASD, high-quality and effective educational programs are needed.

ESSENTIAL FEATURES OF EDUCATION PROGRAM QUALITY

Educational programs vary in quality, as do all human services. To be advocates for children with ASD, it is important for professionals and family members to understand the features of an educational program that reflect quality. Researchers and service providers have developed instruments to measure program quality. In 2001, the New York State Education Department developed the *Autism Program Quality Indicators* guide, which was subsequently adapted by New Jersey (New Jersey Department of Education, 2004). This guide focuses on program characteristics (e.g., personnel and curriculum) and student considerations (e.g., assessment and IEPs). In their research on program efficacy of two comprehensive preschool models, Hume et al. (2011) developed a measure of program quality for preschool programs for children with ASD. Called the PDA Fidelity Form, this rating scale focused on eight features of programs for children with ASD (e.g., teaming, environment, and family involvement). To assist in their work with schools to improve services for children and youth with ASD, investigators with the National Professional Development Center on ASD (NPDC) developed a comprehensive assessment of program quality called the Autism Program Environment Rating Scale (APERS; APERS Research Group, 2014). Similar in content to the PDA Fidelity Form, the APERS conceptual framework contains sections that address teaming, program ecology, and families (Figure 21.1), with subdomains in each section. This framework is used to discuss features of quality in educational programs.

Teaming

Teaming refers to the promotion of collaborative relationships and ongoing interactions among service providers to ensure that the outcomes and goals of students with ASD are being met. High-quality teaming in support of students with ASD is interdisciplinary in nature and includes, in addition to special and general education teachers, any number of

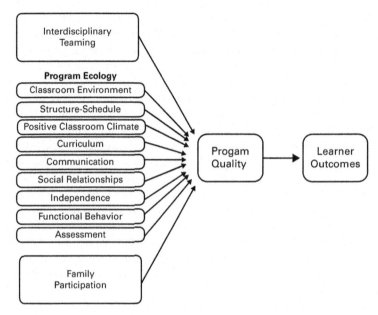

FIGURE 21.1 Conceptualization of quality features of programs for children and youth with autism spectrum disorder.

related service providers, such as speech and language pathologists, occupational therapists, psychologists, counselors, transition coordinators, autism specialists, behavior specialists, and vocational specialists. It is essential that family members are included on the team and, when appropriate, the student should be invited to attend IEP meetings (a requirement beginning no later than age 16 years). Medical professionals may also participate in the team as necessary depending on the individual needs of the student (e.g., related to medications, seizures, and affective behavior). It is important that the team members have training and experience working with students with ASD.

Having a *key* team member who is responsible for the student's program is an essential feature of teaming. The key team member coordinates instructional plans among the team and facilitates frequent communication with and among all relevant team members. Technologies such as e-mail, text, and video conferencing can help facilitate more frequent collaboration. Responsibilities of the team may include assessing needs, identifying problems and problem solving, brainstorming, reaching consensus, setting goals, making plans, and implementing and evaluating plans. A component of particular importance for high-quality teaming includes a system of follow-up to assess the implementation of the team's decisions.

Program Ecology

The ecology of an educational program consists of structural quality and instructional quality (Odom & Bailey, 2001). Structural quality includes the characteristics of the class settings, the structure and schedule, and the social climate of the program. High-quality programs have age and instructionally appropriate materials that are accessible to the learner. They incorporate clearly articulated and predictable schedules, which are often supplemented by visual supports for students (e.g., individual activity schedules). In addition, high-quality programs have a positive instructional "climate," one indicator of which is that the teachers and/or staff direct more positive than negative statements to the students with ASD.

Instructional quality refers to opportunities for students to engage in meaningful learning activities with learning opportunities focusing on areas that are primarily related to individual goals for students with ASD (e.g., communication, social skills, independence, and reduction of challenging behavior). In high-quality programs, staff plan instruction in different formats (e.g., one-on-one instruction and whole class instruction) that fit the learning needs of the students; may use specific behavioral techniques (e.g., reinforce assessment, task analysis, and prompting hierarchy) as appropriate for learner needs; and assess student performance in order to make instructional decisions (i.e., change instructional approach if the student is not making progress). In addition, high-quality programs employ intervention and instructional strategies that focus on communication skills, social skills and peer relationships, independence, and reduction of challenging behavior.

Families

A strong home–school relationship is an important foundation for a positive educational experience for all children with disabilities (Berry & Hardman, 1998). It is for this reason that the IDEA requires that parents have the opportunity to participate in the development of the IEP. The intent is to include the parents as members of the educational team and build a collaborative partnership between parents and educators. Although the legal framework exists, in practice there is great variability in implementation.

In high-quality programs for students with ASD, family involvement is characterized by a strong, positive school–family rapport. To accomplish this, school personnel have a system for regular, frequent, and individualized communication aided by technology (e.g., e-mail and text) as appropriate. It is important that school staff members demonstrate respect for families' knowledge, cultural beliefs, and priorities and avoid jargon and acronyms or technical terms. In addition, schools must be flexible in meeting times to facilitate participation. Throughout the school experience, family involvement is considered an essential support for students with ASD (Test, Smith, & Carter, 2014).

Quality in Early Intervention Programs

As noted previously, early intervention programs differ from most public school-based programs in that they are often administered by a different agency, are more often home-based rather than school- or center-based, more often deliver services through a visiting/consulting therapist or educator, and operate from an IFSP rather than an IEP. In extending their work on the APERS to infant/toddler early intervention programs, NPDC investigators (Cox, Kucharczyk, Shaw, Rogers, & Odom, 2014) created a new program environment measure for infants and toddlers with ASD, their families, and subsequent care providers. Quality features include (1) establishing a positive relationship with the care provider; (2) helping the family organize predictable physical environments, activities, and daily routines; (3) using specific intervention strategies (i.e., as noted in the subsequent section on evidence-based practices); (4) providing ongoing assessment for developing the IFSP and monitoring child progress; (5) addressing behavioral issues when they occur; and (6) leading interdisciplinary teaming.

A Last Note on Intensity

In their 2001 review of educational programs for children with ASD, a National Academy of Sciences committee stated that programs had to be intense to produce positive outcomes for children with ASD (National Research Council, 2001). By intensity, the committee specified 25 hours per week of intervention, and in subsequent years researchers have proposed that student engagement in productive learning experiences during intervention or instruction is also an important feature of intensity (Thompson, 2011). For public school programs, it is reasonable to expect that children and youth with ASD receive at least the same number of service hours as do typically developing children, which usually exceeds 25 hours per week, and that they engage in meaningful learning experiences during the majority of those hours (APERS Research Group, 2014; New York State Education Department, 2001).

EVIDENCE-BASED PRACTICE

The concept of evidence-based practice (EBP) is central to the provision of educational services to children and youth with ASD in the United States. The federal laws governing education (i.e., No Child Left Behind) and special education (i.e., IDEA) emphasize that instruction and intervention for students must be research-based—that is, supported by empirical findings that document efficacy of the approach. This evidence-based education movement emerged from two sources. One source was educational leaders' frustration with the distance between research and practice (Carnine, 1999). Another primary influence was from the field of evidence-based medicine (EBM), which was based on the work of Cochrane (1972) and colleagues in the United Kingdom and led by Sackett (Sackett, Rosenberg, Gray, Haynes, & Richardson, 1996) and colleagues in Canada and the United Kingdom as well. EBM proposes that medical practitioners should use the best available scientific evidence to guide their practice as well as their expert knowledge about the patient and treatment (Sackett et al., 1996). This combination of EBP and professional knowledge of interventions and ASD guides effective education for students with ASD, and it is a theme to which this chapter returns later.

Comprehensive Treatment Models

Beginning early in the history of intervention research for children and youth with ASD, comprehensive treatment models (CTMs) emerged as a form of treatment. CTMs are programs guided by a conceptual model, documented in procedural manuals, and available for adoption or replication (Odom, Boyd, Hall, & Hume, 2014). They are intensive in nature (i.e., often 25 or more hours per week), have a conceptual framework, extend across a long period of time (e.g., school year), focus on the multiple learning needs of students with ASD (e.g., social, communication, and behavior), use assessment and data to make instructional decisions, and have a family component (National Research Council, 2001). Two of the first CTMs were the UCLA Young Autism Project established by Lovaas (1987) and the Treatment and Education of Autistic and Communication Handicapped Children (TEACCH) project established by Schopler, Mesibov, and Hearsey (1995). At least 30 such models have appeared in the professional literature (Odom, Boyd, Hall, & Hume, 2010).

Many CTMs are clinic- or home-based (e.g., Early Start Denver Model; Lovaas Institute). However, some models are amenable to adoption by public schools or specifically designed for use in public school settings. In their research on the TEACCH and Learning Experiences and Alternate Program for Preschoolers and Their Parents (LEAP) CTMs, Boyd et al. (2014) found both types of CTMs implemented in school systems in four states, and research indicates that the STAR model (Arick et al., 2003) has been implemented successfully in public schools. Also, developers have designed school-based versions of the Pivotal Response Treatment Model (Stahmer, Suhrheinrich, Reed, Bolduc, & Schreibman, 2010) and the Social Communication, Emotional Regulation, and Transactional Support (SCERTS) models (Prizant, Wetherby, Rubin, Laurent, & Rydell, 2005). For school system personnel to use these models appropriately, they need to be trained by the developers or authorized trainers and implement them with a high level of fidelity.

A limitation of CTM use in the public schools is that nearly all models have been developed for and validated with preschool and elementary school children. Although schools provide educational services for preschool and elementary children, they also enroll middle and high school students with ASD, and no CTMs have been developed for those groups. A second limitation for the broad CTM literature is that few empirical studies have documented their efficacy and can thus be called evidence-based. The models with randomized controlled trial (RCT) or quasi-experimental design evidence are the Lovaas model (Lovaas, 1987), LEAP (Strain & Bovey, 2011), TEACCH (Boyd et al., 2014), and Early Start Denver Model (Dawson et al., 2010). Although others have accumulated, in some cases, extensive evidence (e.g., single case design studies of individual procedures), it is not in the form of experimental efficacy studies of the model.

A Note on Applied Behavior Analysis

Much confusion now exists over the term "applied behavior analysis" (ABA) and the model of services it implies. ABA represents a wide array of practices based on behavioral principles, although the common erroneous assumption often is that the only practice followed is discrete trial training. The ABA professional community has attempted to ensure some uniformity in the quality of ABA interventions implemented by establishing Board Certificated Behavior Analysis (BCBA) training programs and certification. However, BCBA training does not specifically require any content or supervised experience related to ASD. As mentioned later in the discussion of EBPs, many individual practices have a theoretical ABA foundation.

Focused Intervention Practices

Focused intervention practices are individual interventions that target specific goals for students with ASD. For example, discrete trial training (i.e., a one-on-one form of adult-child instruction) is a focused intervention practice that a teacher might use to address a goal for an individual student, and it is also one of a set of procedures that make up the Lovaas CTM. In most cases, schools do not adopt entire CTMs, but instead teachers design individualized programs for children and youth with ASD, as noted previously. When teachers select evidence-based, focused intervention practices to use with students, they follow a "technical eclectic" model, which is a teaching process that uses instruction/intervention procedures validated by efficacy research (Odom, Hume, Boyd, & Stabel, 2012). The necessary requirement for such an approach is that researchers have identified the EBPs.

Investigators have conducted systematic reviews of the literature to identify EBPs for children and youth with ASD. The National Standards Project (National Autism Center, 2009) conducted an extensive review of the literature that covered multiple decades and followed a systematic procedure for evaluating studies. The project identified 11 practices or sets of practices that it calls treatments. Drawing from a narrower time period (1997–2007), investigators with the NPDC also did a systematic search and evaluation of research articles (Odom, Collet-Klingenberg, Rogers, & Hatton, 2010). They found that 24 practices met their criteria for being classified as evidence-based (i.e., had at least two acceptable RCT or quasi-experimental studies or five single case design studies by two different research groups). In an update of this review, Wong et al. (2014) found support for 27 EBPs. These practices are presented in Table 21.1. The majority of the practices are based on foundational ABA concepts (e.g., prompting, reinforcement, and task analysis) or organized into a multi-component intervention that incorporates the foundational concepts (e.g., functional communication training, pivotal response training, and naturalistic intervention). In addition, there are a set of practices that have been routinely incorporated into a package of positive behavior intervention and support (e.g., functional assessment, extinction, redirection, antecedent interventions, and direct reinforcement of other behavior), which are described later.

Positive Behavior Intervention and Support

The presence of behavior problems poses significant challenges to effective classroom instruction. In school settings, children with ASD demonstrate significantly higher

TABLE 21.1 Evidence-Based Practices Identified by the National Professional Development Center on Autism Spectrum Disorder

Antecedent-based interventions (ABI)	Cognitive–behavior interventions (CBI)	Differential reinforcement (DRA/I/O)
Discrete trial training (DTT)	Exercise (ECE)	Extinction (EXT)
Functional behavior assessment (FBA)	Functional communication training (FCT)	Modeling (MD)
Naturalistic interventions (NI)	Parent-implemented interventions (PII)	Peer-mediated intervention (PMII)
Picture Exchange Communication System (PECS)	Pivotal response training (PRT)	Prompting (PP)
Reinforcement (R+)	Response interruption/ redirection (RIR)	Scripting (SC)
Self-management (SM)	Social narrative (SN)	Social skills training (SST)
Structured play groups (SPG)	Task analysis (TA)	Technology-aided intervention and instruction (TAII)
Time delay (TD)	Video modeling (VM)	Visual supports (VS)

Source: Adapted from Wong, C., Odom, S. L., Hume, K., Cox, A. W., Fettig, A., Kucharczyk, S., . . . Schultz, T. R. (2014). *Evidence-based practices for children, youth, and young adults with autism spectrum disorder.* Chapel Hill, NC: The University of North Carolina, Frank Porter Graham Child Development Institute, Autism Evidence-Based Practice Review Group.

behavioral excesses and deficits, including limited communication, difficulty participating in the school routine, and aggression or self-injurious behavior, compared to typically developing peers (Ashburner, Ziviani, & Rodger, 2010). Educators have taken different approaches to address problematic behavior that occurs in their classroom. Early on, some forms of punishment such as verbal reprimands, school suspension, and even aversive conditioning for more severe problem behavior were used (Friman, 1984). In addition to raising ethical concerns regarding the use of punishment as a primary disciplinary measure, researchers have also found that punishment procedures are generally ineffective over time because they do not address the underlying reasons why the individual may be engaging in the behavior and do not teach students how to engage in more appropriate behavior (Johns, Mather, & McGrath, 2003).

Currently, many school staff members employ a more proactive approach to discipline and behavior management. Positive Behavior Interventions & Supports (PBIS; see http://www.pbis.org) has been widely adopted by schools throughout the United States as a model for dealing with problem behaviors that arise in school. The PBIS model is adapted from public health research on prevention medicine, and it gives educators a systematic process for beginning with prevention strategies and moving to more intensive intervention as needed. The PBIS model depicted in Figure 21.2 identifies preventative strategies

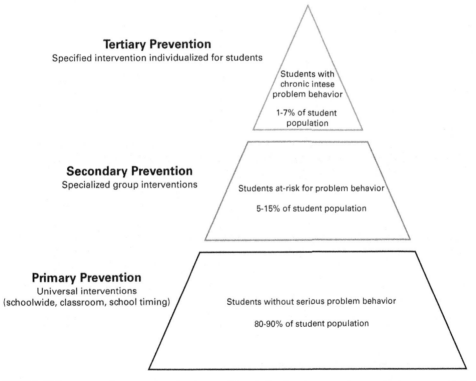

Tertiary Prevention
Specified intervention individualized for students

Students with chronic intese problem behavior

1-7% of student population

Secondary Prevention
Specialized group interventions

Students at-risk for problem behavior

5-15% of student population

Primary Prevention
Universal interventions
(schoolwide, classroom, school timing)

Students without serious problem behavior

80-90% of student population

FIGURE 21.2 Levels of prevention in the positive behavior intervention and support model.
Source: Adapted from Sugai, G., Horner, R. H., Dunlap, G., Hieneman, M., Lewis, T. J., Nelson, C. M., ... Ruef, M. (1999). Applying positive behavior support and functional behavioral assessment in schools. Washington, DC: Office of Special Education Programs, Center on Positive Behavioral Interventions and Supports, p. 11.

taking place at the three tiers of prevention: primary, secondary, and tertiary prevention levels (Sugai et al., 1999).

The goal of *primary prevention* (tier 1/schoolwide positive behavior support) is to prevent challenging behavior for all students by teaching students the behaviors they should demonstrate at school. Prevention efforts at this level involve establishing clear school expectations, designing a system for promoting positive behavior (e.g., incentive programs for following school rules), and manipulating environmental factors that contribute to problem behavior (e.g., increasing supervision in hallways and playgrounds). *Secondary prevention* (tier 2) is used when students continue to engage in challenging behaviors, which requires additional support than is afforded by primary strategies alone. Approaches at this level target students who share common concerns (e.g., family disruption) and who require intensive instruction in a specific area (e.g., social skills groups; Check-in/Check-out with adults). Students who persist in engaging in problem behavior are referred to *tertiary prevention* (tier 3). Interventions at this level involve conducting a functional behavior assessment to identify possible function(s) of the behavior and developing a support plan that includes strategies to address the behavior based on the individualized assessment.

Adopting a Preventative Approach to Reducing Victimization

As previously mentioned, students with ASD are bullied at alarmingly high rates. In one study, 77% of parents reported that their children with ASD (5–21 years old) were bullied within the previous month (Cappadocia, Weiss, & Pepler, 2012). These students have been coined by researchers as "perfect victims" due to their severe deficits in social skills and difficulties establishing and maintaining relationships with peers (Klin & Volkmar, 2000, p. 6). For example, when students with ASD do not adopt similar clothing, hair styles, and mannerisms as those of their peers, they become vulnerable to bullying victimization (Bukowski & Sippola, 2001). In elementary school, bullying is typically expressed physically and verbally. However, as students enter middle and high school and gain better social skills, they begin to manipulate relationships and use more relational forms of victimization. The student with ASD, who likely already has difficulty with social competence and peer relationships, is often easily manipulated by peers and therefore becomes an easy target for perpetrators. PBIS provides a promising approach to reduce the frequency of bullying behaviors. At the primary level, the goal is to reduce new cases of bullying through whole-school and classwide practices. At the secondary level, the goal is to reduce student engagement in bullying behaviors by implementing interventions aimed at bystanders and perpetrators of bullying. At the tertiary level, the goal is to reduce the frequency and severity of bullying behaviors by implementing individualized interventions for students who continue to engage in frequent bullying behaviors (Espelage & Swearer, 2008). The extent to which interventions implemented within the PBIS framework reduce the frequency of bullying victimization and perpetration specifically among youth with ASD is unknown. However, to reduce bullying behaviors among the general population, a coordinated effort between all stakeholders is crucial.

Moving From Goals to Evidence-Based Practices

As in EBM, in which medical care is based on the scientific evidence of treatment effects and clinicians' professional knowledge, a similar process is followed in the evidence-based educational process. The process (as described in Odom et al., 2012) begins with professionals establishing measureable goals for students, as noted previously. Professionals match goals to the types of outcomes researchers have reported in their efficacy studies documenting EBPs. An example of a matrix that describes outcomes (in columns and organized by age level) and EBPs (in rows) is shown in Table 21.2. Practitioners can use this matrix as a tool to begin the process. In most cases, more than one EBP will be available as a possible intervention. In making the final selection of the evidence-based focused intervention to be used with a student, the teacher must use his or her own professional wisdom and judgment. That is, the teacher should consider the student's previous history and response to specific interventions, the current settings and resources, parents' priorities and advice about the student, and possibly the student's choice about intervention type if self-determination is an appropriate option. Last, the teacher should collect data on student performance to determine if the specific EBP results in progress toward the goal and be prepared to select a different approach if there is no progress.

FAMILIES

The structure and definition of families have changed during the past 20 years. Not only are families more culturally diverse but also children with disabilities are being raised with different life experiences. The stereotypical family structure that once consisted of two heterosexual parents with children who are biologically related is no longer the norm (Anyan & Pryor, 2002). These changing dynamics in family structure have significant implications on how health care and education systems provide services to children and youth with ASD.

Families, Schools, and Health Care

Children with ASD present with lifelong challenges that require parents to seek, understand, and act on information from education and health care practitioners. Physicians are often the first to field questions from parents who have concerns and to make referrals to intervention programs. They can also be a source of continuity as children grow and move through the education system. Children from lower socioeconomic status (SES) or minority groups often receive a diagnosis of ASD, and therefore access to intervention services, later in development than their middle-class, Caucasian peers (Mandell, Listerud, Levy, & Pinto-Martin, 2002). Furthermore, parents frequently report frustration with the evaluation and eligibility process, making it critical that physicians acknowledge and are supportive of parents' efforts to access special education services (Osborne & Reed, 2008). Research suggests that families and children experience the most difficulty during points of transition between education service delivery systems (Baer, Davis, McMahan Queen, & Flexer, 2011). When uncertain or vulnerable, families may seek counsel from medical providers on what to expect in the upcoming years, alternative treatments or therapies, and available parent-support groups (Rhoades, Scarpa, & Salley, 2007).

Since the inception of IDEA, parents have been at the forefront of advocacy for children with disabilities. This advocacy resulted in strong provisions for privacy and informed consent in order for schools to release information to those outside the education system. As a result, it is the responsibility of parents to be conduits of information between health care and education providers. Although intervention is primarily delivered by education-based personnel, medical and health care providers may play a significant role as partners in a comprehensive treatment plan. Parents of children with ASD may have concerns related

TABLE 21.2 Matrix of Evidence-Based Practices by Outcome and Age (Years)[a]

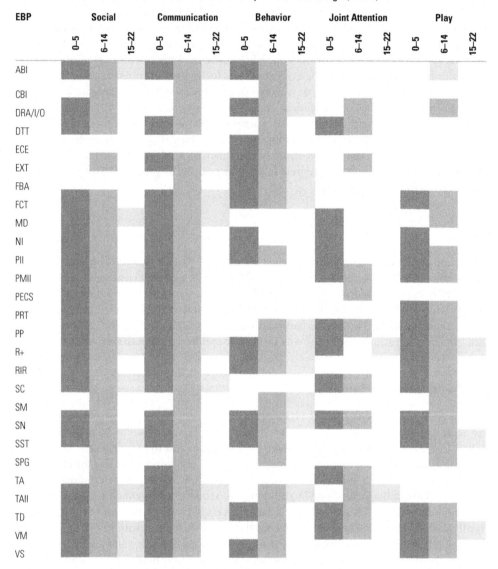

Pink = 0–5 years of age; Yellow = 6–14 years of age; aqua = 15–22 years of age.
[a]Abbreviations for practices are from Table 21.1.

ABI = Antecedent-based interventions; CBI = Cognitive-behavior interventions; DRA/I/O = Differential reinforcement; DTT = Discrete trial training; ECE = Exercise; EXT = Extinction; FBA = Functional behavior assessment; FCT = Functional communication training; MDI = Modeling; NI = Naturalistic interventions; PII = Parent-implemented interventions; PMII = Peer-mediated intervention; PECS = Picture Exchange Communication System; PRT = Pivotal response training; PP = Prompting; R+ = Reinforcement; RIR = Response interruption/redirection; SC = Scripting; SM = Self management; SN = Social narrative; SST = Social skills training; SPG = Structured play groups; TA = Task analysis; TAII = Technology-aided intervention and instruction; TD = Time delay; VM = Video monitoring; VS = Visual supports.

Source: Adapted from Wong, C., Odom, S. L., Hume, K., Cox, A. W., Fettig, A., Kucharczyk, S., ... Schultz, T. R. (2014). *Evidence-based practices for children, youth, and young adults with autism spectrum disorder.* Chapel Hill, NC: The University of North Carolina, Frank Porter Graham Child Development Institute, Autism Evidence-Based Practice Review Group, p. 23.

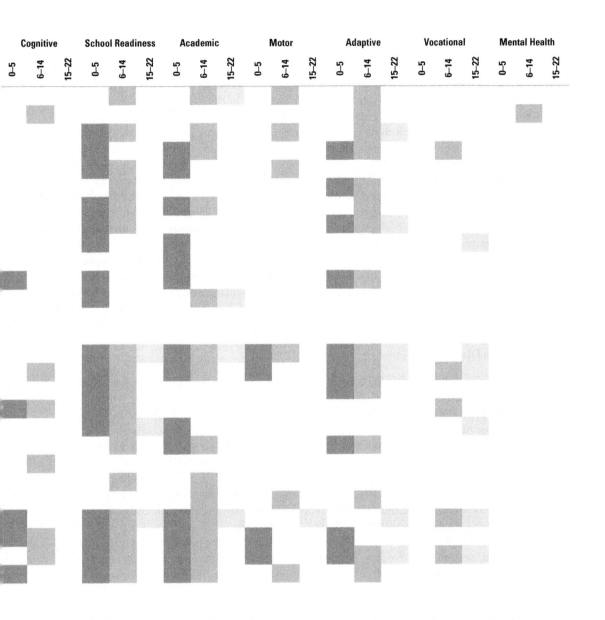

to sensory challenges, sleep disturbances, and diet and food sensitivities that educators and related service providers are not able to address. In addition to the core diagnostic features of social–communication impairment and restricted interests/stereotypic behaviors, individuals with ASD often have comorbid conditions that require medical and pharmacologic intervention. Depression, anxiety, seizure disorders, attention deficit hyperactivity disorder, and oppositional defiant disorder are some of the psychiatric conditions that are prevalent within the ASD population (Simonoff et al., 2008). The side effects of medications prescribed to treat these conditions may negatively impact a child's attention and energy levels in school, resulting in increased hurdles for learning. It is the responsibility of parents to communicate to educators whether or not children are prescribed medications with such side effects. Conversely, parents must also communicate to health care providers any behavioral changes reported by teachers once medications are started or discontinued. Supporting parents as they navigate the benefits and challenges of various treatment options is important for both medical providers and educators if parents are expected to make informed decisions and communicate between the two systems' providers. Parent input and involvement is less emphasized as children age and move through their education programs. Self-determination or the rights of youth and young adults with ASD to choose and refuse services becomes more prominent in IEP discussions and may also be relevant to medical care.

Rights and Advocacy of Families

Families of children with ASD frequently have to advocate for quality services offered through public education systems. Parental and family advocacy can include petitioning for "due process rights" as a result of an IEP meeting or requesting diagnoses and assessment from health care providers. Research suggests that parents who possess the skill set to advocate in the school system also demonstrate the ability to advocate with health care providers (Rehm, Fisher, Fuentes-Afflick, & Chesla, 2013). The availability and types of services may be determined by several factors associated with families, including cultural differences, SES, and marital status. Considering that physicians also have the ability to advocate on behalf of a child with ASD, some of these barriers to access and care can be diminished with proactive physician support of all families.

Finally, the goal of any program or provision of care is to support families and promote independence and self-advocacy. Because there has been continuous change in how families are defined, public schools, like health care organizations, must be responsive to this changing dynamic in family structure if high-quality, comprehensive services are to be provided to individuals with ASD. Sensitivity to language differences and cultural beliefs about special education, disability, labeling, and medication is relevant to both medical and education providers. The objective is the same from both perspectives: that individuals with ASD and their families receive the highest quality of care to support their health, learning, and relationships.

TECHNOLOGY

The use of technology in support of students with ASD is an area showing great promise, but the evidence base remains sparse as researchers struggle to keep up with the rapid pace of innovation (Grynszpan, Weiss, Perez-Diaz, & Gal, 2014). Much of the enthusiasm surrounding the use of new technologies (e.g., tablets and smartphones) to support children with ASD is undoubtedly due to the affinity students with ASD exhibit for screen-based media (Kuo, Orsmond, Coster, & Cohn, 2014). Studies have revealed that screen-based technology use is a primary and preferred activity for the majority of youth with ASD across the spectrum (Mazurek, Shattuck, Wagner, & Cooper, 2012). A possible explanation for this attraction is that individuals with ASD have strengths in the areas of visual perception (Shane & Albert, 2008) and visual search (Kaldy, Giserman, Carter, & Blaser, 2013). A national survey of the post-secondary outcomes of students with ASD found that those students who attend college major in computer science at a rate much higher than the general population (16.22% vs. 6.6%; Wei, Yu, Shattuck, McCracken, & Blackorby, 2013).

There are other reasons for enthusiasm surrounding technology as a support, including the way it can address the core deficits of ASD through its consistency of clearly defined tasks, visually cued instructions, and by providing freedom from social demands (Grynszpan, Weiss, Perez-Diaz, & Gal, 2014). Researchers anticipate potential positive outcomes for students with ASD from technology especially in the areas of motivating task engagement and increasing positive behaviors (Mazurek & Wenstrup, 2013). Social media may help improve social interactions for students with ASD and their peers, as it can be far less intimidating for students who often struggle to engage in face-to-face relations. Virtual reality is showing promise as a way to practice social encounters using avatars (Hopkins et al., 2011). Expensive speech-generating technology that has helped some nonverbal students with ASD to communicate is now available as applications for smartphones, iPods, and tablets, making it more accessible (Kagohara et al., 2013). Adding to the potential of new handheld technologies as a support is the fact that, in addition to being portable and low in price, these tools can be nonstigmatizing for students with ASD because they are now in the hands of the majority of students. Some parents and autism support groups anxious to spread the word have created websites and blogs to share personal technology experiences and recommendations.

Technology can indirectly benefit students with ASD in a variety of additional ways. Texting, e-mail, Skype, and other such tools can improve communication among those who support students with ASD. Teachers can text a parent to help problem solve a youngster's meltdown in real time, or an adolescent who is reluctant to attend an IEP meeting with a room full of adults may feel more comfortable doing so from an adjoining room via Skype. Web-based professional development (e.g., Internet modules and coaching via Skype) can help raise the skill levels of professionals who support students with ASD.

SUMMARY

ASD has the most rapidly advancing prevalence of any disability, and its current impact on the educational system in the United States is substantial. For many children and youth with ASD and their families, the educational system will be the primary mode of behavioral treatment available. This chapter described the core features of ASD and the learning needs that they generate. The process of responding to those needs requires an emphasis on program quality and a technical eclectic approach to selecting evidence-based intervention practices that address individual student goals. A partnership among school personnel, family members, possibly the student him- or herself, and potentially the family physician or health care workers will serve as the foundation for planning and implementing effective and personalized educational programs for students with ASD.

Case Study #1: "Ethan"

Ethan's parents thought that things were finally coming together for their son as he moved through high school with a plan to attend college. Ethan had always loved tinkering with computers and wanted to major in computer engineering. At his IEP meetings, his team talked about college application requirements and deadlines to help Ethan fulfill his goal of attending a 4-year college. Although his critical reading score on the SAT was on the low side, his 750 on the mathematics section was impressive. What the IEP team did not discuss were the skills he would need to be successful in the university setting that may be different from high school. Although he had attended the weekly lunch social group for students with ASD, Ethan rarely saw anyone outside of school for social activities. Throughout the years, his parents had become used to the minimal opportunities for social interaction and thought Ethan seemed content in his room playing video games on his computer. His anxiety and depression, they thought, were well managed with medications. Every morning, Ethan's mom woke him up, made his breakfast, and drove him to the front door of the school. After school, his dad made sure that Ethan completed all his homework assignments and even communicated with his teachers when there were problems. At school, Ethan's resource teacher made sure all of his assignments were written down in his planner at the end of the day and would add in anything that Ethan had forgotten to note. If Ethan came to school without his homework, his teachers would give him an extra day to turn it in. If Ethan had a meltdown, everyone knew that he would get up and run out of the room and go straight to the special education office to see his resource teacher, who would let him put on headphones and watch a movie to calm down. These routines had evolved throughout the years to minimize Ethan's frustrations and maximize his academic performance. What his team was not doing was thinking about the context that Ethan would find himself in when he arrived at university. How was he being prepared for life in a dorm? How was he being prepared for independent learning and management of his work? How would he be able to handle communicating with his professors? Ethan's team members thought they were supporting him for success by focusing on his academic requirements, overlooking some of the areas in which students with ASD need the most help: independence, initiation, self-management, and social communication.

When Ethan arrived at university, he discovered that although there was a disability services department that knew about his ASD diagnosis, the responsibility fell to him to initiate requests for assistance. Despite daily reminders from his parents to go to the disability services office, Ethan could not bring himself to do it. Overwhelmed by all the new demands being placed on him, Ethan began to feel anxious and did not want to get out of bed in the mornings. He started missing classes and missing deadlines. This downward spiral quickly led to Ethan's withdrawal from college. He returned home to live with his parents without a plan for what happens next and without a support system other than his parents.

KEY POINTS

- A continuum of intervention and educational services exist for children and youth with ASD and their families in the United States. The quality and intensity of these services vary, which requires parents to be active consumers for their children.
- Practitioners base interventions and educational services on the specific learning needs of children with ASD. The learning needs are often in the areas of social competence, independence, behavior, and academics.
- Resources are now available that allow educational practitioners and service providers to select and employ intervention/instructional practices that are evidence-based.
- Quality of educational program environments provide the foundation for implementation of evidence-based practices and positive outcomes for children and youth with ASD.
- Educational practitioners' application and utilization of technology in programs for children and youth with ASD holds great promise for the future.

ACKNOWLEDGMENTS

This chapter was supported in part by the Postdoctoral Research Training in Special Education Project funded by the Institute of Education Science (R324C1200C12006) and the Vinnie Ireland Fellowship award to the School of Education at the University of North Carolina at Chapel Hill. The authors thank Ms. Stephanie Ridley for her helpful editing.

DISCLOSURE STATEMENT

Dr. Samuel L. Odom, Dr. Veronica P. Fleury, Dr. Leslie C. Fox, Susan Hedges, Dr. Nigel P. Pierce, and Melissa A. Sreckovic have no conflicts to disclose.

REFERENCES

American Academy of Pediatrics. (2012). *Autism: Caring for children with autism spectrum disorder—A resource toolkit for clinicians.* Washington, DC: Author.

American Psychiatric Association. (2013). *Diagnostic and statistical manual of mental disorders* (5th ed.). Arlington, VA: American Psychiatric Publishing.

Anyan, S. E., & Pryor, J. (2002). What is in a family? Adolescent perceptions. *Children & Society, 16*, 306–317. doi:10.1002/chi.716

APERS Research Group. (2014). *Autism Program Environment Rating Scale–2014.* Chapel Hill, NC: The University of North Carolina, National Professional Development Center on ASD.

Arick, J. R., Young, H. E., Falco, R. A., Loos, L. M., Krug, D. A., Gense, M. H., & Johnson, S. B. (2003). Designing an outcome study to monitor the progress of students with autism spectrum disorders. *Focus on Autism and Other Developmental Disabilities, 18*, 75–87. doi:10.1177/108835760301800201

Ashburner, J., Ziviani, J., & Rodger, S. (2010). Surviving in the mainstream: Capacity of children with autism spectrum disorders to perform academically and regulate their emotions and behavior at school. *Research in Autism Spectrum Disorders, 4*, 18–27. doi:10.1016/j.rasd.2009.07.002

Baer, R. M., Daviso, A., McMahan Queen, R., & Flexer, R. W. (2011). Disproportionality in transition services: A descriptive study. *Education and Training in Autism and Developmental Disabilities, 46*(2), 172–185.

Baron-Cohen, S., Leslie, A. M., & Frith, U. (1985). Does the autistic child have a "theory of mind"? *Cognition,* *21,* 37–46. doi:10.1016/0010-0277(85)90022-8

Berry, J. O., & Hardman, M. L. (1998). *Lifespan perspectives on the family and disability.* Austin, TX: Pro-Ed.

Boyd, B. A., Hume, K., McBee, M. T., Alessandri, M., Gutierrez, A., Johnson, L., . . . Odom, S. L. (2014). Comparative efficacy of LEAP, TEACCH and non-model-specific special education programs for preschoolers with autism spectrum disorders. *Journal of Autism and Developmental Disorders, 44,* 366–380. doi:10.1007/s10803-013-1877-9

Bukowski, W. M., & Sippola, L. K. (2001). Groups, individuals, and victimization: A view of the peer system. In J. Juvonen & S. Graham (Eds.), *Peer harassment in school: The plight of the vulnerable and victimized* (pp. 355–377). New York, NY: Guilford.

Cappadocia, M. C., Weiss, J. A., & Pepler, D. (2012). Bullying experiences among children and youth with autism spectrum disorders. *Journal of Autism and Developmental Disorders, 42,* 266–277. doi:10.1007/s10803-011-1241-x

Carnine, D. (1999). Perspective: Campaigns for moving research into practice. *Remedial and Special Education, 20,* 2–6. doi:10.1177/074193259902000101

Carter, E. W., Common, E. A., Sreckovic, M. A., Huber, H. B., Bottema-Beutel, K., Redding Gustafson, J., . . . Hume, K. (2014). Promoting social competence and peer relationships for adolescents with autism spectrum disorders. *Remedial and Special Education, 35,* 91–101. doi:10.1177/0741932513514618

Cochrane, A. L. (1972). *Effectiveness and efficiency: Random reflections on health services.* London, England: Nuffield Provincial Hospitals Trust.

Cox, A., Kucharczyk, S., Shaw, E., Rogers, S., & Odom, S. L. (2014). *Autism Program Environment Rating Scale–Infant Toddler.* Chapel Hill, NC: The University of North Carolina, National Professional Development Center on ASD.

Dawson, G., Rogers, S., Munson, J., Smith, M., Jamie, W., Greenson, J., . . . Varley, J. (2010). Randomized controlled trial of the Early Start Denver Model: A developmental behavioral intervention for toddlers with autism: Effects on IQ, adaptive behavior, and autism diagnosis. *Pediatrics, 125,* 17–23. doi:10.1542/peds.2009-0958

Espelage, D. L., & Swearer, S. M. (2008). Current perspectives on linking school bullying research to effective prevention strategies. In T. Miller (Ed.), *School violence and primary prevention* (pp. 335–353). New York, NY: Springer.

Estes, A., Rivera, V., Bryan, M., Cali, P., & Dawson, G. (2011). Discrepancies between academic achievement and intellectual ability in higher-functioning school-aged children with autism spectrum disorder. *Journal of Autism and Developmental Disorders, 41,* 1044–1052. doi:10.1007/s10803-010-1127-3

Friman, P. C. (1984). Effects of punishment procedures on the self-stimulating behavior of an autistic child. *Analysis and Intervention in Developmental Disabilities, 4,* 39–46. doi:10.1016/0270-4684(84)90017-X

Grynszpan, O., Weiss, P. L. T., Perez-Diaz, F., & Gal, E. (2014). Innovative technology-based interventions for autism spectrum disorders: A meta-analysis. *Autism, 18,* 346–361. doi:10.1177/1362361313476767

Hopkins, I. M., Gower, M. W., Perez, T. A., Smith, D. S., Amthor, F. R., Wimsalt, F. C., & Biasini, F. J. (2011). Avatar assistant: Improving social skills in students with an ASD through computer-based intervention. *Journal of Autism and Developmental Disorders, 41,* 1543–1555. doi:10.1007/S 10803-011-1179-z

Hume, K., Boyd, B., McBee, M., Coman, D., Gutierrez, A., Shaw, E., . . . Odom, S. (2011). Assessing implementation of comprehensive treatment models for young children with ASD: Reliability and validity of two measures. *Research in Autism Spectrum Disorders, 5,* 1430–1440. doi:10.1016/j.rasd.2011.02.002

Hume, K., Loftin, R., & Lantz, J. (2009). Increasing independence in autism spectrum disorders: A review of three focused interventions. *Journal of Autism and Developmental Disorders, 39,* 1329–1338. doi:10.1007/s10803-009-0751-2

Hume, K., & Odom, S. (2007). Effects of an individual work system on the independent functioning of students with autism. *Journal of Autism and Developmental Disorders, 37,* 1166–1180. doi:10.1007/s10803-006-0260-5

Hurlbutt, K., & Chalmers, L. (2004). Employment and adults with Asperger syndrome. *Focus on Autism and Other Developmental Disabilities, 19,* 215–222. doi:10.1177/10883576040190040301

Individuals With Disabilities Education Improvement Act of 2004, PL 108-466, 20 U.S.C. § 1400, H. R. 1350.

Johns, B., Mather, S., & McGrath, M. (2003). Leadership necessary to promote a call to action. *Beyond Behavior, 13*, 20–22.

Kagohara, D. M., van der Meer, L., Ramdoss, S., O'Reilly, M., Lancioni, G. E., Davis, T. N., … Sigafoos, J. (2013). Using iPods and iPads in teaching programs for individuals with developmental disabilities: A systematic review. *Research in Developmental Disorders, 34*, 147–156. doi:10.1016/j.ridd.2012.07.027

Kaldy, Z., Giserman, I., Carter, A. S., & Blaser, E. (2013). The mechanisms underlying the ASD advantage in visual search. *Journal of Autism and Developmental Disorders* [Epub ahead of print]. doi:10.1007/s10803-013-1957-x

Kasari, C., Locke, J., Gulsrud, A., & Rotheram-Fuller, E. (2011). Social networks and friendships at school: Comparing children with and without ASD. *Journal of Autism and Development Disorders, 41*, 533–544. doi:10.1007/s10803-010-1076-x

Klin, A., & Volkmar, F. R. (2000). Treatment and intervention guidelines for individuals with Asperger syndrome. In A. Klin, F. Volkmar, & S. Sparrow (Eds.), *Asperger syndrome*. New York, NY: Guilford.

Kuo, M. H., Ormsond, G. I., Coster, W. J., & Cohn, E. S. (2014). Media use among adolescents with autism spectrum disorder. *Autism 18*(8), 914–923. doi:10.1177/1362361313497832

Kurth, J. A., & Mastergeorge, A. M. (2010). Academic and cognitive profiles of students with autism: Implications for classroom practice and placement. *International Journal of Special Education, 25*(2), 8–14.

Kurth, J., & Mastergeorge, A. M. (2012). Impact of setting and instructional context for adolescents with autism. *Journal of Special Education, 46*, 36–48. doi:10.1177/0022466910366480

Liptak, G. S., Orlando, M., Yinglin, J. T., Theurer-Kaufman, K. L., Malay, D. P., Tompkins, L. A., & Flynn, J. R. (2006). Satisfaction with primary health care received by families of children with developmental disabilities. *Journal of Pediatric Health Care, 20*(4), 245–252. doi:10.1016/j.pedhc.2005.12.008

Lovaas, I. O. (1987). Behavioral treatment and normal educational and intellectual functioning in young autistic children. *Journal of Consulting and Clinical Psychology, 55*, 3–9.

Machalicek, W., O'Reilly, M. F., Beretvas, N., Sigafoos, J., & Lancioni, G. E. (2007). A review of interventions to reduce challenging behavior in school settings for students with autism spectrum disorders. *Research in Autism Spectrum Disorders, 1*, 229–246. doi:10.1016/j.rasd.2006.10.005

Mandell, D., Listerud, J., Levy, S., & Pinto-Martin, J. (2002). Race differences in the age of diagnosis among Medicaid-eligible children with autism. *Journal of the American Academy of Child & Adolescent Psychiatry, 41*, 1447–1453. doi:10.1097/00004583-200212000-00016

Mazurek, M., Shattuck, P., Wagner, M., & Cooper, B. (2012). Prevalence and correlates of screen-based media use among youths with autism spectrum disorder. *Journal of Autism and Developmental Disorders, 42*, 1757–1767. doi:10.1007/s10803-011-1413-8

Mazurek, M., & Wenstrup, C. (2013). Television, video game and social media use among children with ASD and typically developing siblings. *Journal of Autism and Developmental Disorders, 43*, 1258–1271. doi:10.1007/s10803-012-1659-9

McIntyre, N., Mundy, P. C., Solomon, M., Hatt, N. V., Gwaltney, M., Jarrold, W., & Kim, K. (2013, May). *Reading and oral communication in students with ASD*. Paper presented at the International Meeting on Autism Research, San Sebastian, Spain.

National Autism Center. (2009). *National Standards Project: Findings and conclusions*. Randolph, MA: Author.

National Center for Special Education Research. (2006). *Preschoolers with disabilities: Characteristics, services, and results: Wave 1 overview from the Pre-Elementary Education Longitudinal Study (PEELS)* (NCSER 2006-3003). Washington, DC: Author. Retrieved from http://ies.ed.gov/ncser/pdf/20063003.pdf

National Research Council. (2001). *Educating children with autism*. Washington, DC: National Academy Press.

New Jersey Department of Education. (2004). *Autism program quality indicators*. Trenton, NJ: Author. Retrieved from http://www.nj.gov/education/specialed/info/autism.pdf

New York State Education Department. (2001). *Autism program quality indicators*. Albany, NY: Author. Retrieved from http://www.p12.nysed.gov/specialed/autism/apqi.htm

Newman, L. (2007). *Secondary school experiences of students with autism. Facts from NLTS2* (NCSER 2007-3005). Washington, DC: National Center for Special Education Research.

Newman, L., Wagner, M., Knokey, A.-M., Marder, C., Nagle, K., Shaver, D., & Wei, X. (2011). *The post-high school outcomes of young adults with disabilities up to 8 years after high school: A report from the National Longitudinal Transition Study-2 (NLTS2)* (NCSER 2011-3005). Menlo Park, CA: SRI International.

No Child Left Behind (NCLB) Act of 2001, Pub. L. No. 107-110, § 115, Stat. 1425 (2002).

Odom, S. L., & Bailey, D. B. (2001). Inclusive preschool programs: Ecology and child outcomes. In M. Guralnick (Ed.), *Early childhood inclusion: Focus on change* (pp. 253–276). Baltimore, MD: Brookes.

Odom, S. L., Boyd, B., Hall, L., & Hume, K. (2010). Evaluation of comprehensive treatment models for individuals with autism spectrum disorders. *Journal of Autism and Developmental Disorders, 40,* 425–436. doi:10.1007/s10803-009-0825-1

Odom, S. L., Boyd, B. A., Hall, L. J., & Hume, K. A. (2014). Comprehensive treatment models for children and youth with autism spectrum disorders. In F. Volkmar, S. Rogers, R. Paul, & K. Pelphrey (Eds.), *Handbook of autism and pervasive developmental disorders, Vol. 2* (4th ed., pp. 770–787). Hoboken, NJ: Wiley.

Odom, S. L., Collet-Klingenberg, L., Rogers, S. J., & Hatton, D. D. (2010). Evidence-based practices for children and youth with autism spectrum disorders. *Preventing School Failure, 54,* 275–282. doi:10.1080/10459881003785506

Odom, S., Hume, K., Boyd, B., & Stabel, A. (2012). Moving beyond the intensive behavior treatment versus eclectic dichotomy: Evidence-based and individualized programs for learners with ASD. *Behavior Modification, 36*(3), 270–297. doi:10.1177/0145445512444595

Osborne, L., & Reed, P. (2008). Parents' perceptions of communication with professionals during the diagnosis of autism. *Autism, 12,* 309–324. doi:10.1177/1362361307089517

Plavnick, J. B., & Hume, K. A. (2014). Observational learning by individuals with autism: A review of teaching strategies. *Autism, 18,* 458–466. doi:10.1177/1362361312474373

Prizant, B. M., Wetherby, A. M., Rubin, E., Laurent, A. C., & Rydell, P. J. (2005). *The SCERTS model: A comprehensive educational approach for children with autism spectrum disorders.* Baltimore, MD: Brookes.

Rehm, R. S., Fisher, L. T., Fuentes-Afflick, E., & Chesla, C. A. (2013). Parental advocacy styles for special education students during the transition to adulthood. *Qualitative Health Research, 23,* 1377–1387. doi:10.1177/1049732313505915

Rhoades, R. A., Scarpa, A., & Salley, B. (2007). The importance of physician knowledge of autism spectrum disorder: Results of a parent survey. *Biomedical Central Pediatrics, 7,* 37. doi:10.1186/1471-2431-7-37

Sackett, D. L., Rosenberg, W. M., Gray, J. A., Haynes, R. B., & Richardson, W. S. (1996). Evidence based medicine: What it is and what it isn't. *British Medical Journal, 312,* 71–72. doi:10.1136/bmj.312.7023.71

Schopler, E., Mesibov, G. B., & Hearsey, K. (1995). Structured teaching in the TEACCH system. In E. Schopler & G. Mesibov (Eds.), *Learning and cognition in autism* (pp. 243–268). New York, NY: Plenum.

Shane, H. C., & Albert, P. D. (2008). Electronic screen media for persons with autism spectrum disorders: Results of a survey. *Journal of Autism and Developmental Disorders, 38,* 1499–1508. doi:10.1007/s10803-007-0527-5

Simonoff, E., Pickles, A., Charman, T., Chandler, S., Loucas, T., & Baird, G. (2008). Psychiatric disorders in children with autism spectrum disorders: Prevalence, comorbidity, and associated factors in a population-derived sample. *Journal of the American Academy of Child & Adolescent Psychiatry, 47,* 921–929. doi:10.1097/CHI.0b013e318179964f

Smith, L. E., Maenner, M. J., & Seltzer, M. M. (2012). Developmental trajectories in adolescents and adults with autism: The case of daily living skills. *Journal of the American Academy of Child & Adolescent Psychiatry, 51,* 622–631. doi:10.1016/j.jaac.2012.03.001

Sofronoff, K., Dark, E., & Stone, V. (2011). Social vulnerability and bullying in children with Asperger syndrome. *Autism, 15*(3), 355–372. doi:10.1177/1362361310365070

Sreckovic, M. A., Brunsting, N. C., & Able, H. (2014). Victimization of students with autism spectrum disorder: A review of prevalence and risk factors. *Research in Autism Spectrum Disorders, 8*(9), 1155–1172.

Stahmer, A. C., Suhrheinrich, J., Reed, S., Bolduc, C., & Schreibman, L. (2010). Pivotal response teaching in the classroom setting. *Preventing School Failure, 54,* 265–274. doi:10.1080/10459881003800743

Strain, P. S., & Bovey, E. (2011). Randomized, controlled trial of the LEAP model of early intervention for young children with autism spectrum disorders. *Topics in Early Childhood Special Education, 31,* 133–154. doi:10.1177/0271121411408740

Sugai, G., Horner, R. H., Dunlap, G., Hieneman, M., Lewis, T. J., Nelson, C. M., . . . Ruef, M. (1999). *Applying positive behavior support and functional behavioral assessment in schools.* Washington, DC: Office of Special Education Programs, Center on Positive Behavioral Interventions and Supports.

Test, D. W., Smith, L. E., & Carter, E. W. (2014). Equipping youth with autism spectrum disorders for adulthood: Promoting rigor, relevance, and relationships. *Remedial and Special Education, 35,* 80–90. doi:10.1177/0741932513514857

Thompson, T. (2011). *Individualized autism intervention for young children.* Baltimore, MD: Brookes.

US Department of Education, Office of Civil Rights. (2007). *Students with disabilities preparing for postsecondary education: Know your rights and responsibilities.* Washington, DC: Author.

Wagner, M., Cadwallader, T. W., Garza, N., & Cameto, R. (2004). Social activities of youth with disabilities. *NLTS2 Data Brief, 3*(1), 1–4.

Wei, X., Yu, J., Shattuck, P., McCracken, M., & Blackorby, J. (2013). Science, technology, engineering, and mathematics (STEM) participation among college students with an autism spectrum disorder. *Journal of Autism and Developmental Disorders, 43,* 1539–1546. doi:10.1007/210803-012-1700-z

Wong, C., Odom, S. L., Hume, K., Cox, A. W., Fettig, A., Kucharczyk, S., . . . Schultz, T. R. (2014). *Evidence-based practices for children, youth, and young adults with autism spectrum disorder.* Chapel Hill, NC: The University of North Carolina, Frank Porter Graham Child Development Institute, Autism Evidence-Based Practice Review Group.

World Health Organization. (1992). *Clinical description and diagnostic guidelines.* Geneva, Switzerland: Author.

World Health Organization. (2013). *Meeting report: Autism spectrum disorders and other developmental disorders: From raising awareness to building capacity.* Geneva, Switzerland: Author. Retrieved from http://apps.who.int/iris/bitstream/10665/103312/1/9789241506618_eng.pdf

/// 22 /// VOCATIONAL REHABILITATION AND TRAINING FOR ADULTS WITH AUTISM SPECTRUM DISORDER

History, Practices, and New Directions

MARJI ERICKSON WARFIELD

INTRODUCTION

"What do you do for a living?" This question is often asked when people meet for the first time because employment is a pervasive marker of adulthood. Disparities in obtaining and maintaining employment are stark, however, when examining the extent to which the general population works compared to the population of individuals with disabilities and even more glaring when compared to those with autism spectrum disorder (ASD). Although good jobs can be difficult to find given today's economic climate, various data sources generally are in agreement that whereas more than two-thirds of working-age adults are employed, only between one-fifth and one-third of adults with disabilities are employed. Furthermore, national estimates suggest that although the difference in employment rates has been persistent for more than 30 years, some modest reduction in size of the employment gap has occurred.

Vocational rehabilitation and training programs are designed to maximize employment opportunities for individuals with disabilities by providing a variety of services, such as assessment and diagnosis, counseling, job search assistance, assistive technology, and on-the-job training, in different settings (Escorpizo et al., 2011). Since the Rehabilitation Act of 1973, a variety of programs and policies have used different approaches to try to reduce the persistent disparities in employment between those with and those without disabilities, with little success.

This chapter provides an overview of the current employment picture for adults with disabilities and an introduction to the vocational training and rehabilitation field by defining common terms and approaches. A review of the history of vocational training is presented that outlines the significant pieces of legislation that have attempted to reduce employment disparities, the fragmented system in existence today, and the huge variation in vocational practices across the United States that have resulted from these policies. The chapter then describes the employment picture specifically for individuals with ASD and identifies their unique vocational needs. The chapter concludes with a discussion of successful vocational rehabilitation service models for individuals with ASD and a case example.

THE EMPLOYMENT PICTURE FOR ADULTS WITH DISABILITIES

Various sources of data confirm that there are wide differences between the employment rate for the general population of adults and the employment rate among the population of adults with disabilities. The 2010 Current Population Survey estimates the employment rate for people (aged 21–64 years) with disabilities is 16.2% compared with 75.5% for people without disabilities. Also, according to the Bureau of Labor Statistics, in 2012, 28.4% of individuals with disabilities aged 16 years or older participated in the labor force compared with 71.0% of persons without disabilities. The 2011 American Community Survey estimates that 32.4% of working-age adults with disabilities are employed, compared with 70.5% of people without disabilities (Butterworth et al., 2013). Furthermore, the disparity in employment rates widens when only individuals with intellectual and developmental disabilities (IDD) are considered. Only approximately one in seven (14.7%) adults with IDD was employed in the community based on data from the 2012 National Core Indicators Project (Human Services Research Institute, 2012). These differences persist despite evidence that individuals with disabilities can be employed successfully and that they want to be employed in the community in order to reach goals of self-sufficiency and economic independence (Migliore, Grossi, Mank, & Rogan, 2008; Migliore, Mank, Grossi, & Rogan, 2007). In addition, these differences persist despite evidence of financial gains associated with employment for people with disabilities (Cimera, 2008; Cimera & Cowan, 2009).

INTRODUCTION TO VOCATIONAL REHABILITATION AND TRAINING APPROACHES

The major goal of vocational rehabilitation and training services and supports is to assist individuals with disabilities to become employed in the community (Targett & Wehman, 2011). These services can be provided in a number of different settings, including in schools for youth transitioning out of secondary education and in community-based programs for adults. Vocational support services include two major categories: (1) day programs and sheltered workshops and (2) competitive integrated employment models.

Day Programs and Sheltered Workshops

These programs are often described as "facility-based" because all employment and non-employment services are provided in one location where the vast majority of individuals have a disability (Butterworth et al., 2013). These programs typically operate on a weekday schedule from 9 a.m. to 3 p.m. and can support anywhere between 50 to several hundred individuals with disabilities (Targett & Wehman, 2011). These programs offer skill training, prevocational training, "make-work" vocational activities (i.e., work created to keep a person from being unemployed), field trips, recreation, and other types of special education curricula for people with more severe cognitive, physical, and emotional disabilities (Wehman & Brooke, 2013). Within these facility-based programs, services can be work-focused or non-work-focused or a mix of the two. Work-focused programs are variously referred to as sheltered workshops, work activity centers, or extended employment programs. The premise behind the approach taken by facility-based programs focused on work is that individuals with disabilities must demonstrate that they are employable before moving on to getting assistance finding a job in the community (Targett & Wehman, 2011). However, most programs fail to offer a continuum of services geared toward movement to community-based employment and thus tend to provide only segregated employment where pay is less than the minimum wage (Wehman & Brooke, 2013). Legislation dating from as far back as the National Industrial Recovery Act in 1934 that was part of the New Deal made it permissible to pay individuals with disabilities less than the minimum wage as a way to increase their access to employment (National Disability Rights Network, 2012). As described later in the chapter, more recent legislation and other initiatives are attempting to phase out these programs and replace them with competitive employment models.

Competitive Integrated Employment Models

Competitive employment models focus on attaining "real work for real pay" (Targett & Wehman, 2011). Kiernan, Hoff, Freeze, and Mank (2011) define competitive integrated employment as a job that is compensated by the minimum or prevailing wage, provides similar benefits to all employees, occurs where employees with disabilities interact continuously with employees without disabilities, provides opportunities for advancement, and is full-time unless the employee desires or needs a part-time schedule.

Three approaches to competitive employment are common: (1) supported employment, (2) customized employment, and (3) self-employment (Targett & Wehman, 2011). Supported employment options enable individuals with significant support needs to become employed in the community. When supported employment began in the 1970s and 1980s, groups of individuals with disabilities would work together in a business under the supervision of an adult service provider (Targett & Wehman, 2011). In the past 20 years, however, individualized approaches to supported employment have been developed in which a vocational rehabilitation specialist (also known as a job coach or employment specialist) provides an array of supports (e.g., on-the-job skills training, arranging for assistive technology, and facilitating communications and relationships with coworkers) to assist an individual with significant disabilities to obtain and maintain a competitive job in the community (Targett & Wehman, 2011).

Customized employment shares many features of supported employment but is further characterized by the following principles (Elinson, Frey, Li, Palan, & Horne, 2008; US Department of Labor, 2007): (1) The individual with a disability who is seeking a job decides on the direction of the job search; (2) the individual controls the planning process in order to maximize his or her preferences, interests, and connections in the community; (3) time is taken to explore the individual's unique needs and abilities; (4) the employer negotiates specific job duties and employee expectations; and (5) the job that emerges meets both the needs of the employer and the needs, strengths, and interests of the individual seeking the job. The goal of utilizing these principles is to yield a job that is a good fit and creates the possibility for advancement. Sometimes a personal representative is hired to assist an individual through the customized employment process (Targett & Wehman, 2011).

Finally, pursuing self-employment or entrepreneur opportunities begins with matching a person's talents and desires with a defined product, service, or activity (Targett & Wehman, 2011). Individuals alone or with professional and/or family support will spend time doing person-centered planning to formulate an idea. Then a business plan is developed and a study launched to assess the idea's feasibility and likelihood for success. Implementation then follows on those plans that seem most viable.

HISTORY AND NEW DIRECTIONS

The vocational rehabilitation and training approaches just described have emerged from a history of legal action and legislation related to the general movement of individuals with disabilities from institutional residential settings to community-based settings; changes in educational practices; and efforts to expand employment opportunities through a mix of state and federal disability, workforce development, income maintenance, and health care policies. Thus, the current approach to vocational training for adults with disabilities is fragmented and complex (Wehman, 2013). The patchwork system of vocational training and supports available to individuals with disabilities is described in the following sections. Initiatives to reduce the facility-based options and expand community-based competitive employment opportunities are also discussed.

Overview

The deinstitutionalization movement that occurred in the late 1960s and into the 1970s involved closing residential institutions that housed large numbers of adults with intellectual and developmental disabilities and establishing community-based residences (Stancliffe & Lakin, 2005). Deinstitutionalization was the result of court decisions and new laws that eventually led to the establishment of more than 8000 facility-based day programs and sheltered workshops nationally to care for and support individuals now living in the community (Wehman & Brooke, 2013). From this base of segregated programs, advocacy and legislative efforts during the past 40 years have attempted to build a system of vocational training services that can provide more individualized choices and options for competitive employment to individuals with disabilities (Table 22.1) (Nord, Luecking, Mank, Kiernan, & Wray, 2013). The fragmented system that has resulted is characterized by vast differences across states in terms of the kinds of services and supports available, the use of different eligibility criteria to determine entrance into different systems, and limits on access due to funding restrictions because there is no entitlement to services (Hall, Butterworth, Winsor, Gilmore, & Metzel, 2007; Wehman & Brooke, 2013). Several initiatives are attempting to address this fragmentation and shift resources toward integrated employment options (Butterworth et al., 2013; Kiernan, 2011; Rogan & Rinne, 2011).

Systems Involved in Providing Vocational Training and Employment Supports

Individuals may qualify for publicly funded Vocational Rehabilitation (VR) services if their disability presents a barrier to obtaining competitive employment or maintaining competitive employment (Wehman, 2013). The Rehabilitation legislation provides states with federal grants to operate comprehensive programs of VR services for individuals with disabilities. VR is a federal–state cooperative program operated by the Department of

TABLE 22.1 Federal Legislation Related to Vocational Training and Employment by Policy Area[a]

Year	Legislation	Description of Key Provisions
VOCATIONAL REHABILITATION (VR) PROGRAMS		
1973	Rehabilitation Act of 1973 (PL 93-112)	Extended the authorization of grants to states for vocational rehabilitation services with an emphasis on services to those with the most severe disabilities Included Section 504, which prohibited discrimination on the basis of disability in federal programs and in programs receiving federal funds
1986	Rehabilitation Act Amendments of 1986 (PL 99-506)	Defined supported employment and provided funding for projects and demonstrations in supported employment
1992	Rehabilitation Act Amendments of 1992 (PL 102-569)	Defined the responsibilities of the vocational rehabilitation system as including developing an individualized rehabilitation program with the full participation of the individual with a disability, finding appropriate services and supports to implement the individualized plan, and fostering cooperative relationships with other agencies and programs to unify the system
1998	Rehabilitation Act Amendments of 1998 (PL 105-220)	Promotes the increased employment of individuals with disabilities through the implementation of workforce investment systems under Title I of the Workforce Investment Act Workforce Investment Act—initiated major reform of the nation's job training system primarily through the implementation of One Stop Career Centers
DEVELOPMENTAL DISABILITIES SERVICE SYSTEM		
1984	Developmental Disabilities Act Amendment of 1984 (PL 98-527)	Acknowledged the employability of persons with disabilities and promoted supported employment options
1987	Developmental Disabilities Assistance and Bill of Rights Act of 1987 (PL 100-146)	Put national goals regarding employing persons with disabilities in legislation
EDUCATION		
1990	Individuals with Disabilities Education Act (IDEA) (PL 101-476)	Added language associated with transition planning so that the Individualized Education Plan would include transition goals and linkages to other agencies to support transition prior to leaving school
1997	Individuals with Disabilities Education Act Amendments of 1997 (PL 105-17)	States given permission to use funds to develop and implement transition programs

(continued)

TABLE 22.1 Continued

Year	Legislation	Description of Key Provisions
2004	Individuals with Disabilities Education Improvement Act of 2004 (IDEIA) (PL 108-446)	Established parameters to guide the participation of vocational rehabilitation counselors in the transition planning process

HEALTH CARE

Year	Legislation	Description of Key Provisions
1981	Medicaid Home and Community-Based Services Waiver Program of 1981 (PL 97-35)	Identified supported employment services as an appropriate means for assisting individuals with significant disabilities

INCOME MAINTENANCE

Year	Legislation	Description of Key Provisions
1999	Ticket to Work and Work Incentives Improvement Act of 1999 (PL 106-170)	Established funding for the ticket to work program that is operated under the Social Security Administration to help Social Security disability beneficiaries obtain employment and work toward greater independence and self-sufficiency
		Included work incentives to allow beneficiaries to explore work options while still receiving health care and cash benefits

ᵃThe table utilizes information reported and organized by Wehman (2013).

Education that exists in all 50 states, the District of Columbia, and all territories. Once an individual with a disability applies for support from the VR system, a rehabilitation counselor processes the application for service and determines eligibility. Eligibility is based on the presence of a disability that presents a barrier to employment and an expectation that the provision of VR services will help the individual achieve an employment outcome. After eligibility is determined, an Individualized Plan for Employment (IPE) must be developed. VR counselors have access to funds to be used to purchase services from authorized vendors. Services that can be purchased if they support the goals on the IPE include post-secondary education, training, supported employment, transportation, tools, and uniforms. Reforms to the VR system were enacted in 1998 under the Workforce Investment Act, which set up One Stop Career Centers aimed at consolidating vocational training and employment services and setting standards of performance (Targett et al., 2007).

State developmental disability (DD) agencies operate under a variety of different names and structures. In some states, services are managed locally, whereas in others services are operated by direct state supervision through local providers or offices. Eligibility for these services is usually based on the presence of a disability that meets specific state guidelines that often include standards related to cognitive functioning (Braddock, Hemp, & Rizzolo, 2008). State DD agencies provide, fund, and manage a range of services, including employment supports, as well as facility-based options that include both sheltered workshops and non-work day habilitation programs (Butterworth et al., 2013).

Youth with disabilities who are in the process of transitioning out of the public education system are also eligible for vocational training and employment services under federal legislation. The Individuals with Disabilities Education Act (IDEA) included a focus on transition in 1990, and subsequent amendments added requirements for greater collaboration between school and VR personnel in the community to build stronger linkages to improve post-school outcomes for youth with disabilities.

Policies related to vocational training and employment are also part of legislation emanating from programs under Medicaid and the Social Security Administration (SSA). Medicaid-eligible individuals with disabilities may receive supported employment services under the Medicaid Title XIX Home and Community-Based Waiver Services (HCBS) program. The ability of states to use Medicaid funding for integrated employment services increased under the Balanced Budget Act Amendments of 1997 when eligibility was no longer restricted to individuals who had previously been institutionalized (Hall, Freeze, Butterworth, & Hoff, 2011). Participation in supported employment increased under the waiver but mostly in a small number of states (West et al., 2002).

Finally, the Ticket to Work program is operated under the SSA. The goal is to help Social Security disability beneficiaries obtain employment and work toward greater independence and self-sufficiency (Fraker & Rangarajan, 2009). The SSA issues a ticket to a beneficiary, and the individual then gives the ticket to an employment network or state VR agency. If the ticket is accepted, the agency works with the individual to create an individualized employment plan and, as needed, provides specialized services such as career counseling and job placement. Other provisions include work incentives and work incentive planning and assistance services that enable a beneficiary to explore work options while still receiving health care and cash benefits (Miller, O'Mara, & Getzel, 2009).

Thus, individuals with disabilities have many avenues through which to seek support for vocational training and employment. At the local level, community rehabilitation providers (CRPs) typically contract with these agencies and systems in order to directly assist people with disabilities in obtaining and maintaining employment of various kinds and accessing vocational training and day programs (Wehman, 2013). CRPs can be for-profit or not-for-profit and usually provide services based on a contract or fee-for-service arrangements. Thus, access to these services requires a funding authorization from a VR agency, through the state DD office, through IDEA regulations, through Medicaid, or through the SSA. CRPs that have contracts from all of these sources have a more diversified economic base and thus tend to be more successful (Hall et al., 2011). The different eligibility requirements associated with each system, however, create a difficult maze for individuals and their families to navigate.

In addition, despite the legislative efforts to encourage improved employment outcomes, national surveys of the more than 8000 CRPs that offer vocational and related services to individuals with disabilities reveal that on average, there is little focus on competitive employment (Butterworth et al., 2013). Overall, there are few resources that reward integrated community employment (Niemeic et al., 2009). For example, based on the 2010–2011 National CRP Survey, more than 70% of those served by CRPs are individuals with intellectual and developmental disabilities (Butterworth et al., 2013). Of these, however, only 19% participated in individual, integrated employment services, whereas 25.2% participated in facility-based work and 43% participated in non-work services. The participation in integrated employment services represents a decrease from a high of approximately 25% in 2001. In contrast, participation in non-work services increased approximately 10% from 2002 (Sulewski, 2010).

These low percentages in competitive employment and increases in non-work activities mask the tremendous variation in services delivered in different states. The 2010–2011 National CRP Survey gathered extensive data from 37 states on day and employment services for individuals with intellectual and developmental disabilities every year from 1999 to 2011. More than half (21; 57%) of these 37 states reduced the number of individuals receiving integrated employment services over this time period. The remaining 16 states (43%) changed in the other direction and increased the number of individuals in integrated employment. In 8 of these states, the number of individuals in integrated employment increased by more than 500 individuals (Butterfield et al., 2013).

Research on why there is such variation between states reveals several important factors that are associated with greater systemic change toward more positive employment outcomes. These states, identified as high-performing states, tend to use the flexibility offered in many policies to enable service providers to develop innovative solutions for individuals, make accommodations for individuals as their support needs change, effectively combine funding from multiple sources, use incentives to encourage the implementation of integrated employment services, continuously monitor and evaluate their progress, and invest in the training and development of their professional vocational and employment counseling staff (Butterworth, Migliore, Nord, & Gelb, 2012; Hall et al., 2007, 2011; Migliore, Butterworth, Nord, Cox, & Gelb, 2012).

System Change Initiatives

The persistently low rate of integrated employment among individuals with disabilities has generated several efforts by advocates, self-advocates, providers, and state policymakers to develop new initiatives aimed at system-level change. Twenty-three states that are committed to making integrated employment among individuals with disabilities a priority have formed the State Employment Leadership Network, whose mission is to operate under "a presumption of employability or the option of employment for all persons with disabilities" (Kiernan et al., 2011, p. 300). These states operate under an Employment First principle that demands that employment be the first option offered to any adult with a disability. Other efforts include the US Business Leadership Network and the VR Business Network, which are focused on developing public–private partnerships (Wehman, 2013).

THE EMPLOYMENT PICTURE FOR ADULTS WITH AUTISM SPECTRUM DISORDER

Understanding where adults with ASD fit into the vocational training and employment picture is critical given the size of this population now entering their adolescent and young adult ages and the expectations regarding the increased size of future cohorts. In 2008, approximately 11 children per every 1000 people in the general population received a diagnosis of ASD (Centers for Disease Control and Prevention, 2012). Because 8-year-old children diagnosed with autism in 2008 will reach transition age in 2016, it is likely that the number of youth with ASD seeking vocational training and employment assistance will increase (Migliore & Zalewska, 2012).

Recent data have documented that only between 4.1% and 11.8% of individuals with ASD are employed (Taylor & Seltzer, 2011). Regardless of their level of skills and abilities, individuals with ASD participate less in vocational or technical education and employment than their peers with other types of disabilities, including speech and language impairments, learning disabilities, or intellectual disabilities (Henninger & Taylor, 2012; Shattuck et al., 2012). Even among those youth with ASD who gain employment, the long-term success is poor (Wagner, Newman, Cameto, Levine, & Garza, 2006). Furthermore, youth with ASD have been found to be more likely to have no participation in any post-schooling activities compared to youth with speech and language impairments, learning disabilities, or intellectual disabilities. These differences were greatest during the first 2 years after high school (Shattuck et al., 2012).

Of particular concern among those youth with ASD who had no or few formal day activities after exiting high school were those without intellectual disability (ID) (Taylor & Seltzer, 2011). Youth with ASD but without ID were three times more likely to have no day activities than youth with ASD who also had comorbid ID. These significant group differences raise questions about the ability of the service system to meet the needs of this subgroup.

THE UNIQUE VOCATIONAL NEEDS OF ADULTS WITH AUTISM SPECTRUM DISORDER

Individuals with ASD have markedly different vocational needs than individuals with other developmental disabilities (Hendricks, 2010). The uneven cognitive and social abilities associated with ASD result in a diverse set of vocational needs that are challenging to address with usual practices, create problems with employment stability, and result in isolated work opportunities. Gabriels (2011) identified five unique ASD learning styles that have relevance for vocational training and employment. According to Gabriels, individuals with ASD (1) tend to think concretely and may be confused by social situations or conversations; (2) struggle to understand others' intentions, emotional states, or behaviors; (3) tend to focus on details at the expense of seeing things in context or getting the "big picture"; (4) have difficulty with organization and sequencing; and (5) tend to be very distractible yet able to focus intensely on things of particular interest to them.

Holwerda, van der Klink, Groothoff, and Brouwer (2012) conducted a systematic literature review and identified factors consistently connected with hindering work participation among individuals with ASD. The most consistent factor was limited cognitive ability. Eight other factors were noted, although they were not as consistent across studies. These were (1) severity of the disorder; (2) comorbidity of psychiatric disorders, oppositional personality, or epilepsy; (3) gender, with females being more likely to have a poor outcome; (4) lower speech and language abilities; (5) the presence of maladaptive behavior; (6) the presence of social impairments and poor social skills; (7) lack of drive; and (8) prior institutionalization. Holwerda et al. also identified two factors that had positive impacts on job participation: higher educational attainment and family support for work.

ACCESS TO VOCATIONAL REHABILITATION AND TRAINING BY ADULTS WITH AUTISM SPECTRUM DISORDER

VR programs are struggling to adapt to the unique vocational and employment needs of individuals with ASD (Hendricks, 2010; Lawer, Brusilovskiy, Salzer, & Mandell, 2009; Wehman et al., 2014). This is significant given the finding that between 1995 and 2005, the percentage of people with ASD seeking VR services tripled from 1% to 3% (Migliore & Butterworth, 2008). Lawer et al. (2009) found that relative to other individuals served by the VR system, individuals with ASD were more likely to be denied services because it was believed that their disability was too severe for them to benefit.

Recent data from the US state VR programs from the years 2006–2010 yielded somewhat more promising results for youth with ASD, but overall, more improvement is needed (Migliore, Butterworth, & Zalewska, 2014). Specifically, four key findings emerged. First, although the number of individuals with ASD who utilized the VR system doubled during this time period, it remained small compared to the numbers of other disability groups. Second, although youth with ASD received similar levels of services and reported similar employment outcomes compared with their peers with other disabilities, across all disability groups, only approximately half received services and only approximately half who received services left the VR system with integrated employment. Third, both the percentage receiving services and those who exited with integrated employment declined slightly during the time period studied. Finally, overall the differences in these outcomes were larger across states than across disability groups.

SUCCESSFUL VOCATIONAL REHABILITATION SERVICE MODELS FOR INDIVIDUALS WITH AUTISM SPECTRUM DISORDER

Research and evaluation projects have assessed various vocational training intervention models for individuals with ASD. There is general consensus on the eight critical steps needed to ensure successful employment for individuals with ASD (Schall, Targett, & Wehman, 2013). These eight steps are (1) assess job and task preferences carefully before placement; (2) assess social, communication, and job skill needs; (3) make a careful match between the job, the person's preferences, the social and communication demands in the environment, and the tolerance of coworkers for diversity; (4) teach the social and communication skills required in the job in addition to the actual job skills; (5) prepare employers and coworkers for the diverse behaviors that a person with ASD may display; (6) teach coworker/employee/employer relationship behaviors to the person with ASD; (7) make modifications and adaptations in the job environment to meet the social and communication needs of the worker; and (8) support the person through job challenges and crises.

The job modifications and adaptations that may be needed include providing a consistent schedule, decreasing or developing predictable social interactions, providing visual organizers for job tasks, providing direct supervisory feedback, explaining and preparing the person for changes at the work site before they occur, and encouraging coworkers in initiating interactions with the person (Schall, Targett, & Wehman, 2013).

Finally, the Vocational Rehabilitation Service Models for Individuals with Autism Spectrum Disorders project, an effort funded by the National Institute on Disability and Rehabilitation Research, engaged a national advisory board of experts to identify "best practice" VR service models for individuals with ASD. Ten programs were selected, and their descriptions can be accessed at http://autism.sedl.org/index.php/resources/gep.

SUMMARY

The overview and critique presented in this chapter of the existing vocational training and employment services for individuals with disabilities, and specifically for individuals with ASD, reveals four key themes. First, the vocational system is fragmented and complex, and it struggles to meet the desires of individuals with disabilities and ASD for "real work for real pay." The major difference between the employment rate of the general population and that of people with ASD remains a persistent problem. Second, there is wide variation between states in whether or not their vocational offerings are more or less focused on competitive employment. Third, although access to VR services has improved for individuals with ASD, much more progress is needed. Finally, successful methods for training and employing individuals with ASD have been identified and tested but need to be implemented more widely.

Case Study #1: "J.W."

J.W. is a 21-year-old man with a diagnosis of ASD. He has a full-scale IQ of 133, with the verbal subscale significantly higher than the performance subscale. Despite this above average score on cognitive testing, J.W.'s social–emotional functioning is well below average. J.W. has continued in the community public high school beyond the age of 18 years to participate in a program geared toward providing him with ongoing assistance with his impaired social interaction abilities, preparing him for vocational opportunities, and helping him to develop a resume and practice interviewing skills for possible job interviews. In this extended program, school personnel have been working with J.W. to determine what particular skills he has that might be valuable to potential employers. It was well-known that J.W. has an encyclopedic knowledge of birds native to the United States. He has been interested in this topic since the second grade, when he was required to give an oral presentation on a topic of his interest to his class. Throughout the years, J.W. has continued to learn increasingly more about birds by reading books from the library, searching the Internet, and watching television shows on the National Geographic channel, as well as old reruns of Wild Kingdom.

Despite his cognitive ability and extensive knowledge of birds, J.W. struggles with significant social impairment. He is unable to make eye contact with others without experiencing intense anxiety. His voice is quite loud and monotone. His hair is often unkempt, and he does not show much interest in the clothes he wears, often wearing stripes and plaids together or colors that do not match. When his parents try to help him choose more appropriate outfits, he becomes angry and refuses their assistance.

The majority of the other students in the 18- to 22-year extended program have more significant cognitive impairment than J.W. He told the school personnel that he was not "retarded" and did not understand why he was grouped with these other students. When he tried to initiate conversation with some of the students he considered more like himself, he became frustrated because they did not show great interest in his desire to talk about birds.

The extended school program was to end on J.W.'s 22nd birthday in February, well before the school year ended. Soon after the first of the year, J.W. had an interview for a job as a tour guide for the section on birds at a science and nature history museum at a prominent local university. He was chosen for the position, and a community organization funded a job coach to assist J.W. with the specific duties and responsibilities of his job until the team believed he was able to handle things on his own. The job coach, a woman in her early 20s, was also present to assist J.W. with emotional issues such as anxiety that might arise during times of stress.

For the first 2 weeks, J.W. did reasonably well. He was working only in the mornings from 9 a.m. until noon. During that time, he led three tours, with a 15-minute break between tours. His job coach would gather among those going on the tour and acted as though she was a member of the group. One day, a group of seventh-grade students from a local middle school attended the tour on a field trip. A 13-year-old boy noticed that J.W. dressed in an unusual manner and that he talked loudly and without looking at the members of the tour. He began to tell J.W. that he did not know what he was talking about and that he needed to go back to school to learn more about birds. J.W.'s job coach quietly approached the boy's teacher in an effort to have her intervene. However, J.W. became embarrassed and ran from the corridor and out of the building.

This case study demonstrates the challenges that those with ASD and advanced knowledge of a particular subject can face. In a supportive educational or therapeutic environment, these individuals can be relatively successful. Compared to their peers with cognitive limitations, they often appear more typical and they can be given opportunities to demonstrate their special knowledge to others without excess and with limitations placed by supportive staff. When placed in a public setting among strangers who are usually less knowledgeable about and accepting of those with ASD, however, these individuals may be viewed as odd and unusual. In such settings, despite superior cognitive intelligence, their impaired social–emotional ability can quickly result in overwhelming anxiety, manifest by an angry or tearful outburst or an effort to flee the situation. Although good intentioned, many employers are unable to continue to employ these individuals; and maintaining an available job coach is not always practical or affordable. In many ways, finding successful employment opportunities for "higher functioning" persons with ASD can be more difficult than identifying and supporting those for individuals with ASD and cognitive impairment. Thus, continuing supports are needed to enable individuals such as J.W. to have multiple opportunities to be employed in order to find a sustainable job that fits their skills and abilities.

KEY POINTS

- Adults with ASD are employed at a lower rate than both the general population and the population of adults with other types of disabilities.
- Efforts to expand employment opportunities have occurred through a mix of state and federal disability funding, workforce development, income maintenance, and health care policies, creating an employment service system that is fragmented and difficult to navigate.
- Increasing numbers of adults with ASD are seeking employment supports, but providers are struggling to adapt to their unique vocational and employment needs.
- Investments in the training and development of professional vocational and employment counseling staff have shown promise in improving employment outcomes for adults with ASD.
- There is general consensus on the eight critical steps needed to ensure successful employment for individuals with ASD but these approaches need to be implemented more widely.

DISCLOSURE STATEMENT

Dr. Marji Erickson Warfield has no conflicts to disclose. Her research work is currently funded by National Institute of Child Health and Human Development and two foundations, the Special Hope Foundation and the Deborah Munroe Noonan Memorial Research Fund.

REFERENCES

Braddock, D., Hemp, R., & Rizzolo, M. (2008). *The state of the states in developmental disabilities* (7th ed.). Washington, DC: American Association on Intellectual and Developmental Disabilities.

Butterworth, J., Hall, A. C., Smith, F. A., Migliore, A., Winsor, J., Domin, D., & Sulewski, J. (2013). *StateData: The national report on employment services and outcomes.* Boston, MA: University of Massachusetts Boston, Institute for Community Inclusion. Available at http://www.statedata.info.

Butterworth, J., Migliore, A., Nord, D., & Gelb, A. (2012). Improving the employment outcomes of job seekers with intellectual and developmental disabilities: A training and mentoring intervention for employment consultants. *Journal of Rehabilitation, 78*(2), 20–29.

Centers for Disease Control and Prevention. (2012). Prevalence of autism spectrum disorders—Autism and Developmental Disabilities Monitoring Network, 14 sites, United States, 2008. *Morbidity and Mortality Weekly Report Surveillance Summaries, 61*(3). Available at www.cdc.gov/mmwr/pdf/ss/ss6103.pdf

Cimera, R. E. (2008). The cost-trends of supported employment versus sheltered employment. *Journal of Vocational Rehabilitation, 28,* 15–20.

Cimera, R. E., & Cowan, R. J. (2009). The costs of services and employment outcomes achieved by adults with autism in the US. *Autism, 13*(3), 285–302.

Elinson, L., Frey, W. D., Li, T., Palan, M. A., & Horne, R. L. (2008). Evaluation of customized employment in building the capacity of the workforce development system. *Journal of Vocational Rehabilitation, 28,* 141–158.

Escorpizo, R., Reneman, M. F., Ekholm, J., Fritz, J., Krupa, T., Marnetoft, S., . . . Chan, C. C. (2011). A conceptual definition of vocational rehabilitation based on the ICF: Building a shared global model. *Journal of Occupational Rehabilitation, 21,* 126–133. doi:10.1007/s10926-011-9292-6

Fraker, T., & Rangarajan, A. (2009). The Social Security Administration's youth transition demonstration projects. *Journal of Vocational Rehabilitation, 30,* 223–240.

Gabriels, R. L. (2011). Adolescent transition to adulthood and vocational issues. In D. G. Amaral, G. Dawson, & D. H. Geschwind (Eds.), *Autism spectrum disorders* (pp. 1167–1181). New York, NY: Oxford University Press.

Hall, A. C., Butterworth, J., Winsor, J., Gilmore, D., & Metzel, D. (2007). Pushing the employment agenda: Case study research of high performing states in integrated employment. *Intellectual and Developmental Disabilities, 45*(3), 182–198.

Hall, A. C., Freeze, S., Butterworth, J., & Hoff, D. (2011). Employment funding for intellectual/developmental disability systems. *Journal of Vocational Rehabilitation, 34,* 1–15. doi:10.3233/JVR-2010-0529

Hendricks, D. (2010). Employment and adults with autism spectrum disorders: Challenges and strategies for success. *Journal of Vocational Rehabilitation, 32,* 125–134.

Henninger, N., & Taylor, J. (2012). Outcomes in adults with autism spectrum disorders: A historical perspective. *Autism, 17,* 103–116. doi:10.1177/1362361312441266.

Holwerda, A., van der Klink, J. J. L., Groothoff, J. W., & Brouwer, S. (2012). Predictors for work participation in individuals with an autism spectrum disorder: A systematic review. *Journal of Occupational Rehabilitation, 22,* 333–352.

Human Services Research Institute. (2012). *Working in the community: The status and outcomes of people with intellectual and developmental disabilities in integrated employment* (NCI Data Brief, October 2012). Cambridge, MA: Author.

Kiernan, W. E., Hoff, D., Freeze, S., & Mank, D. M. (2011). Employment first: A beginning not an end. *Intellectual and Developmental Disabilities, 49*(4), 300–304. doi:10.1352/1934-9556-49.4.300

Lawer, L., Brusilovskiy, E., Salzer, M. S., & Mandell, D. S. (2009). Use of vocational rehabilitative services among adults with autism. *Journal of Autism and Developmental Disorders, 39*, 487–494. doi:10.1007/s10803-008-0649-4

Migliore, A., & Butterworth, J. (2008). Trends in outcomes of the vocational rehabilitation program for adults with developmental disabilities: 1995–2005. *Rehabilitation Counseling Bulletin, 52*(1), 35–44. doi:10.1177/0034355208320075

Migliore, A., Butterworth, J., Nord, D., Cox, M., & Gelb, A. (2012). Implementation of job development practices. *Intellectual and Developmental Disabilities, 50*(3), 207–218.

Migliore, A., Butterworth, J., & Zalewska, A. (2014). Trends in vocational rehabilitation services and outcomes of youth with autism: 2006–2010. *Rehabilitation Counseling Bulletin, 57*(2), 80–89. doi:10.1177/0034355213493930

Migliore, A., Grossi, T., Mank, D., & Rogan, P. (2008). Why do adults with intellectual disabilities work in sheltered workshops? *Journal of Vocational Rehabilitation, 28*, 29–40.

Migliore, A., Mank, D., Grossi, T., & Rogan, P. (2007). Integrated employment or sheltered workshops: Preferences of adults with intellectual disabilities, their families, and staff. *Journal of Vocational Rehabilitation, 26*, 5–19.

Migliore, A., & Zalewska, A. (2012). *Prevalence of youth with autism who received vocational rehabilitation services* (DataNote Series, Data Note 42). Boston, MA: University of Massachusetts Boston, Institute for Community Inclusion.

Miller, L., O'Mara, S., & Getzel, E. E. (2009). Saving for postsecondary education: Strategies for individuals with disabilities. *Journal of Vocational Rehabilitation, 31*, 167–174.

National Disability Rights Network. (2012). Segregated and exploited: The failure of the disability service system to provide quality work. *Journal of Vocational Rehabilitation, 36*, 39–64.

Nord, D., Luecking, R., Mank, D., Kiernan, W., & Wray, C. (2013). The state of the science of employment and economic self-sufficiency for people with intellectual and developmental disabilities. *Intellectual and Developmental Disabilities, 51*(5), 376–384. doi:10.1352/1934-9556-51.5.376

Rogan, R., & Rinne, S. (2011). National call for organizational change from sheltered to integrated employment. *Intellectual and Developmental Disabilities, 49*(4), 248–260. doi:10.1352/1934-9556-49.4.248

Schall, C., Targett, P., & Wehman, P. (2013). Applications for youth with autism spectrum disorders. In P. Wehman (Ed.), *Life beyond the classroom: Transition strategies for young people with disabilities* (5th ed., pp. 447–471). Baltimore, MD: Brookes.

Shattuck, P., Narendorf, S., Cooper, B., Sterzing, P., Wagner, M., & Taylor, J. (2012). Postsecondary education and employment among youth with an autism spectrum disorder. *Pediatrics, 6*, 1042–1049. doi:10.1542/peds.2011-2864

Stancliffe, R. J., & Lakin, K. C. (Eds.). (2005). *Costs and outcomes of community services for people with intellectual disabilities.* Baltimore, MD: Brookes.

Sulewski, J. S. (2010). In search of meaningful daytimes: Case studies of community-based non-work supports. *Research & Practice for Persons With Severe Disabilities, 35*(1–2), 39–54.

Targett, P. S., & Wehman, P. (2011). Employment: Community-based choices. In P. Wehman (Ed.), *Essentials of transition planning* (pp. 127–143). Baltimore: Brookes.

Taylor, J. L., & Seltzer, M. M. (2011). Employment and post-secondary educational activities for young adults with autism spectrum disorders during the transition to adulthood. *Journal of Autism and Developmental Disorders, 41*, 566–574. doi:10.1007/s10803-010-1070-3

US Department of Labor, Office of Disability Employment Policy. (2007). *Customized employment: A new competitive edge.* Available at http://www.dol.gov/odep/pubs/custom/edge.htm

Wagner, M., Newman, L., Cameto, R., Levine, P., & Garza, N. (2006). *An overview of findings from Wave 2 of the National Longitudinal Transition Study-2 (NLTS2).* Menlo Park, CA: SRI International.

Wehman, P. (2013). Transition: New horizons and challenges. In P. Wehman (Ed.), *Life beyond the classroom: Transition strategies for young people with disabilities* (5th ed., pp. 3–39). Baltimore, MD: Brookes.

Wehman, P., & Brooke, V. (2013). Securing meaningful work in the community: Vocational internships, placements, and careers. In P. Wehman (Ed.), *Life beyond the classroom: Transition strategies for young people with disabilities* (5th ed., pp. 309–337). Baltimore, MD: Brookes.

Wehman, P., Schall, C. M., McDonough, J., Kregel, J., Brooke, V., Molinelli, A., ... Thiss, W. (2014). Competitive employment for youth with autism spectrum disorders: Early results from a randomized clinical trial. *Journal of Autism and Developmental Disorders, 44*, 487–500. doi:10.1007/s10803-013-1892-x

West, M., Hill, J., Revell, G., Smith, G., Kregel, J., & Campbell, L. (2002). Medicaid HCBS waivers and supported employment pre- and post-Balanced Budget Act of 1997. *Mental Retardation, 40*, 142–147.

/// 23 /// ADULTS WITH AUTISM SPECTRUM DISORDER

Transition Issues

EDWARD S. BRODKIN

INTRODUCTION

The symptoms of autism spectrum disorder (ASD) begin in early childhood and continue throughout life in the vast majority of individuals with ASD (Kanner, 1971), although recent evidence indicates that approximately 8–10% of individuals diagnosed with ASD in childhood do not meet full diagnostic criteria by the time they reach adolescence or adulthood (Anderson, Liang, & Lord, 2014; Orinstein et al., 2014; Seltzer, Shattuck, Abbeduto, & Greenberg, 2004). Given the striking increase in rates of diagnosis of ASD in childhood (Centers for Disease Control and Prevention, 2015), large numbers of youths with ASD are now transitioning to adulthood. As of 2012, approximately 50,000 individuals with ASD per year turn 18 years old in the United States (Shattuck, Narendorf, et al., 2012; Shattuck, Roux, et al., 2012). Therefore, the challenges of transition to adulthood in ASD are now a significant public health issue (Gerhardt & Lainer, 2011; Howlin, 2008).

One of the major challenges in addressing transition to adulthood adequately is the tremendous heterogeneity of ASD, including heterogeneity of underlying etiology, clinical manifestations, levels of cognitive and adaptive functioning, and demographics of individuals with ASD (Taylor, 2009). This heterogeneity makes it difficult to craft "one size fits all" transition plans, and, instead, there is a need for a thorough clinical evaluation and to tailor transition plans, services, and interventions to the goals and needs of the particular individual. Our understanding of the large number of etiological factors (e.g., genes and environmental factors) underlying ASD is still quite limited, but part of transition planning should ideally include a consideration of any potential identifiable etiological factors that may prove useful in understanding prognosis and guiding transition planning, interventions, and services. Approximately 10% or more of individuals with ASD will have an identifiable genetic syndrome, genomic copy number variant, or other mutation that may underlie the ASD and may have associated behavioral or medical implications; others may have had exposure to a teratogen that increased the risk for ASD. A thorough developmental history and modern genetics evaluation, such as a chromosomal microarray analysis, would ideally be included as part of the information to be considered in transition planning (Shen et al., 2010). This can be helpful not only with regard to genetic counseling but also for management of any medical or behavioral comorbidities that are associated with particular genetic syndromes. Also, in order to appropriately tailor a transition plan to each individual's goals and needs, clinicians should conduct a careful evaluation of current symptoms, a neuropsychological evaluation of cognitive and adaptive functioning, and an assessment of the interests and abilities of each individual.

In addition to heterogeneity, another major challenge of transition planning is the relative lack of developed services and lack of evidence base for the efficacy of treatments and services for adults with ASD, although there is increasing recognition of the need for more research in this area (Gerhardt & Lainer, 2011; Howlin, 2008; Howlin & Moss, 2012; Shattuck, Roux, et al., 2012; Taylor, 2009). Despite the limited evidence base, the current chapter makes some recommendations for fostering improved transition to adulthood; these recommendations are based on the available evidence as well as the author's clinical experience.

OUTCOMES FOR ADULTS WITH AUTISM SPECTRUM DISORDER

Despite growing recognition and early intervention for children with ASD, and despite some evidence that ASD symptoms tend to become somewhat less severe from childhood to early adulthood on average (Anderson et al., 2014; Farley et al., 2009; Fecteau, Mottron, Berthiaume, & Burack, 2003; Howlin, Moss, Savage, & Rutter, 2013; McGovern & Sigman, 2005; Seltzer et al., 2003, 2004; Shattuck et al., 2007; Taylor & Seltzer, 2010), most adults with ASD are still left with marked difficulties functioning in various domains, and outcomes for adults with ASD are generally disappointing (Howlin, Goode, Hutton, & Rutter, 2004; Howlin et al., 2013; Seltzer et al., 2004). In a review of published studies from 2000 to 2011 (Howlin & Moss, 2012), on average less than 20% adults with ASD were rated as having good or very good outcomes, or as living independently or semi-independently. Slightly less than 50% were involved in some form of work (paid, sheltered, or volunteer) or educational program.

As individuals on the spectrum go through puberty and enter early adolescence, a subset develops increasing interest in social interactions and in developing friendships or romantic relationships (Rutter, Greenfeld, & Lockeyer, 1967). Despite this, individuals often have ongoing difficulties with social understanding and social skills and, therefore, difficulties in meeting the increasing social subtlety of adolescent interactions (e.g., romantic relationships) relative to childhood social interactions. Most adults with ASD have substantial difficulties with social reciprocity and tend to remain socially isolated (Billstedt, Gillberg, & Gillberg, 2007; Howlin et al., 2013). In one study, only 14% of adults were married or had a long-term intimate relationship, and only 25% had at least one friend (Howlin & Moss, 2012). Several studies have found that approximately 50% of adults with ASD have no friends at all. For example, in one study, more than 50% of adults with ASD had no friendships (Howlin et al., 2004). In a study of 235 adolescents and adults with ASD, 30% reported having at least one friend, whereas almost 50% had no peer friendships (Orsmond, Krauss, & Seltzer, 2004). Another study reported that 16% of young adults with high-functioning autism had at least one friend, whereas 47% had no friends (Mawhood, Howlin, & Rutter, 2000). Of the friendships that adults with ASD do have, some data suggest that the friendships tend to be less close and supportive, on average, than those seen in typically developing adults (Baron-Cohen & Wheelwright, 2003). For another example of data on social relationships in adults with ASD, see Table 23.1. Some evidence indicates

TABLE 23.1 Social Relationships in a Sample of 60 Adults With Autism Spectrum Disorder[a]

Rating	Relationship	n (%)
FRIENDS/ACQUAINTANCES[A] (N = 59)[B]		
0	One or more friends of approximately same age	5 (9)
1	One or more friends but restricted range of interests	9 (15)
2	No specific friendships but seeks contact with others in group situations	8 (14)
3	Never any peer relationships involving selectivity/sharing	37 (63)
CLOSE RELATIONSHIP[A] (N = 60)		
0	Close reciprocal relationship(s) (e.g., sexual relationship/marriage), past or present	4 (7)
1	Some reciprocal relationships but short duration and/or reduced sharing of activities	6 (10)
2	Only ever very brief relationships, involving minimal sharing of activities	4 (7)
3	No reciprocal relationships lasting >1 month or never had relationship	46 (77)

Note: [a]Friends are characterized as individuals seen for outings, visits outside the home but not necessarily invoking emotional intimacy/sharing of feelings. Close relationships are characterized as involving close personal contacts (including sexual); sharing of feelings and activities. [b]One informant could not report on this area.
Source: From Howlin et al. (2013).

that restricted and repetitive behaviors characteristic of ASD tend to become less frequent and less severe as individuals move into adulthood, especially in individuals without intellectual disability (Esbensen, Seltzer, Lam, & Bodfish, 2009; Shattuck et al., 2007), although many adults continue to have unusual responses to sensory stimuli (Billstedt et al., 2007; Howlin et al., 2013).

During adolescence, individuals on the spectrum are at increased risk for periods of aggravation of behavioral symptoms (e.g., aggression, hyperactivity, and insistence on sameness) and for seizures (Gillberg & Steffenburg, 1987; Seltzer et al., 2004), but these symptoms are sometimes transient. Due to these neurobehavioral symptoms, psychotropic medication usage—including use of antipsychotics, antidepressants, mood stabilizers/anticonvulsants, and anxiolytics—tends to increase in individuals with ASD as they enter adolescence and adulthood (Aman, Lam, & Collier-Crespin, 2003), despite the fact that the evidence base for use of medications in adults with ASD is very limited (Dove et al., 2012; Doyle & McDougle, 2012).

Intellectual functioning and language abilities are important prognostic factors that tend to correlate with positive outcomes in adults with ASD, including ability to complete more years of education, ability to live and work independently, and ability to form and maintain relationships (Seltzer et al., 2004). Very few individuals with a childhood IQ below 75 live independently as adults (Howlin & Moss, 2012). Individuals who did not develop speech until after the age of 5 years tend to have poorer outcomes as adults, on average (Howlin & Moss, 2012). However, intellectual disability alone is not the full explanation for the adaptive difficulties of adults with ASD. Adults with ASD appear to have a higher degree of difficulty in some areas than those with intellectual disability without ASD. For example, relative to those with trisomy 21 (Down syndrome), adults with ASD and intellectual disability had less residential independence and more limited social functioning (Esbensen, Bishop, Seltzer, Greenberg, & Taylor, 2010). In a comparison of adolescents and adults with ASD versus adolescents and adults with intellectual disability but no ASD, the group with ASD had significantly more stereotypies, compulsions, and self-injurious behaviors (Bodfish, Symons, Parker, & Lewis, 2000). Moreover, individuals on the autism spectrum with an IQ greater than 70 often still have substantial challenges and difficulties in adulthood (Szatmari, Bartolucci, Bremner, Bond, & Rich, 1989; Howlin & Moss, 2012). A study of individuals with a nonverbal IQ of 70 or greater found that a childhood rating of Reciprocal Social Interaction, a domain of the Autism Diagnostic Interview, was the strongest predictor of adult outcomes (Howlin et al., 2013).

Adolescents and adults with ASD have higher rates of mood disorders, anxiety disorders, obsessive–compulsive disorder, and attention deficit hyperactivity disorder than typically developing individuals, and thus they have higher mental health service needs (Bellini, 2004; Bradley, Summers, Wood, & Bryson, 2004; Ghaziuddin, Ghaziuddin, & Greden, 2002; Ghaziuddin & Zafar, 2008; Hill & Furniss, 2006; Hofvander et al., 2009; Howlin, 2004; Joshi et al., 2013; Kim, Szatmari, Bryson, Streiner, & Wilson, 2000; LoVullo & Matson, 2009; Lugnegard, Hallerback, & Gillberg, 2011; Mouridsen, Rich, Isager, & Nedergaard, 2008; Simonoff et al., 2013). These psychiatric comorbidities often have an adverse effect on general functioning (Ghaziuddin & Zafar, 2008; Howlin & Moss, 2012). The social isolation, social exclusion, and unemployment or underemployment of adults with ASD may contribute to their development of depression and suicidal ideation (Cassidy et al., 2014). Individuals with comorbid psychiatric disorders should be referred for treatment to a psychologist and/or a psychiatrist, ideally one with some experience in treating adolescents or adults on the autism spectrum.

The relatively poor outcomes for adults with ASD may be attributable, at least in part, to the relative lack of services for adults and research on adults with ASD. In many areas of the United States, mandated services and supports for individuals with ASD either disappear or are dramatically reduced after the age of 21–22 years, which is sometimes referred to as "falling off the cliff" (Howlin & Moss, 2012; Taylor & Seltzer, 2010, 2011) or at least an important turning point in the lives of individuals with ASD (Taylor & Seltzer, 2010). The period of time after leaving high school has been associated with a slowing of improvement in symptoms and behaviors, perhaps due to lack of services, daily structure, and engaging daytime activities (Shattuck, Narendorf, et al., 2012). Moreover, relative to the attention that children with ASD have received, much less empirical research has been conducted on treatments, including medication treatments, for adults with ASD, which limits the evidence base for supporting and treating adults (Dove et al., 2012; Howlin & Moss, 2012). Together with the growth of early intervention for children with ASD, there is a growing imperative for more research on transition to adulthood and more service development and reimbursement for adults with ASD, and it is hoped that this will lead to better outcomes for adolescents and adults over time (Gerhardt & Lainer, 2011; Howlin, 2008; Shattuck, Roux, et al., 2012).

STRESS ON FAMILY MEMBERS

The transition to adulthood is often a period of considerable stress and adjustment for close family members of those on the autism spectrum (Seltzer, Krauss, Orsmond, & Vestal, 2001). Many parents serve as primary caregivers and/or care coordinators for adolescent and adult children with ASD, and sustained efforts on the part of parents are needed to coordinate many types of health, educational, and other services. Parents of adolescents on the spectrum often have immediate concerns about challenging behaviors, social and communication skills, behavioral and academic issues with schools, as well as the need for some respite from the stresses of caregiving (Fong, Wilgosh, & Sobsey, 1993; Seltzer et al., 2004). As children grow physically larger in adolescence, certain behaviors that were more manageable in early childhood, such as tantrums, may become more stressful and difficult to manage.

In looking ahead to the near future, parents often have considerable worries about their child's capacity to move out of the home and to function in post-secondary education, employment, and activities of daily living. Also, it may be difficult for some parents to contemplate issues related to their son's or daughter's sexuality and interest in romantic relationships. Parents often have longer term concerns about what will happen to their child when the parents become older, sick, or pass away and questions about how to address those issues, including legal issues about guardianship and financial and health decision-making. Parents of children with ASD tend to experience higher caregiving demands, higher levels of stress, more mental health symptoms, and higher rates of divorce compared to parents of typically developing children or parents of children with trisomy 21 or intellectual disability of unknown etiology (Abbeduto et al., 2004; Dumas, Wolf, Fisman, & Culligan, 1991; Wolf, Noh, Fisman, & Speechley, 1989). Due to the costs of treatments and loss of parent income, raising a child with ASD is also a major financial undertaking that can leave families under severe financial stress (Buescher, Cidav, Knapp, & Mandell, 2014; Ganz, 2007). Lower family socioeconomic status also has been associated with slower improvement in maladaptive behaviors during the transition to adulthood (Taylor & Seltzer, 2010).

Parents should be offered resources for support for themselves, as well as for their child. These include a series of frank and thorough discussions of the many issues involved in transition to adulthood, the particular adaptive strengths and talents of their own child, as well as areas in which their child will need more support and services. Many issues should be addressed in the discussions, such as the following: finding post-secondary educational opportunities when appropriate, as well as educational settings that will be a good match for their young adult son or daughter; preparing as early as possible for vocational development and any services or supports that will be helpful to function in work; options for housing and level of independence that will be sustainable, and finding residential support when necessary; the development of social relationships; ongoing behavioral issues and the potential role of behavioral and medication treatments; planning for emergencies; and finding appropriate legal and financial counseling for longer term planning regarding financial and health care decision-making (Howlin & Moss, 2012; Pilling, Baron-Cohen, Megnin-Viggars, Lee, & Taylor, 2012). There are an increasing number of attorneys with expertise in assisting families of children with special needs regarding guardianship, trusts, education, work, and residential issues. Resources to help individuals and families with transition planning have been developed by various organizations, including Autism Speaks (https:// www.autismspeaks.org/family-services/tool-kits/transition-tool-kit). When necessary, parents should be offered resources for stress management and/or mental health treatment for themselves. Recent research suggests that mindfulness-based stress reduction approaches may be helpful to parents in reducing symptoms of depression and anxiety (Dykens, Fisher, Taylor, Lambert, & Miodrag, 2014). Many parents may also find it helpful to talk with other parents in similar situations or participate in support groups in which experiences and coping strategies can be shared.

It is important to encourage individuals, families, and school systems to plan far ahead for the transition to adulthood because there are numerous complex issues that will take time and planning to address. Planning should begin when the individual is approximately 10–13 years of age, with more effort put into transition planning from 13–16 years of age and older (Hendricks & Wehman, 2009). This transition work should include development of vocational direction and education about independent living skills and adult relationships. Ideally, the student, parents, teachers, and other professionals should all participate in formulating the transition plan, and there should be coordination between efforts of school and community agencies (Everson & Reid, 1999; Hendricks & Wehman, 2009). The transition plan should be paired with an educational program to help students develop necessary skills and reach goals. It is often useful to teach skills in the context in which they will be applied—that is, to teach in community settings, not just in the classroom (Hendricks & Wehman, 2009).

EDUCATION

As measured by high school graduation rates and by performance on academic achievement tests, adolescents with ASD have lower levels of academic achievement, on average, compared with their typically developing peers (Hendricks & Wehman, 2009). A majority of students with ASD have post-school services as part of their transition plan. A study of a nationally representative survey of parents, guardians, and young adults with ASD in the United States found that 34.7% of those with ASD attended college in the first 6 years after high school, and more than 50% of youth who had left high school in the past 2 years had no participation in further education (Shattuck, Narendorf, et al., 2012). Participation rates were lower for individuals who belonged to minority groups or whose family had lower income. These data are generally consistent with previous reports indicating that 40% or fewer individuals with ASD attend college, and a smaller percentage graduate from college, with lower rates among those with more severe symptoms or lack of access to services (Cederlund, Hagberg, Billstedt, Gillberg, & Gillberg, 2008; Eaves & Ho, 2008; Howlin, Alcock, & Burkin, 2005; Howlin, Mawhood, & Rutter, 2000; Taylor & Seltzer, 2011).

For those young adults who have the intellectual ability to attend college and even graduate or pursue professional education, their ability to do so may be thwarted by issues of living away from home, managing their own activities of daily living and finances, managing the unpredictability and inevitable stresses of more independent living, and navigating the relatively complex social environment of higher education. Clinicians should inform individuals and families that there are an increasing number of programs that are designed to prepare and support young adults on the spectrum prior to and during college, as well as an increasing number of colleges that are oriented to the needs of those students on the spectrum. In addition, there are organizations, such as Achieving in Higher Education with Autism and Developmental Disabilities (AHEADD; http://www.aheadd.org) that provide professional support staff and peer mentoring during college, as well as other online resources.

LIVING ARRANGEMENTS AND ACTIVITIES OF DAILY LIVING

Depending on the individual's preferences and independent living skills, various levels of living independence are possible, including living with family, fully supported living, partially supported living, and independent living either by oneself or in a group living setting (Hendricks & Wehman, 2009). Many individuals with ASD do not live independently (Table 23.2). There are advantages and disadvantages to these various living arrangements,

TABLE 23.2 Residential Status of a Sample of 60 Adults With Autism Spectrum Disorder[a]

Rating	Where Living[a]	n (%)
0	Independently	8 (13)
1	Semi-sheltered accommodation (n = 5) or with parents but high degree of autonomy (n = 3)	8 (13)
2	At home, limited autonomy	10 (17)
	Residential home, limited autonomy	12 (20)
3	Specialist autistic placement or another placement with little/no autonomy	20 (33)
	Secure hospital care	2 (3)

Note: [a]All individuals in residential care had been there since early adulthood (age 18–21).
Source: From Howlin et al. (2013).

both to adults on the spectrum and to their families of origin (Hendricks & Wehman, 2009; Krauss, Seltzer, & Jacobson, 2005). Many skills are involved in independent living, including managing safety, cooking, cleaning, laundry, dressing, and personal finances. As with other transition issues, teaching and practice of these independent living skills should be part of behavior and transition plans relatively early on so there is sufficient time for these skills to be acquired. There are an increasing number of agencies and clinicians that can be helpful in implementing plans to teach these skills and providing various levels of supported housing, but access to these services may depend on individuals' and families' particular benefits and entitlements. In addition, groups of parents have worked together to form group homes for their adult children on the spectrum, as well as organizations devoted to housing and residential issues.

VOCATION/EMPLOYMENT

Development of a vocation is a major priority during the transition to adulthood because finding and keeping satisfying work plays an important role in developing a sense of purpose and well-being, self-esteem, social and mental engagement, and financial independence. According to recent studies, only 25–55% of adults with ASD, and perhaps less, participate in any type of paid employment, including competitive or supported employment and full-time or part-time work (Hendricks, 2010; Shattuck, Narendorf, et al., 2012). In some samples, 25–55% of young adults with ASD are not engaged in work of any sort (Cederlund et al., 2008; Eaves & Ho, 2008; Howlin et al., 2013; Taylor & Seltzer, 2011) (see Table 23.3).

Lower levels of cognitive or language skills are associated with lower rates of employment in adults with ASD (Graetz, 2010; Shattuck, Narendorf, et al., 2012). However, intellectual disability is not the full explanation for low rates of employment in this population. In fact, adults with ASD have lower rates of paid employment than adults with intellectual disability without ASD, learning disabilities, or speech/language impairment (Shattuck, Narendorf, et al., 2012). Individuals on the spectrum without intellectual disability are employed at rates lower than one would expect on the basis of their intellectual functioning (Howlin et al., 2004). In fact, in one study, adults with ASD without intellectual disability were three times more likely to have no daytime activities than adults with ASD and an intellectual disability (Taylor & Seltzer, 2011). The authors concluded that there seems

TABLE 23.3 Employment Status of a Sample of 60 Adults With Autism Spectrum Disorder

Highest Occupation	Job Type (*N* = 60)	*n* (%)
Professional or highly skilled	Computer programmer (construction design), engineer (nuclear research)	2 (3)
Non-manual skilled	Project manager (×2) (civil service; telecom), artist (self-employed), accounts clerk (×2), town planner, civil servant	7 (12)
Manual skilled	Electronics work	1 (2)
Partly skilled	Postal workers (×2)	2 (3)
Unskilled and untrained	Postal work (family firm), McDonald's, sales assistant, cleaning/sorting in theatrical costumiers, factory assembly/packing work	5 (8)
PhD student/voluntary lobbying work		1 (2)
Sheltered/voluntary employment	Basic industrial work, cleaning (×2), care–home, charity shop, railway guard, kitchen, gardening work (×2)	9 (15)
Never worked/long-term unemployed		33 (55)

Source: From Howlin et al. (2013).

to be a subgroup of young adults who "fall through the cracks"—those who do not have severe enough symptoms to receive adult day services but who are not able to function independently.

Gaining and keeping competitive employment is very challenging for many individuals on the spectrum, often due, in large part, to the social demands and sensory issues in the workplace. Gaining competitive employment often requires a job interview, which is extremely difficult for many adults with ASD, given their difficulties with social understanding and social skills. Once one has employment, one then has to navigate interactions with bosses, supervisors, and coworkers, as well as workplace "politics," which are very challenging for many adults on the spectrum. Adults with ASD tend to switch jobs more often, and it is more difficult for them to adjust to new job settings (Hendricks & Wehman, 2009; Hurlbutt & Chalmers, 2004; Muller, Schuler, Burton, & Yates, 2003). For those adults on the autism spectrum who are employed, many are underemployed in menial jobs that they find uninteresting and that may pay lower than a living wage (Taylor & Seltzer, 2011; Taylor et al., 2012). Individuals who are able to get competitive employment will likely benefit from continued support outside of the workplace setting in understanding and navigating the social demands and office politics that often are part of the workplace. This support may come from a family member, clinician, or vocational support or rehabilitation program.

Clinicians and others who are caring for or supporting adolescents or young adults on the spectrum should not assume that these individuals, even if they are intellectually disabled, do not have an interest or ability to engage in work. In fact, the vast majority of individuals, including those who are intellectually disabled, prefer to have engaging work or other activities and prefer to play an important role in choosing the type of work (Burchardt, 2004; Shattuck, Roux, et al., 2012). Behavioral problems can worsen when young adults are bored and unstimulated by engaging daytime work or activities.

For individuals with ASD who do want to work, it should be a major goal of transition planning. It is important to give students in high school work experiences and opportunities to explore career options. This can help develop an interest and understanding of work and jobs, develop work skills, and also develop interpersonal skills that can be applied in job settings (Hendricks & Wehman, 2009; Targett, 2006). Many individuals on the autism spectrum have areas of special interest, and rather than viewing these only as pathological symptoms or restricted interests to be treated, these special interests can sometimes by parlayed into a kind of work that is enjoyable and meaningful to individuals (Grandin & Duffy, 2004).

What other strategies can be used to maximize work opportunities and functioning for adults with ASD? Unfortunately, the evidence base on vocational interventions for adolescents and adults with ASD is quite sparse (Taylor et al., 2012). The few studies that have been published mostly focus on supported employment programs, which involve individualized supports, such as a job coach, in a community-based workplace to make employment in community settings more feasible (Taylor et al., 2012). Supported employment programs also may help with writing resumes and job applications, preparing for interviews, job training, matching the person with appropriate jobs, advising employers on making necessary adjustments to the workplace environment, supporting the individual once he or she starts the job, and supporting the employer with advice regarding ASD (Pilling et al., 2012). There is evidence that supported employment increases employment rates (Howlin et al., 2005), quality of life (Garcia-Villamisar, Wehman, & Navarro, 2002), and cognitive functioning (Garcia-Villamisar & Hughes, 2007) for particular sets of individuals on the spectrum, and it may have a long-lasting positive effect on employment (Howlin et al., 2005; Lawer, Brusilovskiy, Salzer, & Mandell, 2009). There is also evidence from a cross-sectional study that supports such as on-the-job training, job search assistance, and assistive technology are associated with a high likelihood of employment in the community (Lawer et al., 2009; Taylor et al., 2012).

Historically, vocational rehabilitation programs have not necessarily been oriented toward helping individuals on the autism spectrum, but there is growing recognition for the need for vocational rehabilitation, or habilitation, for that population, and an increasing number of agencies are providing help customized to adults on the autism spectrum. For those who are not able to participate in supported employment, sheltered workshops or adult day activity centers are options. Sheltered workshops consist of work in a segregated program (not community-based) with coworkers who also have disabilities (Taylor et al., 2012). As a prelude or supplement to paid work, participation on a volunteer work team can help in developing and practicing work and social skills and can give socially isolated individuals a sense of mattering in the world (Fegan & Cook, 2014; Piliavin & Siegel, 2007).

Although ASD is highly heterogeneous, and it is difficult to make generalizations about individuals with ASD, a few rules of thumb are useful regarding work and daytime activities. First, many people on the autism spectrum tend to thrive on a structured and fairly predictable schedule, but they also prefer to have a role in making choices about the types of activities in which they engage. To the extent that work or daytime activities can have a predictable schedule, that is often helpful, and a visual calendar and schedule can often be quite helpful as well so that individuals know what to expect. The areas of work life that are often most difficult for individuals on the spectrum are the social demands (job interviewing, small talk on the job, office politics, communicating with bosses, and tailoring communication to the particular person and context), executive functioning demands (staying organized and timing), and managing stress. One important issue is trying to find the right fit—that is, finding a kind of work that matches as well as possible with the individual's particular interests and strengths. In addition, individuals on the spectrum also may need ongoing support from clinicians, family members, job coaches, peer mentors, or vocational rehabilitation personnel regarding social understanding, social skills, organization, and stress relief in order to make a particular job feasible and sustainable.

INTERFERING BEHAVIORS

Adolescents and adults with ASD may have ongoing difficulties with challenging behaviors, such as tantrums, aggression, or self-injurious behaviors, which can pose safety concerns and interfere with family, social, and occupational functioning. Adults with ASD who are nonverbal or who have severe difficulties with communication may not be able to convey that they feel ill or in pain, and they may only express this through aggressive or self-injurious behaviors (Carr & Owen-DeSchryve, 2007). Therefore, one should first assess the patient for any medical problems, sources of physical pain, or comorbid psychiatric issues (e.g., anxiety and depression) that may be contributing to challenging behaviors and about which the patient may have difficulty communicating, especially if the patient is intellectually disabled or nonverbal. It is typically also very useful to refer the patient to a psychologist, such as a Board Certified Behavior Analyst (BCBA), who can carry out a functional behavior assessment (FBA) to collect data in the patient's natural environment and identify other environmental or social factors (including antecedent and consequent events—that is, events that occur before and after the behavior, respectively) that may be contributing to the behaviors and to identify ways in which the behaviors may be serving a communicative function or function of fulfilling a particular need. The FBA typically should include efforts to manipulate aspects of the environment to determine the effects on the frequency and intensity of the interfering behaviors in order to establish a causal relationship and formulate a strategy for intervention. The BCBA can then implement a behavioral intervention plan to modify aspects of the social environment to try to reduce the frequency and/or intensity of the interfering behaviors and to teach the patient more functional means of communicating his or her needs (National Autism Center, 2009). If the therapeutic response to an adequate trial of a behavioral intervention is not sufficient, and challenging behaviors are still significantly interfering with day-to-day functioning, one should consider treatment with one of the antipsychotic drugs that are approved by the US Food and Drug Administration for this indication, including risperidone or aripiprazole (Dove et al., 2012; Doyle & McDougle, 2012). Medication treatment may also be necessary earlier in the course of treatment if there are more imminent safety concerns, and it can be implemented at the same time as behavioral interventions. More verbal patients may also benefit from regular psychotherapy treatment.

SOCIAL AND COMMUNICATION SKILLS FOR ADULT LIFE

Transition plans should address social and communication skill development and generalization of these skills to a variety of contexts, including home, school, work, and community settings (Hendricks & Wehman, 2009). Speech–language therapy may be necessary in adolescence to improve verbal communication skills. For those who are nonverbal, alternative methods of communication, such as use of the Picture Exchange Communication System (PECS), should be employed for communication. Although much of the evidence base for use of applied behavioral approaches to improve social and communication skills derives from children with ASD, it is likely that similar approaches will be very helpful to adults with ASD in developing social and communication skills (Howlin & Moss, 2012; National Autism Center, 2009).

Social functioning of adolescents and adults with ASD may be adversely affected by low motivation to engage socially, lack of social understanding (social cognition), lack of social skills, anxiety and difficulties with emotion regulation, and/or difficulty in tailoring social behaviors to particular contexts (Chevallier, Kohls, Troiani, Brodkin, & Schultz, 2012; Samson, Huber, & Gross, 2012; Volkmar, 2011). Many adolescents and adults on the autism spectrum spend a very large number of waking hours on solitary activities such as video games and Internet use, and these activities provide few, if any, opportunities to develop social understanding or practice social skills in "live" interactions with others. The "social gap" between individuals on the spectrum and typically developing individuals tends to widen during adolescence and the transition to adulthood (Hendricks & Wehman, 2009). However, many individuals on the autism spectrum express a desire for friendships and intimate relationships and feel lonely, but they do not possess the understanding of social relationships or the social communication skills to form and maintain such relationships (Hendricks & Wehman, 2009). Also, many individuals with ASD have a libido and an interest in romantic and sexual relationships but lack an understanding of the rules of dating and romantic relationships and also lack social skills. This may lead these individuals to engage in behaviors that are misinterpreted or get them into trouble, such as "stalking" behaviors (Stokes, Newton, & Kaur, 2007). Relative to the tolerance for mistakes in childhood, there is reduced tolerance in society for a lack of understanding of social mores in adults, and poor social decision-making in adults with ASD can have severe consequences, including loss of opportunities for employment, social isolation, or even criminal prosecution.

Compared with treatments and services that have been developed for children, relatively few treatments and services have been developed and rigorously tested to improve social functioning for late adolescents and adults with ASD. However, there has been a growing interest in this area and a realization that it is very important, considering the large numbers of individuals transitioning to adulthood. Some social skills groups have been developed for late adolescents and young adults with ASD, and some work has been done in developing video modeling programs to teach social skills (Bishop-Fitzpatrick, Minshew, & Eack, 2013; Day-Watkins, Murray, & Connell, 2014; Gantman, Kapp, Orenski, & Laugeson, 2012; Laugeson, Frankel, Gantman, Dillon, & Mogil, 2012; Turner-Brown, Perry, Dichter, Bodfish, & Penn, 2008). Increasing numbers of social skills groups and programs for adults are being developed by clinicians in various areas of the country. However, much more work is needed in this area to develop evidence-based treatments and services because social and communication skills are vital for virtually all aspects of adult life.

Case Study #1: "John"

Studies of transition to adulthood tend to focus, understandably, on very noticeable and major outcomes of concern in individuals with ASD, such as interrupted education, unemployment, inability to live independently, and repetitive behaviors that may result in injury. However, it is important for clinicians to recognize that even those individuals with ASD with seemingly the very best long-term outcomes according to the usual criteria—excellent cognitive functioning, completed higher education, a well-developed career, independent living, and even marriage—may still have very significant difficulties with social functioning that cause impairments in their relationships and substantial distress in themselves and in their loved ones. Therefore, even if the education, employment, and housing issues of transition to adulthood are navigated very well, many adults still need substantial help with social understanding, emotion regulation, and relationships. This area of need may not be reflected well in studies that present aggregated group data on transition to adulthood, but it is illustrated in this case example.

John is a 47-year-old man with a history of ASD symptoms since childhood, including marked impairment in social–emotional reciprocity, difficulty in using and interpreting non-verbal social communication, very few peer friendships throughout childhood, sensitivities to sound and particular clothing textures, spending many hours per day in pursuing various solitary interests (e.g., video games), and tendency to stick to an inflexible schedule. However, he is very bright intellectually, and he did well academically in school, ultimately graduating from college, where he majored in business and computer engineering. Although his diagnosis of ASD was not made until he was an adult, he realized even before the diagnosis was made that he had some difficulty in understanding social interactions. He compensated for this by teaching himself certain scripts and ways of conversing in structured situations, by reading various sales and self-help books. This has given him sufficient social skill to adequately navigate his workplace for the most part. He has built a career in the computer software field and has been fairly successful financially. Intermittently, however, he has had significant interpersonal difficulties at work related to difficulty in reading and navigating social situations, which has led to multiple changes of jobs and compromised the growth of his career, to some extent, and has recently put his current job in jeopardy.

In his teens and early twenties, he never dated, but in his early thirties he met a woman named Susan at a work meeting who showed an interest in him and whom he ultimately married. Their marriage has lasted for 15 years, and they have a 13-year-old daughter. Susan used to work in the computer field, but she stopped working to raise their daughter. Despite the marriage lasting 15 years, their family life has been marked by great difficulties, and Susan has increasingly considered divorce. She feels that he is emotionally cold and that they are unable to connect. He spends virtually all of his time in his study, working or pursuing his own areas of special interest on the computer—topics that do not interest her at all. After asking her a few standard questions about her day, which seem to her to be scripted, he does not know how to respond to her beyond that. Conversations tend to fall flat. Sometimes John speaks at length about his own areas of interest, but he does not seem to notice that Susan is not interested unless she tells him quite bluntly. He seems to not be aware of his own emotions or hers, unless she expresses them very obviously when she becomes frustrated with their relationship, but then he generally does not understand why she is acting that way and does not know how to respond. He makes little eye contact, and his affect is usually quite constricted. Their teenage daughter feels that she generally cannot connect with her father, and she feels quite distant from him. Susan has become increasingly depressed, and her talk about divorce makes John very anxious, to the point of panic symptoms, because he would feel devastated if he were to lose his marriage, although he has difficulty expressing that to his wife. Although he generally expresses little emotion, he sometimes has yelling temper tantrums when he feels overwhelmed with stress and anxiety, and he does not know how to manage the feelings. Susan brought John to a specialty clinic for adults with ASD, encouraging him to seek help with his social understanding and social skills, in order to have a better chance of saving his job and marriage. If ASD had been recognized earlier in this quite "high-functioning" individual, and John had received help with social functioning in childhood and around the transition to adulthood, he may have had less distress and greater ability to navigate work and relationships.

SUMMARY

Planning for the transition to adulthood should begin early in adolescence, and it should be tailored to the particular goals and needs of the patient and family. Such planning should ideally include input from the patient, family, teachers, clinicians, and other professionals. To optimize functioning and outcomes, various areas need to be addressed, including family stress, education, vocational development, adaptive living skills, interfering behaviors, and social and communication skills. There has been a relative lack of development of treatments and services for adults with ASD, but this is starting to change. Clinicians should become aware of existing or newly developed resources in their area so they can best assist patients and families in navigating the opportunities and challenges of transition and also so that adults with ASD can develop a sense of well-being and higher quality of life in their communities.

KEY POINTS

- Developing plans for transition to adulthood should begin well before the age of 18 years, ideally at the age of 10–13 years, and should involve a collaborative effort of the patient, family, teachers, clinicians, and other professionals.
- Outcomes for adults with ASD have been generally disappointing, including high rates of social isolation, interrupted education, unemployment, and lack of independent living. These outcomes may be attributable, in part, to lack of established services and supports for adults.
- Parents and other family members of adults with ASD tend to be under significant chronic stress, and they may need help from a variety of professionals in managing transition issues.
- The majority of individuals on the autism spectrum, including those who are intellectually disabled, prefer to have engaging work or other activities and prefer to play an important role in choosing the type of work.
- Many adults with ASD feel lonely and have a desire for friendships or romantic relationships, but they may lack the social understanding and skills necessary to initiate and sustain relationships. More treatments and services are needed to help adults with ASD navigate social relationships.

ACKNOWLEDGMENTS

This work was funded by the National Institutes of Health (grants R34MH104407; R34MH100356; and P50MH096891, subproject 6773) and the Autism Services, Education, Resources, and Training (ASERT) Collaborative, Bureau of Autism Services,

Pennsylvania Department of Human Resources. The content of the chapter is solely the responsibility of the author and does not represent the official views of the National Institute of Mental Health, the National Institutes of Health, or the Pennsylvania Department of Human Resources.

DISCLOSURE STATEMENT

Dr. Edward S. Brodkin has no conflicts to disclose.

REFERENCES

Abbeduto, L., Seltzer, M. M., Shattuck, P., Krauss, M. W., Orsmond, G., & Murphy, M. M. (2004). Psychological well-being and coping in mothers of youths with autism, Down syndrome, or fragile X syndrome. *American Journal of Mental Retardation, 109,* 237–254.

Aman, M. G., Lam, K. S. L., & Collier-Crespin, A. (2003). Prevalence and patterns of use of psychoactive medicine among individuals with autism in the Autism Society of Ohio. *Journal of Autism and Developmental Disorders, 33,* 527–534.

Anderson, D. K., Liang, J. W., & Lord, C. (2014). Predicting young adult outcome among more and less cognitively able individuals with autism spectrum disorders. *Journal of Child Psychology and Psychiatry, 55,* 485–494.

Baron-Cohen, S., & Wheelwright, S. (2003). The friendship questionnaire: An investigation of adults with Asperger syndrome or high-functioning autism, and normal sex differences. *Journal of Autism and Developmental Disorders, 33,* 509–517.

Bellini, S. (2004). Social skill deficits and anxiety in high-functioning adolescents with autism spectrum disorders. *Focus on Autism and Other Developmental Disabilities, 19,* 78–86.

Billstedt, E., Gillberg, I. C., & Gillberg, C. (2007). Autism in adults: Symptom patterns and early childhood predictors—Use of the DISCO in a community sample followed from childhood. *Journal of Child Psychology and Psychiatry, 48,* 1102–1110.

Bishop-Fitzpatrick, L., Minshew, N. J., & Eack, S. M. (2013). A systematic review of psychosocial interventions for adults with autism spectrum disorders. *Journal of Autism and Developmental Disorders, 43,* 687–694.

Bodfish, J. W., Symons, F. J., Parker, D. E., & Lewis, M. H. (2000). Varieties of repetitive behavior in autism: Comparisons to mental retardation. *Journal of Autism and Developmental Disorders, 30,* 237–243.

Bradley, E. A., Summers, J. A., Wood, H. L., & Bryson, S. E. (2004). Comparing rates of psychiatric and behavior disorders in adolescents and young adults with severe intellectual disability with and without autism. *Journal of Autism and Developmental Disorders, 34,* 151–161.

Buescher, A. V. S., Cidav, Z., Knapp, M., & Mandell, D. S. (2014). Costs of autism spectrum disorders in the United Kingdom and the United States. *JAMA Pediatrics, 168*(8), 721–728.

Burchardt, T. (2004). Capabilities and disability: The capabilities framework and the social model of disability. *Disability & Society, 19,* 735–751.

Carr, E. G., & Owen-DeSchryve, J. S. (2007). Physical illness, pain, and problem behavior in minimally verbal people with developmental disabilities. *Journal of Autism and Developmental Disorders, 37,* 413–424.

Cassidy, S., Bradley, P., Robinson, J., Allison, C., McHugh, M., & Baron-Cohen, S. (2014). Suicidal ideation or attempts in adults with Asperger's syndrome attending a specialist diagnostic clinic: A clinical cohort study. *Lancet Psychiatry, 1*(2), 142–147.

Cederlund, M., Hagberg, B., Billstedt, E., Gillberg, I. C., & Gillberg, C. (2008). Asperger syndrome and autism: A comparative longitudinal follow-up study more than 5 years after original diagnosis. *Journal of Autism and Developmental Disorders, 38,* 72–85.

Centers for Disease Control and Prevention. (2015). *Autism spectrum disorder (ASD): Data & statistics.* Available at http://www.cdc.gov/ncbddd/autism/data.html

Chevallier, C., Kohls, G., Troiani, V., Brodkin, E. S., & Schultz, R. T. (2012). The social motivation theory of autism. *Trends in Cognitive Sciences, 16,* 231–239.

Day-Watkins, J., Murray, R., & Connell, J. E. (2014). Teaching helping to adolescents with autism. *Journal of Applied Behavior Analysis, 47*(4), 850–855.

Dove, D., Warren, Z., McPheeters, M. L., Taylor, J. L., Sathe, N. A., & Veenstra-VanderWeele, J. (2012). Medications for adolescents and young adults with autism spectrum disorders: A systematic review. *Pediatrics, 130,* 717–726.

Doyle, C. A., & McDougle, C. J. (2012). Pharmacotherapy to control behavioral symptoms in children with autism. *Expert Opinion in Pharmacotherapy, 13,* 1615–1629.

Dumas, J. E., Wolf, L. C., Fisman, S. N., & Culligan, A. (1991). Parenting stress, child behavior problems, and dysphoria in parents of children with autism, Down syndrome, behavior disorders, and normal development. *Exceptionality, 2,* 97–110.

Dykens, E. M., Fisher, M. H., Taylor, J. L., Lambert, W., & Miodrag, N. (2014). Reducing distress in mothers of children with autism and other disabilities: A randomized trial. *Pediatrics, 134*(2), e454.

Eaves, L. C., & Ho, H. H. (2008). Young adult outcome of autism spectrum disorders. *Journal of Autism and Developmental Disorders, 38,* 739–747.

Esbensen, A. J., Bishop, S., Seltzer, M. M., Greenberg, J. S., & Taylor, J. L. (2010). Comparisons between individuals with autism spectrum disorders and individuals with Down syndrome in adulthood. *American Journal on Intellectual and Developmental Disabilities, 115,* 277–290.

Esbensen, A. J., Seltzer, M. M., Lam, K. S. L., & Bodfish, J. W. (2009). Age-related differences in restricted repetitive behaviors in autism spectrum disorders. *Journal of Autism and Developmental Disorders, 39,* 57–66.

Everson, J. M., & Reid, D. H. (1999). A systematic evaluation of preferences identified through person-centered planning for persons with profound multiple disabilities. *Journal of Applied Behavior Analysis, 32,* 467–477.

Farley, M. A., McMahon, W. M., Fombonne, E., Jenson, W. R., Miller, J., Gardner, M., . . . Coon, H. (2009). Twenty-year outcome for individuals with autism and average or near-average cognitive abilities. *Autism Research, 2,* 109–118.

Fecteau, S., Mottron, L., Berthiaume, C., & Burack, J. A. (2003). Developmental changes of autistic symptoms. *Autism, 7,* 255–268.

Fegan, C., & Cook, S. (2014). The therapeutic power of volunteering. *Advances in Psychiatric Treatment, 20,* 217–224.

Fong, L., Wilgosh, L., & Sobsey, D. (1993). The experience of parenting an adolescent with autism. *International Journal of Disability, Development and Education, 40,* 105–113.

Gantman, A., Kapp, S. K., Orenski, K., & Laugeson, E. A. (2012). Social skills training for young adults with high-functioning autism spectrum disorders: A randomized controlled pilot study. *Journal of Autism and Developmental Disorders, 42,* 1094–1103.

Ganz, M. L. (2007). The lifetime distribution of the incremental societal costs of autism. *Archives of Pediatric and Adolescent Medicine, 161,* 343–349.

Garcia-Villamisar, D., & Hughes, C. (2007). Supported employment improves cognitive performance in adults with autism. *Journal of Intellectual Disabilities Research, 51,* 142–150.

Garcia-Villamisar, D., Wehman, P., & Navarro, M. D. (2002). Changes in the quality of autistic people's life that work in supported and sheltered employment: A 5-year follow-up study. *Journal of Vocational Rehabilitation, 17,* 309–312.

Gerhardt, P. F., & Lainer, I. (2011). Addressing the needs of adolescents and adults with autism: A crisis on the horizon. *Journal of Contemporary Psychotherapy, 41,* 37–45.

Ghaziuddin, M., Ghaziuddin, N., & Greden, J. (2002). Depression in persons with autism: Implications for research and clinical care. *Journal of Autism and Developmental Disorders, 32,* 299–306.

Ghaziuddin, M., & Zafar, S. (2008). Psychiatric comorbidity of adults with autism spectrum disorders. *Clinical Neuropsychiatry, 5,* 9–12.

Gillberg, C., & Steffenburg, S. (1987). Outcome and prognostic factors in infantile autism and similar conditions: A population-based study of 46 cases followed through puberty. *Journal of Autism and Developmental Disorders, 17,* 273–287.

Graetz, J. E. (2010). Autism grows up: Opportunities for adults with autism. *Disability & Society, 25,* 33–47.

Grandin, T., & Duffy, K. (2004). *Developing talents: Careers for individuals with Asperger syndrome and high-functioning autism.* Shawnee Mission, KS: Autism Asperger Publishing.

Hendricks, D. (2010). Employment and adults with autism spectrum disorders: Challenges and strategies for success. *Journal of Vocational Rehabilitation, 32,* 125–134.

Hendricks, D. R., & Wehman, P. (2009). Transition from school to adulthood for youth with autism spectrum disorders: Review and recommendations. *Focus on Autism and Other Developmental Disabilities, 24,* 77–88.

Hill, J., & Furniss, F. (2006). Patterns of emotional and behavioural disturbance associated with autistic traits in young people with severe intellectual disabilities and challenging behaviors. *Research in Developmental Disabilities, 27,* 517–528.

Hofvander, B., Delorme, R., Chaste, P., Nyden, A., Wentz, E., Stahlberg, O., . . . Leboyer, M. (2009). Psychiatric and psychosocial problems in adults with normal-intelligence autism spectrum disorders. *BMC Psychiatry, 9,* 35.

Howlin, P. (2004). Psychiatric disturbances in adulthood. In *Autism and Asperger Syndrome: Preparing for Adulthood* (2nd ed., pp. 270–299). New York, NY: Routledge.

Howlin, P. (2008). Redressing the balance in autism research. *Nature Clinical Practice Neurology, 4,* 407.

Howlin, P., Alcock, J., & Burkin, C. (2005). An 8 year follow-up of a specialist supported employment service for high-ability adults with autism or Asperger syndrome. *Autism, 9,* 533–549.

Howlin, P., Goode, S., Hutton, J., & Rutter, M. (2004). Adult outcome for children with autism. *Journal of Child Psychology and Psychiatry, 45,* 212–229.

Howlin, P., Mawhood, L., & Rutter, M. (2000). Autism and developmental receptive language disorder—A follow-up comparison in early adult life. II: Social, behavioural, and psychiatric outcomes. *Journal of Child Psychology and Psychiatry, 41,* 561–578.

Howlin, P., & Moss, P. (2012). Adults with autism spectrum disorders. *Canadian Journal of Psychiatry, 57,* 275–283.

Howlin, P., Moss, P., Savage, S., & Rutter, M. (2013). Social outcomes in mid- to later adulthood among individuals diagnosed with autism and average nonverbal IQ as children. *Journal of the American Academy of Child and Adolescent Psychiatry, 52,* 572–581.

Hurlbutt, K., & Chalmers, L. (2004). Employment and adults with Asperger syndrome. *Focus on Autism and Other Developmental Disabilities, 19,* 215–222.

Joshi, G., Wozniak, J., Petty, C., Martelon, M. K., Fried, R., Bolfek, A., . . . Biederman, J. (2013). Psychiatric comorbidity and functioning in a clinically referred population of adults with autism spectrum disorders: A comparative study. *Journal of Autism and Developmental Disorders, 43,* 1314–1325.

Kanner, L. (1971). Follow-up study of eleven autistic children originally reported in 1943. *Journal of Autism and Child Schizophrenia, 1,* 119–145.

Kim, J. A., Szatmari, P., Bryson, S. E., Streiner, D. L., & Wilson, F. J. (2000). The prevalence of anxiety and mood problems among children with autism and Asperger syndrome. *Autism, 4,* 117–132.

Krauss, M. W., Seltzer, M. M., & Jacobson, H. T. (2005). Adults with autism living at home or in non-family settings: Positive and negative aspects of residential status. *Journal of Intellectual Disability Research, 49,* 111–124.

Laugeson, E. A., Frankel, F., Gantman, A., Dillon, A. R., & Mogil, C. (2012). Evidence-based social skills training program for adolescents with autism spectrum disorders: The UCLA PEERS program. *Journal of Autism and Developmental Disorders, 42,* 1025–1036.

Lawer, L. J., Brusilovskiy, E., Salzer, M. S., & Mandell, D. S. (2009). Use of vocational rehabilitative services among adults with autism. *Journal of Autism and Developmental Disorders, 39,* 487–494.

LoVullo, S. V., & Matson, J. L. (2009). Comorbid psychopathology in adults with autism spectrum disorder and intellectual disabilities. *Research in Developmental Disabilities, 30,* 1288–1296.

Lugnegard, T., Hallerback, M. U., & Gillberg, C. (2011). Psychiatric comorbidity in young adults with a clinical diagnosis of Asperger syndrome. *Research in Developmental Disabilities, 32,* 1910–1917.

Mawhood, L., Howlin, P., & Rutter, M. (2000). Autism and developmental receptive language disorder—A comparative follow-up in early adult life. I: Cognitive and language outcomes. *Journal of Child Psychology and Psychiatry, 41,* 547–559.

McGovern, C. W., & Sigman, M. (2005). Continuity and change from early childhood to adolescence in autism. *Journal of Child Psychology and Psychiatry, 46,* 401–408.

Mouridsen, S. E., Rich, B., Isager, T., & Nedergaard, N. J. (2008). Psychiatric disorders in individuals diagnosed with infantile autism as children: A case–control study. *Journal of Psychiatric Practice, 14,* 5–12.

Muller, E., Schuler, A., Burton, B. A., & Yates, G. B. (2003). Meeting the vocational support needs of individuals with Asperger syndrome and other autism spectrum disorders. *Journal of Vocational Rehabilitation, 18,* 163–175.

National Autism Center. (2009). *National standards report: The National Standards Project—Addressing the need for evidence-based practice guidelines for autism spectrum disorder.* Randolph, MA: Author.

Orinstein, A. J., Helt, M., Troyb, E., Tyson, K. E., Barton, M. L., Eigsti, I. M., . . . Fein, D. A. (2014). Intervention for optimal outcome in children and adolescents with a history of autism. *Journal of Developmental and Behavioral Pediatrics, 35,* 247–256.

Orsmond, G. I., Krauss, M. W., & Seltzer, M. M. (2004). Peer relationships and social and recreational activities among adolescents and adults with autism. *Journal of Autism and Developmental Disorders, 34,* 245–256.

Piliavin, J. A., & Siegel, E. (2007). Health benefits of volunteering in the Wisconsin Longitudinal Study. *Journal of Health and Social Behavior, 48,* 450–464.

Pilling, S., Baron-Cohen, S., Megnin-Viggars, O., Lee, R., & Taylor, C. (2012). Recognition, referral, diagnosis, and management of adults with autism: Summary of NICE guidelines. *British Medical Journal, 344,* e4082.

Rutter, M., Greenfeld, D., & Lockeyer, L. (1967). A five to fifteen year follow-up study of infantile psychosis: II. Social and behavioural outcome. *British Journal of Psychiatry, 113,* 1183–1199.

Samson, A. C., Huber, O., & Gross, J. J. (2012). Emotion regulation in Asperger's syndrome and high-functioning autism. *Emotion, 12,* 659–665.

Seltzer, M. M., Krauss, M. W., Orsmond, G. I., & Vestal, C. (2001). Families of adolescents and adults with autism: Uncharted territory. *International Review of Research in Mental Retardation, 23,* 267–294.

Seltzer, M. M., Krauss, M. W., Shattuck, P. T., Orsmond, G., Swe, A., & Lord, C. (2003). The symptoms of autism spectrum disorders in adolescence and adulthood. *Journal of Autism and Developmental Disorders, 33,* 565–581.

Seltzer, M. M., Shattuck, P., Abbeduto, L., & Greenberg, J. S. (2004). Trajectory of development in adolescents and adults with autism. *Mental Retardation and Developmental Disabilities Research Reviews, 10,* 234–237.

Shattuck, P. T., Narendorf, S. C., Cooper, B., Sterzing, P. R., Wagner, M., & Taylor, J. L. (2012). Postsecondary education and employment among youth with an autism spectrum disorder. *Pediatrics, 129,* 1042–1049.

Shattuck, P. T., Roux, A. M., Hudson, L. E., Taylor, J. L., Maenner, M. J., & Trani, J.-F. (2012). Services for adults with an autism spectrum disorder. *Canadian Journal of Psychiatry, 57,* 284–291.

Shattuck, P. T., Seltzer, M. M., Greenberg, J. S., Orsmond, G. I., Bolt, D., Kring, S., . . . Lord, C. (2007). Change in autism symptoms and maladaptive behaviors in adolescents and adults with an autism spectrum disorder. *Journal of Autism and Developmental Disorders, 37,* 1735–1747.

Shen, Y., Dies, K. A., Holm, I. A., Bridgemohan, C., Sobeih, M. M., Caronna, E. B., . . . Miller, D. T.; Autism Consortium Clinical Genetics/DNA Diagnostics Collaboration. (2010). Clinical genetic testing for patients with autism spectrum disorders. *Pediatrics, 125,* 727–735.

Simonoff, E., Jones, C. R. G., Baird, G., Pickles, A., Happe, F., & Charman, T. (2013). The persistence and stability of psychiatric problems in adolescents with autism spectrum disorders. *Journal of Child Psychology
and Psychiatry, 54*, 186–194.

Stokes, M., Newton, N., & Kaur, A. (2007). Stalking and social and romantic functioning among adolescents and adults with autism spectrum disorder. *Journal of Autism and Developmental Disorders, 37*,
1969–1986.

Szatmari, P., Bartolucci, G., Bremner, R., Bond, S., & Rich, S. (1989). A follow-up study of high-functioning
autistic children. *Journal of Autism and Developmental Disorders, 19*, 213–225.

Targett, P. S. (2006). Finding jobs for young people with disabilities. In P. Wehman (Ed.), *Life beyond the
classroom: Transition strategies for young people with disabilities* (4th ed., (pp. 255–288). Baltimore,
MD: Brookes.

Taylor, J. L. (2009). The transition out of high school and into adulthood for individuals with autism and
their families. *International Review of Research in Mental Retardation, 38*, 2–28.

Taylor, J. L., McPheeters, M. L., Sathe, N. A., Dove, D., Veenstra-VanderWeele, J., & Warren, Z. (2012). A systematic review of vocational interventions for young adults with autism spectrum disorders. *Pediatrics,
130*, 531–538.

Taylor, J. L., & Seltzer, M. M. (2010). Changes in the autism behavioral phenotype during the transition to
adulthood. *Journal of Autism and Developmental Disorders, 40*, 1431–1446.

Taylor, J. L., & Seltzer, M. M. (2011). Employment and post-secondary educational activities for young adults
with autism spectrum disorders during the transition to adulthood. *Journal of Autism and Developmental
Disorders, 41*, 566–574.

Turner-Brown, L. M., Perry, T. D., Dichter, G. S., Bodfish, J. W., & Penn, D. L. (2008). Brief report: Feasibility
of social cognition and interaction training for adults with high functioning autism. *Journal of Autism and
Developmental Disorders, 38*, 1777–1784.

Volkmar, F. (2011). Understanding the social brain in autism. *Developmental Psychobiology, 53*, 428–434.

Wolf, L. C., Noh, S., Fisman, S. N., & Speechley, M. (1989). Brief report: Psychological effects of parenting
stress on parents of autistic children. *Journal of Autism and Developmental Disorders, 19*, 157–166.

/// 24 /// EFFECTIVE COMMUNICATION AND MANAGEMENT WITH THE FAMILY AND IN THE COMMUNITY

NAOMI B. SWIEZY, TIFFANY J. NEAL, DANIELLE WARNER, AND KIMBERLY LO

INTRODUCTION

Collaboration is essential to the care of individuals with autism spectrum disorder (ASD), although it is often an elusive concept. Collaboration is a construct that is understood and conceptualized differently across disciplines (Kelly & Tincani, 2013), making it challenging to contextualize the construct in a cohesive, effective manner. Swiezy, Stuart, and Korzekwa (2008) suggest that

> integration of care across medical, educational, and social service systems is challenging to both families and health care professionals due to the time required, cost of staff time and services, knowledge, training, availability of services, and lack of support for the collaborative effort itself. (p. 1156)

Nevertheless, providing the most effective and integrated care for individuals with ASD and their families involves collaboration across multiple disciplines and domains and is imperative. With this consideration in mind, awareness of the meaning, purpose, and components of collaboration is essential. In addition to this awareness, it is similarly important to have a contextual understanding of selected models of collaboration and the outcomes that can be derived through such context.

In seeking to establish a shared definition of collaboration, reference to various sources serves to pull essential elements together across disciplines. Collaboration in the health care field, according to Kelly and Tincani (2013), is a component of consultation involving voluntary, interpersonal interactions comprising of two or more professionals engaging in communication modalities ... for the purpose of shared decision-making and problem solving toward a common goal. Collaboration results in changes to tasks and solutions that would not have been achieved in isolation. (p. 129)

Collaboration can also be thought of as a partnership, with literature demonstrating the saliency of "mutually agreed upon goals, shared expertise, shared responsibility, ecocultural fit, collaborative problem solving, and a strength-based approach" (Brookman-Frazee & Koegel, 2004, p. 197) in deriving improved outcomes across consumers and providers. Furthermore, the manner in which providers, families, and individuals involved in the care and support of those with ASD work together and collaborate is paramount in strengthening and maintaining integrated and continuous supports to maximize outcomes.

Given the importance of collaboration and the impact it has on the quality of treatment and care for individuals with ASD, this chapter further discusses the necessity and function of collaboration, the components of collaboration, and the way collaboration looks in practice. The chapter aims to provide an understanding of the ways in which professionals and caregivers can facilitate truly effective care for individuals with ASD by considering the necessary components of collaboration and the ways in which such collaboration allows for consistent individually oriented treatment.

NECESSITY FOR COLLABORATION

Individuals with ASD present with a spectrum of abilities and impairments, both physical and psychological. These characteristics vary between individuals and are influenced by multiple factors, including those that are genetic, environmental, and psychosocial. Given the unique presentation of ASD in each individual, the best treatment for one individual may look different from that of another. Therefore, "to ensure that the many needs of these children are met across multiple settings, collaboration among medical, psychological, and educational experts is necessary in order to determine the best course of treatment" (Power, DuPaul, Shapiro, & Kazak, 2003, as cited in Ellis, Lutz, Schaefer, & Woods, 2007, p. 742).

Individuals with ASD may be unable to convey their needs and may therefore rely on others to advocate on their behalf (Vakil & Welton, 2013). Keeping this in mind, it is important to consider how individuals at any level of functioning may present differently across settings. For example, a child's behavior at school with his or her teacher may be very different from his or her behavior at home with parents and/or caregivers due to differences within the environment ranging from the presence of certain persons, tasks requested or demands being placed, time of day, behavioral strategies being used, or disciplinary techniques used by caregivers, among other factors. Therefore, it is crucial to seek input from caregivers across various settings in order to fully understand the scope of functioning, current and historical challenges, strategies or techniques used, supports in place, and strengths of each individual with ASD. This describes a shift from the child-only-focus that continues to be held in certain fields. The importance of seeking to understand a child in the context of his or her family, culture, and community is now well understood. Family context is especially important given the breadth of information that parents can contribute with regard to their children. Parents should be used "as integral members of the care team responsible for coordinating services and disseminating information across settings" (Swiezy et al., 2008, p. 911). Family systems theory supports this premise given the consequent impacts, direct or indirect, that occur across the family system when one family member is affected (Kalyva, 2013). Given that family systems may be significantly affected with the initial diagnosis and resulting course of ASD in one of its family members, family support and collaboration throughout all facets of treatment should be an area of focus.

The incorporation of varying perspectives to inform programming for individuals with ASD, support consistency in program implementation, and evaluate program effectiveness is made possible through collaboration (Swiezy et al., 2008). Many individuals contribute in regard to treatment planning when providing care for an individual with ASD across the lifespan. Such individuals include, but are not limited to, educational and medical professionals, specialists, community service providers, and parents or caregivers. Without collaboration, each party involved may have a different understanding of the individual's needs. Each may be working toward differing goals using varied strategies, thus creating and potentially exacerbating difficulties related to generalization and maintenance of skills for the individual with ASD due to disparate approaches. These issues are minimized when treatment plans develop from a collaborative consultation model, with this approach having increased likelihood to result in more consistent programming across settings (Sheridan & Steck, 1995; Wahler & Fox, 1981).

Evidence shows that collaborative consultation models involving shared decision-making between stakeholders lead to improved outcomes across environments. A review by Kelly and Tincani (2013) demonstrated consistent, increased consumer outcomes with the use of either direct or conjoint behavioral consultation models. With a focus on communication between stakeholders (i.e., providers, family members, and school or community providers) and shared responsibility in decision-making across the problem-solving process, improved outcomes are witnessed with respect to behavioral and academic skills, changes in referral patterns, increased treatment integrity, maintenance of gains, and enhanced consumer acceptability. In addition, collaboration reinforces the intent of foundational special education laws, such as the Individuals With Disabilities Education Improvement Act (IDEIA, 2004), with emphases placed on meaningful parent involvement that fosters opportunities for parents and school personnel alongside or inclusive of medical professionals when opportunity is extended to work together.

Given the aforementioned outcomes, collaboration is essential in providing the best quality care for all individuals on the autism spectrum despite presenting challenges. Models of collaboration built solely on cooperation with professionals assuming the role of experts and with parental participation seen as secondary to care result in disagreement and strife related to treatment plans and goals with decreased adherence and satisfaction (Cunningham & Davis, 1985). Models that account for collaboration in a co-therapy context may fail to consider differences that present in parenting styles, family resources, and cultural context, thereby negating salient elements that result in improved outcomes (Mittler & Mittler, 1983). Furthermore, collaboration models reliant upon parents serving both as the consumer and the primary informant for selection of program elements risk the loss of a more systematic and evidence-based approach that is more appropriately advised and followed with trained professionals guiding the treatment planning and programming (Appleton & Minchom, 1991).

ELEMENTS OF COLLABORATION

Collaboration with parents may look differently depending on their comfort level advocating for their child and ability to express their needs. By validating and empowering the parent, greater trust and ultimately a greater partnership can lead to better outcomes for the child and improve the quality of care provided. However, it is first important to bring the parent to the table. Brookman-Frazee and Koegel (2004) note that

> in a partnership between a parent and a professional, the professional may be the "expert" with regards to particular behavioral intervention procedures, whereas the parent is the "expert" on his or her own child and should be responsible for deciding how the procedures are incorporated into the family's daily routines. (p. 197)

Not only are parents able to provide information about their children but also they are often the primary conduit for dissemination of information across systems (Swiezy et al., 2008).

In order to facilitate individually oriented treatment, certain components of collaboration with families are necessary. These components are explored next. Furthermore, the nature of individually oriented treatment is discussed with an emphasis on its importance in the effort to provide effective care to individuals with ASD.

PROVIDING SUPPORT

Collaboration with parents and caregivers includes supporting the parent as he or she comes to terms with a child's diagnosis and continuing such support as the parent faces the ongoing needs involved with treatment across disciplines. The impact of having a child with a disability has been well documented in the literature. Often, parents initially go through and may cycle back through a mourning period after receipt of the diagnosis of ASD for their child. Such mourning and the consequent emotions are comparable to the five stages of grief—denial, anger, bargaining, depression, and acceptance—put forth by Elizabeth Kübler-Ross (Elder, 2013). In addition to emotional impacts, a qualitative study by Fletcher, Markoulakis, and Bryden (2012) illustrated the substantial financial burden assumed by families in order to cover the costs of treatment and related needs (e.g., dietary needs, child care, private care, and home cleaning and repair) in caring for their child with ASD. Furthermore, it was found that mothers' health was often compromised while they put their child's needs before their own, often resulting in depression, exhaustion, weight gain, and increased stress. Similar health issues have been reported to affect fathers and siblings. Many mothers report a loss of friends and an overall social strain following their child's diagnosis, including strain within marital relationships (Fletcher, Markoulakis, & Bryden, 2012). Consideration of parental needs with respect to support, coordination of care, awareness of increased stress, and potential mental health issues is an aspect that warrants discussion and attention by providers (Stahmer, Brookman-Frazee, Lee, Searcy, & Reed, 2011). Without such attention, a parent's appraisal of communication with professionals is often reported as an area resulting in high levels of stress (Brogan & Knussen, 2003).

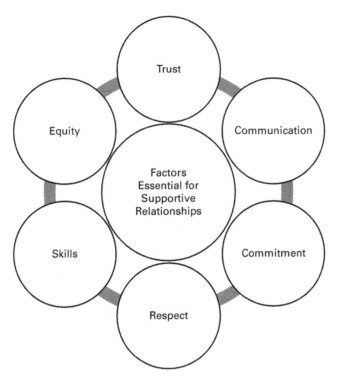

FIGURE 24.1 Six factors essential for supportive relationships. This figure illustrates the components necessary to foster in order to effectively collaborate in a relationship that is supportive.

Given the significant impact that high parental stress can have on the success of early teaching interventions, it is of great importance to take care in all facets of contact and communication with parents leading up to, and during, the diagnostic and/or evaluative process (Osborne & Reed, 2008). Such care includes asking parents questions about their experience and allowing their responses to inform their child's treatment, as well as the supports and resources they are offered. The following factors were listed in Kalyva (2013) as essential components in the development of supportive relationships between parents and mental health professionals (see Figure 24.1):

1. Communication: This should be reciprocal in nature with open, honest, and frequent communication that is free from jargon being fostered across parties.
2. Commitment: Professionals should demonstrate commitment in awareness of and value placed upon the dynamics of the family in serving the whole child.
3. Equity: Conscious effort should be made to seek parental input and empower family members with acknowledgment of the necessary balance between parental input and professional judgment within the therapeutic process.
4. Skills: The professional's skills are highly appreciated by parents when practical help is given both for the care of their child with disabilities and for themselves.
5. Trust: Feelings of trust by parents account for the dimensions of reliability in care and service delivery, physical and emotional security with respect to the care of their children in the presence and planning of providers, and discretion in informational sharing among providers and colleagues.

6. Respect: The individual with a disability should be treated first and foremost as a human being. (pp. 530–531)

The presence and importance of these factors may vary among parents, but they holistically encourage parents and caregivers to feel more supported in their relationship with providers across systems (Brogan & Knussen, 2003).

FACILITATING EMPOWERMENT

Family and parental empowerment is another essential component of effective collaboration. Similar to collaboration, empowerment may have different meanings across disciplines. Within the fields of social work and community psychology, advocacy is posited as a central tenant to empowerment of families and caregivers. However, empowerment within the context of child mental health emphasizes "effective parenting skills, knowledge, parent participation and involvement, and self-efficacy" (Brookman-Frazee & Koegel, 2004, p. 195).

In part, empowerment comes through the delivery and sharing of information. It is important for providers to offer honest answers, refer to other professionals if they do not have the answers, and educate themselves on the presenting disability and effective treatments. The provision of education and support to families of individuals with ASD is one of the treatment goals suggested by the American Academy of Pediatrics' (AAP) Council on Children with Disabilities (Myers & Johnson, 2007). Additional recommendations put forth by the AAP build on such education and support with respect to increasing the child's ability to function independently, maximizing the child's quality of life by minimizing the core features of his or her disability, facilitating the child's development and learning, encouraging socialization, and working toward reduction of behaviors that are maladaptive (Myers & Johnson, 2007). In order to achieve such recommendations, effective collaboration across systems with education, support, and empowerment of parents is of great importance.

As an example of empowering parents through education and support, the HANDS in Autism Interdisciplinary Training and Resource Center (2013) uses the HANDS in Autism *Next Steps* manual and workshop to detail the most salient "next steps" needed after diagnosis and to provide a reference for parents to look to as they navigate their child's care. Within the manual, seven major areas are covered to provide parents and caregivers with information after their child has received a diagnosis, including basic information about ASD; family considerations with respect to how the family system may be affected by the diagnosis; available supports statewide and nationwide to make use of across the child's lifespan; information related to rights and regulations that are in place to protect themselves and their children, including insurance, Medicaid, and other governmental funding; and references and tools to be aware of with regard to the availability and evaluation of interventions and treatments. Last, within the manual and in collaboration contexts, it is essential to provide parents with information regarding "practical strategies that can be applied across the variety of environments and settings that [their] child will be engaged in on a regular basis or will encounter throughout their life" (HANDS in Autism, 2013, p. 5).

INTEGRATING CARE

The integration of care for individuals with ASD and their families requires regular communication and an exchange of ideas. At times, this requires professionals to take the role of student and be willing to listen to and learn from other professionals as well as caregivers to increase the opportunity for effective multidisciplinary intervention efforts. In fact, professionals and all stakeholders need to think of everyone who provides a service to the child as a part of the same team (Vakil & Welton, 2013). Each service provider, educator, specialist, medical professional, and caregiver provides a unique view of the child and needs to be on the same page regarding the child's behaviors, communicative abilities, and functioning level in order to ensure that the type and level of care being provided are consistent across settings. Communication is important not only between the various professionals and caregivers but also between the various disciplines of professionals involved. For example, communication between educators and psychiatrists allows the psychiatrists to have a greater understanding of the child's behaviors while allowing for educators to gain an awareness of changes in medication or other medical issues the child may be dealing with at any point in time (Vakil & Welton, 2013). Such active communication should take place not only during diagnosis but also on an ongoing basis as a child and family adjust to the diagnosis and begin addressing various challenges that may arise.

To illustrate the way integration of care can significantly impact the ability of an interdisciplinary team of professionals to best meet the needs of those on the autism spectrum, consider the following case. A 25-year-old individual with ASD and a long history of anxiety around dental and other medical procedures required general anesthesia in order to be able to undergo even simple medical procedures, including teeth cleaning. Administering the anesthesia required an injection and subsequently several adults' strength to hold the individual down, often resulting in wrestling to sustain grip and administering the injection through the individual's jeans. This struggle to administer the anesthesia was often distressing for all who were involved. Upon the scheduling of a teeth cleaning with an oral surgeon who had previously collaborated with HANDS in Autism, the physician recommended to the family (who had also collaborated previously with HANDS) that HANDS integrate and coordinate care across dentistry, anesthesiology, and the family. In this way, an integrated and coordinated effort served to incorporate all perspectives and components, fostering a sustainable plan that could cultivate increased successes and decreased distress surrounding the process of teeth cleaning in the future. This effort involved preplanning to determine common goals and to outline best practice strategies inclusive of preexposure to the treatment area and staff, development of tools for structure, choice and motivation, as well as video modeling and social narratives for use at home prior to the visit. On the day of the visit, HANDS staff accompanied the individual with ASD to the surgery prep area and supported the culminating acts of a needle stick for anesthesia administration and successful completion of a thorough teeth cleaning. As such, with careful planning, practice, coaching, and mentoring across care providers, family, and the individual, the procedures were successful and were repeated subsequently for an unrelated minor medical procedure a few months later. In this case, when the family contacted HANDS for assistance but learned that HANDS was not available, it opted to go forward with the procedure as planned. The success of this subsequent procedure and those since illustrates the overall successful implementation of interventions once taught and supported through an integrated interdisciplinary approach leading to generalization and success potential of the procedures and the team with progressively increased independence and ease.

INDIVIDUALLY ORIENTED TREATMENT

Regardless of the strategies used across settings, it is essential for professionals to keep in mind that "each intervention needs to be specifically tailored to the individual child for

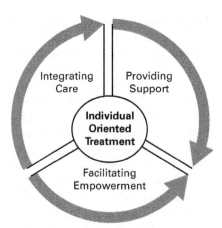

FIGURE 24.2 Components of individual-oriented treatment. This figure illustrates salient components of the collaborative relationship, including the provision of support, facilitation of empowerment, and the integration of care, that allow for individual-oriented treatment.

whom no 'one size fits all' methodology can address" (Swiezy et al., 2008, p. 910). As Figure 24.2 illustrates, the aforementioned provision of support, facilitation of empowerment, and integration of care allow for such individually oriented treatment. The Committee of Educational Interventions for Children with Autism, which was formed by the National Research Council, put forth recommendations that reinforce the need for individually oriented treatment (National Research Council, 2001). Recommendations reflect eligibility for special education services regardless of level of severity or function, as well as support of families through consistent presentation of information by local school systems, ongoing consultation and individualized problem solving, and the opportunity to learn techniques for teaching their children new skills and reducing behavioral problems.

Ongoing measurement of treatment objectives and progress should inform the range of skill areas in which a child may benefit from a particular intervention and that those interventions (educational, behavioral, or other) should always be individualized and adjusted accordingly. Objectives identified for interventions should address observable and measurable behaviors and skills. These objectives should be able to be accomplished within a realistic time period (e.g., 1 year) and be anticipated to affect a child's participation in education, the community, and family life. Services may vary according to a child's chronological age, developmental level, specific strengths and weaknesses, and family needs. However, each child must receive sufficient individualized attention to promote the implementation of objectives with fidelity. Priorities for interventions will include those to address the educational, functional (e.g., communication, social skills, play skills, and independence), and behavioral goals. As further recommended by the National Autism Center (NAC) committee, interventions should include specialized instruction in settings in which ongoing interactions occur with typically developing children and should include coordination across services, systems, and funding at federal and state levels. These efforts should be part of the coordination and collaboration with the already established infrastructure for education, medical and community services, regional resource centers, and technical assistance programs.

When such programming according to best practice and fidelity of implementation is carried out across community systems for a whole child and whole community approach, the practical and very real impact on children and families is positive, pervasive, and far reaching. Communities with this integration and coordination more readily develop the local capacity to best support the consistent use of effective strategies and practices for greatest impact on individual and family potentials. As a case example, HANDS in Autism facilitates community groups called Local Community Cadres (LCCs) composed initially of family, school, and medical representation and eventually encompassing a larger breadth of community participation. As a participant of one of the more vital and active LCCs, a staff psychologist at a local medical center provided an account of a family attending therapy coming to a treatment session one day elated to see some of the visual tools that the psychologist had started incorporating after some training of the LCCs by the HANDS team. As remarked by the enthused parent, she had witnessed the same tools and strategies that the psychologist was using being utilized at the child's school as well. As such, with both the educational and medical system modeling the consistent use of the tools and strategies, the family had consistent models for the process for utilizing the strategies, and the parents were more comfortable and satisfied with the interventions being applied with their child and were more motivated and clear as to how to institute similar strategies at home with fidelity, purpose, and impact on both child and family outcomes.

FOSTERING FAMILY AND PARTNERSHIP CENTEREDNESS

With a focus on educating, supporting, and strengthening family functioning, services and partnerships that focus on family or caregiver needs and strengths foster a positive and proactive rather than deficit-based or categorical approach (Dunst & Deal, 1994). Use of a family-centeredness approach in service delivery ensures services account for family-identified needs, build on family strengths, and work to strengthen social supports. Aligned with the aforementioned need to facilitate empowerment, helping to support families in proactively identifying their needs, mobilizing and connecting them to resources and supports, and setting, monitoring, and accomplishing goals through the identification and strengthening of personal capacities, strengths, and abilities tie together both individualization of care and family centeredness (Dunst, Trivette, Davis, & Cornwall, 1988).

Determination of "where the family is" when beginning or supporting services and treatment rather than solely treating the problem or remediating deficiencies promotes the acquisition of family and individual competencies. If focus is centered on correcting problems without such determination and recognition, results may be limited to short-term resolution of only one presenting concern instead of developing strengths, assets, and skills on behalf of the parent and individual. When such skills are developed, there is increased likelihood that families, caregivers, and individuals will generalize resources and strategies across settings and situations to address a range of presenting challenges at present as well as in the future. Collaborative identification of needs, short- and long-term goals, and immediate and proximal foci for intervention results in more appropriate determination of needed services and supports to facilitate acquisition of skills and commitment to change, resulting in increased treatment adherence and outcomes (Sheridan, Warnes, Cowan, Schemm, & Clarke, 2004).

However, it is important to recognize that family systems represent only one component or system within the entities necessary in coordinated care across systems. Other partners, including, but not limited to, medical providers, mental health professionals, school personnel, community organizations, and advocacy groups, are also contributors within multisystem, coordinated care. Partnership centeredness attends to the need for collaboration, skill acquisition, and strength-based approaches in not only identifying individual needs, strengths, and skills but also building upon the needs and strengths within partnerships to enhance outcomes (Sheridan, Clarke, & Burt, 2008; Sheridan, Eagle, & Dowd, 2005).

Given the necessary components for effective partnerships with families, it is understood that such effectiveness is most readily accomplished when partnering is a fully intentional process. A framework that accommodates this process reflects the relational prerequisites (i.e., approach, attitudes, and atmosphere) to successful collaborative actions (Christenson, 2004) (Figure 24.3). Use of a meaningful approach that accounts for effective communication and shared decision-making, constructive attitudes that begin "where the family is" rather than where providers feel they should or could be, and a positive atmosphere with clearly articulated options for involvement and engagement set the stage for successful implementation of partnership actions and improved outcomes as denoted by the AAP recommendations (Myers & Johnson, 2007).

As a case example of these concepts, impact was realized through interdisciplinary and interagency collaborations to serve the reported and implicit needs of a specific individual and family. Specifically, a family attending therapies at a medical center in an area with an active HANDS/LCC partnership consulted its child's therapist about the family's daughter with ASD. When the therapist, as part of the full medical team, determined the need for an invasive medical procedure, the team had to consider the best course of intervention for the family and child. Although well-versed with the principles and strategies promulgated through HANDS and effectively applied to this individual, the team did not believe that it was best suited to conduct the computed tomography scan at its facility; rather, the recommendation was to visit a partner medical center in a different area of the state. Although the

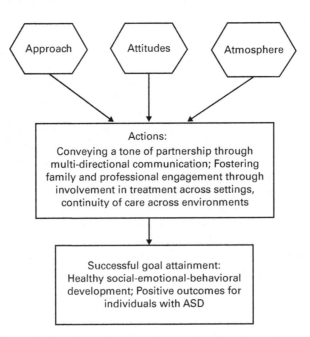

FIGURE 24.3 The four A's. This figure illustrates the way in which the relational prerequisites of approach, attitudes, and atmosphere contribute to the actions of participating stakeholders and ultimately the success of the individual with ASD. *Source: Adapted from* Conjoint Behavioral Consultation: Promoting Family–School Connections and Interventions, 2, *edited by S. M. Sheridan & T. R. Kratochwill, 2007, New York: Springer Science and Business Media.*

family was confident that the staff of the local medical center was effective in utilizing strategies specifically tailored to the child, it concurred that going to a partner medical center where staff was best able to accommodate the needed medical procedures was of highest import. Ultimately, the family opted for the latter and the HANDS team, as the commonality across both medical teams, provided tools and explanation to support the consistent implementation of the intervention successfully despite the new team, new procedure, and new setting. In the end, the procedure was accomplished while accounting for the family's needs, generalizing the use of successful and individualized strategies for the child across settings and providers, and all the while proceeding with minimal stress for staff, family, and child.

COLLABORATION IN PRACTICE

Collaboration while working with individuals with ASD ideally involves families and caretakers, mental health providers, primary care providers, medical subspecialty providers, educators and other school personnel, community organizations, and advocacy groups. An individual's support team may also extend to include employers, residential or group home staff, day program personnel, and other providers or community members. In addition, collaboration with legislators, media, and the public becomes relevant when we move beyond treatment at the individual level to increasing advocacy, awareness, services, and support in relationship to needs related to ASD across the lifespan.

A specific collaboration model is the medical home model. Within this model, specific elements and relationships are detailed that are particularly relevant for psychiatrists and trainees working with children with ASD. Collaboration must occur across all levels and systems, with examples of established and trialed models and practices available to provide guidance in creating programs or developing individual collaborative relationships in practice. Further explanation of the medical home model is detailed next, along with a brief discussion of the other systems involved in the treatment and care of individuals with ASD across their lifetime.

MEDICAL HOME MODEL

The medical home model may be viewed as a broad and overarching model of collaboration. The concept of the medical home was first introduced by the AAP in 1967. In its initial format, the care of children with special health care needs was the primary focus of the medical home concept, although over time the concept has evolved to include all children and adults. Currently, the medical home is a basis for any child's medical and non-medical care and is a cultivated partnership or collaboration between the patient, family, and primary provider in cooperation with specialists and support from the community. According to the AAP (2002), medical home care must be "accessible, continuous, comprehensive, family centered, compassionate, culturally effective, and coordinated with specialized services" (p. 184). In 2007, the AAP joined with the American Academy of Family Physicians, the American College of Physicians, and the American Osteopathic Association to form the Joint Principles of the Patient Centered Medical Home. According to the Joint Principles, a medical home consists of a personal physician, physician-directed medical practice, whole person orientation, coordinated and integrated care, quality and safety, enhanced access to care, and payment for services (Kastner & Walsh, 2012).

Care in a medical home model is associated with improved outcomes with regard to health status, timeliness of care, family centeredness, and family functioning (Homer et al., 2008). Due to the complexities associated with treatment of children with ASD, intuitively, this population benefits from medical home care. Kogan and colleagues (2008) found that medical home care improved health and decreased financial burdens on the family for children with ASD. Golnik, Scal, Wey, and Gaillard (2012) found that ASD-specific medical home intervention resulted in higher satisfaction and shared decision-making, as well as fewer unmet needs, in comparison to controls.

Despite these findings, children with ASD are only half (25% compared to 42%) as likely as children with other special health care needs to have medical care consistent with a medical home model, regardless of condition severity, personal and family characteristics, or insurance status (Brachlow, Ness, McPheeters, & Gurney, 2007). Families of children with ASD are less likely to report that care received was family centered, comprehensive, or coordinated. Families with children with ASD reported 3.39 times more difficulty getting therapeutic services than other children with special health care needs (Montes, Halterman, & Magyar, 2009). In addition, many families of children with ASD remain unfamiliar with the concept of a medical home (Carbone, Behl, Azor, & Murphy, 2010).

Montes et al. (2009) found that parents of children with ASD reported significant difficulty using school and community services (27.6%) and dissatisfaction with services (19.8%). The barriers to obtaining services were reported to be mostly related to challenges in information transfer and communication between health care providers. In a qualitative study by Carbone et al. (2010), parents reported often feeling the need to take on the role of care coordinators themselves and feeling "isolation, anger, frustration, and fatigue in independently identifying, accessing, and financing appropriate services" (p. 320). Half of the families of children with ASD reported that a caregiver had to reduce or stop work because of their child's needs, and more than one-fourth of families spent 10 or more hours per week coordinating care. In the same study, pediatricians reported feeling ill-equipped to meet the needs of families of children with ASD and identified lack of time as a major barrier to the development of expertise and care coordination. Both parents and pediatricians described a need for interdisciplinary models of care (Carbone et al., 2010).

Children with ASD are not the only population for which medical home care is underprovided and underutilized. Strickland, Jones, Ghandour, Kogan, and Newacheck (2011) found significant disparities in receipt of care in medical homes by race, ethnicity, income, as well as health status. Even within the group of children with ASD and other developmental delays, children from immigrant families are more than twice as likely to lack the usual source of care and report physicians not spending enough time with the family (Lin, Yu, & Harwood, 2012). In addition, access to mental health care is universally underserved. In attempts to move toward a medical home, mental health services have worked on increasing accessibility using multiple methods, such as increasing or changing service hours, establishing services within primary care settings, establishing elemental health services, as well as developing innovative consultation services. A major difficulty in implementing the medical home model, particularly in certain populations, is financial viability.

As progress continues to be made toward a medical home model of care for all individuals, it is clear that system-level changes are needed to produce sustainable advancement toward effective community systems of services for families of children in vulnerable populations. Collaboration in advocacy by families, physicians, other health care providers, educators, and community groups is and will continue to be an important piece in driving these changes.

COLLABORATION ACROSS SYSTEMS

Parents and caregivers should be collaborative partners during all phases of planning, implementation, and evaluation of approaches, services, and treatments. The relationship between caregivers and medical professionals should be that of a partnership. In such collaboration, "a partner is a person that one works with in order to achieve a common goal through shared decision-making and risk-taking" (Kalyva, 2013, p. 521). Given that parents and health professionals have their own unique needs, concerns, priorities, and responsibilities within their partnership, a supportive relationship is essential to their communication of realistic goals (Kalyva, 2013).

A study by Kelly and Tincani (2013) found that a majority of behavioral professionals had little or no formal training in the area of collaboration and would have appreciated models to follow. This study also found that current "collaboration" among practicing behavior analysts and nonbehavioral professionals is mostly a unidirectional, didactic process imposed from professional to the lay caregiver. However, many of the state-of-the-art evidence-based practices or services recommended in the treatment of individuals with ASD stress the importance of parental participation in the process. Comprehensive practices evolving from applied behavior analysis, such as the Treatment and Education of Autistic and Related Communication Handicapped Children (TEACCH) and the HANDS in Autism model, emphasize the significance of collaboration with parents or caregivers (Lovaas, 1987; Schopler, Mesibov, & Hearsey, 1995; Swiezy et al., 2006). Additional emphasis regarding collaboration across multiple systems is a significant focus and overarching premise of the HANDS in Autism model for which additional details are provided next.

The HANDS in Autism model is integrative of a number of the aforementioned elements and is novel in its approach, with specific alignment to the following core beliefs:

1. *Strength based:* A focus on building strengths and successes of individuals with an emphasis on proactive planning and teaching practical skills (Iovannone, Dunlap, Huber, & Kincaid, 2003; National Research Council (NRC), 2001)
2. *Collaborative:* Delivery across community stakeholders for consistency, coordination, and positive collaboration for individuals with disabilities (Baker et al., 2005; Swiezy et al., 2008)
3. *Data-driven:* A relationship to data-driven decision-making practices across all settings to affect best outcomes through systematic planning and individualization of efforts (Iovannone et al., 2003; NRC, 2001)
4. *Scientifically based:* A basis from current research in special education, psychology, and related fields with relevance to ASD and other developmental disabilities and a focus on the practical and effective blending of scientifically based strategies (Horner, Carr, Strain, Todd, & Reed, 2002; NAC, 2009; Odom et al., 2003)
5. *Interactive:* An incorporation of implementation and systems training research that indicate the need to appeal to varied learning styles (Fixsen, Naoom, Blase, Friedman, & Wallace, 2005) and the need for more interactive strategies to ensure usage in naturalistic settings (Joyce & Showers, 2002)

6. *Practical and accessible:* Delivery through accessible materials, training, technology, and consultative staff in efforts to decrease barriers, increase support, and improve implementation and utilization of the strategies taught

7. *Process-driven:* An infusion with a fluid and integrated process for effectively educating all individuals by incorporating data-driven strategies, research-based methods, and collaboration and individualized needs to develop effective programming (Iovannone et al., 2003; Kazdin, 2001; NRC, 2001)

The curriculum inherent within the HANDS in Autism model highlights core elements noted for effective practices with focus on "individualized supports and services, systematic instruction, comprehensive and structured learning environments, specific curriculum content, [and a] functional approach to problem behavior and family involvement" (Yell, Drasgow, & Lowrey, 2005) (p. 136, Table 2) (Figure 24.4).

The literature details the evidence-based interventions and practices that are found to be effective strategies and supports for the treatment of individuals with ASD. However, for these practices to be effectively implemented with fidelity to increase the opportunities for success, educators, families, and medical practitioners must understand not only the

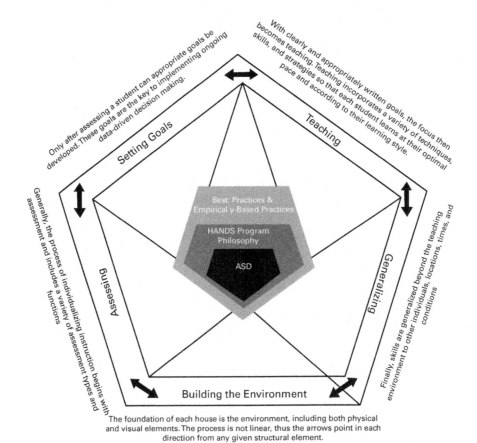

The foundation of each house is the environment, including both physical and visual elements. The process is not linear, thus the arrows point in each direction from any given structural element.

FIGURE 24.4 HANDS in Autism Model: The HOUSE curriculum. This figure illustrates the HANDS in Autism Model, detailing the core components believed to be of greatest importance for the treatment of individuals with ASD, including collaboration.

logistics of the standardized application but also that to be truly effective, interdisciplinary collaboration must occur. Strategies and practices without collaborative efforts cannot be as widely implemented across settings and lack consistency, thus hindering the opportunity for successful generalization of skills and concepts and a shared understanding of goals. However, when collaborative efforts are intentional and made with the aforementioned components in mind, the success and goal attainment that can be achieved are significant.

SUMMARY

Collaborative efforts between medical professionals, parents and other caregivers of individuals with ASD, and community members are essential for the delivery of quality care and programming across settings. In the previous sections, the meaning, purpose, and components of collaboration, as well as models of collaboration that have been shown to be effective, were discussed. Ultimately, a collaborative approach with shared decision-making between professionals and consumers leads to improved outcomes, as well as increased success for individuals with ASD and their families.

KEY POINTS

- ASD includes a wide range of individuals with some commonalities but many differences.
- Individualization is a key aspect to successful treatment planning and management.
- Parents are the experts on their children.
- It is important to empower families with education/knowledge and integrated supports.
- Communities must take shared responsibility for the successful outcomes of individuals with ASD and their families.

DISCLOSURE STATEMENT

Dr. Naomi Swiezy, Dr. Tiffany Neal, Danielle Warner, and Dr. Kimberly Lo have nothing to disclose.

REFERENCES

American Academy of Pediatrics. (2002). The medical home. *Pediatrics, 110*(1), 184–186.

Appleton, P. L., & Minchom, P. E. (1991). Models of parent partnership and child development centres. *Child Care Health Development, 17*(1), 27–38.

Baker, S., Bauman, M., Bishop, M., et al. (2005). Autism spectrum disorders roadmap. Washington, DC: National Institute of Mental Health.

Brachlow, A. E., Ness, K. K., McPheeters, M. L., & Gurney, J. G. (2007). Comparison of indicators for a primary care medical home between children with autism or asthma and other special health care needs. *Archives of Pediatric and Adolescent Medicine, 161*, 399–405.

Brogan, C. A., & Knussen, C. (2003). The disclosure of a diagnosis of an autistic spectrum disorder: Determinants of satisfaction in a sample of Scottish parents. *Autism, 7*(1), 31–46. doi:10.1177/1362361303007001004

Brookman-Frazee, L., & Koegel, R. L. (2004). Using parent/clinician partnerships in parent education pro-grams for children with autism. *Journal of Positive Behavioral Interventions, 6*(4), 195–213. doi:10.1177/10983007040060040201

Carbone, P. S., Behl, D. D., Azor, V., & Murphy, N. A. (2010). The medical home for children with autism spectrum disorders: Parent and pediatrician perspectives. *Journal of Autism and Developmental Disorders, 40,* 317–324. doi:10.1007/s10803-009-0874-5

Christenson, S. L. (2004). The family–school partnership: An opportunity to promote the learning compe-tence of all students. *School Psychology Review, 33,* 83–104.

Cunningham, C., & Davis, H. (1985). *Working with parents: Frameworks for collaboration.* Milton Keynes, England: Open University Press.

Dunst, C., & Deal, A. (1994). A family-centered approach to developing individualized family support plans. In C. Dunst, C. Tirvette, & A. Deal (Eds.), *Supporting and strengthening families: Vol. 1. Methods, strategies, and practices* (pp. 73–89). Cambridge, MA: Brookline.

Dunst, C. J., Trivette, C. M., Davis, M., & Cornwall, J. (1988). Enabling and empowering families of children with health impairments. *Children's Health Care, 17,* 71–81.

Elder, J. (2013). Empowering families in the treatment of autism. In M. Fitzgerald (Ed.), *Recent advances in autism spectrum disorders* (Vol. 1). Rijeka, Croatia: InTech, 503–520.

Ellis, C. R., Lutz, R. E., Schaefer, G. B., & Woods, K. E. (2007). Physician collaboration involving students with autism spectrum disorder. *Psychology in the Schools, 44*(7), 737–747. doi:10.1002/pits.20262

Fixsen, D. L., Naoom, S. F., Blase, K. A., Friedman, R. M., & Wallace, F. (2005). *Implementation research: A syn-thesis of the literature* (FMHI Publication 231). Tampa, FL: University of South Florida, Louis de la Parte Florida Mental Health Institute, The National Implementation Research Network.

Fletcher, P. C., Markoulakis, R., & Bryden, P. J. (2012). The costs of caring for a child with an autism spec-trum disorder. *Issues in Comprehensive Pediatric Nursing, 35,* 45–69. doi:10.3109/01460862.2012.645407

Golnik, A., Scal, P., Wey, A., & Gaillard, P. (2012). Autism-specific primary care medical home intervention. *Journal of Autism and Developmental Disorders, 42*(6), 1087–1093. doi:10.1007/s10803-011-1351-5

HANDS in Autism Interdisciplinary Training and Resource Center. (2013). *Next steps manual: Family guide to autism spectrum disorders.* Unpublished manuscript, Department of Psychiatry, Indiana University School of Medicine, Indianapolis, IN.

Homer, C. J., Klatka, K., Romm, D., Khlthau, K., Bloom, S., Newacheck, P., et al. (2008). A review of the evidence for the medical home for children with special health care needs. *Pediatrics, 122,* e922–e938. doi:10.1542/peds.2007-3762

Horner, R., Carr, E., Strain, P. S., Todd, A., & Reed, H. (2002). Problem behavior interventions for young children with autism: A research synthesis. *Journal of Autism and Developmental Disorders, 32,* 423–446.

Individuals With Disabilities Education Act, 20 U.S.C. § 1400 (2004).

Iovannone, R., Dunlap, G., Huber, H., & Kincaid, D. (2003). Effective educational practices for students with autism spectrum disorders. *Focus on Autism and Other Developmental Disabilities, 18*(3), 150–166.

Joyce, B., & Showers, B. (2002). *Student achievement through staff development* (3rd ed.). Alexandria, VA: Association for Supervision and Curriculum Development.

Kalyva, E. (2013). Collaboration between parents of children with autism spectrum disorders and mental health professionals. In M. Fitzgerald (Ed.), *Recent advances in autism spectrum disorders* (Vol. 1). Rijeka, Croatia: InTech, 521–563.

Kastner, T. A., & Walsh, K. K. (2012). Health care for individuals with intellectual and developmental dis-abilities: An integrated DD health home model. In R. M. Hodapp (Ed.), *International review of research in developmental disabilities* (pp. 2–40). Amsterdam: Academic Press.

Kazdin, A. E. (2001). Bridging the enormous gaps of theory with therapy research and practice. *Journal of Clinical Child Psychology, 30,* 59–66.

Kelly, A., & Tincani, M. (2013). Collaborative training and practice among applied behavior analysts who support individuals with autism spectrum disorder. *Education and Training in Autism and Developmental Disabilities, 48*(1), 120–131.

Kogan, M. D., Strickland, B. B., Blumberg, S. J., Singh, G. K., Perrin, J. M., & van Dyck, P. C. (2008). A national profile of the health care experiences and family impact of autism spectrum disorder among children in the United States, 2005–2006. *Pediatrics, 122*(6), 1149–1158. doi:10.1542/peds.2008-1057

Lin, S. C., Yu, S. M., & Harwood, R. L. (2012). Autism spectrum disorders and developmental disabilities in children from immigrant families in the United States. *Pediatrics, 130,* S191–S197. doi:10.1542/peds.2012-0900R

Lovaas, O. I. (1987). Behavioral treatment and normal educational and intellectual functioning in young autistic children. *Journal of Consulting and Clinical Psychology, 55,* 3–9.

Mittler, P., & Mittler, H. (1983). The transitional relationship. In P. Mittler & H. McConachie (Eds.), *Parents, professionals, and mentally handicapped people: Approaches to partnership* (pp. 221–240). London, England: Croom Helm.

Montes, G., Halterman, J. S., & Magyar, C. I. (2009). Access to and satisfaction with school and community health services for US children with ASD. *Pediatrics, 124,* 407–413. doi:10.1542/peds.2009-1255L

Myers, S. M., & Johnson, C. P. (2007). Management of children with autism spectrum disorders. *Pediatrics, 120*(5), 1162–1182. doi:10.1542/peds.2007-2362

National Autism Center. (2009). *National Standards Project—Addressing the need for evidence based practice guidelines for autism spectrum disorders.* Randolph, MA: Author.

National Research Council. (2001). *Educating children with autism.* Washington, DC: National Academies Press.

Odom, S. L., Brown, W. H., Frey, T., Karasu, N., Smith-Carter, L., & Strain, P. (2003). Evidence-based practices for young children with autism: Evidence from single-subject research design. *Focus on Autism and Other Developmental Disabilities, 18,* 176–181.

Osborne, L. A., & Reed, P. (2008). Parents' perceptions of communication with professionals during the diagnosis of autism. *Autism, 12*(3), 309–324. doi:10.1177/1362361307089517

Schopler, E., Mesibov, G. B., & Hearsey, K. (1995). *Learning and cognition in autism.* New York: Plenum.

Sheridan, S. M., Clarke, B. L., & Burt, J. D. (2008). Conjoint behavioral consultation: What do we know and what do we need to know? In W. P. Erchul & S. M. Sheridan (Eds.), *Handbook of research in school consultation: Empirical foundations for the field* (pp. 171–202). Mahwah, NJ: Erlbaum.

Sheridan, S. M., Eagle, J. W., & Dowd, S. E. (2005). Families as contexts for children's adaptation. In S. Goldstein & R. Brooks (Eds.), *Handbook of resiliency in children* (pp. 165–180). New York, NY: Springer.

Sheridan, S. M., & Kratochwill, T. R. (2007). *Conjoint behavioral consultation: Promoting family–school connections and interventions* (2nd ed.). New York: Springer.

Sheridan, S. M., & Steck, M. C. (1995). Acceptability of conjoint behavioral consultation: A national survey of school psychologists. *School Psychology Review, 24*(4), 633.

Sheridan, S. M., Warnes, E. D., Cowan, R. J., Schemm, A., & Clarke, B. L. (2004). Family-centered positive psychology: Focusing on strengths to build student success. *Psychology in the Schools, 41,* 7–17.

Stahmer, A. C., Brookman-Frazee, L., Lee, E., Searcy, K., & Reed, S. (2011). Parent and multidisciplinary provider perspectives on earliest intervention for children at risk for autism spectrum disorders. *Infants & Young Children, 24*(4), 344–363. doi:10.1097/IYC.0b013e31822cf700

Strickland, B. B., Jones, J. R., Ghandour, R. M., Kogan, M. D., & Newacheck, P. W. (2011). The medical home: Health care access and impact for children and youth in the United States. *Pediatrics, 127,* 604–611. doi:10.1542/peds.2009-3555

Swiezy, N., Stuart, M., & Korzekwa, P. (2008). Bridging for success in autism: Training and collaboration across medical, educational, and community systems. *Child and Adolescent Psychiatric Clinics of North America, 17*(4), 907–922.

Swiezy, N. B., Grothe, M., Maynard, M. L., Korzekwa, P., Pozdol, S., Anderson, P., Hume, K., et al. (May 2006). *Helping answer needs by developing specialists in autism: Program development.* Poster presented at the 2006 Association for Behavior Analysis convention, Atlanta, GA.

Vakil, S., & Welton, E. (2013). Autism spectrum disorders: The collaborative roles of the psychiatrists, educators and parents. *Open Journal of Psychiatry, 3*(2), 1–4. doi:10.4236/ojpsych.2013.32A001

Wahler, R. G., & Fox, J. J. (1981). Setting events in applied behavior analysis: Toward a conceptual and methodological expansion. *Journal of Applied Behavior Analysis, 14*(3), 327–338. doi:10.1901/jaba.1981.14-327

Yell, M. L., Drasgow, E., & Lowrey, K. A. (2005). No Child Left Behind and students with autism spectrum disorders. *Focus on Autism and Other Developmental Disabilities, 20*(3), 130–139.

/// 25 /// AUTISM SPECTRUM DISORDER FROM A FAMILY PERSPECTIVE

NANCY LURIE MARKS, CATHY LURIE, AND CLARENCE E. SCHUTT

INTRODUCTION

It is often said that when one meets one person with autism spectrum disorder (ASD), one has simply met one person with ASD. This disarmingly simple statement, wrought with meaning, conveys what is known not only from decades of clinical observation but also from the revelations of the many studies underway to understand the genetics and systems biology of ASD. Perhaps the same is true with families, and even within a family, where each member sees ASD through the prism of one person, and each family presents a unique challenge to the medical profession. Certainly the viewpoint of a parent raising a child is far different from that of a sibling, and each family constellation poses different challenges.

Many families are torn apart as parents struggle with one income, diminished career expectations, loss of intimacy, and social isolation (Smith et al., 2010). If asked for one word to describe their lives, the answer is invariably "stressful" (Barker et al., 2011), often followed by fears of "what happens when we are gone?" However, remarkably, while bravely accepting their situation and often finding extreme ways to adapt—moving to another state to find services, taking on part-time work to pay for early intervention, developing therapies on their own, and giving up vacations—the majority of family members show great resiliency and creativity in seeking ways to channel their talents and abilities to create better lives for their own as well as others with ASD.

The family perspective presented here is based on experiences over many years during which the authors have had the privilege of living with, meeting, and hearing from many individuals with ASD, their families, and numerous dedicated professionals, clinicians, and researchers. The purpose of this chapter is to offer medical practitioners new to the field a way to appreciate how profoundly ASD impacts the rhythms and patterns of family life.

THE PHYSICIAN AND THE FAMILY

The great range of behaviors and medical issues associated with ASD presents a challenge for the physician meeting with the family of a person with ASD for the first time. However, as with every medical encounter, a physician, trained over many years in the practice of close clinical examination, chooses what information to privilege, a subtle aspect of the doctor's art, and the choice of frames into which to formulate a treatment plan.

Parents arrive at an examination ready to give detailed reports on eating behavior; seizures; gastrointestinal complaints; self-injurious and other-directed scratching, biting, and pinching; as well as obsessions with all manner of systems and structures. Self-injurious behavior is not uncommon: It includes hand biting, head banging, and face scratching as well as other unusual and incomprehensible behaviors, such as spinning, hand flapping, and bouncing. Parents are wondering what they might have done to bring this ASD on—something in their diet during pregnancy, or a stressful event, obstetric complication, or a family history of psychiatric illness—and they are hopeful that the physician has some answers.

Each individual case may appear to fit the broad definition of ASD in terms of deficits in social communication, and obsessive and repetitive behaviors, that the doctor has undoubtedly encountered in the medical literature or from the *Diagnostic and Statistical Manual of Mental Disorders*, fifth edition (American Psychiatric Association, 2013). But parents entertain a hope that their individual experiences might offer important clues leading to a more physiological or neurological explanation for the obvious distress their child is feeling, and often with no means, other than "aggressive behavior," to communicate where it is coming from. During the examination, the person with ASD may have little or no speech or may be highly talkative; he or she might be hyperkinetic—biting a wrist, flapping hands, spinning about, shrieking, and exhibiting various tics—or might just sit quietly staring off into middle space.

Fortunately, physicians are now in a position to give a more informed response to families in the examination room. This is because it is becoming accepted that ASD in most cases is caused by some event during development that may have affected the nervous, endocrine, or immune systems and their mutual interactions. As a result of these scientific advances, it is becoming more common for teams of medical professionals to make the first diagnosis of ASD and to set the agenda for integrated treatment and care.

Nevertheless, it is not a simple matter to connect the possibility that someone's synaptic machinery may be leaky, one explanation for ASD based on genetic findings, to the behavior of the person in the office who is darting to the cupboard to liberate bandages, surgical gloves, and syringes from their sterile wrappings or to another person sitting calmly, perhaps silently, observing with subtle sideways glances the events around him or her. For the physician, fashionable ideas about ASD from the neurocognitive sciences, such as the notion that these individuals lack "a theory of mind" or that they have strong local brain connectivity but weak global or "central" coherence, seem to lose relevance and serve up little in the way of wisdom that can be imparted to the anxious family member sitting opposite, or even to help structure the information the family brings. It would behoove a physician treating this population to become acquainted with the full range of treatments and remedies that a family might be considering, as well as to develop some sensitivity to the idea that ASD is not only about the brain (Herbert & Weintraub, 2013).

There was a time when it was common for doctors to assume that poor parenting caused ASD and to recommend that the parents see a psychiatrist. In that era, ASD, if viewed at all, was seen by experts as a psychiatric disorder, and the child was viewed as being lost in his or her own world, "choosing" isolation where, in reality, the child might be working hard to free him- or herself from it. These views still persist, having migrated to other forms of ostracism and insulting, sometimes abusive, treatment by those who have no comprehension of ASD, adding to the anxiety and stress on family members. Recently, more attention is being paid to treating primary caregivers with "mindfulness" training and other forms of relaxation therapy. It is reported in a study from Vanderbilt University that mothers of individuals with neurodevelopmental disorders have significantly elevated levels of stress and clinical depression (Dykens, Fisher, Taylor, & Miodrag, 2014).

PERSONAL NARRATIVES

A good way for physicians to educate themselves about the impact of ASD on families is to read parent narratives (Greenfeld, 1970; Iversen, 2007; Parks, 1982), often written by professional writers (Savarese, 2007) or academics (Grinker, 2007). Although each describes unique and unforgettable scenes from everyday life, they share a nearly universal expression of love, commitment, and fear for the future beyond their own lives, reflecting the reality that ASD is a lifelong condition, not a lifespan-limiting disease. A theme running through many of these stories is the questioning of the assumptions behind the facile classification of persons with ASD as "low-functioning" and "high-functioning," as if human beings are appliances that break down in the workplace and are not covered by a warranty. A careful reading of these books is probably the best introduction a young physician can have to the full range of devastation and adaptation experienced by a family.

Parents of children with ASD, already stressed emotionally and financially, are also beset by worries about the future of their child, a long adulthood and perhaps an old age without the emotional anchorage provided by their parents during their middle age. A valuable lesson to be shared with young parents is that some things do get better, especially after adolescence, as individuals with ASD develop an understanding of the world and achieve, in some cases, greater calmness and self-sufficiency in personal care and choice-making in daily life. Parents will be concerned about how to help their growing adults form friendships; safely learn about their sexuality and potential desire for intimacy; and deal with normative human experiences of loneliness, loss, and rejection.

It is important to realize that a person with ASD is not a closed book but, rather, capable of growth and change in many dimensions like the rest of us. Many adults with ASD, and not only those more recognizably labeled as "savants," engage in the visual and musical arts, poetry, and writing—sometimes producing work of commercial value, but always with a sense of self-satisfaction and accomplishment. A few pioneers have gone on to college, with some earning degrees and some with aims to be advocates for others with ASD. One may see adults working today in supermarkets, warehouses, and local businesses; in libraries; and even in the computer and technology sectors, where their spatial and systems recognition abilities may hold special value.

We know a little about the internal world(s) of persons labeled autistic from the writings of Donna Williams (1992, 1994, 1996), Temple Grandin (1995), Tito Mukhopadhyay (2000), Naoki Higashida (2013), and others. Reading these four narratives should be enough to convince anyone that the human brain, fed by the senses, moved by the emotions, and experiencing muscular activity, can produce a staggering range of metaphors, artistic creations, and insights, even though it may be connected to a somewhat uncooperative body. Yet, many somehow see fit to attribute internal states to the outward appearances of behaviors and difficulties and to interpret severe problems in communication and social behaviors, or apparent misunderstanding, as a lack of interest in, or a paucity of emotional feeling for, others.

It is difficult to ignore the surface appearances and behavioral manifestations of ASD to get to the feeling, thinking person beneath, but confusing these outward signs and impairments with definitive conclusions about affection, motivation, and capacity is a mistake. Inevitably, the result is to dehumanize the person with ASD, adding a veil of isolation to the person's already isolating difficulties.

One attempt to redefine ASD (Markram & Markram, 2010), by neuroscientists who are parents of an individual with ASD, posits that each person with ASD inhabits a unique, but almost unbearably intense, world in which each sensation or memory contributes to conscious thought with a weight, influence, or affinity outside what is considered normal. This causes one to wonder why anyone should be valued simply by how they fit into our everyday world of consumption, constant electronic bombardment, and frenetic movement when the novel combinations formed in isolated human minds, given means of expression, can give rise to delight, invention, and insight into what we all are or could be.

Increasingly, individuals with ASD are playing more active roles in planning their lives and defining their interests. As they become confident in creating new avenues for themselves, they begin to engage more in their own communities. These efforts are leading to an increase in activities for both young and old in sports (e.g., skiing, bowling, golf, and swimming), theater-going (including relaxed performance opportunities), hobbies (crafts, gardening, computers, yoga, and cooking), and interests in continuing education or participation in their religious or social communities.

A meaningful life need not be one of only working for a living, not always possible, or of achieving professional success but, rather, of having projects and involvement that offer opportunities for self-expression and participation in their communities.

THE CENTRAL IMPORTANCE OF COMMUNICATION

Opening any door to communication can change the life of the 30% of those with ASD who lack speech or have only minimally verbal means of expression. Throughout the 1960s, 1970s, and 1980s, there was very little expectation placed on these persons, and little in the way of hope—even the use of sign language was discouraged because it was thought to offer an easy way out of learning to speak. Today, we are learning much from the experiences of those who, either as children or as adults, have been taught new ways and methods to access communication through technologies such as computers, voice output devices, structured interfaces, and haptic anticipation. This may take years of hard work to accomplish, but it is of immense importance to family members who hope (and often awake from sleep with this dream fresh) to one day hear their silenced child or sibling express thoughts, feelings, and personality. New interests, educational opportunities, and relationships with others will evolve, opening up a world for that person and the lives of those around him or her.

Perhaps, with the means to express themselves for the first time, these individuals can explain where they feel pain to a doctor or describe aspects of their ASD such as noise sensitivities, or problems with certain clothing, or how their outward appearance may or may not match what they feel is going on inside them. Indeed, some clinicians (Robinson, 2011) conduct examinations in situations in which augmentative communications are encouraged and used as the patient types answers to questions posed by the doctor.

They may be treated for the first time in life as a "you" rather than spoken about in the third person, or over their heads, in their presence, as if they are not there; all the while, they may be listening and taking in the conversations, whether distortedly or clearly, even if their appearance may be distracted and nontypical. Achieving communication does not mean that the individual is no longer autistic by any means, but it does diminish the possibility that it is not ASD alone that defines him or her as a person. This view is strengthened by the growing literature produced by writers with ASD, once classified as "low-functioning" and "retarded" (Biklen et al., 2005). Some professionals will acknowledge, if not publicly then privately, that the old assessments of intelligence are, or at least may be, mistaken; that testing methods are inadequate for those who poorly respond to tests or who cannot speak; and that the capacities and potentials of those with ASD may be often quite underestimated.

It is to be hoped that every school, clinic, doctor, or family involved in the life of an individual with ASD endeavor to solve this often central predicament for each and every child or adult in their lifetimes, whether through augmentative and alternative communication approaches or others. Technology holds the promise to deliver better means to enable communication and meet the challenge of unlocking the doors to the inner person. Although someday research will uncover the internal biological and systemic processes that interfere with the ability to communicate, and offer interventions or solutions at the source, there remain, in the meantime, lives that are being intensely lived, and the possibility of redirecting real-life trajectories sooner rather than later. By not acting, lives are being circumscribed and consigned to an isolation and loneliness few of us can imagine enduring, even if surrounded by the most caring people.

SIBLING PERSPECTIVES

Although parent narratives, and increasingly self-reports from individuals with ASD, appear regularly, the stories and experiences of siblings are less rarely seen. A notable exception (Greenfeld, 2009), by the brother of Noah, whose story and his family's adaptive reaction were so movingly told by his father (Greenfeld, 1970) a generation ago, powerfully chronicles his and his brother's transition to adulthood. Siblings who are close in age, such as Jonah and Karl, bring a very different perspective on ASD than a parent or an older sibling.

Young children, unlike parents, enter a world with no a priori expectation that the newborn or young child is anything but "normal." They gradually come to realize that their sibling acts significantly different from themselves and their peers. A young sibling grows and experiences life with an autistic brother or sister, like any other family, first with all the joy and pleasure of playful growth and shared learning and then with love and affection, and the creation of private worlds. Gradually, awareness that something might be different, but not "wrong," with their sibling appears, and they find themselves adapting inexorably, somewhat confusedly, and not always smoothly.

Young siblings today may be exposed earlier to what is happening as early diagnosis, specialized interventions, and altered household routines, such as the machinery of applied behavioral analysis, descend and family tensions increase (Orsmond & Seltzer, 2009). Autism spectrum disorder was once a term rarely heard, unlike today when it is often in the media and public mind, as well as firmly situated within a growing body, even enterprise, of professional approaches and research. At one point, children if asked about their own siblings were told to say "he is autistic," and often heard back, "Oh, he is artistic, how nice!" This had to be disconcerting for a young person beginning to engage the social world outside of the home. Later, ASD came to be called "retarded" or "emotionally disturbed." What was not appreciated in those times was that siblings may have lacked a framework to understand what those odd words meant and were unable to grasp fully the derogatory or sometimes sinister import of these labels, resulting in an uncomfortable, gnawing, realization that something is not right with the little person growing next to them.

The sibling may bring no notion of disability, judgments, prejudices, deficits, or any notions whatsoever of ASD or anything else; it is simply one's own brother or sister—a very real person both alike and different than oneself, endowed with all the intriguing, delightful, messy, irritating, and curious facts of personhood, even if he or she may well express him- or herself differently, as becomes more apparent over time. There can be a window of acceptance and relatedness, which one later learns is not necessarily the window the larger world has. Unencumbered by the responsibilities and worries of a parent, the child may find natural ways to relate to his or her sibling. In many cases, it is through activities enjoyed by both, whether through song, music, dancing, swimming, or other novel ways and games. This childhood oasis of ignorance can, in a sense, be a blessing. Strong childhood bonds are formed, even if they appear atypical compared to bonds with other peers.

But the outside world intrudes and forces upon a sibling what may be the most troubling aspect of all in growing up with ASD in the form of bullying, teasing, and taunting of a sibling because of the unusual sounds they make, things they say, or their preoccupations, generating an early stance of protectiveness. These episodes are not lost on the child with ASD, and they fall back on their brother or sister for comfort and understanding, even if it is not apparent. Adult siblings today report incidences of bullying or outright prejudice and intolerance from adults, sometimes on hospital wards, but most often in supermarkets, malls, and convenience stores. This is relatively new because ASD was once pretty invisible and the spectrum very much more narrowly defined; there were no special education mandates, and children with ASD were usually rarely seen or included in social gatherings, religious institutions, community life, and in family celebrations of weddings or religious holidays. Adults with ASD were a complete absence, perhaps hidden away or institutionalized, with visits from aged parents and siblings, portrayed with great impact in the movie "Rain Man" (Johnson & Levinson, 1988).

Despite all the positive changes that have occurred socially today, it would be helpful for parents (and professionals counseling them) to find good explanations and language, geared to a child's age and maturation, to help a "typically" developing sibling not only understand more about his or her brother or sister with ASD but also offer the sibling a way to explain to his or her friends, who may be curious or fearful about the child with ASD, what is going on. It is essential, however, to shape these explanations in terms that give the child an opportunity to relate (and help others relate) to his or her sibling rather than teaching the child to diminish the value of his or her sibling due to differences or difficulties. This can be a tall order in a society in which a person with ASD is more generally seen as alien, an outsider or less than fully human, even though that too is changing (Murray, 2008).

As one grows into adulthood, there can be a push–pull between the personal need to move beyond the family—entering into a more independent existence, going off to college, starting a career, or getting married—and the needs of the grownup sibling with ASD, which require ongoing strong family focus and involvement. Some siblings have spoken of feeling of guilt as they move on and out into life arenas their sibling did not enter. These are complicated emotions, involving feelings of leaving the parents to deal alone with issues at home but also the pain of separating from one so loved and so close. Some siblings feel the necessity of appraising future life mates, in part, in terms of how they relate to the sibling with ASD, knowing this relationship is both a valued part of life and one that the future mate would share in. As parents grow old and die, siblings often take on the role of supporting or navigating life planning for their maturing brother or sister with ASD, often putting stress on their own resources, both emotional and financial.

THE FAMILY AND THE SYSTEM

The physician treating a person with ASD will, of course, be well aware of the import of an ASD diagnosis, including the insurance and reimbursement practices in the community and state in which they practice. But what happens for the parents post diagnosis? What else in their lives demands attention beyond what the medical profession can give?

Many feel they are stepping off of a cliff, with few clear supports in place to help navigate the world with and for their child. First and foremost, they must figure out how to care for their child, often at home and with few extra resources to help in this care. They must learn about and engage in negotiations for appropriate therapies and interventions and determine how to pay for them after insurance coverage ends. The search for an appropriate school placement can be daunting, at times involving battles with administrators and teachers to secure a good educational setting. Extended family and social circles may or may not provide a welcoming atmosphere for the family with a child with ASD. Holiday celebrations and other family events (e.g., weddings, birthdays, and graduations) can be especially stressful.

Preparing for young adulthood, a time when educational benefits and supports end, requires extensive planning for employment training and exploring of options. Securing a residential placement or working out how to live at home well into middle age is a major concern. Arranging for ongoing supports and services for their family member often puts them into confrontational and contentious situations with social service systems and case workers who barely know the person with ASD. The tasks of financial planning and the securing of government benefits in those situations in which the autistic adult may not be self-supporting can be a full-time job unto itself. All the while parents must worry about who will care about and advocate for their young adult when they grow old or pass away. Siblings, if they exist, may or may not be able to provide continuity of support and emotional care as the parents have done, and themselves must carry on with life planning needs as they unfold, often with no professional or other network of support. Finally, all must think about the aging adult and what kinds of living, medical, and social supports should and will be in place when the immediate family may not be around.

FAMILIES RISING

These life challenges can be met with resiliency, compassion, and, often, an ethic and value placed on caring, empathy, and open-mindedness to the differences, vulnerabilities, and capacities of others with significant challenges, not just those with ASD. As in many aspects of life, sometimes seemingly difficult or nontypical experiences thrust in one's way prove to be instructive in surprisingly positive ways. This "silver lining" in no way diminishes the pain, uncertainty, and doubt experienced by the family, nor does it alleviate the sometimes difficult emotional and practical problems with which the family members grapple and that often cannot be shared with peers who have no such life experiences.

Parents, families, individuals with ASD, and the diverse networks they form can be a great inspiration and often driving forces in pushing the envelope for what is possible in the world of ASD, whether opening up new scientific directions, paving the way for new medical treatments and educational therapies, or in the social realm in terms of searching for new life options. Families often do not give up on the potentials that may unfold in a person's life, nor take as final or determinative "expert" pronouncements as to future capacities and growth in their own lives, and they often seek to drive progress in their communities or in public advocacy. Of course, they do not necessarily see eye to eye on what form this progress should take because there is no one path applicable to all, and professionals should take heed and even embrace the open-mindedness of the families in their quest for a better life. A recent gripping account of human nature and variation situates ASD in the context of the disability movement and presents a comprehensive picture of what families face and how they are coping (Solomon, 2012).

SUMMARY

Over many years and many encounters, whether with families, those with ASD, or professionals, the authors have encountered multiple views of ASD as a concept, with some viewing it as a tragedy in need of cure and elimination; others perceiving ASD as a scientific, medical, or societal challenge; many seeing ASD as containing talents to be discovered and nurtured in the face of real and tough obstacles; some who value their ASD and have no wish to exchange it (or only parts of it) for another place in the world; those who see the "neurotypical world" as in need of change; and any number of variations in a wide arc of vantage points. As our understanding of ASD unfolds, this arc will no doubt shift and broaden with much to teach us all about our common human family.

KEY POINTS

- Parents often wonder what they might have done or how the environment might have caused ASD in their child. They are hopeful that the physician has some answers. As a result of recent scientific advances, it is becoming more common for teams of medical professionals to make the first diagnosis of ASD and to set the agenda for integrated treatment and care.
- A good way for physicians to educate themselves about the impact of ASD on families is to read parent accounts and personal narratives by individuals with ASD. These books are probably the best introduction a young physician can have to the full range of devastation and adaptation experienced by a family.
- The most pressing, central, and frustrating aspect of ASD is the difficulty of communicating. This has a profound effect on the family, especially for siblings, who construct a social consciousness for themselves that might be without parallel among their peers.
- Parents need to determine appropriate therapies and interventions, supports and services, and educational settings, as well as meet financial challenges related to residential planning for adulthood and prepare for a time when the immediate family may not be around.
- Families confronting ASD show great resiliency in adapting to the realities they face in providing a home environment, seeking schooling, employment, recreation, and medical care while at the same time trying to look after their own emotional and marital health. Many still manage to find time and energy to advocate for others and share their experiences.

DISCLOSURE STATEMENT

Dr. Nancy Lurie Marks, Cathy Lurie, and Dr. Clarence E. Schutt have nothing to disclose.

REFERENCES

American Psychiatric Association. (2013). *Diagnostic and statistical manual of mental disorders* (5th ed.). Arlington, VA: American Psychiatric Publishing.

Barker, E. T., Hartley, S. L., Seltzer, M. M., Floyd, F. J., Greenberg, J. S., & Orsmond, G. I. (2011). Trajectories of emotional well-being in mothers of adolescents and adults with autism. *Developmental Psychology, 47*(2), 551–561.

Biklen, D. P., Attfield, R., Bissonnette, L., Blackman, L., Frugone, A., Mukhopadhyay, T. R., . . . Burke, J. (2005). *Autism and the myth of the person alone.* New York, NY: New York University Press.

Dykens, E. M., Fisher, M. H., Taylor, J. L., & Miodrag, N. (2014). Reducing distress in mothers of children with autism and other disabilities: A randomized trial. *Pediatrics, 134,* 2.

Grandin, T. (1995). *Thinking in pictures: And other reports from my life with autism.* New York, NY: Doubleday.

Greenfeld, J. (1970). *A child called Noah: A family journey.* New York, NY: Harcourt Brace Jovanovich.

Greenfeld, T. J. (2009). *Boy alone: A brother's memoir.* New York, NY: HarperCollins.

Grinker, R. (2007). *Unstrange minds: Remapping the world of autism.* New York, NY: Basic Books.

Herbert, M., & Weintraub, K. (2013). *The autism revolution: Whole-body strategies for making life all it can be.* New York, NY: Ballantine.

Higashida, N. (2013). *The reason I jump: The inner voice of a thirteen-year-old boy with autism* (K. A. Yoshida & D. Mitchell, Trans.). New York, NY: Random House.

Iversen, P. (2007). *Strange son: Two mothers, two sons, and the quest to unlock the hidden world of autism.* New York, NY: Riverhead Books.

Johnson, M. (Producer) & Levinson, B. (Director). (1988.) *Rain man* [Motion Picture]. Beverly Hills, CA: United Artists.

Markram, K., & Markram, H. (2010). The intense world theory—A unifying theory of the neurobiology of autism. *Frontiers in Human Neuroscience, 4*(224), 1–29.

Mukhopadhyay, T. R. (2000). *Beyond the silence: My life, the world and Autism.* London, England: National Autistic Society.

Murray, S. (2008). *Representing autism: Culture, narrative, fascination.* Liverpool, England: Liverpool University Press.

Orsmond, G. I., & Seltzer, M. M. (2009). Adolescent siblings of individuals with an autism spectrum disorder: Testing a diathesis-stress model of sibling well-being. *Journal of Autism and Developmental Disorders, 39*(7), 1053–1065.

Parks, C. C. (1982). *The siege: A family's journey into the world of an autistic child.* Boston, MA: Little, Brown.

Robinson, R. G. (2011). *Autism solutions: How to create a healthy and meaningful life for your child.* Ontario, Quebec, Canada: Harlequin.

Savarese, R. J. (2007). *Reasonable people: A memoir of autism & adoption.* New York, NY: Other Press.

Smith, L. E., Hong, J., Seltzer, M. M., Greenberg, J. S., Almeida, D. M., & Bishop, S. L. (2010). Daily experiences among mothers of adolescents and adults with autism spectrum disorder. *Journal of Autism and Developmental Disorders, 40*(2), 167–178.

Solomon, A. (2012). *Far from the tree.* New York, NY. Scribner.

Williams, D. (1992). *Nobody nowhere.* New York, NY: Times Books.

Williams, D. (1994). *Somebody somewhere: Breaking free from the world of autism.* New York, NY: Three Rivers Press.

Williams, D. (1996). *Autism: An inside-out approach.* London, England: Kingsley.

FROM THE PERSPECTIVE OF A PERSON WITH AUTISM SPECTRUM DISORDER

JOHN M. WILLIAMS

INTRODUCTION

Living with autism feels like there is a TV turned on in your head with the channel changer broken, constantly cycling through all the channels, bombarding your head with stimuli. Every sense is on fire at the same time. Thoughts swirl endlessly and every type of stimuli hits with the same intensity—sounds, sights, smells, and the feel of the fabric in your clothes. The whole world feels out of control. You just feel like screaming!

GROWING UP AUTISTIC

To escape the chaos as a child, I withdrew into my own world. It was easier to spend time alone with my own thoughts. It was like living in a bubble of my own creation. I was self-absorbed, perseverating on subjects I was interested in such as dinosaurs, cartoons, or movies that I watched over and over. I easily memorized the names of all the dinosaurs by age 4 years and the script of entire movies by age 7 years. This gave me a pretty impressive-sounding vocabulary, but it was all rote learning. I sounded smart but did not really understand the context and certainly had no feel for conversation. I used the memorized material as a way of starting a conversation with peers, trying to get them interested in me since I had no idea how to have a "normal" conversation.

I enjoyed spending time outdoors, wandering around the yard and engaging in repetitive behaviors such as stripping twigs off the bushes. I talked out loud to myself, often just repeating the dialogue from favorite movies. I was unaware of others and what they might think about this behavior. There were also a series of "tics" through the years, from picking my face to flapping my arms and hands, the latter continuing through middle school. This was all part of the self-absorbed, perseverative behavior pattern that has persisted throughout my life. I guess it was a way of comforting me.

In social settings, I have always been extremely anxious and uncomfortable. Auditory processing deficits make it hard to understand language and, as a result, I was resistant to learning in school. Transitions and changes in schedule were so hard to process that I might throw tantrums or punch the wall with frustration. I needed a very steady, dependable schedule with lots of structure in order to function.

I was not very aware of my peers and made little effort to engage them, although my mother says my interactions at home with my brother were pretty normal when we were small. It was not until age 4 years when I attended nursery school that my social deficits became obvious. That is when I began attending special classes designed for kids like me. The teachers were very good at providing a structured environment where I could learn to focus. They used behavior modification techniques for rewarding achievement and appropriate behavior. My mom remembers how they employed techniques to help my brain function better and to desensitize my nerves. For example, every morning before class I spent time on a swing or marched around swinging my arms. Holding a pencil was very uncomfortable, so my occupational therapist massaged my shoulder and elbow joints and then rolled a heavily bristled brush down my arms, which calmed my nerves and allowed me to hold a pencil with a large grip. Eventually, the grips were reduced in size until I didn't need them anymore.

The breakthrough in school came for me when I finally learned to read around age 8 years. After that I learned quickly and was eventually mainstreamed for math class with an aide. I attended the Concord Area Special Collaborative (CASE) in Massachusetts, which has separate classrooms in regular schools so kids like me can interact with neurotypical kids and join in regular activities such as assemblies or recess. Through the years I was mainstreamed more, although the CASE classroom was always my home base.

Auditory learning is an ongoing challenge for me. When the teacher talks, I can't process the words and find the context or main idea. I need visual tools such as pictures, storyboards, and assignments written on the blackboard. It is hard to hear the words and create a picture of their meaning in my head. Visual learning works best. I look for books with photos to help process the subject matter. Much of my historical knowledge is gained by watching DVDs or documentaries. I can watch them repeatedly, processing the pictures and gradually assimilating the dialogue.

In junior high, I began interacting more with my peers through my talent for memorizing. By memorizing movie dialogue, I could make them laugh. Since conversation was hard for me, I became more of an entertainer. I still use this technique today when I can, especially in relating to younger kids. I feel more comfortable relating to younger people, probably because my development was delayed. Emotionally, I feel I am in early adolescence even though I am now over 30 years old.

Eventually I left the CASE program and went to a regular high school with an aide for support. High school was scary! The kids were tall and loud. There was graffiti in the bathrooms. All the sensations bothered me—noise, hustle bustle, body odors. To help me cope, my aide arranged modifications such as letting me pass classes early and have extra time for tests. If I melted down in class, I could escape to the resource center where it was quiet, like an oasis. As I became more comfortable in later years, I stayed in class more and needed my aide less. My favorite class was drama. This may seem surprising but my memorization skills really gave me an edge. The teacher was reassuring and the other students were nice to me and appreciated my skills.

For the last 2 years of high school, I was invited to join the swim team. It was a small group so I felt more at ease. This was the most interaction I can recall having with peers. I felt "part of it" for the first time. Swimming is an individual sport and everyone just tried to do their best. The environment was more congenial than competitive. I was elected co-captain in my senior year and received a trophy and two varsity letters. I always felt I lagged behind my brother in sports, but later I realized that I had two varsity letters and he had none. For once I was not second-string. I'm not a boastful person, but this still made me feel proud.

In high school, I was becoming aware of sexuality but it was confusing. I did not know how to talk to girls and never had physical contact with anyone. I maintained a safety blanket by developing a routine, working at the resource center during school hours and then coming directly home. That kept me out of trouble. Luckily, I was never bullied in school, but I was glad to get out of there all the same.

After graduation at age 19 years, I was lucky enough to be accepted into college. First I attended a community college where there was a resource room and extra help similar to high school. I took my tests in the resource center and had extra time to finish. I could talk to a counselor when I felt out of control. My class load was reduced to three courses per semester. After graduation I moved on to the state university and eventually earned a bachelor's in fine arts. It took 7 years in total but I made it! Graduation day was one of the happiest of my life.

FAMILY RELATIONSHIPS

The person who has guided and supported me most is my mom. She was always there when I needed help with homework, not to mention love and support. Although my parents were divorced when I was 4 years old, they both stayed connected to me. Dad taught me to ride a bike and encouraged me to learn to drive. Along the way, Dad explained that he had symptoms similar to mine, as did his father even though they were not diagnosed with autism. His sister has bipolar disorder. I know autism has a familial connection, so this helps to explain my disability. It was good to know where it came from and that I was not the first "oddball" in the family.

My brother, James, is 2 years younger. He is not autistic, although he admitted to me that he feels anxious at times. When we were very young, we played together, but as we grew older our relationship became more problematic. Looking back, I would not expect him to understand, but I wanted to be left alone and he talked too much and teased me. I wish someone had sat us down and explained things to him from my perspective, how challenging interactions can be. Maybe we could have been better friends. Now that we're both grown, we have a friendlier relationship, although James still finds it hard to interact easily with me. I know he is proud of me, and I am counting on him to help me in the future when my parents are gone.

FEELINGS

Anxiety is the biggest issue for me. I have many fears and they can often be overwhelming. The scariest things are those beyond my control. For example, I worry on a daily basis about bad weather and climate change. I become very upset when severe weather is forecast, especially tornadoes or hurricanes. The constant news about climate change drives me crazy. I avoid hearing the nightly news because so much of it is negative and frightening. My concerns about the future seem much more pronounced than other people's. Maybe it's that difficulty with screening out the extraneous stimuli. My mother tells me to focus on the things I can control in the next few weeks or months, but the old fears keep looming up. My anxiety was seriously heightened after 9/11, and I have felt much more insecure since then. I have focused a lot of attention on learning about other parts of the world, especially the Middle East, in an effort to understand their cultures and worldviews, hoping to find some thread of commonality that may lead to peace in the future.

Although other people tell me they feel anxious at times, my feelings are overwhelming. My pulse races, my nerves are jittery, and the veins feel like they are jumping out of my head. The scariest feeling is that I may lose control and spin away. Even though I take medicine (a selective serotonin reuptake inhibitor (SSRI) that helps with anxiety, I still feel anxious at some time almost every day. This really affects my ability to function and interact with others. When anxiety or frustration gets the best of me, I have meltdowns where I scream and hit the wall with my fist. As a child, I needed to be restrained physically at times to help me calm down. As I got older, the need was to vent verbally for extended periods to anyone who would listen. Through this process, I eventually calm down and start to feel better.

One thing that leads to a feeling of extreme frustration is an unexpected change to the schedule. I need to know what will happen, when, and with whom. If a change is required, I need lots of time to process it. My mom tries to prepare me when changes are coming, which helps a lot. I know change is inevitable, but it is still very unsettling. This goes along with my perfectionist tendencies—wanting things to be done a certain way. I am neat and orderly, often imposing my needs on others—by organizing my brother's bedroom, for example, and throwing away things that seem extraneous. This has led to lots of conflicts in the household, but I take pride in keeping myself and my belongings well-organized.

Another feeling I experience is loneliness. I stay to myself as a means of self-protection, causing people to think of me of as a loner but this is not totally true. My auditory processing challenges inhibit my conversational ability. With the help of language therapy, I am gradually learning conversational skills. My therapist is helping me to understand how conversations flow and how to appropriately engage with other people. I need help knowing what to say once the conversation gets going. It does not come naturally for me to focus on the other person's interest, to ask questions to draw him or her out, to stay focused on the other person's side of the conversation. As a result, I tend to use one-sided monologues rather than engaging in dialogue. Sometimes I start my thoughts in the middle and circle around to the point I want to make so people tend to get lost and stop listening. This really inhibits my ability to interact successfully, even with my own family members. Learning better conversational skills is a major goal that will significantly improve my life.

ADULTHOOD

How do I feel now that I am an autistic adult? I remember hoping when I was younger that somehow I would grow out of autism when I grew up—that I could be normal like everyone else in my family. Unfortunately, that did not happen, and life still feels scary much of the time, especially in new situations. Even changes at home can be upsetting—for example, when the schedule is changed or when the house is being renovated. I feel really stressed out when forced into a social situation I did not expect or where I do not feel comfortable. A good example is the Asperger's Artist Collaborative meetings that my mom facilitates every month. The other members seem to be able to participate in the meeting discussion, but I feel lost, not able to follow the discussion. I just want to escape and often refuse to attend.

From a behavioral perspective, I am more self-aware today but I still fall back on old mannerisms at times, such as talking out loud even outside the house, pacing the floor at night, and trying to lead conversations by sharing information rather than really engaging with the other person. I still find comfort in staying in my own space, watching movies and producing my art. This gives me some control over my environment. For physical comfort,

I often tie a sweatshirt around my waist or hold a blanket on my lap at home. I yearn for the blissful days of childhood when I was oblivious to the world around me.

My dreams for the future are to continue producing art and to find a safe, comfortable place to live with a dog to keep me company. I can drive and take care of my basic needs, but it is scary to think about the time when my parents are gone. I will need help with finances, for example. Although I would like to have female companionship, I am fearful of having children. I can barely take care of myself, let alone others. Hopefully my brother will have kids because I would be a terrific uncle.

CLINICAL EXPERIENCE AND MEDICATIONS

From age 4 years when my disability was first noted by my nursery school teachers until age 11 years when I received a formal diagnosis of Asperger's disorder, the doctors didn't seem to know exactly how to describe my condition (Asperger's disorder no longer exists as a specific diagnosis. All forms of autism are now called Autism Spectrum Disorder—ASD) (American Psychiatric Association, 2013). Although I had autistic tendencies such as perseverative behavior, I was verbal and bright. Tests for fragile X syndrome were negative. I often had staring spells, as if I were in a trance. As a result, I was tested at Children's Hospital in Boston for seizures, but the tests were negative. It was unclear whether this behavior was willful or organic in origin, but it stopped after a few years. I would guess it was a means of retreating from the stimuli bombarding me.

I took methylphenidate (a Ritalin-type medication) for most of my childhood during the school week. It seemed to help me focus, but my mom thought it made me more isolated socially. When I stopped taking it as a freshman in high school, I felt more sociable. I tried paroxetine (an SSRI) for a month or so, but I could not sleep and had suicidal thoughts, so the doctor switched me to buspirone for anxiety. It seemed to help some, so I stayed on it through high school and college. When I let it lapse, I did not feel much different, so I tried going without medication for a few years.

When I was 30 years old, I wanted to try something new for anxiety to help slow down my racing thoughts. My new psychiatrist recommended sertraline, which I am now taking. It took a while to get to the right dosage, and even then it took a while to feel the effect. It does seem to be calming me down, and I am doing better with social interactions, eye contact, and conversation. My old anxiety is still there in the background, and it flares up from time to time, but overall I am feeling less intense, a little happier with less mood swings, and more focused.

Through my childhood, I visited a psychologist periodically. He has known me since age 4 years and was the consulting psychologist in my school program so he has watched me grow up. I enjoyed going to see him as he was always calm and a good listener. He encouraged me to talk about how I was feeling and gave me ideas on ways to manage my anxiety. I did not see him continuously but episodically when my anxiety became overwhelming or when a tough subject such as sexuality was on my mind. It is a comfort knowing he is available when I need his support, and we already have an established connection so it's not like starting over every time.

I need doctors who are calm, quiet, soft-spoken, and understanding. It is very nerve-wracking to go to the doctor, making it hard to interact and stay calm. At the beginning of the appointment, the doctor should speak slowly in a soft voice, engaging me in general conversation to help settle my nerves before proceeding with medical questions. I can be slow to respond, so the doctor needs to be patient to allow me to express my thoughts my way. I find it hard to take criticism from the doctor, especially about my weight gain, which has increased due to medications. This criticism makes me feel defensive and I don't process it well. It is certainly not motivating.

Before any procedures begin, the doctor should explain what will be done—for example, taking my blood pressure or drawing blood—and what it will feel like if it is invasive or new to me. I am not afraid of having shots or blood tests. I can be defensive about being touched unexpectedly, but its fine when I know what to expect. Recently I underwent a lengthy (1 hour) MRI and PET scan. Since the staff had taken me through a dry run and explained all of the steps involved, including an IV of radioactive material, the scanner noises, the time required for each step, and a communication process, I was able to control my nerves and get through it in one session. I was pretty nervous but felt well prepared and the staff consisted of young people approximately my age who showed a lot of interest in me and were very supportive through the whole procedure. I felt really proud when it was over.

Sometimes my mother is present during medical appointments to make sure all the necessary information is provided and to help me process the instructions, but I am not afraid to go alone, especially for routine appointments with doctors I know. However, if there is something complicated or negative coming out of the examination, I would prefer to have this information provided first to my mother, who will share it with me in a way I can process.

One of the best things for medical people to talk to me about is my art. I really enjoy hearing their feedback on my work, and I like to chat about my new projects. This interest provides a great basis for a positive conversation and puts me at ease.

THE ROLE OF ART IN MY LIFE

Artistic creation has played an integral role in my life and development. I began modeling with clay when I was 4 years old, and my talent began to blossom. I could lose myself in my creative activity. It was harmonious compared to the chaotic world around me. My first creations were copied from TV shows, such as Godzilla, or from books, such as dinosaurs. The combination of visual images and my imagination played out in my head, leading me to add my own twists, creating entirely unique characters. Like a writer who gets an idea and just can't stop until he gets it down on paper, I felt compelled to create my clay models. I did what came naturally without thinking about other's opinions of my work, and I still do this.

All through school, I continued clay modeling and excelling in art classes. In college, I focused mostly on sculpting, but at the end of my senior year I began experimenting with producing collage portraits and landscapes using small pieces of paper cut from magazines. This has become my specialty.

In high school, a friend gave me a book about the Civil War and it became my passion. I began reading everything about it, looking at pictures, photos, maps, movies, and documentaries about that period in our history. Over time, I became very knowledgeable about the Civil War and other eras of history. This is a consuming interest for me, and my strong memorization skills help me retain all the details. Once I landed on the collage process, I focused on creating historical art pieces such as the Civil War generals, US presidents, and the War in the Pacific in World War II. The combination of my passion for history, my art skills, and a vivid imagination is a winning formula.

Art is more than self-expression for me. It is a way of exploring and understanding the world. I study my subjects in great detail before beginning a collage to find out what kind of personality and character they had. For example, how did a Civil War general treat his troops? Was he well-liked? Was he grumpy? What effect did his actions have on the course of events? This all effects how I present the person's face in a portrait. I often include background elements to tell the person's story. I consider this an important aspect of my work—telling a story visually, sharing my knowledge with others.

My concern about the Middle East led me to reading a biography about the Shah of Iran. I learned that much of what we see in Iran today was an outgrowth of his reign. To help people understand this, I made a collage of the Shah with a tapestry background showing the influences on him and his era. He was a pivotal person of his time. I learned he was an insecure man, so I tried to reflect that in his face. He put on a good front by wearing fancy uniforms, but deep inside he was indecisive and weak. I can relate to him because I often have to put up a front, pretending to be braver or more social than I feel. Maybe that's why I spent more time on this portrait than any other so far.

Fairness is important to me. In my artwork, I try to represent my subjects in a fair and balanced way. Sometimes I choose to depict people who were not popular, such as the Shah or Richard Nixon, because I am curious about what made them tick. They are complex characters, not easy to understand. In representing them, I try to be fair, not lionizing or demonizing them but showing both their good and bad features. I try to pierce through the subject, to capture the essence or soul of the real person, leaving the viewer to draw his or her own judgment.

As most people know, autistics have great difficulty making eye contact. We do not learn this naturally as most people do. Looking directly at someone is really challenging, although I don't know why. I am learning to do better, but it takes conscious effort and practice. It is ironic that in my portraits eyes play a central role, usually looking directly at the viewer. Everyone who sees my work comments on the eyes. It seems that through my art I have learned to compensate for this aspect of my disability.

I often describe my artistic process as an analogy for living with autism: trying to make sense of the world by sorting out the chaos. In my collages, I place hundreds of small pieces of paper together to create a unified image. The end product, while recognizable, presents an entirely new perspective on the subject. When I am working, I do not envision the end product. The piece designs itself through a discovery process as the paper is applied. It is like breathing life into the subject. I don't know how it happens. It just comes naturally to me, imparting a new vitality to my subjects. Perhaps the one good thing about having autism is that I have a unique way of seeing the world and passing on my vision through art.

MY LEGACY

I would like my life to have meaning and to leave a legacy. I would like to impart my knowledge to others through teaching in some way. Through my artwork, I tell the stories of my subjects, illuminating their lives. I hope the story of my life will be meaningful to others and inspire them to use their gifts to create meaningful lives of their own.

SUMMARY

In this chapter, I have done my best to describe what it is like to have autism from my personal perspective. As a child, the world was a confusing place. I was self-absorbed and generally unaware of others. Over time, I found myself begin bombarded by sensory stimuli and felt almost hyper-aware of things. I became extremely anxious in social settings.

Predictability and structure allow me to function better. Yet the world is a very free-flowing, spontaneous place filled with transitions and constant change. I am doing my best to adapt, but it remains a day-to-day challenge.

My interest in the Civil War and leaders of different nations, in the context of my artwork, serves as a consistent safe base for me. Because of the confidence I have in my knowledge of these topics, they serve as a platform from which I can interact with others. I have been fortunate to be able to develop my knowledge of these topics into a passion and vocation. Transforming what I know about Civil War generals into visual images that reflect their personality and characteristics, for example, brings me great joy; I hope the same is true for those who view my work.

It is somewhat unusual for a person with autism to accomplish many of the things I have in my life. Most do not graduate from high school, let alone college. Not many are awarded letters in a varsity sport. Very few are able to drive. Despite these accomplishments, of which I am proud, I am lonely. I worry about my future. Society needs to make significant strides in the way it views adults with autism. We need the same opportunities that are available to typical people. I am hopeful things will improve during my lifetime.

I have tried to provide some tips for medical providers caring for individuals with autism in this chapter. It has been helpful to me for the doctor to be calm, soft spoken, understanding, and a good listener. Sometimes, especially when I am anxious, it takes me some time to respond to a question. I have appreciated the times when the doctor doesn't rush me or try to speak for me in order to hurry through the appointment. If any medical procedures or tests are to be scheduled, it is useful if the doctor and staff can create a visual image of what this will look like rather than simply providing a verbal explanation. Finally, it is terrific if the doctor remembers me as John Williams, not just a young man with autism. Having the doctor ask me about my recent art projects and showing interest in me as a person, not just a patient, is quite important to me.

KEY POINTS

- Anxiety rules my life. Constant worries and fears plague me, sometimes leading to dysfunction. Managing these feelings is the biggest challenge I face.
- My most severe observable deficit is in social skills—comprehending conversation, figuring out how to respond appropriately, staying on topic, and making eye contact. Improving conversational skills is a major goal.
- Adulthood is very challenging for me. Gone is the carefree childhood freedom to withdraw and live in my own world. The fears loom larger now as my view expands and the world seems so out of control. It is scary!
- Medications have so far been moderately helpful in reducing anxiety—not the silver bullet I was hoping for. Behavior modification has been most helpful in managing anxiety and improving social skills.
- Through my artistic process, I try to explore and understand the world—dissecting my subject and reassembling the pieces to create a new perspective. The one good thing about autism is my unique way of seeing the world and passing on my vision through art.

ENDNOTE

John Williams' artwork can be viewed at the John M. Williams Fine Art website at http:// johnmwilliamsfineart.com.

DISCLOSURE STATEMENT

John M. Williams has nothing to disclose.

REFERENCE

American Psychiatric Association. (2013). *Diagnostic and statistical manual of mental disorders* (5th ed.). Arlington, VA: American Psychiatric Publishing.

INDEX

CPSIA information can be obtained
at www.ICGtesting.com
Printed in the USA
BVOW09s1204101217
502013BV00011B/15/P